Oracle JDeveloper 10g for Forms & PL/SQL Developers

p xxi – on-line doco + other resources
p 26 – high-volume data entry
p 63 – use of workspace vs project

Peter Koletzke
Duncan Mills

New York   Chicago   San Francisco
Lisbon   London   Madrid   Mexico City   Milan
New Delhi   San Juan   Seoul   Singapore   Sydney   Toronto

McGraw-Hill books are available at special quantity discounts to use as premiums and sales promotions, or for use in corporate training programs. For more information, please write to the Director of Special Sales, Professional Publishing, McGraw-Hill, Two Penn Plaza, New York, NY 10121-2298. Or contact your local bookstore.

Oracle JDeveloper 10*g* for Forms & PL/SQL Developers

1234567890 CUS CUS 019876

ISBN-13:   978-0-07-225960-5
ISBN-10:   0-07-225960-4

Sponsoring Editor
Lisa McLain

Editorial Supervisor
Jody McKenzie

Acquisitions Coordinator
Alex McDonald

Technical Editors
Leslie Tierstein
Didier Laurent

Technical Contributor
Steven Davelaar

Technical Review Coordinator
Simon Day

Technical Reviewers
Simon Day
Peter Ebell
Caryl Lee Fisher
Pam Gamer
Ann Horton
Jonas Jacobi
Sandra Muller
Frank Nimphius
Blaise Ribet
Grant Ronald
Avrom Roy-Faderman
Frank van der Borden
Ton van Kooten

Copy Editor
Lisa McCoy

Proofreaders
Paul Tyler
Susie Elkind

Indexer
Jack Lewis

Production Supervisor
George Anderson

Composition
International Typesetting
and Composition

Illustration
International Typesetting
and Composition

Art Director, Cover
Jeff Weeks

For Anne, who reintroduced me to the finches.
—Peter Koletzke

For my wife, Amanda, and the rest of the gang: Josh, Sam, and Hissy.
—Duncan Mills

About the Authors

Peter Koletzke is a technical director and principal instructor for the Enterprise e-Commerce Solutions practice at Quovera, in Mountain View, California, and has worked in the database industry since 1984. Peter has presented at various Oracle users group conferences more than 170 times and has won awards such as Pinnacle Publishing's Technical Achievement, Oracle Development Tools Users Group (ODTUG) Editor's Choice, ECO/SEOUC Oracle Designer Award, ODTUG Volunteer of the Year, and NYOUG Editor's Choice. He is an Oracle Fusion Middleware Regional Director and Oracle Certified Master. Peter is coauthor, with Dr. Paul Dorsey, of the Oracle Press books: *Oracle JDeveloper 10g Handbook and Oracle 9i JDeveloper Handbook* (also co-authored with Avrom Roy-Faderman), *Oracle JDeveloper 3 Handbook, Oracle Developer Advanced Forms and Reports, Oracle Designer Handbook,* 2nd Edition, and *Oracle Designer/2000 Handbook.*

Quovera (www.quovera.com) is a business consulting and technology integration firm that specializes in delivering solutions to the high technology, telecommunications, semiconductor, manufacturing, software and services, public sector, and financial services industries. Quovera deploys solutions that deliver optimized business processes quickly and economically, driving increased productivity and improved operational efficiency. Founded in 1995, the company has a track record of delivering hundreds of strategy, design, and implementation projects to over 250 Fortune 2000 and high-growth middle market companies. Quovera's client list includes notable organizations such as Cisco Systems, ON Semiconductor, New York state, Sun Microsystems, Lawrence Livermore National Laboratory, Seagate, Toyota, Fujitsu, Visa, and Cendant.

Duncan Mills is a Java evangelist and Senior Principal Product Manager at Oracle, specializing in JavaServer Faces, the Oracle ADF Framework, and related J2EE technologies. He has been working with Java and Oracle products in a variety of application development and DBA roles since 1988. For the past 13 years, he has been working at Oracle, and is currently working as part of the JDeveloper Java IDE development team. Duncan is a frequent presenter at Oracle User Groups and Java events around the world, achieving awards such as Best Oracle Presentation from the annual conference of the UK Oracle User Group and Contributor of the Year from ODTUG. He is an Oracle Technology Network ACE, and publishes frequently on the OTN site, as well as in the Oracle Development Tools User Group Journal and the Java Developers Journal.

For nearly three decades, Oracle, the world's largest enterprise software company, has provided the software and services that let organizations get the most up-to-date and accurate information from their business systems. With over 275,000 customers—including 98 of the Fortune 100—Oracle supports customers in more than 145 countries. For more information about Oracle, visit www.oracle.com.

Contents

v

PART II
Developing the Application

PART III
Additional Techniques

Foreword

I was recently talking to a developer, wondering how well developers knew their software development tools. He made the point that he was spending more time with his tool than with his wife and therefore felt he had a deep knowledge of it. I thought that was funny until I realized it was probably true. I am not sure what it says about the quality of the relationship between our users and their better halves, but beyond the fiscal responsibility that we have toward our management, our employees, and finally our stock holders, this discussion drove home that there is nothing more daunting than the responsibility we have toward our users and the potential disruption of the relationship they have with their software development tools.

I became Vice President of Application Development Tools at a time when the Internet and J2EE were nascent while the penetration of our PL/SQL-oriented tools (Oracle Forms and Designer) had never been so high. This meant that my biggest challenge was to make sure that our customers and our tools would be relevant in this new landscape.

It was, and still is, not easy. Developers are a passionate bunch, and one thing we are never short of is opinions from customers. To this day, one of the most difficult aspects of my job is explaining to people the reasoning behind the things we do or, more importantly, chose not to do.

One of these controversial decisions we took early on was not to tackle the task of migrating Forms and PL/SQL applications to J2EE. We did not think that in the long term, it was the right for thing for our customers and, consequently, it was not the right thing for Oracle. There is a long list of reasons for this, but the top two were:

■ We knew we would not be able to provide a complete migration, and manual modifications would have been required for all but the simplest application.

■ The applications resulting from any automated migration would not have had the structure of an architecturally sound J2EE application (which requires separation of the UI from the business logic).

xi

However, something that is important to us is to make sure that our users could leverage all of the skills they garnered while away from their spouses. We wanted JDeveloper and ADF to expose concepts similar to the one used to build Forms and PL/SQL applications.

What Peter and Duncan have done in this book is leverage their combined experience on the subject to jumpstart Forms and PL/SQL developers on their way to building J2EE applications.

This is Peter's fourth book on JDeveloper and ADF; he is a regular speaker at Oracle Tools events and is widely regarded as an expert in his field. Not being on the Oracle payroll, he also brings a fresh and unbiased perspective to the topic.

Duncan started working on Oracle Tools before I knew Oracle had tools—he brings tremendous expertise to this book. In his role at Oracle, he deals on a daily basis with customers facing the difficult road of wanting to move their environments to J2EE while preserving as much as possible of their current investments in PL/SQL. He is instrumental in defining the evolution of our tool set and making sure that our J2EE tools are a natural evolution of our PL/SQL tools.

There is no cookie-cutter answer to the question of what to do. Oracle, for its own E-Business Suite, chose to leverage the expertise of its development team; however, in building the Fusion applications, we are re-writing everything from the schema up rather than attempting an automatic migration of the code. No matter which approach you choose, I highly recommend you pick up this book. Beyond the chosen words of wisdom at the start of each chapter, ranging from Confucius to Edgar Allan Poe by way of Albert Einstein, the book will help you better understand the pros and cons of the different approaches.

Ultimately, it is our goal to make sure that developers are more productive and, therefore, have the option of spending less time with their tools and more time with their spouses. This book is a tremendous help along the way.

Christophe Job
Vice President, Application Development Tools
Oracle Corporation

Acknowledgments

"You shouldn't be working on vacation," said a fellow bicycle tour participant as I sat working on this book in the front lawn of our Loire Valley hotel in France. I was focused on meeting a chapter deadline at the end of that day's ride. I replied that having the luxury of only doing book work without other consulting duties was definitely a vacation. I think there was a subsequent mention of Type A behavior, but I was so engrossed in the chapter that I don't recall exactly.

The process of writing this book was a lot like that Loire Valley bike tour. The tour was a slow but scenic ride through territory that was new to me. To be the most effective when interacting with residents, the tour required knowledge of a language with which I was mostly unfamiliar (French). The road offered many challenges along the way, but also offered as many rewards.

So it was with this book—new territory, an unfamiliar environment and language (J2EE and Java), many challenges, and many rewards. As we started writing in the early stages of JDeveloper 10.1.3 and discovered many new and exciting features, we came to the realization that this new release of JDeveloper offered more J2EE web development productivity for Oracle Forms and PL/SQL developers than previous releases.

One of the key success factors for a bike tour (as well as for a book) is a knowledgeable guide. Our Loire Valley tour was blessed in that respect and this book was, too. Along with his writing duties as coauthor of this book, Duncan Mills served as J2EE Tour Guide. Duncan is not only fluent in the J2EE technologies and how best to use them in an Oracle environment, but also is a renowned expert on every aspect of Oracle Forms. Therefore, he was able to help me understand the sticky points of JDeveloper web development in terms that an old Oracle Forms developer could understand. Many thanks to Duncan for his patience and persistence in answering basic questions, as well as for supplying and maintaining the hardware and software that allowed us to co-develop the sample application over the distance of an ocean and a continent. I also appreciate Duncan's tutelage on the nuances of UK English and fun features of instant messaging.

Leslie Tierstein has assisted as technical editor for most of the Oracle Press books I have worked on, and she served this role again for this book. Leslie's insight helped guide the book to its intended audience. Her honest opinions about deleting extra material and willingness to supply additional or reworked text was helpful. Thanks once again, Leslie.

I've used the JHeadstart extension to JDeveloper on several projects and found it to be extremely useful. Features of the new version were not familiar to Duncan or me, but Steven Davelaar generously agreed to supply the material for that chapter. Steven, I greatly appreciate that important information and all your hard work. I also greatly appreciate the insights offered by Christophe Job in the foreword to this book.

In addition to those members of our core support team, many technical reviewers kept us pedaling in the right direction. Thanks to all the experts at Oracle Corporation who reviewed one or more chapters, tried out the hands-on practices, and provided helpful comments, suggestions, challenges, ideas, and even some text: Simon Day, Peter Ebell, Pam Gamer, Jonas Jacobi, Sandra Muller, Frank Nimphius, Blaise Ribet, Grant Ronald, Frank van der Borden, and Ton van Kooten. Ann Horton volunteered to review a set of chapters and was able to find and fix several bugs in the practices, as well as to fine-tune the instructions. Thanks, Ann! A special thanks to Didier Laurent, who stepped in during the later stages of the process to do a review of the entire book and who provided many critical technical corrections and clarifications. In addition, Avrom Roy-Faderman, one of my coauthors on the *Oracle 9i JDeveloper Handbook* and *Oracle JDeveloper 10g Handbook* and fellow Quovera employee, supplied some useful tips for improving the material. I deeply appreciate all the help from those reviewers.

Dr. Paul Dorsey, coauthor of the other Oracle Press titles I have worked on, was busy during this time working on another book, but his administrative assistant, Caryl Lee Fisher, somehow carved out time to work through our hands-on practices many times. Thanks, Caryl Lee, for your patience and for all the suggestions about how to improve that text.

I also appreciate the professionalism and friendliness of the Oracle Press staff who helped this book project manifest, especially Lisa McClain, Jody McKenzie, Alex McDonald, Lisa McCoy, and Jack Lewis.

Thanks also go to my boss, Guy Wilnai, for the flexibility in schedule required to balance book work with client work. Also, thanks to the staff at my long-term client project, the New York State Office of Alcoholism and Substance Abuse Services, for gracefully handling my strange work schedule and helping me understand what Oracle Forms developers would expect to see in a book like this. I also appreciate the techniques and tips I learned from others working on my client projects during this time: Igor Gorbunov, Mohamed Javid, and Sean Kim. You will see some of your techniques and ideas reflected herein.

As always, Mom, Dad, and Marilyn, thank you for sympathizing with and showing a constant interest in the struggles of the book process.

Most importantly, thanks to my wife, Anne, for her understanding and support. Anne, I foresee a vacation in the near future without the laptop.

Peter Koletzke
San Carlos, CA, USA
May 2006

It's been a long road from that first email that Peter sent back in May 2004 suggesting that this book might be a good idea. We've wrestled the pre-production software hydra—after each screen shot was taken and each behavior noted, another change would spring up to take its place. So thanks to Lisa McClain and Alex McDonald at McGraw-Hill for putting up with such a slippery schedule!

Throughout this whole process, immense credit has to go to my co-author Peter whose mentoring guided me through the darkness and out the other side. Without Peter's editorial skills, organization abilities, and, most importantly, constant curiosity as to "why," the book would never have made it and would certainly not be as good. So, Peter, thank you (but I would still like to slip the word "bespoke" in somewhere).

We've been through many revisions and rewrites during the birth of this book, all the while helped along by an able and extremely thorough team of reviewers. Particular mention must go to Leslie Tierstein, who along with Peter, put up with the worst of my British dialect and phrasing.

Everyone at Oracle has been immensely supportive of the project and gratifyingly impatient to see the results. So thanks to Roel Stalman for giving the green light, Christophe Job for the Foreword, and Simon Day for managing the Oracle review process. A special mention must go to my buddies at Oracle: Didier Laurent, Grant Ronald, Blaise Ribet, Frank van Der Borden, Frank Nimphius, and Pam Gamer who reviewed more than their fair share of material. Thanks especially to my friend and colleague Jonas Jacobi, who not only helped with the review process, but, more importantly, also proved to me that books do eventually get printed. Finally, but by no means least, a big thanks must go to Steven Davelaar from the JHeadstart Team in the Netherlands who produced the JHeadstart chapter for us. We all owe Steven and the whole JHeadstart team a debt of gratitude, not only for the package itself, but also for the essential check-and-balance function they provide by stretching the products just that little bit more.

Writing a book and doing a full-time job at the same time doesn't make for much of a work-life balance. Throughout the whole process, my family has been an inspiration and constant support. So, Amanda, Josh, Sam, and little Zoë, thank you most of all, and I make no apologies to Sam Gamgee in saying "Well, I'm back."

Duncan Mills
Winchester, UK
May 2006

Introduction

Learning without thought is labor lost;
thought without learning is perilous

—Confucius (551 BC–479 BC), *The Confucian Analects*

Kicking and screaming. That's what most Oracle Forms and PL/SQL developers feel like doing when told they need to convert their skills to Java 2 Platform, Enterprise Edition (J2EE). We don't mean to imply that long-time Oracle Forms and PL/SQL developers like us are an immature lot—only that J2EE is so new and, seemingly, so complex that traditional Oracle developers fear a severe loss in productivity, a painful learning curve, and an ensuing failure of their first J2EE project. These are valid concerns, and addressing these concerns was the main motivation for writing this book.

The motivation for writing this introduction was to provide you with our vision of the book's objectives, purpose, and contents so you can decide whether it will be useful for you and, if the answer is "Yes," how best to use the book's contents. This introduction includes details about the book's intended audience, objectives, contents, and scope. It also provides tips and advice about how best to follow the practical examples (hands-on practices) in the second part of the book.

Who Is This Book For?

As the title states, we address the material in this book to Oracle Forms and PL/SQL developers. Even an experienced Java developer, who needs to know more about how to create JavaServer Faces (JSF) applications with Application Development Framework (ADF) in JDeveloper, will find material of interest in this book. If you are experienced with J2EE and JavaServer Faces (JSF) and do not think you need JDeveloper 10*g* and ADF, while we may disagree with that opinion, we also think you may want to put this book back on the shelf and browse more advanced books about JSF and J2EE development.

Although it may be erring on the conservative side, we assume that readers who are Oracle Forms and PL/SQL developers have no knowledge of or experience in J2EE web development. We do assume that you have some experience at least with browsing web applications and are familiar with the tasks required to develop a database application. Although not a prerequisite, if you have worked on a J2EE web development project, you will be more quickly able to absorb the concepts needed to understand web application work. You will gain knowledge of best practices and solid techniques for JDeveloper work.

Do I Need Oracle Forms Skills to Read This Book?

The parallels between development in the traditional Oracle development world and the J2EE web development are easy to draw between Oracle Forms and JDeveloper because both are fully featured development tools. Parallels between PL/SQL work (or work in the *PL/SQL Web Toolkit*, an API that allows you to output to a browser) are not as easy to draw because PL/SQL is a language, not a tool. Therefore, where we feel that explaining a concept in terms of a known technology is important, we most often refer to Oracle Forms.

These references are not intended to slight traditional Oracle developers who know PL/SQL but have little or no knowledge of Oracle Forms. If you are in this category, you do not need to study Oracle Forms to understand the material in this book; you can safely ignore the references to Oracle Forms and the material in this book will still sufficiently orient you regarding J2EE development techniques.

Objectives

No book can teach you all possible techniques that you will need when you face a real application development task. If it could, this would take away much of the challenge, excitement, and creativity that developers face and often take pride in handling every day. However, a book can empower you with knowledge about the underlying principles; this knowledge will help you face future application challenges presented to you.

Therefore, the book's objectives are as follows:

- **To explain in some detail the technology** behind the code you create in *JDeveloper 10g, Release 3* (JDeveloper 10.1.3) with ADF Business Components, ADF Faces, and JSF. This information will give you a context for understanding what you are doing in the tool and how to address development requirements and any problems that may occur.

- **To demonstrate development** of a somewhat real-world application that contains functionality requiring work at different levels of development: wizards, declarative and visual tools, and raw coding (explained a bit more in the "Levels of Coding" section later on).

- **To show you some of the basic techniques** required for a typical application. We provide gentle introductions and explanations of some techniques so that you can fully understand why you are performing certain actions in JDeveloper.

- **To present some best practices** for approaching requirements for a web application. There are always many paths to a goal, and this is true of J2EE development. We provide opinions about specific paths with reasons for those opinions.

- **To guide you towards additional sources of information** for more details. These sources include those that have helped us, as well as others, understand aspects of J2EE web development. These references are scattered throughout the body of the book in context of the applicable subjects.

The J2EE Knowledge Problem

You likely have read or heard material about J2EE web development and JDeveloper, but still may not be comfortable with it. In fact, so-called introductions to J2EE often leave you with more questions than understanding. This is a natural effect of learning new material, but it seems to be particularly true with J2EE, which already has a well-established and expert-level user community. That user community is highly qualified to present J2EE concepts and examples to others and is quite generous in doing so. However, as is true with any instructor, J2EE writers many times assume that readers have understood more than they actually have mastered. This assumption means that new content is not properly assimilated because the reader has an incomplete understanding of that content's foundation.

You can obtain any information about the technologies behind J2EE web development from the Internet. The wealth of available information actually contributes to the steep learning curve for Oracle Forms and PL/SQL developers. When trying to learn a technology, you need to search for the right source, decide which sources are reliable and correct, read and understand multiple explanations (because one explanation is rarely complete for your purpose), and integrate them into a comprehensive picture. However, you are not sure whether the knowledge you gain in this way is essential. You would like to reduce the knowledge to only that which is essential. Providing you with the essentials is one of the goals of this book.

The JDeveloper 10.1.3 Solution

When you run JDeveloper, you will see the splash screen motto—"Productivity with Choice," as shown in the following illustration.

This motto means that JDeveloper supports different ways of creating code (for example, typing code text, declaring property values, and performing visual layout). It also correctly implies that

JDeveloper supports development work using any J2EE technology. You will not need more than one tool—JDeveloper handles it all. However, this same motto has frustrated some Oracle Forms and PL/SQL developers in the past, because it means that they need to be aware of the ins and outs of various technologies, and they need to make the choice with little direction from Oracle.

Unlike Oracle Forms, which provides a single technology suite for deploying web applications and a defined path for development, with JDeveloper, you need to string together various J2EE technologies for a final solution. The danger of a wrong selection exists unless you study carefully and obtain some help from those with experience.

With JDeveloper 10.1.3, you can still select from any J2EE technology, and JDeveloper will support your development work. However, with this release, Oracle has provided a defined path that makes the most sense for developers with a background in Oracle Forms and PL/SQL—ADF Business Components with JSF and ADF Faces. The development experience using these technologies consists mainly of declarative and visual editing of components and events, much like the Oracle Forms 4GL experience. This path requires much less Java and HTML coding than any previous technology combination. Although this technology stack is still just one of many choices to which the JDeveloper motto refers, it is likely to be the choice for Oracle Forms and PL/SQL developers.

Levels of Coding

When you first learn how to develop a user interface of a certain style—for example, Oracle Forms—you need to quickly master the techniques that provide you with a starting point for the application. You work in the following levels within Oracle Forms:

1. **Using the wizards,** such as the Data Block Wizard, Layout Wizard, and LOV Wizard, to create a working application. You can develop a fully functional user-interface application using these wizards, but it is almost certain that your design requires more functionality than the wizards provide.

2. **Using declarative and visual coding tools,** such as the Layout Editor and Property Palette, to define additional components, modify the layout, and customize existing components.

3. **Writing 3GL code** for triggers (and supporting program units) that fine-tune the interaction with users and fulfill the business needs for the application.

4. **Extending the framework** by calling external Java programs or plug-ins (in web environments), using Foreign Function Interface programs (in client/server environments), or writing transactional triggers (such as ON-INSERT and ON-UPDATE) that add to or replace the default runtime functionality or component set.

Naturally, you will move back and forth among these levels as you create the finished application. You will also write database code and define database objects to complete the project.

NOTE
If you are writing front-end application code using the PL/SQL Web Toolkit or other purely PL/SQL application environments, you are working in the third and fourth levels.

Each of these development levels requires more expertise and experience than the preceding level; to be most productive, you try to spend the most time working in levels 1 and 2. If you are like most developers, who acquire most of their skills by developing applications, your early projects in Oracle Forms likely had some challenging moments. You needed to learn the tool and its best practices (and work around its bugs) while producing useful code.

Using JDeveloper 10.1.3 for the first project is likely to follow similar patterns; development work in JDeveloper and ADF requires time and knowledge of the tool in the same four levels. We strongly feel that if you have a background in a declarative development environment such as Oracle Forms, your experience with the technologies we emphasize in this release of JDeveloper will be the closest possible to that of Oracle Forms. We also feel that JDeveloper releases before the 10*g* line required more work in the third and fourth levels and that this was a stumbling point or showstopper for many Oracle Forms and PL/SQL developers.

Information in This Book and Other Sources

A small number of readers may worry that a book in the Oracle Press series might repeat material found elsewhere. Therefore, it is necessary to assure this group that the material in this book is original and unique, although it is thankfully not the only information available about JDeveloper. JDeveloper has an active user community and wide support within the Oracle development world. Much material has been written about JDeveloper 10.1.3 already, and most is available from the following sources:

Oracle Technology Network (OTN)   This website (www.oracle.com/technology) contains many pages devoted to work with JDeveloper, ADF Business Components, and ADF Faces. Most OTN articles focus on a specific application-development feature and usually assume you can research J2EE technologies from other sources. This type of material is a critical source of practical information about techniques. It can save you much time in researching how to solve a particular programming problem. Start browsing for information from the JDeveloper home page (www.oracle.com/technology/products/jdev/).

Oracle ADF Learning Center   As of this writing, an OTN website page called "Oracle ADF Learning Center" (www.oracle.com/technology/products/adf/learnadf.html) provides useful information including demos, tutorials, developer's guides, and sample applications to experienced Java developers as well as 4GL developers.

ADF Developer's Guide   The *Oracle Application Development Framework Developer's Guide for Forms/4GL Developers—10g Release 3 (10.1.3)* online book is available in the Oracle ADF Learning Center as well as the JDeveloper Help Center. It targets the same audience as this book and contains some similar techniques. However, it provides many more examples of different types of code you may need to write. We think that the developer's guide is a perfect follow-on book to this book. Once you come to an understanding about the J2EE web technologies and development techniques here, you can use the developer's guide to round out your understanding or to provide you with specific techniques not discussed here.

JDeveloper Help Center   In addition to detailed (and some overview) information on OTN, the JDeveloper *Help Center* (online help system) provides more tool-oriented information about accomplishing specific tasks. For example, JDeveloper 10.1.3 contains several useful features, such as *Cue Cards* that provide step-by-step instructions for performing a certain task or for developing a certain type of page, Favorites that allow you to create a list of help topics of interest, and Dynamic

Links that display a list of help topics relevant to the task at hand. The entry point for the Help Center is the Help menu in the JDeveloper IDE or the Help Center window (**View** | **Help Center**).

NOTE
Menu selections from right-click menus or the JDeveloper main menu are marked in boldface throughout the book with "|" symbols separating submenu selections.

What's Different About This Book?

Although a wealth of material about web development using JDeveloper is available from various sources, much of it assumes you have some background in the basics of Java and J2EE. This book helps you better assimilate that material by providing the necessary background information for your web development work.

In addition, although many techniques and white papers you will find on the Web provide clear steps for creation of all types of web application code, this book has the luxury of spending many pages on a technique as well as on the background material you need to understand the technique more fully.

Coming up with best practices from the many information sources available to you can be daunting. This book guides you down a development path using specific technologies, and at the same time, states best practices for this path at appropriate points in the discussion.

The Hands-On Practices

In addition to the explanations of technologies and best practices, this book walks you through the creation of a sample application using business services from ADF Business Components—a natural choice for Oracle Forms and PL/SQL developers.

The hands-on practices in Part II of this book explain the task at hand before walking through how to accomplish it in JDeveloper. They are divided into major phases of work, and these phases are divided into sections, each of which contains a logical unit of work. At the end of each major phase of development, the practice contains a section called "What Did You Just Do?," which explains again the result of the steps you followed. Some practices contain an additional section called "What Could You Do Next?," which provides guidance about variations or enhancements on the code you just wrote.

We took inspiration for these sections from similar sections in the hands-on practices for the *Oracle JDeveloper 10g Handbook* (Roy-Faderman, Koletzke, and Dorsey, 2004, McGraw-Hill/ Osborne). It is important not only to complete a series of steps by following the instructions, but also to comprehend exactly what occurred in those steps. The detailed explanations and summaries at the end of each phase will help with that comprehension.

Contents of the Chapters

To provide you with a better idea of the subjects we think you need to know about J2EE web development using JDeveloper and ADF, it is useful to briefly examine the contents of each chapter. The chapters are organized into three parts: Technology Overviews, Developing the Application, and Additional Techniques.

Part I: Technology Overviews

Developing J2EE web applications using JDeveloper and ADF requires familiarity with concepts that will be new to you if you have previously worked mainly in the Oracle Forms and PL/SQL environments. You may have heard about and learned about some of these concepts before. However, so many J2EE technologies are available that you may be at a loss to know which technologies you need to learn most thoroughly. Part I of this book introduces you to the concepts you will run into when developing J2EE web applications with ADF in JDeveloper 10*g*.

The chapters in this part are structured around questions listed at the beginning of each chapter. This should make finding an answer for a particular question easier later on, but the chapters are also intended to be read from start to finish. Although Part II is dedicated to hands-on practices that provide step-by-step instructions about how to complete tasks, some of the chapters in Part I provide general instructions for JDeveloper work that illustrate the concepts discussed in the chapters. While understanding the concepts is not dependent upon working in JDeveloper while you are reading, you might find that following along using JDeveloper helps you understand these concepts better.

J2EE is a set of specifications and best practices for developing and deploying a Java-oriented application. Chapter 1 explains the components of J2EE and how J2EE web technologies work.

Chapter 2 briefly explores the basic communication path of Hypertext Transfer Protocol (HTTP). The knowledge about what occurs when the client browser and server layers of a web application exchange messages provides a context for the code you create and helps when you need to debug problems.

Although JDeveloper 10*g* is the subject of entire books (such as the *Oracle JDeveloper 10*g *Handbook* mentioned before), it is useful to approach the tool from the standpoint of how it can serve a Rapid Application Development (RAD) role. RAD is second nature to Oracle Forms, so knowledge of how this works in JDeveloper and ADF will be of keen interest to Oracle Forms developers. This is the subject of Chapter 3.

J2EE web applications require coding in several languages. Even though Java is the core language used for J2EE technologies, with tools such as JDeveloper 10*g* 10.1.3 and frameworks such as ADF, you will not spend all your application development time coding Java. Chapter 4 discusses which languages you need to know and how much of each language you will likely end up using. Since Java works differently from PL/SQL and is the hardest language to shift to for a PL/SQL developer, Chapter 4 also spends some time introducing Java concepts. This introduction is not intended to substitute for further study on Java, but it should allow you to read the code examples in the book with no previous Java knowledge. In addition, this chapter can serve as a review for those who already understand Java.

A relatively new J2EE technology, JavaServer Faces (JSF), is gaining popularity within the Java community and is the focus of many of the new features in JDeveloper 10.1.3. Chapter 5 introduces JSF and an Oracle component library, ADF Faces, which provides basic components with functionality close to that of Oracle Forms' components.

Chapter 6 explains the business services of ADF Business Components (ADF BC). You will use ADF BC to communicate with the database, so this is an important concept for traditional Oracle developers.

ADF Model features perform the previously daunting task of *binding*—connecting user interface code to data supplied by the business services layer. Chapter 7 introduces the ADF Model layer and the files it uses for binding data on the page. Chapter 8 explores the ADF Model bindings topic in more depth and explains the available binding types, as well as how to create and use them.

Part II: Developing the Application

There is absolutely nothing like the practical application of concepts to help them sink in; in addition to helping you absorb concepts, it is often easier to explain a technical concept with real code that implements a real-life requirement. Therefore, we dedicate roughly 40 percent of the book to walking you through hands-on practices that develop sample applications. After a practice that introduces you to JSF code in Chapter 9, we spend the rest of Part II guiding you though development of sample applications using JDeveloper, ADF Business Components, ADF Faces, and JSF.

The main application you create in this part of the book contains elements you would usually build into a real-world system. The application consists of five main pages, two of which you will fill with typical query, browse, sort, add, and update capabilities, including LOVs, poplists loaded from tables, and display items. The remaining three pages are stubbed (created without content) so that you can test navigation. You will also add security features to all the pages. Unlike the general instructions provided in the conceptual material of Part I, the practices in Part II provide more detail about the tasks you are completing. Sidebars and additional information paragraphs anticipate questions you might have while completing the development steps.

Chapter 9 follows up on Chapter 5's JSF introduction by walking you through the creation of a basic two-page JSF application that is not connected to a database. The hands-on practice in this chapter provides a gentle introduction to techniques you will use in the rest of this part of the book.

When starting a project, you will use a technique such as structured analysis or use-case modeling to identify the business needs. Then you will make design decisions about the application. Chapter 10 presents some principles and best practices that can help guide your decisions about application design. It also explains the design of the sample application you create in the rest of Part II. A short hands-on practice at the end of this chapter begins this application development effort.

NOTE
As mentioned throughout the book, completed code for the sample application, as well as some additional features, is provided on the websites mentioned in the "Websites for Sample Code" section later in this introduction. You can use this code to check your work or to view additional techniques not detailed in the book.

In Chapter 11, you begin to fill out the sample application's projects, template, tab menu system, and files for five main pages. Chapter 12 continues the work by adding business components to represent the database objects and by developing a search-and-browse page. The application allows you to navigate from the search-and-browse page to an edit page containing a dropdown list and LOVs (lists of values), which you will develop in Chapter 13.

Chapter 14 explores the basics of a security facility provided by the Oracle Application Server and walks you through adding users, groups, and code to handle security in the application.

It is not our intention in these chapters to provide you with all techniques you will ever need to build applications with similar functionality to Forms applications. Rather, the intention is to guide you through some basic techniques that go far beyond the defaults provided by the JDeveloper wizards. This type of work should make you think about how ADF and the other frameworks work, and this will help you solve programming problems in future projects.

Part III: Additional Techniques

Part III provides some other techniques you can use when developing a web application using JDeveloper. Chapter 15 describes techniques for functionality, such as a common message file, a special filter that adds security to your queries, and how to record the logged-in user name into audit columns in a table. Some of these techniques use a hands-on practice format so that you can add their features to the sample application and test the technique.

To close out the book, Chapter 16 introduces JHeadstart—an add-on to JDeveloper that allows you to generate sophisticated screens with various page flows from the data model. The screens you generate are used as starting points, and, after generating them, you work with the code using the same techniques you learn in the earlier sections of the book.

Subjects Not Discussed in This Book

As mentioned, this book does not intend to provide you with every technique you will ever need when developing an application. We do discuss most of the technology concepts and basic techniques you will require in a real project. However, you will need to refer to other sources for information on other essential topics, such as:

Life Cycle Phases Other Than Development   Although we mention some database and application design principles, the Design phase, along with the Analysis phase of the project life cycle, are not demonstrated or discussed. The book focuses on the Development phase of a typical project.

Deployment Techniques   Deployment is a necessary stage in an application's life cycle. J2EE application files are packaged together into archive files—the web application archive (WAR) file and enterprise application archive (EAR) file—and copied to the application server. JDeveloper contains a robust deployment strategy that consists of a deployment profile file, which you define for a ViewController project. Settings in the deployment profile guide how the EAR file is created. With the proper application server connection, you can even copy the EAR file to the server from the JDeveloper Integrated Development Environment (IDE). This book does not describe this process further, but more information and examples appear in the *Oracle JDeveloper 10g Handbook*, the JDeveloper help system, and online at otn.oracle.com.

Details About the JDeveloper IDE   Chapter 3 explains the main areas of JDeveloper that you will use to create J2EE web applications. However, this book does not intend to introduce all JDeveloper features. By following the hands-on practices, you will have a good idea of how to use the various IDE areas required for J2EE web development.

Should you require more information about other IDE tools and some best practices for using them, the JDeveloper help system contains material introducing various areas of the IDE. Moreover, the JDeveloper 10.1.3 Start Page (**Help | Start Page**) contains a "What's new" link to a web page that explains new features added after version 10.1.2.

In addition, we highly recommend (because we were involved with authoring and the technical reviewing of) the *Oracle 10g JDeveloper Handbook* mentioned before. Although this book describes the first release of JDeveloper 10g, its explanations of the tools available in JDeveloper are still a good introduction to the features of the IDE.

Reporting   Application development is not complete without a reporting system. Some reporting needs can easily be handled by read-only JSF screens that are formatted in a printer-friendly way. ADF Faces provides container components that can assist in the layout, but for the most flexibility, Oracle Reports is our tool of choice. It can output HTML (for on-screen needs) or PDF (for printing needs) and allows you to fulfill the most complex layout needs. Oracle shops that do not use Oracle Reports may already write reports in Oracle Application Express (formerly called "HTML DB") or the PL/SQL Web Toolkit, and they can continue to use those tools for reporting needs.

Third-Party Migration Tools   Chapter 16 introduces JHeadstart. Since some people use JHeadstart to assist with migrating Oracle Forms (or Oracle Designer definitions) to J2EE, Chapter 16 also includes some guidelines for selecting migration tools. However, we do not attempt to compare or recommend migration tools. We realize that circumstances arise where migration tools are required, and can be useful if used correctly. Nonetheless, we firmly believe that building an application from scratch will result in code that is the easiest to maintain and enhance.

Additional Development Tools—Ant, JUnit, and CVS   Development efforts with JDeveloper often employ other tools, such as Ant (ant.apache.org) for building deployment files or running scripts; JUnit (www.junit.org) for testing Java code; and CVS (www.nongnu.org/cvs) for software configuration and source control management. These (and many other) useful tools integrate well with JDeveloper and complement its features; in fact, the authors used JUnit and CVS for developing the sample application in Part II. However, this book contains no specific discussion of features or techniques for these tools.

NOTE
JDeveloper supports team development work better now than ever before, and source control products such as CVS are tightly integrated with the JDeveloper IDE.

A Complete Sample Application   Although the hands-on practices in Part II take you through development techniques for some of the most common types of screens—query, browse, add, delete, and edit, with security features—you will need many more techniques to complete a real enterprise-level application. As mentioned, some of these additional techniques appear in Chapter 15, on the sample code websites, and on otn.oracle.com. For a more complete sample application, look for SR Demo on OTN or in the Check for Updates list in JDeveloper.

Web Application System Development Life Cycle (SDLC)   This book focuses on the Development phase of a full SDLC. Along the way, it provides tips and best practices for work you would perform in the Design phase, and many of the techniques you learn in the book will guide how you design your application. However, other than this implied support, the selection and design of an SDLC for a web application project is beyond the scope pf this book.

Getting the Most Out of This Book

The chapters in this book are intended to be read in a sequential order. We have included material that we think will help you when developing J2EE web applications and think you will gain something from each chapter.

However, we realize that you may need information about a certain subject before reviewing the entire book. You can find subjects in the book using the following features:

- Contents
- Index
- Questions in the beginning of the Part I chapters
- List of phases and sections in the hands-on practice chapters

You may be able to skim through a chapter that addresses a subject already within your comfort zone. For example, if you have a working knowledge of Java language basics, scan through that material in Chapter 4 and pay attention only to information about any unfamiliar languages that the chapter describes.

Following the Hands-On Practices

We highly recommend that you perform the steps in the hands-on practices in Part II using JDeveloper 10.1.3. Although these chapters contain some standalone explanations, merely reading them will provide minimal benefit. The hands-on practices provide experience with concepts introduced in Part I, and new and more detailed concepts are provided in the practices. Therefore, it is useful to stop and read these concepts embedded inside the hands-on practices so that you can have a context for the task at hand.

CAUTION
The material in this book has been tested with build 3673 (the first production release) and all service updates up to and including Service Update 4. If you are using a later version of JDeveloper 10.1.3, you may need to adjust some of the instructions, although the principles and best practices should remain accurate.

Preparing for the Hands-On Practices

You will need JDeveloper and access to sample HR schema, as described next.

Installing JDeveloper

You will need to install JDeveloper 10.1.3 (production build 3673 or later). For computers running Windows, navigate to the JDeveloper home page at www.oracle.com/technology/products/jdev and find the download link. For Windows, download the Studio Edition, complete installation version for your operating system; this version includes the Java Development Kit that is compatible with this release of JDeveloper.

NOTE
To install JDeveloper on operating systems other than Windows, refer to the install guides available after navigating to the JDeveloper download page.

JDeveloper's installation does not use Oracle Installer. After you have downloaded the archive file, unzip it into a local directory (for example, C:\JDev1013 in a Windows operating system). Be sure the directory name does not contain spaces; this can cause problems when deploying applications.

We call this directory *JDEV_HOME* throughout the book because its location may be different on your computer.

TIP
After installing JDeveloper, create a shortcut on your desktop or taskbar toolbar to the JDeveloper executable, jdeveloper.exe, located in JDEV_HOME. This will allow you to start up JDeveloper quickly and easily.

JDeveloper System Requirements

The file JDEV_HOME\jdev\install.html describes system requirements. Oracle recommends running JDeveloper in one of the following operating systems: Windows XP (SP 2), 2000 (SP 4), and NT (SP 6a); Red Hat Enterprise Linux 3.0; or Mac OS X 10.4.x (dual CPU) operating system. As with most software, the more memory you have, the better, but the recommendation is at least 1 GB (2 GB for Mac OS X). If you are running a database on the same computer as JDeveloper, add the database's requirements to those numbers. JDeveloper Studio Edition requires about 500 MB of hard disk space.

It is always useful to review the Release Notes for any Oracle product for known limitations and issues. JDeveloper is no exception. You can access the Release Notes in the file JDEV_HOME\jdev\readme.html.

NOTE
This book was prepared with and provides examples in the Microsoft Windows operating system. If you run JDeveloper on another operating system, you will need to translate the instructions (particularly about file directory access) to that other operating system. In addition, we tested the code with the latest versions of Microsoft Internet Explorer and Mozilla Firefox browsers.

Accessing the Sample Database Schema

Although JDeveloper supports connecting to any database with a JDBC driver, we focus on some specific features of the Oracle database. This book builds examples using database objects installed in the HR schema of an Oracle9*i* or Oracle 10*g* database. Oracle8*i* also offers the HR schema, but its tables are slightly different. Should you not have access to the HR schema, you can download an installation script from the sample code websites. In later versions of the database, the HR schema is locked and you (or a DBA) will need to unlock it (using the SQL statement "ALTER USER hr ACCOUNT UNLOCK;").

If you do not have access to an Oracle database and would like to install one on a desktop or other computer for non-production purposes, we highly recommend Oracle 10*g* Express Edition. Oracle 10*g* Express Edition is available in a production version from OTN (www.oracle.com/technology/products/database/xe). This database is limited to 4 GB of data (1 GB for database memory), and the HR schema is preinstalled with the database.

NOTE
Should you need to run Oracle 10g Express Edition on the same computer as JDeveloper, read its requirements (in the readme file on otn.oracle.com) to be sure your hardware can handle the additional load gracefully. Also, be sure your operating system is supported.

Ensuring Success with the Hands-On Practices

Your experience with development in the hands-on practices should be trouble-free. However, it is possible that you will run into problems that are not easy to debug. Although problems are a natural part of any development effort, and solving problems that arise is an excellent learning tool, we want you to ultimately be successful in completing the practices. Therefore, we offer the following tips:

Test the Application when the Instructions Indicate   If you run into a problem, backtrack through the steps you followed after the last successful run, and look for typos or missed techniques.

Slow Down   We have found ourselves, at times, wanting to quickly complete an exercise. However, in this haste, we miss (or misread) a critical step or part of a step.

Check the Errata   The websites mentioned later in the Introduction in the section "Websites for Sample Code" contain corrections and updates for the practices and other parts of the book. The problem you are experiencing may be documented in the errata.

Debug the Code   Although code that JDeveloper creates is not likely to cause problems, you should check the values of properties you set by typing the values, especially property values with expressions and Java code. In addition, double-check the order and contents of the nodes in the Structure window for the files you are working with. You can compare these with the sample solutions visually in the Structure window or using the comparison utility mentioned next.

Compare Your Code with the Sample Application Files   The sample code websites contain a starting or ending application for each chapter. You can download the working code and compare it with your code using the file comparison utilities available from the right-click menu on a file in the navigator, as shown here:

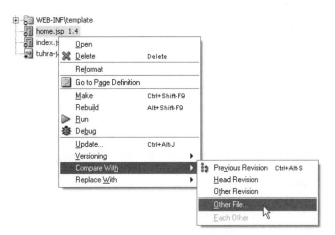

Frequently Back Up the Application Directory   We (and our reviewers) advise that you back up the application directory after a successful test for application functionality (at least at the end of each chapter in Part II, or even after each phase or section that concludes with a test). That way, if you experience problems in a later stage, you can restore the backup and reapply the changes you made after the backup. Use a file manager, such as Microsoft Windows Explorer, to copy the top-level directory (containing the application workspace .jws file and the project subdirectories), and paste it to another location (optionally renaming it to indicate the save point).

Although the practices in Part II are intended to be run sequentially, you can use the sample starting or ending application files to skip chapters. For example, if you wanted to start with the hands-on practice in Chapter 12, you could install the Chapter 11 ending application and use it to work through the steps in Chapter 12.

Authors' Availability

Unfortunately, the authors are not able to help you with problems encountered in the hands-on practices. However, you can use the OTN JDeveloper forum (accessible from the JDeveloper home page) to post questions for the JDeveloper community. This resource is also useful for questions that occur when working in JDeveloper outside of the book.

We intend to post updated files, corrections, and additional techniques on the sample code websites mentioned in the next section.

Websites for Sample Code

Sample files and errata for this book may be found at www.tuhra.com—named after the sample application you develop in Part II of this book called "The Ultimate Human Resources Application" (TUHRA). In addition, the authors' websites contain information about this book and other topics of interest to Oracle developers—ourworld.compuserve.com/homepages/Peter_Koletzke for Peter Koletzke and www.groundside.com/blog/ for Duncan Mills. (Check the tuhra.com website for updates to the authors' website addresses.)

The Downloads page of the McGraw-Hill/Osborne website also hosts sample files for this book—www.oraclepressbooks.com.

Further Study

You will need more information than this book contains to learn fully the subject of application development in JDeveloper. Most developers agree that the best learning experience is gained from focusing efforts on a real development project. Books can help you get started learning about a technology and can serve as one source of reference material for when you get stuck in development. For this extra information, we again point you towards all the sources mentioned before in this Introduction—the JDeveloper help system; the *Oracle JDeveloper 10*g *Handbook*; technical articles, tips, how-to's, forums, and blogs linked from the OTN JDeveloper home page (www.oracle.com/technology/products/jdev); and other sources mentioned in the chapters that follow.

In addition, we strongly urge you to take advantage of information available from independent Oracle user groups. These groups meet at local, regional, national, and international levels. Some offer newsletters or journals in addition to online forums. For example, the Oracle Development Tools User Group (ODTUG, www.odtug.com) offers free electronic mailing lists, conferences, and white papers, all geared towards sharing information gained by experience in business environments. The Independent Oracle Users Group (IOUG, www.ioug.org) also offers key technical tips and contains information about many local Oracle user groups in the Americas. A web search engine will also assist you in finding a group near you.

PART
I

Technology Overviews

*One pill makes you taller
And one pill makes you small
And the ones that mother gave you
Don't do anything at all.
Go ask Alice
When she's ten feet tall.*

—Grace Slick (1939–), *White Rabbit* (1967)

CHAPTER
1

J2EE Basics

What has been is what will be,
And what has been done is what will be done;
There is nothing new under the sun.
Is there a thing of which it is said, "See, this is new?"
It has already been, in the ages before us.

                                         —Ecclesiastes 1:9–10

n recent times, IT organizations have been tasked more and more with charting a course for writing new applications and migrating existing applications to a Java 2 Platform, Enterprise Edition (J2EE) environment. On the surface, this task might seem to be a matter of using predetermined methods, as was the case with the migration to client/server technology. However, one major aspect of J2EE is its variety and breadth. There is no one way to create a J2EE system; in fact, there are probably hundreds of combinations of J2EE technologies that could serve any one purpose. This makes the decision of selecting the proper technology combination daunting, especially if the J2EE environment is new to the organization.

When making a decision, you need to collect as much information about the choices as possible. Information about J2EE is certainly prominent in the Oracle world, as it is across the IT industry. However, information about what J2EE actually consists of is rare. Literature available in trade publications and on the Web often assumes that the reader is familiar with at least some of the J2EE basics and buzzwords. Grasping these basics is essential to assimilating and understanding any specific J2EE technology. In turn, understanding the technologies will help in making the decisions needed to collect these technologies into the proper environment for a particular application, as well as in the work performed during development of the application.

This part of the book provides overviews of the technology concepts you will need to know when developing J2EE web applications. It starts in this chapter, with an explanation of the J2EE basics and the main technologies that it offers for implementing database applications. Chapter 2 fills in the picture by explaining how the Hypertext Transfer Protocol (HTTP) communication process works in a web application. The next chapter introduces JDeveloper and the features it offers for Rapid Application Development. Chapters 4 and 5 introduce some of the tools you will use to create J2EE web applications in JDeveloper—programming languages including Java and JavaServer Faces technology. This part of the book continues with explanations of the ADF Business Services layer (Chapter 6) and the ADF Model layer (Chapters 7 and 8), which allow you to access database objects and easily represent data in your web applications.

The objective of this chapter is to provide a bit of background in the popular J2EE technologies to prepare you for the details of these technologies discussed in the rest of this book. The discussions in this chapter focus around these questions:

- **What do I need to know about database application architecture?**
- **What is J2EE?**
- **What non-J2EE web technologies are popular in J2EE environments?**

After explaining those foundation subjects in some detail, we will then draw some conclusions by briefly answering the following questions:

- **How do J2EE architectures differ from traditional architectures?**
- **How do I choose between J2EE and Oracle Forms and Reports?**
- **Should I pay attention to .NET?**
- **How does Oracle Forms Services fit into J2EE?**

What Do I Need to Know About Database Application Architecture?

The authors, along with many Oracle technologists, have experienced technology shifts from mainframe to mini-computer, from mini-computer to microcomputer client/server, and from microcomputer client/server (two-tier) to microcomputer multi-tier, as well as its recent variation of web browser clients and web servers. Each shift requires a retooling of decision processes for architectures, system design methodologies, and best practices for development. However, there is a common thread in the architectures that has appeared throughout the years, and it is worth reviewing this common aspect to help understand J2EE architectures.

The main actions in a database system are interacting with the data—inputting and outputting it—and managing the data—storing and serving requests for input and output. Data is kept and managed by a specific program—in the case of relational systems, a *relational database management system* (RDBMS). Users or systems requiring access to the data use another program, the *application* (or interface). The application program recognizes and interprets user input to be sent to the RDBMS and also receives data and message results from the RDBMS. A *communications network* transmits data and messages between the RDBMS and the user access layer. J2EE is no different in these basic characteristics. The difference in technologies through the years has been where (on which computer) the various programs are located and how communication between the computers is provided, as described in the following examples.

NOTE
For the sake of clarity in the examples in this section, the client computers with which the user interacts are described and diagrammed in a singular way, but most enterprise database application systems are set up to serve more than one user simultaneously.

Mainframe   In a *mainframe architecture* (shown in Figure 1-1a), the application program and the database management program often reside on a single computer—the *mainframe*. All processing occurs on that computer. The user interacts with the application program using a *dumb terminal* session. No communication lines are required other than to connect the dumb terminal to the mainframe.

Client/Server   *Client/server* (two-tier) *architecture* divides the processing, as shown in Figure 1-1b. The application program resides on a client's desktop computer (often a microcomputer). The database management program resides on a centralized server computer, and a communications network connects the database server with all client computers. Application processing occurs on the client computer; data management processing occurs on the database server.

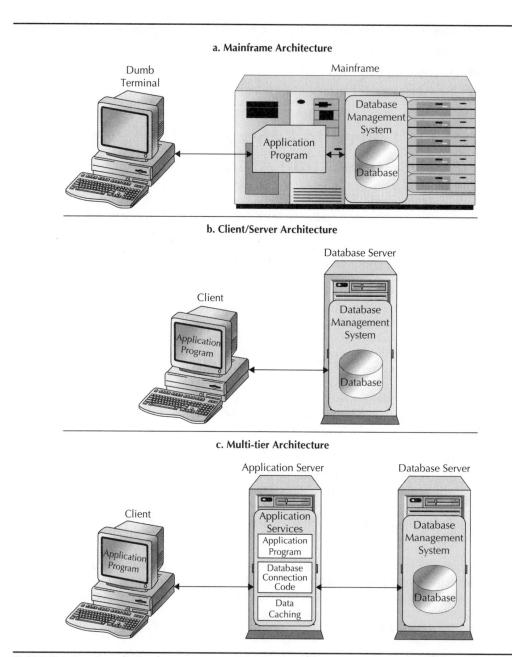

FIGURE 1-1.   *Sample database system architectures*

Multi-Tier   A *multi-tier architecture* places program components on different computers, each of which is a *tier*, that is, a location for a specific type of processing. Figure 1-1c shows a sample multi-tier architecture. This architecture is also called *n-tier*, because, unlike client/server, which always runs programs on only two tiers (client and server), multi-tier systems can operate on any number of computers. In the example shown in Figure 1-1c, the client computer runs part of an application program that communicates with application services running on an application server.

The application services consist of parts of the application that can be shared among programs and among client users—for example, code to manage and maintain connections to the database server, as well as data-caching software that offloads processing from the database for frequently accessed data.

The database server operates the same type of database management system as in the other architectures. The only difference is that the database server communicates with the application server (*middle tier*) programs, not directly with the client computer.

Oracle Forms Services (Oracle Forms 9*i* and later versions running on the Web) is an example of a multi-tier architecture. The client runs inside a web browser; the application code runs mainly on the application server (but partially on the client); and the application server communicates with the database server.

If these concepts are not new, you already have a basis for understanding J2EE architectures. J2EE offers the same types of architectures, variations on familiar architectures, and new architectures. Before discussing how J2EE architectures differ from those just described, a discussion of the J2EE basics is in order.

NOTE
Multi-tier environments often separate the web server, which handles requests from web clients and returns results to those clients, and the application server, which runs the application code.

What Is J2EE?

Java 2 Platform, Enterprise Edition (J2EE) is a set of standards and specifications (called a *platform*) created and maintained by Sun Microsystems. It is not a product. This means that vendors can create a J2EE-compliant product by implementing the J2EE specifications. As the *enterprise platform*, J2EE describes components for software applications intended to serve an entire organization. Two other platforms describe architectures and technologies used for applications running in different environments:

- *Java 2 Platform, Micro Edition* (J2ME) describes components used for applications that run on small, portable devices that have minimal memory, such as cell phones or personal digital assistants (PDAs).

- *Java 2 Platform, Standard Edition* (J2SE) describes components used for applications running on a desktop computer. This platform also includes the Java language distributed as the *J2SE Development Kit* (JDK).

J2EE contains all components in J2SE, such as the Java language. The additional functionality that J2EE adds to J2SE is in the realm of multi-tier deployment and web technology. This makes J2EE popular with organizations that need to develop applications that will be run on the Web.

J2EE and Java EE 5

The "Java 2" part of J2EE refers to versions 1.2 through 1.4 of the language. The last version of J2EE was version 1.4. At this writing, a new Java platform specification was recently ratified by the *Java*

Community Process (JCP)—the means by which new and revised features and technologies are added to the Java realm. The Java language is in production in version 1.5 (also called 5.0) and the platform specification (formerly called "J2EE") has been renamed to "Java EE 5." The industry will take some time to adopt this new moniker. In addition, JDeveloper 10.1.3 is certified for creating any type of J2EE 1.4 code (in addition to some Java EE 5 code, such as JavaServer Faces). This book refers to the enterprise Java platform as "J2EE" throughout.

TIP
To track the progress of any JCP, look on the jcp.org website.

J2EE Parts

J2EE is comprised of the following parts:

- **The Java platform**   This part of J2EE defines the environment under which various components used to create application solutions run (java.sun.com/j2ee/).

- **The Compatibility Test Suite (CTS)**   You can verify that a particular product or application complies with J2EE standards by running compatibility tests. You can use one of the tests, the *Application Verification Kit* (AVK), to check your application's J2EE compatibility (java.sun.com/j2ee/verified/).

- **A reference implementation**   This part of J2EE supplies code that uses J2EE-compatible components and standards. You can use this code to assist in writing parts of your application (java.sun.com/j2ee/sdk_1.2.1).

- **BluePrints**   This part of J2EE supplies a set of best practices and guidelines for various uses of Java—for example, enterprise applications, web services, and performance tuning (java.sun.com/blueprints).

In addition to high-level best practices, BluePrints also offers *design patterns,* low-level code solutions for solving common problems. Model-View-Controller (MVC) is a popular design pattern that is used extensively in Oracle Application Development Framework (ADF) and in JDeveloper.

NOTE
"Frameworks" are high-level architectures focused on providing a specific service, such as controller code or database access. Frameworks usually consist of code libraries, a development method, and tools to assist in creating code for that service. Chapter 3 describes frameworks in more detail.

Model-View-Controller

Model-View-Controller is a frequently used design pattern (originally developed for Smalltalk, an object-oriented programming language) that defines a separation of application code into three layers, as shown here.

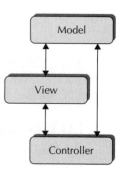

- **Model** The Model layer defines and validates the data used by the application. It includes code to validate business rules and to communicate data to and from the database. It interacts with the View layer to notify it of changes in the data. It interacts with the Controller layer by receiving and processing requests to update data in the application.

- **View** The View layer provides the user interface that displays data from the Model layer. It interacts with the Controller layer by receiving requests for a specific view (page) and by sending it user events (for example, a button press).

- **Controller** Code in the Controller layer determines what happens after a user event in the View layer. It interacts with the View layer to request a page; it sends requests to the Model layer when data needs to be updated. The Controller layer determines *page flow*—the definition of which page in the View layer will appear after a certain data or user event.

The intention of MVC is to allow the code that implements a particular area of the application to be reused by many implementations of another area. For example, you could use the same Model code to supply data to a desktop web browser application, as well as to an application displayed on a cell phone. These two display devices might not be able to share the Controller layer, but reusing just the Model layer code can save a great deal of work and many maintenance worries. Whatever the level of reuse possible between layers, MVC is still a valid guide.

Other than the MVC design pattern, the J2EE platform is the most important, most frequently used, and most referenced part of J2EE; therefore, it is important to understand it in a bit more depth.

J2EE Platform

Although J2EE is not a product, it defines components that are software products and technologies. When you use J2EE to guide your application, you assemble these components into a software and hardware architecture solution.

JRE and JVM

The Java runtime, called the *Java Runtime Environment* (JRE), consists of an executable file (such as java.exe) and a number of library files, which it requires to interpret and run the code in an application. A *Java Virtual Machine* (JVM) refers to both the executable file and to an instance of this executable running as an operating system process. Sometimes, the terms "JRE" and "JVM" are used interchangeably to refer to a Java runtime process.

Component Architecture

To understand some of the popular components and how they are assembled into a complete solution, it is necessary to understand the J2EE component architecture. Each component fits into a *tier*, or layer, of this architecture. Often, a tier represents a single computer (or multiple computers in a distributed processing or grid system), but more than one tier can also exist on a single computer. J2EE components are divided into the following four tiers:

Client Tier User interface code runs on this tier (usually a desktop computer or mobile client device). A web browser displays a Hypertext Markup Language (HTML) user interface, or a JVM presents the interface. These interfaces interact with the user.

Web Tier The Web Tier runs user interface code on a remote server. This tier is responsible for running application code inside a JVM and outputting user interface code (such as HTML) to the Client Tier device.

NOTE
HTML was created so that plain-text files displayed in a web browser could be formatted with colors, fonts, graphics, and links to other pages. HTML also contains a set of user interface controls, such as fields and forms, so that information can be sent to the application server for processing. Chapter 5 describes HTML in more detail.

Business Tier   A JVM on this tier runs validation and business logic code, as well as code that accesses the database. It connects the Web Tier or Client Tier to the Enterprise Information System (EIS) Tier.

EIS Tier   The EIS Tier represents the database for business data. The EIS Tier also represents pre-existing database applications that are out of J2EE's scope. This book assumes that you are using a single Oracle database, but that database could be distributed across a grid or a series of servers. The sidebar "Accessing the Database with JDBC" describes briefly how this kind of database access is accomplished.

NOTE
You can create code in JDeveloper to access any database that offers a JDBC driver.

Popular Component Assemblies

Instead of offering a laundry list of the components of the J2EE component architecture, it is more useful to examine the components in context of how they are assembled into the following styles of code:

- **Application client**   The application's JVM runs on the client computer.
- **Web client**   The application's JVM runs on a J2EE (application) server.

The discussion of these solutions assumes, and therefore does not further discuss, an EIS Tier supplied by an Oracle database. The main discussion will be about the other three tiers. All examples show one of two types of components in the Business Tier: Enterprise JavaBeans or ADF Business Components.

Accessing the Database with JDBC
Java Database Connectivity (JDBC) is a library of Java classes included with the JDK that allows you to easily access a relational database from a Java program in the same way that SQL*Net allows easy access to the database from an Oracle Forms (or other client) application. You do not need to use SQL*Net if you are using JDBC.

JDBC is the most frequently used database access method because it is implemented in Java class files and, therefore, allows you to embed standard SQL inside Java code. JDBC is defined in the J2EE specifications but many frameworks have been built on top of JDBC to make it easier to use.

Enterprise JavaBeans   *Enterprise JavaBeans* (EJBs) are Java class files that provide access, through JDBC, to specific database objects, such as tables or database views, located on the Business Tier. They can be used for validation and other business rules code and, in this way, are an alternative to running business logic in the database. EJBs are another J2EE standard and are used heavily by Java developers.

NOTE
EJBs are discussed more in Chapter 3.

ADF Business Components   ADF in JDeveloper offers an alternative to EJBs: *ADF Business Components* (ADF BC), which also supply access, through JDBC, to database objects. ADF BC was invented and developed by Oracle. Although it was written using J2EE design patterns, ADF BC offers some powerful advantages to EJBs, and ADF in JDeveloper is oriented towards using ADF BC. Therefore, we focus on ADF BC for our examples in this book. ADF BC fits into the Business Tier because it offers a place for validation and business rule code, as well as access to database objects. ADF BC has no client interface, so, in addition to creating ADF BC code, you need to create code for the Client Tier. Chapter 6 discusses ADF BC in more detail.

Application Client

The *application client* coding style runs Java application code in the Client Tier. J2EE defines two types of clients that run in the Client Tier: Java applications and applets.

Java Applications   A *Java application* (also known in the Java world as an *application*) consists of compiled Java code that runs in a JVM on the client computer. The Java runtime code and the compiled Java application files must be installed on the client computer (or on a network computer accessible by the client computer). Figure 1-2 shows this component in the J2EE tiers. In this application client example, the application program running in the JVM on the Client Tier communicates with Enterprise JavaBeans on the Business Tier. The EJBs supply business rules logic and the JDBC connection to the EIS Tier database.

EJBs are shown on the Business Tier, which is often on an application server computer; locating the EJBs on a separate server allows multiple client applications (and multiple users) to access the same code. Alternatively, this code could be placed on the client computer. In this situation, J2EE Client Tier and Business Tier code would reside on the client computer and the computer architecture would be two-tier (client/server)—the same as Oracle Forms code running in client/server (non-web) mode.

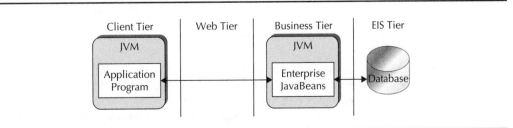

FIGURE 1-2.   *J2EE application client architecture*

Windowed Java applications are written using code objects derived from the Java *Swing* library such as panels, text fields, labels, pulldown lists, and checkboxes that result in a standard Windows look and feel, as shown next. JDeveloper is another example of a fully featured Java application.

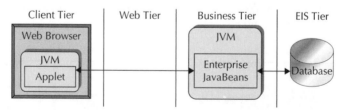

A Java application is useful when the system requires highly interactive and controllable user-interface components that offer immediate event processing and design-time support. Swing is a standard J2SE UI component library, but other third-party libraries also offer this type of control set. The number of properties and events you can modify for these controls is similar to the controls used in the Oracle Forms environment.

NOTE
Another Sun Microsystems technology, "Java Web Start," allows you to distribute application code from an application server to the client. This eases the burden of installing the application code manually on each client computer. The client installs Java Web Start using a link in a browser window. Java Web Start then downloads and installs the Java application code. After this installation, the application can be run as a normal Java application, without using a web browser.

Applets   An *applet* is a Java program running on the Client Tier within the JVM of a web browser, as shown in the J2EE tiers here:

Client Tier	Web Tier	Business Tier	EIS Tier
Web Browser — JVM — Applet		JVM — Enterprise JavaBeans	Database

An applet can be displayed as a window embedded inside the browser's window; it can also be displayed as a separate window that is part of the browser session. Applets use the same highly interactive controls (for example, those from the Swing library) as Java applications, and their appearance and behavior is the same as Java applications written using those controls.

An applet and its supporting libraries need to be installed on the client computer. It is started when the user issues a Hypertext Transfer Protocol (HTTP) request using a web browser HTML control, such as a link or button. The request is for the web server to return an HTML page to the browser. The HTML page contains an APPLET tag that signals the browser to open a JVM session. The APPLET tag also includes a reference to the Java applet file that the session will run. If the Java applet file does not exist on the client computer, it is downloaded from the application server. Then, the JVM takes control and runs the applet.

Both Java applications and applets access compiled Java files on the client and run them in a JVM on the client. The main difference between Java applications and applets is that an applet runs in a web browser session. If the web browser session is closed, the applet closes.

One benefit of using applets is that you can distribute the application code centrally on a web server; all clients will download the application code if it does not already exist. (Applets can also be distributed using Java Web Start.) One drawback of applets is that they run in the browser session, which normally cannot read and write to the client computer file system. Security signature files allow client file system access to occur, but this is viewed by some organizations as a potential security risk because a program distributed from the Web in this way can access the local, and perhaps the network, file systems. Applications that use applet technology are, therefore, prohibited in some locations.

This book focuses on developing web applications, so methods for designing and developing Java applications and applets are not discussed further.

Web Client

A J2EE *web client* presents an interface on the Client Tier and runs application code in the Web Tier. For example, an application can execute Java code on an application server; this application code queries or otherwise interacts with the Business Tier for data needs; it then assembles an HTML page and returns it to a web browser. The user interacts with the browser page and sends data access and update requests to the application running on the application server. This is another example of J2EE multi-tier server architecture: the Client Tier runs a web browser on the client's desktop (or mobile) computer, and the Web Tier runs the application code, as depicted in Figure 1-3.

Running application code on a centralized server offers easier maintenance than the application client, because the application is located on a central server and it can be updated or patched in one location. Clients access a single installation, so there is no requirement to maintain client-side installations other than the web browser. This architectural style places the burden of processing on the application server, but as the number of application users grows, servers can be added or upgraded to handle the increased load.

One limitation to web client architecture is its controls—elements defined using HTML. Although HTML offers basic user interface controls, such as text fields, buttons, checkboxes, pulldown lists, and radio button groups, the range of controls does not match those offered by the application client.

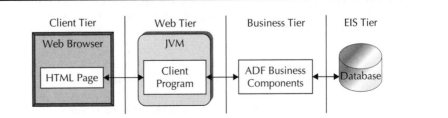

FIGURE 1-3. *J2EE web client architecture*

For example, the Swing library available for application clients includes hierarchical tree, grid (table), slider, menu, and other controls that are not native controls in HTML. The default rendering of HTML elements is basic, although you can apply colors, fonts, and sizes to change this default. For example, a page with a default table, heading, and text might appear as follows:

Job History

| First | Previous | Next | Last |

EmployeeId	101
StartDate	1989-09-21
EndDate	1993-10-27
JobId	AC_ACCOUNT
DepartmentId	110

You could apply color, font, and border attributes and make the same elements appear as follows:

Job History

| First | Previous | Next | Last |

EmployeeId	101
StartDate	1989-09-21
EndDate	1993-10-27
JobId	AC_ACCOUNT
DepartmentId	110

Another limitation of the HTML control set is the limited event model. For example, while application client Swing controls can capture and interpret keypress and button-click events within the client session, by default, user interactions with web client controls are interpreted only when the page is submitted to the server. The use of JavaScript within an HTML page can mitigate this limitation, because JavaScript can run procedural operations in an HTML page without server submits. Chapter 5 explains JavaScript a bit further.

As is true of the J2EE application client, a number of web client technologies offer alternatives for coding and functionality. The two main J2EE alternatives are servlets and JavaServer Pages (JSPs).

All of these technologies fill the role of the client program, as depicted in Figure 1-3. Before examining these technologies in more detail, it is necessary to introduce the web client runtime environment that is supplied in general by J2EE containers and specifically within the Oracle Application Server by Oracle Application Server Containers for J2EE (OC4J).

NOTE
Much of the discussion in this book concentrates on how to write programs that output to a web browser. Most of the technologies are capable of output to other devices, such as PDAs and cell phones. A switch in client hardware usually requires modification of the code, however.

J2EE Containers   J2EE services called *containers* provide the ability for the code in a component to run on a server. The Web Tier and Business Tier code runs inside JVMs located on a remote server (an *application server*). Thus, the *Web Tier container* is basically a JVM on an application server that is customized to run Web Tier components. Similarly, the *Business Tier container* is also a JVM on an application server that runs Business Tier components such as EJBs. J2EE-compliant application server programs, such as Oracle Application Server 10*g*, must supply these container processes as standard features. In addition to runtime services, these containers offer services such as connection pooling (so that many clients can share the same database connection) and transaction support (so that database commit and rollback operations can be associated with a particular user session).

Oracle Application Server Containers for J2EE (OC4J)   *Oracle Application Server Containers for J2EE* (OC4J), originally called *Oracle Containers for J2EE*, supplies J2EE-compatible container services to the Oracle Application Server. OC4J runs within the Oracle Application Server environment, but can also be run as a standalone server. JDeveloper includes a copy of OC4J with which you can run web client applications inside of JDeveloper. This copy can also be started as a standalone process outside of JDeveloper.

Servlet   In general, a *servlet* is a program that extends the capabilities of a server. In the case of J2EE code, the term "servlet" usually refers to an *HTTP servlet* that extends the capabilities of an HTTP server. You can use *back-end servlets* to perform server-level operations that do not interact with or display to the user. The examples in this chapter are servlets used for user interfaces. The following shows how this process works:

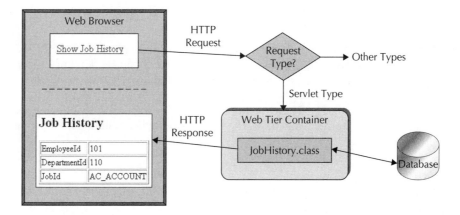

An HTTP server receives a request for content or processing, the *HTTP request*, from a client, such as a web browser. The request is transmitted from the client through the network using the HTTP protocol. A standard HTTP request causes the server to find a resource such as an HTML page in the file system and return it to the web browser (as an *HTTP response*). (Chapter 2 discusses details of this exchange.) If the request is not for an HTML page or other standard resource, the server interprets the HTTP request and determines (by the directory or file name) what type of file it should process. If the request is for a servlet, the Client Tier container on the server runs a Java program (the servlet) that assembles the page dynamically based on parameters sent in the request. The Java program can then query and send data to the database and format the resulting data or message into the HTTP response—in this case, an HTML page.

The servlet is coded in pure Java. That is, all code is contained in a Java class file that is compiled and available in the file system of the server. Java class files use a .java extension for the source code and a .class extension for the compiled, runtime code. The Java class file can contain database access code as well as print statements that will be output to the HTTP stream (and that eventually will be rendered in the web browser). For example, the following code snippet might appear in a servlet:

```java
out.println("<html><body>");
out.println("  <h2>Job History</h2>");
out.println("  <table border='1'>");
out.println("    <tr><td>");
out.println("      EmployeeId");
out.println("    </td><td>");
out.println(getJobHistoryEmployeeId());
out.println("    </td></tr><tr><td>");
out.println("      DepartmentId");
out.println("    </td><td>");
out.println(getJobHistoryDepartmentId());
out.println("    </td></tr><tr><td>");
out.println("      JobId");
out.println("    </td><td>");
out.println(getJobHistoryJobId());
out.println("    </td></tr>");
out.println("  </table>");
out.println("</body></html>");
```

This code would send each print statement to the HTTP response stream. Since Java is a full-featured programming language, the Java file can contain any kind of logic to manipulate the data and the page. Three lines in this example include calls to Java methods in the servlet file: `getJobHistoryEmployeeId()`, `getJobHistoryDepartmentId()`, and `getJobHistoryJobId()`. These methods are simplified versions of code in a servlet that would retrieve data from the database. The servlet would then output the following HTML to the browser:

```html
<html><body>
   <h2>Job History</h2>
   <table border='1'>
     <tr><td>
       EmployeeId
     </td><td>
101
     </td></tr><tr><td>
       DepartmentId
     </td><td>
110
     </td></tr><tr><td>
       JobId
     </td><td>
```

```
AC_ACCOUNT
     </td></tr>
  </table>
</body></html>
```

The browser would render this HTML as shown in the previous illustration.

In summary, servlets are written in Java, run in a container (JVM) on the server, and output HTML to the browser.

JavaServer Pages   *JavaServer Pages* (JSP) technology is a variation on servlet technology. A *JSP page* is a web client file that is written in a combination of HTML and JSP tags. It is saved in a file with a .jsp extension; an HTTP request to the application server that contains this extension indicates that the file should be processed as a JSP page. JSP page processing is demonstrated in the following illustration:

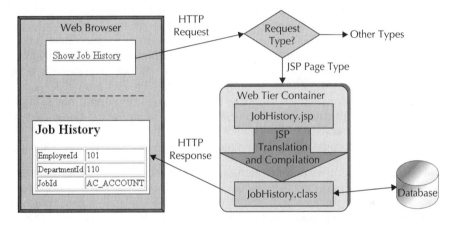

The communication flows are similar to those of a servlet. As with the servlet, the web server runs the JSP file in the Web Tier container. The first time a JSP page is run on a server, the Web Tier container converts it to a servlet file (.java) in a process called *JSP translation*. It then compiles the servlet file into a .class file. Once the .class file is available on the server, it can be run for future requests from any client without the translation and compilation processes. If the .jsp file is changed and copied to the server, the server will sense that the .jsp file is out of sync with the .class file and will translate and compile it into a new .class file.

Then, the .class file is run in the same way as a normal servlet, because it is a normal servlet at that point in the process. The only difference between servlets and JSP pages is the additional JSP translation process and the style of code. JSP source code contains a mixture of HTML tags and JSP tags. For example, the JSP source code that would create the same HTML code as the example servlet shown before would be this:

```
<html><body>
  <h2>Job History</h2>
  <table border="1">
    <tr><td>
      EmployeeId
```

```
  </td><td>
    <%= getJobHistoryEmployeeId() %>
  </td></tr><tr><td>
    DepartmentId
  </td><td>
    <%= getJobHistoryDepartmentId() %>
  </td></tr><tr><td>
    JobId
  </td><td>
    <%= getJobHistoryJobId() %>
  </td></tr>
</table>
</body></html>
```

This source code is not that much different from the servlet's HTML result. HTML elements are coded in the JSP file without print statements. The JSP translator wraps the HTML tags in print statements when it creates the servlet file. JSP coding style is different from the servlet use of pure Java because of these raw HTML tags. It is also different from a static HTML page because it contains dynamic, Java-like elements, such as the lines containing the method calls to obtain data from the database. The JSP specification defines standard JSP tags. You can also write Java class files to implement the custom functionality that you need to call from a JSP page. You then declare the files as a *tag library*, a set of files that is cataloged in an XML file called a *tag library descriptor* (.tld file). After including in the JSP code a reference to the tag library descriptor, you can then use these custom tags.

Other than HTML tags, a JSP file can contain the following standard JSP elements:

- **Directives** A *directive* affects the structure of the servlet code; it uses the delimiters "<%@ %>". Three directives are available: *page* (to supply file-level commands, such as code imports for the class), *include* (to cause elements from another file to be embedded inside the current page), and *taglib* (to specify the location, name, and alias of a tag library). Here is an example:

  ```
  <%@ taglib uri="/WEB-INF/struts-html.tld" prefix="html"%>
  ```

- **Actions** *Actions* use the syntax "<*prefix: tagname*>" where "prefix" is the name given the tag library in the taglib directive for the JSP page, and "tagname" is the name of the tag you are calling from that tag library. Actions allow you to call code written in another Java class file from the JSP file. Custom tags that you or a third party has written are action tags. The following is an example that calls a tag, "form," in the tag library referred to by the prefix "html."

  ```
  <html:form action="/locDP.do">
  ```

  The JSP page would also contain the taglib directive shown in the previous example to define the prefix.

- **Scripting elements** *Scripting elements* are snippets of Java code that you can embed inside the JSP file. They can supply logical processing inside the JSP page. Three types of scripting elements are available:

  - **Scriptlets** *Scriptlets* are excerpts of Java code logic that are embedded directly in a tag. The scriptlet appears inside "<% %>" tag delimiters. For example, to print a message conditionally, you would code the following:

```
<% if (getEmployeeId() == 101)
    { out.print('Employee 101');
    } %>
```

■ **Expressions** In the earlier example, the result of a method call is displayed in the HTML output using an expression tag ("<%= %>"). An *expression* will be placed inside a print statement in the servlet so you can place in an expression any Java code that you would place in the argument of a print statement, such as the following:

```
<%= "The employee ID is " + getEmployeeId() %>
```

■ **Declarations** *Declarations* contain code snippets that you need to call from within a scriptlet or expression. They are delimited with "<%! %>" characters. For example, you could code in a declaration the getEmployeeId() method in the previous example. It would then be available to the other scripting tags. You can also declare variables that are required throughout the JSP page, for example:

```
<%! int empStartingSalary; %>
```

Currently, most J2EE experts agree that overuse of scripting elements in the JSP page can make the code less reusable and harder to maintain. Therefore, the preference is to use libraries or custom action tags when complex logic is required.

In summary, JSP pages allow you to write code that will translate into a servlet when it is run. The source code makes use of raw HTML tags as well as JSP tags. Many non-Java experts find this style easier to code and work with than servlets.

What Non-J2EE Web Technologies Are Popular in J2EE Environments?

In addition to the J2EE servlet and JavaServer Pages web client alternatives, three other web client user interface technologies are worth mentioning: JavaServer Faces technology, ADF UIX, and ADF Faces. Although they are not part of the J2EE 1.4 specification, they are solid alternatives for creating web-deployed, light-client applications. In later discussions of how to develop web applications, this book provides examples using JSF and the successor to ADF UIX, ADF Faces. In addition, web services provide supplemental functionality for J2EE client and server environments. All of these technologies are worth a brief mention here to round out the view of J2EE basics.

User Interface Technologies

Although JavaServer Faces, ADF UIX, and ADF Faces are not part of the J2EE 1.4 specification, they are J2EE 1.4–compliant and can, therefore, be run in a J2EE 1.4 environment.

JavaServer Faces Technology

JavaServer Faces (JSF) technology is a Sun Microsystems framework that provides View and Controller layer functionality to J2EE applications. Although it was not included with the J2EE 1.4 specification, JSF is part of the new platform specification (Java EE 5), mentioned before. The JSF tag libraries offer components that contain a rich set of properties and events that manage user interactions and the state of the data inside the component. JSF components also include the capability to easily bind the data in the elements to database objects and other data sources.

In addition to these rich components, JSF offers controller classes and tags that manage page flow and handle events to and from the components.

For Oracle Forms developers, JSF tags offer a development model that is more familiar than other J2EE-based technologies—that is, user interface components and the page provide events to which programming code for validation and navigation can be attached. Without a technology such as JSF, events occur at the page level, that is, when the page is submitted to the server, and component-level event handling is limited to the code you add using JavaScript. However, JavaScript is an add-on to HTML that is not well integrated with the controller.

Since JSF tags are usually embedded inside a JSP page, the runtime architecture for JSF is the same as for JSP pages. The difference between JSP pages and JSP pages with JSF is the additional functionality and built-in components, events, and controller code that JSF provides.

NOTE
Chapters 3 and 5 describe JSF technology in more detail.

ADF UIX

ADF UIX (formerly called UIX or User Interface XML) is a user interface framework created by Oracle Corporation. It has been used extensively in the Oracle E-Business Suite self-service applications for over four years. Since ADF UIX is not discussed elsewhere in this book and since it is a basis for ADF Faces, which is used for examples elsewhere in this book, it is appropriate to examine ADF UIX in a bit more depth here.

ADF UIX is coded in XML, in contrast to JSP pages, which are coded using HTML and servlet tags. The XML elements represent Java classes that render HTML elements in the same way as a JSP tag renders HTML elements. ADF UIX offers a well-evolved and rich set of user interface components and other features that allow you to easily implement functionality that is not native to JSP pages, for example:

- **Layouts**   ADF UIX ships with a set of tags that can be used as containers for components. For example, the `pageLayout` tag draws an HTML table with a set of prebuilt areas for various components, such as branding graphics, a tab header, global navigation buttons, a content area, and a copyright area. Including this tag on a UIX page allows you to plug components into those areas without having to worry about how the HTML table cells and rows are drawn around those components.

- **Rich components**   One example from the extensive set of ADF UIX components is `listOfValues`, which you can use as the basis for a popup LOV window. This single component draws a number of user interface items, as shown in the example here:

Search and Select: Employee

      (Cancel) (Select)

Search

Search [   ]
(Go)

Results

      (Cancel) (Select)

The user would enter a query value in the Search field and click Go; query results would appear in the Results area. Then, the user would select a record and click Select to return the value to the screen. This component includes a number of properties that you can use to specify its appearance and behavior (such as *title*, which appears as "Employee" in this example). listOfValues is displayed as a number of HTML tags when the page is run. Implementing this control in a JSP page without a tag library would require coding individual HTML tags, as well as custom code, to handle the action of querying and returning a selection (all of which is built into the UIX control).

■ **Partial page rendering** Several ADF UIX components offer *partial page rendering* (PPR)— a combination of prebuilt JavaScript and frames that allow just a section of the page to be redrawn. A good example of a PPR component is table. This component draws a standard HTML table, but adds column headings that allow the user to click and automatically sort the rows by the values in the column. When sorting in this way or scrolling through sets of records, only the table data area is redrawn. The rest of the page remains static. This results in an interface that can enhance user productivity because the new page is ready more quickly than it would be with a full page redraw.

■ **Automatic graphics file generation** Some components, such as the tabBar, create graphics files when run. This eliminates the need to create and manage separate files for standard decorative elements. The *text* property of the tag specifies the text that will appear on the graphics file. For example, the following code will be rendered as shown in the illustration following it.

```
<tabBar>
  <contents>
    <link text="ADF UIX" destination="http://oracle.com" />
    <link text="ADF Faces" destination="http://oracle.com" selected="true" />
    <link text="JavaServer Faces" destination="http://java.sun.com"/>
  </contents>
</tabBar>
```

The server architecture used for ADF UIX is similar to that used by JSP pages, but ADF UIX pages run under a servlet process, the UIX servlet. The *UIX servlet* is a Java class run inside the Web Tier container; it interprets the ADF UIX XML code, runs the Java class files referenced by ADF UIX tags, and assembles an HTML result page that is sent to the browser.

Since ADF UIX is an Oracle technology, it is not part of the J2EE specification. However, it uses J2EE design patterns, and its successor, ADF Faces, is used as an extension to JSF, which is part of the new J2EE specification.

ADF Faces

ADF Faces is a set of JSF components that add to JSP pages with JSF the same kind of rich user interface controls available in ADF UIX. As mentioned, examples throughout this book use ADF Faces as the underlying technology because ADF Faces is highly integrated with JDeveloper, and the development experience is closer to the experience in Oracle Forms than anything else that has come before.

Most of the ADF UIX controls have ADF Faces equivalents. For example, the `tabBar` control described and shown previously has an ADF Faces equivalent—`menuTabs`. Features such as PPR and automatic graphics file generation have also been rewritten into ADF Faces. ADF Faces components are handled in the same way as all other JSF components, which provides a consistent way to handle both JSF and ADF Faces components. More than 100 ADF Faces components are available including the following:

- **chooseDate** This component displays a control that opens in the same window as the main page. `chooseDate` allows the user to scroll between months in a calendar display and select a date to be returned to a field on the page.

- **selectOrderShuttle** This component displays a *shuttle* control—two text areas filled with selections—that allows the user to select more than one value for a single field. All required headings, graphic buttons, and text areas are built into a single control.

- **menuButtons** This component displays a set of buttons that navigate to another page.

- **panelPage** This container component provides a number of areas that you can use to place other components.

You can think of ADF Faces as being a merge of JSF technology, which supplies the underlying J2EE architecture and development methods, with ADF UIX components, which offer highly evolved and extremely rich user-interface controls.

Web Services

Web services are application components served from a host provider that allow client applications to tap into the provider's data and functions through the Web. For example, Amazon.com offers a web service that allows associates and vendors outside of the company to search its product database. An application created by outside organizations can, among other things, allow users to perform searches on Amazon.com without leaving the organization's application. The Amazon web service provides an ability that the organization's application would otherwise not include or would include only after a great deal of development effort.

Web services have two aspects: server and client. The server aspect requires creating an application that provides the function (such as searching a product database). The provider develops a standard interface to the service so that the service details are easily accessible. The function is then published to a registry so that it can be available to Internet users.

The client aspect of web services consists of application calls to the web service interface. Data is transmitted from the server to the client using a standard protocol. The web service is a black box to the client. That is, the client does not know specifics about how the web service performs the functionality; it only needs to know how to call the service.

Figure 1-4 shows the components and communication flow for a web service. In this diagram, the user's browser sends an HTTP request for the organization's local application. This request is handled by the organization's local application server that runs the local application. The application consists of normal application code that accesses the organization's services and databases in addition to calling the web service to retrieve or modify data from that source. When the web service returns a result, the application combines it with the rest of its data and sends a result back to the browser.

In addition, a web service stub is created in the application code to call the web service. The stub is built using information retrieved at design-time from a descriptor document in the registry.

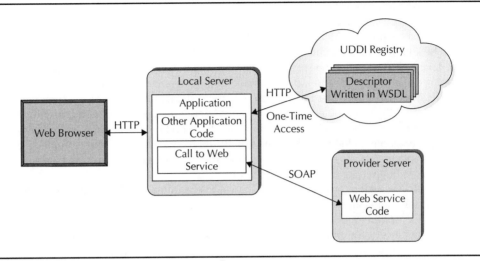

FIGURE 1-4. *Web service communication flow*

Web Services Technologies

4 JAN 08

Universal Description, Discovery and Integration (UDDI) is the registry technology used to hold the web services information. A public UDDI registry, the *UDDI Business Registry* (UBR), holds information about web services available on the Internet. Organizations may also create private UDDI registries that hold web services information for their own and their customers' use. UDDI registries can be likened to telephone yellow page books, because both contain a list of services and a method for accessing those services.

The web services descriptor (API) is written in a standard format using *Web Services Definition Language* (WSDL), an XML language. It contains information about the provider's host, the call interface, and the format in which the data will be returned. The application calls the web service code using *Simple Object Access Protocol* (SOAP)—a lightweight communications protocol used for web services requests and responses in conjunction with HTTP.

How Do J2EE Architectures Differ from Traditional Architectures?

Now that we have discussed traditional database application architectures and details about J2EE, we can draw some conclusions about how J2EE fits into the molds of previous architectures. As discussed earlier in this chapter, the mainframe architecture places the application and data management programs on a central server. The user accesses the application program using a dumb terminal, a computer that collects information input by the user and sends this information to the central computer a block at a time. This model has some similarities to the J2EE web client architecture because very little, if any, processing occurs on the client computer. The client computer is responsible for displaying the application interface assembled by the server and for sending the user's requests to the server on a form-level basis.

The J2EE application client architecture fits into the client/server architecture also discussed earlier in this chapter. The client computer in both models runs the application program and accesses data from a central server that runs the data management system.

The J2EE web client architecture fits into the multi-tier architecture described in the chapter. The J2EE web client relies on some client processing occurring on one tier, application code running on another tier, and a data management program running on a third tier. Multi-tier usually describes three roles for computers in the system: client, application server, and database server. Naturally, a computer system often serves more than one user, so many computers fill the role of the client in this model. In addition, variations on how the application server divides its work (for example, in the J2EE Web Tier and Business Tier) can add more computers to the middle tier. Distributed databases, database links, and grid computing strategies can cause more than one computer to be used for the database server tier.

As this discussion implies, the real answer to the question of how J2EE architecture differs from the traditional architectures is that it really does not differ at all. J2EE architectures fit into the standard computing models that you are likely accustomed to using. The way that code is divided among the tiers in these models may be slightly different, but we can conclude that J2EE web client architectures, at least, are really no different from the traditional multi-tier architecture.

In addition, as web application interface components become more sophisticated (and they have made a large jump in this direction recently with ADF Faces), J2EE web application technologies will be able to serve the highly interactive application styles associated with traditional tools such as Oracle Forms.

How Do I Choose Between J2EE and Oracle Forms and Reports?

The requirement for applications to run on the Web is nearly assumed these days. A lightweight web client (web browser) requires little installation and maintenance on the hardware and software sides. In addition, web browsing is popular and users are quickly able to learn new applications that use a browser front-end. Long gone are the days of special training and manuals, such as *SQL*Forms Operator's Guide* (old Oracle part number 3301), to teach computer operators how to perform system functions using keyboard function keys. The requirement for building a user-friendly, intuitive interface, which took some effort with traditional tools, is handled nearly automatically now. Deploying applications to the Web is common practice.

Applications developed using J2EE web technologies are an alternative to Oracle Forms and Reports applications running on the Web. Since Oracle Forms and Reports are mature products, many Oracle customers have significant amounts of application code and development expertise in these products. They need to be careful when moving to any new environment, especially one that requires retraining and retooling for both infrastructure and development resources.

Oracle's Direction

Oracle's statement of direction for applications built with Oracle Forms and Reports is to move them to the web environment. Although support for Oracle Forms and Reports has no planned ending, Oracle has set a future direction towards J2EE because it offers flexibility, wide industry support, and greatly increased openness. For example, although many Oracle Forms developers invented ways to fill extraordinary requirements, they ultimately ran into a limitation—Oracle Forms design-time and runtime code cannot be modified. In J2EE technologies, the base Java classes that correspond to Oracle Forms runtime are extendable and replaceable. This opens a world of possibilities to the developer.

NOTE
You can find the plan for support of Oracle tools in the statements of direction on otn.oracle.com. These documents change periodically, so it is worthwhile to check the latest statement before making decisions that rely on Oracle tools support. At this writing, the statement of direction for Oracle Forms and Reports states that "Oracle has no plan to desupport these products."

The cost of this type of development derives from the classic difference between working in a 3GL environment, such as those based on Java, and a 4GL environment, such as Oracle Forms. Less work is done by the base runtime in a 3GL, so the developer is responsible for much more code. With Java frameworks (discussed further in Chapter 3), this responsibility is lessened, with little loss of flexibility. With fully featured tools, such as JDeveloper 10.1.3, that assist in generating and managing basic code, the responsibility is lessened even further.

Oracle customers are often satisfied with the functionality of 4GL applications, and they have significant investments in applications built with the traditional Oracle development tools. Applications built with these tools are stable and user-friendly. However, they have some serious drawbacks beyond the client/server and intranet web environments. One of these major drawbacks is that Oracle Forms uses Java applet technology, which requires a Java runtime and an applet viewer (JInitiator) to be installed on the client. Although mechanisms exist to make this requirement manageable, it can be unmanageable with a large Internet user base. Applets also have the security drawback mentioned before, and their use in some environments might be prohibited by an enterprise-level policy.

Although support and development is continuing for Oracle Forms and Reports, Oracle is concentrating on guiding customers towards J2EE and is spending much time and effort on new and competitive features for JDeveloper. This trend is a natural reflection of Oracle's direction towards J2EE for the application server and the database, which are based upon or well integrated with J2EE technologies.

Oracle Forms or J2EE?

The preceding discussion has mentioned both Oracle Forms and Oracle Reports as examples of traditional development environments. However, the considerations for weighing each tool against J2EE alternatives are different. The decision of whether to use Oracle Forms or J2EE forms is more difficult than the decision of whether to use Oracle Reports or J2EE reports. Although Oracle Reports on the Web requires only a browser on the client computer, as do J2EE web applications, Oracle Forms requires a Java runtime and the applet viewer on the client computer.

NOTE
The Oracle Application Server provides robust runtime environments for both Oracle Forms and J2EE applications, and you can definitely run both types of applications simultaneously. The questions in this section apply to decisions you will make for individual applications. Mixing Oracle Forms and J2EE within the same application may require some workarounds and additional coding.

When making the decision whether to use Oracle Forms or J2EE, you need to answer at least the following questions:

Are Users Familiar with Web Browser Applications?   Most users are now accustomed to web browser applications. Even if they do not interact with a web browser for business applications, it is likely they do so outside of the work environment. However, your user base may not have such familiarity, and you will need to plan time for training, as you would for any new environment. If this time or the required training resources are not available, you may be better off creating a traditional-style application that is more familiar to users.

Do I Need to Migrate an Existing Application to J2EE?   If you are considering a new application, you can go on to other questions. If the application does exist and is not deployed to a light client (web browser), you need to first confirm that users will be able to adjust to the new front-end, as just discussed. However, you need to ask why you want to rewrite it in the first place. If the application is written in Oracle Forms, you are not risking nonsupport in the foreseeable future, so moving it to J2EE may not be necessary at this time.

Does the Application Require High Interactivity?   Oracle Forms offers a highly productive data entry environment. Users can quickly enter data and have data validated before committing it. This allows them to quickly enter a large volume of data. Nothing in the web client J2EE stack yet rivals this ability for high-volume data entry. If the application requires this type of high interactivity, Oracle Forms (or a thick J2EE client that uses a Java application or applet) is indicated. As web technologies mature, this type of interactivity will become more possible. For example, features such as the UIX and ADF Faces partial page rendering mentioned before allow the user to scroll through records without refreshing the entire screen.

If universal access and other benefits of thin client applications are more important than high interactivity, a J2EE solution may be appropriate.

Are Your Infrastructure and Development Teams Ready for the J2EE Technology Stack?   If you have already developed applications using J2EE technologies, this answer will most probably be "Yes" and your decision will not need to weigh this factor. However, if this is the first or an early J2EE project, the IT personnel will require training and more time than usual to develop the application.

You will also need to weigh into the budget the costs of training, development and application server software, hardware (for application servers), and loss of staff time while being trained.

If you have an in-house, experienced J2EE expert in the position of architect, that person will be able to spearhead the effort and direct staff, and the project, effectively towards the goal. If you do not have such a person, it might be necessary to hire one as an employee or to use the consulting services of an outside vendor who has experience in bringing Oracle Forms shops into J2EE development. Often, an arrangement that schedules project work close to training is more effective because development staff will be able to use what they learn immediately. It is also helpful to assign an experienced Java architect (employee or consultant) to the role of technical lead, which would include the role of mentor.

NOTE

When leading a group into J2EE, any development tool that can assist in generating code will be helpful. Oracle Consulting offers a product, JHeadstart, that generates a starting set of controller and front-end code files based on database tables. This product can also migrate definitions from an Oracle Designer repository to create J2EE code. Chapter 16 introduces this product and mentions some guidelines that you can use for selecting third-party vendor tools that can create J2EE applications directly from Oracle Forms code.

Is the Application Large, Mission-Critical, or Time-Sensitive?   Actually, most applications are mission-critical, but there are degrees of importance. The application might be mission-critical to a smaller team of IT staff, or it may be mission-critical to a multi-thousand member user organization. The size of an application is relative, but a small application with few screens and a small data model is a better test bed for learning a new technology stack than is a large application. You will then be able to spend more time learning than coding. Also, a smaller application will be faster to rewrite if a wrong direction was taken due to incomplete knowledge of the solution.

Since you will need to incorporate time to learn and absorb new technologies and potentially to set up new servers, the time factor will be greater for the first application that uses J2EE. The amount of time for ramping up on the new technology must be factored into the project. If there is no time for that ramp up, the decision will probably be made to wait on the new technology.

You rarely have a choice of the importance or size of the application, but you might have a choice about when to start using J2EE. A smaller, less widely deployed application will be a better first effort for a team that is not accustomed to J2EE development. If your shop is a traditional Oracle Forms shop, you still might choose Oracle Forms for a mission-critical application with a tight deadline. If you have a small application with a limited number of (hopefully adaptable) users and have time at hand to learn and set up a new environment, J2EE might be indicated.

NOTE

As with any IT decision, you will probably also need to weigh organizational politics and directives from management into the mix when deciding when and how to move to J2EE.

Oracle Reports or J2EE?

J2EE technologies have few alternatives for reporting that match the flexibility and robustness of Oracle Reports. Oracle Reports contains features for exact placement of text that are unrivaled by J2EE alternatives. It also provides multiple output styles (HTML, PDF, Excel, and delimited text) more easily than other tools. Oracle Reports integrates easily with Oracle's J2EE application server; this makes it an automatic choice for organizations that license that server. If the organization does not use Oracle's application server, it would not be using Oracle Forms and Reports, and would probably have its own reporting solution in place.

Naturally, the question of support needs to be answered for Oracle Reports, as it does for Oracle Forms, but the urgency of migration is almost nonexistent because Oracle Reports runs in a lightweight client (web browser) application server environment already. In addition, Oracle does not currently offer a clear J2EE alternative to Oracle Reports as it does for Oracle Forms.

Should I Pay Attention to .NET?

We assume that since you have gotten this far in the book, you have some leaning toward at least exploring the capabilities and coding styles of J2EE. However, you may be curious about or already be considering an alternative offering by Microsoft called .NET.

.NET is a set of standards and architectures published by Microsoft Corporation. It is an alternative to J2EE and does not use J2EE components. .NET has at its core a number of Microsoft products, such as the following:

- **Windows** as the operating system
- **Internet Information Services** (IIS) as the application server
- **SQL Server** for the database
- **Visual Studio** as the development environment for programming languages such as Visual Basic and C#

.NET offers all of the major services and strategies offered by J2EE and is popular in corporations that have a large existing investment in Microsoft products. Oracle products support the use of .NET and several pages on otn.oracle.com discuss using .NET with Oracle products. However, Oracle is not developing mainstream tools or products to create .NET applications. .NET is looked at with caution by those who do not have heavy investments in Microsoft products, because .NET is a single-vendor solution, is less mature, and requires a specific operating system and, therefore, specific hardware.

Java and J2EE are designed to be platform-independent. An attractive benefit of J2EE to an organization is Java's multivendor support. In addition, shops that are heavily invested in the Oracle database prefer J2EE over .NET because of Oracle Corporation's interest in Java as a flexible, cross-platform solution. .NET is still a strong competitor to J2EE, however, and may be the right choice for some IT shops. In addition, as suggested before, the choice of technology sometimes has political motivations instead of purely technical considerations.

How Does Oracle Forms Services Fit into J2EE?

Although the architecture of *Oracle Forms Services* (Oracle Forms running on the Web) does not fit into the standard configurations mentioned in this chapter, it relies solely on mechanisms defined by J2EE to start and run the form. It is deployed in a J2EE application server, run in a J2EE Web Tier container, and displayed through a web browser on the J2EE Client Tier.

Oracle Forms Services contains the Forms Servlet and Forms Listener Servlet, both of which are standard Java servlet files run in the J2EE Web Tier container (OC4J). These servlets are back-end servlets (as mentioned before) configured using standard J2EE property files. The client interface runs within a JVM in the browser session and, therefore, fits into the category of application client (applet) as defined by J2EE. Thus, Oracle Forms Services uses both the Web Tier (the servlets) and the Client Tier (the applet) to run a form. J2EE applications usually run the application code in one of these tiers.

For example, the front-end J2EE servlet architecture mentioned before runs the application in the Web Tier and sends the application's output to a web browser in the Client Tier. In the case of Oracle Forms, the Forms Servlet running on the Web Tier communicates with the applet running in the Client Tier. Therefore, Oracle Forms Services requires both tiers to run the form and, in that respect, its architecture fits into both the J2EE application client and web client styles.

NOTE
Although J2EE applications can be deployed on any J2EE-compliant application server, Oracle Forms Services must be run under the Oracle Application Server.

CHAPTER
2

Web Communications

It is true that I may not find
An opportunity of transmitting it to the world,
But I will not fail to make the endeavor.
At the last moment I will enclose the MS. in a bottle
And cast it within the sea.

—Edgar Allan Poe (1809–1849), *MS. Found in a Bottle*

 ow that you have a basic understanding about the J2EE web environment and web technologies, it is appropriate to introduce how communication is accomplished to and from the web server. Most of the details of this communication are hidden from users. In most situations, these details are also hidden from developers. However, knowing the capabilities and mechanics of the communications to and from the browser will serve you well while you develop and debug web applications.

In computer systems, *communications protocols* are guidelines for formatting the messages sent from one hardware or software component to another. Since effective communications cannot occur without an agreed-upon format, the communications protocol is the key to any successful interaction involving computer systems.

The most important communications protocol for all web applications, including those built in J2EE architectures, is *Hypertext Transfer Protocol* (HTTP). In fact, web servers are HTTP servers, so HTTP is at the heart of the World Wide Web. This chapter presents an overview of HTTP and explains how the communication process works between the client and web server. The chapter addresses these subjects by answering the following questions:

- **How does HTTP work?**
- **What are the steps in a web application roundtrip?**
- **How does Oracle Forms Services use HTTP?**

 NOTE
A web browser is capable of issuing requests in other protocols, such as File Transfer Protocol (FTP), Lightweight Directory Access Protocol (LDAP), mailto, and Hypertext Transfer Protocol Secure (HTTPS). Web servers can only handle HTTP, and sometimes HTTPS, so web applications are written for those protocols.

How Does HTTP Work?

Web applications use HTTP for communications between the client's web browser and the application code running on an application server. As with all communication protocols, a round-trip communication process consists of a request and a response. The *request* (also called an *HTTP request*) is a message asking for resources (such as an HTML page or image file) or an action from another computer. A *response* (also called an *HTTP response*) is a return message from the computer to which a request was sent. These messages often include browser content, such as HTML text or images. Figure 2-1 shows these two messages with some of their contents. Descriptions of the contents of the request and response messages, as well as methods and other features, follow.

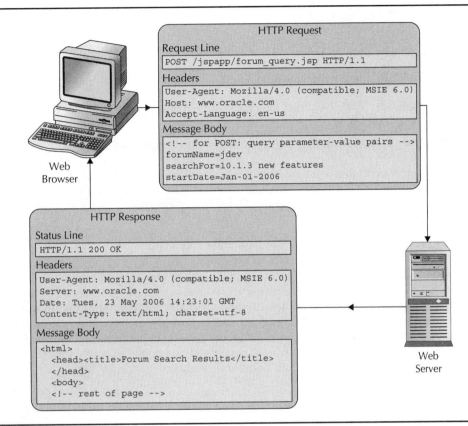

FIGURE 2-1.   *An HTTP communication session*

NOTE
*HTTP uses TCP/IP (Transmission Control Protocol/Internet Protocol).
TCP/IP is a lower-level protocol that defines how the hardware
communicates. When you develop web applications, you interface
with HTTP, not directly with TCP/IP.*

HTTP Request

The browser sends an HTTP request message when the user clicks a link or button on the page or
enters an address in the browser's address (location) field. As shown in Figure 2-1, the request
consists of a request line, headers, and a message body.

NOTE
*A detailed explanation of HTTP appears on the TCP/IP Guide website,
www.tcpipguide.com.*

Request Line

A sample request line follows:

```
POST /app/jobhist.jsp HTTP/1.1
```

This example consists of the following values:

- **Method**   "POST" signifies the method, a command to the server for a specific operation (described later).

- **URI**   "/app/jobhist.jsp" indicates the *Uniform Resource Identifier* (URI), which uniquely identifies a resource on the Web, in this case, a JavaServer Pages (JSP) file. URIs contain components that uniquely identify a file available on the Web. A *Uniform Resource Locator* (URL), a subset of the URI standard, is used to find files using HTTP. URLs are described further in the sidebar "About the Uniform Resource Locator (URL)."

About the Uniform Resource Locator (URL)

As mentioned, the Web uses the URL format, a subset of the URI standard, to uniquely locate a web resource (such as a file) in HTTP communications. URLs contain the protocol (HTTP), host name and port of the web server, the path (directory structure) in which the resource may be found and the resource name, *query parameters* (name and value pairs used by the server application), and an optional bookmark name (called a *named anchor* in HTML) that scrolls the browser to a specific location on the page. Here is an example using the Oracle website's domain and some fictitious details:

```
http://www.oracle.com:8080/jspapp/forum_query.jsp?forum_name=jdev&
    searchFor=10.1.3%20new%20features&startDate=Jan-01-2006
```

This URL identifies the following components:

- **Host** (www.oracle.com). This name uses dot separators between components.

- **Web server listener port** (8080). No port identifier declares that the default port assigned to the server, usually 80, will be used.

- **Context root** (/jspapp), also called the *application directory* (or *virtual directory*), the top-level directory for a web application. This part of the URL may be mapped to a physical directory on the application server. It also may be translated to a servlet or other service through an entry in the web deployment descriptor, web.xml (described later in the sidebar "About server.xml and web.xml").

- **File name** (forum_query.jsp). This file is processed by the Web Tier container, as described in Chapter 1. If this had been a static HTML file, you could add an anchor name with a "#" delimiter (for example, "#response3") to cause the browser to scroll to the point on the page where the anchor ("a" tag) with that name is coded.

- **Query parameters and values** (forum_name with a value of "jdev," searchFor with a value of "10.1.3 new features"—"%20" translates to a space character—and startDate with a value of "Jan-01-2006). These values are processed by the JSP file.

- **HTTP version** "HTTP/1.1" refers to HTTP version 1.1. The version of HTTP used is meaningful to both client and server, because different versions offer different features. For example, HTTP version 1.1—the most recent and most popular version—allows multiple requests to be served in the same connection session.

Headers

Headers identify the requestor and indicate how the content will be obtained. Headers consist of a series of header fields. Each header field consists of the name of the header entry followed by either a value or a directive, for example:

```
Accept: */*
Accept-Language: en-us
Accept-Encoding: gzip, deflate
Connection: Keep-Alive
Host: otn.oracle.com
User-Agent: Mozilla/4.0 (compatible; MSIE 6.0; Windows NT 5.1)
```

These headers hold the following information:

- **Accept** This header field indicates the media types that the client will receive. Media types are defined by another standard, *Multipurpose Internet Mail Extensions* (MIME). For example, image/jpeg and plain/text are MIME types that a browser can accept. (Refer to the sidebar "About MIME Types" for more information.) The "*/*" in the previous Accept example means that all types of content will be accepted.

- **Accept-Language** This header field defines the language that will be accepted in the request (in this example, U.S. English).

- **Accept-Encoding** This line indicates the compression algorithms that are acceptable. A server uses *compression* methods to reduce the response message size. *Deflate* and *gzip* are two common compression algorithms. The order indicates that gzip is preferred over deflate.

- **Connection** A *persistent HTTP connection* allows a TCP protocol connection established by a browser to the web server to be reused for additional request/response roundtrips. For HTTP 1.0, the Connection field value "Keep-Alive" specifies a persistent connection. *Persistent connections* are a default in HTTP 1.1; in both versions, they save the time and resources required to open a new connection for each request. They allow the server to send multiple responses (for example, a set of image files displayed in an HTML page) within the same connection session. The session is closed when the request has been completely fulfilled, that is, when all files requested as part of the request have been sent as responses.

- **Host** This header defines the computer to which the request is sent—in this example, otn.oracle.com. The host header is the only required header field for a request.

- **User-Agent** The user-agent header field declares the software used by the web browser, including the name and version. The server can use this for statistics and for modifying the content to take advantage of a featured offered by a specific type of browser.

About MIME Types

Multipurpose Internet Mail Extensions (MIME) declares the format (encoding scheme) of a file. The MIME identifier consists of a type and subtype (with optional parameters). Here are some examples:

```
image/gif
image/jpg
text/html
text/plain
application/msword
application/pdf
```

These strings identify types of images, text, and applications, each of which has two subtypes. Both client and server can process the content, depending upon its type. For example, if the type is "text," the browser renders it using HTML processing (for the "text/html" type) or as unformatted text (for the "text/plain" type). If the type is "image," the browser displays the image file using the appropriate image renderer for the page (GIF and JPG are the two most common image formats). If the type is "application," the browser opens up a helper program to assist in the display of the file (in these examples, Microsoft Word for "msword" or Adobe Reader for "pdf").

NOTE
Standard headers are documented in the HTTP specifications on the W3C website (www.w3.org/Protocols/rfc2616/rfc2616.html).

Message Body

The request can also send a message body to the server. The message body is typically used in a POST method request (described later) to supply parameter values to the server application. It is typically not used with a GET method request, because the information in the URL provides parameter values to the server application.

HTTP Response

When the web server receives the HTTP request, it gathers content and sends it back to the browser as an HTTP response. As shown in Figure 2-1, the response consists of the status line, headers, and message body.

Status Line

The status line contains values that indicate success or failure of the request. The following shows an example:

```
HTTP/1.1 200 OK
```

This status line contains the following parts:

- **HTTP version**   "HTTP/1.1" indicates the HTTP version. This helps the browser interpret the content in the response.

- **Status code**   "200" is the status code that represents success in handling the request. Codes in the 100s indicate that the server is still processing the request; 200s indicate that the request was processed; 300s indicate a redirection problem; 400s indicate an error with the client request (such as authorization failure); and 500s indicate a server error.

- **Reason phrase**   "OK" is a message unique to the status code. It repeats the information of the code in a friendlier format.

NOTE
You can find a listing of all status codes at
www.w3.org/Protocols/rfc2616/rfc2616-sec10.html.

Headers

The response header fields are formatted in the same way as the request headers. A sample response header follows:

```
Cache-Control: no-cache
Content-Length: 2748
Content-Type: image/gif
Date: Tues, 20 Dec 2005 12:00:00 GMT
Expires: -1
Server: Microsoft-IIS/5.1
Set-Cookie: <cookie information>
```

These header fields provide the following information:

- **Cache-Control**   This header field signifies whether the browser or other means can *cache* the content; if so, the client stores the content so that a subsequent request can be filled from the local cache and not from a server response; the "no-cache" directive disables caching, which is useful for responses whose contents can change over time. Caching is also affected by the headers Expires and Last-Modified.

- **Content-Length**   This header field designates the length in bytes of the message body sent after the headers.

- **Content-Type**   This header field defines the MIME format of the content. In this example, the file is a GIF image file.

- **Date**   This header field indicates the date and time on the web server.

- **Expires**   This header field defines the date and time when the content should be considered out of date. If the cache is enabled for the content (using the Cache-Control header described previously), the browser can obtain the content from the cache until the date indicated in this header. "-1" means that the content expires immediately so the content will never be retrieved from a local cache.

- **Server** This header is the type and version of the web server.

- **Set-Cookie** This header writes a cookie to the client machine so that the server can determine later what requests the client previously sent. The upcoming section, "State Management and Cookies," explains cookies in more detail.

Message Body

After the headers, the HTTP response includes the actual content (message body) requested by the client. This is usually the file (also called an *entity*) requested by the client.

State Management and Cookies

HTTP defines a *stateless connection* consisting of a standalone request and a standalone response. A stateless connection is one where the server does not know that a particular request was issued by the client that issued a previous request. This interaction works for a situation that only requires requesting and returning a file, but it is unsuited for e-commerce and database transaction situations, where the server needs to tie a number of requests together.

HTTP was not originally designed to retain state information on the server to tie one request to another. However, a feature called *cookies* allows the server to store information about the client session in the browser session's memory; optionally, the response can specify a *persistent cookie*, which stores cookie information in a file on the client's computer (in a directory maintained by the browser; for example, C:\Documents and Settings\<username>\ Local Settings\Temporary Internet Files). Then, when another request is issued to the same server, this information will be sent in the request header. The cookie contains the host name and path, a cookie name, value, and expiration date, as shown next in the cookie information after a request from the Sun Microsystems' website:

Cookie Information – http://java.sun.com/

http://java.sun.com/

NAME	SUN_ID
VALUE	18.108.4.68:16804:5468649354:16864
HOST	sun.com
PATH	/
EXPIRES	Wednesday, December 31, 2025 3:58:47 PM

NOTE
This illustration shows cookie information using the Firefox Web Developer Toolbar available at addons.mozilla.org/firefox. This toolbar also allows you to view the response headers and other useful information about a browser session.

For example, you could cause the application to write a cookie that stores the last page visited. Then, when the same user issues a subsequent request, the application code can process the request based on the page the user last viewed.

Another example of cookie usage is the session ID. The session ID ties one request from a particular browser to a subsequent request. This is useful for many database transactions whose life cycle spans multiple HTTP requests, for example, if the user issued one request to update a record, another to insert a record, and yet another to commit the update and insert. The application can write a cookie (in a persistent file or in client memory) that stores the session ID retrieved from the application server, and this information can be sent with each request so that the application server can tie the requests to a particular database session.

However, users can disable cookies and break the mechanism that stores the session ID. If this could be a problem in an application, the application can use a technique called *URL rewriting* to circumvent this problem. URL rewriting consists of writing the session ID directly into the HTTP response message body. Then, the browser can send this session ID back to the application server in subsequent requests. URL rewriting is a service of most modern controller frameworks, such as Struts or the JSF controller. If your application does not use one of these frameworks, you will need to implement URL rewriting if you need to maintain the session ID.

URL rewriting is different from the HTTP persistent connection concept mentioned before; in persistent connections, multiple files can be sent in one request-response communication session.

The J2EE environment has added to HTTP communications an API called the *HTTP Session* that allows developers to maintain state. HTTP Session consists of a Java class containing methods that can be used to create and read information about the application user session.

Methods

An HTTP method specified in the HTTP request commands the server to perform a particular task. The most frequently used methods are GET, POST, and HEAD, although several other methods are available.

GET

The *GET method* retrieves content from the server based on the URL. It can only supply parameters coded into the URL (the query parameters mentioned before); the URL is usually specified using a link or entered using the URL field of the browser. The URL can also be constructed from an HTML form submission (described in Chapter 5). Large amounts of data cannot be passed to the server this way because the *URL size limitation* is 2,083 characters for most browsers.

Another limitation of the GET method is that the query parameters are visible to the user in the URL (address or location) field of the browser. Users could potentially figure out the calling syntax for a server action and make an unintended request by sending different parameter values.

GET is used for requests that can be repeated safely without side effects—usually, just retrieving a file. The request could be resubmitted without causing a change of data. For example, when ordering books online, viewing your shopping cart has no effect on your order. If you refresh the shopping cart page and therefore send the same request to the server to display the shopping cart, your order will not change.

POST

POST sends information to the server. The parameter values are coded into the request's message body, as depicted in Figure 2-1; this hides the calling mechanism from the user and is a bit more secure. A POST request is most often sent from a button or image click after filling out fields in an HTML form (described later).

POST is best for requests that cannot be repeated safely. For example, if you were ordering one copy of the *Oracle JDeveloper 10g Handbook*, you would navigate to the description page for that book, fill in the quantity of "1," and click the submit button. This adds one book to your order.

If that page were to use a GET request and then that page were refreshed, the quantity of books would increase. This is an undesirable side effect.

HEAD

The HEAD method works the same way as the GET method, but it requests the server to send only the response headers, not the message body. This allows the client to determine the existence or size of a resource before requesting that the server send the resource.

Other Methods

The following HTTP methods are used less frequently:

- **OPTIONS** This method requests the server to send information about a resource or the server.

- **PUT** The PUT method is used when you want to allow the user to copy a file to the web server.

- **DELETE** This method removes an object, such as a file, from the server. Obviously, this command must be carefully used, but it is handy if you allow users to maintain files on the website.

- **TRACE** This method requests the server to send the entire request back to the browser. Normally, the server processes the request but does not allow the browser to see it. TRACE is useful for debugging a problematic request.

Other HTTP Features

You may run into several other features of HTTP as you work with web applications:

- **Redirection** Servers can send a request to another location. This will return a status code in the 300s to the client. One use of redirection is to instruct the client to show a page from its cache.

- **HTTPS** HTTP Secure (HTTPS) is used in an encrypted Secure Sockets Layer (SSL) session. The request and response messages are encrypted and considered secure, because only a key shared between client and server will allow the messages to be read. Otherwise, it works the same way as HTTP.

What Are the Steps in a Web Application Roundtrip?

Using the concepts from the preceding overview of how HTTP works, we can now examine the steps an application goes through in a request-response communication roundtrip, as shown in Figure 2-2. This discussion assumes that the host computer domain has been assigned a domain name on the client computer or on a server, as described in the sidebar "About Domain Name System and Domains." It also assumes that the HTTP request is sent through the Internet instead of being handled by the client or a local network.

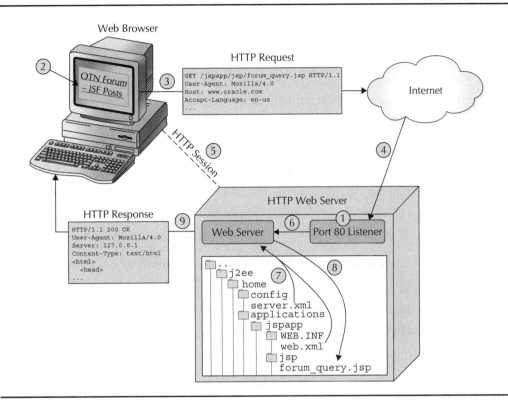

FIGURE 2-2. *HTTP request-response roundtrip*

About Domain Name System and Domains

HTTP supports locating a web server by using an IP address, such as 141.146.8.66 (currently assigned to otn.oracle.com). Numbers, such as those that comprise an IP address, are not very user-friendly. In addition, they are subject to change based on hardware and network architectures. Therefore, an important part of a typical roundtrip is resolution of the domain name.

The client computer may contain a list of domains and IP addresses; on a computer running Windows, it is usually in the C:\Windows\drivers\system32\drivers\etc\hosts file. If this file does not contain the IP address, the address must be supplied by a *Domain Name System (DNS) server*—a network server that translates a domain name (such as www.oracle .com) to the Internet Protocol (IP) address that represents an actual host computer. This DNS (sometimes expanded to *Domain Name Service*) server could be located on the local network or on the Web. This name resolution process is not part of HTTP.

A domain name on the Web is assigned a unique IP address by a "domain registration service," which has access to the means to copy a domain/IP pair to DNS servers on the Internet.

1. A process on the HTTP web server—called the *listener* or *HTTP daemon (HTTPD)*—listens for a request from the network on a specific port (by default, port 80).

2. The user clicks a link on an HTML page that contains the following reference:

   ```
   http://www.oracle.com/jspapp/jsp/forum_query.jsp?forum_name=jdev&
        searchFor=10.1.3%20new%20features&startDate=Jan-01-2006
   ```

3. The browser assembles an HTTP request (specifying a GET method in this case) and sends it to the network (the Internet, in this example).

4. A DNS server on the network translates the domain name to an IP address and sends the message to the web server.

5. The port 80 listener accepts the request and allows the client to set up a connection session so that data communication can occur.

6. The listener passes control to the web server program.

7. The web server parses the request and determines if the request is for static content that can be retrieved from the file system or for dynamic content, which requires another process to build the content. If the request is for dynamic J2EE content, the web server uses values in the server.xml and web.xml files to determine the location of the application files. The *context root* (in this example, jspapp) is associated either with the location of the static content or with the process that will supply the content. Some examples follow:

   - **For a static HTML file**, the server locates the file within the physical directory mapped to the context root. No additional program (other than retrieving the file) is needed.

   - **For a J2EE application file**, such as forum_query.jsp in this example, the file requested in the URL is found in the physical directory that maps to the context root. The sidebar "About server.xml and web.xml" describes the mapping mechanism in more detail.

   - **For a URL without a file name**, such as http://www.oracle.com/jspapp, the web server finds the welcome file for the application and returns its content. The sidebar "About server.xml and web.xml" provides more detail about how the web server determines the welcome file.

8. The web server runs the code associated with the file (if it is a J2EE program, such as a servlet or the JSP page in this example) or opens the file (if it is an HTML or other type of nonprogram file).

9. The web server constructs a response comprised of the status line, headers, and message body (containing the requested content) and then sends that response to the browser. The browser then renders the content and closes the connection.

NOTE
Tim Berners-Lee, the inventor of the World Wide Web, tells the story of how web communications work to "kids of various ages (6–96)" at his W3C website page, www.w3.org/People/Berners-Lee/Kids.html.

About server.xml and web.xml

J2EE specifies the standards used to write and place the descriptor files the web server uses for fulfilling requests. When the web server needs to find a J2EE web application file to satisfy an HTTP request, it parses the context root from the URL. It then looks in the *server.xml* file (an XML configuration file located in the web server's ../j2ee/home/config directory) for an entry, such as the following:

```
<application name="jspapp" path="../applications/jspapp" />
```

This entry identifies the application (the *name* attribute) and associates it with the physical directory (the *path* attribute). The file mentioned in the URL will be located in a subdirectory (for example, /jsp) of the context root directory. Therefore, the URL www.oracle.com/jspapp/jsp/forum_query.jsp may point to the forum_query.jsp file in the Oracle Application Server 10*g* (web server) directory, O:\Oracle\Product\mtier10g\j2ee\home\applications\jspapp\jsp.

If the URL contains no file name, the application server determines which file to open based on an entry in *web.xml*—the *web module deployment descriptor*. Web.xml is another XML file, which is located in the context root's WEB-INF directory. Web.xml contains, among other entries, an entry that defines the startup page for the application, for example:

```
<welcome-file-list>
  <welcome-file>forum_query.jsp</welcome-file>
</welcome-file-list>
```

The web server determines from this entry that a URL containing only the application context root will start the forum_query.jsp file.

How Does Oracle Forms Services Use HTTP?

If you are accustomed to working with *Oracle Forms Services* (Oracle Forms applications running on the Web), the HTTP web application communication mechanism may seem a bit foreign and complex. However, communications within Oracle Forms Services uses the same HTTP request and response steps, as well as the same application server (Oracle Application Server), as J2EE web applications. Although it is not useful at this point to fully explain the process and communications path for an Oracle Forms application running on the Web, a brief description should provide a further understanding of the HTTP mechanisms explained in this chapter.

The process of starting up an Oracle Forms application on the Web begins with a standard HTTP request for a file from the browser. The file is returned to the browser in the corresponding HTTP response; the browser then starts an applet session (running in a JVM—Java Virtual Machine) in the web browser; the Forms Servlet also initiates a Forms runtime session on the application server. The form displays in the browser's applet session. The applet collects messages based on interactions with the user and sends them as an HTTP request to the Forms Servlet running on the application server. The Forms Servlet passes these messages to the Forms runtime session. The Forms runtime session collects messages and sends them to the Forms Servlet, which formats them as an HTTP response.

The servlet then sends the HTTP response to the browser, and the applet interprets the message so that it can update its display when appropriate. Therefore, HTTP is used throughout the Oracle Forms runtime session.

NOTE
You can find more information about how Oracle Forms runs on the Web in Chapter 3 of the "Oracle Application Server Forms Services Deployment Guide 10g Release 2 (10.1.2)" online documentation available after logging into OTN at otn.oracle.com (for example, at download-east.oracle.com/docs/cd/B25016_04/doc/dl/web.htm).

CHAPTER
3

JDeveloper and ADF
as RAD Tools

Although the whole trend of modern engineering progress
is towards the elimination of hand labour by machinery
in the production of metal articles,
nevertheless, there still is—and always will be—
a certain amount of hand work necessary
in fabricating many engineering parts.

—Arthur W. Judge (1887–?), *Engineering Workshop Practice* (1936)

 apid Application Development (RAD) is a somewhat abused term. There is no formal definition of what constitutes a RAD technique or environment, so vendors have used the term to encompass everything from What You See Is What You Get (WYSIWYG) editing facilities to model-driven code generation.

This chapter starts out by defining what we mean by RAD and then looks at the implications of implementing RAD in the context of J2EE:

■ **What do we mean by RAD?**

■ **What is a framework?**

■ **What is Oracle ADF?**

■ **Why is JDeveloper an IDE for RAD?**

What Do We Mean by RAD?

Wikipedia (en.wikipedia.org/wiki/Rapid_Application_Development) defines *Rapid Application Development* as a methodology involving iterative development, the construction of prototypes, and the use of computer-aided software engineering (CASE) tools, which capture details about requirements and generate code.

Coming from an Oracle Forms or PL/SQL background, you will have your own idea of what RAD methodology is all about, but we think it includes these key characteristics:

■ **Visually oriented development**   We expect RAD methodology to be supported by an *Integrated Development Environment* (IDE) that will provide an interactive and easy-to-use environment for defining and coding the application. This applies particularly to the development of user interfaces, where it will be much more productive to draw a screen in some kind of visual editor than to lay it out with code that references X and Y coordinates.

■ **An infrastructure**   In a RAD environment, we expect the basic low-level application tasks to be handled by some sort of infrastructure. Such operations as interacting with a database or the rendering of user interfaces are common to any application. RAD development is largely about configuring this infrastructure rather than programming it. This is something we'll look at in detail when we discuss *frameworks*. Such an infrastructure is generally exposed to the developer as high-level components that encapsulate the underlying common functionality.

■ **Guided development**   The RAD development environment should both help and constrain the developer to work within the defined boundaries of the infrastructure. This can take several guises; for example, the code editor may provide popup help on matters of syntax and application programming interfaces (APIs), and property inspectors may provide help in configuring components.

■ **Reduced coding**   Ideally, RAD should involve as little handwritten code as possible. Any code you write either will focus on implementing the core business function of the application or will configure and glue together infrastructure components.

■ **Focus on maintenance as well as creation**   Anything written using a RAD tool should be maintainable through that tool. Code generators that create low-level code from a high-level model do not really implement RAD principles, unless they provide the ability to reverse-engineer and subsequently maintain the code throughout its existence. This is not to say that a RAD tool cannot involve a code generation step. The point is that the results of generation or compilation would never be touched by the RAD developer; the higher-level abstraction will be the source of truth.

In light of the preceding definition, we can see how a tool like Oracle Forms can be defined as a RAD tool. The core of an application is defined using form modules, blocks, and canvases. These abstract components represent convenient building blocks. The developer does not type code to define instances and properties of the components; instead, the developer configures the components using the Oracle Forms Property Palette to define their appearance and behaviors. At runtime, the Oracle Forms infrastructure interprets this developer's configuration to create a form that can be executed. The programmer goes on to write small fragments of code in triggers to coordinate these components and manage the behavior and presentation of the application user interface. The RAD characteristics just described are the core of the Oracle Forms architecture.

Therefore, we can sum up RAD as being based around a component paradigm at design time to provide abstraction from low-level coding and some kind of runtime infrastructure or framework to interpret the components and their configuration data.

Lately, *agile methodologies* have become popular because of their potential for cost savings and accuracy in filling business requirements. Although RAD and agile development methods are fundamentally different, they share the characteristic that the software is developed iteratively and quickly. Therefore, RAD tools such as JDeveloper can fit projects that are focused on agile methods. You can start learning about agile methodologies at en.wikipedia.org/wiki/Agile_software_development.

This design pattern for RAD is successful, but does have a flaw. RAD environments have historically been based around vendor-specific development environments, components, and the runtime frameworks required to implement the running application. As such, RAD environments, such as Oracle Forms, Delphi, and Visual Basic, are classed as proprietary and closed. Openness and compliance with standards are essential features to the J2EE development community, and traditional, vendor-driven RAD environments are viewed with suspicion.

Furthermore, the genesis of a typical proprietary RAD environment has been driven primarily from the development environments themselves. Each of the popular RAD methodologies has an associated IDE and specialized scripting language. The runtime infrastructure required to support the design-time abstraction is a secondary concern. This does not fit naturally into the J2EE environment, where the language and runtime APIs are established and the community frowns upon any kind of specialization or proprietary extension that is not part of a preestablished framework.

Rapid Application Development is not impossible within the context of J2EE, but it is molded and constrained by the need to produce a result that is not tied to a particular vendor's development environment or implementation of the *J2EE APIs* (code libraries that offer access to Java-based functions, such as database access, messaging, and XML file access). The result of this restriction is that no single RAD-focused tool dominates the J2EE development space. The majority of IDEs for Java and J2EE are general tools that concentrate on key low-level functionality, such as writing Java code or Extensible Markup Language (XML) —a text-based coding language consisting of tag elements and attributes (described in Chapter 4).

In contrast, the real strides in the J2EE space towards improving developer productivity have come from the opposite direction. The runtime infrastructure or frameworks have evolved independently from the tools and have had a major effect on the way that J2EE applications are constructed.

What Is a Framework?

When confronted with a set of low-level APIs, such as the J2EE APIs, programmers naturally start to develop common patterns and convenience methods for dealing with requirements that come up again and again. After a while, most developers will build up their own personal toolkit of handy code and techniques that they can reuse whenever they encounter a familiar use case. Sometimes, problems are so common across the industry that formal recipes or design patterns are recognized for dealing with the scenario.

TIP
As we mentioned in Chapter 1, BluePrints forms an important part of the J2EE platform. An extensive catalog of these design patterns and related information for J2EE can be found on the Sun BluePrints site (java.sun.com/blueprints/).

Frameworks evolve as concrete implementations of such patterns, factoring out the repeated portion of the task, and leaving programmers with a much more limited exercise of configuring the parameters of the framework to their needs. The scope of a framework can vary. Some frameworks address specific parts of the application development problem. For example, *object-relational mapping (O/R mapping)*, used to convert between object-oriented and relational structures (such as class instances and database tables), is an important but constrained task. Many O/R mapping frameworks have evolved and compete. Some, such as Hibernate, are from the open-source community; others, such as ADF Business Components or Oracle TopLink, are from the commercial world. As we will see, using one of these existing frameworks for O/R mapping is a sensible thing; the skill comes in choosing a framework that will be best for implementing a particular project profile.

Frameworks are not confined to point solutions (addressing one and only one task), such as O/R mapping. Some have evolved to cover a much larger range of the functionality needed to provide the infrastructure for a complete application. For example, the Apache Struts framework handles user interface creation, page flow control, and a certain amount of security. Inevitably, this has led to the development of larger frameworks, such as Oracle Application Development Framework (ADF), Apache Beehive, and Spring, which directly provide infrastructure for some tasks as well as inheriting functionally by aggregating smaller frameworks, such as the O/R mapping solutions or Struts. These conglomerates are referred to as *meta-frameworks*, described further in the sidebar "About Meta-Frameworks."

The Anatomy of a Framework

We explained how frameworks evolve out of standardized solutions to common tasks, in the process implementing the best practice for solving that particular problem. What is it, however, that transforms a programmer's toolkit of simple APIs into a framework? Part of this, of course, is

About Meta-Frameworks

We've just started to define a framework and already we've introduced a twist in the form of meta-frameworks. What's this all about? A meta-framework is a convenient term used to describe an end-to-end application development framework that covers a wide range of functionality. The meta-framework not only provides functionality, but may also encapsulate or subsume multiple single-solution frameworks. If a single-solution framework is a screwdriver, a meta-framework is the whole toolbox.

Furthermore, the definition of meta-frameworks includes the idea that they offer choice and pluggability in response to any particular task. For the O/R mapping example, meta-frameworks, such as Oracle ADF or Spring, allow the developer to choose one out of a whole range of O/R mapping solutions to implement the data access function. The important distinction is that the actual choice of implementation will not have an effect on the rest of the application. The user interface, for example, will be unaware of the actual O/R mapping mechanism being used. This allows for much more flexibility in the development of the application.

determined by the scope of the problem being solved; beyond that, the following attributes imply framework status:

- **Configured, not coded** By definition, a framework performs most boilerplating and plumbing tasks for you. In order for that to happen, there must be a way to define configuration data that provides the framework with the information it needs. This configuration data, or *metadata*, is sometimes injected through code, but more often through some sort of configuration file. XML is typically used for such metadata files in modern frameworks, although this does not have to be the case. As a familiar example, Oracle Forms is completely metadata-driven; all of those properties entered through the Form Builder are compiled into compact binary metadata in the Forms runtime (.fmx) file. The metadata is then interpreted by the runtime engine to create the running form instance.

- **Runtime component** Applications written using frameworks rely on the framework infrastructure code being available at runtime. This infrastructure code may be deployed with the application as libraries, or it may exist as some kind of runtime engine that the application runs on top of. (This is how Oracle Forms works.)

- **Design-time component** Since frameworks need to be configured with your business domain's profile, they need to have some way of helping you create that configuration. This facility may take the form of complete IDE support, including graphical editors and syntax checkers; or it may be a more manual process, for instance, a *Document Type Descriptor* (DTD) containing XML element and attribute names used to verify that an XML configuration file is valid.

If you review the many frameworks available within the J2EE universe, you'll see a vast spectrum of pretenders to the framework title. Many open-source frameworks, for instance, are weak on the design-time support or concentrate too much on coded configuration rather than on metadata-driven configuration. (See the sidebar "The Importance of Metadata" for details.). So let's look at what turns "just another framework" into something that you might actually want to use.

The Importance of Metadata

Although you can usually configure frameworks using both code and metadata, metadata has some advantages. First, you achieve a clean separation of framework configuration from application logic; second, you have the potential for customization without recompiling.

The first point is perhaps obvious. We all can understand the sense in keeping code that configures the basic framework operation separate from the code that implements the business logic so that updates are easier in case either layer changes. The second point, however, has implications that are more profound. The ability to customize an application through metadata can make the initial installation and setup of an application easier. For example, you can develop code while pointing the application database connection to a development database. Then, when you need to install the application in a production situation, you change a configuration file that points to the production database. The change is small and contained, and requires minimal testing.

Further, the metadata may be manipulated at runtime to customize an application. For example, your code can change metadata for security rules at runtime if the application has to adapt based on the credentials of the connected user.

The management and storage of such complex metadata is a problem. To this end, Oracle ADF has a complete set of services for managing and storing metadata called *Metadata Services* (MDS). The presence of MDS is largely transparent to a developer using ADF, but its services underlie all of the framework metadata handling in the JDeveloper IDE.

What Characterizes a Good Framework?

Although we've defined a framework as a best-practice implementation that includes runtime, design time, and a little configuration thrown in, there is much more to a framework than that. Let's consider the factors that make a framework truly useful:

- **Functional depth** The framework must provide all features needed for a particular functional area. This is the one area when a well-thought-out commercial framework can outshine an in-house toolkit. The framework must be able to handle every eventuality in the problem domain. Take, for example, an O/R mapping framework that handles basic query syntax but cannot map outer joins. Such a limitation may not have mattered to the original developer, but if you suddenly need that capability in your application, what do you do? You certainly don't want to employ a second framework just to fulfill that niche requirement.

- **Functional scope** The functional depth argument works the other way, too. A framework can be too specialized to a particular domain. An O/R mapping framework that specializes in only the query of data and that does not manage updates is of limited use in most applications, no matter how deep its query functionality. Learning to use a framework well takes time; you don't want to have to repeat that exercise for every piece of point functionality in a system.

- **As declarative as possible** We expect that a framework will relieve us of coding burden, and this implies that most of the interaction with the framework will be in configuring it with the relevant metadata, rather than writing lower-level code.

■ **Clean APIs**   Frameworks must provide a clean separation between the underlying code and the programming interface that the framework exposes to the developer. The framework's authors should be able to change its implementation without affecting the code in existing business applications. This problem is particularly difficult in the J2EE world, as the frameworks and code written using them are generally both written in Java. In Java, it is fairly simple for a developer to inadvertently call an internal function by mistake or to override an internal-only class accidentally (or even deliberately to obtain some extra functionality). An update to the framework can break that type of code.

■ **Tooling**   Many frameworks attempt to make your life easier by allowing you to configure them using metadata. However, if this involves having to manually write XML files, for example, you may well lose many of the productivity gains that the framework promises, because XML coding is prone to syntax errors that are difficult to debug. A framework does not need associated IDE support to make it successful, but such support will certainly boost adoption by flattening the learning curve. A good example of this is the Apache Struts framework. The Struts framework was popular before any kind of visual Struts tool was available, but with the introduction of diagrammatic representations of Struts page flows in IDEs, such as JDeveloper and Eclipse, Struts use has grown immensely. Developers using Struts in such graphical environments need never learn the syntax of the Struts XML configuration file or, indeed, the in-depth mechanics of how Struts works.

■ **Acceptance**   Frameworks evolve in a Darwinian environment; that is, widespread adoption is more a key to survival than technical brilliance. Particularly with open-source frameworks, the framework will survive and evolve only as long as people feel that it's worthwhile and are prepared to give their time to both using and maintaining it. Successful frameworks tend to have a snowball effect: they are discussed more on the Web; more books are written about them; and because more information is available, the framework becomes even more popular. An active user community is another natural result of wide acceptance. An active user community can offer support and experience in real solutions that are not available from the framework's author. A user community, therefore, adds to the snowball.

■ **Support**   The most expensive part of using a framework is never the purchase price (if there is one); it's the investment in time to learn and use the framework and the maintenance of that system down the line. With open-source frameworks, you have access to the source code, but in many cases, you may not have the expertise or desire to understand that code well enough to fix bugs yourself. As soon as you make a change, you can contribute it back to the open-source community. Legal restrictions within many organizations may, however, present a significant barrier to the transfer of code into the public domain. Alternatively, you can keep the change to yourself, but then you're stuck with a custom implementation of the framework.

The fashionable business models in the open-source world recognize this issue. Much open-source software is now directly funded by companies looking to profit from support or consulting services in those frameworks. This is the ultimate loss-leader. Of course, this provides a loose coupling in terms of support, because those vendors can just walk away if something better comes along. Commercial frameworks like Oracle Forms and ADF at least offer a degree of service level, with commitments to error correction and so on. This is what gives them such tremendous longevity (for example, more than 18 years for the Forms framework) and makes them a surer bet for typically long-lived commercial applications.

■ **Documentation** The learning curve for a framework is greatly reduced if it offers complete documentation in several categories: reference for the APIs and framework classes, development guides with examples, and IDE documentation with task-oriented explanations. The more documentation the framework offers, the better the perception of its ease-of-use. This adds to its popularity as well as to its usefulness.

Oracle Forms as a Framework

The framework that you may already be most familiar with is Oracle Forms. Take, for example, the task of building a form for querying and updating a record in a table. In Forms, you define a data block in the Data Block Wizard and Layout Wizard or in the Property Palette using some key information: the table upon which the block is based, the columns you want to see, the WHERE clause, and so on. When you run the form, you know that the framework will take care of the basic plumbing for you, establishing the database connection, creating the database cursor, fetching from the cursor, and displaying the data. All of these tasks take a lot of code internally, but it is code in the Forms framework that is written generically enough for universal reuse. Most Forms developers have no exposure to, or understanding of, the underlying C programming interfaces that Forms actually uses—the framework's abstraction layer is the platform they code against. So, if each of these functional areas (connecting to the database, retrieving data, and displaying data to the user) is a framework, we can regard Forms as a meta-framework, providing an end-to-end programming abstraction for the programmer.

Forms programmers have been able to take all the functionality provided by this meta-framework for granted without having to think of the underlying mechanics. But you can't do this in the J2EE world without framework help. If we examine the Forms services in more depth, you should see the correspondence to J2EE and Oracle ADF.

Oracle Forms Architecture

Figure 3-1 shows a logical representation of an Oracle Forms application with an emphasis on the related internal structures. Oracle Forms Services is a multi-tiered application with three layers, working from the bottom:

■ **The Database Tier** is the *persistence store*, the location where data is kept between data access requests, and often is also a repository of business logic in the form of stored procedures.

■ **The Application Server Tier** *or middle tier* is where the Oracle Forms runtime engine executes and provides the runtime framework infrastructure. This is where the metadata in the runtime .fmx file is actually interpreted to create the running application.

■ **The Client Tier** represents the user interface rendering of a forms application. As mentioned in Chapter 2, this tier uses a Java applet, generic to all Oracle Forms files, that runs within a web browser, hosted in a Java Virtual Machine—usually the JInitiator plug-in.

From the framework point of view, the interesting component is the application running in the middle tier. You can view this as an encompassing runtime session encapsulating one or more data blocks. Let's look at the key elements within that tier.

The Runtime Session The concept of a runtime session is not an explicit artifact in Forms application development. With many J2EE-based frameworks, you will find yourself having to engage with some kind of session or context object before you do anything. In Oracle Forms,

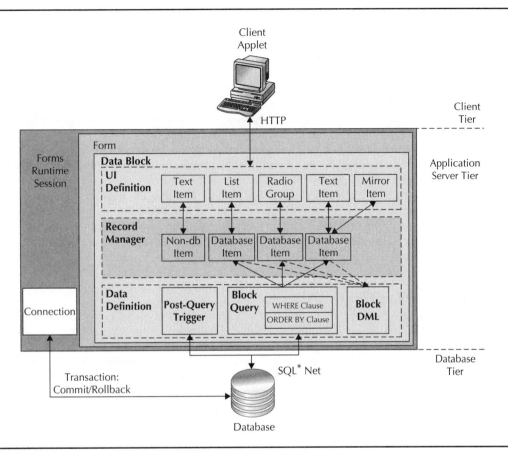

FIGURE 3-1.   *The Oracle Forms logical architecture*

however, you just take the session for granted. The database connection is automatically created and Oracle Forms knows how to handle database transactions. These factors make a programmer's life much simpler. However, the price for that simplicity is a comparative lack of flexibility. For example, it is only possible to base a block on one connection to the database, albeit with multiple sessions.

Within the session, you can open one or more forms, and within each of those forms, the data block (or just "block") is the significant component. The form module does little more than encapsulate a set of data blocks.

The Block   The main message that Figure 3-1 conveys is the way in which a block object can be split into logical layers. If Oracle Forms were designed from scratch today, it is likely that the Data Definition portion of the block metadata would be defined separately from the UI Definition portion of the block (as is the case in Oracle Reports today with the data model and layout model). This would expose two objects in the navigator for the block rather than one, and would allow certain capabilities, such as forming two UI blocks from the same data block definition. This split is not a reality today, but it does help to view a block as layered in this way. It is mentally possible to divide all of the block and item properties up into UI attributes or data attributes.

In Figure 3-1, the Data Definition layer interacts with the database through SQL*Net. It executes POST-QUERY and other triggers that load data for non–base table items. In addition, it loads data from the database for base table items. This layer also prepares block DML statements—INSERT, UPDATE, or DELETE statements—based on data in the base table items. These statements are then sent to the database.

The UI Definition for the block is derived from the properties of the items in the block. It is not an implementation of the user interface; instead, it is an abstract description, which the Oracle Forms runtime engine will turn into instructions used to drive the Forms Java applet, which will then render user interface items based on UI Definition properties.

Figure 3-1 includes a middle layer within the block—the Record Manager, which is part of the Forms runtime engine. Most Forms programmers are unaware of the existence of the Record Manager, although they interact with it all the time using the various Forms built-ins, such as SET_BLOCK_PROPERTY and SET_RECORD_PROPERTY. Record Manager is the key part of the Forms runtime framework. As records are required by the UI, the Record Manager handles the query process and maintains a cache of the rows—some in memory and some on disk. The Record Manager also performs the vital job of tracking changes to the block data and issuing corresponding locks, inserts, updates, and deletes based upon the block's Data Definition.

Core Framework Functions

With this image of the Oracle Forms architecture in mind, we can summarize the standard functionalities that we use in Forms, and that we would expect any framework of this nature to handle, in Table 3-1.

In addition to these stock functions, Forms provides a set of simple extension points and framework override points in the form of triggers. To Forms programmers, these are really the core of the whole RAD framework, and this is where they really invest their time and skills to add value. One of the most common issues in converting to the J2EE world is the logical mapping of the functionality that would have been placed in those triggers.

The whole purpose of this exercise in deconstructing Forms is to highlight the logical functions that make up the Forms infrastructure. As we look at the ADF framework and the whole application development process throughout the rest of the book, we'll be carrying out exactly the same tasks, albeit with different implementations.

What Is Oracle ADF?

Like Forms, *Oracle Application Development Framework* (Oracle ADF or just ADF) is a meta-framework that fulfills the same set of core functions outlined in the preceding section. One of the major differences between ADF and Oracle Forms, however, is in how those functional pieces are provided. As a framework, Oracle Forms provides all of the functions in a monolithic whole. ADF, on the other hand, relies on a mix of sub-frameworks to provide the key functions, along with the functional glue to hold it all together. That sounds complex, but the end result is the same. Nearly everything that an application needs is already encapsulated within ADF. And if something is not available, you can add external packages and libraries to extend the meta-framework still further to cover the new requirement. A great example of this is the JHeadstart package, which is discussed in Chapter 16.

Figure 3-2 shows some of the available technologies within the overall Model-View-Controller (MVC) design pattern used by ADF. (Chapter 1 describes MVC further.)

Framework Function	Fulfilled By
Database connection	Managed by the Forms runtime engine automatically as part of the runtime session state.
Transactions: Commit, rollback, and save pointing	Handled by the Forms runtime session state and mostly managed automatically, although you can manually manage transactions through PL/SQL calls.
Database interaction: queries and DML	Defined by the block definitions (Data Definition layer) or manually coded in Forms triggers.
Middle-tier data caching and transactional integrity	Provided by the Record Manager, which handles state management and database interaction on the programmer's behalf.
User interface generation	Defined by the programmer in the layout of the block items in the visual editor. This information is stored in the Forms (UI Definition layer) metadata and interpreted at runtime to generate the correct UI for the data.
Navigation	Most navigation between screens within a Forms application results from the programmer's logic. No framework piece really provides an abstract representation of a complete application flow. However, the Forms engine introduces a degree of abstraction by allowing the programmer to specify a field to navigate to without having to work out what window or canvas that field is actually on.
Security	Forms hooks into both *Single Sign-On* (SSO) (a feature of the Oracle Application Server that allows the user name and password used to log on to the server to be used in all applications within the session) and the database security definitions for the connected user. The programmer can customize item and menu display based on this.
Validation	Items and blocks expose declarative validation and integrity rules, and provide established trigger hook points for more sophisticated requirements.

TABLE 3-1. *Framework Functions and Oracle Forms Features*

Since this book focuses on a certain combination of technologies (ADF Faces and JSF with ADF Business Components), we will not discuss all details of the ADF architecture, but Figure 3-2 highlights the pluggability of ADF as a meta-framework. ADF coordinates your selections from a range of technologies that fulfills various logical functions, such as interacting with the database and generating user interfaces. The key component is a layer provided by the ADF framework, the ADF Model (or ADFm). The *ADF Model* layer (depicted as the Model section of Figure 3-2) acts as the glue between the various business service providers, such as Enterprise JavaBeans (EJB) or web services, and the consumers of those services, generally the user interface that you are building. We discuss the ADF Model layer in detail in Chapter 7.

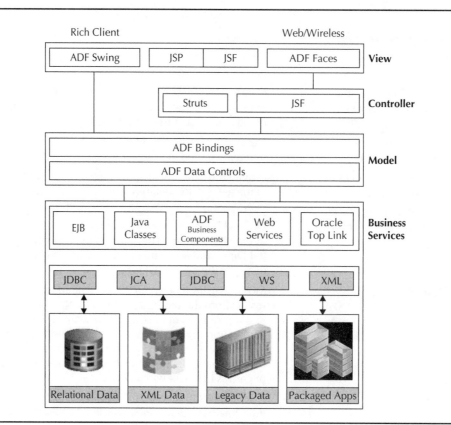

FIGURE 3-2. *The Oracle ADF architecture showing the available technologies*

NOTE
The ADF Model binding layer has been proposed to the Java Community Process as an extension to the J2EE standard. The proposal is covered in the Java Specification Request (JSR) 227, which can be found using the JSR search feature at www.jcp.org.

How Do I Choose Technologies?

ADF is a great offering, but the capability to plug in several different solutions into each functional area gives rise to a problem—there is almost too much choice. If the technologies to be used for an application have not been predefined for you, what slice through the available technology stack should be used?

Things are simple in Oracle Forms. There is only one way to access the database, and there is only one way to define the UI. Probably the most complex architectural decision to be made when coding a Forms application is how much logic to implement in the database and how much in the module.

When starting out on your first J2EE project using ADF, you are going to come up against this technology question right away. The first step when creating an application presents the *Create Application* dialog, which asks you to select an application template, as shown, and each template consists of a different combination of technologies.

Create Application dialog box

If you make a wrong choice, you can always change your mind later on, but it's better to get it right from the start.

When building a traditional data entry–style application of the type you would build with Oracle Forms or the PL/SQL Web Toolkit, you need to make a technology choice for two main functional areas: user interface and database integration.

User Interface Technology

This book concentrates on building web applications for delivery through a standard browser, without the use of plug-ins or Java applets. This means we concentrate on UI technologies that can generate standard HTML, and maybe some JavaScript to create the screens. A large number of technologies available in the J2EE world address this task, for example, JavaServer Pages (JSP), servlets, Velocity, Tapestry, Wicket, and JavaServer Faces (JSF). However, JDeveloper best supports JSP and JSF. A third technology, ADF UIX, is supported in JDeveloper 10.1.2 as well, but is being deprecated in favor of JSF and is not recommended as a technology for new builds.

NOTE
Chapter 2 describes JSP, servlet, and ADF UIX technologies a bit further.

Before the advent of JSF (introduced in Chapter 1), the user interface was a difficult area in which to make a decision; JSP technology has the benefits of being widely used, but it provides a rather low level of UI capabilities. ADF UIX, on the other hand, comes with a large set of rich components, such as tabbed menus, tree controls, and grids, but it's harder to learn and not widely used outside of the Oracle E-Business Suite. Other frameworks, such as Tapestry, are popular in the open-source community, but suffer from a lack of design-time support.

JSF has changed this picture considerably, and we feel that it will provide the easiest transition for Forms developers to the J2EE world. In the next section, we examine some of the reasons for this opinion.

NOTE
Chapter 5 describes JSF in more detail.

Why JSF?

JavaServer Faces has really changed the playing field for web user interface development. Published as a standard in May 2004, JSF is now, like JSP, a formal part of the new Java platform specification (Java EE 5), and J2EE container engines, such as Oracle's OC4J (Oracle Application Server Containers for J2EE), will need to implement a JSF service in order to conform to this standard.

JSF technology is attractive for several reasons:

■ **Component-based** All UI elements within JSF are components, and are written to a standard specification. These components can be complex and can consist of many sub-elements. For example, a tree control consists of images to connect the nodes, hyperlinks for the nodes, buttons to expand and collapse all, and some dedicated JavaScript. Because components are standardized, you can pick and choose from multiple open-source or commercial sets of widgets and create your own if required. They will all work together and be consistent to use.

■ **Programming model** Each JSF component is able to register action handlers and listeners for events. Put simply, for something such as carrying out an action in reaction to a button press, the programmer just has to write a piece of what we'll call "trigger" code that is associated with the button definition in the UI and automatically executed by JSF when that button is pressed. Contrast this to JSP or servlet development, where the programmer has to decode the request object to determine if a button was pressed and, if so, which one was pressed. So JSF makes the whole process of wiring up code to UI events much simpler and more familiar to a 4GL programmer.

■ **Page layout** In the same way that each UI element in JSF is a component, screens collect and organize those components within specialized layout components. This removes the requirement from the developer to code low-level screen layout tasks using tables and style sheets. It also requires much less code to define a single screen, since the boilerplate HTML elements used to generate a particular layout are created only at runtime. Some JSF component sets, such as *ADF Faces*, also support the concept of multiple look and feel—custom *skins*, templates, and other definition files that enforce a common look and feel within an application. These capabilities allow the whole graphical aspect of an application to be changed after creation without having to change each and every page.

■ **Device-independent** Through the use of components and layout containers, the programmer is actually coding an abstracted definition of a page rather than hard-coding the actual HTML tags. JSF includes a mechanism called *render kits* that can enable a single page definition to be rendered in a device-specific way at runtime. For example, render kits allow a JSF page to run unchanged in a normal browser or on a handheld device. The JSF component and its render kit, rather than the developer, have the responsibility for creating the correct markup tags for the target device.

■ **Built-in Controller layer** Page flow or Controller functionality within the MVC design pattern is often discussed as a separate technology layer in J2EE applications. However, in practical terms, the choice of a controller is tightly bound to the choice of user interface technology. In the case of JSF, page flow control is built in, so we won't need to consider a separate technology to handle this function.

Therefore, with the advent of JSF, the problem of choosing the correct UI technology—and, by implication, the technology that you use to link pages together into a flow—has been greatly simplified.

Database Integration

In PL/SQL, you may take it for granted that you can just embed a SQL statement without thinking about how it will be actually issued or how the data will be handled. However, in the J2EE world, things are different. You cannot just embed SQL within the code; you need to use specific APIs to handle the SQL. Low-level Java Database Connectivity (JDBC) APIs (introduced in Chapter 1) are available for accessing the database. However, using these APIs would be like coding to the Oracle Call Interface (OCI) in order to build Oracle Forms applications—this is not something you really want to be doing. Therefore, with Java, you need to use one of the higher-level O/R mapping frameworks supported by ADF.

Your Choices for Database Integration

ADF offers three primary choices for mapping database objects to Java code. Each choice exhibits a slightly different focus and suits different communities of developers. The choices are as follows:

- ADF Business Components
- Oracle TopLink
- Enterprise JavaBeans (EJB)

In addition, the technologies in question support a degree of mixing and matching among themselves to further add to the confusion. For instance, you will see examples such as one version of the Oracle SRDemo sample application that uses a combination of TopLink persistence and EJB.

ADF Business Components   ADF Business Components (ADF BC) is a powerful and rich framework for mapping database objects into Java. It forms one of the core frameworks of the ADF stack of technologies (as shown in Figure 3-2). It is widely used in the Oracle community and as one of the key technologies for the E-Business Suite.

ADF BC is the O/R mapping layer that we concentrate on in the rest of this book (for reasons discussed later in the section "Selecting the O/R Mapping Tool"). It is well suited to what we call the *relational viewpoint*, where you approach the design process after creating a well-formed relational database design. This, after all, is the way that most PL/SQL and Oracle Forms developments are run—with the database designer, DBA, and coders working closely. We'll look at the similarities between ADF Business Components and Oracle Forms in greater detail in Chapter 6.

Oracle TopLink   TopLink is Oracle's flagship object-relational and object-to-XML persistence architecture. Like ADF BC, TopLink has a long pedigree, having survived and evolved over the last 10 years (a sure sign of a good framework). TopLink's strength is in approaching the object-relational mapping problem from the opposite side as ADF Business Components. Starting from a well-formed object model, TopLink gives you the tools to create highly sophisticated mappings into a relational database (or an XML database).

You could use TopLink to perform the relatively simple mapping that ADF Business Components performs, but this would not really exploit its core competency, and you'd lose out on some of the added value that you gain from the declarative aspects of Business Components. TopLink is ideal for use when, as a Java developer, you don't have control over the database schema. TopLink allows you to design the middle tier object model which does not have to be compromised to fit into a relational model.

Enterprise JavaBeans (EJB)   The Enterprise JavaBeans standard defines a server-side component architecture for J2EE loosely based (conceptually, at least) on the JavaBeans standard used for Java GUI components. The EJB standard defines a series of services for handling database persistence and transactions using an EJB container, which is usually, although not always, provided by the application server's J2EE container. EJBs have had such bad press in the past that they've become somewhat of a cliché. However, things are changing in the EJB world with the latest revision of the specification—EJB 3.0. The Java Community Process expert group driving this latest revision of the standard (JSR 220) received the message that EJB was unnecessarily complex, so 3.0 is about simplification. EJB 3.0 also defines entity beans as *Plain Old Java Objects* (POJOs)—standard Java class files—without having to implement all of the interfaces and artifacts required by earlier standards. The EJB standard is turning into a usable way to handle data, having learned from its past mistakes.

On the positive side, using EJB does have some advantages: all of the major development IDEs can help you build them, and every vendor's EJB/J2EE container provides all of the EJB services required for persistence and transactional support at runtime.

However, to a traditional Oracle developer, EJBs are still going to be the least attractive option for the following reasons:

■ **You do not write "normal" SQL,** but a slightly different dialect using EJB Query Language.

■ **The EJB container generally handles persistence and querying.** Embedded hints in the form of code annotations define the management of data and relationships in data, such as sequence-number generation and master-detail queries. Most Oracle developers are accustomed to writing this code themselves and will probably feel that EJBs lack the degree of control that they require.

■ **EJB is a bare-bones framework.** You need to write your own code to add capabilities, such as validation in the EJB layer.

NOTE
Oracle's implementation of EJB 3.0 within the Oracle Application Server and the OC4J J2EE container uses TopLink under the covers. This foundation opens the way for users of Oracle's particular implementation to use native SQL, and to gain all of the benefits in performance and resource usage that TopLink provides.

Selecting the O/R Mapping Tool

This book assumes that you're approaching J2EE development from a relational and PL/SQL perspective. As such, we don't have any hesitation in recommending that you use ADF Business Components. This recommendation is not intended to minimize the effectiveness of other options, but experience has shown that Oracle Forms developers in particular adapt to ADF Business Components fairly quickly. We'll look at some of the reasons for that next. However, one of the benefits of using the ADF framework is that, should you choose to use any of the other options, such a decision won't really affect the user interface of the project; it will just affect the mechanics of the model or database integration layer and the amount of code that you have to write.

ADF Business Components is attractive for several reasons:

- **It emphasizes declarative definition.** It's possible to build a relatively sophisticated database integration layer without a single line of handwritten code. You can generate default mappings to database tables using a wizard, much as you would generate a default block in a form. JDeveloper will *introspect* (automatically examine properties of) the database schema and not only generate the table mappings, but also put in place all of the artifacts and rules required to enforce referential integrity.

- **It provides the ability to define basic validation rules** in a declarative fashion, just as with declarative O/R mapping. This type of declaration includes validating an attribute based on a database lookup—something which we find relatively easy in PL/SQL and Oracle Forms but which is generally not an off-the-shelf function in O/R mapping frameworks.

- **It exploits the power of the database.** ADF Business Components will run against non-Oracle databases, but Oracle is its core competency, and this allows it to support functionality such as *inter*Media types and direct integration with PL/SQL.

- **It provides a rich event model,** much like the trigger points available in Forms or database triggers.

As we look at ADF Business Components in detail in Chapter 6, we'll continue to draw parallels with the Forms world in particular, since so many things are similar.

Why Is JDeveloper an IDE for RAD?

As the title of this book states, we use Oracle's JDeveloper as our working environment throughout the book. This is not to say that anything we'll be talking about has to be done in that particular IDE; however, there are several reasons for choosing JDeveloper:

- **It is specifically designed as a complete, integrated, and productive environment for end-to-end development.** Competing IDEs do not have the full range of tools that you are likely to need (at least, not without paying for additional plug-ins).

- **You can code more than just Java in JDeveloper.** You can also model database schemas, and develop and debug PL/SQL and SQL—all tasks that are likely to be needed at some stage in a typical database application development life cycle.

- **It fully supports Oracle ADF,** up to and including deployment of the finished application.

- **It is the best tool for creating an application that uses Oracle database and middleware suite.**

Although this book is primarily about application development, providing a complete rundown on all the JDeveloper functions and features would consume a book in its own right. As mentioned in the introduction, you can refer to the *Oracle JDeveloper 10g Handbook* (Roy-Faderman, Koletzke, and Dorsey, 2004, McGraw-Hill/Osborne, ISBN 0-07-225583-8) for a more comprehensive introduction to the product.

A Familiar IDE?

All modern IDEs, irrespective of the languages or methodologies they support, tend to resemble one another to a certain degree. Although the look and feel of the windows and controls in JDeveloper may be somewhat more modern than the Oracle Forms or Designer interfaces, these key windows are the same:

- Application Navigator
- Property Inspector
- Code editors and visual editors
- Component Palette

Several other key panels might be less familiar to someone from a Forms background, for example:

- Connections Navigator
- Structure window
- Message area
- Thumbnail view for diagrams
- Data Control Palette

Before we take a brief look at each of these areas, let's discuss the realities of J2EE application development. There are a lot of files to manage. In a Forms or Web PL/SQL Toolkit application, you are accustomed to coding a single module or script to define multiple screens as well as most of the logic required to hold them together, including the database access. In the J2EE world, this is turned on its head. A single screen may consist of multiple files of different flavors. For instance, to fully define a JSF page, you might well have:

- A JSP file defining the UI layout
- A Java file containing all of the event handlers (triggers) for the page
- One or more entries in an XML configuration file that defines the navigation rules between all pages of the application
- An XML file defining all of the data bindings used by the page

Moreover, that list doesn't even consider the files that will make up the business logic and database access portion of the JSF page.

Therefore, where a medium-sized Oracle Forms application with 12 blocks, 12 windows, and six master-detail relationships can be contained in one .fmb file, a similar set of features implemented in J2EE web technologies might require over a hundred files. In addition to the sheer number of files, the location of those files is also important. Unlike conventional PL/SQL or Forms development, where the location of the source scripts or files is largely immaterial to the application, J2EE applications require discipline for locating the files on disk. The J2EE standards require that files be placed in specific directories. Therefore, you need help so all of these bits fit together and are deployed correctly.

The JDeveloper IDE will, of course, help with this by placing files in the correct places by default, and even generating some of the key deployment files for you, such as the *web.xml*, the web module deployment descriptor file (introduced in Chapter 2 and discussed later in this chapter).

TIP

As you are starting out, take the time to look at how JDeveloper lays out your projects on disk. Should the day come that you have to merge someone else's code into your project or recover a lost file, knowing where the files are located can make that task much simpler.

Getting Started with JDeveloper

The introduction to this book provides information on downloading and installing JDeveloper. You can then start it by running the jdeveloper.exe file in the root install folder (if you are on Windows), the application icon (on Macintosh), or the /jdev/bin/jdev script (on Unix and Linux computers). The IDE displays as a single window containing multiple child windows. Some of the windows may not be immediately visible in the IDE. However, the View menu provides a way to access each one. Shortcut keys also allow you to access these windows.

TIP

If you have problems finding one of these windows, or you just corrupt your layout beyond recovery, delete (or rename) the file windowinglayout.xml, which you'll find under the jdev\system\ oracle.ide.10.1.3.n.n\ folder. When you next start JDeveloper, it will revert to the default layout.

The Application Navigator and System Navigator

The Application Navigator (CTRL-SHIFT-A) provides an overview of all of your programming work, much like the Oracle Forms Object Navigator does. The top-level nodes represent logical *applications* (*workspaces*), which are collections of projects represented as .jws files on disk. Each workspace contains one or more *projects*, which encapsulate the actual coding of the application. The workspace itself has no real properties or attributes. The project as a logical entity points to a source tree of code and metadata, and you deploy all files in the project at the same time.

Convention has it that projects within an application are split along architectural lines. For instance, in a typical web application that uses the MVC architecture, the default application template creates two projects: one project called "Model," which will contain your application business logic, and a second project called "ViewController," which will contain the user interface (View) and page flow (Controller) code. There is nothing to stop you from creating more projects to subdivide an application further, for example, for functional areas of the UI.

Within each project, you'll see one or more nodes, which subdivide the files within the project directory structure into logical groups based on the project contents—for example, Application Sources, Web Content, and Resources.

The System Navigator (CTRL-SHIFT-N) is an alternative view onto the workspace; it provides an on-disk, file-based view of a project rather than the logical view provided by the Application Navigator, as shown here:

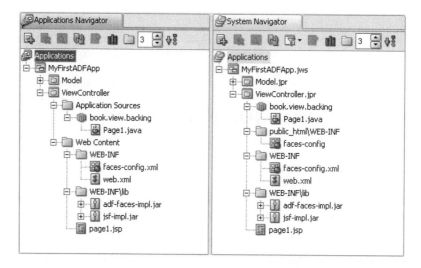

As you can see from this illustration, the implications of choosing one navigator style over another will depend on the types of objects within the project. Basic file types, such as .jsp or .java source files, are represented in an identical manner. Many of the objects represented within the IDE, such as a JSF configuration file or a web-service definition file, are actually complex and composed of several physical files. These compound objects are represented differently in the two navigators. As an example, faces-config.xml (the JSF configuration file) is represented as a single node in the Application Navigator. In the System Navigator, it is shown to be composed of two physical files: faces-config.xml, which is in the /WEB-INF directory, and faces-config.oxd_faces in the /public_html/WEB-INF directory. In this case, the former file is the XML metadata file that configures JSF, and the latter is the diagram file that the IDE uses to draw the page flow.

The System Navigator is most useful when you are actively source-controlling a project and need to work at the physical file level to manage differences. For day-to-day use, you will probably find the Application Navigator view sufficient. The sidebar "Dynamic Projects in JDeveloper 10.1.3" describes the contents of the navigators in more detail.

The Property Inspector

Another familiar friend for Oracle Forms users is the Property Inspector (CTRL-SHIFT-I). The Property Inspector, shown next, operates just as you would expect it to, although some of the visual hints it provides are slightly different.

InputText - Employee Name - Property Inspector

General	
Label	Employee Name
Columns	
RequiredMessageDetail	
Rows	1
Validator	
Value	#{bindings.EmployeesView1LastName.inputValue}
ValueChangeListener	
AccessKey	

Go to Page Definition.   Edit Binding...

Character used to gain quick access to the form element specified by the for, if set (or this component itself, if it is a "non-simple" form element). For accessibility reasons, this functionality is not supported in screen reader mode. If the same access key appears in multiple locations in the same page of output, the rendering user agent will cycle among

Dynamic Projects in JDeveloper 10.1.3

The JDeveloper project file (.jpr) on disk does not list the explicit contents of a project. Instead, it defines all of the source directories for a project and a series of filters that are used to actively configure the display in the navigators. (You can define filters by double clicking a project node to display the Project Properties editor and selecting the Project Contents node.) Any files within the mapped directories that pass the filters are automatically and dynamically included in the project, hence the term *dynamic project*. To add a file to a project, you just have to create it in, or copy it to, one of these mapped source directories. Conversely, you can exclude files from a project, either by deleting them or by adding a filter to the project properties that excludes that particular file or file pattern.

A common case for using a filter is for source control management files and subdirectories, such as those used by CVS or Subversion. You need these source control files present in the correct directories, but you do not want to see them within the navigator or use them in the build process. Filters hide them from view in a nondestructive way. By default, the projects will automatically have a default set of filters to exclude these common cases from view.

The dynamic project concept also allows for creating multiple *working sets*—view ports into the same source code tree. Working sets allow the developer to define a series of named filters, which can be applied to simplify the structure in the Application Navigator for a particular task. Use the **View | Options | Manage Working Sets** menu option or the Working Sets button in the System Navigator toolbar to define, select, and manage working sets.

The Property Inspector contains three sub-panels:

■ **Properties**   This area displays property names and values that you can edit.

■ **Tasks**   *Tasks* are hyperlinked shortcuts to actions associated with the object you are editing, in this case, "Go to Page Definition" and "Edit Binding."

■ **Property hint**   The area at the bottom of the Property Inspector shows an explanation of property currently selected in the properties area.

You can resize the tasks and hint areas by moving the splitter bars.

TIP
A green box next to a property label (as shown for the Label property in the illustration) indicates that the property has been overridden from its default value. The blue database-style drum symbol (as shown for the "Value" property in the illustration) indicates that the property is data-bound in some way and that a special bindings editor is available to help you edit the binding expression.

Code Editors and Visual Editors

You have the option of working with more than one kind of editor in JDeveloper. Some editors are code-based, such as those for Java, PL/SQL, or XML; others are UI designers or visual modelers. All of these editors will appear in the central region (document area) of the IDE (as described in the "Laying Out the IDE" section later). The available views on a particular editor are shown as *editor tabs* along the base of the editor panel, whereas the *document tabs* along the top of the editor panel represent all of the objects being edited. The visual UI editors and diagrams also have an editor-specific toolbar within the editor tab, as shown here for the JSF Navigation Diagram:

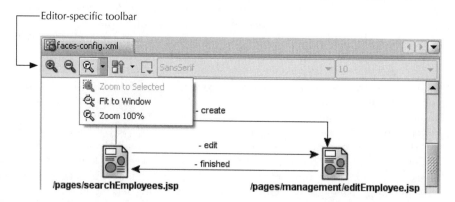

All of the editors in JDeveloper 10.1.3 offer a History editor tab. This view allows you to examine the changes that have been made to the file. If you are using a source control system such as CVS, this history will include the version history from the repository. If you are not using source control, it will just reflect the local history of the file that JDeveloper maintains for a development session. An example file history when CVS is being used is shown in the following illustration:

You can use this editor history view in three ways:

- **As a convenient way to review changes made to a file**   These changes, or *diffs* (differences), are highlighted when you select a version of the file in the revision frame.

- **As a super-undo facility**   When you find a diff that you want to undo, you can select it and reapply the old version of this statement. This contrasts with conventional Undo, for which you have to undo all of the intermediate steps to return to the prior desired state.

- **As a way of generating patches**   If you have made changes to a version of a file, perhaps to fix a bug, you can generate a patch file to apply to the original version of the file. This is most useful in environments where fixes and changes to source code files are controlled or have to be approved.

Component Palette

The Component Palette (CTRL-SHIFT-P) dynamically changes to reflect the current editor in focus. When you are editing a user interface definition, such as a JSP file, the Component Palette will, of course, contain the widgets and tags that can be dropped into that UI. When editing a piece of code, however, the available components may be code snippets, and with an XML file, they will be the valid XML elements.

At the top of the Component Palette, you will also see a dropdown list of palette pages. This list allows you to select different sets of configured components based on the type of document in the editor area. Some of these pages will allow you to add or remove components (for example, the Code Snippets page), and you can always add extra pages to the palette for anything you need frequently. The following illustration shows different views of the Component Palette that appear for the JSF configuration file and JSF pages, respectively:

NOTE
The Component Palette pages are displayed based upon selected files and the Technology Scope selections you define in the Project Properties dialog. Double click the project to display the Project Properties dialog.

The Connection Navigator

The Connection Navigator (CTRL-SHIFT-O) provides a view of the IDE's links to external resources. You are initially concerned with connections to databases, but connections to application servers will become important when you need to deploy an application. All connections nodes work in a similar way: You select New from the right-click menu on the top-level node to display a creation wizard; then you follow the wizard to create a connection definition. Once connections are established, you expand the tree nodes to explore the contents of the external resources. The illustration on the right shows an expanded view of a database connection; this allows you to browse the objects within that schema. The connection node for database connections is similar to Form Builder's Database Objects node, except that JDeveloper also allows you to create and edit more objects, and provides a SQL worksheet for constructing ad hoc queries. This database connection area allows you to use JDeveloper for PL/SQL and SQL programming and debugging, as well.

The Structure Window

Many of the objects that we edit within the IDE are complex and are either made up of several files combined into one logical entity or have some internal hierarchical document structure that can be represented as a tree. The Structure window (CTRL-SHIFT-S) provides a drilldown into the internal makeup of a particular node in the main navigator, and is a powerful tool for understanding and editing the object. The following illustration shows a structural view of a Java source file. You can quickly navigate around the source by double clicking the nodes in the Structure window.

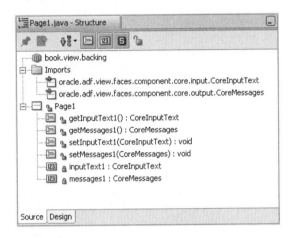

Like the editors or the Component Palette, the Structure window contents will change, depending on the type of object selected. It offers various options to filter or order its contents to suit the required use. It's always worth exploring the context menu on the Structure window just to see the available options.

Much as the main Application Navigator and System Navigator provide alternate views on the files involved within the project, so, too, does the Structure window provide both logical and physical views of a single file—in tabs at the bottom of the panel. In the illustrated example of a .java file, the Design view is available for developers building Swing user interfaces using Java code. As you would expect, different file types expose different views appropriate to the function of that file and its complexity.

The Log Window

Throughout the development process, JDeveloper will keep you informed about progress on tasks such as compiling, deployment, and code generation using various tabs in the Log window message area. When you debug your applications, many of the debug windows will also appear in this area.

Diagram Thumbnail

The Thumbnail window is a useful facility. It displays a miniature view of any diagram (such as a JSF page flow diagram) that is active in the editor area. You can position a view port box in the Thumbnail window to reposition the view port in the visual editor. You can then use the mouse to zoom in and out on the main diagram using the scrolling wheel (if you have one). So if you have a large and complex diagram, you can use the thumbnail view to provide an overview, while keeping the main diagram in the editor at a comfortable zoom level and focused on the area of interest. The following illustration shows this window floating over the JSF Navigation Diagram window.

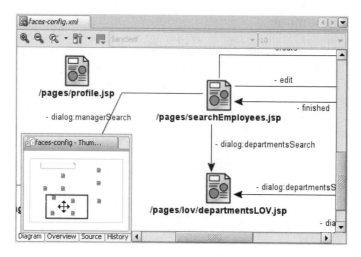

Data Control Palette

Finally, in our lightning roundup of the primary windows in the IDE interface, we come to the Data Control Palette (CTRL-SHIFT-D). This palette exposes one of the key RAD features of the ADF framework—the available data controls. We'll discuss data controls in much more detail in Chapter 7, but in summary, this palette exposes all collections of data (such as the results of database queries) that you can bind into your application user interface. The IDE allows the developer to drag and drop data objects from this palette onto a screen editor. The IDE then creates all of the runtime ADF Model bindings. This simple method of binding means that the developer usually does not have to be concerned with any of the mechanics of actually interacting with the data. The ADF Model layer in the framework handles the mundane tasks, such as establishing the database connections, issuing the query, caching, paging, and so on. The following illustration shows an example collections hierarchy in the Data Control Palette.

Laying Out the IDE

As you have seen, the IDE offers many different windows that convey various bits of useful information. In addition, JDeveloper is exceedingly flexible in its screen layout; you can move windows around within the main IDE window and dock them into a layout that makes sense. Docking a window fixes it to one of the sides of the IDE window frame. There are five layout zones for dockable windows, as shown in the following illustration. The preferences screen shown (accessed through **Tools | Preferences** and then selecting the Environment\Dockable Windows node) allows you to change the relative shapes of these zones.

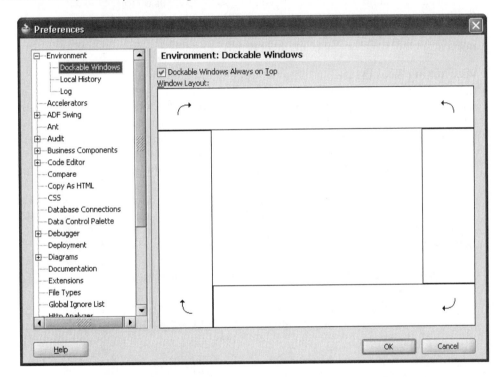

You control the position of a dockable window by dragging and dropping it onto one of these zones (in the IDE). The central zone, or document space, is reserved for the main editors. You cannot move the editors from this central position. You can place the other windows we mentioned before in the left-hand, right-hand, or bottom zones. The top docking zone is also available to some of the panels, but only really makes sense for the Component Palette, where it will lay out the available components like a toolbar.

Within each of the docking zones, you can place windows next to each other on any edge, or you can drop them on top of each other. In the latter case, the panels will share the same area in the docking zone and you can use the panel's tabs to switch focus between them.

TIP
JDeveloper borrowed a convenient shortcut from the Mozilla Firefox browser. If you have a mouse with a scrolling wheel, you can close any window by clicking the wheel button on the window's tab. You can of course also close the panel by clicking the conventional close control icon that will appear when the mouse hovers over the tab or by using the relevant keyboard shortcut.

You can also undock any dockable window so that it floats on top of the IDE window. You can also drag them together to create a floating window with several windows (tabs) in it. This works particularly well on a system with multiple monitors, where you can use one screen for the editor area and another screen for all of the other panels.

Maximizing Real Estate

There is an unwritten law that a programmer can never have enough screen space, no matter how many monitors he or she has. It is equally true that most purchasing managers fail to appreciate the vast productivity enhancements that dual or triple screens can introduce into the development process. You lose a significant amount of time resizing, moving, and otherwise manipulating the windows in a complex IDE such as JDeveloper. This requires time and thought you could be spending on the development tasks at hand instead, if all windows were already open and sized reasonably.

Undocking panels and moving them away to provide a larger editing area works best when you have multiple monitors. Also, you can minimize (collapse) windows to the edges of the screen (using the minus button in the window's top-right corner), in a style somewhat like the Windows taskbar. These minimized panels will pop up as the mouse hovers over them. The next illustration shows the Property Inspector window expanded after being minimized into the IDE frame. Pointing the cursor at the minimized icon expands the window until the cursor is no longer within the borders of the window, which causes the window to minimize again.

General	
GlobalOnly	false
Message	
AttributeChangeListener	
Id	messages1

Go to Page Definition

Inspector   Log   Tasks

JDeveloper also provides a quick-maximize feature. Double click the tab label of any window (including the editor window), and the panel will expand to fill the IDE window. Double click it again to restore it to normal. If you need access to the Property Inspector or the Component Palette while in maximized mode, you'll need to toggle back to see those panels, or already have them undocked and floating.

Splitting and Pinning

As you start to use the IDE in earnest, you will learn what works best for you. There are many other subtle features for manipulating the layouts of panels and windows to exactly suit your needs.

Many of these features are also present in the Forms Builder, if somewhat underused. You can, for example, split a panel into multiple views. This is particularly useful in the visual editors, where you can split the pane and display both the visual and source code views of the same screen definition. To activate this feature, drag the split panel bar next to the right-hand arrow on the horizontal scrollbar or above the up arrow on the vertical scrollbar.

You can also open multiple copies of some windows, such as the Property Inspector, by clicking the New View icon on their toolbars and then using the Freeze View icon (pin) to fix the view of one of the panels to a particular object.

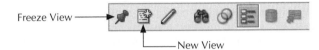

This is handy if you need to compare the properties of two objects side by side.

In summary, the IDE is highly flexible and offers many options you can explore to make it work the way you need it to. Take some time to explore the IDE to see what works for you.

Where Are the Wizards?

You might expect one trademark of a RAD tool to be the availability of wizards. Wizards often help you get started with a basic application skeleton, but thus far we have not mentioned them. Wizards exist within JDeveloper. Some are restricted to creating objects (files), and are not re-entrant; others are used for both creating and editing files. For example, the Create JSF JSP Wizard gathers information such as the tag libraries and page style that you want to use. When you exit the wizard, JDeveloper creates the page, but from there, you're on your own. You will use editors and the Property Inspector to modify the code and will not return to the wizard for that page.

The one area in JDeveloper where you will see a more traditional wizard-enabled environment is in the creation of ADF Business Components. Here, you use wizards for the initial creation of multiple interrelated objects as a default skeleton application. ADF Business Components offers this approach because much of that framework is declarative. As such, wizard-type UIs are the most efficient way of gathering all of the configuration information. In addition, the wizards reappear (as property editors) when you need to modify the ADF BC definitions. We'll look at this in more detail in Chapter 6.

A Different Approach to RAD

It is important at this stage to understand the philosophy of JDeveloper as a product. The "Productivity with Choice" banner that you see on the splash screen extends not only to the technologies that you can select to implement the various layers of your application, but also to the development techniques that you use. JDeveloper offers you a choice of visual, declarative, or raw source code views on a particular object.

Let's consider a JSF page, for example. When you open a page in the navigator, you'll initially see a visual editor, which shows a preview of the JSF screen with the components rendered and with placeholders to represent bound information, such as the results of a query. This is a RAD view of the page. You can edit the page in this view using drag-and-drop techniques to add and move components or keypresses to copy and remove them.

The Structure window provides an alternative perspective on the same page. This window provides a hierarchical representation of the components on the page, with the nesting of components within their parents and containers. Again, you can edit the contents of the page in this view, although in this case, you are altering the logical structure of the page to change the visualization rather than changing the UI layout directly.

At first, this structural view of an object like a page may seem less useful than the visual layout editing. However, you will find that the one benefit that it does offer on complex screens is the precise placement of components. Often, in the visual view, it can be tricky to drop a component in the correct place. The Structure window view provides a much simpler way of ensuring that an object ends up where you want it. In both the visual editor view and the structural view, you use the Property Inspector to set individual attributes of the object you are editing.

TIP
The Structure window is the quickest way to reorder or reposition components. For example, changing the visual order of a set of fields is just a matter of dragging and dropping their nodes in the Structure window hierarchy. This technique is akin to, but much more flexible than, dragging and dropping items within Form Builder's Object Navigator.

JDeveloper also provides a source code view of the page, where you can directly edit the markup code for the JSF page. The other views will synchronize with your code changes in real time.

JDeveloper tries to present these three types of editors for any source or metadata file, not just for UI pages. For example, the JSF application configuration information (in faces-config.xml) is stored as an XML file and contains several subsets of configuration information, such as the application navigation model and the JavaBeans that JSF is managing. The editor for this configuration file has the following views to enable editing in both visual and nonvisual ways:

■ **Diagram view** of just the page flow navigation metadata, as shown here:

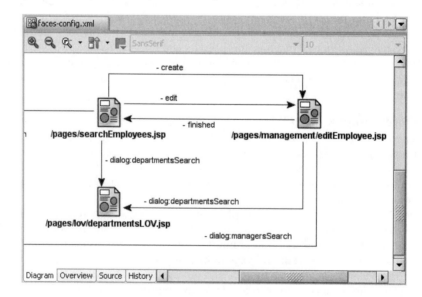

■ **Dialog-based view**, on the Overview page shown next, which provides a structured editing interface for the various subsets of JSF configuration information; this gives you more feedback and validation than you would receive from editing the raw XML.

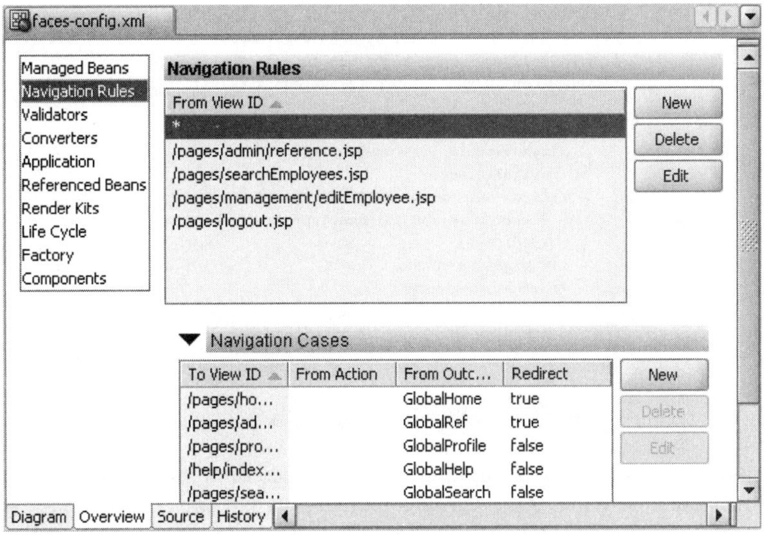

■ **Structural view** of the configuration XML provided within the Structure window, shown here:

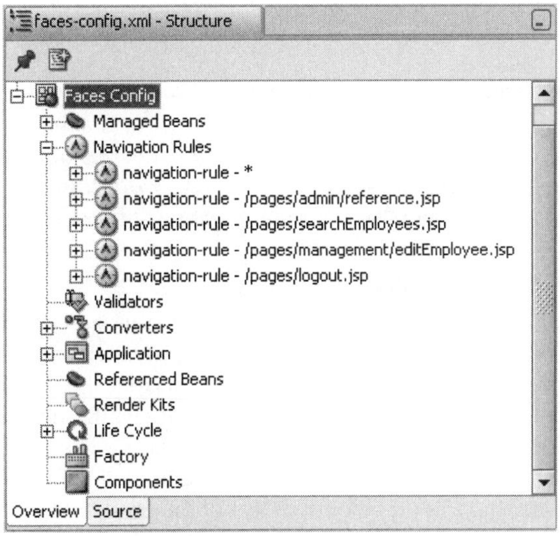

■ **XML source**, editable in the code editor (Source tab), shown here:

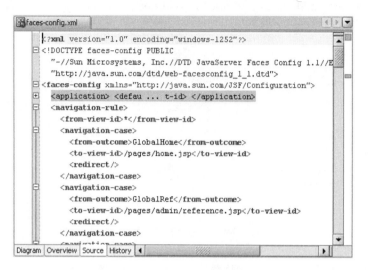

This approach of providing multiple synchronized editor views means that a developer can choose the most productive approach for a particular task. For example, an experienced developer might find it faster to work directly with familiar source code, benefiting from the control that typing provides (particularly to a touch typist). On the other hand, as a developer starts work on a new technology, the visual editor and diagram-based editor will provide a quick leg up to producing content and will also help in the learning process for that technology. The choice of development approach then, is very much up to you, the developer.

NOTE
In Part II of this book, you will step through creating sample applications in JDeveloper. In those steps, we demonstrate various techniques we have found useful. You will have a chance to try different techniques and get a sense of which one works best. Often a combination of techniques is required to be the most productive.

The RAD Is in the Frameworks

Although the traditional face of RAD has been the design-time availability of wizards or visual editing, in the J2EE world, this really doesn't work that well. If a tool attempts to provide a RAD interface for the raw low-level J2EE APIs, it may well make it simple to generate a basic application from a wizard, but the developer then hits a complexity wall. This was particularly obvious in versions of JDeveloper prior to the first release of 10*g* (9.0.5). The product at this stage offered some one-click application wizards that would generate a complete JSP application as a UI to a business components project. This was great for demos, but the problem then came when the developer wanted to customize or alter the wizard-generated code. The code was highly genericized to make the code generation steps simpler for the tool, but it was hard to understand as a result. For any serious application, it was generally easier to start from scratch rather than attempt to customize the generated code.

Effective RAD within the J2EE development process is not exposed as a feature of the tool, but rather is in the implementation of the runtime frameworks. Frameworks in the J2EE world are all about providing convenience and abstraction on top of low-level APIs, making for accelerated development cycles by shielding the developer from having to operate at that level. Meta-frameworks like ADF add an additional layer of abstraction by providing tooling that gives you a visualization of those frameworks in some form.

If we ignore the obvious visual screen editors and modelers within JDeveloper, the key RAD feature in the IDE is the Data Control Palette and its creation of the abstraction metadata used by the ADF Model. This abstraction saves you from having to write a huge amount of low-level code. This represents the largest opportunity for productivity gains within the development process. In Chapters 7 and 8, we examine exactly what is happening in this ADF Model layer and how it works.

CHAPTER
4

Required Web Languages
and Java Language Basics

Out beyond ideas of wrongdoing and rightdoing there is a field.
I will meet you there.
When the soul lies down in that grass the world is too full to talk about.
Ideas, language, even the phrase "each other" doesn't make any sense.

—Jelaluddin Rumi (1207–1273), *A Great Wagon*
(translated by Coleman Barks)

 raditional Oracle application developers, such as this book's authors, had it easy for many years. We were able to create complete applications coded mostly in one language—PL/SQL. In rare situations, we sprinkled our software solutions with snippets of other languages, such as Unix shell and Visual Basic; and, if we felt adventurous, we may have written extensions in the form of user exits in C or Pluggable Java Components in Java. However, PL/SQL was still the language with which we spent most of our development time. Even work with the PL/SQL Web Toolkit (mod_plsql) was performed primarily in PL/SQL, although this tool also requires fluency in Hypertext Markup Language (HTML).

In case you hadn't noticed, the days of the application written in a single development language are gone. For better or worse, J2EE web development work these days relies on many languages to create a full-featured application. Although tools such as JDeveloper 10.1.3 help greatly, web developers still need a working knowledge of multiple languages. This chapter discusses which languages you really need to know for J2EE web development in JDeveloper 10.1.3 and provides the basic language concepts for one of them—Java. In addition to introducing JavaServer Faces, Chapter 5 continues the discussion of J2EE web languages by providing the basics of HTML, cascading style sheets, and JavaScript. Chapter 9 provides a brief introduction to Expression Language. This chapter is structured around three main questions:

- **Which languages do I really need to know?**
- **What do I need to know about XML?**
- **Which Java concepts are important?**

Although this chapter and Chapters 5 and 9 provide basic concepts for some languages in an overview form, these overviews are not intended to replace more formal classroom training or self-guided training. Training in these languages will be much more extensive and should include programming problems that you must solve. Moreover, you become proficient in a programming language by applying the knowledge you gain from training to a real-world development project. The overviews in this chapter and the next are intended to get you started thinking about the languages and to point you to other references that can assist in the learning process.

Which Languages Do I Really Need to Know?

In the early days of Java, web development consisted of coding Java applets—user interface code written purely in Java that runs in the JVM (Java Virtual Machine) of the web browser. This style of coding was essentially done in a single language—Java. The next major Java-oriented web development solution was servlets—code also written purely in Java that runs in the JVM of an application server and returns HTML to the web browser. This style is closer to the style used with the PL/SQL Web Toolkit, because you embed HTML inside the main language's logic; therefore, even though the code is written in Java, a thorough understanding of HTML is required.

NOTE
Regardless of the web technology, whenever you create applications to be displayed in a web browser, HTML is a highly recommended skill. In addition, knowing about the languages that extend the capabilities of HTML—Cascading Style Sheets (CSS) and JavaScript— is also helpful.

The more modern J2EE technologies used for web development, JavaServer Pages (JSP) and JavaServer Faces (JSF) applications, rely less on code written purely in Java than the previous alternatives do. In fact, Java is not actually used at an advanced level in everyday J2EE web development. Naturally, the more you know about Java, the better, but you can be quite productive with a knowledge of Java on the level required for *scripting* (code snippets rather than full systems of Java classes); at this level, you are familiar with the basic Java concepts and language constructs, and can write logic to solve problems. The reason that Java is used less in JSP and JSF applications is that you program using JSP and XML tags rather than Java. The tags point to a tag library that lists Java class files. These class files implement the tag functionality, but you do not usually work directly with these class files.

In some cases, when creating a J2EE web user interface, you need to write Java code to implement custom business logic or page navigation. In this case, the IDEs, such as JDeveloper, handle much of the mechanics of creating and maintaining these files. In addition, the IDEs handle the *plumbing* (infrastructure code that connects all parts of the application) for you; you do not need to write Java code specifically for that purpose. Your main time is spent in writing the business-specific application logic that defines data validation and transformation and user interaction (page flow and events).

The level of Java skills required for web applications these days is akin to the level of PL/SQL knowledge required to be productive in Oracle Forms. You use PL/SQL in Oracle Forms to define what happens when trigger code is executed in response to a form event such as a button click. Additional PL/SQL skills may be required if you need to write more sophisticated database code to support Oracle Forms triggers, but the majority of development work performed in Oracle Forms uses PL/SQL as a scripting language.

CAUTION
Although it is possible to be productive developing a web application by using Java for scripting purposes, a web project cannot easily succeed using developers who only know this level of Java. An enterprise-class application will also require at least one expert-level J2EE architect who can set directions and standards, and who can either code or guide the coding of framework extensions.

How Much Code Will I Need to Write?

Modern IDEs and technologies such as JDeveloper 10.1.3 and ADF Faces reduce the need to write as much code as with previous Java web technologies. Since HTML is used for displaying content in the browser, a good understanding of HTML is important, even though the tools generate most of the HTML that you will need. Dragging and dropping components into a visual editor creates HTML and JSP tags that you can view and modify in the source code editor. At runtime, the Web Tier container assembles an HTML file with output from the tags and sends the file in an HTTP response message.

For example, you can use a single component from the ADF Faces library (`af:table`) and its child column component (`af:column`) to display an HTML table containing rows and columns of data (in addition to some user interface features, such as navigation buttons and sort buttons). You code this component by dropping it into the visual editor from the Data Control Palette (or Component Palette) and setting its properties using the Property Inspector. Setting properties, especially properties that bind the component to data sources, may require Expression Language. The internal workings of the Java, JavaScript, and XML code (used for the look and feel) that make up the component are not usually important; you are just using prewritten library code when you include its tag. However, should you need to modify the component's behavior in a way that the property interface does not provide, you will need to write some Java code.

More details about ADF Faces and JDeveloper 10.1.3 appear in later chapters of this book. The important point for this discussion of languages is that the style of coding using ADF Faces and JDeveloper 10.1.3 is different from previous versions of JDeveloper. Development with ADF Faces and JDeveloper 10.1.3 consists more of declarative programming (dragging and dropping components and setting their properties) than it does of writing lines of code. This means that the burden of mastering the many languages used in a J2EE web application is lessened.

How Much of Which Languages Do I Need to Know?

This book concentrates on explaining how to develop JSF-based applications, since these applications are easiest for a traditional Oracle programmer. The language skills required for JSF development in JDeveloper 10.1.3 are listed, with corresponding levels and uses, in Table 4-1. In this table, the Level Needed column designates one of the following skill levels:

- **Basic**   This level refers to an understanding of all language fundamentals, such as syntax, logic constructs, datatypes, code assembly, compilation, and library usage. A developer at a basic level will need to refer to code examples frequently but knows how to code the solution to a programming problem using the language. A developer will need to study the language formally or informally to achieve this level. Novice developers without this level will not be as useful for project work.

- **Intermediate**   This level includes all the basic skills plus the ability to quickly write basic code without having to refer to samples or reference material. Developers will quickly progress to this level from the basic level during the first project in which they use the language.

- **Expert**   This level includes all the intermediate skills plus a good understanding of how to modify framework functionality. This level requires a high-level of experience and facility with the particular language. A developer will progress to this level after assisting another expert developer with this type of code or after spending time coding a framework extension.

A prerequisite with all skill levels is the ability to find examples of code usages for the particular level; these reference sources are usually available on the Web or in books. The following discussion mentions websites available at the time of writing.

After a brief section about another language not shown in Table 4-1, XML, the rest of this chapter introduces Java at the basic level. Chapter 5 introduces HTML, CSS, and JavaScript; Chapter 9 introduces Expression Language.

Language (Use)	Level Needed	Primary Use
Java (using frameworks such as ADF Faces)	Basic	Writing specific business components code for validation and special handling of model objects, as well as coding conditional page flow.
Java (extending framework features)	Expert	Supplementing or replacing functionality supplied by the framework. This requires research into the framework's capabilities and architecture, as well as writing framework-level code.
HTML	Basic	Modifying code generated with component drag-and-drop operations; infrequently constructing new pages from scratch with no IDE support. You can (and should) code JSF pages without any HTML. The JSF tags and the HTML renderer take care of the HTML for you, but knowledge of HTML helps you understand the HTML they generate.
CSS	Basic/None	Defining, modifying, or using cascading style sheets for making the appearance of application pages consistent. If you use prebuilt look-and-feel templates, no CSS coding is needed.
JavaScript	Basic/None	Providing customized user interaction functionality, for example, special handling of a checkbox selection.
Expression Language	Basic/Intermediate	Supplying data to components from properties or methods in the application.

TABLE 4-1.   *Languages Needed for JSF Web Development in JDeveloper 10.1.3*

What Do I Need to Know About XML?

Extensible Markup Language (XML) is an omnipresent language in J2EE web applications. It is used whenever a hierarchical description is needed, for example, to store property values or to define the structure of a web page. The main aspects of XML that you need to know when developing web applications follow.

XML Is a Tag Language   XML uses the same syntax elements and structure as other tag languages, such as HTML. Like HTML, XML uses tag elements expressed with opening ("< tag >") and closing ("</tag>") tags; each tag element can have multiple properties to make its behavior explicit and customized; some tag elements can be embedded within the opening and closing tags of other tag elements. Therefore, if you understand how to read and write HTML, you understand how to read and write XML.

NOTE
XML requires "well-formed code," whereas in some cases, HTML does not. Well-formed code means that each start tag has a corresponding end tag.

XML Has No Standard Tags   The primary purpose and characteristic of XML is extensibility—that is, anyone can define an *XML schema*, which defines the *elements* (tags) available for a particular use and the properties for those elements. The XML schema declares the name of the elements, the properties each element offers, and how the elements are nested hierarchically. An XML schema is stored in an XML file; an older type of tag definition file, called *Document Tag Definition* (DTD), used a different syntax to store the allowable tags and attributes, but its use is rare these days. To prevent conflicts between XML schemas that define the same tags names but use them for different purposes, an XML schema is assigned a *namespace*, a general name for a set of XML tags. An XML document can reference tags from more than one namespace. You often see XML tags prefixed with a letter or two, for example, af:column; these prefixes specify the namespace (abbreviated as "xmlns") to which they belong.

TIP
You can find more information about XML at the w3c.org website and also in tutorials at www.w3schools.com.

Since the schema designer defines tags for a specific purpose, unlike HTML, there is no single set of XML tags that you can learn. Each XML schema has its own set of tags and rules for using them. Once you understand the concepts of opening and closing a tag element, of tag elements having properties, and of the hierarchical arrangements of tag elements, you have enough background in XML for the purposes of XML development.

NOTE
An example of hierarchical tags in HTML is the "title" tag, which can only be used between the "head" beginning and end tags, which, in turn, can only be used inside the "html" start and end tags. The "html" tag is the top of the HTML tag hierarchy.

JDeveloper Wizards and Editors Write and Maintain the XML for You   In JDeveloper 10.1.3, XML needed by some frameworks, such as Application Development Framework Business Components (ADF BC), is created and modified by interaction with property editors and wizards. All properties set in the wizards for ADF BC (and some other frameworks) are written into an XML file that you cannot edit using the JDeveloper Code Editor. Instead, you edit the XML file by reopening its property editor and interacting with the editor's pages.

JDeveloper offers property editors for some other XML files, such as the *faces-config.xml* file (which defines page flow and file locations for a JSF-based application), although you can also edit its source code in the Code Editor. Using the Code Editor to modify an XML file requires knowledge of the framework service the file defines. The Code Editor and Structure window in JDeveloper assist with syntax checking, but XML code is not compiled so you need to be careful when using the Code Editor. Since XML files are used for core definitions in many frameworks, making an error when editing an XML file in the Code Editor could cause an entire system to fail.

NOTE
*As mentioned before, this book focuses on development of JSF files
for the user interface layer. JSF is an XML-style tag language that,
combined with another layer called a render kit, outputs HTML tags
for a web application. Best practices state that, to make JSF files most
generic, you should not use HTML (or other markup language) tags in
conjunction with JSF tags.*

Which Java Concepts Are Important?

If you want to use Java at the basic level for J2EE web development work, it helps to know the
language foundations, control structures, datatypes, and operators. This section introduces some
of the basics in these categories, including some of the terms you will run into when reading
about Java code. For more examples, consult the resources mentioned in the "Resources" section
at the end of this chapter.

Java Foundations

Java is defined by J2SE specifications (explained briefly in Chapter 1) outlined in the *J2SE
Development Kit* (JDK), previously called Software Development Kit (SDK). Java was released in
May 1995, and is considered to be an evolution of C++. Compiled C++ code is specific to an
operating system and requires the developer to manage the memory used by the program, for
example, by allocating and de-allocating memory and by addressing data using memory locations.
Compiled Java code is portable, which means that it will work in any operating system that can run
a Java interpreter.

Java and C++
Java shares the following characteristics with C++:

- **Java uses most of the same commands, operators, datatypes, and syntax characters**
  (such as the end of command ";" and comment delimiters "//").

- **Java is case sensitive.** This is important for those accustomed to writing code in PL/SQL,
  which is not case sensitive.

- **Java is multithreaded.** You can spawn threads that execute at the same time as other
  threads within a single operating system process. This saves memory and execution time.
  Although this feature is not used in code that you write for J2EE applications, it is used by
  the server and development tools.

- **Java is an object-orientated language.** Object orientation (OO) is explored later in
  this chapter.

However, you need to be aware of some differences. If you do not have experience with
C++, these differences are merely academic. In Java, there is no need (and no way) to explicitly
manage program memory. Another difference is that Boolean values (true and false) do not
evaluate to a number, as they do in C++.

The foundational concepts you need to know when starting to work with Java are code
organization, code units, object orientation, a few other Java concepts, and the Java code life cycle.

Code Organization

Java code is located in class files, and class files appear inside packages. The class path and import statements ensure that code is accessible. Libraries store collections of classes oriented towards a common function.

Classes All Java code is stored in a named container called a *class*. Java does not offer the ability provided by PL/SQL to execute code from anonymous blocks. One Java class usually corresponds to a single file. The class is declared as in the following example:

```
public class Employee
{
}
```

The class declaration starts with an *access modifier* (or access specifier), public, that defines which class files can reference this class; in this case, all class files can refer to this class. The name of the class appears after the word "class." The curly brackets "{ }" define the *code block* that encloses the code units (not shown). Curly brackets are used throughout Java to enclose code blocks in the same way that PL/SQL uses BEGIN and END to enclose its code blocks. A Java class can contain a number of code units, just as a PL/SQL package contains a number of code units (cursors, functions, and procedures).

Packages Java class files that have some functionality in common are assigned to a *package*, which usually represents a file system directory. Class files and their packages can be placed in *archive* files that use a .jar or .zip extension (also called *JAR files*). The Java runtime can find and run class files inside these archive files. Archive files facilitate the handling of the many files that make up an application.

Class Path The Java runtime looks for files by navigating the directory list stored in an operating system (environment or shell) variable, *CLASSPATH*. This variable keeps the *class path*, a list of the JAR files used for an application. The class path can also include physical file system directories if the Java files are not archived; that is, they are separate files in the file system. For example, the class path in a Windows environment could mix JAR file and directory names, as shown here:

```
CLASSPATH=C:\JDev\jdk\jre\lib\rt.jar;C:\app\project;C:\app\project\lib\app.zip
```

In this example, the Java interpreter will look for class files inside the JAR file, the C:\app\project directory, and the Zip file.

Imports In order for the Java runtime to find class files within the class path, Java code must reference the exact location in the same way that PL/SQL must refer to the schema name of a package or procedure referenced in the code. For example, a PL/SQL procedure might contain the following snippet:

```
DECLARE
    v_employee_record    employees%ROWTYPE;
BEGIN
    v_employee_record := hr.employee_pkg.employee(v_emp_id,
        v_hire_date, v_dept_id);
```

The `employee_pkg.employee` function assigns variable values to a PL/SQL record.
`hr.employee_pkg` refers to the location of the employee function: the package, `employee_pkg`,
owned by the schema, `hr`.

Although the following snippet does not represent an exact translation of this PL/SQL code,
code that performs a similar function in Java might appear as follows:

```
app.project.employee.Employee newEmployee;
newEmployee = new app.project.employee.Employee(employeeId, hireDate, deptId);
```

Just as the PL/SQL variable, `v_employee_record`, was typed from the EMPLOYEES table,
the Java variable, `newEmployee`, is typed from the Employee class. The symbol
`app.project.employee` in the first line signifies the location of the code for the Employee
class—in the package (directory), `employee`, that is located within the app/project directory. In the
second line, the Java runtime will look within the directories or archives in the class path for the
app/project/employee directory and will execute the code found in the `Employee` class, in this
case, the constructor (discussed later). Although Java code has no concept of a schema owner, the
Java package is a loose parallel because it represents the parent location of the code object.

You can create a synonym for PL/SQL code that allows you to call the code without the
schema prefix, for example:

```
CREATE SYNONYM employee_pkg FOR hr.employee_pkg;
```

You then use the synonym in your code:

```
DECLARE
    v_employee_record    employees%ROWTYPE;
BEGIN
    v_employee_record := employee_pkg.employee(v_emp_id,
        v_hire_date, v_dept_id);
```

In Java, instead of a creating a synonym, you *import* classes used within the code so that the
interpreter knows the exact location of the file, for example:

```
import app.project.employee.Employee;
// more code here
Employee newEmployee;
newEmployee = new Employee(employeeId, hireDate, deptId);
```

The complete path to the class file, `app.project.employee`, added to the class name is called
the *fully qualified name*. The import must include this fully qualified name so that the class name
can be used by itself in the code. The employee package within the app\project directory would be
found in one of the directories or archives listed in the class path. The `import` statement must be
included in each class file that needs to use the `Employee` class without its fully qualified name.

NOTE
*A fully qualified name is relative to a directory or archive in the class
path list. This allows you to place the application and supporting files
inside any file system directory structure and adjust the class path
accordingly.*

Libraries   JAR files such as the ADF Business Components core classes can be collected into *libraries*, which usually provide a certain function such as database access. JDeveloper assigns libraries to projects automatically when you select an application workspace template to create an application workspace. At runtime, JDeveloper constructs a class path containing all the JAR files that make up the libraries assigned to the project.

Often, these default assignments are sufficient, but you may need to add libraries to the project definition for special requirements. You can add libraries using the Project Properties dialog in JDeveloper, as shown in Figure 4-1, which is available from the right-click menu on the project node.

Code Units

Java code appears in two types of code units within the class: methods and constructors. These code units can be overloaded in the class file. Accessors are special methods that manage variables in the class.

Methods   A method is declared much in the same way as a PL/SQL function or procedure. For example, you could declare a PL/SQL function in the following way:

```
FUNCTION calculate_commission(
    p_base_rate    NUMBER)
    RETURN NUMBER;
```

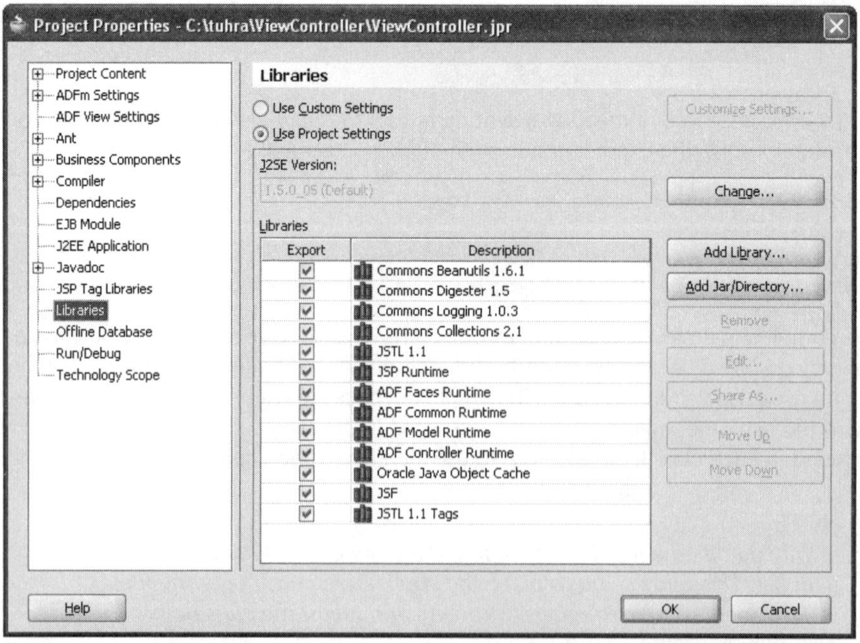

FIGURE 4-1.   *Libraries page of the Project Properties dialog*

In Java, a method is declared using similar elements, as in the following example:

```
public int calculateCommission(int baseRate)
```

Just as the declaration of a PL/SQL code unit is referred to as a *signature*, this declaration line in Java is called the *method signature*. The method signature in this example includes the same access specifier as mentioned in the class example before—`public`. The method signature also declares the return type, in this case, an `int` (integer). It also lists a parameter (argument)—`baseRate`—with its datatype (`int`).

Methods must be declared with a return type. If the method does not return anything (as with PL/SQL procedures), the `void` return type is used, as in the following example:

```
public void removeCommission(int empId)
```

Method code must appear with the class. At this level of organization, a Java class is similar to a PL/SQL package, where procedures and functions appear in the package body. Unlike PL/SQL packages, Java does not require a separate specification and body section, so the method signature only appears once in the class file. In addition, Java does not allow you to code standalone methods whereas PL/SQL allows you to code standalone procedures and functions.

Constructors Another type of Java code unit is the constructor. Like methods, its code must appear in the class. A constructor signature looks much like a method signature, except that it is missing the return type, for example:

```
public Employee(int empNo, int deptNo)
```

In this example, the word "public" represents the access modifier, as in the example methods. The name of the constructor, `Employee()`, is followed by its arguments. The constructor must have the same name as the class (including the same spelling and case usage). Therefore, the preceding example would be part of the `Employee` class. You can always identify constructors within a class file because they have no return type and because they have the same name as the class.

You use a constructor to create an object programmatically, as shown here:

```
newEmployee = new Employee(101, 200);
```

In this code, `Employee()` represents the constructor shown in the previous example. The idea of creating objects is described in the section "Object Orientation."

A constructor is a standard aspect of a class. If you do not code a constructor, you can still call the *default constructor*, which the Java compiler supplies; the default constructor uses no arguments.

TIP
It is good programming practice to write an empty, no-argument constructor in your class even if you do not need a constructor. That way, you and others reading your code know that you intend for the constructor to be empty.

The closest parallel to a constructor in PL/SQL is the optional default block in a package body (between the BEGIN and END keywords at the end of the package body), because this block of code executes when the package is first accessed in a database session. This code block is unnamed in PL/SQL, whereas in Java, a constructor must be named.

Overloading Java code may be overloaded. That is, more than one method or constructor with the same name can be coded in the same class file if those methods contain different argument lists (regardless of whether the return types are the same). This is similar in concept to the way that procedures and functions can have the same name in a single PL/SQL package if they have different parameter lists.

Accessors Another standard feature of a Java class file is the use of methods called *accessors* (or *getters and setters*), which assign the value of a variable at the class level, in the case of a *getter* method, or retrieve the value of such a variable, in the case of a *setter* method. By convention, these methods are named by prefixing the variable name with the words "set" or "get." For example, you might create a class file as follows:

```
public class Employee
{
  private int mEmpNo = 0;

  public Employee()
  {
  }

  public void setEmpNo(int newEmpNo)
  {
    mEmpNo = newEmpNo;
  }

  public int getEmpNo()
  {
    return mEmpNo;
  }
}
```

The mEmpNo variable is declared as a *member variable* or *class variable* at the class level, outside any method or constructor, just as you would declare a PL/SQL package variable outside any function or procedure. (Member variable names are often prefixed with an "m" although the root name is used for the accessor, as in this example.) This variable is declared with a default value of "0" and an access modifier of "private," which means that only code units within the class can access this variable. The setEmpNo() accessor method is responsible for changing the value of this variable. This method is public, which means that any class file can use it. The getEmpNo() accessor method is responsible for retrieving the value of the mEmpNo variable. It, too, is public, so any class file can call it.

NOTE
Boolean getter methods are usually prefixed with "is" instead of "get" to make their return value more explicit and to make the name more readable.

Accessors can hide logic that needs to be attached to a variable. For example, the setter could be written as follows:

```
public void setEmpNo(int newEmpNo)
{
  if (newEmpNo > 0)
  {
    mEmpNo = newEmpNo;
  } else
  {
    // throw an exception
  }
}
```

In this example, the setEmpNo() method validates the value passed to it before setting the variable. A business rule states that EmpNo values must be greater than 0. The setter not only sets the value of this variable based on the input, but also enforces the business rule. If the value is less than or equal to 0, it throws an exception (discussed in the "Exceptions" section later).

> **NOTE**
> *Naturally, the code example just shown is not complete. This class could also contain member variables for all other columns in the EMPLOYEES table. In a database-oriented application, after setting all variable values, the values would be written to the database.*

Object Orientation

PL/SQL's roots are in the Ada language, which is very different from Java's C++ roots. Understanding syntactical and keyword differences between PL/SQL and Java is usually not much of a transition for a PL/SQL developer, because structured programming control structures (conditionals and loops), datatypes, and variables are similar in any language. However, PL/SQL developers uninitiated in object orientation (OO) also need to understand OO concepts. This is probably the hardest hurdle to leap when learning Java. Fortunately, for the novice, the object-oriented concepts used most often in the basic level of Java programming needed for J2EE web development are easily grasped.

> **NOTE**
> *This section assumes you have little or no experience with PL/SQL's object extensions and, therefore, does not draw parallels between Java and PL/SQL object extensions. If you do have such experience, you will recognize many close parallels, since PL/SQL object extensions are based on principles of object orientation.*

Java incorporates the three basic principles of *object orientation* (OO): inheritance, encapsulation, and polymorphism.

Inheritance   The inheritance principle means that a class can be designated as a child of another class using the keyword extends, as in the following example:

```
class Employee extends People
{
}
```

In this example, the child class, Employee, will have available to it all the data (public variables) and behavior (methods) of the parent class, People, and can add to or replace that data and behavior as required. A *subclass* (child class) is considered a *specialization* of the parent class (the *generalization* of the child), because it refines or adds something to the parent.

NOTE
The "Object class" (java.lang.Object) is the main class from which all classes inherit. That is, if you follow the class hierarchy for any class up to the top level, you will find the Object class. Object is the default superclass. If you do not write an extends clause for a class declaration, that class is a subclass of Object.

As another example, when you create an ADF Business Components object to represent the DEPARTMENTS table, you can generate a Java class called DepartmentsImpl.java. This file serves as a location for code that you want to write to validate attributes (corresponding to columns in the table). It extends the ADF BC base class, EntityImpl, which supplies default behavior for accessing database objects. Here is an example of part of the DepartmentsImpl class:

```
// required import statements
public class DepartmentsImpl extends EntityImpl
{
  public static final int DEPARTMENTID = 0;
  public static final int DEPARTMENTNAME = 1;
  //... other attributes
  /**This is the default constructor (do not remove)
   */
  public DepartmentsImpl()
  {
  }
  public Number getDepartmentId()
  {
    return (Number)getAttributeInternal(DEPARTMENTID);
  }
  public void setDepartmentId(Number value)
  {
    setAttributeInternal(DEPARTMENTID, value);
  }
  public String getDepartmentName()
  {
    return (String)getAttributeInternal(DEPARTMENTNAME);
  }
  public void setDepartmentName(String value)
  {
    setAttributeInternal(DEPARTMENTNAME, value);
  }
  // ... more accessors
}
```

The class declaration states that DepartmentsImpl is subclassed from EntityImpl. Therefore, it inherits all methods and data (nonprivate class variables) from EntityImpl. The file also declares some *final variables* (*constants*), a default constructor, and accessors for each attribute in the class. The accessors call methods in EntityImpl, such as setAttributeInternal() and getAttributeInternal(). You could write your own code for validating data (in the case of the setters) or processing data before returning it (in the case of the getters). DepartmentsImpl, therefore, allows you to use the superclass's methods, but also allows you to specialize the standard methods provided in the superclass for the specific purpose of handling data from the DEPARTMENTS table.

You can only specify one parent for each Java class, but that parent can have a parent, and so on, up to an unlimited number of steps. Therefore, the functionality available to a particular class from its *class hierarchy* (the line of classes from the parent up to the Object class) can be substantial.

Inheritance is the most important of the three OO principles for Java work at the basic level, because you need to understand that a class file takes many of its characteristics from its parent. Other than its object extensions, PL/SQL does not offer features that parallel object-oriented inheritance.

Encapsulation   The encapsulation principle means that the details of the program being called are hidden from the caller. A good example of encapsulation is the member variable discussed previously (mEmpNo). Member variables are usually assigned a private access modifier so that no program unit outside the class in which they are declared has direct access to them. They are only accessed using getter and setter methods. This allows a caller to use the variable but hides the details about the variable from the caller, because any logic can be built into the getter and setter to protect the variable value.

You will use getter and setter methods frequently. For example, you write code in these methods when extending the ADF BC database access mechanism.

In PL/SQL, you can emulate encapsulation with a table API (and Virtual Private Database policies) that requires the user to access a table for SELECT, INSERT, UPDATE, and DELETE using PL/SQL procedures and functions. Triggers and policies can block or modify normal SQL operations to the table, so the user must use the PL/SQL procedures and functions for those operations. In this example, the table's data is like the private class variables in the Java class and the PL/SQL procedures and functions of the table API are like the Java class's accessors.

Polymorphism   The polymorphism principle means that a class can modify or override aspects of any class from which it inherits. A program that calls a method may not know which class from the class hierarchy is servicing the call.

This principle is applied most frequently at the advanced Java level when subclassing framework classes for specialized requirements. It is also used when creating template classes that will serve as a basis for other classes.

Classes and Objects   In object-orientated thinking, the *class* is a blueprint or pattern from which you will build something. The "something" you build from a class is an *object*. The preceding discussion has presented the Java class as the container for code units; the class also acts as the pattern on which code objects are built. In Java, an object looks much like a variable in PL/SQL; in fact, you will sometimes see an object referred to as a variable. An example of creating an object follows:

```
Object anObject;
anObject = new Object();
```

In this code, the symbol, anObject, is declared from the class Object. The second line of code *instantiates*, or makes, an object from the Object class using the new operator and calling the Object() constructor. Both lines are required to fully create the object, just as, in PL/SQL, you declare a variable and assign it separately. As in PL/SQL, you can collapse the declaration and instantiation into one line, as follows:

```
Object anObject = new Object();
```

After this code, anObject can use methods and variables coded into Object. Calling a method from the class hierarchy for an object uses the "." operator, for example:

```
anObject.toString()
```

In this case, the Object class contains a toString() method that is available to all objects built from it. The preceding expression would return a character representation of the class name and a hash number (for example, "java.lang.Object@3e86d0").

NOTE
The Javadoc for java.lang.Object recommends that you write a specific toString( ) method for classes you create. This is particularly important for classes that have variable contents that you would like to display. Otherwise, toString( ) will return only the class name and hash number, which is not very useful.

You can use the System.out.println() method to display the expression in the Java console (or JDeveloper message window), as follows:

```
System.out.println(anObject.toString());
```

In this same way, anObject has available to it all methods coded in its pattern class, or in any class in the pattern class's hierarchy (although, in this case, Object is the top level of the class hierarchy).

Other Java Concepts
Several other Java concepts will help your work at the basic level.

Access Modifiers   As shown in the preceding examples, you can place access modifiers on methods and class variables. Examples in the preceding discussion have used the public (available to any class) and private (available only to the current class) access modifiers. Two other access modifiers are available:

- **(no access modifier)**   If you do not specify an access modifier, the code unit will be available to other classes in the same package. This is called the *default access modifier*.
- **protected**   If you specify an access modifier of protected, the code unit is accessible from any class within the same package (as with the default access modifier) or from any subclass.

Static Variables and Static Methods   Class variables in the examples up to this point have been *instance variables*, which are accessible (through getters and setters) as separate copies in each object created from the class. *Static variables* are class-level variables that do not require an object. Consider the following Java class snippet:

```
public class Employee
{
    int mEmpNo = 0;
    static int globalEmpNo = 100;
```

This class declares an instance variable, `mEmpNo`, which would be accessible using the "object.variable" syntax. It also declares a static variable, `globalEmpNo`, that acts like a global variable (in a PL/SQL package specification, for example). Access to this variable does not require an object and is accessible using the "class.variable" syntax. For example, you might create the following code to assign the static variable:

```
Employee.globalEmpNo = 200;
```

Notice that this variable uses the class name instead of an object name as a prefix. Static variables are independent of any object, so no object name is appropriate.

Methods can also be marked as static, as in the following method signature:

```
public static void main(String[] args)
```

The `static` keyword indicates that the `main()` method can be executed without an object. Another example of a static method used in the preceding examples is `System.out.println()`. No object is required to call the `println()` method.

NOTE
The main( ) method is the method run when you start a class file from the command line. It must always be declared as the example shown, although the name of the argument may vary and, as with any array, you can define the String array argument with "String args[]" or with "String[] args".

Static methods cannot use nonstatic variables (instance variables). Any type of method can use static variables.

Interfaces   An *interface* is a list of method signatures that acts as a pattern for classes that you build. When you implement an interface, you must write code for all methods declared in the interface. The *implements* keyword declares that a class is built from an interface, as shown here:

```
class Employee implements Human
```

A class file can implement more than one interface, for example:

```
class Employee implements Human, Staff
```

An interface is somewhat like a PL/SQL package specification, which contains program unit declarations without code logic. The PL/SQL package body must contain all the program units declared in the package specification, just as a class implementing an interface must contain all methods declared in the interface.

You will find many examples of interfaces in framework code, although beginning-level Java developers will probably not need to create interfaces for their code.

Exceptions   Exceptions in Java can be raised by the runtime code or by code you create. Code that might cause an exception must be included in a block, starting with `try`. You can use the keyword `throw` to explicitly create the exception. Here is a small example:

```
try
{
  if (globalDeptId <= 0)
  {
    throw new RuntimeException("I must be positive today.");
  }
} catch (Exception empExcept)
{
  empExcept.printStackTrace();
}
```

If `globalDeptId` were negative or zero, the code would throw the exception, and the exception would print the message with the *stack trace*—details about the methods called including line numbers and class file names. A try block must have a catch block (or a *finally* block containing code that executes regardless of whether exceptions occurred) so that processing can occur after the exception. If you do not catch exceptions in this way, they will be passed back to the calling program (or command line, if you started the code from the command line). The try and catch blocks can also catch errors that are implicitly thrown. For example, if variable or expression values cause a divide-by-zero error in your code, a catch block could handle the exception even if you did not explicitly throw the divide-by-zero exception.

Naming Conventions   Names in Java code (for example, classes, methods, and variables) may be any number of characters. They can consist of any letter (uppercase or lowercase), any numeric character, an underscore (_), and the dollar sign ($). Names may not start with a numeric character. As mentioned, Java is case sensitive, so the use of uppercase and lowercase for a particular name must be consistent. So that your Java code is easily readable, it is best to follow these naming conventions generally recognized by the Java community:

- **Methods and variables (objects)** use the *CamelCase* naming convention, which defines identifiers as mixed-case names, with the first letter of each word uppercased. For methods and variables, the first letter is lowercased, for example, `salary`, `empCommission`, and `newHireDate`.

- **Classes, interfaces, and constructors** are also named with CamelCase but the first letter is uppercased, for example, `Employee`, `SalaryHistory`, and `AdfbcEntityObject`.

- **Constants** are named with all uppercase letters containing underscores to separate words, for example, `DISCOUNT`, `BASE_SALARY`, and `DEFAULT_DEPT_NO`.

Commenting   Java provides the following types of comments:

- **Single-line**   These comments are preceded by the "//" characters in the same way as PL/SQL uses the "--" (double dash) characters. You can also place these comments at the end of a line containing a Java statement, as with the PL/SQL single-line comment.

- **Multi-line**   These comments are delimited by "/*" at the start and "*/" at the end, the same as with PL/SQL.

■ **Javadoc**   These comments are also multi-line comments, but start with the "/**" characters and end with the "*/" characters. You can place these comments before a method or class to explain the purpose of the code. You then run the Javadoc executable (javadoc.exe in Windows) on the class file. The Javadoc executable extracts the Javadoc comments and writes them into an HTML file that uses a standard format. You will also see this format used for all third-party libraries, all core class documentation, and for the Java language.

Java Code Life Cycle

The code life cycle consists of four main steps that are common to most language environments, including Oracle Forms:

1. **Development**   Java source code files are separate from runtime files. Java code is written into plain text files (with a .java extension) that can be edited in any text editor.

2. **Compilation**   You run the javac compiler (in Windows, javac.exe) to compile the .java file into a .class file (the *bytecodes* file). The bytecodes (or *bytecode*) file is not executable on its own; it must be run using the Java interpreter (java.exe in Windows environments).

3. **Runtime (Test)**   You test the .class file using the *Java Runtime Environment* (JRE), a runtime interpreter (java.exe in Windows). The Java runtime session is called the *Java Virtual Machine* (JVM), although the terms JRE and JVM are often used synonymously. The JVM is like the Oracle Forms runtime for running .fmx files or the PL/SQL runtime engine in the database for running PL/SQL code.

4. **Deployment**   If you want to run the class file on another computer, you *deploy* the code—copy it to another computer that is set up with the required libraries, correct class path, and compatible Java runtime version. You can then run the Java code on that computer in a similar way to running it in test mode. Compiled Java code is portable between operating systems, so you do not need to recompile the source code file after copying it to a computer using a different operating system.

These descriptions of development, compilation, runtime, and deployment apply both to code run on the client computer—described in Chapter 1 as an application client architecture—as well as to code run on an application server—described in Chapter 1 as a web client architecture.

Control Structures

The normal flow of code runtime is for one line of code to run after the line directly before it. This implements the structured programming concept of *sequence*. Programming language control structures cause the code to execute in a nonsequential way so that the next code line to be run is not necessarily the next line in the source code file. The two main control structures to discuss are branching (selection) and iterative processing (the two other main concepts in structured programming). Since these concepts are familiar to PL/SQL developers, the Java control structures can be summarized with simple examples, as shown in Table 4-2 (for branching) and Table 4-3 (for iteration).

Java	PL/SQL	Java Example/Notes

if …
else
	IF … THEN …
	ELSIF …
	THEN …
	ELSE …
	END IF;
		`if (empNo <= 10)`
		`{`
		`   System.out.println("empno is <= 10");`
		`} else {`
		`   System.out.println("empno is > 10");`
		`}`
		The parentheses in the evaluation clause are mandatory. A single statement may appear after the evaluation clause without using curly brackets, but the use of curly brackets will help ensure that the logic is preserved when changes are made to the code. There is no single Java keyword corresponding to the PL/SQL ELSIF keyword, but you can nest if statements after the else clause (for example, "else if { }") as shown in this code snippet to create the same logic.

switch	(no parallel, but similar to CASE)	`switch (deptNo) {`
		`   case 101:`
		`      deptName = "Accounting";`
		`      break;`
		`   case 102: case 103: case 104:`
		`      deptName = "Also Accounting";`
		`      break;`
		`   default:`
		`      deptName = "Not Accounting";`
		`}`
		The break statement is required at the end of each paragraph so that the code does not flow into the next evaluation. The switch statement can only evaluate integer or *enum* (fixed set of constants) types.

TABLE 4-2. *Java Branching Statements*

Jump Statements

In addition to the loop structures, Java offers several *jump statements*—statements that break the sequential, branching, or iterative flow of the program, as follows:

Java	PL/SQL	Meaning
return	RETURN	Pass control back to the caller (the command line, if the statement appears in the first method started from the command line, or method that called the method containing this statement).
break	EXIT	Pass control out of the loop or switch structure. The PL/SQL equivalent, EXIT, only works within a loop structure.

Java	PL/SQL	Meaning
`continue`	(no parallel)	Within a loop structure, pass control back to the top of the loop, ignoring all statements in the loop after the `continue` statement.
(no parallel)	GOTO	Although Java offers no `goto` statement, the `break` and `continue` statements can reference a label (a word followed by a colon, such as `startHere:`) and accomplish an unstructured jump. As in PL/SQL, taking advantage of this feature is considered bad coding practice (unless there is no alternative) because it makes the code difficult to follow.

Java	PL/SQL	Java Example / Notes

`for`	`FOR ... LOOP ... END LOOP;`	<pre>for (int i = 0; i <= 10; i++){
		    System.out.println("i is " + i);
		}</pre> This loop will show a message for the numbers 0 through 10. The `for` statement includes sections for *initialization* (to assign the loop variable), *evaluation* (to determine whether the loop should continue), and *incrementing* (to increase the loop variable value).

`while`	`WHILE ... LOOP ... END LOOP;`	<pre>while (i <= 10){
		    System.out.println("i is " + i);
		    i++;
		}</pre> Assuming the `i` variable is initialized as 0 before the loop, this code prints a message for each number from 0 to 10. The variable in the evaluation expression must change during the loop to prevent an endless loop.

`do...while`	(no parallel)	<pre>do {
		    System.out.println("i is " + i);
		    i++;
		} while (i <= 10);</pre> This is the same as the `while` loop, except the evaluation is performed at the end. This means that the loop code is executed at least once (the first time through the loop).

TABLE 4-3. *Java Iteration Statements*

Datatypes

Java variables can be typed from classes, as discussed before. Although common usage of the word "variable" includes the idea of variables typed from classes, technically, variables typed from classes are *objects* (also called *reference variables*). True variables are typed using primitive datatypes that represent single data values with no methods. Variables typed from primitive datatypes are good for arithmetic and comparison operations because they are faster. Reference variables that evaluate to a number must usually be converted to a primitive before applying the arithmetic operator (although this requirement was relaxed in Java 5.0, it is still better for performance to convert to primitives). The overhead of the class instantiation (with its class hierarchy lookups) and conversion adds time to operations using reference variables. Therefore, it is best to type variables from primitive datatypes if you expect to be using their values for calculations or comparisons. Table 4-4 shows the primitive datatypes with their value ranges and includes notes about some of the corresponding PL/SQL types.

Wrapper Classes   Java offers *wrapper classes* that allow you to store primitive values: Byte, Short, Integer, Long, Character, Float, Double, and Boolean. These classes offer the ability to manipulate the value with methods.

Character String and Date Types

Java primitives do not provide for storage of more than one character. In addition, Java has no primitive datatype for storing date or date-time data. Therefore, storage of character string and date values must be handled by classes, such as String and Date (or others with similar features,

Primitive Type	Value Range
Whole Numbers	Correspond to PL/SQL's BINARY_INTEGER, PLS_INTEGER, NUMBER (with no precision definition), or any of their aliases (such as INTEGER and INT)
byte	−128 to 127
short	−32,768 to 32,767
int	−2,147,483,648 to 2,147,483,647
long	−9,223,372,036,854,775,808 to 9,223,372,036,854,775,807
char	integer of 16 bytes, 0 to 65,536 (this can represent a single character's ASCII value)
Decimal Place	Corresponds to PL/SQL's NUMBER (with precision) or its aliases (such as DEC, DECIMAL, FLOAT, DOUBLE PRECISION, and NUMERIC)
float	3.4e−038 to 3.4e+038
double	(1.7e−308 to 1.7e+308)
Logical	Corresponds to PL/SQL's BOOLEAN
boolean	true or false (not a number or a character string; no null value)

TABLE 4-4.   *Java Primitive Datatypes*

such as `StringBuffer` and `java.sql.Date`), corresponding to the PL/SQL datatypes `VARCHAR2` and `DATE` (or `DATETIME`), respectively.

String The `String` class holds multi-character values and includes methods such as `charAt()` and `length()` to operate on the value. You can create a `String` object using the `new` operator, as with any object, which the following example shows:

```
String someString = new String("This is a string");
```

This example creates the `someString` object and assigns to it the value "This is a string." You can also use a shortcut syntax to create a `String` object, as in the following example:

```
String someString = "This is a string";
```

Strings are *immutable*, which means that once a value is assigned, reassigning another value will create a different object in memory. The new value will be accessible, but the memory taken by the old object will not be released until the JVM's garbage collection process runs. In addition, the old object will not be accessible. Although you can reassign `String` variables on an infrequent basis, it is better practice to use the `StringBuffer` (in Java versions before 1.5) or `StringBuilder` (in Java versions 1.5 and later) classes for character values that will change frequently. `StringBuffer` and `StringBuilder` offer methods for removing, inserting, and concatenating characters to the variable without causing extra memory to be used.

Date The `Date` class, which is available in several varieties from different libraries, stores a date and time to the millisecond. You can assign a date using a long value representing the number of milliseconds from January 1, 1970. You can retrieve the long value associated with the date using the `getTime()` method. If you need to format the date object for display purposes, you need to create an object from the `DateFormat` or `SimpleDateFormat` classes and apply that format, as in the following snippet:

```
Date today = new Date(); // import java.util.Date before this
DateFormat dateFormat = new SimpleDateFormat(
    "EEEE MM/dd/yyyy hh:mm:ss.SSS aa zzz");
System.out.println("Today is " + dateFormat.format(today));
System.out.println("Milliseconds: " + today.getTime());
```

This will show something like the following:

```
Today is Tuesday 12/20/2005 09:23:46.846 PM EST
Milliseconds: 1135131826846
```

Date calculations require manipulating the long values that represent the dates or, preferably, using the `Calendar` class that contains methods for easily parsing out year, month, and day information. ADF Business Components contains its own `Date` class (`oracle.jbo.domain.Date`) that is used to represent date columns in the database.

NOTE
The Javadoc for SimpleDateFormat provides details about format mask letters, as shown in the preceding example. The DateFormat class also includes static constants that you can use for some prebuilt masks, such as DateFormat.LONG.

Datatype Matching and Casting

PL/SQL provides automatic type conversions (for example, from a VARCHAR2 to a NUMBER) if the values are compatible. Java enforces stricter type matching, but it does allow a value to be assigned to a nonmatching variable type if that type is *wider*—that is, it allows larger values or is a superclass of the value being assigned. For example, the following snippet will work:

```
int value1 = 1000;
long value3 = value1;
```

In this example, value3 is a `long` and it can be assigned an `int` variable because a `long` is wider than an `int`. The same principle applies to classes, although a class is wider if it appears higher in the other class's hierarchy. For example, an object created from a class could be assigned to an object created from the class's parent class.

You can also force Java to perform a type conversion using *casting*, which temporarily changes the type of a variable for a particular statement. Consider the following code:

```
byte numA1 = 50;
byte result = numA1 * 2;
```

This will cause a "possible loss of precision: int, required: byte" compiler error. All literal numbers are treated as `int` types. The multiplication of the `int` (2) with the `byte` (numA1) could exceed the allowed range of the `byte` result (although it will not with these particular values). You can cause the compiler to allow the statement by casting the entire multiplication expression to a byte, as shown here:

```
byte numA1 = 50;
byte result = (byte) (numA1 * 2);
```

The symbol "(byte)" defines the type you intend for the expression. This is a narrowing conversion, but it will work with the values in this example. This idea of casting variables applies to reference variables as well. You will see this type of casting in ADF BC code, as shown in the following code snippet from the `DepartmentsImpl` class, which casts into a `String` the output from a framework class method (`getAttributeInternal()`) that returns an `Object`:

```
Return (String)getAttributeInternal(DEPARTMENTNAME);
```

Arrays and Collections

As is true with most languages, Java provides a way to store more than one value in a single variable. *Arrays* in Java are multiple-row structures consisting of a single datatype (primitive or reference type). They correspond roughly to PL/SQL table variables. You can create multi-dimensional arrays in Java that correspond to PL/SQL tables of records, although Java arrays can be any number of dimensions. An array index number refers to a single row in the array. Java index numbers start with 0, as shown in this example:

```
int[] iList = {1,3,5};  // declare and initialize the array
for (int j = 0; j < iList.length; j++)
{
   System.out.println(j + ": " + iList[j]);
}
```

This will show the following:

```
0: 1
1: 3
2: 5
```

Collections in Java are classes that allow objects created from them to store multiple values (rows). As with all classes, collections offer methods that assist in iterating through the rows. Various collection classes exist for storing different kinds of objects, for example, `ArrayList`, `HashSet`, and `LinkedList`.

Operators

Operators act upon one or more values. Java operators are similar to operators in other languages like PL/SQL; in fact, some of the operators are the same, so not much discussion is required. Table 4-5 summarizes some of the Java operators that are different from their PL/SQL equivalents. Most of these operators are inherited from the C and C++ languages.

Name	Java Operator	PL/SQL Equivalent
Modulus (remainder)	`%`	`MOD()` function
Assignment	`=`	`:=`
Increment	`++`	(none)
Decrement	`--`	(none)
Addition assignment	`+=`	(none)
Subtraction assignment	`-=`	(none)
Multiplication assignment	`*=`	(none)
Division assignment	`/=`	(none)
Modulus assignment	`%=`	(none)
Equal to (for primitives)	`==`	`=`
AND	`&&`	`AND`
OR	`||`	`OR`
XOR (exclusive OR)	`^`	(none)
AND assignment	`&=`	(none)
OR assignment	`|=`	(none)
XOR assignment	`^=`	(none)
Ternary if-then-else	`?:`	`DECODE()` function
Concatenation	`+`	`||`
Creation	`new`	(none)

TABLE 4-5. *Some Java Operators and Their PL/SQL Equivalents*

Table 4-5 omits the bitwise operators that move or modify bits in a byte. These operators have no equivalents in PL/SQL and are not used frequently for business applications. The arithmetic assignment operators (such as addition assignment) assign a value to a variable with a shortcut syntax. For example, you can add 5 to num1 as follows:

```
num1 += 5;
```

The relational operators && (AND) and || (OR) are called *short-circuit* versions of & (AND) and | (OR), respectively. The short-circuit versions evaluate the Boolean expression on the left side of the operator. If the outcome of the operator is determined by that evaluation, the remainder of the expression is not evaluated. For example:

```
(1 > 0) || (5 < 6)
```

Since the first expression (1 > 0) is true, the second expression does not need to be evaluated. This saves a bit of time.

Resources

When learning and using Java, you will need to rely on websites as well as books.

Websites

As with all topics, a simple web search engine search for the word "Java" will provide more results than you will be able to read. A better way to use the Web is to look up examples or try to answer a question that you have about the language. This is not the best way to learn Java, however, because you may spend more time searching than learning. The best option for learning is to go to the source.

Since Sun Microsystems invented, maintains, and owns Java, the java.sun.com website is the first resource for information about the language. At this site, you will find the J2SE Development Kit (JDK) in various versions, discussion forums, and articles relating to Java. In addition, you will find the Java Tutorial, which explains the language basics and gives examples that you can try on your own. This tutorial is also available in book format should you want to refer to a hard copy.

In addition, *Thinking in Java*, by Bruce Eckel, is a well-established, popular, complete guide to Java that is available online at www.mindview.net/Books/TIJ. You can also purchase hard-copy versions of *Thinking in Java* from links on that website.

CAUTION
Anyone can publish anything on the Web, regardless of whether it is true, so it is always good to verify that the source you are referring to supplies accurate information. Gravitate towards sites that seem to be well established and favorably reviewed.

Books

Even though websites can provide useful information, you will have a better chance at grasping Java more fully if you also rely on printed reference books. Books often have been reviewed and corrected more thoroughly than content on the Web. Therefore, although errors can appear in any medium, you have a better chance at obtaining accurate information from a book. The Java Tutorial website mentioned in the "Websites" section can count as one of the books you refer to (since it has a printed version as well).

TIP
Chapter 5 from the Oracle JDeveloper 10g Handbook *(McGraw-Hill/ Osborne, by Roy-Faderman, Koletzke, and Dorsey) contains more introductory information about Java including longer code examples and hands-on practices; this chapter is available in the downloadable files for this book on the websites mentioned in the "Websites for Sample Code" section of the Introduction.*

In addition to the Java Tutorial, you will need at least four other books. This statement may seem a bit like self-promotion in a printed book, but we have found that, although nearly all information you need about Java is available on the Web, finding the correct information with code examples on the Web can take more time than just opening a book and flipping to the appropriate page.

The number of books you should have is a bit arbitrary, but, in our experience, one book, however good it may be, will not be able to answer all your questions or contain all the examples that you will need. Therefore, it is good to obtain multiple books that you can grab from the shelf and read when you have a question about a topic. Hundreds of books on the language exist, and it is difficult to select among them. Browsing the books at a local bookshop is helpful, even if you eventually purchase them from a discount source on the Web.

The actual titles you select are not as important as the quantity, but we have found *Java 2, The Complete Reference, 5th Edition* by Herb Schildt (McGraw-Hill/Osborne) a good place to start. Be sure to look for books that seem to discuss most of the basics, that are written in a style that is comfortable to you, and that contain understandable examples.

CHAPTER
5

JavaServer Faces Basics

There are three things I always forget.
Names, faces, and—the third I can't remember.

—Italo Svevo (1861–1928)

he purpose of frameworks, and of new development technologies in general, is to make development within a complex environment easier. Technologies evolve so that development can be faster, cheaper, and more accurate. It is one thing to develop a technology and create guidelines about how best to use it. It is another to actually apply that theory to a real-world application development project. The proof of the technology and its methods comes from applying it. Therefore, as a natural course in the evolution of a technology or framework, features and methods are added that improve development productivity. At some point, needs arise that require core changes to the original technology. At this point, the technology's authors must decide to evolve it with a rewrite or to replace it with another technology and end the life cycle of the original technology.

This kind of evolution has occurred with J2EE web technology. As mentioned in Chapter 1, J2EE web technology evolved from Java applets to HTTP servlet code written in pure Java. This evolution was a major shift in development and deployment environments. The next major shift was from servlets to JavaServer Pages technology, which mixes HTML and Java tags. JSP pages are translated into and run as servlets, so they share the deployment environment, but the code is different and requires less hands-on work with Java. The next major evolution in J2EE web technology was from JSP pages to JavaServer Faces (JSF) pages. JSF technology was ratified as a standard in March 2004 through the *Java Community Process* (JCP), which Sun Microsystems uses to obtain the participation of Java experts when introducing new technologies and existing technology upgrades (jcp.org).

Since this book focuses on J2EE web development using JSF technology, we need to provide some more details about JSF concepts. This chapter explains the basics of JSF and an Oracle JSF extension, ADF Faces. Material about JSF architecture and design principles abounds on the Web. Therefore, this chapter will focus on what you, as a PL/SQL or an Oracle Forms developer, need to know to be productive in creating JSF-based code. The chapter answers the following questions:

- **Why was JSF developed?**
- **What languages other than Java are important to JSF work?**
- **What JSF concepts do I really need to know now?**
- **Where can I find additional information about JSF?**

Part II of this book provides hands-on practices so that you can get a taste of development work using JSF technology. Chapter 9 consists of a hands-on practice that introduces you to some of the JSF concepts this chapter discusses. It is intended as a precursor to your work in the other hands-on practices in Part II, but you also may want to jump directly into it after reviewing the concepts in this chapter. (If you do jump to Chapter 9, naturally, we do advise that you read Chapters 6, 7, and 8 before continuing with Part II.)

NOTE
This chapter assumes that you have been exposed to the J2EE, JSP, JSF, and ADF Faces material in Chapter 1 and the JSF introduction in Chapter 3.

Why Was JSF Developed?

The popularity of JSP technology grew rapidly because it was easier to use than the preceding technologies. Instead of building up an HTML page using print statements and coding low-level details of the HTTP communication in a servlet file, developers could concentrate on creating the HTML page using HTML tags and JSP (Java-oriented) tags. They could use HTML visual editors for the visual design and Java tools for the required Java logic. In the early days of JSP technology, developers used the core JSP tags with Java scriptlets added for custom functionality. However, they found themselves writing the same scriptlets in each application and so started creating their own custom tags to perform the same function as those scriptlets (for example, drawing an HTML table containing rows and columns of data). They then stored the tags in tag libraries and referenced these tags in each application.

This served the Java community up to a point, but, even though frameworks supplied many of the custom tag libraries required for an application, the Java platform standards (J2EE) did not regulate these libraries. In addition to problems with design consistency, developers found JSP custom tag libraries lacking consistency in a number of areas. JSF grew out of the need to address inconsistencies and inefficiencies in areas such as these:

- **Components** The days of writing JSP files that included large amounts of JSP scriptlet tags and JSP expression tags came to an end when developers found that approach nonproductive for code modifications and framework usage. Wrapping complex functionality and display characteristics into a single tag was a goal for most tag libraries. As mentioned before, a single tag could query a database table and present an HTML table structure, with data from the query arranged into rows and columns in the table. JSF supplies similar, high-level controls and supports them with a standard. Developers concentrate less on HTML layout tags and more on the arrangement of components.

- **Layout Container Components** When you add components to a JSF page, you plug them into areas inside *container components* (or *layout components*), which maintain the relative position of the components within it when the window is resized. In this way, container components act somewhat like frames in Form Builder. Another benefit of using containers is that you do not need to worry about coding HTML tables to position components in specific locations in the page. The HTML tables are created for you based on the functionality and areas defined for the container. Another benefit of layout containers is that they abstract the component arrangements from the specific markup language. For example, you can stack components into an `af:panelForm` layout container. If the JSF page appears in a web browser, the components will appear inside an HTML table. If the display is in a wireless device, the components will appear inside the corresponding table structure specific to the wireless markup language.

- **Support for Different Display Devices** Before JSF, running an application on different display devices, such as a web browser, PDA, or TELNET character-mode client, usually required rewriting the View layer code to use different view tags. Tag libraries that supported multiple display devices were, again, not standard. JSF separates the View layer components from their display using a render kit that outputs a certain style of code.

- **Controller** The J2EE MVC design pattern specifies that a separate code layer (the Controller) defines page flow and data communications. In addition, the J2EE Front Controller design pattern describes a single handler for all requests in an application. The patterns are clear, but in the past, the developer was responsible for implementing them. Open-source controller frameworks, the most popular being Apache Struts, removed the need for developers to implement custom controllers and provided the infrastructure needed to manipulate page flow. However, these controller frameworks did not tie the Controller layer to View layer tag libraries in a standard way. JSF includes a Controller layer that is integrated with the JSF View layer tag libraries.

- **Event Processing** User events, such as a button press, had no standard handling mechanism in web technologies before JSF. JSF defines an event model for its tags using listeners and actions.

NOTE
Although it is not part of the J2EE version 1.4 specification, JSF is part of the new version of the newly ratified specification—Java EE 5.

What Languages Other than Java Are Important to JSF Work?

In addition to having a grasp of Java at the basic, scripting level, a familiarity with other languages, such as the following, is important for JSF work as well as for work in any web application:

- **Hypertext Markup Language (HTML)**
- **JavaScript**
- **Cascading style sheets (CSS)**

In most JSF and ADF Faces applications, you will use these languages less than you would with other web application styles, such as Java servlet and traditional JSP without JSF. However, they are used by tags in the tag libraries, and understanding their basics will help you understand the environment in which JSF applications run. Although each of these languages is a subject for an entire book, the introductions that follow will help you get started in case you have not worked with the languages before.

HTML Basics
As you will notice when developing the JSF application in Chapter 9, using JSF and ADF Faces components requires very little, if any, Hypertext Markup Language (HTML). In fact, the example in Chapter 9 does not require any manual HTML coding. However, all JSF and ADF Faces code generates HTML code at runtime if the intended client is a web browser, because the web browser displays HTML. Therefore, it is useful to have a grasp of basic HTML concepts.

HTML is a display language that does not support processing on the client side. All processing for values sent from an HTML form to the server must be performed on the server. However, a popular add-on to HTML—JavaScript—provides a programmatic way to handle user interactions without requiring server roundtrips. (JavaScript is described further in the "JavaScript Basics" section.)

HTML was developed primarily to display formatted text and graphics inside a web browser and to allow navigation to other web pages using text, graphics links, or submit buttons. HTML has evolved and its capabilities have been extended beyond the initial purposes, but it remains focused on displaying content sent from a web server.

Tags, Attributes, and the Tag Hierarchy HTML surrounds text to be formatted with *tags*, keywords inside less-than and greater-than symbols, for example, "<html>." The tag that ends a format or structure begins with a slash; for example, to boldface text, you can surround it with the "strong" tag (formerly "b"): "The next word is bold." The browser will display the text with the word "bold" in boldface.

HTML tags offer *attributes*, which refine their actions. For example, the anchor tag "a" is used to link to another website or page using an attribute, href, that defines the linked page, for example, <a href="www.oracle.com">Oracle Corporation</a>. In this example, the words "Oracle Corporation" would appear specially formatted (underlined by default) in the browser. If the user clicks "Oracle Corporation," the browser would load the requested page—in this case, the Oracle home page.

NOTE
HTML code is not case sensitive. Also, the browser ignores multiple spaces and blank lines embedded in the body. If you want to add a blank line, use the "p" (paragraph) or "br" (line break) tags. If you want to add multiple spaces, add the "entity" (code representation of a special character) for the nonbreaking space, " " (without quotation marks but including the semicolon).

HTML tags are arranged hierarchically on the page with the html tag appearing as the root tag that surrounds all other tags. The child tags for the html tag are head (for heading, nonprinting content) and body for content that usually appears in the browser window. Both head and body have child tags. The most popular child tags for body are table (used to show text and graphics arranged in a set of rows and columns) and p (used to define a new paragraph). The following HTML shows some of these principles and, through the code indentation, suggests how the HTML tags appear in a hierarchy.

```
<html>
  <head>
    <title>Sample HTML File</title>
  </head>
  <body>
    <h1>Sample Body Text</h1>
    The next word is <strong>bold</strong>.
    <p />
    <a href="http://www.oracle.com">Oracle Corporation</a>
  </body>
</html>
```

This file would display in the browser as follows:

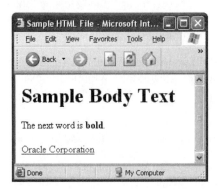

NOTE
Notice that the paragraph ("p") tag is formatted as a combination of a start tag and end tag (including the slash). This is a shortcut for coding the start and end tags—"<p></p>." Browsers may interpret some tags, such as the paragraph tag, correctly even if the end tag is not present, but it is good practice to include both start and end tags (or the shortcut) for each tag.

The JDeveloper Structure window representation of this page shows the tag hierarchy a little more clearly, as shown here:

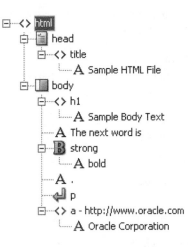

NOTE
Since browsers ignore blank spaces in HTML, as is true of most programming languages, indenting source code is useful only for those who need to read the source code. As with all programming languages, indenting code is considered a good practice because it makes the code easier to read.

The HTML Form   The HTML form, `form` tag, is another child element of the `body` tag. It is the primary tool the browser offers for the user to communicate with the server.

The form holds all user interaction tags, such as input fields (`input type="text"`) and buttons (`input type="button"`). An HTML page may contain more than one form. Each form is named, for example:

```
<form name="deptdata">
```

The form is also associated with an *action*, such as a JSP file, that is run when the form is submitted to the server, as in this example:

```
<form name="deptdata" action="deptmodify.jsp">
```

The form tag can also specify which HTTP method will be used to send data to the server, for example, GET or POST (explained in Chapter 2), as shown here:

```
<form name="deptdata" action="deptmodify.jsp" method="get">
```

A typical life cycle for an HTML form follows:

1. The user fills in values for fields defined inside the form tag.
2. The user clicks a submit button that is also defined inside the form tag.
3. The browser assembles the values and names of all fields inside the HTML form containing the submit button.
4. If the HTTP method defined for the form is GET, the browser writes the name-value pairs into the URL that is sent to the server. If the HTTP method defined for the form is POST, the browser embeds the name-value pairs in the HTTP request message body.
5. The browser adds to the end of the URL the name of the file referenced by the *action* attribute of the form tag.
6. The browser sends the HTTP request message to the network and waits for a reply.
7. The server finds the target file referenced in the URL and passes the name-value pairs to it as parameters.
8. The target file processes the parameters and sends an HTTP response message to the browser, which displays the response content.

More Information   The source for all HTML standards, and a good starting point for reference material and examples, is the custodian and owner of HTML standards—the World Wide Web Consortium (www.w3c.org). In addition, examining source code for any web page (in Internet Explorer, select **View | Source** from the menu or **View Source** from the right-click menu on the page) can give you ideas for your HTML code.

JavaScript Basics

HTML is a text-and-graphics display language that has no capability for processing on the client side. Processing an HTML page occurs only on a server after the page is submitted. HTML supports embedding *JavaScript*, a scripting language (that has no relationship to Java) that provides procedural processing when the page is loaded (like the WHEN-NEW-FORM-INSTANCE trigger in Oracle Forms) or when the user interacts with elements on the page. JavaScript, developed by Netscape Communications Corporation, is the most popular HTML embedded scripting language.

CAUTION
JavaScript is interpreted by browsers in a relatively standard way, but it is a good idea to test the application with each browser you intend to support to be sure the JavaScript you use is supported by those browsers.

Events JavaScript executes in response to user events, and you can write code in the HTML page (usually in the head section or in a separate file accessed from the head section) that is called from event attributes on form objects. JavaScript events are similar to Oracle Forms triggers. For example, you can code *JavaScript functions* (the JavaScript code unit) and call this code from input fields using the attributes onMouseOver (when the mouse cursor hovers over an object—like WHEN-MOUSE-ENTER), onChange (when the user selects a value from a pulldown, like WHEN-LIST-CHANGED), onLoad (when the page is first rendered, like WHEN-NEW-FORM-INSTANCE), and onClick (when the user clicks an object, like WHEN-MOUSE-CLICK). You have probably seen websites that display a pulldown menu as the mouse cursor hovers over an image or word. JavaScript can supply this kind of functionality.

The following shows a single-field HTML form (actionForm) with an embedded call to a JavaScript function in an onChange event attribute:

```
<form name="actionForm">
    Last Name: <input type="text" name="lastName"
      onChange="return validUpperAlpha('Last Name', this.value);" />
</form>
```

NOTE
The symbol "this.value" in the preceding code is a reference to the value of the lastName field. If you needed to reference the lastName field from a script called from another field or button, you would use the fully qualified name of the field, including the document reference and form name, for example, "document.actionForm.lastName."

This example calls a function, validUpperAlpha(), that is written in a file referenced in the HTML head section. This function runs when the onChange event fires (the user presses TAB or clicks out of the input field). The function might be written as follows:

```
function validUpperAlpha(fieldLabel, fieldValue) {
    var validChars = "ABCDEFGHIJKLMNOPQRSTUVWXYZ";
    var isValid = true;
    var oneChar;
    for (i = 0; i < fieldValue.length && isValid == true; i++) {
      oneChar = fieldValue.charAt(i);
      if (validChars.indexOf(oneChar) == -1) {
```

```
        isValid = false;
        alert (fieldLabel + " may only contain uppercase letters.");
    }
  }
  return isValid;
}
```

The code checks if the text passed to it (represented by `this.value` in the input tag) contains only uppercase letters. If it contains something other than uppercase letters, the function displays an alert dialog containing the field label and returns "false" to the `onChange` event. The `onChange` event failure will cause the cursor to stay in the field. If the validation succeeds, the function returns "true" and the `onChange` event allows the cursor to leave the field.

Before coding a JavaScript validation such as this, check the built-in validators for the JSF or ADF Faces component you need to validate. For example, JSF offers standard validation for a required value. The sidebar "About Validators" provides additional explanation.

Page Objects and Attributes   JavaScript uses a *Document Object Model* (DOM) to address objects on the page. In the preceding example, the symbol "this" referred to the object (the input field). The *value* attribute for that object represented the contents of the field. A fully qualified object name in JavaScript includes the name of the form (much like addressing an item in Oracle Forms using "block.item" syntax). For example, a field called "empName" in a form called "empForm" would be referenced as `document.empForm.empName` in JavaScript. Other object attributes, such as *style*, can supply other information—for example, whether the object is displayed. You can also set these attributes; the following example will hide the `userName` field in the `actionForm` form:

```
document.actionForm.userName.style.display = "none";
```

JavaScript syntax is much like C language syntax. Since Java is patterned from the C and C++ languages, you will find many keywords the same in Java and JavaScript. However, JavaScript

About Validators

The JSF framework supports the concept of validation code in backing beans for pages and declarative validators in the user interface definition. You can code a declarative validator by dropping the item (such as `ValidateLength`) from the JSF Core page of the Component Palette onto the field that needs validation support. You then set the validator's properties in the Property Inspector. You can use these validators to perform basic checks, such as the length of entered data. The ADF Faces Core page of the Component Palette offers additional validator components to supplement the JSF Core page components. You can also create validator methods in the page's backing bean. The JDeveloper help system topic "Using Validation and Conversion" (also in the *ADF Developer's Guide*) provides details.

uses loosely defined datatypes and is not arranged in classes, so you will still need to understand JavaScript-specific coding rules.

NOTE
Since embedding programming logic in JavaScript means that the application has another layer for business rules functionality, business rules enforcement (such as value checking) is often implemented in the application or the database layer (or both).

More Information Many examples of JavaScript are available from various websites. You can start your research about JavaScript at javascript.internet.com. As with most languages, the best way to learn this language is to find examples for a particular need using web searches. In addition, you may find a JavaScript reference book useful.

NOTE
Just as with HTML, some JavaScript code is built into JSF and ADF Faces components if they are displayed in a web browser. You do not modify that code, but you can write JavaScript for events on the components.

CSS Basics

HTML relies on the browser to specify the fonts, sizes, and colors used to display text. You can add a `font` tag and its attributes to specify a font, but this tag is *deprecated*—supported now but targeted to be removed from future releases of HTML. Cascading style sheets are preferred over the `font` tag for specifying fonts and colors for text on an HTML page.

CSS Files *Cascading Style Sheets* (CSS) is a language that specifies how an HTML component or area will be displayed. CSS definitions may be stored in the head section of an HTML file, the same as with JavaScript. However, CSS are more often stored in a file that is referenced in the HTML page head section so that the file can be accessed by many HTML pages.

Selectors (Styles) The CSS file contains *selectors* (named definitions of style-oriented attributes, such as font, color, and size) that act much in the same way as a style in a word processing program, such as Microsoft Word. The selector is also the same as a Visual Attribute Group in Oracle Forms. For example, you can apply a heading level 1 tag to a paragraph on your page and specify that this tag use a CSS selector that presents the text in red, Arial, 24 point. You can apply the same selector to many objects on your page and those objects will all take the characteristics of the selector.

You can use CSS to achieve a common look and feel for your application's pages. Each page can refer to the same selectors in a common CSS file.

A selector definition contains a selector name followed by an attribute value pair separated by a colon. Attributes are delimited by semicolons, and the list of attributes is surrounded with curly brackets.

CSS selectors are coded in a number of varieties, the most important of which are these:

- **Universal selector** This type of selector can be applied to any HTML tag using the `class` attribute of the HTML element. For example, a universal tag named BlueBold can be applied to any tag, such as p or td (table cell), using `<p class="BlueBold" />`.

- **Class selector**   This variety of selector is written for a specific HTML tag, such as td. You name the selector with <tag_name>.<selector_name>. For example, a style called "td.highlight" can only be applied to td (table cell) tags using <td class="highlight">

- **Type selector**   This variety of selector is written for a specific tag and redefines the default way in which the browser displays this tag throughout the document. For example, a selector called "p" will be applied to all p (paragraph) tags without the need for a class attribute on each tag. The p tag would appear as only "<p>" with no class attribute. The p type selector style will be applied automatically to any p tags.

The following example of a simple CSS demonstrates the syntax for the universal, class, and type specifiers in the tinytext, p.warning, and H1 selectors, respectively:

```
*.tinytext {
    font-size:70%;
}
p.warning {
    display: block;
    font-family: Arial, Helvetica, Geneva, sans-serif;
    font-size: 95%;
}
H1 {
    font-family: Arial, Helvetica, sans-serif;
    font-size:170%;
    color:#336699;
}
```

Applying a Selector   HTML tags contain an attribute, class, that you use to specify a universal or class selector from a style sheet attached to the HTML file. For example, the following will specify that the p tag use the selector "warning":

```
<p class="warning">
```

If more than one warning selector is available to a page (for example, from multiple CSS files attached to the page and from selectors defined in the page head area), the styles will *cascade*, or add to each other. If the selectors conflict for any given attribute, a single value is selected using the *CSS precedence order* based on location (from low to high precedence: browser default, external style sheet, style inside the head tag, and style inside the element tag).

CAUTION
The type selector that replaces a tag style is not intended for use with the class attribute. The browser will ignore any type selector names coded as class attribute values (such as H2, P, or BODY).

More Information   As with HTML, the custodian of CSS specifications and the first stop to make when learning the language is the World Wide Web Consortium, www.w3c.org. You can open and edit CSS files in JDeveloper. JDeveloper shows styles in the Structure window and Property Inspector. In addition, you can view sample text formatted using some of the CSS styles in the Preview window of the editor when a CSS file is open.

NOTE
JSF and ADF Faces components have default style assignments. You can apply a different style to a component by specifying the styleClass property.

What JSF Concepts Do I Really Need to Know Now?

Fortunately, just as with most other modern frameworks, you only need to know a subset of everything there is to know about JSF concepts to start creating JSF pages. However, as is true of any technology, the more you know, the more creative you can be when faced with a development challenge. The resources mentioned in the later section "Where Can I Find Additional Information About JSF?" will continue your JSF education.

What Is JSF?

JSF is comprised mainly of specifications that resulted from the JCP (jcp.org), focused on Java Specification Request (JSR) 127. The specification was revised as JSR 252 and is included in the new Java platform specifications, Java EE 5. In principle, JSF technology supports any type of client device and coding style. However, as of this writing, Sun Microsystems offers a *Reference Implementation* (RI)—code libraries that prove that the standard supports real code—for servlets (as class libraries) and JSP technology (as tag libraries). These libraries contain classes and tags for the components and functionality described later in this section. Since RI libraries are tested and proven implementations of the standard, you can use them as a basis for your own code. The RI also includes a *render kit* (a code layer that writes a particular kind of output format) for HTML output from JSP components.

NOTE
MyFaces, an open-source, non-Sun reference JSF implementation is available at myfaces.apache.org. You can use this as an alternative to the Sun RI, but examples in this book focus on the Sun RI with the addition of Oracle's ADF Faces (now also part of the MyFaces project).

Understanding JSF requires knowing a little about each of these concepts:

■ Runtime architecture

■ JSF-oriented files

■ Components

■ Designing cross-platform interfaces

NOTE
Many of the principles discussed in this section are exemplified in the application you will develop in the hands-on practice in Chapter 9.

Runtime Architecture

JSF code runs in a Web Tier container (discussed in Chapter 1) in the same way as servlet code. Figure 5-1 shows the main actors in the request-response round-trip communication for a JSF file. JSP files are the standard view technology used for JSF components, and you usually code JSF inside a JSP file (although JSF, theoretically, supports multiple-view layer technologies). The browser issues an HTTP request to the web server. The web server finds the URL's virtual directory name in the web.xml file and passes the request to the Faces Servlet that is running (or that will be started) on the web server. The Faces Servlet handles the request by passing control to an object created using the life cycle class (`javax.faces.lifecycle.Lifecycle`). This `Lifecycle` class manages a preset series of steps called the *JSF Life Cycle* (described later in this section).

NOTE
The Faces Servlet initializes an object typed from the FacesContext class that stores state information and data pertaining to the user interface elements, as well as information about the request session. You can tap into the FacesContext object in your code, as shown in the practice in Chapter 9.

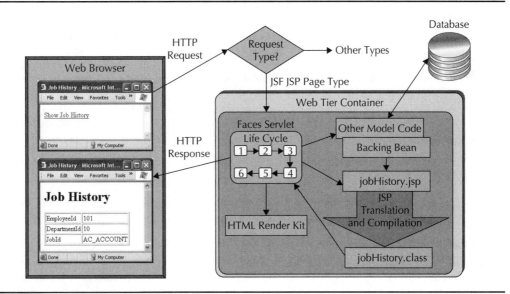

FIGURE 5-1.   *JSF JSP runtime*

> ### About Managed Beans and Backing Beans
> A *bean* in Java (also called a *"JavaBean"*) is a class file that has a standard set of methods. A *managed bean* (*MBean*) is a Java file containing code used to handle operations and data for a resource (in this case, for components on the page). In JSF work, a managed bean can contain code for one or more pages or code that is shared between pages (for example, a logout action available on many pages). The convention is to use one managed bean for each JSF page. The term *backing bean* is used to denote a managed bean assigned to a single page. A JSF page may not require special code for its components; in this case, you would not create a managed bean for that page. Examples in this book follow the usual convention of using backing beans (one managed bean for each page) when necessary, but use both terms interchangeably when referring to this file.

The servlet accesses any necessary Model layer code to obtain values from the database. The servlet instantiates the bean if a component property value refers to an element in a backing bean (described in the "About Managed Beans and Backing Beans" sidebar). The Faces Servlet then assembles the page (shown here with a .jsp extension identifying it as a JSP page). The file runs through the normal JSP translate and compile steps. The application then assembles an HTTP response using a render kit (in this case, the HTML render kit), which converts the display elements to an HTML page. It then sends the response to the web browser. The process for other display types, such as PDA, cell phone, or TELNET client, is similar, although their render kits are different.

JSF Life Cycle
The `FacesServlet` and `Lifecycle` objects work together to process the HTTP request and assemble an HTTP response using the steps described in this section. A JSF application can support requests to non-JSF components, but processing of a non-JSF request follows an abbreviated version of the life cycle. This description focuses on the process for requests that address JSF components.

In most of these steps, the servlet processes events that may bypass one or more steps. For example, if there is an error in step 2, an error message would normally be queued for display later in the life cycle. However, the JSF code can be written to jump directly to step 6 (Render Response) and bypass the intermediate steps.

NOTE
Various sources, including some from Oracle, refer to "JSF life cycle" as "JSF lifecycle." Although this book adopts the classical term ("life cycle"), the two forms of the term are synonymous.

1. Restore the Component Tree   A JSF request triggers this step. The components used in a JSF application are arranged in the file in a hierarchical way. This hierarchy, the *component tree* (also called the *UI tree*), corresponds to the tag hierarchy you would see in an HTML file. For example, the following illustration shows the JDeveloper Structure window view of the JSF login page you will create in the hands-on practice in Chapter 9:

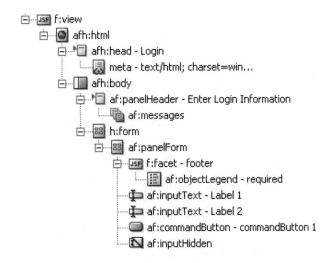

For a *postback*—a repeated request of the same page—the component tree is already created in the `FacesContext` object. It is stored there when the page is first rendered (in step 6). The first time the page is requested, the component tree has not been created in the `FacesContext`, so processing passes from this step directly to step 6 to render the content.

NOTE
The root component in a JSF file is f:view. All other JSF tags will appear within this tag. A JSP file may have element tags outside the f:view tag (such as taglib directives) but these are used to assist in processing the JSP file.

2. Apply Request Values   In this step, the Lifecycle instance populates the components in the component tree with data from the request parameters. These values are held in a buffer area and the process does not validate the assigned datatypes yet. Events that apply to this step are also processed.

3. Process Validations   This step applies *conversions* (defined in *converter* components) that translate the plain-string value loaded into the buffer for each component in the preceding step to the datatype assigned to that component.

You can define *validation* (using validators, as described previously)—for a component that checks the value assigned to it. For example, you can define a minimum and maximum value validator, like the *Lowest Allowed Value* and *Highest Allowed Value* properties of an item in Oracle Forms. This step applies these validations.

Validations and conversions are bypassed for a particular component if that component is assigned an *immediate* property value of "true." You would set this value for a component that you would not want to validate, such as a button.

If any validation or conversion fails, the error messages are queued and the process jumps to step 6 for rendering the response. In addition, event code written for this step is executed. Errors or messages from these events are also sent to the message queue.

4. Update Model Values Just as step 2 set values for the components in the component tree from the request, this step sets the values for the corresponding components in the Model layer code. As before, if errors occur in validations or conversions, the messages are queued and the process jumps to step 6 for rendering the response. As with all phases, appropriate events are also processed or queued.

5. Invoke Application This step performs application-level tasks, such as form submission or page navigation, as appropriate to the request. Events are handled if the page being restored contains components that fired events. Therefore, this step runs any event code you have written.

6. Render Response If this is the first request to a page, control is passed from step 1. The `FacesServlet` object builds the component tree as specified in the JSF file and stores the tree in the `FacesContext` object. The framework then requests components in the tree to be rendered; this results in the components using the appropriate render kit to output markup text (such as HTML), which the JSF servlet buffers into the final page definition.

Messages that were queued from previous steps are written to the output as well. In addition, the state of the page (for example, the component data values) is also stored so that subsequent requests can use it for the Restore the Component Tree step. This step ends with the Faces Servlet sending an HTTP response to the browser containing the buffered page output.

> **NOTE**
> *During most JSF development work that you perform, the life cycle is transparent. However, knowing a bit about the life cycle steps should give you an idea about the richness of the environment. It can also assist when debugging or when you need to write specialized code to alter the normal runtime behavior (as described in Chapter 8). You have much more control over the JSF runtime process than you do of the Forms runtime process.*

JSF-Oriented Files

When you set up a project for JSF work in JDeveloper by including the JSF technology scope in the project (or using a JSF application template), the web deployment descriptor file (web.xml) is modified so that it contains a pointer to the Faces Servlet for requests that contain a designated virtual directory (such as "/faces/"). In addition, you work with the following files when developing a JSF application.

Managed Beans

As mentioned in the "Runtime Architecture" section previously, a managed bean may be associated with the JSF JSP page file. For example, a login.jsp page file would use a managed bean file, Login.java. The Java file contains the code needed to process events that are outside of the declarative framework. (You will write code to handle button-click events in Chapter 9.)

The managed bean also contains accessors (getters and setters) for the objects on the page (for example, text fields), so you can manipulate the values of these objects programmatically.

In addition, the managed bean contains a private object (variable) for each object in the JSF file. This object and its accessors can be used to change the characteristics of the object in the same way that you use Oracle Forms built-ins to manipulate an item in a form.

For example, if your JSF file contains a text input field, `lastName`, the managed bean would contain a `lastName HtmlTextInput` object as well as a `getLastName()` method to retrieve the value and other properties of the object, and a `setLastName()` method to assign the object's properties. If you had an Oracle Forms item, EMPLOYEES.LAST_NAME, you would be able to hide the item with the following code:

```
SET_ITEM_PROPERTY('EMPLOYEES.LAST_NAME', DISPLAYED, PROPERTY_FALSE);
```

In a corresponding JSF file, you would perform the same action using this code:

```
getLastName().setRendered(false);
```

In this code, the getter, `getLastName()`, provides access to the component and `setRendered()` changes the *rendered* property value.

Writing a managed bean in JDeveloper is a code-intensive task. However, JDeveloper adds accessor stubs and component objects to the bean automatically and maintains the synchronization between the JSF JSP file component names and the method and object names in the backing bean.

Events and Action Listeners   One of the strengths of the JSF framework is its rich model for event handling. Events occur due to some user interaction, such as a button click or list selection. You write *action listener* methods in the managed bean to handle these events. For example, an OK button called "okButton" in a JSF page could have a corresponding action listener method called `okButton_action()` written in the managed bean. When the user clicks the OK button, the code in this method would be run. This is a perfect parallel with Oracle Forms, where you code triggers that fire in response to a user interaction with an Oracle Forms object or database event. Oracle Forms supplies triggers with standard names, whereas JSF action listener methods are, by convention, named with a prefix of the component they work for. A single-action method can be reused to provide the event handler for many components.

The action listener name is associated with the component using a property, such as *Action* for a button component. Alternatively, you can code a separate listener class (that implements the `ActionListener` interface). You then associate that class with the component using a different property, such as *ActionListener* for a button component.

NOTE
Since JSF components render as HTML controls in a web browser, you can set event properties, such as onClick, on JSF components to run JavaScript code you have written.

faces-config.xml

This XML file, called the *application configuration resource file*, contains definitions that specify the following:

- **Navigation rules** for defining flow from one page to another.
- **Managed bean definitions** for making JavaBean code accessible in the application.

- **Render kits** that are used to display the page in a certain encoding, such as HTML or WML.

- **Converters**, mentioned before, which change the type of data from the plain-vanilla string supplied by the HTTP request parameter value to a specific datatype for a component value.

- **Validators**, mentioned earlier, which check the value of the data (for example, the range of the value or its length).

Although this file is coded in XML, JDeveloper offers a visual representation of the navigation rules in the JSF Navigation Diagram. You can code other entries in this file using the code editor or a property editor available on the Overview tab. The practice in Chapter 9 demonstrates both methods.

A Note About Struts   The open-source, highly evolved Apache Struts framework has become popular for the Controller layer of a JSP or servlet application. Struts is not supported by the J2EE standards, but due to its widespread use, Struts was an industry standard before JSF technology was released. The JSF controller serves the same purpose for JSF applications as Struts served for JSP applications. Therefore, you do not need to use Struts when creating a JSF application.

JSF JSP file

The JSP file contains all user interface components (discussed next) arranged in the same kind of hierarchy as with any HTML or JSP file. When developing a JSF application, you write View layer code in the JSF JSP file, and you write Model and Controller code in the managed bean and faces-config.xml file. When working with the JSF JSP file in JDeveloper, you can use declarative and visual tools, such as the Visual Editor, Property Inspector, and Structure window. You can also use the Code Editor to write or modify code outside of the declarative tools.

NOTE
As mentioned in Chapter 3, the Structure window allows you to position components more precisely than is possible in the Visual Editor. You can drag and drop components from any node to any applicable node. You can also add components by dragging them from the Component Palette or from the right-click menu on the structure node.

Oracle Forms developers will find using the declarative tools used to develop JSF JSP code in JDeveloper similar to using the corresponding Oracle Forms tools. For example, both sets of tools contain a Property Inspector (called the "Property Palette" in Oracle Forms) where you set the values of properties for any component in the application. Both have a visual layout tool (Oracle Forms uses the Layout Editor; JDeveloper offers the Visual Editor) for positioning components on the page. You will get a taste for these tools in the hands-on practices in Part II of this book.

TIP
To quickly navigate and expand the Structure window hierarchy to a particular component, select it in the Visual Editor.

Components

Just as the experience of JSF development in JDeveloper is similar to the experience of developing Oracle Forms applications, you will find many parallels between Oracle Forms components and JSF components. JSF components for JSP work are contained in two tag libraries:

- **JSF Core**   This tag library contains components, such as validators and converters, that are used in conjunction with other components. Components in this library use the "f" prefix; for example, `f:loadbundle`.

- **JSF HTML**   This tag library contains HTML user interface components, such as text input, buttons, labels, and radio options. You refer to these components using the "h" prefix; for example, `h:datatable`, `h:column`, and `h:form`.

NOTE
As mentioned, the JSF standard supports multiple output device styles through the use of render kits, but the initial RI only offers an HTML render kit for JSP files. ADF Faces also provides a render kit for JSP as well as other render kits for wireless and TELNET clients.

Facets

In addition to the component hierarchy, you can nest a JSF component inside another JSF component using the *facet*, a named subcomponent. For example, the JSF `h:column` component contains facets for a header and a footer. It is up to the component to determine where to render the contents of a particular facet. For example, the ADF Faces `af:panelPage` component supports `menu1`, `menu2`, and `menu3` facets. Items in these facets will appear in specific positions within the page, as shown in Figure 5-2.

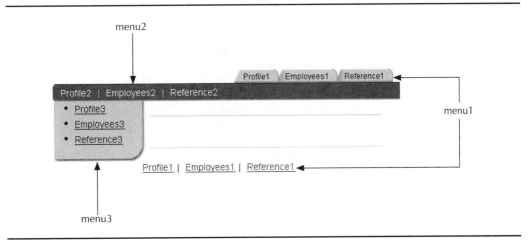

FIGURE 5-2.   *af:panelPage component showing menu1, menu2, and menu3 facet items*

NOTE
A facet can only contain one component, but that one component can be a container component (such as af:panelForm), which can contain more than one component.

Although you would not normally repeat menu choices in this way, this figure shows the different positions for the menu facets. The code within the `af:pagePanel` component that creates this display is as follows:

```
<f:facet name="menu1">
   <af:menuTabs>
     <af:commandMenuItem text="Profile1"/>
     <af:commandMenuItem text="Employees1"/>
     <af:commandMenuItem text="Reference1"/>
   </af:menuTabs>
</f:facet>
<f:facet name="menu2">
   <af:menuBar>
     <af:commandMenuItem text="Profile2"/>
     <af:commandMenuItem text="Employees2"/>
     <af:commandMenuItem text="Reference2"/>
   </af:menuBar>
</f:facet>
<f:facet name="menu3">
   <af:menuList>
     <af:commandMenuItem text="Profile3"/>
     <af:commandMenuItem text="Employees3"/>
     <af:commandMenuItem text="Reference3"/>
   </af:menuList>
</f:facet>
```

Notice that menu1, menu2, and menu3 facets each hold a different *container component* (a component that only holds other components)—af:menuTabs, af:menuBar, and af:menuList, respectively. However, each of these container components contains the same af:commandMenuItem component. The context of the af:commandMenuItem within a specific container and facet determines its appearance. You will also notice that links appear in the bottom area of the layout. These links appear as a result of the menu1 facet.

Facets are important in controlling and adapting standardized layouts (skins) within JSF applications, because they provide a type of named API for component children that can be changed without having to recode the page.

JDeveloper provides special support for facets in a component by displaying facet drop zones in the Visual Editor, as shown here for the af:panelPage component:

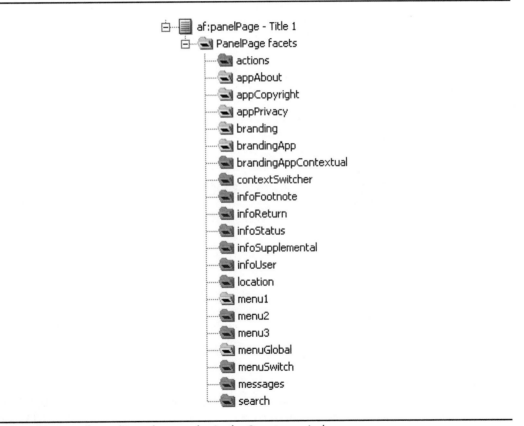

The branding, brandingApp, menuGlobal, menu1, appCopyright, appAbout, and appPrivacy facets display these drop zones by default, but you can drop components into the Structure window for other af:panelPage facets (or for the default facets), as shown in Figure 5-3.

FIGURE 5-3. *af:panelPage facet nodes in the Structure window*

You can control the facets displayed in the Visual Editor by checking the relevant facet names in the right-click submenu selection, "Facets - <component>," on the component, as shown here:

ADF Faces

As mentioned in Chapter 1, ADF Faces consists of class libraries and tag libraries. ADF Faces evolved to allow access to the enhanced component set offered previously as ADF UIX (also explained in Chapter 1) in JSF code.

NOTE
Oracle donated ADF Faces to the open-source Apache MyFaces Project (myfaces.apache.org) in early 2006. This places its source code in the public domain, which means that, although Oracle will enhance and support ADF Faces for its customers, the larger Java community will also contribute to its functionality. The name of the ADF Faces part of the MyFaces project is "Trinidad."

The examples in the applications developed in Part II of this book focus on use of ADF Faces components. ADF Faces is designed to be displayed on different devices. The tags or other language required to display a component in a specific device are generated by the render kit. ADF Faces also contains a much richer set of components than the JSF RI.

When working with ADF Faces, you do not code HTML tags directly. Instead, you use ADF Faces components that will be rendered in a web browser using HTML tags. For example, ADF Faces offers a component, `af:inputText`, which renders an HTML form input item when displayed in a web browser.

Container Components As mentioned before, some ADF Faces tags act as containers, which hold other components. The process of creating a file with ADF Faces consists of adding container component tags, and then inserting components within the containers. ADF Faces offers containers, such as `af:panelPage`, that contain a number of predefined areas, as shown in Figure 5-3. These predefined areas use JSF facets to provide default positions for objects such as navigation buttons, copyright information, and branding logos. After dragging this component onto the page, you can drag other components to each of the facet areas you need to use.

ADF Faces containers have a parallel concept in Oracle Forms, where, before adding user interaction objects such as items and checkboxes, you create windows to contain canvases that, in turn, hold the user interaction objects. All ADF Faces containers provide automatic layout capabilities that reposition child components when the container is resized. This capability is somewhat like that of frames in Oracle Forms, although in the case of ADF Faces, the container's automatic layout applies at runtime as well as at design time.

Tag Libraries Just as the JSF RI offers Core and HTML tag libraries, ADF Faces offers Core and HTML tag libraries (prefixed with "af" and "afh," respectively). Some of the ADF Faces components are parallel to JSF components. For example, the JSF RI component `h:inputText` has an ADF Faces equivalent, `af:inputText`, used to present a text entry field. You can distinguish between these components in code by their prefixes ("h" for JSF RI and "af" for ADF Faces). Also, the ADF Faces tags offer more properties than the RI tags.

The prefixes for JSF RI and ADF Faces are defined in `taglib` directive tags in the beginning of the JSF JSP file, as follows:

```
<%@ taglib uri="http://java.sun.com/jsf/html" prefix="h"%>
<%@ taglib uri="http://java.sun.com/jsf/core" prefix="f"%>
<%@ taglib uri="http://xmlns.oracle.com/adf/faces" prefix="af"%>
<%@ taglib uri="http://xmlns.oracle.com/adf/faces/html" prefix="afh"%>
```

NOTE
JDeveloper automatically adds the appropriate taglib directive for a tag library the first time you drag a component from that library onto the page.

ADF Faces Properties   In general, ADF Faces components offer more properties and built-in functionality than the JSF RI components. For example, the ADF Faces af:inputText component includes a label property (for a prompt) that is not included with the comparable JSF RI component. This property is much like the *Prompt* property of an Oracle Forms item because it is a property of the object, not a separate boilerplate object. Also, unlike the JSF RI component, the ADF Faces component validates items marked as required using JavaScript, which does not require a communications trip to the server.

Figure 5-4 shows a property list (divided into two columns) for an ADF Faces component, af:inputText, that corresponds to an Oracle Forms text item with *Item Type* of "Text Item." If you are an Oracle Forms developer, you will see many familiar properties (described in Table 5-1) just as you will find other familiar features as you continue to work with ADF Faces and JSF.

General	
Value	
Columns	15
Label	Label 1
RequiredMessageDetail	this is required
Rows	1
Validator	
ValueChangeListener	
AccessKey	
AttributeChangeListener	
AutoSubmit	false
Disabled	false
Id	usernameField
Immediate	false
LabelAndAccessKey	&Username
MaximumLength	20
PartialTriggers	
ReadOnly	false
Required	true
Secret	false
Simple	false
Valign	
Wrap	

Core	
Converter	
InlineStyle	
Rendered	true
ShortDesc	
StyleClass	
Events	
Onblur	
Onchange	
Onclick	
Ondblclick	
Onfocus	
Onkeydown	
Onkeypress	
Onkeyup	
Onmousedown	
Onmousemove	
Onmouseout	
Onmouseover	
Onmouseup	
Onselect	
Message	
Tip	Your name
MessageDescUrl	
MessageTargetFrame	
ShowRequired	false

FIGURE 5-4.   *Property list for af:inputText ADF Faces component*

ADF Faces af:inputText Property	Oracle Forms Item Property
Value	(:BLOCK.ITEM represents the value)
Columns	Width
Label or LabelAndAccessKey	Prompt
Rows	Height
Access Key	Access Key (only for a push button or radio group)
Disabled	Enabled
ReadOnly	Insert Allowed and Update Allowed
Required	Required
Secret	Conceal Data
Valign (for items) or HAlign (for containers)	Justification
Wrap	Wrap Style
InlineStyle	Properties in the Color and Font sections
Rendered	Visible
StyleClass	Visual Attribute Group
Events	(Item-level triggers)
Tip (appears under the item)	Tooltip (pops up over the item)

TABLE 5-1.   *ADF Faces af:inputText Properties Compared With Oracle Forms Item Properties*

NOTE
*Some Oracle Forms properties contain database-oriented functionality.
This functionality may be implemented in properties on the ADF BC
objects used in the Model project code.*

Several features of ADF Faces improve on the already rich feature set of the JSF RI:

■ **A larger component set**   ADF Faces offers container and basic components for various styles of layout, such as panel components, menus, shuttle controls, button bars, and selection lists. In addition, ADF Faces also includes date and color pickers.

■ **More properties**   ADF Faces adds properties for features such as *Hint* and *Label* on an `af:inputText` item. Without using ADF Faces, you would need to add output text items for both the hint and the label.

■ **Partial Page Rendering (PPR)**   Several ADF Faces components, such as `af:tree`, `af:treeTable`, `af:menuTree`, and `af:showDetail`, may be refreshed individually without affecting the rest of the page. This yields a smoother user session because the page does not redraw as often. PPR uses the same core technologies as *Asynchronous JavaScript and XML (AJAX)*, which currently has much Java industry attention because of its enhanced user experience.

■ **ADF BC support** As with any standard J2EE view layer technology, ADF Faces work well with ADF Business Components. You can quickly bind values from ADF BC to ADF Faces components. Also, the Data Control Palette in JDeveloper provides automatic binding of some components, such as master-details layouts.

NOTE
otn.oracle.com offers a visual guide to ADF Faces components. Currently, you navigate from the JDeveloper home page to the ADF Faces home page. A link on that page refers to the ADF Faces list.

Messages

As the application runtime proceeds, messages are written to the `FacesContext` object. They are placed into a queue until the last step of the life cycle renders a response. You can programmatically add messages to a component (`af:messages`) using managed bean code.

JSF messages support the idea of specific text for specific locales and languages. To implement this feature, you abstract the messages out of the JSF JSP file into *message bundle* files that hold all text for the application (one message bundle for each location or language). The JSF controller matches the correct language file and uses it to supply messages for the application. Chapter 9 contains more information and a hands-on practice for creating and using message bundles.

Designing Cross-Platform Interfaces

ADF Faces and JSF support the concept of displaying the user interface on different types of client devices. The render kit used to display the application is specific to each device's needs, but the same JSF code can display a user interface in a web browser, cell phone or other wireless device, or a TELNET window. As mentioned, currently, the JSF reference implementation only offers a render kit for HTML and the preferred code container is a JSP file. However, ADF Faces offers other render kits and its code is not dependent upon HTML.

If the application needs to support multiple client platforms, you would work this requirement in from the starting point. You would need to set a standard that code in the application avoids the use of tags from the HTML libraries, such as `afh:html`, `afh:head`, and `h:dataTable`. In addition, you would create a standard to avoid use of JavaScript and CSS, both of which are add-ins to HTML browser code that may not work on other display devices.

When you create a template for a cross-platform application, you would change the default HTML tags generated into the JSP file. For example, the wizard creates a default JSF JSP file containing `html`, `head`, and `body` tags. When you drop an ADF Faces component into this page, the HTML tags automatically change to the ADF Faces versions of these HTML components: `afh:html`, `afh:head`, and `afh:body`, respectively. Like pure HTML, ADF Faces HTML tags are specific to a web browser and would not work for other devices. Therefore, to be cross-platform-compliant, you would replace the HTML-specific tags with `af:document`, an ADF Faces component that draws the `html`, `head`, and `body` tags for a web browser but that can also be used with other client devices.

NOTE

Enterprise applications target web browsers more frequently than any other style. Therefore, the examples in this book assume that the application will be running in a web browser.

Where Can I Find Additional Information About JSF?

This chapter describes most of the JSF basics you will need to know to start working with JSF technology. You will likely need other resources for learning about JSF. The authors have found the following resources useful.

Websites

Information about JSF concepts abounds on the Internet. The following websites are good places to begin further research:

- **JavaServer Faces home page**, at java.sun.com, currently at java.sun.com/j2ee/javaserverfaces. Look for the "An Introduction to JavaServer Faces" article as a starting point.

- **JSFCentral.com.** This website contains many articles and discussions about JSF.

- ***JSF Tutorial.*** This is an online book by Marty Hall, at www.coreservlets.com, currently at www.coreservlets.com/JSF-Tutorial.

- ***JavaServer Faces Resources,*** by James Holmes, www.jamesholmes.com/JavaServerFaces.

- ***J2EE v.1.4 Tutorial (JavaServer Faces chapter).*** This is an online book at java.sun.com, currently at java.sun.com/j2ee/1.4/docs/tutorial/doc/.

- **JSF Technology Theme,** at java.sun.com, currently at developers.sun.com/prodtech/javatools/jscreator/reference/themes.

- **JSF Tutorials** at www.jsftutorials.net.

- **OnJava,** at www.onjava.com, by O'Reilly Media, Inc. (search for "JSF").

- **JSF Home Page,** on Oracle Technology Network (OTN), currently at www.oracle.com/technology/tech/java/jsf.html and linked from Java Developer home page; also perform a search on OTN for ADF Faces for articles about that subject.

- **J2EE Application Development for Forms and Designer Developers home page,** on OTN, currently at www.oracle.com/technology/products/jdev/collateral/4gl/formsdesignerj2ee.html.

- **Dhruva Online Books—Oracle JDeveloper News,** www.dhruvaraj.com/fdstr/oracle_jdev.htm.

CAUTION

The website addresses presented are current as this chapter is being written. If your requests to these addresses fail, use a web search engine to look for their new locations.

Printed Books

As mentioned in Chapter 4, you will probably need to supplement your available JSF information with printed books, such as the following:

- *JavaServer Faces in Action*, by Kito D. Mann, Manning Publications, 2004. This is a good book for overall JSF learning and reference.

- *Core JavaServer Faces*, by David Geary and Cay Horstmann, Sun Microsystems Java Press, Prentice Hall PTR, 2004. Some chapters of this book are also available online at www.horstmann.com/corejsf/.

- *JavaServer Faces: The Complete Reference*, by Christian Schalk and Ed Burns, McGraw-Hill, 2006. This book is an in-depth look at JSF technology.

- *JavaServer Faces Programming*, by Budi Kurniawan, McGraw-Hill/Osborne, 2004. This is a good book about basic JSF concepts.

- *Pro JSF and Ajax: Building Rich Internet Components*, by Jonas Jacobi and John Fallows, APress, 2006. This is an advanced book, which is useful for those who need to know how to create their own JSF components that use Asynchronous JavaScript and XML (AJAX) technology for a highly interactive user interface.

CHAPTER
6

Business Services in ADF

"What is the use of repeating all that stuff,"
the Mock Turtle interrupted,
"if you don't explain it as you go on?"
"It's by far the most confusing thing I ever heard!"
—Lewis Carroll (1832–1898), *Alice's Adventures in Wonderland*

 s we explained in Chapter 3, ADF Business Components provides the best fit for relational-minded developers who need to wire the database to Java programs. Conventional descriptions of and discussions about ADF Business Components often focus on its major objects: view objects, entity objects, and so on. This approach doesn't really deliver the information that you need and the questions that you probably want answered from the start. This chapter takes a different approach; it presents ADF Business Components essentials and key components in a task-oriented manner.

This chapter answers the questions you will ask during the development of a typical database application:

- **How do I issue a query to the database?**
- **How can I update data?**
- **How do I generate a primary key value?**
- **How do I handle transactions?**
- **How does record locking work?**
- **Where is the login dialog?**
- **How do I define business rules?**
- **How can I dynamically change a query?**
- **How can I interface ADF BC with PL/SQL?**

In answering these questions, we'll necessarily have to cover some related topics, such as validation and key generation.

How Do I Issue a Query to the Database?

Coming from a PL/SQL background, it seems like executing a query on the database should be the simplest thing in the world. In PL/SQL, you just embed the query inside the code and provide variables for the return values. Unfortunately, in Java, this is not a trivial task at all. Unlike PL/SQL, Java has no native understanding of SQL and you have to do a lot of work to just get to the point where you can start submitting a statement to the database. ADF Business Components, of course, is designed to carry out a lot of the low-level work and makes the whole process more straightforward. So, knowing this, if you want to create a query using ADF Business Components, what do you do?

To illustrate the process, we'll provide some high-level steps you would use in JDeveloper to create a query that populates a list of values from the Departments table in the Oracle HR schema.

1. Set up an Application Workspace and Project for ADF Business Components

Chapter 3 highlights the use of application templates through the Create Application dialog. You reach this dialog using the **File | New** menu option to display the New Gallery, and then selecting the Application option from the General category. The template to use in this case is called "Web Application [JSF, ADF BC]." Creating such an application produces a workspace containing two projects: Model and ViewController. The Model project is set up for ADF Business Components objects; the ViewController project is used to define the application user interface, so you can ignore it for now.

2. Create the Query Object

With the Model project selected, we open the New Gallery again. Under the Business Tier category, select ADF Business Components, as shown in Figure 6-1.

The gallery is sensitive to the technology scope of the project and filters the display of categories accordingly. If you change the *Filter By* value to "All Technologies," several other options, such as Web Services and EJBs, will appear in the Business Tier category.

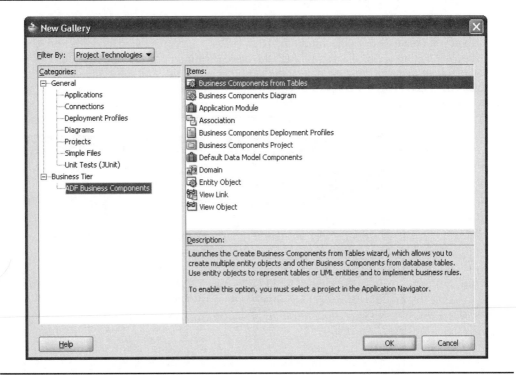

FIGURE 6-1. *The New Gallery for an ADF Business Components project*

With the ADF Business Components category selected, the list of possible items shown in Figure 6-1 is displayed. The first item we need is "View Object." The best way to think of a *view object* is as a query definition, rather like a conventional database view (a full SELECT statement) or the *Query Data Source Name* property of an Oracle Forms data block definition (that defines the database source for the query data). As you go through the process of defining a view object, you'll see the similarity in the information that is being collected to the kind of information that would be used to define an Oracle Forms data block. For example, the information in a view object includes:

- The SELECT clause, used to define the data elements
- The data source (FROM clause)
- The WHERE clause, used to filter the results
- The ORDER BY clause for the query
- The number of rows to fetch when populating the query
- Optimizer hints

The similarity does not end there. As in Oracle Forms, the WHERE clause and the ORDER BY clause can be manipulated at runtime using code.

3. Define the Query

When you create a view object from the New Gallery, after specifying a connection, a wizard (shown in Figure 6-2) walks you through the basic definition process. This wizard does not expose all of the attributes of the view object; the attributes properties and some advanced features, such as the tuning options, can only be accessed after you create the view object.

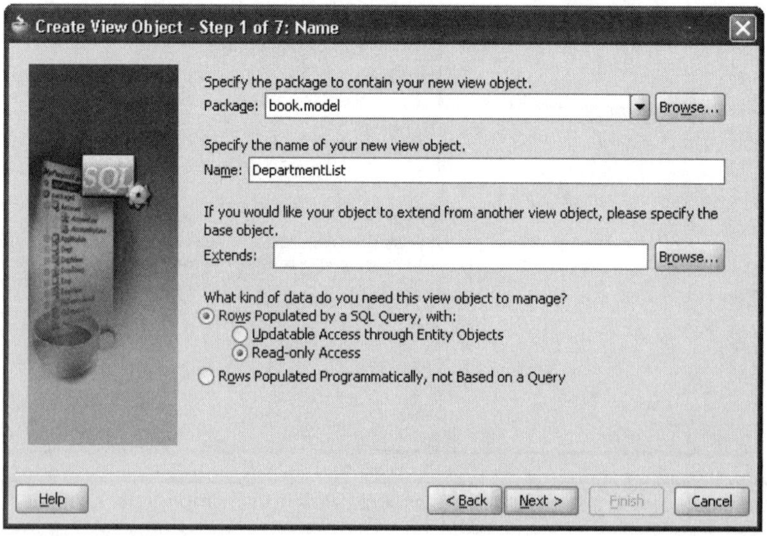

FIGURE 6-2. *Create View Object dialog; Step 1 of 7: Name*

In the first screen of the wizard, you provide a descriptive name, for example, "DepartmentList," and specify a package for the view object. The package is the Java package name, which is used to help organize the code, both logically in code references and also physically on disk. The package defines the directory structure used to store all of the code and metadata files that make up the view object that you're creating.

TIP
Although it is fine to accept the default package names suggested by JDeveloper, it is a good idea to fully define package names early on to help maintain your code as it evolves. For example, you may choose to place all of the read-only view objects (queries) used for list-of-values lookups in a separate package from those used for updateable access.

Also on this screen, we'll select the *Read-only Access* radio button within the *Rows Populated by a SQL Query, with* option. This radio button declares that we will be supplying a SQL statement to populate the view object at runtime.

The next screen in the wizard gives us the opportunity to define the SQL statement, as shown here:

```
Create View Object - Step 2 of 7: SQL Statement                    [X]

Enter your custom SELECT statement and click Test to check its syntax. Provide the
ORDER BY clause separately.

Query Statement
  select depts.DEPARTMENT_ID,
         depts.DEPARTMENT_NAME
  from DEPARTMENTS depts
  where depts.LOCATION_ID = :location




Query Clauses
  Order By: DEPARTMENT_NAME                                   Edit...

  [✓] Expert Mode              Query Builder...  Explain Plan...  Test
  Binding Style: Oracle Named  ▼

Help                                    < Back   Next >   Finish   Cancel
```

This screen should represent familiar territory. A *Query Statement* and *Order By* clause can be entered directly in property fields, or you can invoke the Query Builder (just as in Oracle Reports). The query defined here can use joins, subqueries, aggregations, set operators, and so forth. There is no restriction confining the query to a single table or database view.

If you are likely to reuse a query statement with variations in the query criteria, you should use bind variables to represent the changeable conditions in the query. This is an alternative to using several similar statements with hard-coded values. The bind variables can then be dynamically set at runtime to customize the query results. This approach of using bind variables bestows several benefits:

- **Database scalability** The statement is cached as a single reusable cursor in the database shared SQL area rather than a separate cursor being created for each combination of query and criteria.

- **Project size** For a database application of any complexity, many queries will be needed. Reusing the same statements with the aid of bind variables will help to keep view object proliferation under control. This makes it both easier to manage the project at design time and reduces the memory requirements at runtime, as fewer object definitions will have to be managed by the framework.

You define embedded bind variables using one of three notations, selected by the *Binding Style* drop-down list:

- **Oracle Named** This bind variable reference uses a meaningful name, for example, location, prefixed with colon.

- **Oracle Positional** Bind variable placeholders are indicated by a colon, followed by a zero indexed number, for example :0, :1, :2, and so on. These numbers are expected to be sequential.

- **JDBC Positional** Bind variables are represented as question marks in the statement.

Coming from a PL/SQL background, using named bind variables will no doubt be the most familiar approach. This feature is specific to the Oracle JDBC drivers and so can only be used when Oracle is your target database. Named bind variables also allow you to reuse variables within the same statement, rather than having to resupply the same value again, as JDBC-style question mark placeholders require.

CAUTION
The Oracle Positional style of numbered bind variables seems to promise bind variable reuse in the same way that the Oracle Named style does. However, this turns out not to be the case, and reuse of the bind references will not work. We recommend that you use Oracle Named as a binding style unless database portability is required, in which case, the JDBC Positional style should be used.

If you do use bind variables in a particular query, be sure to define some default values for them. This is defined in Step 3 of the Create View Object Wizard, as shown here:

This page is used to define the name, datatype, and default value of any bind variables used by the query. The Custom Properties and Control Hints tabs allow additional metadata to be added to the bind variable definition. At runtime, ADF uses this metadata to create default labels and other user interface features, such as date formatting for the bind variable if it appears in a screen as a field. This extra metadata is optional.

At this point, we have everything that is needed in the query definition. Clicking the Next button again in the wizard displays a list of the attributes defined by the query. Click Finish to complete the wizard. To change the definition of the view object after it has been created, double click the view object node in the navigator or select **Edit Department** from its right-click menu. The View Object Editor will present the same pages found in the wizard, plus a few extra pages for advanced features.

4. Expose the Query

There is no obvious way of running or testing the query that we've just defined, other than through the syntactical check offered by the Test button on Step 2 of the wizard. In order to test the query and see the resulting data, a second type of object is required to represent a runable service interface.

To run this object, we need to create another object called an "Application Module." You can return to the New Gallery and choose "Application Module" from the ADF Business Components category, or you can display the right-click menu on the package node of the Model project and select **New Application Module**.

The *application module* is the service façade (see the sidebar "What is a Service Façade?" if that term is not familiar) for an ADF Business Components project. Everything that needs to be visible to the consumers of the service has to be exposed through this object. In principle, the

---

What Is a Service Façade?

The term *service façade*, or *service interface*, is used to describe the public functions that a module, typically one that interacts with a database, exposes. You program consumers of this service to use this external API, but these consumer programs have no knowledge of the service's internal implementation. A parallel in the PL/SQL world is the specification portion of a PL/SQL package, which acts as the façade for the body. The details of the code in the package body are hidden from the consumers (calling program units).

---

application module acts a little like the Oracle Forms runtime session, as both the entry point to the application and the thing that maintains the database connection and the transactional state (something we'll cover a little later on).

Creating an application module displays the Create Application Module Wizard shown here (after dismissing the Welcome page):

The next page of this wizard (Step 2 of 4: Data Model, shown in the next illustration) is the important one. It allows us to specify which view objects should be exposed to the outside world through the application module. The view objects defined in an application module are called *view object instances*. In this case, we only have a single query to run, so that can be shuttled to the right side of the selection control. You do not need to use the application module to expose view objects for queries that are only used within your business logic. You can still access these view objects within the business services layer, but they are essentially private to that scope.

Notice that when the DepartmentList view object is selected and exposed through the data model, it is given the name "DepartmentList1." The numerical suffix is automatically added to the name of the view object instance to ensure unique naming if the view object is reused in several different contexts. You can alter this name by changing the value in the *Instance Name* field beneath the *Data Model* list.

Once you define the view object instance, you can click Finish to complete the wizard.

5. Test the Query

So far, you've created an object that defines a query—the view object—and a way of exposing it to the outside world through the application module. Despite all of this, we still don't appear to be much closer to seeing a list of departments. Consider an analogy with Oracle Forms here. When you define a block with the wizards, the Data Block Wizard runs first and defines the query part of the block definition. Then, the Layout Wizard (optionally) runs to define the layout of the user interface.

In the process described so far, we have effectively run that first wizard, but not the second. It would be inconvenient if we now had to go and build a user interface just to test this query. Fortunately, however, ADF Business Components provides a built-in testing utility (the *Oracle Business Component Browser*), which you can invoke by selecting **Test** from the right-click menu on the application module in the Application Navigator, as shown next.

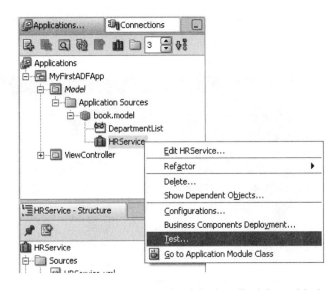

This testing utility will examine the application module for all of the publicly exposed view objects and generate a simple screen to allow you to run the query and test any embedded business logic.

The first screen of the tester (shown next) defines the connection and the configuration that the tester should use.

In most cases, you just accept the default, which will use the same database connection used for creating the objects in the first place.

Once connected, the tester displays a list of available view objects. To view the results of the query, double click the name of the view object. The right pane will then show the records for the query. If one or more bind variables are defined for the view object, as in this case, an intermediate dialog (shown here) will pop up, allowing a suitable test value to be entered.

After you enter a query value and click OK, the query will be run and the records displayed, as shown next:

The fields for the view object are disabled in this case because we are testing a read-only view object, but you can scroll through the records to view the query results.

How Can I Update Data?

The process of defining a simple read-only query has introduced two of the five major ADF Business Components artifacts: view objects and application modules.

Now we need to explain how data can be queried from the database, changed, and then put back—essentially the basic functionality of an Oracle Forms data block. If we think of the view object as defining the block's *Query Data Source*, how does the corresponding block property *DML Data Source* get defined?

1. Create an Entity Object

In order to implement update functionality, a new object type needs to be created: the entity object. *Entity objects* have a one-to-one mapping relationship with database objects, for example, a table or a view. They represent a sort of business-tier local cache of the rows from that database artifact. In Chapter 3, we looked at the logical structure of an Oracle Forms block and discussed the Record Manager. In Oracle Forms, the Record Manager keeps a local cache of rows and enables the engine to track updates and manage scrolling. Entity objects fulfill basically the same role and offer some additional functionality, such as validation.

Like the view object, an entity object can be created from the New Gallery or the package right-click menu. This launches the Create Entity Object Wizard, shown here (after dismissing the Welcome page):

The wizard page for selecting a source database object (EMPLOYEES in this example) is about what you'd expect. The additional pages in the wizard allow you to select the columns required from the source table or view, and then to further refine these with properties, such as a primary key flag. Columns are mapped to entity object *attributes* that combine information about the underlying database column with additional metadata about validation and user interface properties.

When creating an entity object based on an object in an Oracle database (such as the EMPLOYEES table), the wizard is smart enough to query the data dictionary for the key properties of each attribute, such as size and data type. Therefore, you are finished once the source object has been selected, since everything else will be set to intelligent defaults based on definitions in the data dictionary.

2. Create an Updateable View Object

How does the existence of an entity object help for updating data? To retrieve the records to be updated, you need to create a view object (called EmployeesUpdateable, for example) that is associated with that entity object. In Figure 6-2, you'll notice that the other option within the *Rows Populated by a SQL Query with* radio group was *Updatable Access through Entity Objects*. If you select this option when creating a view object, the following wizard screen (Step 2 of 7: Entity Objects) will be shown:

We are not confined to selecting just a single source entity object here. View objects can literally be a "view" over several tables as represented by several entity objects. At this point, things begin to diverge from the viewpoint that we might have as Oracle Forms programmers. One of the conventions of Oracle Forms programming is that a block can, for the purposes of update anyway, only be based upon a single database object. (The *DML Data Target Name* block property can only hold one name.) Creative use of transactional triggers or updateable join views or procedure-based targets can circumvent this restriction, but it is not an out-of-the-box experience. On the other hand, a view object may be based upon several entity objects and all of them can be made updateable if required.

NOTE
Unlike the situation with Oracle Forms where the Record Manager maintains a separate cache for each data block, the entity object row cache is shared among all view objects that use that particular entity object. This means that all of the view objects see any local uncommitted changes in the cache, and you are spared some of the self-locking issues that can occur in a form with multiple data blocks containing the same records.

3. Define the View Object Attributes

The next screen of the Create View Object Wizard (Step 3 of 7: Attributes), shown next, allows you to select attributes from the entity object(s) that are to be exposed through this view object.

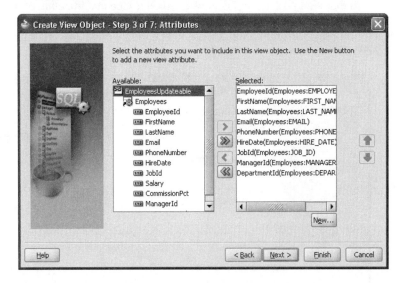

Any or all of the attributes can be selected. The only restriction is that the attributes representing primary key columns of the underlying tables must be included.

TIP
A view object can also contain "nondatabase" attributes that are not directly based on fields from the underlying entity objects. These attributes function in the same way as "non-base table items" in an Oracle Forms block. These view object attributes may be indirectly based on entity attributes, for example, in the form of a calculation, in which case they are referred to as "entity-derived attributes." Alternately, they may be unrelated to the entity cache in any way, in which case, they are referred to as transient attributes. *The New button in the Attributes page is used to create both of these.*

Once the columns are chosen, the next screen (Step 4 of 7: Attribute Settings) allows us to further define the field attributes. The properties for the initial field settings are inherited from the base entity object, so the default selections are usually sufficient.

4. Refine the View Object Query

The information gathered so far, in the selection of entities and columns, is enough for a view object's query to be generated. Again, this is similar to a base table query in Oracle Forms where the text of the query statement is generated (by the Oracle Forms runtime) from the selected table and columns. The next page of the wizard (Step 5 of 7: SQL Statement) allows the definition of WHERE and ORDER BY clauses for the query, as shown here:

NOTE

The query statement generated from properties you set in the wizard's pages appears in the "Generated Statement" pane. As you type in the WHERE clause, this statement is updated. In addition, adding or deleting attributes or changing the entity object assignments in preceding pages will update this query statement.

That is all that you need for the updateable view object to function, so you can complete the wizard at this point.

5. Test the View Object

The view object can be exposed through the application module (by including the EmployeesUpdateable view object in the data model) and tested. This time, the fields in the tester are enabled, and we are able to make updates to the Employees object. Just like Oracle Forms, any data changes are held in the cache (the entity object cache, in this case) and will be applied to the database when a commit is issued. The tester provides a toolbar containing functions such as "Commit" to help you to test view object functionality comprehensively, as shown in Figure 6-3.

How Do I Generate a Primary Key Value?

If an entity object is updateable, chances are that new records will be inserted through it, and that being the case, it may well need to have a primary key value allocated to it. In Oracle Forms or

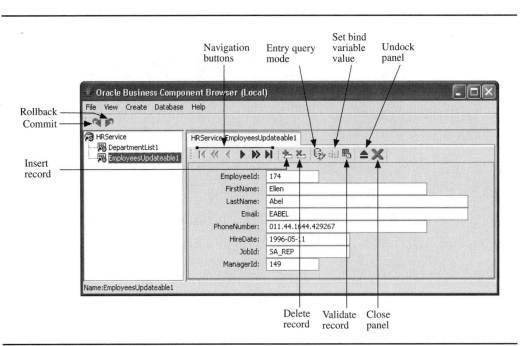

FIGURE 6-3. *The ADF Business Component Browser*

PL/SQL, this is generally achieved using a database sequence to provide the unique key value, which can then be used in one of three ways:

- **In the insert statement** Including a reference to <sequence name>.NEXTVAL directly as the value of the key column

- **In a trigger** Either an Oracle Forms PRE-INSERT trigger or a database BEFORE INSERT row-level trigger on the table

- **By reference** Oracle Forms can reference a sequence number in the initial value for a key field, and the framework will generate the correct insert SQL to load the field from the database sequence.

In ADF Business Components, there are two ways of carrying out this function:

- **Using a database trigger** and some declarative properties on the entity object
- **Writing code** in the entity object create method

We will look at the second of these two techniques later in the chapter when we cover adding code to the entity object. For now, let's look at the more common declarative technique.

Using a Database Trigger to Allocate Sequences

Using a database table trigger is a common approach to allocating a unique sequence number to a record as it is created in the database. The problem with this method is that the actual primary

d until the record is committed, and that can lead to difficulties if
l records are committed to the database as part of the same transaction.
or each master means that the associated detail records have no parent
associated.

ients solves this problem by using a specialized data type or *domain*
)F BC Domains" for more detail) called a *DBSequence*. When an entity
s being of this type, it will gain two useful behaviors:

object instance is created, it is allocated a temporary (negative) value.
t hang off this record will refer to that temporary value, maintaining
the master record.

key value in the master (and the master's detail records) is
ied with the correct value from the database after the commit

tion for the Employees entity object in our example, therefore,

Jence (if one does not exist already) to be the source of the unique
key (using "CREATE SEQUENCE employees_seq;").

2.   Define a BEFORE INSERT row-level trigger on the EMPLOYEES table to allocate a value
     to the EMPLOYEE_ID column from the sequence when a record is created.

3.   Set EmployeeId, the primary key attribute (based on the EMPLOYEE_ID column) in the
     Employees entity object, to be of type DBSequence.

NOTE
*Chapter 13 provides steps for using DBSequence to implement a
primary key value based on a database sequence in the context of
developing a sample application. This will give you more practice in
implementing this frequent requirement and will allow you to test the
code within a J2EE web application page.*

Create the BEFORE INSERT Trigger   The following code provides an example of the database
trigger that would be used to load the EMPLOYEE_ID of the EMPLOYEES table. The sequence
object in this case is called EMPLOYEES_SEQ. Triggers can be defined in SQL*Plus or from within

About ADF BC Domains
Domains within ADF Business Components are specialized data types that can be allocated to
entity and view object attributes. The domain you will encounter most often is DBSequence.
A domain can define both a standard set of properties for the datatype (for example, the length,
whether required, and so on) and behaviors, such as validation rules. Using domains for
commonly occurring datatypes that always have the same validation logic—for example,
a postal code or telephone number—promotes consistency and reduces the amount of code in
the application.

JDeveloper by opening the connection to the database in the Connection Navigator and selecting **New Trigger** from the right-click menu on the Triggers node. The resulting screen will allow you to create a skeleton BEFORE INSERT trigger on the Employees table, which should then be filled out with the following code:

```
TRIGGER employees_bi BEFORE INSERT ON employees
FOR EACH ROW
BEGIN
    SELECT EMPLOYEES_SEQ.nextval
    INTO :new.employee_id
    FROM dual;
END;
```

This trigger loads a generated number into the EMPLOYEE_ID column from the sequence regardless of whether the INSERT statement contains an EMPLOYEE_ID value. This ensures that the value is always loaded from the sequence and that it will be unique.

Set the Data Type of the Entity Attribute   The attribute definition panel on the entity is used to set the attribute type to DBSequence. This screen is displayed as Step 3 of the Create Entity Object Wizard, and you can also access it after an entity object has been created by double clicking the entity object node in the Application Navigator, expanding the Attributes page, and selecting the EmployeeId node in the Property Navigator, as shown in Figure 6-4. Here, the default Number data type for EmployeeId has been replaced with the DBSequence type.

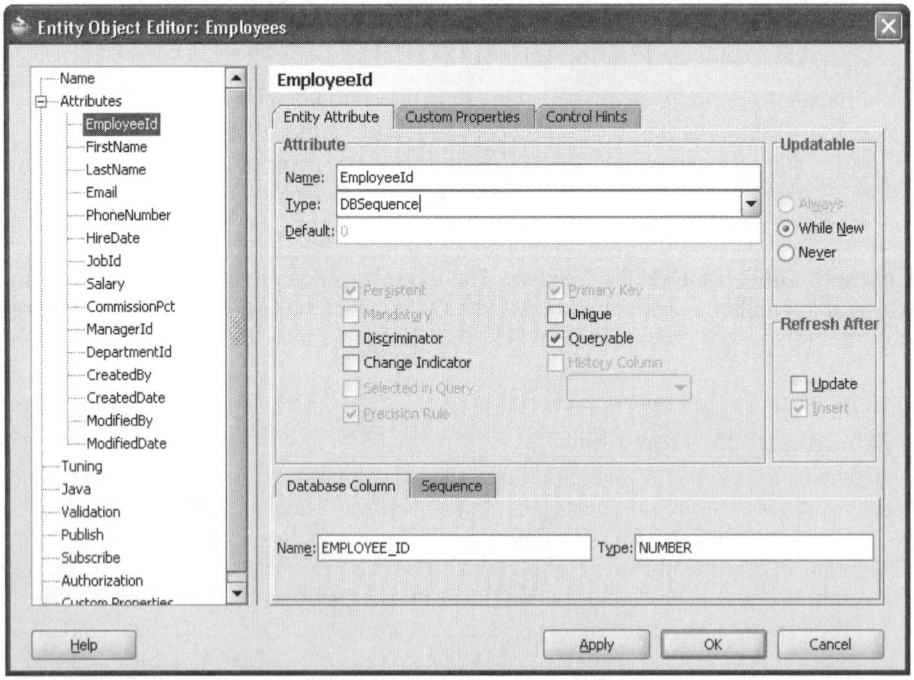

FIGURE 6-4.   *The Entity Object Editor attributes page*

CAUTION
Do not be fooled by the Sequence tab at the bottom of this page. This allows you to define a sequence name to associate with the attribute. However, the sequence name, as defined, is only used if a schema is forward-engineered (to create database objects) from the ADF Business Components definition. It is not used to generate sequence values for new entities.

Mutating Data

Primary key generation is a situation where the data that is posted to the database is changed within the database transaction before being committed. Such mutating data has always posed a problem to frameworks such as Oracle Forms that maintain a local cache of data. The changes made in the database transaction are out of view of the framework. Both ADF Business Components and Oracle Forms solve this in the same way by allowing attributes to be flagged for "refresh after commit." When this is set, the framework is alerted that the data may be changed and that any change needs to be synchronized with the local cache.

If you refer to Figure 6-4, the area on the right side of the page labeled "Refresh After" contains two checkboxes offering the options *Update* and *Insert*. In the case of the Employee attribute shown in Figure 6-4, the value will only be mutated by an insert, so that checkbox is selected and disabled automatically when you enter the type as DBSequence.

If your application makes use of database triggers that could mutate data in the same way, you should set these options according to the operations that cause the mutation.

History Columns

While on the subject of data changes made by database triggers, the entity object *history column* feature is worth a mention. In Figure 6-4, this can be seen but it is disabled because the column has already been marked as a primary key.

The history column feature provides a declarative way to carry out auditing operations that you would often achieve through database or Oracle Forms trigger code. When an entry object attribute is marked as a particular history column, ADF BC automatically populates it for you, removing the need to write code to do the same thing. Table 6-1 lists the available history columns and their functions.

History Column	Purpose
created on	This value causes the entity object to store the date and time of the record's creation. It can only be used for an entity attribute that is associated with a date or timestamp database column.
modified on	This value stores the date and time of the last update to the record. Again, this must be mapped to a date or timestamp column.
created by	This value stores the identity of the user that created the row. It must be mapped to a character column of some type (CHAR or VARCHAR2).
modified by	This value stores the identity of the user that last updated the record. It also must be mapped to a character column.
version number	This value specifies a number that will be automatically incremented when the record is updated. This is not a sequence number in the sense of generating a primary key, but rather is a value that indicates the version of the record itself. Applications can compare the value of this column held in cache with the value in the database to see if another session has updated the record since it was queried. It must be mapped to a number column in the database.

TABLE 6-1. *History Column Meanings for Entity Attributes*

NOTE
History columns require that you use J2EE application security. The identity mentioned in reference to "created by" and "modified by" is the J2EE login, not the database account being used. We discuss J2EE application security in Chapters 10 and 14.

How Do I Handle Transactions?

Now that we've explained the basics of querying and updating, it is time to see how ADF BC handles some of the key transactional concepts, such as committing and locking.

The ADF Business Components tester provides Commit and Rollback buttons, but what are they doing and what is their scope? In order to explore this, we'll need to look at a little code.

The Transaction Object

In ADF Business Components, the application module is the unit of transactional scope. When a commit is issued, that event will affect all entity objects encapsulated within view objects instantiated in that application module. Additionally, if you have nested application modules (See the sidebar "Nested Application Modules"), then these will commit as well.

Commit (or rollback) events are issued in one of two ways. Most simply, the ADF Model layer can issue a commit in response to a user interface event. This is normal and involves no coding at the ADF Business Components level. Another option, however, is to interact with the transaction directly in Java code. This approach is useful if you want to produce an application with discrete transactions carrying out defined units of work exposed through functional interfaces, such as web services.

Programmatic access to operations such as Commit takes place through a `Transaction` object. The following fragment of code shows a simple function in an application module file (for example, HRServiceImpl.java) that issues a COMMIT:

```
public void myCustomMethod() {
   //Do some work
   ...
   //Commit any changes
   getTransaction().commit();
}
```

Nested Application Modules

When we introduced application modules as a service façade for an application, the implication was that there would only ever be one application module to represent the interface of the entire business service. This is partially correct in that an application will usually only expose one top-level module. However, an ADF BC project may contain multiple application modules, which can be nested within the master application module. Any view objects or methods exposed by these child application modules are exposed through the Application Modules page of the application module properties.

Nested application modules provide a convenient way of organizing large projects into functional areas. The child modules can be developed and tested in separate projects and then combined under a master application module for deployment.

The transaction object is available using a getter method, `getTransaction()`. But where did this code come from? It is provided by the `ApplicationModuleImpl` class that this application module .java file has subclassed. The `Transaction` object exposes methods to commit and rollback, as well as many other transaction-related functions.

Extending Application Modules with Custom Code

Now we need to examine some Java source code. The application module .java file was created automatically in the Create Application Module Wizard (on Step 4, a page which was skipped over by clicking Finish earlier). The same options are included on the Java page of the Application Module Editor, as shown in the following illustration:

If both of these checkboxes are unselected, the application module will only exist as an XML definition file with no place to add code. However, the "Application Module Class: <name>Impl" option is selected by default, so that file will be created unless you have changed the base preferences, as explained in the sidebar "Altering the Defaults."

Altering the Defaults

ADF Business Components is designed to provide a set of default behaviors, such as generating a .java file for the application module, which makes sense in the majority of circumstances. These default behaviors can be configured if they are not suitable. Like other preferences in the Integrated Development Environment (IDE), these settings, and many others for ADF BC, are defined in the Preferences dialog (**Tools | Preferences**).

This application module *Impl* (short for Implementation) class is where we can add extra methods to the public service interface exposed by the application module.

The second class mentioned on this screen, the `HRServiceDefImpl`, is used to customize the XML metadata that the application module uses. This class is an advanced usage, and you should not worry about creating it at this stage. To see if the application module Impl file has been created, select the application module in the Application Navigator, and then view the Structure window. The result should look something like this:

Here we see the XML definition for the application module in the HRService.xml file, the Java Impl class file (HRServiceImpl.java), and a third file—bc4j.xcfg, which contains runtime configuration information used by the application module. We will examine this configuration file later in this chapter.

You can access the Java Impl file in two ways:

■ Double click the Impl Java node in the Structure window, or select **Open** from the right-click menu.

■ On the application module object in the Application Navigator, select **Go to Application Module Class** from the right-click menu.

NOTE
If you use the System Navigator to view the project rather than the Application Navigator, you will see the .xml and .java files listed separately. You do not need to look at the Structure window.

However, creating the Impl file and adding some code is only half the story. You also need to specially flag methods that will be exposed as part of the application module service interface so that they can be used by a UI client. In typical Java development, you would just mark the methods as "public." In ADF Business Components, however, you need to complete an additional step to ensure that methods are exposed correctly. This step exposes the method through the ADF Model layer for use in user interfaces, and also makes the methods available as remote method calls. This is important, because the business service provided by the application module may not be co-located in the same JVM (Java Virtual Machine) as the web interface or Swing UI that is calling it.

Publishing these methods is handled in the Client Interface page of the Application Module Editor, as shown here:

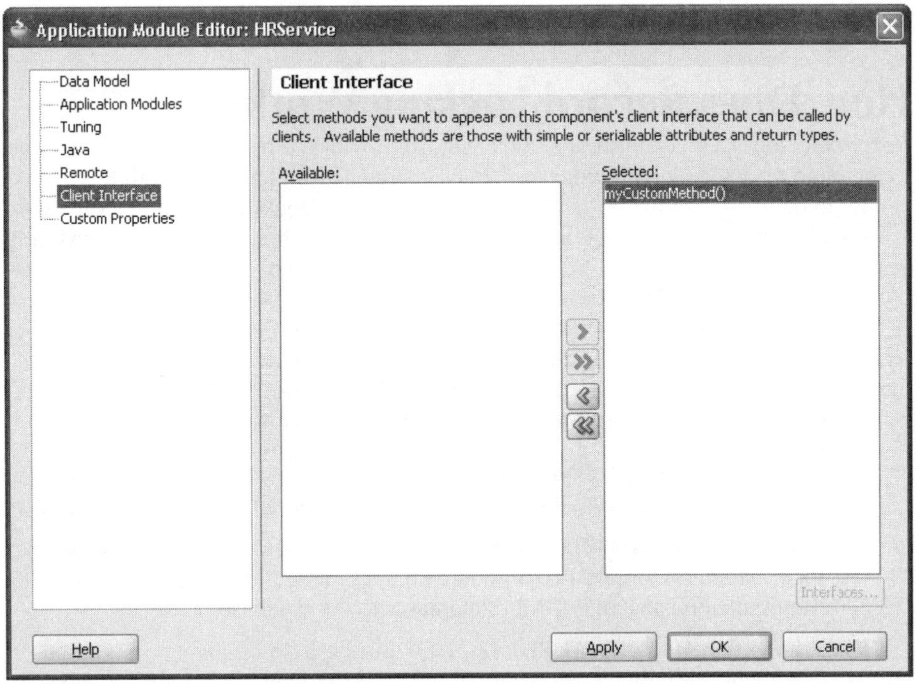

Once one or more custom methods are published in this way, a number of extra files are generated into the project. These include an interface that represents the service's contract (that is, the signatures of the methods that have been published) and a client-side proxy Java file. This is used to handle the remote invocation of the method across the network. This simple publishing stage actually generates extra code to allow you to access the service effectively in an *n*-tier environment. Again, the extra Java files that have been created will appear in the Structure window for the application module, as shown here:

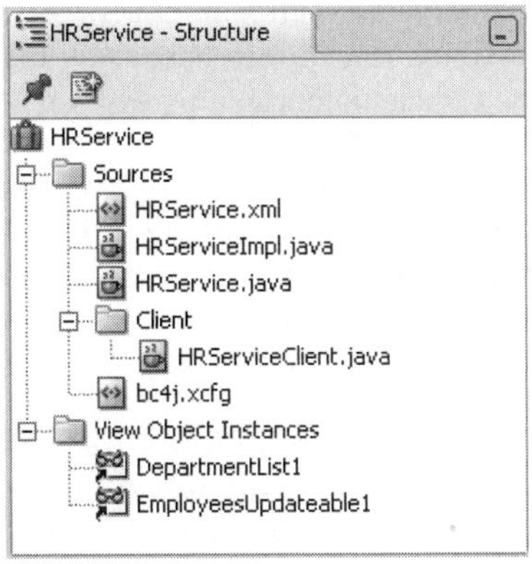

Once a method has been published through the Client Interface page in the application module, it will also be exposed through the Data Control Palette as a custom operation that can be bound into the user interface using drag and drop. Chapter 7 discusses how such methods can be used.

How Does Record Locking Work?

Record locking is a mechanism that the database provides to prevent simultaneous update access to the same resource by multiple users. Locking strategies and granularity differs from database vendor to database vendor, but with the Oracle database, locks are taken out on a row-level basis.

Just like Oracle Forms, ADF BC automatically handles the day-to-day process of issuing locks to protect updates in progress. You do not have to write code to issue locks. However, you can configure the way that these locks are managed.

Within ADF Business Components, the `Transaction` object, which we encountered earlier as a home for COMMIT and ROLLBACK operations, also provides a way to configure the locking mode of the application. This is achieved through the `setLockingMode()` method of the `Transaction` object. You need to pass this method one of the following constants:

- **Transaction.LOCK_NONE**   ADF Business Components should not issue any explicit lock statements, leaving it to the underlying database mechanisms to manage locking.

- **Transaction.LOCK_OPTIMISTIC**   ADF Business Components should issue explicit lock statements for updated and deleted data immediately prior to issuing those Data Manipulation Language (DML) statements to the database.

- **Transaction.LOCK_OPTUPDATE**   ADF Business Components should issue explicit lock statements for updates only (partial optimistic locking). Deletions are the responsibility of the database.

- **Transaction.LOCK_PESSIMISTIC**   ADF Business Components should issue explicit lock statements for updates and deletions as soon as the row is modified in the cache.

Ignoring the case of no locking, there are two basic modes: pessimistic and optimistic.

Pessimistic Locking

Pessimistic, as the name suggests, assumes that the row that has just been modified may also be vulnerable to change by someone else in the lifetime of the transaction. So, the pessimistic view is to immediately issue an explicit row lock to make sure that no other session can change the same row. In the case of the Oracle database, this will not prevent other users from reading the locked row.

Pessimistic locking occurs when you make normal updates through server-side PL/SQL. In this case, however, it is the database that carries out the locking rather than any mid-tier framework. Pessimistic locking is the default locking mode in ADF BC. It is also the default locking mode for Oracle Forms applications, although it is disguised as the "Immediate" value for the data-block property *Locking Mode*.

Optimistic Locking

Optimistic locking, on the other hand, makes the assumption that the changed rows will probably not be changed by anyone else in the immediate future, and the lock is deferred until the last possible moment. This is equivalent to the Oracle Forms setting "Delayed" for the *Locking Mode* property. Optimistic locking differs from no locking, because all locks will be issued before the actual rows are touched in the database. This means that no DML will be issued if one or more of the locks fail.

In the case of no locking at all, the DML will be issued against the database until an implicit lock fails, and then all the work done so far will have to be rolled back.

Which Mode to Use?

The main reason that Oracle Forms applications primarily use pessimistic locking is that it provides much earlier feedback to the user about a locking problem. The alternative (optimistic) allows the user to enter the whole transaction's worth of data and commit before issuing a locking error.

Web-deployed J2EE applications generally exhibit block-mode characteristics for Online Transaction Processing (OLTP) data entry. In block mode, data is entered or updated a screen at a time and then submitted to the middle tier to process and pass to the database, if required. As such, the immediate feedback of pessimistic locking is not really applicable, because the user has already filled in a whole page of data. In fact, pessimistic mode is seen as a universally bad thing in web-deployed J2EE applications because of the asynchronous nature of browser-based interfaces. If the application secures locks in this way, there is no real guarantee that the user will issue a commit or rollback to complete the transaction and release the locks. It is not unusual for users to simply exit the browser, leaving hanging transactions and consuming resources, both on the application server and the database. Although both of these tiers will eventually clean up after the relevant timeout, in the meantime, other users may be blocked from changing the data. Therefore, the best practice for locking is to use optimistic mode.

This topic was introduced by showing the programmatic calls required to configure the locking mode, but surely there is a simpler way. In Oracle Forms, there is a declarative setting on the block. Does ADF Business Components have something similar? It turns out that it does, but the setting is effectively buried. To find it, we need to learn about configurations.

ADF Business Component Configurations

In logical terms, ADF Business Components uses two distinct sets of metadata:

- **XML object definitions** are created in the design time environment. These files define the essential properties of artifacts, such as entity objects and view objects.

- **Configurations** are runtime settings for the ADF Business Components framework as a whole, defining session-level information, such as the database connection.

Configurations control the runtime behavior of the framework. An application may have several configurations defined for it, but at runtime, only one configuration can be active. When an application is installed into an application server, the configuration file will usually be customized as a post-deployment step. For example, the administrator may configure the database connection and various application-tuning parameters, such as application module pooling and failover settings. The configuration file differs in this way from the basic XML object definition metadata, which would not be customized after deployment.

Accessing the Configurations

The configuration file is an XML file named "bc4j.xcfg," which is visible in the Structure window for the application module. In physical terms, it is located in a subdirectory called "common" underneath the directory that stores the application module XML definition. You use the Configuration Manager to view and edit configurations. This is accessed by selecting **Configurations** from the application module right-click menu.

The first screen of the Configuration Manager shows the defined configurations and a summary of their properties—mainly the database connection information, as shown next:

	Property	Value
	AppModuleJndiName	book.model.HRService
	ApplicationName	book.model.HRService
	DeployPlatform	LOCAL
	JDBCName	hr
	java.naming.factory.initial	oracle.jbo.common.JboInitialContext...
	jbo.project	Model

Configuration Manager — Names: HRServiceLocal. Buttons: New..., Copy, Edit..., Delete, Help, OK, Cancel.

The default configuration shown here will be named with the application module name plus "Local" The word "Local" in this context indicates that this default configuration operates in local deployment mode, where the ADF Business Components module and its client are co-located in the same JVM.

Although only one configuration is created initially, you can add others with different settings. It is not unusual to have one configuration for development use, another for acceptance testing and QA, and yet another for live deployment.

TIP
Although the most obvious difference between development and deployment configurations will be the database connection, other settings may also differ. For example, it is unlikely that enabling application module pooling and failover will be useful during development. However, these features may well be needed for production deployment.

Clicking the Edit button displays the following tabbed dialog:

Here you can change the name of the configuration and, more importantly, define the connection information. There are two approaches to defining the connection:

- **JDBC URL** This uses a hard-coded reference to a connection as defined in the Connection Navigator.

- **JDBC DataSource** This looks the connection up from the application server at runtime. In this case, the connection information will be resolved at runtime using a Java Naming and Directory Interface (JNDI) look-up on the generic data sources defined by the application server administrator. Each servlet container uses a slightly different method of defining these data sources. In the Oracle Application Server OC4J case, data sources are defined in a file called "data-sources.xml" in the OC4J configuration directory. The administrator can set up data sources in the Oracle Application Server Control web application (also called "EM").

For design-time purposes, you will use the JDBC URL connection type. For production deployments, you will probably want the flexibility provided by the named data source. An application server administrator can configure such a data source without having to touch any of the application files.

The second tab of the Configuration Manager (Pooling and Scalability) contains information concerned with runtime tuning. However, the third tab (Properties) is of interest right now, as it gives the ability to change the locking mode (the reason we are looking at configurations). This page provides the expert mode view of ADF Business Components configuration, including several options, most of which will never need to be changed in normal operation. The property we're looking for is *jbo.locking.mode*, shown here:

You can set locking mode to "none," "optimistic," or "pessimistic." You can only set it to OPTUPDATE programmatically. Note that "none" is valid even though it is not mentioned as a valid value in the tooltip. Also note that you need to type in this value, so be careful of spelling. Once you make that change and click OK, the Configuration Manager summary screen displays the changed property, indicating that it has been assigned a nondefault value.

Looking at the underlying XML file for the configuration—bc4j.xcfg—you will see that a new jbo.locking.mode entry has been added, as shown in this code listing:

```
<BC4JConfig>
  <AppModuleConfigBag>
    <AppModuleConfig name="HRServiceLocal">
      <DeployPlatform>LOCAL</DeployPlatform>
      <JDBCName>hr</JDBCName>
      <jbo.project>Model</jbo.project>
      <jbo.locking.mode>optimistic</jbo.locking.mode>
      <AppModuleJndiName>book.model.HRService</AppModuleJndiName>
      <ApplicationName>book.model.HRService</ApplicationName>
```

```
      </AppModuleConfig>
    </AppModuleConfigBag>
    <ConnectionDefinition name="hr"/>
  </BC4JConfig>
```

TIP
As mentioned, the default locking mode in ADF Business Components is pessimistic. This can lead to problems in a development environment, where a lot of testing and incomplete transactions can take place on a limited set of records. To prevent frustrating locking problems, make the switch to optimistic mode in the configuration early on in the project life cycle.

Where Is the Login Dialog?

In discussing configurations, we mentioned the database connection definition, so at this point, it's probably a good idea to think about how the database login works. Many PL/SQL and Oracle Forms developers find this area rather confusing when dealing with an ADF Business Components application because they never see a login dialog.

Authenticating a user login for Oracle Forms and PL/SQL developers will nearly always mean the use of one of two methodologies. Either the user logs in with an individual database account or the user logs in as some shared database user account (usually automatically), but then has to authenticate through an application security layer, which maintains its own concept of users and roles.

Connection Pooling

J2EE applications usually take the latter approach—a shared database account. This approach helps in maximizing scalability. Most J2EE applications are designed for high transaction rates and are not necessarily stateful. That is, database transactions may be autonomous and short-lived, and the end user does not have a continuous connection to the database. Most frameworks provide maximum scalability for this scenario by using a single database account for the connection. A single account means that a pool of identical connections can be created and allocated by the application server to each session that needs to carry out a database transaction. Connections to the database are expensive to create because they require network and database server resources. This way, if multiple sessions share the same credentials, they can just borrow a connection from the pool for a short time and return it when they are done. If every session used its own user name and password, this would not be possible, and the cost of connecting to the database server would have to be incurred for every session.

As we have already seen, in ADF Business Components, the information about the database account to use is maintained in the runtime configuration file, bc4j.xcfg.

Security the J2EE Way

We have seen how best practice dictates the use of a shared database account to increase scalability. However, applications still need security. How is that achieved?

The best solution is to leverage the built-in security that is defined for J2EE—J2EE container security. This is a standard security mechanism that web-deployed applications can use to protect sets of pages within an application. We will spend more time on container-managed security in Chapter 14 as part of developing a sample application.

How Do I Define Business Rules?

So far, this chapter has covered the basics of ADF Business Components. It has tackled the core issues of both read-only and updateable queries, but it has not discussed the definition of any rules or logic associated with that basic activity. For most applications, we can consider three levels of business logic:

- **Database referential integrity constraints**   These are referential integrity rules defined through relationships in the database that enforce structural aspects of the relational data itself, for example, "Each employee must be assigned to a department that actually exists."

- **Basic data content validations**   This is logic, which, like the referential constraints, may be defined by hard rules defined or coded within the database (in check constraints, unique constraints, and triggers), but which checks the content of the data rather than its relationships, for example, "Salary cannot be less than zero."

- **Complex validations and rules**   These are higher-level functions that perform validation across a row or between rows of data, or that implement other rules, such as setting default attribute values.

Chapter 10 examines application logic design. For now, we will look at how each of these rule categories is addressed within the ADF Business Components framework.

Database Referential Integrity Constraints

We assume that the database has been built using good relational design and that referential integrity constraints have been created in the database. At the very least, these will define the primary and foreign keys of the related tables. The database will validate these constraints automatically when rows are inserted, but it is also possible to apply the same rules in the ADF Business Components layer using associations.

Associations

Associations define the relationship between two entity objects. If the entity objects are created using the Create Business Components from Tables Wizard, the IDE will automatically create associations based on the foreign key constraints defined in the data dictionary. For example, when creating the Employees entity object earlier in this chapter, an association called "EmpManagerFKAssoc" is created to implement the constraint enforcing that an employee's manager should be a valid employee. You can examine the association in the Association Editor (shown next) by selecting **Edit** from the right-click menu on the association node:

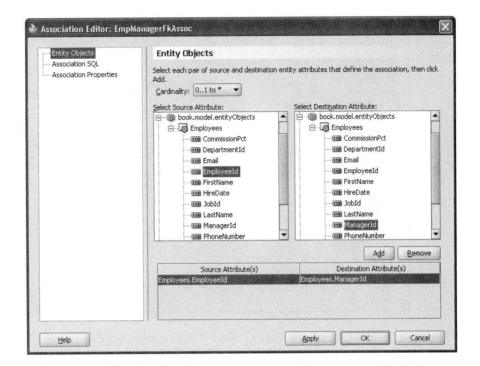

Why Use Associations?   Given the information so far, it seems that an association is not giving you much more than a foreign key relationship on the database. Remember, however, that ADF BC maintains relationships between entity objects, and entity objects are detached from the database. Some of the entity object instances will have been created and cached by ADF BC and not yet committed to the database. Other entity object instances may not be derived from a table at all. For example, an entity object may be mapped to a PL/SQL collection (as we explain later). In this case, associations can enforce relationship constraints that cannot exist in the database.

In addition to being a basis for referential integrity, associations manage the process of cascading deletions and updated keys through the object tree; they also provide programmatic access in Java from the master records to the details and from the details to the master. We've already seen an implicit example of this mechanism in action with the DBSequence mechanism, where the primary key generated for the master record is propagated to all of the detail records. Programmatic access might also be useful in a scenario where a value on the master record needed to be calculated based on information from all of the children—for example, an order total attribute.

Associations are also somewhat richer than foreign key relationships on the database, because you can declare the precise cardinality of the relationship, for example, 1 to * (one-to-many), 0..1 to *(optional one-to-many), 1 to 0..1 (one-to-optional-one), and so on. An association can even define a direct * to * (many-to-many) association by mapping through a third, intersection entity, as in this example, which maps the association between Countries and Departments:

Notice the two relationships declared in the bottom panes. These many-to-many relationships are useful from a programmatic point of view. When an association is created, it will (by default) expose an accessor method in the Impl file for the either or both entity objects. This accessor method will allow you to follow the relationship to access the detail (or conversely the master) entity object instance in code should you need to. You define these accessors on the Association Properties page of the Association Editor, shown here:

View Links

Associations define the relationship between two entity objects and its cardinality. However, they don't address the issue of querying related data to answer a question like, "Can you give me a list of all employees within a certain department?"

Writing code to traverse a list of departments and view the employees in each one is not a scalable approach. Oracle Forms already has a solution to this—the relation object. A *relation* is a declarative join between two data blocks so that the contents of the detail block are automatically synchronized with the current row in the master block (using triggers created when you define the relation). In fact, as well as providing this function, the relation also handles cascading deletions much like an association.

Not surprisingly, ADF Business Components also has a relation-like construct: the view link. Just like the association, the *view link* defines a relationship between objects, in this case, between view objects rather than entity objects. When creating a view link, you select the master and detail view objects and the joining columns in the Create View Link Wizard, shown here:

View links provide a way to access the contents of a view object in a filtered way. For example, in the case of Departments and Employees, the Employees view object may be accessed as is, that is, to retrieve the entire list of employees based on the view object's WHERE clause. Alternatively, it may be accessed through a view link from the Departments view object. In this case, the WHERE clause of the EmployeesUpdateable view object will be refined to restrict the results to employees within the currently selected row in the DepartmentList view object. Therefore, we have two possible usages of the EmployeesUpdeatable view object.

At runtime, if a view object is accessed through a view link, the relationship defined between the two view objects is applied in the form of an additional WHERE clause predicate for the detail. By the same token, if the detail view object is updateable, then any rows inserted through it will automatically contain the correct foreign key value to reference the selected master record.

This is a powerful feature that you should leverage rather than trying to maintain key relationships manually in your own code.

If you are following along with creating the Business Components project discussed in this chapter, create a view link between EmployeesUpdateable and DepartmentList, as shown previously, and call it "EmpDeptFkLink." We'll be using this in Chapters 7 and 8 when we discuss binding.

View Links in the Application Module   Once view links are in the picture, we have to revise our idea of what is going on when we expose view objects through the "Application Module Data Model" screen. This screen is all about defining instances of view objects to expose. Where there are view links, you can see the master-detail relationships through the nesting of the view objects in the "Available View Objects" panel of the dialog:

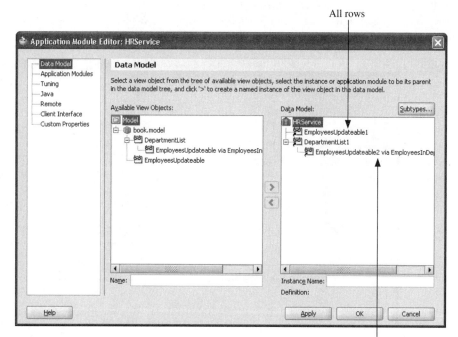

At the bottom of the Data Model page is a field you can use to rename the view object instances. It is a good idea to use this field to provide a name that describes the query. The default names are somewhat meaningless, as you can see in this illustration. The EmployeesUpdateable view object instances could be renamed to *AllEmployees* (for the unbound query) and *EmployeesByDepartment* (for the employees in the current department) to make their function clearer. These names will identify queries exposed through the Data Control Palette, which you will use to construct a UI for this data.

Data Content Validations

Now we need to discuss validation at the attribute or field level—this covers the kinds of validation that you might define within the database using check constraints and possibly database triggers as well.

Constraints

We have seen that associations and view objects provide a way of defining relational constraints within ADF BC, but in database terms, constraints can also act on the content of data. The most familiar manifestation of this is the NOT NULL constraint applied to a column when it is created. Check constraints are common, too, as a way of performing basic validation against constant values. For example, the SALARY column in the HR schema EMPLOYEES table has a check constraint to ensure that the salary value is greater than zero.

When discussing the creation of entity objects, we mentioned how ADF BC uses the data dictionary to intelligently select default properties, such as the primary key for entity object attributes. Once you have created an entity object in this way, if you look in the Structure window, you will see the following top-level nodes: Sources, Attributes, Association Accessors, and Constraints. The Constraints node shows a list of all of the rules that have been extracted from the data dictionary for this entity object. You might be forgiven for thinking that these would therefore implement your validation for these simple conditions (such as the aforementioned check on SALARY). But it's another trap—just like the sequence name mentioned in relation to the DBSequence domain that we looked at when generating primary keys. The constraints defined here in the entity object are only used if you generate a table from the entity object.

To implement basic validation rules and constraint equivalents in the entity object, you actually use declarative validation rules.

Declarative Validation Rules

You can define one or more declarative validation rules in ADF BC for each attribute in an entity object. *Declarative validation rules* are simple validations declared in the Entity Object Editor (accessed by double clicking the entity object in the Navigator). The Validation page of this editor will display a list of attributes with any declarative validation rules you declare, as shown here:

To add a declarative validation rule for a particular attribute (such as Salary) in the Entity Object Editor, select it in the list and click New.

The Add Validation Rule For dialog (shown in Figure 6-5) appears. You can use this to select from the following range of predefined validations:

- **Compare Validator** Allows you to compare (using operations such as equals, greater than, and so on) the new value for an attribute with a single value of various types: a literal value, the result of a SQL query, or the value of a view object attribute.

- **List Validator** Like the compare validator, this allows you to use literals, the results of queries, or other view objects, but this validator compares with a set of values rather than with a single value. The operator can be either In or Not In as required. This validator can act much like the *Use LOV for Validation* flag on an Oracle Forms item.

- **Range Validator** Provides a Between or Not Between comparison with high and low literal values.

- **Length Validator** Checks the length of the value. You can base the check on the number of characters or the number of bytes.

- **Regular Expression Validator** Gives an immense amount of power within a declarative context. It allows you to use regular expressions to validate formatted strings, such as email addresses, URLs, or postal codes.

- **Method Validator** If all else fails, you can write your own code as a custom method. This method has access to the other attributes within this row (and potentially across the entire row set). Unlike the other validators, a method validator is not fully declarative, because you write your own validation code. This means that you have the freedom to create a complex validator, which can be reused throughout the application. You create the method in the entity object Impl class with a `boolean` return and an argument of the attribute for which this rule is defined.

A particular attribute can have multiple declarative validation rules defined for it. The rules are evaluated in the order of definition. The actual rules, with the exception of the method validators, are stored inside the XML definition file for the entity object. No code is generated for them.

As shown in Figure 6-5, each rule can also have an associated error message, defined through the rules dialog. These messages are stored in a message bundle .java file (described and demonstrated in Chapter 9) that is listed as a child of the entity object in the Structure window. The advantage of storing the messages in a separate class rather than putting the message into the XML file is that you can create files for multiple translations of the message bundle class.

Complex Validations and Rules

We have seen how the method validator allows the creation of more complex rules in Java code. In most cases, this will be sufficient for single attribute validations, but as we discussed at the start of this section, applications generally have more complex requirements than this, such as validation across sets of attributes or records. To handle such requirements, custom code needs to be added to the entity object Impl file.

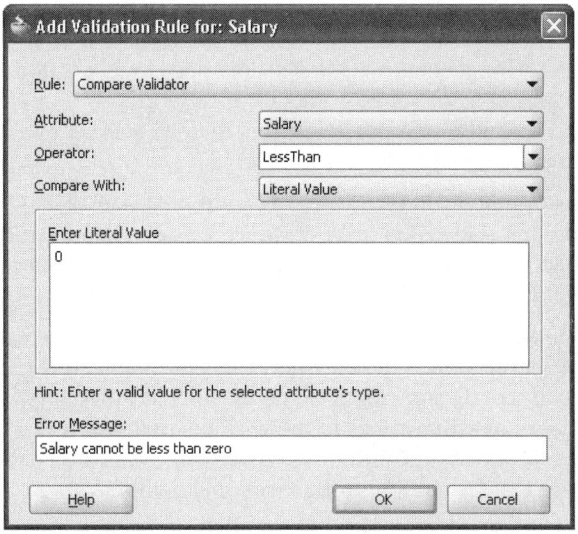

FIGURE 6-5. *Creating a validation rule in the Add Validation Rule For dialog*

Just as in the case of the application module, the Impl file for an entity object is usually created automatically. If not, you can force its creation from the Entity Object Editor's Java page, shown next.

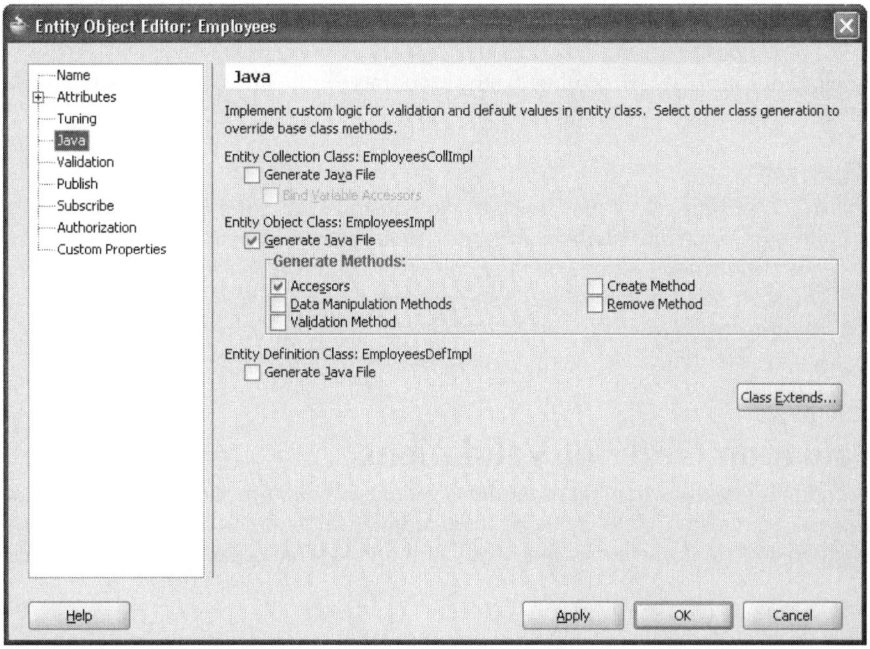

Notice that the "Generate Java File" selection for the entity object class offers several options. Selecting each of these will generate extra code stubs (or trigger points) into the Impl .java file:

■ **Accessors** This generates get and set methods for each attribute. For example, it will generate a getFirstName() and a setFirstName() method for the *FirstName* attribute. You can write code to each of these to supplement, or occasionally replace, the default functionality.

■ **Validation Method** In Oracle Forms terms, this is a WHEN-VALIDATE-RECORD trigger. If this option is selected, a validateEntity() method will be created in the Impl file. This method executes once per entity object that is updated or created, allowing you to define validations that operate across all the attributes.

■ **Create Method** The create() method is not a place for validation, but it is a place for initialization code for a new entity object instance (row). This is ideal for setting the default values of dynamic data elements, such as timestamps and user information, that cannot be set as static values in the attribute definitions. This is similar to the Oracle Forms WHEN-NEW-RECORD-INSTANCE trigger. See the sidebar "Using the create( ) Method for Key Generation" for an example of this.

■ **Remove Method** The remove() method is triggered as the entity is marked as deleted from the entity object cache. This is more or less equivalent to the WHEN-REMOVE-RECORD trigger in an Oracle Forms application.

■ **Data Manipulation Methods** This checkbox will generate a lock() method and a doDML() method. These act just like the Oracle Forms "ON-" transactional triggers (for example, ON-LOCK, ON-INSERT, ON-DELETE, and so on), and you can use them to override default entity object behavior. Although these methods are not normally needed, they do provide a way of basing an entity object on a PL/SQL package rather than on a table, as we will see later.

These options provide a rich set of extension points for the basic entity object, allowing you to customize the default functionality.

CAUTION
Just as checking one of the Generate Methods options in the Entity Object Editor creates method stubs for you, unchecking them will delete the methods, along with any code that you've added inside of them. As a precaution, it is wise to put any custom code into your own user-named methods and call those from the generated stubs. In this way, should you inadvertently uncheck an option, the damage will be minimal.

Evaluation Order of Validations

It is important to know in what order these validations will fire. Consider an entity object, which has a validateEntity() method, a declarative validation on an attribute, and some custom validation code in the setter for that same attribute. In what order will these validations occur?

Using the create( ) Method for Key Generation

Earlier in the chapter, we saw how you can use a database trigger and the DBSequence domain to manage sequence number allocation into entity primary keys. At that point, it was also mentioned that you could use code to achieve the same thing. The create() method is the place to do this. It is such a common operation that ADF BC provides a helper class to simplify the code. Here is the typical code to carry out the operation:

```
01: protected void create(AttributeList attributeList)
02: {
03:    super.create(attributeList);
04:    DBTransaction trans = getDBTransaction();
05:    SequenceImpl seq = new SequenceImpl("EMPLOYEES_SEQ",trans);
06:    setEmployeeId(seq.getSequenceNumber());
07: }
```

- **Line 03** calls the entity object superclass to create the new row.

- **Line 05** creates a new `oracle.jbo.server.SequenceImpl` object, passing the name of the database sequence to use and a reference to the `DBTransaction` obtained in **Line 04**.

- **Line 06** calls the setter for the key column on the new row (`setEmployeeId()`), passing the next sequence number for the key obtained by calling the `getSequenceNumber()` method on the `SequenceImpl`.

Unlike the DBSequence technique discussed earlier, allocating a sequence number in this way does not require a database trigger to manage the allocation of the new key. The key is also allocated as soon as the new entity object instance (row) is created, so any user interface item bound to the key column will reflect the new value before the record is committed. However, the side effect of this is that key wastage increases as users create and then abandon new records.

The entity object `validateEntity()` method will always execute at the end. But the execution order of the other two depends on how the setter method has been defined. Here is a sample setter method:

```
public void setFirstName(String value)
{
  setAttributeInternal(FIRSTNAME, value);
  checkCustomRule(value);
}
```

In this case, the `checkCustomRule()` method will perform additional validation and may fail by raising an exception. The declarative validation rule will fire before `checkCustomRule()` because the `setAttributeInternal()` call within the setter is the application point for the declarative rules. Therefore, if `checkCustomRule()` was placed before the `setAttributeInternal()` call, it would fire first. The implication here is that you can define custom validation in the setter, both before and after the declarative rules are applied.

Raising Errors in Code

We've looked at how code can be added to define validation rules in various places. The question then arises about how to generate error conditions if something goes wrong. In the case of a method validator, the method just needs to return "false" to indicate that all is not well. The `validateEntity()` and `lock()` method signatures define no return type, so something else is needed. In these cases, the solution is to raise an exception—specifically, an `oracle.jbo .JboException`. This will signal to the framework that something has gone wrong, and the framework can pass a suitable error message back. For example:

```
public void lock()
{
  if (!auditLockingChange(key, user))
  {
    throw new JboException("Unable to audit record lock");
  }
  super.lock();
}
```

In this example, if the audit activity fails, the locking process is aborted by throwing a JboException. From the Oracle Forms perspective, this is much like coding RAISE FORM_TRIGGER_FAILURE to abort a trigger.

How Can I Dynamically Change a Query?

We've seen how view objects can be created to define multiple queries of records cached in the entity objects, but we know that fixed queries will not suffice. Most applications require functions, which need to be customized at runtime, for example, a search function where the results are based on the criteria specified through the UI.

> **TIP**
> *The rest of this chapter requires writing Java code to interface with the ADF Business Components APIs. You can find more information about these APIs in the JDeveloper help system. Search the Contents tab for the topic "Reference\ Oracle ADF Business Components Java API Reference."*

Fortunately, you can customize the view object to accommodate this requirement. As you saw earlier, you can define bind variables for substitution into the statement. Like entity objects and application modules, you can also define a Java Impl file for the view object as a place to put your own code for functions such as rewriting the WHERE and ORDER BY clauses.

Here is an example method, which sets the value of the `:location` bind variable in the DepartmentList view object (DepartmentListImpl.java) we created earlier:

```
public void searchByLocationId(Number locationId)
{
  setNamedWhereClauseParam("location",locationId);
}
```

In this example, the code just sets the value of the :location named bind variable to whatever value is passed into the method. Here is another example for the same file that will toggle the sort order for DEPARTMENT_NAME in the view object between ASC and DESC:

```
public void toggleOrdering()
{
  String orderBy = getOrderByClause();
  StringBuffer newOrderBy = new StringBuffer("Depts.DEPARTMENT_NAME ");

  //Append the correct new order indicator
  if (orderBy.endsWith(" ASC"))
  {
    newOrderBy.append("DESC");
  }
  else
  {
    newOrderBy.append("ASC");
  }

  //Set the new order by
  setOrderByClause(newOrderBy.toString());
}
```

TIP
If you're not sure what methods are available within a particular context, press CTRL-SPACEBAR to display a list. Press F1 after selecting a variable or method to display the relevant Javadoc. Finally, use CTRL- - (the CTRL and minus keys) to display the "Go To Java Class" dialog. This dialog provides a search facility to locate a class, even if you only know part of its name. You can then view the code or the Javadoc for that class.

In both of these examples, the code alters the view object definition but does not re-execute the query to apply those changes. The alterations will be used the next time ADF BC internally executes the view object. You can explicitly force a view object to requery using the executeQuery() method. For example, you might add a method, toggleDepartmentSorting(), to the application module Impl file to call the toggleOrdering() method defined previously and then re-execute the query to obtain the new order. Here is a sample call (the line numbers are to aid explanation and do not appear in the code):

```
01: public void toggleDepartmentSorting()
02: {
03:    DepartmentListImpl deptVO = getDepartmentList1();
04:    deptVO.toggleOrdering();
05:    deptVO.executeQuery();
06: }
```

- **Line 03** calls a method `getDepartmentList1()`. This method is one that ADF BC automatically generates when a view object (in this case, DepartmentList) is exposed in the data model of the application module. Recall the discussion earlier about the default names generated for view object instances on the Data Model page of the Application Module Editor. The `findViewObject()` function is provided by the application module to look up a view object instance by name, which is then cast to the appropriate implementation type of DepartmentListImpl.

The generated function to access the view object instance is as follows:

```
public DepartmentListImpl getDepartmentList1() {
  return (DepartmentListImpl)findViewObject("DepartmentList1");
}
```

- **Line 04** calls the `toggleOrdering()` custom method on the view object Impl file.
- **Line 05** calls `executeQuery()` to refresh the data in the view object, and in this case re-sort the rows according to the new ORDER BY.

Exposing View Object Methods on the Façade

Earlier in this chapter, we discussed how methods defined in the application module can be made available to clients using the Client Interface page of the Application Module Editor. We've also just looked at an example method (`toggleDepartmentSorting()`) that is exposed in this way. View object methods can be directly exposed to UI clients as well. This is done using the Client Interface page of the View Object Editor, as shown here:

In this case, the searchByLocationId() function that we defined at the beginning of this section is published as a view object method.

Such methods are shown as custom operations in the Data Control Palette for that view object instance, provided that the view object itself is exposed for client use. In Chapter 8, we'll look at how such methods can be used in your application code. For example, after exposing the searchByLocationId() method, you will be able to drop it into the user interface as a button and pass a new location to customize the query.

NOTE
Configuring bind variables for a view object at runtime is such a frequent operation that the ADF framework provides a shortcut called ExecuteWithParams, saving you from frequently having to write code to manage the task. We also discuss ExecuteWithParams in Chapter 8.

How Can I Interface ADF BC with PL/SQL?

As the final topic in this chapter, we will look at a key requirement: how do you call PL/SQL from ADF BC? We'll break this question down into three different usages of PL/SQL:

- **Calling a stored PL/SQL procedure** as a standalone operation, for example, from validation code.

- **Returning data from PL/SQL to ADF BC** as a variation on the preceding technique. You can use this technique for PL/SQL functions that return a value or for PL/SQL functions or procedures that contain OUT (or IN OUT) parameters.

- **Basing an entity object on PL/SQL** for DML operations—similar to basing an Oracle Forms data block on a stored package rather than directly on a table.

Calling a Stored PL/SQL Procedure

The Transaction object introduced earlier in the chapter provides the hooks we need to execute a PL/SQL procedure or function or, for that matter, any SQL statement. This technique will use a JDBC construct called a *prepared statement* (java.sql.PreparedStatement), an object into which you define a PL/SQL block or SQL statement; you then execute the statement within the context of the Transaction object. The following sections step through the code required to call a PL/SQL procedure that has the following signature:

```
PROCEDURE update_department_name(
            p_department_id IN PLS_INTEGER,
            p_new_dept_name  IN VARCHAR2)
```

And here is the Java code that will be needed to call it (line numbers for reference purposes only):

```
01: import java.sql.PreparedStatement;
02: import java.sql.SQLException;
03: import oracle.jbo.CSMessageBundle;
04: import oracle.jbo.SQLStmtException;
05:
```

```
06: // other application module Impl code omitted
07:
08: public void callUpdateDepartmentName (int deptNo,
09:                                         String newName)
10: {
11:    PreparedStatement plsqlBlock = null;
12:    String statement = "BEGIN update_department_name(:1,:2); END;";
13:    plsqlBlock = getDBTransaction().createPreparedStatement(statement,0);
14:    try
15:    {
16:      plsqlBlock.setInt(1,deptNo);
17:      plsqlBlock.setString(2,newName);
18:      plsqlBlock.execute();
19:    }
20:    catch (SQLException sqlException)
21:    {
22:      throw new SQLStmtException(CSMessageBundle.class,
23:                                 CSMessageBundle.EXC_SQL_EXECUTE_COMMAND,
24:                                 statement,
25:                                 sqlException);
26:    }
27:    finally
28:    {
29:      try
30:      {
31:        plsqlBlock.close();
32:      }
33:      catch (SQLException e)
34:      {
35:        // We don't really care if this fails, so just print to the console
36:        e.printStackTrace();
37:      }
38:    }
39: }
```

1. Define the Java Method (Lines 08-09)   The previous sample code represents an extract from an application module Impl file. The entire code for the class is not included, just the salient points for the task of calling PL/SQL. The interesting section begins with the declaration of a method that will encapsulate the PL/SQL call. Such methods are generally referred to as *wrapper methods* since they wrap a convenient interface around something more complex—in this case, a call out to PL/SQL:

- **Line 08** defines the name of the Java method that contains the PL/SQL call as `callUpdateDepartmentName()`.

- **Lines 08-09** specify the two arguments, `deptNo` and `newName`, that will be passed through to the PL/SQL function.

In addition to this method declaration, the application module Impl will have to contain various import statements (as shown by **Lines 01-04**) to make all of the required classes available in code.

JDeveloper will pop up hints as to when import statements are needed. You use the ALT-ENTER keyboard shortcut to add these imports as you go along.

2. Create the Prepared Statement (Lines 11-13) The first part of the PL/SQL wrapper method creates a prepared statement:

- **Line 11** declares a variable (`plsqlBlock`) to hold the `PreparedStatement` object that will be created.

- **Line 12** defines the text of the actual PL/SQL call. The statement is written as an anonymous PL/SQL block with BEGIN and END keywords. Parameters that will be passed to the PL/SQL procedure are represented by the bind variable references :1 and :2.

CAUTION
The PreparedStatement syntax expects bind placeholder variables to be in this numbered style and based on a one-indexed scheme (that starts at :1 not :0). Do not confuse this with the Oracle Number style of bind variables used for view object queries, which are zero-indexed. The style of bind variable placeholders in prepared statements cannot be changed.

NOTE
If you were calling a packaged procedure, you would use the package_name.procedure_name syntax within the prepared statement just as in normal PL/SQL.

- **Line 13** creates the prepared statement and assigns it to the `plsqlBlock` variable defined in line 11. The transaction object that we discussed earlier in relation to locking and commits is responsible for creating the `PreparedStatement` object. It uses the method `createPreparedStatement()`, passing a String representation of the PL/SQL block (defined in line 14) as the first argument.

  The second argument to `createPreparedStatement()` is only used when the statement being executed is a query that returns values. It can be left as zero (indicating no return values) in this case. The technique for calling PL/SQL functions with return values is discussed later on in this section.

3. Set the Arguments (Lines 16-17) Now that the statement is prepared, the parameter values to pass to the PL/SQL procedure are defined:

- **Line 16** calls a method `setInt()` on the prepared statement. The first argument to `setInt()` indicates the index number of the placeholder bind variable that is being set with this call. In this case, the code is setting the first parameter to the PL/SQL procedure— p_department_id. The second argument to `setInt()` is the actual value to substitute into the p_department_id parameter. The underlying PL/SQL type for the parameter is PLS_INTEGER, so using `setInt()`, which expects a Java int type, ensures that only a valid value can be passed through to PL/SQL.

- **Line 17** calls `setString()` to set the value of the second PL/SQL procedure argument, which is of type VARCHAR2.

The `PreparedStatement` interface defines a whole set of these type-safe methods for converting from Java types to the equivalent SQL types. Use CTRL- - (Ctrl and minus) to display the "Go To Java Class" dialog, and enter "java.sql.PreparedStatement" to view them

4. Execute the Statement (Line 18) Now that the arguments are set, you can execute the statement using the call to `execute()` shown on **Line 18**.

5. Handle Errors (Lines 14, 20-26) In the code listing, the call to set the `PreparedStatement` arguments and execution are enclosed in a Java try-catch block. If the setting of the parameters or the execution of the statement fails, the catch statement in **Line 20** passes control to **Lines 22-25**. This section of code throws a new `SQLStmtException` exception, passing the text of the offending PL/SQL block and the actual error that was raised. The references to `CSMessageBundle` in this new exception refer to the framework class `oracle.jbo.CSMessageBundle`. This class is a resource bundle class provided by ADF BC that contains strings and error constants used by the `SQLStmtException` exception.

6. Clean Up (Line 31) The prepared statement must be cleaned up when it is complete. If the statement will only be called once, you can clean up after the `execute()` call. However, if the statement will be reused several times within the lifetime of the application module, the `PreparedStatement` object can be stored as an instance attribute in the Impl class; you can then clean up in the application module's `remove()` method. The clean-up code just calls `close()` on the `PreparedStatement`, as shown on **Line 31**.

In this case, the statement is cleaned up as soon as it is finished with, so this `close()` statement is called within the `finally` clause of the `try-catch` block that you used to enclose the `execute()`. Putting the `close()` call in the `finally` block ensures that the statement will be cleaned up, even if the `execute()` statement raised an exception.

7. Run the Code In Step 1, the wrapper function for the PL/SQL method was declared. It can be run from Java passing the required arguments:

```
callUpdateDepartmentName(99,"Offshore Telesales");
```

This Java code can now be called internally from any code in the application module or through the service façade, if the method is exposed through the Client Interface panel in the application module properties editor.

Returning Data from PL/SQL to ADF BC

The previous example called a procedure with no return value. What if you want to call a PL/SQL function or a procedure with IN OUT or OUT parameters? The procedure is essentially the same, except you use a `CallableStatement` rather than a `PreparedStatement`; also, you need to define variables for the return values.

For example, let's rework the same PL/SQL to be a function with a BOOLEAN return value to indicate success or failure, as in the following signature:

```
FUNCTION update_department_name(
            p_department_id IN NUMBER,
            p_new_dept_name  IN VARCHAR2)
            RETURN BOOLEAN
```

Here are the changed and extra steps to call this function from Java:

1. Create a CallableStatement   Like the prepared statement, the `CallableStatement` object is also created by a call to the `DBTransaction` object. This time, an extra bind variable is added to the PL/SQL block to hold the return value from the function call, as shown here:

```
CallableStatement plsqlBlock = null;
String statement = "BEGIN :1 = update_department_name(:2,:3); END;";
plsqlBlock = getDBTransaction().createCallableStatement(statement,0);
```

2. Register the OUT Parameter   With a `CallableStatement`, the `registerOutParameter()` method is used to indicate which of the bind variables will return a value and the variable's datatype. This applies to both the return value of a function and the OUT or IN OUT parameters in the PL/SQL signature:

```
plsqlBlock.registerOutParameter(1,OracleTypes.BOOLEAN);
```

In this case, the first bind variable in the statement (`:1`) will hold the result of the function call, and its type is BOOLEAN. The types of the variables are defined in the class `oracle.jdbc` `.driver.OracleTypes` when using the Oracle JDBC drivers. (As before, you can review all possible datatypes using the Javadoc for that class.)

3. Set the Arguments and Executing   The arguments for a `CallableStatement` are set in the same way as for a `PreparedStatement`; the only difference is the numbering of the bind variables to account for the first return parameter, as shown here:

```
plsqlBlock.setInt(2, deptNo);
plsqlBlock.setString(3,newName);
```

Likewise, execution is identical, as in this call:

```
plsqlBlock.execute();
```

4. Get the Result Back   The `CallableStatement` offers type-safe getters to retrieve the values of those return bind variables registered earlier. Therefore, we make this call:

```
boolean result = plsqlBlock.getBoolean(1);
```

5. Put It All Together   The following is a version of the function excluding the error handling:

```
public boolean callUpdateDepartmentName (int deptNo,
                                         String newName)
{
  boolean result = false;
  CallableStatement plsqlBlock = null;
  String statement = "BEGIN :1 = update_department_name(:2,:3); END;";
  plsqlBlock = getDBTransaction().createCallableStatement(statement,0);
  try
  {
    plsqlBlock.registerOutParameter(1,OracleTypes.BOOLEAN);
    plsqlBlock.setInt(2,deptNo);
    plsqlBlock.setString(3,newName);
```

```
        plsqlBlock.execute();
        result = plsqlBlock.getBoolean;
   }
   //catch and finally blocks omitted

   return result;
}
```

Basing a Entity Object on PL/SQL

Oracle Forms programmers are familiar with the technique of combining a database view for retrieving data and a PL/SQL package to handle inserts, updates, deletions, and locks. This method simplifies the coding required in the form because the data block is based on a single data source (the view); the use of PL/SQL as the DML interface affords a lot of flexibility to manipulate and validate the data changes. You have the following two choices when using PL/SQL as a data source:

■ **Base the business components on a database view with INSTEAD OF triggers.** Using this technique, you need to code the INSTEAD OF trigger to perform all logic that you want to occur for INSERT, UPDATE, and DELETE operations. The view serves as the query object. The work in ADF BC is nothing more than basing an entity object and view object on the database view. The database view can be arbitrarily complex.

■ **Base the business components on a database view, and call PL/SQL procedures from ADF BC for INSERT, UPDATE, and DELETE operations.** This strategy uses the database view for the query but replaces the normal ADF BC operations for INSERT, UPDATE, and DELETE.

Since the first of these techniques requires no additional code in ADF BC, we will not explain it further. However, the second technique demonstrates how to fulfill a common requirement. In addition, if you have already defined these PL/SQL APIs, this technique will show how to leverage them from ADF Business Components. Therefore, we will explain the second one here.

We have already discussed how to call PL/SQL from within Java, and that is exactly the technique that you would use to perform the DML calls to your PL/SQL APIs. The key question is, of course, where to put the prepared statement calls that will interface with PL/SQL.

In Oracle Forms, you can use the transactional triggers mechanism to replace the default DML calls. Likewise, in ADF Business Components, you can replace the default functionality in the doDML() method in the entity object Impl class. Recall how this method can be generated by selecting the *Data Manipulation Methods* option in the Java panel of the Entity Object Editor.

The doDML() method handles INSERT, UPDATE, and DELETE. Locking is handled by the separate lock() method, which is also created if the Data Manipulation Methods option is selected.

Overriding Insert, Update, and Delete

Each instance of the entity object Impl file represents a single row, and the framework passes an operation argument to doDML() that indicates if this row operation is to be an insert, update, or delete. The doDML() method uses a switch/case statement to carry out code appropriate to the operation argument. This argument is passed as an integer value that corresponds to a constant, such as DML_INSERT. A typical doDML() method will look like this:

```
public void doDML(int operation,
                      TransactionEvent e)
{
  switch (operation)
  {
    case DML_INSERT:
    {
      plsqlProcInsert();
      break;
    }
    case DML_UPDATE:
    {
      plsqlProcUpdate();
      break;
    }
    case DML_DELETE:
    {
      plsqlProcDelete();
      break;
    }
  }
}
```

In this code, each DML operation is handled by a call to a method elsewhere in the Impl method, for example, `plsqlProcUpdate()`. These methods are coded to call PL/SQL in the same way as the techniques shown before. Because they are coded within the Impl file, they have direct access to the contents of the entity object through the appropriate getter methods. As an illustration, here is the `plsqlProcInsert()` method for a view based on the Departments table:

```
private void plsqlProcInsert()
{
  CallableStatement plsqlBlock = null;
  Integer generatedDepartmentId = null;
  String statement = "BEGIN deptv_api.do_insert(:1,:2,:3,:4); END;";
  plsqlBlock = getDBTransaction().createCallableStatement(statement, 0);
  try
  {
    plsqlBlock.registerOutParameter(1, Types.INTEGER);
    plsqlBlock.setInt(1,
                       getDepartmentId().getSequenceNumber().intValue());
    plsqlBlock.setString(2, getDepartmentName());
    plsqlBlock.setInt(3, getManagerId().intValue());
    plsqlBlock.setInt(4, getLocationId().intValue());
    plsqlBlock.execute();

    // The PL/SQL will generate a new Dept Id so get it
    generatedDepartmentId = new Integer(plsqlBlock.getInt(1));

    // Reset the local value
    populateAttribute(DEPARTMENTID,
```

```
                        new DBSequence(generatedDepartmentId),
                        true, false, false);
    }

// catch and finally blocks ommitted
}
```

The insert method is the most interesting to look at because the corresponding PL/SQL procedure (DO_INSERT in the DEPTV_API package) declares the `p_department_id` parameter as an IN OUT variable.

```
PROCEDURE do_insert(p_department_id    IN OUT PLS_INTEGER,
                    p_department_name  IN     VARCHAR2,
                    p_manager_id       IN     PLS_INTEGER,
                    p_location_id      IN     PLS_INTEGER);
```

In this example, the PL/SQL procedure allocates a new sequence number for inserted records. The new department ID then is passed back to ADF Business Components. Therefore, the first argument (bind variable) is registered as an OUT parameter. Once the statement has been executed, the key value generated by the procedure is retrieved so that the mid-tier version of the DepartmentId can be reset in the entity object using the `populateAttribute()` method.

The code required for the other methods—`plsqlProcUpdate()` and `plsqlProcDelete()`— follows the same pattern as the prepared statement example before.

A complete example of both the PL/SQL and Java code required for overriding the DML is available in JDeveloper's online help for ADF Business Components.

> **TIP**
> *To find the Java and PL/SQL examples we refer to, navigate to the Help system Search tab and look for "calling stored procedures." Open the topic "Calling Stored Procedures."*

Overriding the lock( ) Method

In a similar way to Oracle Forms, when the DML is being overridden, the programmer needs to supply a lock procedure in the PL/SQL. This can be called from the entity object `lock()` method. The generated `lock()` method will look like this:

```
public void lock() {
    super.lock();
}
```

Your implementation would replace the call to `super.lock()`, with a suitable PL/SQL call to lock the required objects for this transaction.

This chapter has covered a huge amount of ground in relation to ADF Business Components. There is, of course, much more that we could have covered, because ADF BC is a rich and mature framework. However, the material that we presented here will hopefully address many of your initial needs when using the framework, and will help you understand enough to explore its more complex aspects as your knowledge grows more sophisticated. We'll revisit ADF Business Components and show some more complex code examples in Chapter 15.

CHAPTER
7

The ADF Model Layer

I don't pretend we have all the answers.
But the questions are certainly worth thinking about.

—Arthur C. Clark (1917–)

ow that we've discussed the basic technologies for defining business services and user interfaces, we now are ready to address the thorny issue of gluing the two together. In traditional J2EE applications, this implies creating a large amount of Java code to carry out tasks such as managing the location of and connection to business services, obtaining collections of data, mapping that data into the UI layer, and so on. One major benefit of using the ADF framework is that this task of binding the UI to the back-end business services is handled by the *ADF Model* (abbreviated in this book as *ADFm*) layer. In this chapter, we will discuss ADFm binding by answering the following questions:

- **How do I create data-bound pages?**
- **What files are involved in data binding?**

How Do I Create Data-Bound Pages?

The Data Control Palette provides the basic design-time user interface to ADFm. This palette exposes all of the data and public functions (operations) that the UI developer can use in an application's screens. The following illustration shows the Data Control Palette structure from the ADF Business Components project that we created in Chapter 6:

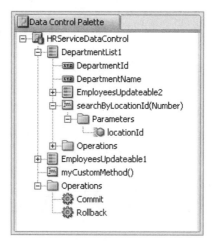

NOTE
If you followed along with the creation of the project in Chapter 6, you may not have implemented the custom method myCustomMethod() *shown in the illustration. This method was the example that we used to illustrate the use of the* Transaction *object.*

The nodes that represent view objects within that project are displayed, as are the attributes of the DepartmentList1 view object instance. Other types of elements are also represented, and we'll look at those in the next section.

If you created the ADF Business Components objects that we discussed in Chapter 6, you will be able to see the illustrated palette for yourself. Select the Model project and select **View** | **Data Control Palette** (or press the shortcut key CTRL-SHIFT-D). The palette appears automatically when you edit a JSF page.

The Data Control Palette

Let's take a closer look at the palette. Figure 7-1 provides a detailed look at the elements that are exposed as nodes in the tree:

- **Data control** The top-level nodes of the tree exposed in the palette are the data controls. Each *data control* represents a separate source of data; in this case, the *HRServiceDataControl* is an ADF Business Components application module. Other possible sources of data controls include EJB (Enterprise JavaBean) session beans and web services.

- **Data collection** The Data Control Palette may expose *data collections* (sets of rows). When the data control represents an application module, each view object instance in the application module will be represented as a data collection node. Recall that a view object corresponds to a query and, therefore, represents a set of rows. Some user interface components, such as table controls, can be bound to a whole collection of data.

- **Attribute** Individual data elements (representing column data) are exposed either at the top level of a data control or by expanding data collections. These can be dragged onto the page to bind the individual attributes to the user interface (UI).

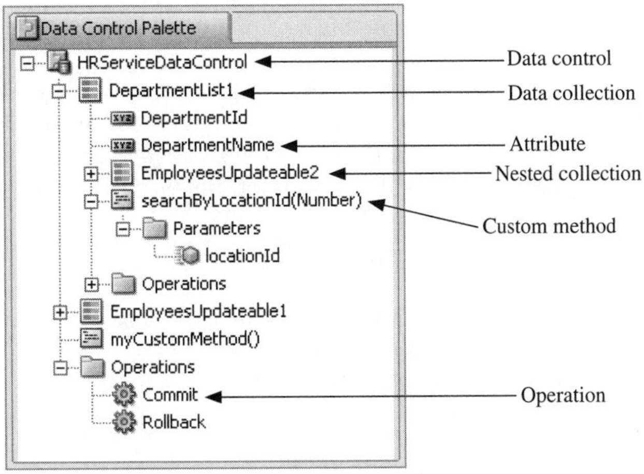

FIGURE 7-1. *Data Control Palette elements*

- **Nested collection** Where a master detail relationship exists, as is shown in Figure 7-1 for employees within departments, that *nested collection* (the detail of the master) can be accessed and bound into the UI. In this case, the EmployeesUpdateable2 collection represents the EmployeesUpdateable view object accessed through a view link from the DepartmentList. The important feature here is that any nested collection (or attributes of that collection) will reveal data only within the context of, and coordinated with, the associated master row in the master collection.

- **Custom method** Any data control may expose custom methods that can be executed from the UI. Methods can be bound in different ways: to provide a way to run them, to provide any *parameters* (arguments), and to gain access to their results. The method displayed in the Data Control Palette can be expanded as shown to give the developer access to these parameters and results. In Figure 7-1, you can see that searchByLocationId() takes a single Number parameter, called "locationId."

- **Operation** This is a special method type provided by the framework itself rather than being written by you. Operations are common across one or more types of data controls and may apply at the data control level (as shown here with Commit and Rollback) or at the collection level. We will look at operations in more detail later.

Before we look at the characteristics of data controls and how data controls are created, we will look at how the UI developer can use the Data Control Palette to build data-bound screens.

Using the Data Control Palette

The Data Control Palette represents the data and methods that developers can use, or bind to, in their pages. The act of creating a usage of data by a user interface element is, therefore, referred to as *data binding*. The primary use of the Data Control Palette is to create bindings by dragging and dropping a node from the Data Control Palette onto the page. For example, if you need to create a page showing an editable table of Employee information, you would drag and drop the EmployeesUpdateable1 collection icon in the Data Control Palette onto the page. When you release the mouse button, a menu will pop up so that you can choose the kind of user interface element (or elements) to create, as shown in Figure 7-2.

The list of UI options displayed when the mouse button is released is dependent on the page technology, the available components, and the type of object dragged from the palette (that is, a collection, attribute, method, or operation). As mentioned in Chapter 5, two JSF component libraries are shipped with JDeveloper: the Sun Reference Implementation (RI) libraries and the ADF Faces libraries.

TIP
Although we generally discuss drag-and-drop data binding onto a page, you can also drop bindings onto the Structure window for the page. This technique is useful when you want to place a UI component in a precise position.

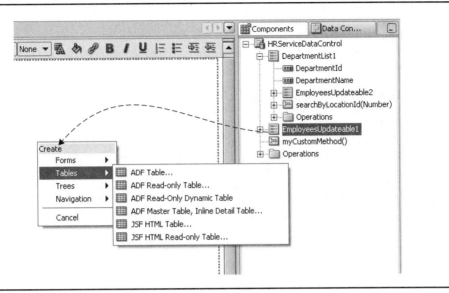

FIGURE 7-2. *Data binding a collection onto a JSF page*

"Drop as" UI Options

In this section, we'll explore the various "drop as" UI options you can create using drag and drop from the Data Control Palette. By default, if you select all of the available tag libraries when creating a page, the Component Palette will list both JSF RI components and ADF Faces components; however, only ADF Faces-based UI options will be used when you drop from the Data Control Palette. The sidebar "Showing All the Options" explains how to make RI components available as well. Throughout the rest of this book, we'll be focusing on the ADF Faces components. The additional choices offered by the RI components overlap and are a subset of what we'll be covering.

"Drop as" Options for Collections

Although you have the option to drag and drop one component onto the page at a time (from the attribute nodes), you will probably want to bind a whole set of attributes at once to create a form or tabular layout. Think of this as like the Layout Wizard in Oracle Forms. It is much quicker in

---

Showing All the Options

If you want to view the alternative "drop as" UI options that use the Sun RI components, you need to change the project properties.

In the ViewController project, display the project properties dialog (**Tools | Project Properties**), and then select the ADF View Settings node in the property navigator. Select the *Include JSF HTML Widgets for JSF Databinding* checkbox so that options will be offered that use both the RI components and the ADF Faces component set.

Oracle Forms to run that wizard and then tweak the layout and item properties afterwards, rather than creating each item individually. Figure 7-3 shows the options available for collections when dropping onto a JSF page.

The drop options for the collection are divided into five groups: forms, tables, master-details, trees, and navigation.

Form Style "Drop as" Options for Collections   Table 7-1 lists the options available for form layouts. In most cases, choosing one of the form options will display the Edit Form Fields dialog shown in Figure 7-4.

Each field in the source collection is listed, allowing you to add or delete fields or to change the field order using the buttons around the field list. The *Include Navigation Controls* checkbox adds navigation buttons used to scroll through the records. The *Include Submit Button* checkbox places a Submit button on the form. This button allows the user to apply any changes made in the screen to the Model layer. The navigation buttons can also be added later by individually binding the relevant operations or by dragging and dropping the collection again and selecting **Navigation |** **Navigation Buttons** in the appropriate style. The Submit button can also be added later by dropping in a normal CommandButton from the Component Palette.

In the list of fields displayed by the dialog shown in Figure 7-4, you can control how each field is represented in the generated form. The *Value Binding* column in the center lists the attributes that are available in the collection. The *Display Label* column controls the label for the field that is created to represent that attribute. If this is left to the default value of "<bound to attr label>," the *Label Text* control hint or attribute name (if there is no control hint) defined for the underlying ADF BC entity object or view object attribute will be used at runtime. Alternatively, you can hard-code your own label value here (in the same way you modify the default prompt text in the Oracle Forms Layout Wizard).

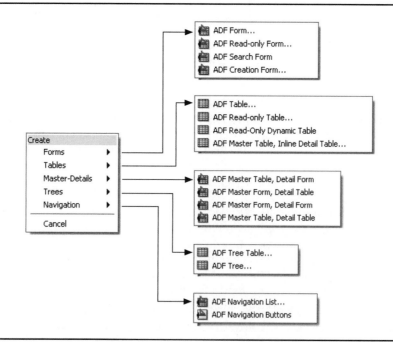

FIGURE 7-3.   *"Drop as" options for collections in ADF Faces*

Edit Form Fields

Select the columns or fields that you want to add/modify below. For each component, you can elect to choose the default label binding, or supply your own. For components that do not have labels, this choice is ignored.

Items:

Display Label	Value Binding	Component To Use	
<bound to attr label>	DepartmentId	ADF Input Text w/ L...	Top
<bound to attr label>	DepartmentName	ADF Input Text w/ L...	Up
<bound to attr label>	ManagerId	ADF Input Text w/ L...	Down
<bound to attr label>	LocationId	ADF Input Text w/ L...	Bottom

New   Delete

☐ Include Navigation Controls
☐ Include Submit Button

Help   OK   Cancel

FIGURE 7-4. *Edit Form Fields dialog*

"Drop as" Option	Description
ADF Form	Dropping this form displays the Edit Form Fields dialog. The attributes of the collection are created by default as input fields using `af:inputText`, with the label property bound to the ADF BC *Label Text* control hint. The following illustration shows a form based on the DEPARTMENTS table:

Fields created from ADF BC attributes marked as "mandatory" are displayed at runtime with an asterisk indicating a required value. The components are automatically aligned within an `af:panelForm` container component. JSF validators are also automatically defined for the fields to implement any validation defined in the model. If the user clicks the supplied Submit button, the controller will update the model but not commit any changes.

TABLE 7-1. *"Drop as" Form Options with ADF Faces*

"Drop as" Option	Description
ADF Read-Only Form	Dropping this form on the page also displays the Edit Form Fields dialog. The only difference from the previous option is that the default components selected are ADF output text (af:outputText) rather than input text. Assuming all of the fields are left as af:outputText components, the result looks like this:

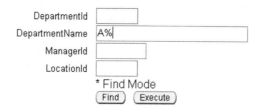

ADF Search Form	A *search form* provides a *Query-by-Example* (QBE) interface for a data collection. This form provides similar functionality to Enter Query mode in Oracle Forms. Just like an Oracle Forms data block, this form can be used to update and input records as well as query records. The drag-and-drop operation from the Data Control Palette defines buttons to place the form into Find (Query) mode and execute the query. When the form is in Find mode, an additional text flag appears at the bottom of the form, alerting the user that the form is in Find mode. This form is shown in the next illustration:

	In this case, when the data collection is dropped, the Edit Form Fields dialog shown in Figure 7-4 does not appear. Any changes to layout and labeling need to be made later.
ADF Creation Form	Dropping a creation form pops up the Edit Form Fields dialog. The only difference is that the navigation buttons option is not available. The idea is that this form is used on a separate screen of the application to only create new records (not to browse existing records). Once the form is created, it looks exactly the same as the ADF Form option. However, behind the scenes, there is a difference. Adding this form to a page will also bind in a Create operation for that data collection; the Create operation will add a row to the view object, and the form will display this blank record when the page is loaded.

TABLE 7-1. *"Drop as" Form Options with ADF Faces* (continued)

The *Component To Use* column will use a specific type by default based on the type of form and the selected component library. For example, if a read-only form is dropped, the *Component To Use* will select af:outputText components by default. You use the pulldown list on this field to change the component type created. However, the choices offered in the dialog are limited. To create UI elements such as lists and radio groups, you will need to carry out a separate binding operation using the individual attributes after the form has been created.

Table Style "Drop as" Options for Collections   As an alternative layout to the conventional single row form, you can drop in various types of tabular layouts, in both writable and read-only alternatives. This ability to implement multi-row editing with no extra coding is one of the benefits of JSF. Table 7-2 shows the options available for tabular layouts when using the ADF libraries.

"Drop as" Option	**Description**
ADF Table	Dropping a data collection as "ADF Table…" displays an Edit Table Columns dialog, with all fields designated as input fields by default. This will create an af:table component (see the sidebar "About af:table"), containing one af:column for each field and then an af:inputText within the column. The attribute label control hint (or the attribute name) is automatically used as the column header, as shown here:

	The example table shown in this illustration was created with the sortable and selection options selected in the dialog.
ADF Read-only Table	Using the Edit Table Columns dialog, this option creates a table control identical to the editable table example, except that each column contains a read-only af:outputText component rather than an input field. This type of table is shown in the following illustration with no selection and no sorting.

TABLE 7-2.   *"Drop as" Table Options with ADF Faces*

"Drop as" Option	Description
	TIP *It is possible to have a table that contains a mixture of read-only fields and input fields. To define this effect, set the component types as required in the Edit Table Columns dialog.*
ADF Read-Only Dynamic Table	The output from this option is identical to a read-only table, except that the columns in this option are not explicitly created in the page. Instead, an `af:forEach` loop is used to dynamically list the columns at runtime. This is advantageous, because if the number of attributes in the data collection (or the actual data collection used) changes, the table will adjust automatically.
ADF Master Table, Inline Detail Table	This visualization of a data collection will allow the read-only display of the collection's rows and a related detail collection. A Show/Hide control at the left of the row can be expanded to display the detail table. The developer needs to define a tree binding to correctly populate this type of table. We discuss how to define a tree binding in Chapter 8. Here is an example of this option with the detail table for Department 110 displayed inline under the Department 110 row:

Details	DepartmentId		DepartmentName	
▼ Hide	110		Accounting	
	EmployeeId	**FirstName**	**LastName**	**Email**
	206	William	Gietz	WGIETZ
	205	Shelley	Higgins	SHIGGINS
▶ Show	10		Administration	
▶ Show	160		Benefits	
▶ Show	180		Construction	

TABLE 7-2. *"Drop as" Table Options with ADF Faces* (continued)

In a fashion similar to the form layouts discussed before, dropping a collection as a table can display an Edit Table Columns dialog, as shown in Figure 7-5. This dialog is similar to the Edit Form Fields dialog, except that the navigation and Submit button check options are replaced by options to make the table sortable and enable record selection.

Master-Detail "Drop as" Options for Collections   When a collection that is a nested within another collection is dropped onto the page, four master detail options will be available. Unlike the inline master detail offered as part of the table options, these master detail options create multiple components and bindings on the page. Selecting one of these options is a shortcut for

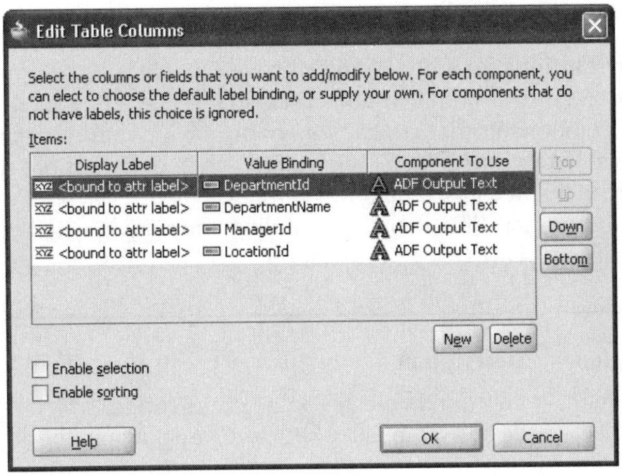

FIGURE 7-5. *Edit Table Columns dialog*

dropping an option for the master collection, followed by a second drop from the detail collection. The shortcut combinations available are as follows:

- ADF Master Table, Detail Form
- ADF Master Form, Detail Table
- ADF Master Form, Detail Form
- ADF Master Table, Detail Table

About af:table

The ADF Faces table component used for creating tabular layouts is quite powerful. It supports features such as sorting by column headers, paging control, row selection, banding (coloring columns or rows at repeating intervals), and nested detail tables.

You bind a data collection to the af:table component. The individual attributes within the collection are then referenced using an alias (usually "row"), which is defined using the *var* attribute of the table tag. For example, the value for Department Name in a table column is bound using the expression #{row.DepartmentName}.

Notice also the "Select and …" section in the header and footer of the tables shown in Table 7-2. This section is defined by a facet of the table control called *selection*. This facet contains a row selection control, af:tableSelectOne, which renders the radio button next to each row. Any command button nested within the af:tableSelectOne, such as the Submit command button, will operate in the context of the row that is marked with a selected radio button. For example, the ability to delete a row from a table can be defined by dragging and dropping the Delete operation from the relevant collection into this facet. The currently selected row is then deleted when the Delete button is clicked.

The forms and tables created using these options are identical to the read-only forms and tables that we covered earlier.

Tree "Drop as" Options for Collections As we saw with the master table with an inline detail table and the master-detail combinations in the preceding section, ADF Faces includes some complex components that are capable of displaying master-detail relationships in another way. If a collection contains such a relationship to another collection, such as employees within a department, then the tree-based bindings will be available. These components require you to define the relationship by filling in the tree binding information when you drop the control onto the page. This process is discussed in Chapter 8. Table 7-3 lists the tree options.

"Drop as" Option	**Description**
ADF Tree Table	This option creates an `af:treeTable`, which represents hierarchical data in a table like structure, as shown in this illustration:  Tree-specific events—such as *DisclosureEvent*, an event that fires when the user expands a node in the tree—are supported by this control. This component is complex, and you will need to consult the ADF Faces documentation in the JDeveloper help system for the full list of attributes and events. The tree table is covered by the help system topic "Using the ADF Tree Component."
ADF Tree	An ADF Tree provides a more conventional navigator or explorer tree control, as shown in the next illustration. Again, events are raised when the user clicks or expands a node.  This tree component functions in much the same way as the tree in Oracle Forms. One weakness with the ADF Faces tree is that you have no ability to change the icons used for the nodes. However, you can display different types of labels, such as hyperlinks in place of the default plain text.

TABLE 7-3. *"Drop as" Tree Options with ADF Faces*

"Drop as" Option	Description
ADF Navigation List	Dropping a navigation list will create an af:panelGroup containing a specialized dropdown list item, as shown in the following illustration:  The list is bound to the rows in the collection in such a way that selecting a particular row in the list will set the row currency in the collection. This effectively "jumps" you to the selected record. This kind of navigation is best restricted to small collections of records; otherwise, the dropdown list will be too long. The panel group is labeled with a default header value of "Details." This can be changed by editing the properties of the embedded af:panelHeader that the drag-and-drop action creates. If you want to display detail fields after selecting a record in the dropdown list, you drop a form onto the page. This will automatically show the row as it is selected from the navigation list.
ADF Navigation Buttons	This option will create and arrange buttons for the First, Previous, Next, and Last operations, as shown here: (First) (Previous) (Next) (Last) These buttons are set up with expressions to automatically enable and disable the buttons. For example, when you are on the first record of the collection, the Previous and First buttons are disabled.

TABLE 7-4. *"Drop as" Navigation Options with ADF Faces*

Navigation "Drop as" Options for Collections   We have already been introduced to the concept of navigational buttons. These buttons can be created using a checkbox in the Edit Form Fields dialog used to create forms from a collection. You can also create these buttons separately by dragging and dropping a data collection. Table 7-4 shows the types of navigational user interfaces that you can create by dragging and dropping a collection as a navigation type.

"Drop as" Options for Attributes

In many cases, it will not be enough to just drop a collection as a form or table onto the page. You cannot specify display types of dropdown lists and checkboxes in the collection dialogs, so you need to create these types individually by dragging and dropping the individual attributes. Although dragging and dropping a collection creates a group of components, when you drag and drop an attribute, you will usually create a single component.

As shown in Figure 7-6, you can create three classes of components from the Data Control Palette: Dates (date components), Texts (text-based-components), and Single Selections (list-based components).

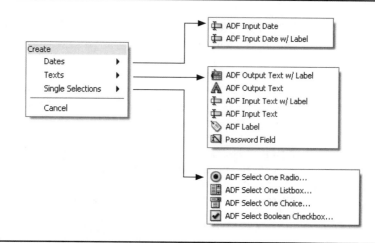

FIGURE 7-6. *"Drop as" options for single attributes*

The Dates submenu is only shown when the attribute being dropped is a date type. This submenu offers the ADF Input Date (`af:selectInputDate`) component, an input field with a built-in pop-up calendar.

The various components shown on the Texts menu are all self-explanatory. The Input Text and Output Text options come in two flavors: plain or with a label (labeled as "w/ Label" in the menu). Selecting the "w/ Label" version will set the relevant component property to be bound to the label UI hint defined in ADF BC.

With the Single Selections options, you need to do extra work after dropping the attribute to define the values to display, as well as the attribute to which the underlying value is bound. When these components are dropped, the List Binding Editor pops up to gather the extra information needed to define the contents of the list options. This dialog is described in more detail in Chapter 8.

"Drop as" Options for Operations and Methods

You can also drag and drop operations and methods from the Data Control Palette. Operations and custom methods are essentially the same thing: code that the user will activate rather than data to edit or view. As a result, the same binding options are offered for both operations and custom methods, as illustrated here:

After dropping the command button or command link, the framework will create a UI component on the page with the correct expressions to ensure that it is only enabled when the underlying operation is available. For example, if the Commit operation is dropped as a button onto the page, it will be disabled until a change has been applied to ADF BC. Once there is something to commit to the database, the button will be enabled. We have already seen another example of this auto-enabling and disabling behavior for the navigation bars created from a collection. For example, the following navigation bar would be used for the first record in the collection; its Previous and First buttons are disabled because they are not appropriate.

TIP
The commit operation is not enabled until a change has been submitted. This can be inconvenient, because you will often want a single button that will both submit a change to ADF BC and commit that change. To enable a Commit button to carry out both functions at once, you need to change its "Disabled" property from "#{!bindings. Commit.enabled}" to "false". Then the button will always be available to the user.

Operations and Methods with Parameters   Custom methods and a small subset of operations may have arguments and return values. As shown under the custom method in Figure 7-1, those arguments are exposed through the Data Control Palette as parameters. This Parameters node can be expanded, and each parameter is treated like a normal data attribute. When such parameters are dropped onto the page, the same options as those in Figure 7-6 for normal data attributes are shown. Behind the scenes, JDeveloper will create slightly different binding information in order to correctly wire these input fields to the method calls, but this does not affect the UI creation activity.

When you drop a method or operation with parameters, the standard list of command items (button or link) are available for binding, as well as extra options to create a parameter form, as shown here:

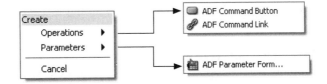

If a parameter form is dropped, the Edit Form Fields dialog appears. After interacting with that dialog, a basic input form will be laid out with one field for each parameter and a command button (named after the operation or method) to execute the method or operation call. The developer can add extra functionality to this parameter form—for example, to validate the input—before calling the custom method.

Method Results   Just as custom methods may take parameters, they may also return one or more values. If the values returned are single-value attributes (such as a `String`), they can be bound to the UI just like any other attribute using the types of bindings shown in Figure 7-6. If the method call returns a collection (with multiple objects, such as an `ArrayList`), that collection can be bound to a table or a form in the normal way.

UI First Binding
So far, we've looked at data binding using the drag-and-drop operation onto an empty area on the page or into the Structure window. There is, however, an alternative approach. You can start

by building the user interface with unbound components from the Component Palette and then bind them later. This technique is referred to as *UI first binding* and is useful when you are prototyping a screen, since the layout can be perfected before the business service is completed and the components bound later.

To bind the unbound components, all you have to do is drag and drop an element from the Data Control Palette on top of the component rather than into empty space. The standard context menu will appear, with an additional operation "Bind Existing…." Selecting this will set up the binding on that component rather than creating a new component.

What Files Are Involved in Data Binding?

So far, we've looked at the results of data binding within the design-time environment, but you might be wondering what is actually going on here? How does the ADF Model actually work and what files are used?

At a high level, the binding model is represented by a series of XML files, which we will examine shortly. At runtime, these XML files are translated by the framework into instances of lightweight Java classes (binding objects) that work with the framework to coordinate the requested business service with the UI.

As was the case with ADF Business Components in Chapter 6, the best way to understand how the ADF model works is to build a simple example and examine all these XML files as they are created. Recall that ADF allows the developer to use multiple service providers: ADF Business Components, EJB, web services, and plain Java classes, among others. To simplify the example and help build up an understanding of the files involved in defining the bindings, we'll look at how to create bindings to a single Java class.

Defining the Data Control

The following sections step through creating a data control that will be displayed in the Data Control Palette.

1. Set Up a Workspace and Java Class

This exercise will require a new application workspace; for example, "DataControlTest." Create this as in Chapter 6, but use the "Web Application [JSF, EJB]" template.

In the Model project, create a Java class called User (press CTRL-N to display the New Gallery, and double click Java Class in the Simple Files category, accepting all defaults except the name, and using "book.model" as the package name).

Enter the following code. To code the getters and setters, after typing the name and birthday variable declarations, select **Generate Accessors** from the right-click menu in the Code Editor, select the User checkbox, and click OK.

```
package book.model;
import java.util.Date;

public class User
{
  private String name;
  private Date birthday;
```

```
public long userAge(int fudgeFactor)
{
  return (long)(21 + fudgeFactor);
}
public void setName(String name)
{
  this.name = name;
}

public String getName()
{
  return name;
}

public void setBirthday(Date birthday)
{
  this.birthday = birthday;
}

public Date getBirthday()
{
  return birthday;
}
}
```

This Java class conforms to the JavaBean standard, which states that member variables (attributes) of a class should be private and have accessors (as described in Chapter 4). By using this standard convention, JDeveloper can distinguish the accessor methods from the one real method in the class: userAge(). This userAge() method returns a fake result for the sake of brevity, but does provide a method that both takes a parameter and returns a result.

Compile the class file (by clicking Make in the toolbar), and fix any errors.

2. Create the Data Control

Now that you have a basic business service in the User class, JDeveloper needs to know that it can be used for binding. With ADF Business Components, you skip this step, because the IDE (integrated development environment) understands that application modules are a valid service and populates the Data Control Palette automatically. However, with Java classes and other service types, you will need to create the data control.

There are two ways to make the User class available in the Data Control Palette:

- **Drag and Drop** From the application navigator, drag the Java class and drop it into the open Data Control Palette.

- **Right-Click Menu** On the User class file in the navigator, select **Create Data Control** from the right-click menu.

Remember that you can display the Data Control Palette by selecting it from the View menu. Use either method, and display and expand the nodes of the Data Control Palette. It will look like this:

Notice how the content is similar to Figure 7-1, even though the implementing technology for the business service is different. This similarity is the whole point of the Data Control Palette. You do not have to know, or even care, where the data comes from; you can just bind to the data that you need and leave the rest to the framework.

When developers consume data from a service, they are not required to write code to access the resources. Instead, the runtime ADF Model framework manages the infrastructure associated with gaining access to the business service and retrieving the correct data or executing the correct method. ADF Model, in theory, allows the actual implementation of the business service to be switched to something totally different without needing any changes in the UI.

Naturally, different service providers have different capabilities. A plain Java class, as in the example you've created here, can be exposed as a data control, but it will not have the same transactional facilities as an ADF BC-based control. Commit and Rollback, for example, mean nothing to a normal Java class and will not be shown as operations in the tree structure for that data control.

The Data Control Definition   In addition to the change to the Data Control Palette, notice that two files have appeared in the Model project: User.xml and DataControls.dcx.

Open the User.xml file in the editor. This file is a description of the User service. The XML will look something like this:

```
<?xml version="1.0" encoding="UTF-8" ?>
<JavaBean xmlns="http://xmlns.oracle.com/adfm/beanmodel"
          version="10.1.3.36.73"
          id="User" BeanClass="book.model.User"
          Package="book.model"
          isJavaBased="true">
  <Attribute Name="birthday" Type="java.util.Date"/>
  <Attribute Name="name" Type="java.lang.String"/>
  <MethodAccessor IsCollection="false" Type="long" id="userAge"
                  ReturnNodeName="Return">
    <ParameterInfo id="fudgeFactor" Type="int" isStructured="false"/>
  </MethodAccessor>
  <ConstructorMethod IsCollection="false" Type="void" id="User"/>
</JavaBean>
```

This XML file contains all of the information needed to describe the User class. The full package and name of the class is defined in the JavaBean element, each of the attributes with getters and setters is listed as a nested `Attribute` element, and the `userAge()` method with its input and output is fully described.

Not only does this file provide the information needed to draw the tree structure of the Data Control Palette, but it will also be used at runtime by the framework to generate an instance of the `User` class for the UI.

In most circumstances, you will never need to edit this file. If you make a change in the `User` class—for example, by adding an attribute or a new method—rather than trying to change the XML to match the new version, just regenerate the data control definition again.

The DataControls.dcx File   The second file added to the Model project is another XML metadata file with a .dcx extension, DataControls.dcx. Open this file in the editor; it will look something like this:

```
<?xml version="1.0" encoding="UTF-8" ?>
<DataControlConfigs xmlns="http://xmlns.oracle.com/adfm/configuration"
                    version="10.1.3.36.73"
                    Package="book.model"
                    id="DataControls">
    <JavaBeanDataControl
             SupportsTransactions="false"
             SupportsFindMode="false"
             SupportsResetState="false"
             SupportsRangesize="true"
             SupportsSortCollection="true"
             SupportsUpdates="false"
             id="UserDataControl"
             xmlns=http://xmlns.oracle.com/adfm/datacontrol
             FactoryClass="oracle.adf.model.generic.DataControlFactoryImpl"
             Definition="book.model.User"
             BeanClass="book.model.User"/>
</DataControlConfigs>
```

The DataControls.dcx is the index file for all data controls contained within a project. Each data control will have its own XML description file (like User.xml), but there will only be one DataControls.dcx file to summarize them all. Your DataControls.dcx, of course, only has one entry that describes the `User` class data control.

Looking at the XML for the control, you can see how the capabilities of the service are declared using attributes such as `SupportsTransactions`. Different service providers have different capabilities. `SupportsTransactions` is set to "false" in your plain Java class-based control because it does not know how to perform the Commit and Rollback operations.

As an exercise, try setting some of these flags (like `SupportsTransaction`) to "true," save the DataControls.dcx, and then refresh the Data Control Palette using the **Refresh** option on the right-click menu. You will see extra operations made available. Remember to undo any changes you make when testing this. The newly available operations will not function because the underlying service will not have any code to implement them.

3. Enhance the Data Control

In addition to serving as an abstract description of a service, the data control definition allows you to add default values, control hints (such as field labels and tooltips), and simple declarative validation rules on top of the service definition.

To add this type of functionality, select the User.xml file in the navigator and look at the Structure window. If you double click one of the available attributes, for example, `birthday`, the Attribute Editor dialog will display. This dialog allows you to set up extra metadata, such as control hints, as shown in the following illustration:

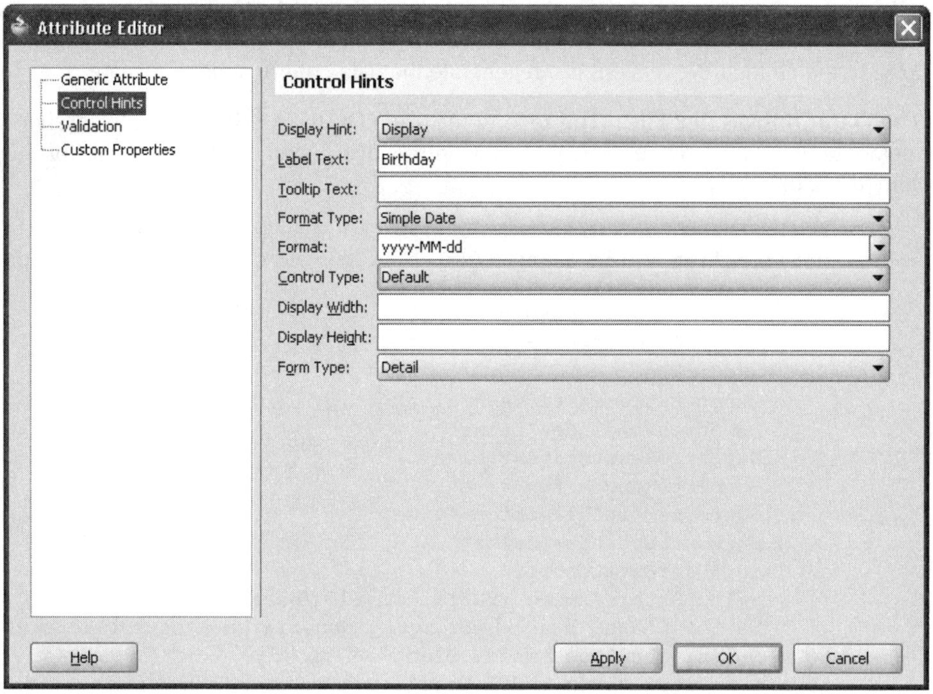

You might notice at this point that this property editor looks remarkably similar to the Entity Object Attribute Editor in ADF Business Components. This facility adds a layer of declarative metadata on top of the service definition, and it mirrors the capabilities that are already available as a core part of ADF Business Components. Some of the functionality is not as rich, however. For example, the List Validator can only work off of a static list rather than having the option to work off of the results of a database query or view object.

To illustrate the effect that adding control hints and declarative validation rules has on the XML, edit the properties of the *birthday* attribute to add a validation for birthday greater than or equal to "1900-01-01" with an error message. (Select Validation and click New to get started. Click OK and click OK again when you're done.) Also, add control hints for *Label Text* ("Birthday") and *Format Type* ("Simple Date"). Click OK.

The XML for that attribute in the User.xml will look something like this:

```
<Attribute Name="birthday"
           Type="java.util.Date" DefaultValue=""
           PrecisionRule="false" Precision="0" Scale="0">
```

```
<CompareValidationBean xmlns=http://xmlns.oracle.com/adfm/validation
                       OnAttribute="birthday"
                       ResId="birthday_Rule_0"
                       OperandType="LITERAL"
                       Inverse="false"
                       CompareValue="1900-01-01"
                       CompareType="GREATERTHANEQUALTO"/>
</Attribute>
```

The XML code shows the declarative validation rule that has been added. The validation error message (and any definition for control hints) is not in this file.

ADF Model Resource Bundles   As soon as you add any kind of string to the data control definition, a Java resource bundle file, UserMsgBundle.java, is created. This file can be translated into multiple languages and shipped as part of the application code. Each translation will use a file suffix, such as "_de" for German (UserMsgBundle_de.java), to indicate the language it contains. The framework will automatically use the correct resource bundle based on the language that the browser indicates the user is using.

The strings used for the control hints and declarative validation rules are all contained within an array of name value pairs, sMessageStrings, within that Java class. For example:

```
static final Object[][] sMessageStrings = {
    { "birthday_FMT_FORMAT", "yyyy-MM-dd" },
    { "birthday_Rule_0", "I doubt that you are that old!" },
    { "birthday_FMT_FORMATTER", "oracle.jbo.format.DefaultDateFormatter" },
    { "birthday_LABEL", "Birthday:" }};
```

In this case, you can see how the label control hint for the *birthday* attribute has been set to "Birthday:."

When you add control hints and declarative validation rules to ADF Business Components, similar resource bundles are generated to hold the string values.

Using the Data Control

You have just seen how a basic data control is built. As we mentioned, you'll only ever need to explicitly create data controls for services that are not written using ADF Business Components; however, it is useful to understand how they are defined and what they contain.

What happens when you drag and drop from the Data Control Palette onto a page? Let's do that and see what happens.

1. Create an Empty Page
On the ViewController project, create a JSF page called "binding.jsp" by selecting JSF JSP from the Web Tier\JSF category in the New Gallery. Make sure you select all ADF Faces libraries in Step 3 of the wizard and accept the default selections for everything else.

2. Bind the Attributes
Drag a PanelForm from the ADF Faces Core Component Palette page onto the new JSF file. This component will help organize the fields. Then, from the Data Control Palette, drag the *name* attribute and drop it as "ADF Input Text w/ Label" inside of the af:panelForm.

Repeat this operation for the *birthday* attribute. This time, you will see the Dates selection, as shown here:

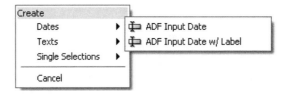

The data control definition informed the IDE that the *birthday* attribute is a Data datatype, so the drop operation offers date options. Again, select **ADF Input Date w/ Label**. The fields in the visual editor will now look something like this:

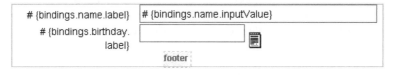

Switch to the Source tab for the page. The field definitions will look something like this:

```
<af:panelForm>
  <f:facet name="footer"/>
  <af:inputText value="#{bindings.name.inputValue}"
                label="#{bindings.name.label}"
                required="#{bindings.name.mandatory}"
                columns="#{bindings.name.displayWidth}">
    <af:validator binding="#{bindings.name.validator}"/>
  </af:inputText>
  <af:selectInputDate
                value="#{bindings.birthday.inputValue}"
                label="#{bindings.birthday.label}"
                required="#{bindings.birthday.mandatory}">
    <af:validator binding="#{bindings.birthday.validator}"/>
    <f:convertDateTime pattern="#{bindings.birthday.format}"/>
  </af:selectInputDate>
</af:panelForm>
```

You will notice the use of expression language to set the value of each of the attributes, and specifically the use of expressions beginning with "#{bindings." You will also see references to validators and a converter (`f:convertDateTime`), which refer to these expressions using the "bindings" object. What is the bindings object and where does it come from?

3. Examine the Bindings
The reference to "bindings" in the JSF page is a reference to data that is being managed by the ADF Model. When a page is displayed, any attributes required on that page are exposed in a specific object called bindings on the HTTP request. You can think of this *bindings object* as a bucket

containing all the data that this particular page needs. The bucket is emptied and refilled with a new set of data as the user navigates between pages. The interesting part is how the framework knows what data to put into this bucket. Looking at your example, you can see references to the name and birthday attributes in the page, but on their own that is not enough information to link back to the ADF Model `UserDataControl` object.

In the JSF Visual Editor (Design tab), on the *name* field, select **Edit Binding** from the right-click menu; this will display the Attribute Binding Editor for the field, showing that it is indeed linked with the `UserDataControl`, as shown here:

The information that defines the mapping shown in this dialog is not held in the JSF page; it exists in another XML metadata file that is paired with the page. This file is referred to as a *Page Definition File* or a *PageDef* for short. Dismiss the dialog, and in the Visual Editor, select **Go To Page Definition** from the right-click menu.

TIP
Clicking a UI component and selecting Edit Binding is a shortcut for choosing Go To Page Definition, locating the relevant binding in the Structure window, and then editing the binding in the Property Inspector.

The PageDef file (in this case, called bindingPageDef.xml) will open in the editor area and will look something like this:

```xml
<?xml version="1.0" encoding="UTF-8" ?>
<pageDefinition xmlns=http://xmlns.oracle.com/adfm/uimodel
                version="10.1.3.36.73"
                id="bindingPageDef"
                Package="book.view.pageDefs">
  <parameters/>
  <executables>
    <iterator id="UserDataControl_rootIter"
              RangeSize="10"
              Binds="root"
              DataControl="UserDataControl"/>
  </executables>
  <bindings>
    <attributeValues id="name"
                     IterBinding="UserDataControl_rootIter">
      <AttrNames>
        <Item Value="name"/>
      </AttrNames>
    </attributeValues>
    <attributeValues id="birthday"
                     IterBinding="UserDataControl_rootIter">
      <AttrNames>
        <Item Value="birthday"/>
      </AttrNames>
    </attributeValues>
  </bindings>
</pageDefinition>
```

TIP
The PageDef file will always be called <pageName>PageDef.xml. By default, it will be created in the application top-level package (relative to the project) called "pageDefs"; you will find it under Application Sources\book.view.pageDefs in this example. You can control the location of this package by selecting ADFm Settings in the project properties and changing the "PageDef sub-package" value.

How Do I Read the EL Binding Expression? In the next section, we'll spend more time looking at this file, but for now look at one of the `attributeValues` elements, for example, `birthday`, in the bindings section. The *id* of this element contains the name of the attribute as referred to by the expression on the page—"#{bindings.birthday.inputValue}." Notice that the `attributeValue` element also has an attribute called *IterBinding* with a value of "UserDataControl_rootIter." This value is a reference to an iterator tag in the executables section of the same XML file. Again, we'll look at exactly what an iterator is in Chapter 8, but for now observe that the iterator has an attribute called *DataControl* containing the name of the data control that you created from the User Java class.

So, the linkage from the page to the service providing the data is through the following sequence: Binding expression to `AttributeValues` to `Iterator` to Data Control.

So far, in an expression such as `#{bindings.birthday.inputValue}`, you've seen how "bindings" refers to data managed by ADFm. The "birthday" part refers to an attribute mapped in the PageDef file. What about "inputValue" in this expression?

You would rightly guess that "inputValue" relates to the actual data of the attribute in the runtime instance of the `User` class. However, there are several other suffixes used in the code that you have generated, such as `#{bindings.birthday.label}` and `#{bindings.birthday .validator}`. These are references to the additional metadata you can add to the data control for control hints and declarative validation rules. For example, `#{bindings.birthday.label}` evaluates to the entry you made in the *birthday* attribute's Label Text control hint, and `#{bindings.birthday.validator}` evaluates to a method call that will implement the declarative validation rules you entered through the attribute editor.

Most of the expressions are fairly obvious based on their naming. For reference purposes, you can find the full list of expressions in the JDeveloper help topic "About the Properties of the ADF Bindings."

Bind to Data Dialog   If you need to manually create expressions that refer to binding objects, you can use the Bind to Data dialog. Select a bound property, such as the *Label* of the name field in the Property Inspector. In that property's value field, click the [...] button or the "Bind to data" button on the Property Inspector's toolbar; the expression builder dialog will appear. You can expand the nodes so that the dialog appears as shown here:

CAUTION
The "Bind to data" toolbar button on the Property Inspector works as a toggle. If a property is already populated with a binding expression, the button function changes to "Remove data binding." To edit an existing binding expression, use the [...] button in the value area of the property in the Property Inspector.

The Bind to Data dialog displays a title of the property you are editing. It allows you to browse the available objects that can be bound to an attribute (property) value in a JSF component. In most cases, you will be interested in data listed under the ADF Bindings\bindings node. This node contains the available data in the context of the current page. However, this dialog also gives you access to any JSF managed beans, as well as the general expression scopes available to JSPs, such as sessionScope, cookies, and so on.

In addition to allowing the selection of attribute values and metadata, this dialog also provides help in composing compound expressions using the operators shown on the right side of the dialog.

CAUTION
In addition to the bindings node, the ADF Bindings branch also contains a "data" node that you can use to access the bound data elements of any page within the application. However, caution is required here. Such references are only valid if the target page has been visited within the current session, and the lifetime of the binding reference is not guaranteed beyond the initial request. If data is required on a specific page, it is a best practice to bind it directly for use on that page and only use expressions based on the "bindings" node.

4. Examine the Binding Master File

Just as all of the data controls in a project are summarized in the DataControls.dcx index file, the same is true of the PageDef files. In the Application Sources\book\view node of the ViewController project, open the DataBindings.cpx file. You will see something like the following (the line numbers are added for explanatory purposes):

```
01: <?xml version="1.0" encoding="UTF-8" ?>
02: <Application xmlns=http://xmlns.oracle.com/adfm/application
            version="10.1.3.36.73"
            id="DataBindings"
            SeparateXMLFiles="false"
            Package="book.view"
            ClientType="Generic">
03:    <pageMap>
04:      <page path="/binding.jsp" usageId="bindingPageDef"/>
05:    </pageMap>
06:    <pageDefinitionUsages>
07:      <page id="bindingPageDef"
               path="book.view.pageDefs.bindingPageDef"/>
08:    </pageDefinitionUsages>
09:    <dataControlUsages>
```

```
10:        <dc id="UserDataControl" path="book.model.UserDataControl"/>
11:     </dataControlUsages>
12: </Application>
```

The DataBindings.cpx file is the master mapping file that the framework uses to associate a page (binding.jsp, in our case) with the PageDef file that contains the data required for the page. All pages in the same project are mapped in this one file.

If you examine the XML of this file, you will see the following:

- **Line 03** defines the start of a section called the pageMap. This section lists one or more URL paths. When a page is about to be displayed, ADF looks up the URL path of that page in this section.

- **Line 04** contains the page entry with the *path* value ("/binding.jsp"). It also contains the *usageId* value associated with that path—in this case, the value "bindingPageDef."

- **Line 06** defines a section called pageDefinitionUsages. This section contains a list of references to the PageDef files.

- **Line 07** is a match for the *id* we require—"bindingPageDef." This matches the *usageId* value from the pageMap section (Line 04). The *path* attribute of the PageDef file (book.view.pageDefs.bindingPageDef, in this case) points to the actual PageDef file that contains all of the bindings to be set up.

In the example we've been working through, all of this mapping hardly seems worthwhile; it seems that naming alone would be enough to provide the relationship between the page and the associated PageDef file. However, for a naming system to work, the framework would have to be rather strict about file locations, and could experience problems using multiple pages with the same name. The reality is that the names don't have to match, the PageDef files don't have to be in a fixed location, and several pages could share the same PageDef file if their data needs are the same. So this mapping file is necessary to provide the degree of flexibility required.

5. Find Where DataBindings.cpx Is Referenced

When you create an ADF application, everything is set up to use binding automatically. However, it is useful to know how everything connects. The job of defining the name and location of the DataBindings.cpx file is a parameter in the application web.xml file.

Open the web.xml file from the Web Content\WEB-INF node in the navigator. A context parameter will be defined towards the top of that file, as follows:

```
<context-param>
   <param-name>CpxFileName</param-name>
   <param-value>book.view.DataBindings</param-value>
</context-param>
```

The parameter defined here, *CpxFileName*, is used by the ADF Binding Servlet filter, which does all of the hard work for you. Note that the DataBindings.cpx does not need to be called DataBindings, but the .cpx extension is required. For example, the following value would be valid and would direct the ADF binding filter to use a file called DataBindingMasterFile.cpx in the view.bindings package:

```
<param-value>view.bindings.DataBindingMasterFile</param-value>
```

NOTE
A future version of ADF should contain the ability to use multiple .cpx files so that many developers working in the same project can more easily add pages without affecting each other's work.

A Binding File Summary

Before diving into the details of bindings themselves in the next chapter, let's list the key files that we've discussed:

- **DataControls.dcx**   This file defines any data controls in a project that are not implemented in ADF Business Components. Only one DataControls.dcx file appears in each project.

- **<pagename>PageDef.xml**   In a project, this file defines the bindings used on a particular page. One PageDef.xml file is available for each page file.

- **DataBindings.cpx**   In a project, this file defines the relationship between PageDef files and the page files that use them; it also defines the data controls used within the project. One DataBindings.cpx file is present in each user interface project.

CHAPTER
8

ADF Model
Advanced Bindings

Dig within.
Within is the wellspring of good;
and it is always ready to bubble up,
if you just dig.

—Marcus Aurelius (121–180), *Meditations, Book VII*

 n Chapter 7, we looked at the mechanics of and files used in binding. Now we'll spend some more time understanding the various types of bindings, how to edit them, and how to work with the ADF Model in code. We'll structure this chapter around the following questions:

- **How can I edit data bindings?**
- **What is an iterator?**
- **How can I control execution in the ADF Model?**
- **What are parameters?**
- **How do I write code using the ADF Model?**

How Can I Edit Data Bindings?

We have looked at the act of creating bindings through drag-and-drop actions and seen that the binding information for a page is stored in the PageDef file. Now we need to examine those bindings in more detail and see how they can be edited. As you become more familiar with ADF, you will find yourself spending more and more time in the PageDef file. Familiarity with manually creating and editing bindings is the key to success with the framework.

To view the bindings, you can open the PageDef file from the navigator, or, as we saw in Chapter 7, there are two shortcuts to the binding information, as follows:

- **Selecting Go To Page Definition** from the right-click menu on a page displays the entire PageDef file.
- **Selecting Edit Binding** from the right-click menu on a bound item displays the item's binding editor.

Another way to work with bindings is from the Property Inspector for a bound item. Hyperlinks at the bottom of the Property Inspector provide shortcuts to common actions, as shown here:

InputText - #{bindings.DepartmentN... - Property Inspector ✕

General	
🔲 Label	#{bindings.DepartmentName.label}
🔲 Columns	#{bindings.DepartmentName.displayWidth}
RequiredMessageDetail	
Rows	1
Validator	
🔲 Value	#{bindings.DepartmentName.inputValue}
ValueChangeListener	
AccessKey	
AttributeChangeListener	
AutoSubmit	false
Binding	
Disabled	false
Id	
Immediate	false

Shortcut area — Go to Page Definition, Edit Binding...

If a table component is selected, this shortcut area also provides a link to redisplay the Edit Table Columns dialog (discussed in Chapter 7).

For this chapter, we'll use the ADF Business Components from the ADFBindingExample application we created in Chapter 6 as a business service provider.

NOTE
As mentioned before, you can download starting files for any chapter that needs them from the authors' websites mentioned in the section "Websites for Sample Code" in the Introduction.

We will discuss the following types of bindings:

- **Attribute bindings**, more specifically called *attribute value bindings*, are used to define the binding for a single attribute in a collection.

- **Table bindings** are used to define the contents of table components bound to collections.

- **Action bindings** are used to define the binding of standard operations, such as Commit.

- **Method bindings** are similar to Action bindings, but are used to bind custom methods rather than standard operations.

- **List bindings** (also referred to as list value bindings) are used to define the contents of data-bound list components, such as radio groups and dropdown lists.

- **Navigation list bindings** are used to manipulate and identify the current row in a row set.

- **Boolean bindings** (also called button bindings or boolean value bindings) are used to define a set of Boolean options. This binding is used for checkboxes in JSF pages.

- **Tree bindings** are the most complicated type of binding. They define a set of master-detail data used to populate hierarchical controls such as trees or tree tables.

ADFm supports another type of binding called a *graph binding*. However, this binding type is not currently used for JSF applications, so it does not apply to this discussion.

In addition to bindings, we will need to discuss iterators, which are referenced by the bindings mentioned previously. The JDeveloper documentation refers in places to "iterator bindings," implying that they are just another binding type. Although this is strictly true (because they bind to a row set iterator in the underlying collection or view object), iterators have a very different function from the other binding types. Iterators are covered in the section "What Is an Iterator?" but as a brief introduction, we've included a sidebar, "Introducing the Iterator," later on in this chapter.

Attribute Bindings

Figure 8-1 shows a default screen created by dragging the EmployeesUpdateable1 collection (view object instance) onto the page and dropping it as an ADF Form.

Each of the fields shown on the page has a matching attribute binding in the PageDef file. Selecting **Edit Binding** from the right-click menu on one of the fields, such as *EmployeeId*, displays the Attribute Binding Editor, as shown in Figure 8-2.

The left side of this dialog mirrors the contents of the structure in the Data Control Palette, complete with nested collections. One of the collections—in this case, EmployeesUpdateable1— is selected in this list. On the right side, the *EmployeeId* attribute is selected. Therefore, this dialog is telling us that the *EmployeeId* attribute from the EmployeesUpdateable1 collection is bound to this field in the UI.

If you edit this binding, for example, by selecting the *FirstName* attribute and clicking OK, the reference to the binding will not change on the page. The expression in the component will still read #{bindings.EmployeeId.inputValue}. However, when the page runs, the "FirstName" information will be displayed in the field. This makes an important point: the name of the attribute used in the binding expression is an abstraction. Just because a field is bound to an expression containing the word "EmployeeId", does not mean that the Employee ID value will be displayed; the value depends on the PageDef file entry that you can see in this Attribute Binding Editor.

Manually Creating an Attribute Binding

The bindings we have looked at so far were all created by drag and drop from the Data Control Palette. You can also create bindings manually in the PageDef file, either by editing the XML

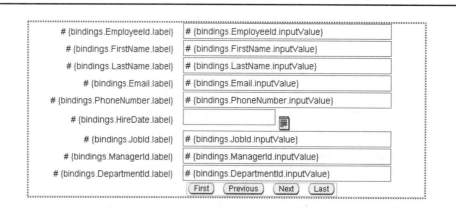

FIGURE 8-1. *A form created from an ADF BC view object*

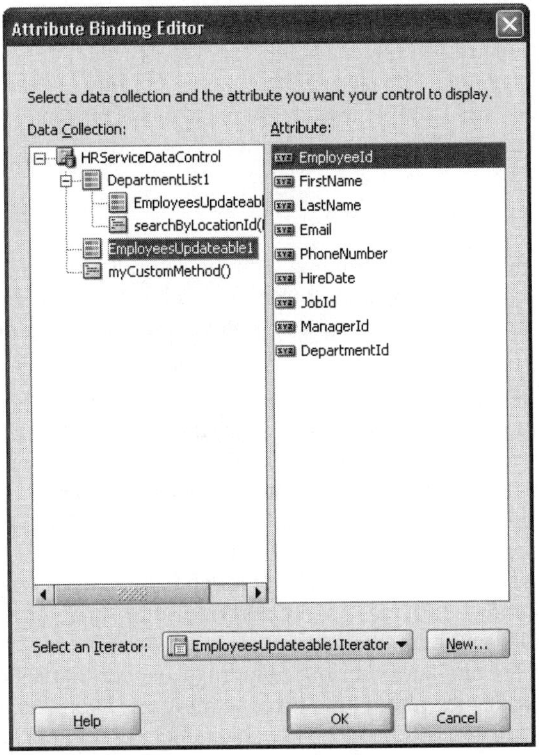

Attribute Binding Editor

Select a data collection and the attribute you want your control to display.

Data Collection:

- HRServiceDataControl
  - DepartmentList1
    - EmployeesUpdateabl
    - searchByLocationId(
  - EmployeesUpdateable1
  - myCustomMethod()

Attribute:

- EmployeeId
- FirstName
- LastName
- Email
- PhoneNumber
- HireDate
- JobId
- ManagerId
- DepartmentId

Select an Iterator: EmployeesUpdateable1Iterator   New...

Help   OK   Cancel

FIGURE 8-2. *The Attribute Binding Editor*

directly in the code editor, if you are familiar with its structure, or by using menu options offered in the Structure window's right-click menus.

All binding types can be manually created using the Structure window by following these steps:

1. Open the PageDef file that needs the new binding.

2. Ensure that the Structure window is visible and select **Insert inside bindings** from the right-click menu on the bindings node.

A submenu then displays the various binding types that can be created.

If you follow these steps and choose "attributeValues" as the binding type, the Attribute Binding Editor shown in Figure 8-2 displays.

TIP
You can also show the editor for an existing binding in the PageDef file's Structure window by expanding the bindings node to locate the binding you want and then double clicking it. Alternatively, you can select the binding in the Structure window and edit the properties in the Property Inspector.

Introducing the Iterator

We haven't explained the concept of iterators yet. They are described more fully in the section "What Is an Iterator?" later in the chapter. For now, we will say that an iterator is an element used to navigate a row set, much like a cursor navigates a query result in PL/SQL.

When you create an attribute binding with the Attribute Binding Editor shown in Figure 8-2, you can either select an existing iterator (see the sidebar "Introducing the Iterator") from the Select an Iterator pulldown or you can create an iterator using the New button.

Table Bindings

After single-attribute bindings, table bindings are the binding most frequently used in ADF applications. The primary use of *table bindings* is, of course, to populate table controls in the user interface, but they can also be used to create sets of data for other list UI components. For example, you can generate a bulleted list of records using a table binding and the `af:forEach` component (that loops through the collection).

You can think of a table binding as being much like the visible records displayed in an Oracle Forms block—the binding provides a view port or display range on top of the complete list of the records returned from the source collection.

Table bindings are similar to attribute bindings, except that a single binding encapsulates a set of attributes for display rather than just one attribute. Dragging the EmployeesUpdateable1 collection onto a page and dropping it as a table generates the following binding in the PageDef file (with line numbers added to aid explanation):

```
01: <table id="EmployeesUpdateable1"
02:        IterBinding="EmployeesUpdateable1Iterator">
03:   <AttrNames>
04:     <Item Value="EmployeeId"/>
05:     <Item Value="FirstName"/>
06:     <Item Value="LastName"/>
07:     <Item Value="Email"/>
08:     <Item Value="PhoneNumber"/>
09:     <Item Value="HireDate"/>
10:     <Item Value="JobId"/>
11:     <Item Value="ManagerId"/>
12:     <Item Value="DepartmentId"/>
13:   </AttrNames>
14: </table>
```

Line 01 defines the ID of the table binding used in the expression that binds the value of the table control. By default, the table binding will have the same name as the source collection.

Line 02 links the table binding to an iterator using the iterator's ID.

Lines 04–12 define the attributes within the collection that are available through this binding. In this case, we are seeing all of the attributes of the EmployeesUpdateable view object. Alternately, a table binding can define only a subset of columns.

Like other binding types, a table binding can be created or edited through a specialized editor, the *Table Binding Editor*, invoked from the Structure window of the PageDef file. This editor, shown in the following illustration, opens from the right-click menu (or by double clicking the binding node) in the Structure window:

This Table Binding Editor exposes the standard list of data collections on the left side and allows for the selection of an iterator in the dropdown list at the bottom of the dialog. With an iterator (and therefore a collection) selected, the attributes required for the table binding can be shuttled between the *Available Attributes* and *Display Attributes* lists. The ordering of attributes in the binding is controlled using the buttons on the far right side of the dialog.

Using a Table Binding

A table tag that references a table binding will use the expression "#{bindings.[Table Binding Name].collectionModel}" as the tag's value attribute—for example, #{bindings .EmployeesUpdateable1.collectionModel}. The exposed attributes can be accessed through the row alias, defined by the *var* attribute of the table tag, which defaults to the current row. For example, #{row.FirstName} used within the context of a table would reference the *FirstName* attribute associated with the current row in the table.

The following JSF UI snippet shows a fragment of a table component based on the EmployeesUpdateable1 collection (in this listing, the name of the table binding has been abbreviated from "EmployeesUpdateable1" to "EU1" to save space):

```
<af:table value="#{bindings.EU1.collectionModel}"
          var="row"
          rows="#{bindings.EU1.rangeSize}"
          first="#{bindings.EU1.rangeStart}"
          emptyText=
              "#{bindings.EU1.viewable?'No rows yet':'Access Denied.'}"
          selectionState="#{bindings.EU1.collectionModel.selectedRow}"
          selectionListener="#{bindings.EU1.collectionModel.makeCurrent}">
  <af:column sortProperty="FirstName"
             headerText="#{bindings.EU1.labels.FirstName}">
    <af:inputText
      value="#{row.FirstName}"
      simple="true"
      required="#{bindings.EU1.attrDefs.FirstName.mandatory}"
      columns="#{bindings.EU1.attrHints.FirstName.displayWidth}"/>
  </af:column>
```

The snippet shows several references to the table binding `EU1` in the context of column headers (`af:column` components) and the input item (`af:inputText`), as well as the `af:table` component itself. We explained how the *collectionModel* property of the table binding provides a JSF table control with its value. In this listing, the emptyText value uses a ternary expression as explained in the sidebar "What Is a Ternary Expression." Table 8-1 lists the other properties supported by the binding.

What Is a Ternary Expression?

As introduced in Chapter 4, a *ternary expression* is a Java operator. It is also available for Expression Language constructs; it acts very much like the PL/SQL DECODE function. A ternary expression consists of three parts:

Evaluation An expression, which evaluates to a `Boolean`.

True value The value to return for the whole expression if the evaluation is true.

False value The value to return for the whole expression if the evaluation is false.

The expression is written in the form: (evaluation)?(true value):(false value). Consider the following expression:

```
#{(1==2)? 'One does equal two':'One and two are different'}
```

This expression will print "One and two are different" because (1==2) evaluates to false. In JSF work, be careful with ternary expressions and null values. If the subject of the evaluation is null and you compare it to something other than null, the result will evaluate to false.

Table Binding Attribute	Use
collectionModel	This attribute adapts the table binding to a form that any JSF table component can use. The collectionModel object supports additional properties and functions—for example, collectionModel .selectedRow, which helps the table to mark the current record in the table, and collectionModel.makeCurrent, a function reference, which synchronizes the iterator with the selection that the user makes in the table UI.
rangeSize	This attribute indicates how many rows the table should display at once. It maps directly to the *RangeSize* attribute of the iterator that the table binding uses (see "What Is an Iterator?").
rangeStart	Based on information provided by the iterator, this attribute will tell the table which record within the collection is currently at the top of the table. In Oracle Forms terms, this attribute corresponds to the block property TOP_RECORD.
viewable	If security is being used on the collection, this property of the table binding indicates if the user is actually able to view data from this collection. The expression that uses this attribute is a ternary expression as explained in the sidebar "What Is a Ternary Expression?" We discuss security concerns in Chapter 14.
labels	Most of the control hints defined in the underlying view object or entity objects are accessible through Expression Language. The *labels* property of the table binding is an example of this. It is a Map (a list indexed by the attribute name) of the labels for the bound attributes. The expression #{bindings.EU1.labels.FirstName} means to display the label of the attribute called *FirstName*. This label will be extracted from the control hint *Label Text*; if that control hint is not set, the label will be the attribute name. Attribute bindings also support a *label* (singular) property, which provides the same information on a single-attribute basis (as opposed to being a collection of labels).
attrDefs	Provides more generic access to control (UI) hints. Again, like labels, it points to a map of information indexed using the name of the column. The attrDefs object can be used to get UI hints, such as *displayWidth* and *mandatory* (required) for that column.
rangeSet	Although not used in the previous example of a table, the rangeSet property of a table binding is useful, so it deserves a mention. This property is similar to the collectionModel property, but rather than adapting the table binding to a form acceptable to a JSF table control, it exposes the rows in the binding as an array that can be used inside af:forEach loops.

TABLE 8-1. *Table Binding Properties Accessible Through Expression Language*

Action Bindings

In addition to the data-bound fields shown in the JSF page in Figure 8-1, there are also a series of buttons used for navigating between records. Just like the fields, these buttons are bound and defined in the PageDef file. The buttons are bound to operations using an action binding.

Operations are data control items that do something to the data model. Available operations appear in the Data Control Palette, and you can drop them onto the page as buttons or links (or, in some cases, as forms). *Action bindings* connect the UI element (button or link) on the page (View layer) to the operation function in the Model layer. Action bindings (actions) are defined in the PageDef file.

If you have an Oracle Forms background, the best way to think of operations is that they are like the Oracle Forms built-ins. *Operations* are standard infrastructure functions that operate at the collection level (like the block level in triggers) or at the data control level (like Form-level triggers). Some operations are shown in the following illustration:

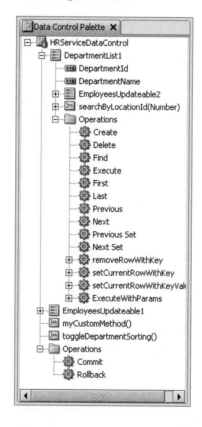

Available Operations

Operations are part of the abstraction provided by the ADFm layer, and different business services will support a different subset of operations, depending on the capabilities of that service. With ADF BC-based data controls, the full set of operations is supported. At the other extreme, a data control like the `UserDataControl` we created in Chapter 7, which is based on JavaBeans, may support no operations.

Data Control-Level Operations The data control-level operations (shown in Table 8-2) are only exposed by ADF BC–based data controls and any other data controls that have the *supportsTransactions* property set to "true" in the DataControls.dcx file.

In the PageDef file, a data control-level action binding for Commit will look like this:

```
<action id="Commit"
        InstanceName="HRServiceDataControl"
        DataControl="HRServiceDataControl"
        RequiresUpdateModel="true"
        Action="100"/>
```

The properties used in the action binding have the following meanings:

■ **id** This property defines a name for the operation. This ID is used when binding the action into the UI. It matches the logical name of the operation by default, but does not need to match.

■ **InstanceName** This property is set to the name of the data control for ADF BC work.

■ **DataControl** This property defines the data control that this operation acts on.

■ **RequiresModelUpdate** This Boolean value indicates to the framework if any changes on the page should be applied to the Model layer before the operation executes.

■ **Action** This numerical code tells the framework what to do. Each operation has a unique number. For example, Commit is 100, and Rollback is 101. This numbers are fixed within the framework.

Collection Operations Most operations are associated with a collection or, more strictly, are associated with an iterator. Table 8-3 lists the collection operations and the codes associated with them. Unlike the data control-level operations, collection operations are available to any business service type.

An action binding for a collection-level operation has similar attributes to the data control-level operation bindings. The following code listing shows the binding of the First button shown in Figure 8-1:

```
<action id="First"
        RequiresUpdateModel="true"
        Action="12"
        IterBinding="EmployeesUpdateable1Iterator"/>
```

Operation	Description
Commit	This operation tells the data control to issue a database COMMIT to save changes in the transaction.
Rollback	This operation issues a database ROLLBACK to undo any changes posted after the last COMMIT. This operation also clears out the record caches in ADF Business Components and resets the iterators to the first record.

TABLE 8-2. *Data Control-Level Transactional Operations*

Operation (code)	Description
Create (41)	This operation opens a slot for a new record in the collection. The new record is added to the collection after the page is submitted. Therefore, if the user abandons the page by navigating away, an empty record is not left orphaned. The new record opened by Create is inserted before the current record in the iterator.
CreateInsert (40)	This operation is the same as Create, except that the new empty record is inserted into the collection as part of the operation. This means that even if the user never submits the page, the row will still be in the collection. See the sidebar "Create or CreateInsert?" for details about how to decide between these operations. Unlike Create and the other operations listed in this table, CreateInsert is not displayed in the Operations node of the Data Control Palette. A CreateInsert binding can only be created manually in the PageDef file.
Delete (30)	This operation removes the current row from the collection. It is similar to the removeRowWithKey operation.
Execute (2 or 0)	This operation refreshes the current collection. This is like requerying the database, although it works with data in the mid-tier cache rather than data from the database.
ExecuteWithParams (95)	This operation will be available if the source view object for a collection contains bind variable references. ExecuteWithParams combines the tasks of setting the bind variable values and refreshing the collection. We'll be using this when we build a list-of-values screen in Chapter 13.
Find (3 or 1)	This operation places the collection into Query-By-Example mode. Be careful when using this mode. The kind of query block interface that you might construct with Oracle Forms is not a usual construct for web applications, where a Google-like single search field is the norm. The Create and Delete operations take on overloaded meanings when in Find mode. They add and remove from the list of query criteria rather than adding and deleting rows.
First (12)	This operation repositions the current row, as defined by the iterator, to the initial record in the collection.
Last (13)	This operation repositions the current row to the final record in the collection.
Next (10)	Next moves the current row down one.

TABLE 8-3.   *Operations Available on a Collection*

Operation (code)	Description
Next Set (14)	This operation scrolls the current record location down a number of rows specified by the iterator's *RangeSize* property.
Previous (11)	Previous moves the current row up one record.
Previous Set (15)	This operation scrolls the current record location up by the number of rows specified by the iterator's *RangeSize* property.
removeRowWithKey (99)	This operation deletes a specified row in the collection. This operation takes a parameter of the row identifier generated by ADFm and accessed through the binding attribute *rowKeyStr*. This attribute is available when iterating through a collection as a special attribute that is always present, rather like ROWNUM in a SQL query. It is unlikely that you will need to use this operation in a JSF-based application since JSF tables manage row currency for you.
setCurrentRowWithKey (96)	Like removeRowWithKey, this operation takes a row identifier parameter and uses it to set the iterator currency (focus) onto a specific row. It does not remove the row, however. Again, you are unlikely to need this in JSF applications.
setCurrentRowWithKeyValue (98)	This operation is a version of setCurrentRowWithKey that takes a parameter of the primary key value rather than the ADFm-generated key.
<custom methods> (999)	As shown in Chapter 7, methods you create in the application module or view object Impl classes can appear in a similar way to operations.

TABLE 8-3.   *Operations Available on a Collection* (continued)

Create or CreateInsert?

The two different create operations provided by ADF, Create and CreateInsert, can be a little confusing because they seem to accomplish the same task. Although the Create behavior is generally more useful, there are still some circumstances where CreateInsert should be used. Typically, this will be when the side effects of entity object creation are desirable. For example, the `create()` method on the entity object adds information defined as defaults for attributes such as dates and reference numbers. With CreateInsert, this default information will be visible to the user on the created (blank) record. If the new Create operation is used, the defaults will not be set until after the user submits the new record.

The *id, Action,* and *RequiresModelUpdate* properties have the same meaning as the data control-level operations. In this case, the binding is associated with an iterator though the *IterBinding* property, rather than directly with a data control.

Manually Creating Action Bindings

The most convenient way of creating an action binding is to drag and drop the operation from the Data Control Palette onto the page. Like the other binding types, action bindings can be created from within the PageDef file. As we discussed, this is the only way to create some bindings, such as the CreateInsert operation binding.

To create action bindings in the PageDef file, you display the Structure window and, on the *bindings* node, select **Insert inside bindings | action** from the right-click menu. The Action Binding Editor will appear. Expanding the *Data Collection* nodes and displaying the *Select an Action* dropdown list will display the following:

The Action Binding Editor shows the standard list of data collections on the left side and offers a dropdown list of actions on the right. Selecting the top-level data control node will configure the *Select an Action* list to show the data control-level operations (Commit and Rollback), if they are available for the selected data control. When a collection is selected, the list reconfigures to display the valid operations for a collection.

Scoped Action Bindings   If you scroll through the collection-level actions to the Execute and Find operations, you'll see the dialog reconfigure slightly. A radio group appears containing two options—*Binding Container Level* and *Iterator Level*. Execute and Find have special scopes of operation; the default level is *iterator level*, where the operation is associated explicitly with an iterator. The alternative, *binding container level*, operates at the page level. Clicking a button bound to a Find operation scoped at the binding container level will put all forms on the page into Query mode. If the button's operation were defined on the iterator level, only the form associated with the same iterator as the Find action would be placed into Query mode.

If you create both types of bindings (iterator and binding container) and compare them, you will see that the only difference is the numerical action code. Iterator-level Find, for example, has an *Action* attribute of "3." The same operation bound at binding container level has an *Action* attribute of "1." So although we call these two scopes or levels for the same operation, in reality, we are dealing with two separate operations. Table 8-3 shows both action codes when applicable. The lower numbered code of any pair operates at the whole-page level.

NOTE
The term "binding container" is the formal name for the set of bindings on a page. All bindings defined within a PageDef file are within the same binding container. When building JSF user interfaces, there is generally a one-to-one relationship between a binding container and a page.

Action Bindings in the UI

When we looked at table bindings, we saw that the binding exposes extra features though Expression Language. The same is true of action bindings. For example, here is the markup for the First button shown in Figure 8-1:

```
<af:commandButton actionListener="#{bindings.First.execute}"
                  text="First"
                  disabled="#{!bindings.First.enabled}"/>
```

The key property here is *actionListener*. An *actionListener* in JSF is code that will execute before the main *action* for a commandItem. For example, consider the following code:

```
<af:commandButton actionListener="#{bindings.Commit.execute}"
                  action="Home"
                  text="Save and return"/>
```

The actionListener operation of a commit is processed, and then the navigation implied by the "Home" outcome takes place. The expression "#{bindings.[operation].execute}" is a JSF method binding. In the section "How Do I Write Code Using the ADF Model?," we'll look at how you can override or enhance these built-in operation calls.

The second feature exposed by the operation is the enabled attribute in the expression `#{!bindings.First.enabled}`. This expression implements a framework behavior that we mentioned earlier in the chapter. Operation UI elements, such as buttons, are enabled or disabled automatically by the framework to reflect if the operation is available. You saw examples of the button-disabling effect in the illustrated data control listings in Chapter 7.

TIP
You can use this "enabled" attribute within Expression Language to partially emulate the Oracle Forms system variable :SYSTEM.FORM_ STATUS by binding the Commit operation into the PageDef file. The expression "#{bindings.Commit.enabled}" can then be used to flag if there are outstanding changes.

Operations with Parameters

A subset of operations, most importantly ExecuteWithParams, takes arguments (parameters). The three operations named with "WithKey" suffixes (in Table 8-3) take a single argument value. ExecuteWithParams will take as many arguments as there are bind variables in the view object SQL statement. For operations with arguments, you can expand the operation's node in the Data Control Palette to reveal a Parameters node. This node contains the arguments.

Recall from Chapter 7 that dropping an operation such as ExecuteWithParams onto the page allows you to create a parameter form as well as a command button or a command link.

Dropping a parameter form onto the page creates the binding to the operation in the PageDef file; it also creates one input field in the page file for each argument to the operation, along with a Command Button to execute it. As an example, let's take a look at the markup generated by dropping the ExecuteWithParams operation for the DepartmentList1 collection that we created in Chapter 6. The underlying view object has a single bind variable—":location." Dropping this operation as a parameter form creates the following JSF tags:

```
<af:inputText value="#{bindings.location.inputValue}"
              label="#{bindings.location.label}"
              required="#{bindings.location.mandatory}"
              columns="#{bindings.location.displayWidth}">
  <af:validator binding="#{bindings.location.validator}"/>
  <f:convertNumber groupingUsed="false"
                   pattern="#{bindings.location.format}"/>
</af:inputText>
<af:commandButton actionListener="#{bindings.ExecuteWithParams.execute}"
                  text="ExecuteWithParams"
                  disabled="#{!bindings.ExecuteWithParams.enabled}"/>
```

Notice that the af:inputText uses value bindings to retrieve several of its UI attributes, such as the *label, columns* (width), and *required* attributes. It also has nested validators and converters. All of the information powering these bindings is coming from the view object. In Chapter 6, we talked about defining view object bind variables, control hints, and datatypes. That information is used here to configure the parameter form.

TIP
The af:validator tag nested within the af:inputText will connect the parameter to any validation rules that you define for that binding. Unlike attributes from a view object, which will have declarative validation rules defined on the underlying entity object definition, the declarative validation rules for parameters are defined in the binding layer. To create such validations, switch to the PageDef file, select the parameter's attribute binding in the Structure window, and choose **Edit Validation Rule** *from the right-click menu.*

Notice that the `af:inputText` item used to enter the bind variable value has been bound to an attribute binding called "location" (in the PageDef file). To find out about this binding, on the field, select **Edit Binding** from the right-click menu. The Attribute Binding Editor appears as follows:

Observe that an iterator called "variables" is selected. The variables iterator is a special iterator that provides access to local variables defined in the PageDef file. In this case, the input field is bound to a variable called `DepartmentList1_location`, using an attribute binding called "location."

The `af:commandButton` tag created by dropping the parameter form is identical to the examples that we've seen before. Its binding definition in the PageDef file, as shown in the following listing, should be relatively familiar:

```
<action id="ExecuteWithParams"
        IterBinding="DepartmentList1Iterator"
        InstanceName="HRServiceDataControl.DepartmentList1"
        DataControl="HRServiceDataControl"
        RequiresUpdateModel="true"
        Action="95">
  <NamedData NDName="location"
             NDType="oracle.jbo.domain.Number"
             NDValue="${bindings.DepartmentList1_location}"/>
</action>
```

You will see that the ExecuteWithParams operation has an action number of "95" and that it is bound to the DepartmentList1 Iterator. In addition, you will see a child element of the action tag, the *NamedData* element.

NamedData is used to define arguments that the framework needs to pass to operations and methods that have arguments. This element has the following attributes:

- **NDName**   This attribute is the name of the argument. It is important to assign a name if you need to programmatically set this value before calling the bound method.

- **NDType**   This attribute identifies the datatype of the parameter.

- **NDValue**   This attribute is the value to pass to the parameter. This can be set to a literal value, or, as in this example, it can be set to an expression.

The ability to pass an expression to the parameter's value attribute is immensely powerful. The programmer can use any EL expression here, including conditional expressions using the ternary operator we discussed earlier. In this case, the drag-and-drop operation has set up the expression as `${bindings.DepartmentList1_location}`. This expression binds the value of the DepartmentList1_location local variable as the argument to the operation call. Thus, we can see the relationship between the input field in the parameter form and the operation call. The input field sets the value of the local variable, and the operation passes that same value up to the model.

TIP
Expressions in the PageDef file can use either the dollar "$" or hash (pound) "#" symbol to mark the start of the expression. Expressions in the JSF page can only use the "#" symbol.

Method Bindings

In principle, method bindings are virtually identical to the action bindings used to access operations. When a custom method is dropped into the UI as a parameter form, for example, input fields are created and bound to variables in the same way as for operations with parameters. The only difference between custom methods and operations is that custom methods may yield results. These results can then be bound into the page and treated just like any other normal attribute.

Editing Method Bindings

Custom methods are bound using a binding type called a *methodAction* binding. You create a methodAction binding by dropping the method onto the page as a command button, command link, or parameter form. If you select either of the command options, the Action Binding Editor will appear to allow you to define the values to pass to any method parameters. The next illustration shows the Action Binding Editor dialog for a method called `searchByLocation()`, which is exposed as a client method on the DepartmentList1 view object instance.

Action Binding Editor

Select a data collection and the action you want your control to initiate. The control initiates the action on the data objects of the selected collection.

Data Collection:

- HRServiceDataControl
  - DepartmentList1
  - EmployeesUpdateable1

Select an Action

searchByLocationId(Number)

Parameters :

Name	Type	Value	Option
locationId	oracle.jbo....	${bindings.searchByLoca...	

Select an Iterator: DepartmentList1Iterator

Help   OK   Cancel

This method takes a single argument in this case (`locationId`), and the Action Binding Editor provides a place to set the value of the argument. The parameter can be set to a literal value or an expression. Double clicking the *Value* field in the dialog causes a button to appear; this button will display the Expression Language dialog, which will allow you to set an expression for the value.

The dropdown list labeled *Option* is only operational in Swing-based applications, so you can ignore it for JSF applications.

The XML for a method binding in the PageDef file looks similar to that of an operation binding:

```
<methodAction id="searchByLocationId"
              InstanceName="HRServiceDataControl.DepartmentList1"
              DataControl="HRServiceDataControl"
              MethodName="searchByLocationId"
              RequiresUpdateModel="true"
              Action="999"
              IsViewObjectMethod="true"
              IterBinding="DepartmentList1Iterator">
  <NamedData NDName="locationId"
             NDValue="10"
             NDType="oracle.jbo.domain.Number"/>
</methodAction>
```

In this case, the binding is to a method exposed by a view object instance, so there is little information required to map that relationship. You can see that custom methods use the *Action* property in the same way that operation bindings do. However, custom methods always use the magic value of "999" for that property. The framework interprets this as a call to the service.

NOTE
If you reproduce this example, you may or may not see the IterBinding
property in the methodAction definition. In this kind of binding, the
InstanceName *property provides the runtime with enough information*
to locate and execute the method. JDeveloper is not consistent about
adding iterator references for view object methods, and what you see
in the binding will depend on what other binding operations have
been carried out on the same page.

This listing also shows how method parameters are defined as they are for operations—using
NamedData elements. In this case, the value to pass to the method is a literal value ("10"), but it
could alternatively be set to an expression.

List Bindings

List bindings are a specialized subset of bindings used for populating lists, radio groups, and
checkbox groups. These components need to be bound to two items—the actual attribute in the
underlying dataset that is being populated and the set of data that makes up the options. This set of
data could be a static list of values, such as "Male" or "Female" for a radio group, or it could be fully
dynamic and driven from a collection managed by a data control, for example, a list of departments.

You can create a list binding by dragging and dropping a suitable attribute from the Data
Control Palette. When you drop the attribute and choose a UI widget from the Single Selections
submenu, the List Binding Editor dialog (shown in Figure 8-3) will appear. You can also invoke

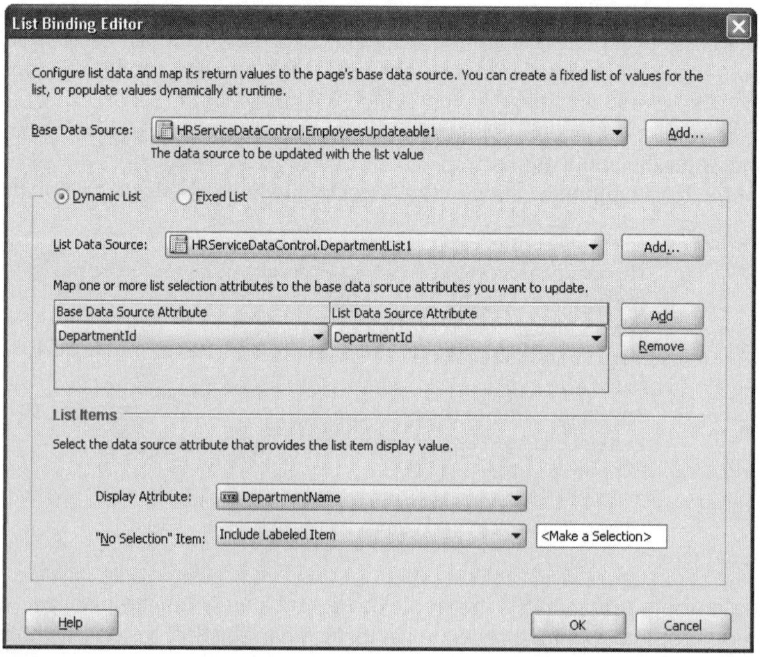

FIGURE 8-3. *The List Binding Editor*

this dialog by selecting **Insert Inside Bindings | list** from the context menu on the bindings node of the page definition structure and then selecting "Create Dynamic/Fixed List Binding."

The two forms of lists that can be created, dynamic and static, present different interfaces through this editor.

NOTE
*List bindings offer similar functionality to Oracle Forms record groups.
In Oracle Forms, you can define a static record group, for which
you specify literal values; this corresponds to a static list binding.
Alternatively, in Oracle Forms, you can define a record group that is
populated from a query, like the dynamic list binding. Just as you can
base a JSF UI dropdown list on a list binding, you can programmatically
populate an Oracle Forms poplist from a record group.*

Dynamic List Bindings

Dynamic list bindings are one of the best features of ADF binding. ADF takes care of a lot of data management to correctly populate the list and manage the type conversions that are required. Figure 8-3 shows how the *DepartmentId* attribute in the EmployeesUpdateable1 collection is bound to a list that is populated with the departments from DepartmentList1.

To define a dynamic list, you carry out the following steps:

1. **Define the *Base Data Source*.** If the editor popped up after a drag-and-drop operation, this dropdown list will contain the correct iterator. If you are creating a binding from the Structure window, all existing iterators in the PageDef file will be listed; you can also create an iterator using the Add button that is adjacent to this field. The base data source in a list binding is the target of the list—the iterator that holds the attribute for which you are setting the value using the list.

2. **Select the *Dynamic List* option**, as shown in Figure 8-3.

3. **Define the *List Data Source*** as the name of the iterator that will supply the data in the list. Again, you can use the Add button, which causes a dialog to appear, so you can create an iterator if required.

4. **Map the key attribute(s) that define the relationship** between the list options and the value you are selecting. After you select both iterators, the lists labeled *Base Data Source Attribute* and *List Data Source Attribute* will be populated for you. Use these lists to define the relationship between the collections. The *Base Data Source Attribute* is the attribute that will be populated. The *List Data Source Attribute* is the attribute that will supply the value when the user selects from the list. The attribute you use will usually be the foreign key that links the table on which the page is based with the table that supplies values to the list, but a foreign key is not required. You can define more than one pair of attributes to populate more than one value on the page by clicking the Add button next to the attribute pulldowns.

5. **Define the value to display in the list.** The *Display Attribute* dropdown list allows you to specify an attribute from the list data source that will be used as the label for the list entries. In Figure 8-3, we are selecting DepartmentId for the value attribute, but the list label (*Display Attribute*) will display the DepartmentName.

6. **Set up the "no selection" option.** Dropdown lists can display a blank item that can signify various values. The *No Selection Item* dropdown list allows you to declare how to handle this blank selection. Setting this property to "Selection Required" means that the populated list will have no blank item. Alternatively, you can allow nulls, either with an empty label ("Include Blank Item") or a custom label ("Include Labeled Item"), as is shown in Figure 8-3. If you select "Include Labeled Item," the string that is entered in the dialog is stored in a message bundle .java file in the same directory as the PageDef file; this Java file uses the same name as the PageDef file, but with the MsgBundle suffix (for example, listPageDefMsgBundle.java for the list.jsp file).

This definition will create a dropdown list for the employee department ID item on the page. The dropdown list will offer all department names. When the user selects a department name from the list, the department ID will become the value for that item. Similarly, when the record is queried, the list will display the department name corresponding to the department ID value of the list item's attribute. The following code listing shows the XML in the PageDef file generated by the values selected for the binding in Figure 8-3:

```
<list id="EmployeesUpdateable1DepartmentId"
      IterBinding="EmployeesUpdateable1Iterator"
      StaticList="false"
      ListOperMode="0"
      ListIter="DepartmentList1Iterator"
      NullValueFlag="1"
      NullValueId="EmployeesUpdateable1DepartmentId_null">
  <AttrNames>
    <Item Value="DepartmentId"/>
  </AttrNames>
  <ListAttrNames>
    <Item Value="DepartmentId"/>
  </ListAttrNames>
  <ListDisplayAttrNames>
    <Item Value="DepartmentName"/>
  </ListDisplayAttrNames>
</list>
```

You can easily spot the mapping between the values selected in Figure 8-3 and the corresponding XML definition. Notice the *NullValueFlag* property and the *NullValueId* property. In this example, these properties specify that a null value is allowed on the list, and the NullValueId names the resource that contains the null value label (in the message bundle file). If you look at the top of the PageDef file, you'll also see that a reference to the message bundle file has been added:

```
<pageDefinition xmlns="http://xmlns.oracle.com/adfm/uimodel"
                version="10.1.3.36.73"
                id="listPageDef"
                Package="book.view.pageDefs"
                MsgBundleClass="book.view.pageDefs.listPageDefMsgBundle">
```

CAUTION
*If you manually create a dynamic list binding in the PageDef
file, be sure to set the "RangeSize" attribute of the iterator that is
populating the list values to minus one (–1). This will ensure that all
of the possible list items will appear in the list. Failure to do this will
restrict your lists to a maximum of 10 entries, the default value of the
"RangeSize" property.*

Fixed Lists

In some circumstances, lists only require a set of static values. Fixed lists are defined through the
same List Binding Editor as dynamic lists. The following illustration shows such a definition:

When defining a fixed list binding, the target iterator is defined in the same way as for a
dynamic list. The *Fixed List* option must be selected, and then the attribute within the target iterator
that will take the selected value is selected. In this example, the *FirstName* attribute has been
selected, and the values to display as options have been entered into the *Set of Values* field. As
before, the list can be configured to display a null entry, or not, using the *"No Selection" Item* list.

Switching to the PageDef file, we can see that the list-binding definition is slightly different,
indicating that this is a static list (using the *StaticList* attribute) and containing the literal values
that will appear in the list.

```
<list id="EmployeesUpdateable1FirstName"
      IterBinding="EmployeesUpdateable1Iterator"
      ListOperMode="0"
      StaticList="true">
```

```
<AttrNames>
  <Item Value="FirstName"/>
</AttrNames>
<ValueList>
  <Item Value="John"/>
  <Item Value="Paul"/>
  <Item Value="Ringo"/>
  <Item Value="George"/>
</ValueList>
</list>
```

NOTE
As you can see in this listing, the values for the list items are hard-coded into the PageDef file. The strings are not translatable to another language, and the value and label of each item is the same. If you need flexibility, such as multiple languages in a static list, you could use a conventional attribute binding for the target attribute and build the list using JSF f:selectItem components (one per option) nested inside the selection component rather than populating it out of a list binding.

Lists in the UI

The List Binding Editor defines a list binding that can be used from several types of user interface components: af:selectOneChoice (a dropdown list known as "poplists" to Oracle Forms developers), af:selectOneList (a multiline selection item, known as a "T-List" in Oracle Forms), and af:selectOneRadio (a radio group). As an example, here is the tag markup for a dropdown list:

```
<af:selectOneChoice value=
    "#{bindings.EmployeesUpdateable1DepartmentId.inputValue}"
                label=
    "#{bindings.EmployeesUpdateable1DepartmentId.label}">
  <f:selectItems  value=
      "#{bindings.EmployeesUpdateable1DepartmentId.items}"/>
</af:selectOneChoice>
```

And a radio group:

```
<af:selectOneRadio value=
    "#{bindings.EmployeesUpdateable1DepartmentId.inputValue}"
                label=
    "#{bindings.EmployeesUpdateable1DepartmentId.label}">
  <f:selectItems value=
      "#{bindings.EmployeesUpdateable1DepartmentId.items}"/>
</af:selectOneRadio>
```

These sets of markup are identical, apart from the type of top-level component. The value that the component is bound to and the set of options (the f:selectItems tag) are the same for both.

Navigation List Bindings

A *navigation list binding* is used less often than list bindings, and is really unrelated to it, except that it is displayed in a list-style UI component. Rather than setting the value of a bound attribute, the navigation is used to change the row currency within the collection. Selecting a value from a navigation list will navigate to that row. Since all rows in the collection appear in the list, navigation list bindings are of minimal use unless the number of records in the collection is small.

Recall that the navigation list is one of the options offered when you drop a collection onto a page. The following illustration shows the slightly different version of the List Binding Editor that displays after dropping the collection as a navigation list:

The attributes shuttled into the Display Attributes column will be used to create the label for the list entries. The value of the list control is not selected because the function of the list is to set the row currency; it does not bind a value to a control.

If you take a look at the XML created in the PageDef file, you will see the distinguishing feature of this binding is the value of the *ListOperMode* attribute, which is set to "1," unlike the dynamic list and fixed list, which have a mode of "0." This value indicates the purpose of the list binding to the framework.

```
<list StaticList="false"
      ListOperMode="1"
      id="DepartmentList1"
      IterBinding="DepartmentList1Iterator">
  <AttrNames>
    <Item Value="DepartmentName"/>
  </AttrNames>
</list>
```

CAUTION
Just like dynamic list bindings, navigation list bindings are constrained by the default range size of the iterator. Of course, it may be a good idea to use an upper limit for the "RangeSize" property for the navigation list, because showing a navigation list containing every row in a huge table is of minimal use.

Boolean Bindings

As a complement to list bindings, we have the specialized binding called *boolean bindings* that offer two choices and no option for null. Checkboxes are the usual UI component for this kind of binding. However, toggle buttons (which represent a boolean value and display either as depressed or not) in ADF Swing also use it. Therefore, this binding is also known as a *button binding.* You can create a boolean binding by dragging an attribute onto the page and dropping it as a checkbox (ADF Select Boolean Checkbox). You can also create it in the PageDef file's Structure window by selecting the bindings node and selecting **Insert Inside Bindings | button** from the right-click menu. The Boolean Binding Editor shown here will display:

Boolean Binding Editor

Select a data collection and attribute you want your control to operate on. The value to return to the bound attribute is determined when the user changes the control's selection state. You must know what values the bound attribute takes in order to supply meaningful selection state values.

Data Collection:
- HRServiceDataControl
  - DepartmentList1
  - EmployeesUpdatea
  - myCustomMethod(

Attribute:

Selected State Value:

Unselected State Value:

Select an Iterator: New...

Help   OK   Cancel

The elements should be familiar. You can select an iterator from the dropdown list (or create one with the New button) to be a target of the binding. The collection will then automatically be selected. You can also select the target attribute within that collection (in the *Attribute* column). You need to type in the *Selected State Value* and *Unselected State Value* fields the values that the database expects for those states. These fields correspond directly to the *Value When Checked* and *Value When Unchecked* properties of an Oracle Forms checkbox item.

The following listing shows what a boolean binding looks like. As you can see, it's remarkably similar to a fixed list binding. (This listing assumes that an *EmailContactAllowed* attribute has been added to the EmployeesUpdateable view object.)

```
<button id="EmailContactAllowed"
        IterBinding="EmployeesUpdateable1Iterator">
  <AttrNames>
    <Item Value="EmailContactAllowed"/>
  </AttrNames>
  <ValueList>
    <Item Value="Y"/>
    <Item Value="N"/>
  </ValueList>
</button>
```

In the `ValueList` element, the first child element represents the true (checked) value and the second represents the false (unchecked) value.

Tree Bindings

Tree bindings provide access to master-detail information within a single binding definition. The most common use for this binding is to serve UI components, such as tree controls or master-detail nested tables. With a little imagination, however, tree bindings can also be handy for any data representation requiring a nested structure; for example, organizational chart data.

Because the tree binding exposes a relationship, it is a little tricky to grasp how to actually create one the first time that you encounter it. For example, if you drag a collection from the Data Control Palette and drop as an ADF Tree control, you will see the Tree Binding Editor shown in Figure 8-4.

The key term to understand is *rule,* which represents one level in the tree hierarchy. For example, in a tree that needs to display employees within departments, you will need two rules. The first rule will define the master data—the departments—and a second rule defines the employees within each department. As part of this definition, the rule also defines the relationship between each level and the next. The tree binding uses the relationships defined by view links as we have used to define the master-detail relationships in data.

Each rule requires three essential pieces of information:

- **The collection that populates this level of the tree** This is selected in the *Data Collection Definition* list in the dialog. This selection, of course, will use an iterator, so the *Select an Iterator* dropdown list appears at the bottom of the screen. You would use this if you display this dialog from the Structure window. If you drag and drop from the Data Control Palette, the top-level iterator is created (if it does not exist) and selected for you.

- **The attributes from the selected collection for the tree branch** These attributes are selected using the *Display Attribute* list. If multiple attributes are selected, they will be displayed in the order shown in the list on the same line with a space between each attribute value. This display can be customized, and we look at this in the section "Customizing the Tree."

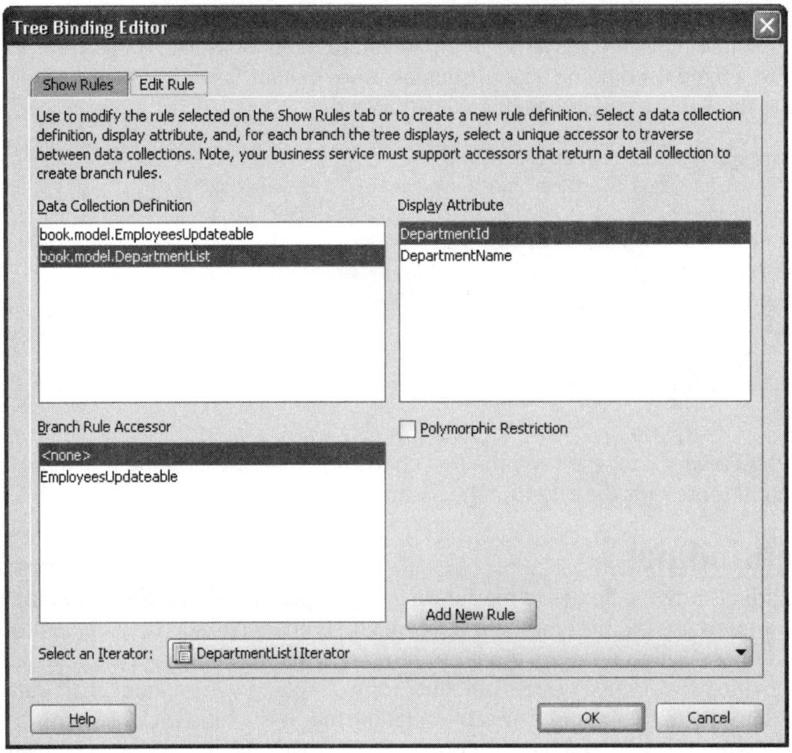

FIGURE 8-4. *Tree Binding Editor*

■ **The relationship between this level of the tree and its children** If you are defining a parent node, set *Branch Rule Accessor* to the child collection. If the rule you are defining will build the leaf (last-level) nodes of the tree, set the *Branch Rule Accessor* to "<none>." The editor will automatically list any valid relationships.

Creating a Tree Binding Step by Step

Let us run through the steps required to define a tree binding for employees by department using the starting point shown in Figure 8-4 (after dragging the master collection as an ADF Tree onto the page).

NOTE
If you follow along with this exercise using the application created in Chapter 6, you will need to create a version of the DepartmentList view object that does not have a bind variable and so returns all rows in the DEPARTMENTS table. Create a corresponding view link to EmployeesUpdateable, and expose both of these through the application module data model screen. Follow the instructions provided, substituting in the new objects that you've created.

1. On the Edit Rule tab, in the *Data Collection Definition* list, select the master node for Departments—book.model.DepartmentList.

2. In the *Display Attribute* list, select the label for each node at this level, the DepartmentName, in this example.

3. Each department branch of the tree needs to show the related employees within that department, so set the *Branch Rule Accessor* to EmployeesUpdateable.

4. Click Add New Rule. (This is important.) A dialog will confirm that the rule has been entered, as shown in the following illustration:

Additional Information: The first level of the tree is now defined and the view in the dialog will automatically switch to the Show Rules tab, as shown here:

The Show Rules tab allows you to delete or reorder the rules as required. However, note that the dropdown lists shown in the *Icon*, *OpenIcon*, and *ClosedIcon* columns have no effect in a JSF application. They are only used for ADF Swing tree controls.

5. Switch back to the Edit Rule tab in the dialog.

6. Now select book.model.EmployeesUpdateable in the *Data Collection Definition* list. Notice that the Select an Iterator dropdown list still indicates the DepartmentsList collection. Access to the children within the hierarchy is managed internally by the binding and does not use extra iterators.

7. In the *Display Attribute* list, select FirstName and LastName (using CTRL-click).

8. Select "<none>" in the *Branch Rule Accessor* list, because this is the last node level in the hierarchy.

9. Click Add New Rule again. Click OK to dismiss the dialog and create the tree component.

Running the page after following these steps results in a tree control that looks like this:

```
⊟🗁 Accounting
  │  ⊞🗁 William Gietz
  │  ⊞🗁 Shelley Higgins
⊟🗁 Administration
  │  ⊞🗁 Jennifer Whalen
  ⊞🗁 Construction
  ⊞🗁 Contracting
  ⊞🗁 Control And Credit
  ⊞🗁 Corporate Tax
  ⊞🗁 Executive
  ⊞🗁 Finance
  ⊞🗁 Government Sales
  ⊞🗁 IT Helpdesk
```

The Edit Rule tab in the dialog can also be used to modify a rule. If you are modifying a rule, select it in the Show Rules tab, click Edit Rule, and make changes to the rule. Then, be sure to click Modify Current Rule rather than Add New Rule or OK. You will see the following dialog to confirm the change:

The Tree Binding in the PageDef File
The code that represents the tree binding is as follows:

```
<tree id="DepartmentList1"
      IterBinding="DepartmentList1Iterator">
  <AttrNames>
    <Item Value="DepartmentId"/>
    <Item Value="DepartmentName"/>
  </AttrNames>
```

```
<nodeDefinition DefName="book.model.DepartmentList"
                id="DepartmentListNode">
  <AttrNames>
    <Item Value="DepartmentName"/>
  </AttrNames>
  <Accessors>
    <Item Value="EmployeesUpdateable"/>
  </Accessors>
</nodeDefinition>
<nodeDefinition DefName="book.model.EmployeesUpdateable"
                id="EmployeesUpdateableNode">
  <AttrNames>
    <Item Value="FirstName"/>
    <Item Value="LastName"/>
  </AttrNames>
</nodeDefinition>
</tree>
```

At the highest level, the tree is bound to a single iterator; each level of the tree is defined in a `nodeDefinition` child element of the tree. The `AttrNames` child element of the `nodeDefinition` lists the display attributes for that level of the tree.

TIP
Given the complexity of the binding information for a tree binding, it's wise to use the supplied editing dialog to create or edit one.

Polymorphic Restrictions

The Tree Binding Editor dialog shown in Figure 8-4 displays a *Polymorphic Restriction* checkbox. This is rarely used, but is worth explaining. This option allows you to populate a particular level in the tree with more than one set of data, thus contradicting the previous statement that a rule defines a single level in the tree hierarchy. This data could be loaded from different child collections based on a discriminator column in the master collection, or it can be used to filter a single child collection by only displaying rows that match the entered criteria.

When *Polymorphic Restriction* is selected, a dropdown list of attributes is displayed, allowing you to select an attribute from a list and add a string value in the field below, as shown here:

> ☑ Polymorphic Restriction
> Define a polymorphic definition (attribute/value)
> | ManagerId ▾ |
> | 101| |

At runtime, as this rule is processed, the indicated attribute will be compared with the fixed value and the node only returned if they match.

Customizing the Tree

A common question about the `af:tree` control is how to customize the look of the tree. Unfortunately, some aspects, such as icons and the open and closed indicators, cannot be changed, unless you use a custom skin for ADF Faces. Custom skins are beyond the scope of this book.

However, you can change the label of the leaf nodes. As we explained, all of the selected display attributes are presented in the node label separated by spaces by default. Sometimes, you will need access to data in the tree programmatically but do not want to display that data. For example, if the tree is used as a navigation device for selecting a department, the label of the tree node will only need to contain the department name, not the ID; however, the ID will need to be available in the binding definition for use in the drilldown.

If we examine the markup generated in the JSP file by an ADF tree drag-and-drop operation, it is not immediately obvious how we can accomplish conditional display of data. Here is part of the generated code:

```
<af:tree value="#{bindings.DepartmentList1.treeModel}"
         var="node">
  <f:facet name="nodeStamp">
<af:outputText value="#{node}"/>
</f:facet>
</af:tree>
```

As you can see, the UI tree definition is simple; the value of the tree is the model that is defined by the tree binding (the *treeModel* attribute). The tree uses a facet called "nodeStamp" to "stamp" out each row in the tree which displays a value referenced through an object called `node`.

It is important to understand that this `node` object encapsulates all of the attributes that you selected for display (as represented in the tree binding). This means that you can access those attributes explicitly using EL. If left on its own, the `node` will resolve to a string that carries the correct label for that level of the tree. If you take over and start to define exactly what you want printed, you also need to take responsibility for that decision-making process. This is all possible, but the Expression Language is a little complicated. Here is an example from the sample application reference screen where a tree is used to list departments by city, cities by country, and countries by region. At runtime, the tree looks like this:

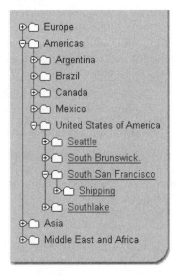

Notice that the nodes of the tree representing the city and department are shown as hyperlinks and the other nodes are shown as plain text. Here is the markup used to create the tree (with line numbers added for explanatory purposes):

```
01: <af:tree value="#{bindings.AllRegions.treeModel}"
02:          var="node"
03:          immediate="true">
04:   <f:facet name="nodeStamp">
05:     <af:panelHorizontal>
06:       <af:outputText
07:           rendered="#{node.RegionId != null}"
08:           value="#{node.RegionName}"/>
09:       <af:outputText
10:           rendered="#{node.CountryId != null}"
11:           value="#{node.CountryName}"/>
12:       <af:commandLink
13:           rendered="#{node.LocationId != null}"
14:           text="#{node.City}"
15:           action="#{backing_reference.treeLocationSelect_action}"
16:           immediate="true"/>
17:       <af:commandLink
18:           rendered=        le.DepartmentId != null}"
19:           text="#{n        partmentName}"
20:           action="           ng_reference.treeDepartmentSelect_action}"
21:           immediate     ue"/>
22:     </af:panelHorizon    >
23:   </f:facet>
24: </af:tree>
```

Line 01 shows that the af:tree control is bound to a tree binding called AllRegions.

Line 02 defines the variable (*var*) name used for each branch of the tree as node. This reference is just like the default "row" variable we use to access the rows of a table binding. The name can be changed, but there is no reason to do so.

Line 03 shows that this tree is in immediate mode. *Immediate mode* means that expanding and collapsing the tree nodes should not cause validation on the screen. The tree will automatically use partial page rendering to update the tree UI without a full page refresh.

Line 04 defines the nodeStamp facet that will loop through every displayed branch in the tree. The binding remembers which nodes are currently visible.

Line 05 defines a container component. Facets (nodeStamp, in this example) can only have one child component. In this case, we need to put a number of output items inside the facet. To allow this, we make a container—af:panelHorizontal—the immediate child of the facet and put everything else inside it. This is a common practice with facets.

Lines 06 and 09 define the node labels for region and country as display items (af:outputText components).

Lines 07, 10, 13, and 18 use the *rendered* attribute of the components to control which component is displayed on which level of the tree. For example, we need to display the region on the top level of the tree. The *rendered* property tests the RegionId property; if it's not null, this is a region node, so the component can be displayed. Notice how we can use expressions such as #{node.RegionName} to access the display attributes of the tree binding. Every display attribute selected in the Tree Binding Editor can be accessed in this way. This is the way that the output on the tree labels is controlled.

> **NOTE**
> *This code uses the principle that all attributes displayed in the tree are available in the single tree binding. This is the reason that you only need one iterator for any number of tree levels.*

Lines 12 and 17 show that you are not restricted to output text items. In this case, two levels of the tree are shown as hyperlinks. Clicking these links executes the associated actions defined in Lines 15 and 20. In this case, the action is to drilldown into an edit form for the selected record.

Cleaning Up Bindings

If a bound item is deleted from the Design view of the visual editor, the corresponding binding will be deleted from the PageDef automatically. When all bindings associated with a particular iterator are removed, JDeveloper will display a dialog (like that shown in the next illustration) asking if it can automatically remove the corresponding iterator binding from the PageDef file. Deleting components from the Source view of the visual editor, however, will bypass the clean-up mechanism and will leave bindings orphaned in the PageDef file.

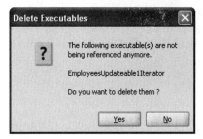

This behavior can be desirable. For example, to create a binding for programmatic purposes, it can be quicker to drag and drop the component onto the page and then delete the UI element, leaving the binding behind. If you take this approach, be sure to delete the component from the source view so that the clean-up process is bypassed.

If you need to clean up bindings manually, open the PageDef file and edit the XML, or use the Structure window to locate the binding and press the DELETE key.

What Is an Iterator?

Data access for attributes in a binding, as well as most operations and method bindings, requires iterators. You can think of an *iterator* as a current record pointer on a collection; for example, the expression #{bindings.EmployeeId.inputValue} actually evaluates to "the Employee Id of whatever record in EmployeesUpdateable1 collection is currently pointed to by the Employees Updateable1Iterator." This link from EmployeeId to EmployeesUpdateable1Iterator is defined in the PageDef file.

In normal circumstances, a particular collection of records would maintain a single iterator to track the *row currency* (record marked as current) in the user interface. However, secondary iterators on the same collection are possible and not uncommon. Specifically this is used to allow one iterator, and therefore components associated with it, to be in Find mode while the other tracks the contents of the view object. We'll use two iterators on the same collection to build the Search screen in Chapter 12.

The primary iterator for a collection is automatically created when binding data to the page in a drag-and-drop operation. The default name is made up of the name of the collection suffixed with the word "Iterator," for example, "EmployeesUpdateable1Iterator." Once an iterator is defined for a collection, any subsequent bindings to attributes, operations, or methods associated with that collection will reuse the same iterator.

Editing the Iterator

Iterators are defined in the PageDef file within the executables section before the bindings section. The sidebar "Why Are Iterators Called 'Executables'?" provides details about this designation.

To examine or edit an iterator, open the PageDef file and locate the iterator's node within the executables section of the Structure window. In the editor, the code associated with this section looks like the following for EmployeesUpdateable1Iterator (without the line numbers):

```
01: <executables>
02:    <iterator id="EmployeesUpdateable1Iterator"
03:             RangeSize="10"
04:             Binds="EmployeesUpdateable1"
05:             DataControl="HRServiceDataControl"/>
06: </executables>
```

Lines 01 and 06 mark the beginning and end of the executables section.

Line 02 defines the iterator and gives the iterator its identifier (`EmployeesUpdateable1Iterator`).

Line 03 declares how many rows should be pulled from the view object into the bindings at one time. This value controls how many rows are displayed in a table that is bound to data managed by the iterator. In this case, the table will display up to ten rows (the default).

Line 04 defines the collection (view object instance) that this iterator works with.

Line 05 completes the definition by indicating which data control supplies the collection named in the *Binds* property (Line 04).

Why Are Iterators Called "Executables"?

If the iterator is a current record pointer, why is it defined in a section called "executables" in the PageDef file?

The executables section defines work that is done when the PageDef file is loaded at runtime. The framework processes each entry in the order in which it appears in the PageDef file. In the case of the iterator, as ADFm processes the definition, it automatically fetches the collection data so that the iterator has something to work with. So, a side effect of executing (or refreshing) the iterator is to execute the query on the underlying view object (when using ADF BC) and put the contents of that query into the bindings object, ready for display on the page. The framework automatically manages fetching from the view object as the user scrolls through the data.

If more than one iterator is defined for a collection, only the first will invoke the side effect of executing the query on the view object.

A single PageDef file may contain multiple iterator definitions, depending on the data sources required to service all of the bindings in the page.

A Note on Range Size   The *RangeSize* property is somewhat like the *Records Fetched* property in Oracle Forms. It defines the number of records to retrieve in the first batch, and the framework handles the fetching of extra batches as required. As mentioned, ten rows is the default value for the RangeSize, and this should be adjusted depending on the requirements of the application. RangeSize supports a magic value of minus 1 (–1), which declares that all rows will be retrieved in the first batch. This is useful for dropdown lists and other cases where all records need to be visible at once. This property value is like the Oracle Forms EXECUTE_QUERY(ALL_RECORDS) built-in.

Making Changes to the Iterator   Once you are familiar with the XML schema syntax, you can edit and create iterators directly in the XML file. You can also use the following more-structured approaches to editing existing definitions:

■ **Using the Property Inspector**   Select the iterator to edit in the Structure window, and the Property Inspector will display all of the iterator properties for editing, as shown in the following illustration:

■ **Using the Iterator Binding Editor**   This is a specialized editor that is invoked for an existing iterator by double clicking the iterator name in the Structure window or by choosing **Properties** from its right-click menu. This editor is useful for new iterators, but is of limited use for editing existing definitions, as it does not expose the key properties such as *RangeSize*.

To create an iterator in the Structure window, on the executables node in the Structure window, select **Insert inside executables | iterator** from the right-click menu. The Iterator Binding Editor displays, as shown in the following illustration (with the nodes expanded to show all available collections):

As shown here, the editing dialog displays all of the available collections in the data control. Select one, provide a name for the iterator, and click OK.

NOTE
When the Iterator Binding Editor is displayed for an existing iterator, it contains a Sort Criteria *tab. This tab can be ignored for ADF BC because sorting is managed for you.*

In the Attribute Binding Editor shown in Figure 8-2, you saw that you can also create an iterator using the New button. This button is available in the other binding editors available for objects in the bindings node.

Controlling Iterator Execution

By default, an iterator will refresh when the user first enters the page. ADFm will then manage the collection when the user carries out actions such as scrolling through a table or inserting and deleting rows.

There are some circumstances, however, when you need to control exactly when (and if) an iterator is refreshed. For example, you call an application module method that recalculates the summary value in a record accessed through the iterator. You need to somehow refresh the iterator to display the updated value.

Iterator execution is controlled by the two optional iterator properties *Refresh* and *RefreshCondition*. We look at what these properties do and what they can be set to in the section "How Can I Control Execution in the ADF Model?"

Types of Iterators

So far, we've explained the plain iterator used to manage a view object collection. If you choose **Insert inside executables** from the right-click menu on the executables node in the Structure window, you'll see four iterator types. These are described in the following table:

Iterator Type	Description
accessorIterator	Accessor iterators give access to secondary (detail) sets of data, based on the selection in a master iterator. These iterators are not needed in ADF Business Components-based applications, since the view link mechanism handles master-detail coordination automatically.
iterator	The plain iterator acts as the current record pointer for a collection (view object instance). This is the type you will normally use.
methodIterator	When a custom method that returns data is bound to a page, a method iterator provides access to the results of that method. It works just like a plain iterator and is created automatically if the return value of a custom method is dragged onto the page. Refreshing a method iterator will cause the associated method to be executed. Method iterators are used to access method call results, regardless of whether the results returned are a collection or a single value.
	Because a method iterator acts just like a plain iterator, user interface elements such as tables and lists can be bound to the results returned from a method call; this type of data source is like basing an Oracle Forms block on a PL/SQL package. Like accessor iterators, method iterators are used frequently with service providers such as EJB, but you will encounter them in ADF BC-based applications if you use custom application module methods or view object methods.
variableIterator	The PageDef file supports the definition of local variables that are not bound to the business service, but rather are a convenient holder for temporary state. This iterator provides access to these variables. We saw the variableIterator in use when we looked at method bindings earlier in the chapter.

In most cases, you will only create iterators implicitly by dragging and dropping or by using one of the binding dialogs; in both cases, the correct type will be created for you.

How Can I Control Execution in the ADF Model?

So far in this chapter, we've been looking at the results of drag-and-drop operations and basic binding. In this section, we'll dig into how the ADF Model can be controlled and extended. As a basis for this investigation, we'll look at how code can be executed as a page is loaded. This particular task touches on all of the key aspects of controlling ADFm.

We'll start by looking at how bound operations or methods can be called when the page loads. For example, the page may need to switch into Enter Query mode when the user navigates to the page. In Oracle Forms, various triggers, such as WHEN-NEW-FORM-INSTANCE, provide the location for this kind of code. Let's see how you would achieve the same thing with ADF.

Another Look at Executables

Everything that we've discussed so far in this chapter has been based around creating bindings in association with user interface elements and the iterators to support that. One thing you may have noticed when you bind a collection onto a page is that the data appears as soon as you navigate to the page. So, although you've just been concerned about creating bound fields, somehow the collection has been populated by the framework automatically.

This automatic population is a default behavior of iterators. Recall that iterators are defined in a section of the PageDef file called executables. Anything defined in the executables section will be executed by the framework when the page is loaded. We'll look at how this process is controlled a little later.

The executables section of the PageDef file can contain either iterators, as we've discussed, or an *invokeAction*, which calls an existing action or method binding defined in the action bindings. The invokeAction executable is created in the Structure window of the PageDef file on the executables node by selecting **Insert inside executables | invokeAction** from the right-click menu. The invokeAction needs to be associated with an existing action (operation) or method binding in the PageDef file. For example, to create an insert form that creates a new record automatically, you would need to create a binding to the Create operation for the relevant iterator, and then create an invokeAction on that Create binding. When you create an invokeAction executable, the following Insert invokeAction dialog will appear; in this illustration, the *Binds* dropdown list shows all of the operations or methods that are already defined in the PageDef file. The *id* field can be set to any string value.

For clarity, adopt a naming convention that clearly identifies the purpose of the invokeAction executable. For example, call the invokeAction that calls Create "invokeCreate."

Controlling the Execution Order

The elements defined in the executables section of the PageDef file will be processed from top to bottom in the order in which they appear in the file. This means that you can control the order of execution by reordering the elements. This can be done in the PageDef file or, more conveniently, by dragging and dropping the elements in the Structure window. An example where ordering might be important is where a custom method is used to set up the context on which a view object query might rely. For example, when drilling down into a detail page, a record key from the calling page has to be passed to a method that customizes the WHERE clause used by the called page.

Clearly, the simple ordering of the elements can provide an amount of control. However, the framework actually offers more flexibility than this. If you inspect an iterator or invokeAction definition, you'll see two properties within the Property Inspector for the elements: *Refresh* and *RefreshCondition*. By default, neither of these properties will exist in the XML code, but the Property Inspector will show the default value of *Refresh* as "ifNeeded." The dropdown list for that property will show the following options:

- **always** This option will invoke the action or refresh the collection of data every time the page is invoked. Page invocation occurs upon the initial navigation to the page or when the user submits the page using a command item.

- **deferred** This setting indicates that the executable should only be invoked if a binding that is associated with it is used in the UI. You might use this mode to prevent the refresh of an iterator when regions of the page are dynamically hidden or displayed using the *rendered* property present on all JSF components.

- **ifNeeded** This value, the default, allows the framework to decide when to refresh the collection or execute the method. When using ADF BC as the service layer, the framework only refreshes the collection or method when it knows changes have been applied to the ADF Model.

- **never** This option stops the framework from calling this executable. You would use this when you're explicitly managing execution from code. (The section "How Do I Write Code Using the ADF Model?" explains this subject further.)

- **prepareModel** This value provides more precise control over when in the life cycle the executable should be invoked. (We will provide an overview of the life cycle later.) An invokeAction with the *refresh* property set to "prepareModel" will be invoked before any changes posted by the user have been applied to the model.

- **prepareModelIfNeeded** This selection refreshes the executable only if the framework has detected that is required. If the refresh is required, then it takes place during the prepareModel phase, just as the prepareModel option does.

- **renderModel** Like the prepareModel option, this option offers more precise control over when the executable is invoked. In this case, any changes made to the ADF Model by the user will have been applied before this invokeAction is called.

- **renderModelIfNeeded** This value also allows the framework to decide if execution is actually required, and if that is the case, executes during renderModel.

In most cases, when using ADF Business Components, the default "ifNeeded" is a sensible *Refresh* value for iterators. The value "ifNeeded" specifies that the refresh of the iterator can take place either during the prepareModel phase or in the renderModel phase as the framework sees fit. (These life cycle phases are explained further later in this chapter.)

However, with invokeAction executables, you should be more explicit about defining the phase in which the method or operation should be executed. The decision here comes down to whether the function you are calling needs access to any incoming changes that the user has just made on the screen. For example, an invokeAction is declared to execute an ExecuteWithParams operation. That operation passes the value of an orderId to populate a collection of order lines. If the user selects another orderId, refreshing the ExecuteWithParams in the prepareModel stage would pass the old orderId to the ExecuteWithParams operation. Instead, if the invokeAction refresh were set to the renderModel stage, the orderId selected by the user would be processed and applied; the new orderId would then be used as the basis for the bind parameter (and the resulting query of order lines).

Refining Execution Further with RefreshCondition

The most powerful feature of the executables' mechanism is the ability to conditionally control the execution. We've explained how both ordering and the *Refresh* property can be used to control when an executable is called or refreshed. *RefreshCondition* adds an "if" dimension to the refresh execution.

In the earlier sections on action and method bindings, we discussed how expressions can be used to define arguments. Expressions can also be used to control execution using the *RefreshCondition* property. For example, here is a fragment of a PageDef that ensures that a particular iterator is always kept in Find mode (Enter Query mode). We'll see this example in action in Chapter 12.

```
<invokeAction
    id="AlwaysFind"
    binds="Find"
    refreshCondition="${! bindings.DeptViewIter.findMode}"/>
```

The Find operation in this case is associated with an iterator `DeptViewIter`. Iterators expose an attribute called *findMode* which returns a boolean value. So in this example, if the iterator is not in Find mode, the *refreshCondition* will evaluate to "true" and the Find action will be invoked.

The conditions used in the expressions can refer to any bound data, or even any valid EL for JSF. Therefore, information held in managed beans or cookies can be used to control execution.

Handling Postback   One condition that deserves special mention is that of page postback. As mentioned briefly in Chapter 5, *postback* is a request from one page to the same page. In a JSF page, all events are handled by posting back to the same page (view). Usually, you will want to carry out an operation when the user first enters the page but not repeat that operation every time a button or link is clicked. In JSF work, it is tricky to detect this situation, even though it is often essential to know, because JSF provides no simple expression that can be used from within the PageDef to distinguish the initial page display from a postback. However, ADF Faces does provide that information through the expression `adfFacesContext.postback`. This is often used in an inverted way, as shown here:

```
<invokeAction id="ExecuteClearQuery"
              Binds="ClearQueryCritera"
              RefreshCondition="${!adfFacesContext.postback}"/>
```

This code declares that the custom method, ClearQueryCriteria, should only be called when postback is false, that is, when the page is initially loaded.

Overriding and Adding to the ADFm Life Cycle

We've shown how executables in the PageDef file can be used to automatically invoke operations and custom methods exposed by the business service, for example, through an ADF BC application module. However, sometimes you need to carry out work that does not involve the ADF Model. An example of this is setting a cookie after login to remember the name of the user who last logged in to the system. You can achieve this by using the extension mechanisms that ADFm supplies in creating a customized life cycle for the page.

NOTE
The example of controlling the ADFm life cycle later in this section is kept very basic to give an idea of the required code. However, the ability to override and customize the ADFm life cycle is extremely powerful, and you will use this ability more and more as you become more proficient at building ADF applications.

The ADFm Life Cycle

As we've seen with the various refresh values for an executable, preparing the bindings for a page proceeds through a fixed set of steps—the *ADFm life cycle*. This life cycle is an abstraction mechanism that allows the same sequence of events to take place no matter what UI technology is used. The ADFm life cycle corresponds quite closely to the JSF page life cycle, as shown in Figure 8-5. This figure also shows how the ADFm life cycle phases map to the refresh options used by executables.

NOTE
Figure 8-5 shows the life cycle used specifically during a postback to a page. This life cycle is truncated when a page is initially loaded, because there are no changes to apply from user input. In this case, a shortened version of the ADFm life cycle also runs with the initContext, prepareModel, and prepareRender squeezed before the RenderResponse phase in the JSF life cycle.

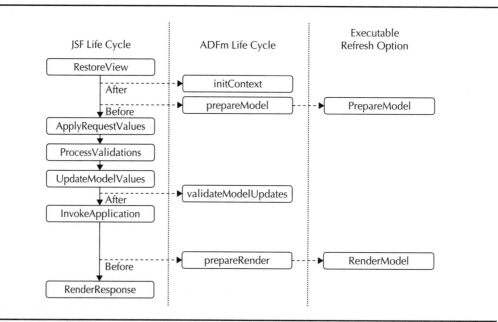

FIGURE 8-5. *The ADF Model life cycle in relation to the JSF life cycle and executable refresh options*

In Figure 8-5, the ADFm life cycle is shown in the context of the JSF life cycle that we introduced in Chapter 5. The dashed lines show at which point each of the ADFm life cycle methods is executed in relation to the JSF life cycle. Likewise, the dashed lines to the Executable Refresh Option column shows how the Refresh option on executables that we discussed earlier relates to the ADFm life cycle. The ADFm life cycle consists of more phases than are actually shown in Figure 8-5; however, the phases shown are the key integration points and have the following functions:

- **initContext** sets up the life cycle.

- **prepareModel** creates the bindings object and adds it to the HTTP request.

- **validateModelUpdates** manages validation errors from the Model layer. For example, an inserted record may violate a primary key constraint. This phase will capture and report that error.

- **prepareRender** is the last phase to execute before the page is displayed.

A useful feature of the ADFm life cycle is that we can customize it on a page-by-page basis. This allows us to add extra functionality that will be called automatically. ADFm offers two ways to add functionality to the life cycle: using a life cycle listener and using a custom page controller.

ADFm Life Cycle Listener   A *life cycle listener* allows you to add code to specific phases of the ADFm life cycle without changing the basic life cycle. A life cycle listener must implement the interface `oracle.adf.controller.v2.lifecycle.PagePhaseListener`. This interface defines two methods—`beforePhase()` and `afterPhase()`—which the life cycle will automatically call before and after each phase, respectively. You can see from Figure 8-5 that you could define code to execute after the prepareRender phase. This code would look something like this:

```
public class CookieSettingListener implements PagePhaseListener
{
  public void beforePhase(PagePhaseEvent event) { }

  public void afterPhase(PagePhaseEvent event)
  {
    if (event.getPhaseId() == Lifecycle.PREPARE_RENDER_ID)
    {
      setCookie();
    }
  }
}
```

Our intention is to call the `setCookie()` method (implementation not shown) in the afterPhase handler for the prepareRender phase in the life cycle, that is, just before the page is displayed to the end user. In this example, no events fire in the beforePhase handler, so the implementation is empty. The standard life cycle process will still occur before the phase; this empty method just fulfills the requirement that methods defined in an interface must be implemented in the class built from the interface. Each of these methods can handle events from each phase of the life cycle. When the framework calls the methods in this class at the appropriate time in the life cycle, it passes in a `PagePhaseEvent` object that represents the phase of the life cycle. As shown in the sample code, this `PagePhaseEvent` object offers a `getPhaseId()` method that indicates the life cycle phase that called the method (in this example, prepareRender).

The listener must be attached to the page life cycle so that the life cycle knows to raise the events. This attachment occurs in the PageDef file for the page that needs the customized life cycle. The top-level element of the PageDef file is the `pageDefintion` element. This element offers a *ControllerClass* property, in which you would indicate the custom listener class to use:

```
<pageDefinition xmlns="http://xmlns.oracle.com/adfm/uimodel"
                version="10.1.3.35.59"
                id="homePageDef"
                Package="book.view.pageDefs"
                ControllerClass="book.view.framework.CookieSettingListener">
```

You would add this reference to any PageDef files that need the same customization.

Custom ADFm Page Controller   The listener approach just described is probably sufficient for most purposes. However, it is also possible to customize the ADFm life cycle by creating a custom page controller subclass from `oracle.adf.controller.v2.lifecycle.PageController`. A custom page controller that emulates the preceding life cycle listener example would look like this:

```
public class HomeSetup extends PageController
{
  public void prepareRender(LifecycleContext context)
  {
    super.prepareRender(context);
    setCookie( );
  }
}
```

In this case, the subclass of the PageContoller only overrides one method—the `prepareRender()` method. The first line of `prepareRender()` calls the superclass's `prepareRender()` method so that the normal action for this phase occurs. Then, the custom code calls the cookie setting method (implementation not shown). The `LifecycleContext` object that is passed into this method provides access to the HTTP request and response, which is usually enough external information for most purposes. As you might expect, if you want code to execute before the life cycle phase, you would place this code before the call to the superclass's method.

CAUTION
Be sure to include the call to the superclass code when you are replacing the life cycle phase. Otherwise, the normal life cycle code will not be called.

You can consult the Javadoc for that class for details about the methods and objects you will use when replacing the page controller. (Press CTRL-MINUS to display the Go To Class dialog, which will help you to locate the Javadoc.) In most cases, you will override the `prepareRender()` method if you want to execute code before the page renders.

You register a custom page controller using the same *ControllerClass* attribute in the `pageDefinition` element of the PageDef file. The framework will understand by the type of code if the class that you specify in this attribute is a listener (implementation of `PagePhaseListener`) or a custom page controller (subclass of `PageController`).

NOTE
The PageController class provides a comprehensive way to customize the life cycle for a page. It is also possible to provide a further level of customization in the form of a custom life cycle. Unlike the custom page controller (shown in the sample), which has to be applied individually to each page, a custom life cycle can be used by all pages. Consult the online help within JDeveloper for information on this. The help topic "Customizing the Oracle ADF Lifecycle for an Application" is a good place to start.

What Are Parameters?

Parameters are another set of elements that can appear in the PageDef file. They provide public API for a page. A common-use case for parameters is when a value needs to be passed to a method in the PageDef file as an argument. For example, a page that displays information for a given stock ticker symbol could define the stock symbol as a PageDef file parameter. The method binding would then refer to the page parameter directly using the syntax `#{bindings.parameterName}`. Unlike variables, parameters can be accessed directly in EL without having to go through an attribute binding. However, as a trade-off, parameters are read-only at runtime.

Populating Parameters

Parameters can be defined from the parameters node in the Structure window for the PageDef file using hard-coded values or EL in their value attribute. A common approach is to map the value of the parameter to the EL expression, which will insert a URL parameter into the value. Here is an example:

```
<parameter id="status"
           value="${param.status}"/>
```

If the page was called with a URL, such as "http://tuhra.com/hr/mypage.jsp?status=open," the status parameter in the PageDef file would evaluate to "open."

Parameters are coded into the URL created from a command link or command button using the `f:param` tag nested inside those items. Alternatively, parameters may be defined in a hard-coded URL that identifies a resource external to an application. For example, you might generate an email as part of your application and require the user to click a link within the email to carry out some action. The combination of URL parameters and parameters within the PageDef file can then be used to set the data context correctly for the page being loaded.

CAUTION
Parameters are not a way to routinely pass context information around the application. JSF-managed beans provide a simpler way to manage such tasks. Restrict your use of PageDef file parameters to application entry points where information needs to be passed in from outside the application.

How Do I Write Code Using the ADF Model?

Much of what needs to be achieved in an ADF application can be handled declaratively through the various bindings and use of Expression Language in those binding definitions, as we have already discussed. For example, conditionally executing a method exposed by an application module or carrying out a task in addition to a bound operation on a button click can all be handled without having to replace the default invocation mechanism. However, it is inevitable that you will need to write code that will interact with the bindings, either in the form of accessing bound data values or manually executing operations and methods.

Access to Data and Methods

When programming with JSF, it is possible to access any managed bean using Expression Language, both in the PageDef file and also from within the code. This maintains a loose coupling between the page, its associated code, and any ADF Model objects that it uses.

Therefore, you can use standard JSF Expression Language to access a bound data value using something like this in a page-backing bean (line numbers added):

```
01:   FacesContext ctx = FacesContext.getCurrentInstance();
02:   Application app = ctx.getApplication();
03:   ValueBinding bind =
      app.createValueBinding("#{bindings.DepartmentName.inputValue}");
04:   String departmentName = (String)bind.getValue(ctx);
```

In JSF terms, this code translates an EL expression into an actual object that can be called from Java.

Lines 02–03 obtain a reference to the JSF `Application` object that is needed to resolve references to EL. This reference is created from the `FacesContext` object created in line 01.

Line 03 shows the `Application` object creating a `ValueBinding` object based on the required EL expression.

Line 04 extracts the underlying value from the `ValueBinding` by calling its `getValue()` method.

You have seen this expression `#{bindings.DepartmentName.inputValue}` already in the expressions that JDeveloper generates for you when dragging and dropping from the Data Control Palette. These four lines of code are the programmatic way to obtain the same data.

More Direct Access to the Bindings

When you implement a JSF page that contains ADF Bindings and you double click a bound command button or command link to create some code, the Bind Action Property dialog will appear, as shown here:

Selecting the *Generate ADF Binding Code* checkbox will set up shortcut access to your data bindings. The backing bean for the page will gain two new methods, getBindings() and setBindings(), and the managed bean definition for the backing bean in the faces-config.xml will be altered to inject the binding object value into your backing bean through the setBindings() method. The result is that you will now have access to the binding object directly in Java without having to use the expression-resolving facilities provided by createValueBinding() (as shown in the preceding code example).

Manually Defining the Bindings Object JDeveloper will only show the Bind Action Property dialog if you attempt to override an existing command component that is bound to a custom method or operation by double clicking the component in the visual editor or selecting **Create Method Binding for Action** from the right-click menu on the component.

In some cases, you will want access to the bindings object without overriding an existing bound component. In this situation, you need to use the following steps to manually configure the managed bean:

1. In the backing bean, for example, CustomerEdit.java, add a private variable called bindings of type oracle.binding.BindingContainer, as follows:

    ```
    private BindingContainer bindings;
    ```

2. Create getBindings() and setBindings() methods by selecting the **Generate Accessors** option from the right-click menu and selecting the bindings checkbox. This action will generate the following code:

    ```
    public BindingContainer getBindings()
    {
      return this.bindings;
    }

    public void setBindings(BindingContainer bindings)
    {
      this.bindings = bindings;
    }
    ```

3. Edit the definition of the managed bean in the faces-config.xml to add the bindings value, as shown in the following code:

    ```
    <managed-bean>
      <managed-bean-name>CustomerEdit</managed-bean-name>
      <managed-bean-class>book.view.backing.CustomerEdit</managed-bean-class>
        <managed-bean-scope>request</managed-bean-scope>
        <managed-property>
          <property-name>bindings</property-name>
          <value>#{bindings}</value>
        </managed-property>
      </managed-bean>
    ```

These steps are identical for any managed bean that needs to access bindings information.

Getting and Setting Attribute Values Using getBindings()

The following code uses the bindings object we just created to access the department name:

```
AttributeBinding deptBinding =
     (AttributeBinding)getBindings().getControlBinding("DepartmentName");
String departmentName = (String)deptBinding.getInputValue();
```

This code is a little simpler than the code shown earlier, although with this code, we need to cast the `ControlBinding` returned by the `getControlBinding()` to an `AttributeBinding`.

CAUTION
Although they might seem similar, the `ValueBinding` and `AttributeBinding` objects are different. ValueBindings are integral to JSF, whereas AttributeBindings are part of ADFm and apply to multiple UI types.

This technique gives us access to all properties of the attribute binding, the most important of which is the underlying value, accessed through the `inputValue()` attribute.

You can similarly set the values of attributes using the `setInputValue()` method. Here is an example:

```
AttributeBinding deptBinding =
     (AttributeBinding)getBindings().getControlBinding("DepartmentName");
deptBinding.setInputValue("Special Projects");
```

Refreshing the UI   When you change the value of a bound attribute in code, you are directly changing the Model layer. For output items, such as `af:outputText`, the new value that you've defined will be displayed (as you would expect) when the page is next rendered. However, for input items, you do not see the value when the page is next rendered, because JSF input components maintain their own version of the bound value and will continue to display that version. For input items to show the changed data immediately, you have to cause them to refresh from the model.

To cause this value refresh, you need to have a reference to the item in the page's backing bean so that you can call methods on the component. If you elected not to have JDeveloper create and manage a backing bean for you, you can create the required class file object and reference to it by selecting the component in the visual editor and clicking the "..." button in the *Binding* property in the Property Inspector. Clicking this button displays the Binding dialog, which allows you to select an existing managed bean to use as the backing bean or to create one if necessary. The dialog also allows you to specify a name for the component in that bean.

After clicking OK in this dialog, JDeveloper will create a component variable in the page-backing bean using the name you have specified and of the appropriate type based on the selected component in the UI. It also generates a getter and setter method for that component, along with the binding reference in the JSF page to the component in the backing bean.

CAUTION
The "binding" property supported by JSF components has nothing to do with the bindings object that we've been discussing in this chapter. "Binding" in this context means the binding of a component definition in the UI to a component reference in the page backing bean. This component reference can then be used to programmatically change the UI object. For example, you can set the "rendered" property from code to display or hide the component.

Once you have created a reference to the object that represents the input field, you can call its `resetValue()` method to force it to refresh its internal state from the new model value. So to extend our earlier example with the `DepartmentName`:

```
AttributeBinding deptBinding =
        (AttributeBinding)getBindings().getControlBinding("DepartmentName");
deptBinding.setInputValue("Special Projects");
this.getDepartmentNameField().resetValue();
```

NOTE
The resetValue() method is supported only by the ADF Faces components, not the Sun RI components. However, in JSF version 1.2, it will become a standard part of the JSF API and will be available for any component set.

Accessing PageDef File Parameters
You can access parameters directly from the bindings object that is generated into the page backing file and obtained through the `getBindings()` method. The only twist here is that you need to cast the binding up to an `oracle.adf.model.DCBindingContainer` (see the sidebar "Which Binding Container Do I Use?"), which supports the `findParameter()` method. An example follows:

```
DCBindingContainer dcBindings = (DCBindingContainer)getBindings();
DCParameter param = dcBindings().findParameter("deptno");
String paramValue = (String)param.getValue();
```

Note that the exact return type of `param.getValue()` depends on what is stored in the parameter. Unlike variables, you do not declare the type of parameters up front, so if you map an object into a parameter using EL, the type of the parameter will be the type of that object; it is your responsibility to cast the return from `getValue()` correctly.

Executing Methods and Operations
Now that we have mastered basic access to get and set bound attributes, what about calling methods? This is similar, and it uses the same `getBindings()` method as a starting point. The method or operation is retrieved into an `OperationBinding` object using a lookup-by name, and then its `execute()` method is called, as shown here for the First operation:

```
BindingContainer bindings = getBindings();
OperationBinding operationBinding =
    bindings.getOperationBinding("First");
Object result = operationBinding.execute();
```

> ### Which Binding Container Do I Use?
> When you are writing code using these binding classes, you may notice import insight displaying two alternatives for many of the classes. For example, `oracle.adf.model.BindingContainer` and `oracle.binding.BindingContainer`.
>   The classes in the oracle.binding package make up the generic data-binding APIs. The classes in the `oracle.adf.model` package extend the generic classes and add extra functionality to support some of the additional features found in ADF. In most cases, it is best to use the `oracle.binding.*` versions; if you need the extra functionality of the ADF-specific types, you can cast as required. The `BindingContainer` class itself is an interface, and `DCBindingContainer` is a concrete implementation of it. You would generally code to the interface unless you need a capability only found in the specific implementation, such as `findParameter()` in `DCBindingContainer`.

When you choose to override a method call by double clicking a command item bound to a method, the previously shown code will be generated into the backing bean for you. Of course, a single command button could be coded to call multiple operations, looking each up by name and executing as required.

Method Results   You will note in the example used to show how to execute an operation that the `execute()` call returns an `Object` type. If the method that you are calling returns a value, you will need to cast the object to the correct type. If the method or operation you are calling does not return a value, you can ignore this value.

Setting Method Arguments   In many cases, a method that is called programmatically will have its arguments set in the PageDef file, either as bindings to input fields or as EL expressions. However, in some cases, you will want to explicitly set the argument values from code.

You could, of course, add the data into the relevant PageDef file variables using the methods we just discussed, but there is a simpler way. The `oracle.adf.model` version of `OperationBinding` exposes a `getParamsMap()` method that returns a `Map`, allowing you to set the values of arguments using the `put()` method of the `Map` interface. Here is an example that sets an argument (`searchTerm`) on a method called `findDepartmentManagerId`:

```
OperationBinding operationBinding =
    getBindings().getOperationBinding("findDepartmentManagerId");
Map params = operationBinding.getParamsMap();
params.put("searchTerm","Sales");
Number deptManager = operationBinding.execute();
```

This chapter has explained one of the key moving parts of any ADF-based application. Although you can do a lot with drag-and-drop operations within the IDE, they are never enough. It is important that you are comfortable both with editing the metadata and writing the code to interact with it. This really is the key knowledge required to build effective ADF-based applications.

PART
II

Developing the Application

We learn by example and by direct experience
because there are real limits
to the adequacy of verbal instruction.

—Malcolm Gladwell (1963–),
Blink: The Power of Thinking Without Thinking (2005)

CHAPTER
9

Your First JSF

By nature, men are nearly alike;
by practice, they get to be wide apart.

—Confucius (551–479 B.C.), *The Confucian Analects*

An ounce of practice is worth more than tons of preaching.

—Mahatma Gandhi (1869–1948)

his part of the book continues your learning process by providing hands-on practices where you experience the technologies, languages, frameworks, and concepts introduced in Part I. This chapter builds on the introductions to JavaServer Faces technology in Chapters 1, 3, and 5 and provides a hands-on practice that creates a simple, two-page, non-data-aware JSF application. Chapters 10–14 build another simple application that interacts with the database. Chapter 10 discusses basic application design principles, as well as the design of the sample application, and gets you started by creating the application workspace and its projects. Chapters 11–13 prepare the data model and build templates, home pages, a menu system, a query-browse page, and an edit page for adding and updating records. Chapter 14 discusses security concepts and provides a hands-on practice to add login and logout pages as well as to define users and roles for the application.

In all chapters in Part II, the hands-on practices assume that you have read the material in Part I. Part II provides more detailed discussions of some topics along with the steps for creating the application. The guiding principle in this part of the book is that you will absorb these detailed concepts better if you use them right away in code that builds an application. The applications created in this book do not provide all possible techniques you will ever need when creating a real-world application. They do make you think about how to perform basic web development tasks in JDeveloper 10g, but to master the basic concepts, you will need to solve various programming problems in a production development effort. The hands-on practices also point you towards external resources that can be useful when you are stuck in a programming situation.

Although the chapters in this part of the book illustrate concepts from Part I, they also introduce new topics. As mentioned in the Introduction, merely reading the text in these chapters will not benefit you as much as reading the text and following the steps in JDeveloper to create the applications.

The JSF coding example that dominates this chapter provides annotated examples of concepts discussed in Chapter 5. In addition, woven into the JSF discussions in this chapter are introductions to some other languages required for J2EE web development using this technology stack. After developing a simple, two-page application, the discussion and hands-on practice at the end of this chapter explains how to centralize messages in message bundle files.

TIP
The Introduction section "Ensuring Success with the Hands-on Practices" provides some advice about how to handle errors and solve problems that may occur during this work.

Hands-on Practice: Create a JSF Login and JSF Home Page

This hands-on practice shows how you can create a pair of simple JSF pages that emulate login and home page screens. This is really just an enhanced version of the standard "Hello World" application you would code when learning any new language.

To allow the example to focus on JSF concepts, this application does not connect to a database or pay much attention to real-world security needs. You will build this application to implement the following features:

- **A login page** with user name and password fields marked as required.
- **Validation** of the user name and password fields. Both are required, and can be from one to 20 characters long. The password must be "JSF." (The required password is hard-coded in the application, although it would never be hard-coded in a real-world application.) Error messages are displayed for invalid or missing entries.
- **Additional logic** on the login page to display the password after three unsuccessful attempts. (Again, you would never code a real-world application to show a password.)
- **A login button** that submits the form to the server, which will validate the data and pass control to the home page if validation succeeds.
- **A home page** that displays the user name and the number of login attempts.
- **A logout button** on the home page that returns to the login page and removes the password.

Developing these pages consists of the following phases:

I. Create the application workspace and project

II. Diagram the page flow

III. Create the login and home pages

IV. Add components to the login page

- Add the container components
- Add the form components
- Test the page

V. Add components to the home page

- Add ADF Faces components
- Set the component properties and test the page

VI. Add navigation and validation logic to the application

- Add the navigation and validation code
- Test the validation and navigation logic

As with all practices in this book, sample code and code snippets for long code examples are available on the websites mentioned in the "Websites for Sample Code" section of the Introduction.

 NOTE
Although this section does not use database data, it assumes that you have read the installation notes and installed JDeveloper as mentioned in the Introduction section "Preparing for the Hands-on Practices."

I. Create the Application Workspace and Project

In this phase of the practice, you create the JDeveloper code containers—an application workspace and projects.

1. Open JDeveloper using the shortcut that points to jdeveloper.exe in the JDEV_HOME directory.

   Additional Information: If you have not created a shortcut, create one now for the jdeveloper.exe file in JDEV_HOME. As mentioned in the Introduction, *JDEV_HOME* is the operating system directory into which you installed JDeveloper.

2. On the Applications node in the Navigation window, select **New Application** from the right-click menu. The Create Application dialog will appear, as shown here (although the *Application Package Prefix* and *Application Template* fields may contain values from a previously created application):

3. Fill in the *Application Name* as "LoginJSF," and leave the default directory name. Change the *Application Package Prefix* to "login" and the *Application Template* to "No Template [All Technologies]."

   Additional Information: The "*No Template [All Technologies]*" option creates a project that is not assigned any specific *technology* (also called "*technology scope*")—a selection of libraries oriented to a specific type of development, such as ADF BC and JSF. Some technology scope selections create specific project names in specific directories. However, if you use the "No Template [All Technologies]" selection, JDeveloper will prompt you for a project name and directory. We will add technologies in another step so that you can see how the process works. This selection is useful for demonstration purposes, such as this simple application, but for production applications, you would select a template that contains projects with specific technologies, such as ADF Business Components.

4. Click OK. The Create Project dialog will appear. Enter the project name as "ViewController." The directory name will be rewritten to include the new project name. Leave this directory name, and click OK. The application workspace and project will appear in the navigator. Notice that no files appear under the ViewController project.

5. Associating technologies with a project is an optional step, but it allows JDeveloper to further filter selections in the New Gallery. This step is usually performed automatically when you select an application template. Since we chose not to use a template, we now need to associate technologies with this project. Double click the ViewController project to open the Project Properties dialog, and select the Technology Scope node, as shown next.

6. Notice that no technologies are selected because no template was selected. This means that all technologies will be available in the New Gallery. However, we'd like to have the list in the New Gallery filtered down to only the applicable items. Double click JSF in the *Available Technologies* text area. This action will move JSF to the *Selected Technologies* area. It will also move the Java and JSP and Servlets technologies, both of which are required for JSF development.

7. Click OK. Click Save All (in the JDeveloper main toolbar).

Additional Information: Notice in the navigator that a Web Content node appeared under the ViewController project. This node contains a WEB-INF node for *faces-config.xml* (the *application configuration resource*, also called *application configuration file*) and *web.xml* (the web module deployment descriptor introduced in Chapter 2). The Web Content node also contains a WEB-INF\lib node that holds the jsf-impl.jar file (the library of all JSF components and supporting files).

What Did You Just Do? You just created the JDeveloper application workspace that organizes the projects you are working on. You also created the project that is used for deployment of application files. For this example, you just needed a single project, so you used the "No Template" option when creating the application workspace. This option does not assign technology scopes to the project, although all technology scopes are still available. Since you wanted to display a filtered New Gallery list, you added the JSF technology and its required parent technologies to the project. It is time to look at the files that have been created: faces-config.xml and web.xml.

faces-config.xml

Adding the JSF technology to the project properties created the application configuration resource, faces-config.xml. Open faces-config.xml in the editor (on the ViewController node in the navigator, select **Open JSF Navigation** from the right-click menu). Click the Source tab. Other than the XML definition tags at the beginning of the file, this file contains an empty root node, faces-config, as shown here (the line numbers do not appear in the Code Editor):

```
01: <?xml version="1.0" encoding="windows-1252"?>
02: <!DOCTYPE faces-config PUBLIC
03:   "-//Sun Microsystems, Inc.//DTD JavaServer Faces Config 1.1//EN"
04:   "http://java.sun.com/dtd/web-facesconfig_1_1.dtd">
05: <faces-config xmlns="http://java.sun.com/JSF/Configuration">
06:
07: </faces-config>
```

- **Lines 01–04** define this file as a specific type of XML file (faces-config) and reference the Document Tag Definition. As mentioned in Chapter 4, a *Document Tag Definition (DTD)* identifies the tag set available to the document. DTDs contain the names of the tag elements and a list of available attributes for each tag.

- **Lines 05 and 07** declare the root element for the file, faces-config. All other elements will be contained inside this root element.

NOTE
You can turn line numbers on or off in the Code Editor by selecting **Toggle Line Numbers** *from the right-click menu in the left-hand margin.*

web.xml

JDeveloper generates the web.xml file automatically when you create a web project or associate the project with the web technology scope (such as JSF or JSP). The entire web.xml file that is created by default is shown next. As before, the line numbers do not appear in the actual file.

```
01: <?xml version = '1.0' encoding = 'windows-1252'?>
02: <web-app xmlns:xsi="http://www.w3.org/2001/XMLSchema-instance"
    xsi:schemaLocation="http://java.sun.com/xml/ns/j2ee
    http://java.sun.com/xml/ns/j2ee/web-app_2_4.xsd" version="2.4"
    xmlns="http://java.sun.com/xml/ns/j2ee">
```

```
03:     <description>Empty web.xml file for Web Application</description>
04:     <servlet>
05:       <servlet-name>Faces Servlet</servlet-name>
06:       <servlet-class>javax.faces.webapp.FacesServlet</servlet-class>
07:       <load-on-startup>1</load-on-startup>
08:     </servlet>
09:     <servlet-mapping>
10:       <servlet-name>Faces Servlet</servlet-name>
11:       <url-pattern>/faces/*</url-pattern>
12:     </servlet-mapping>
13:     <session-config>
14:       <session-timeout>35</session-timeout>
15:     </session-config>
16:     <mime-mapping>
17:       <extension>html</extension>
18:       <mime-type>text/html</mime-type>
19:     </mime-mapping>
20:     <mime-mapping>
21:       <extension>txt</extension>
22:       <mime-type>text/plain</mime-type>
23:     </mime-mapping>
24:   </web-app>
```

This code defines the following elements:

- **Lines 01 and 02** define this file as XML and start the root element (web-app) that encloses the other elements in this file.

- **Line 03** provides the optional description element that explains the contents of the file.

- **Lines 04–08** associate a name, "Faces Servlet," with the FacesServlet class file. This file is used to process JSF files.

- **Lines 09–12** direct the web server to send requests containing the /faces/ virtual directory to the Faces servlet for processing.

- **Lines 13–15** describe session parameters for this application. In this case, the timeout is set to 35 minutes.

- **Lines 16–23** define two MIME mappings that direct the web server to treat files with extensions html and txt as specific MIME types—text/html and text/plain, respectively. MIME types are introduced in Chapter 2.

Normally, you do not need to modify this file, but if you want to add or change elements in this file, you use the Code Editor that is now open. You can also interact with this file using the Web Application Deployment Descriptor editor, shown next.

Web Application Deployment Descriptor

- General
- Context Initialization
- Filters
- Filter Mappings
- Listeners
- Servlets/JSPs
  - Faces Servlet
- Servlet Mappings
- MIME Mappings
- Tag Libraries
- JSP Property Groups
- Welcome File Lists
- Locale Encoding Mapping Lists
- Message Destinations
- Message Destination Refs
- Resource Environment Refere
- Resource References
- Security Constraints
- Login Configuration
- Security Roles
- Environment Entries

Faces Servlet

General | Initialization Parameters | Security

Servlet Name: Faces Servlet

◉ Servlet Class: javax.faces.webapp.FacesServlet

○ JSP File:

Tool Support

Display Name:

Description:

☑ Load This Servlet When the Web Application is Started

Positive Integer Specifying Load Order (Optional): 1

New... | Delete | Help | OK | Cancel

On the web.xml node in the Applications Navigator, select **Properties** from the right-click menu to access this editor.

II. Diagram the Page Flow

Since this application contains only two pages, you will define a very simple page flow. This phase will demonstrate how to design the page flow in the JSF Navigation Diagram before adding any code for the pages. The application you develop in Chapters 11–14 will demonstrate a slightly more complex page flow, but for this example, you only need navigation from the login page to the home page and from the home page back to the login page.

1. Open the faces-config.xml file, if it is not already open (on the ViewController project node in the Applications Navigator, select **Open JSF Navigation** from the right-click menu). If the file is open, click the Diagram tab to display the empty diagram page.

TIP
You can also open the JSF Navigation Diagram by double clicking the faces-config.xml file in the navigator (under Web Content\WEB-INF).

2. Drag a JSF Page from the Component Palette to the diagram. (If the Component Palette is not visible, select it from the View menu.) After you drop it onto the page, the name will

become editable. Change the name to "login" and press ENTER. JDeveloper will add a .jsp file extension and a "/" prefix, so the page icon will appear as follows:

Additional Information: The icon appears with a yellow alert triangle, indicating that no file has been associated with this diagram element.

3. Click the Source tab to examine the code in faces-config.xml. Notice that nothing has been added since you looked before, because no file has been linked to the diagramed page element. You are only interacting with the diagram in design mode. Click the Diagram tab again.

4. Drop another JSF Page from the Component Palette to the right of the login.jsp symbol. Enter the name as "home" and press ENTER. As before, JDeveloper will add a .jsp extension and "/" prefix to the file name.

5. In the Diagram view of the faces-config.xml file, select JSF Navigation Case from the Component Palette, click the login.jsp symbol, and click the home.jsp symbol to draw the navigation case line. Click the navigation case name, and change it to "login." Press ENTER. JDeveloper will add a dash as a prefix.

Additional Information: *Navigation cases* define the flow of control from one page to another. Chapter 11 explains more about navigation cases. Navigation cases are named "success" by default, but it is a best practice to rename them so that you can more easily distinguish between them within your code.

6. Under the navigation case line, draw another navigation case from home.jsp to login.jsp in the same way. Name the navigation case "logout."

7. Drag the center of the new navigation line straight down to create right-angle lines. The diagram should now appear as follows:

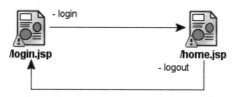

TIP
You can also add drawing points by holding SHIFT and dragging a point on the line. Remove these points by holding SHIFT and clicking the point. Experiment with these techniques now to see how they work. Then restore the diagram so it appears as shown before.

8. Notice that the navigation cases are also displayed in the Structure window.

9. Click Save All.

What Did You Just Do?   You used the JSF Navigation Diagram to depict the two pages and the flows between them. This example application starts with page design. Alternatively, you could start by coding the (.jsp) page files and then work out the navigation diagram. The finished application will include a page design diagram, where each page symbol has an associated page file. It doesn't matter whether you create the page file code or diagram the pages first. In fact, since design and development are often performed iteratively, you will probably find yourself working in both ways to complete an application.

Some code was added to faces-config.xml, so it is worthwhile taking a quick look at it.

Application Configuration Resource (faces-config.xml)

Click the Source tab of the faces-config.xml file. You will see the following listing inside the tags shown earlier (again, without the line numbers):

```
06: <navigation-rule>
07:    <from-view-id>/login.jsp</from-view-id>
08:    <navigation-case>
09:      <from-outcome>login</from-outcome>
10:      <to-view-id>/home.jsp</to-view-id>
11:    </navigation-case>
12: </navigation-rule>
13: <navigation-rule>
14:    <from-view-id>/home.jsp</from-view-id>
15:    <navigation-case>
16:      <from-outcome>logout</from-outcome>
17:      <to-view-id>/login.jsp</to-view-id>
18:    </navigation-case>
19: </navigation-rule>
```

The first `navigation-rule` element (lines 06–12) specifies that navigation flows from login.jsp to home.jsp if the outcome is "login" (the name you assigned to the navigation case in the diagram). You can define when you want the navigation to occur by setting the outcome string in backing bean code or in the *action* property of a command button or link.

The second `navigation-rule` element (lines 13–19) specifies flow from home.jsp to login.jsp if the backing bean or the action property indicates "logout." The `from-view-id` and `to-view-id` elements identify the start and end of the navigation.

III. Create the Login and Home Pages

You are now ready to create the JSP files. You can run the Create JSF JSP Wizard from the New Gallery to create a JSP page file, and add that file to the JSF Navigation Diagram afterwards. Alternatively, you can start the Create JSF JSP Wizard from the JSF Navigation Diagram by double clicking a JSF page symbol that has no page file associated with it (and displays a yellow triangle icon). You can code JSP files in two styles: the JSP page and the JSP document. This hands-on practice, and the others in this book, uses the JSP page style. Since it is better to use one style throughout an application, it is worthwhile discussing these two choices at this point.

JSP Page and JSP Document

The *JSP page* is a file with a .jsp extension that contains both HTML tags and JSP-oriented tags. It is the traditional style used for JSP files. The benefit of this file type is that it allows you to use HTML tags, which you can display and design in an HTML editor such as Dreamweaver. JDeveloper also provides HTML editing and viewing capabilities, including a formatting toolbar that helps you enter HTML tags in a visual way.

The *JSP document* is a file with a .jspx extension that contains only well-formed XML code (mentioned in Chapter 4). In this case, *well-formed code* means that all start tags have corresponding end tags and all tag elements are named with lowercase names. Although some browsers can interpret HTML tags without closing tags, XML parsers are stricter than browsers about requiring well-formed code.

JDeveloper provides a way to view JSP document code in a visual way and to edit it using the Property Inspector and some drag-and-drop functions. However, other tools such as Dreamweaver may not be able to interpret the XML tags you use in a visual way.

Should I Use a .jsp or a .jspx File?   You can use either JSP pages or JSP documents for creating JSP code that contains JSF tags. However, ADF Faces does not rely on HTML. In fact, it wraps most of the HTML you would normally write for formatting the page into its components. Therefore, you do not code as much, if any, HTML and so the separation of HTML and JSP tags that a JSP page offers is not as important. Page design consists more of selecting which ADF Faces tags to use and of setting their properties using the Property Inspector. Those tags will draw major areas of the page without the requirement for HTML design.

In addition, HTML is appropriate only for users who run your application in a web browser. If they run the application in a wireless device or a TELNET display device, HTML would be ineffective, because these display devices require a different markup set. JSF ADF Faces tags are portable between display devices if you do not use HTML. Therefore, if you know you need to support multiple display device types (or think you will in the future), you would avoid the use of HTML tags.

Whether your application will support multiple display devices is still not a firm decision point for using either JSP pages or JSP documents because you can code both JSP pages and JSP documents without HTML. However, it is more difficult to write HTML within a JSP document, and selecting this type as a standard may help enforce portability. It is a natural choice for files you will be editing only in JDeveloper, because JDeveloper is built to help you lay out and maintain JSF tags and ADF Faces in a visual way. Other HTML editing tools support layout with JSP pages better, and if you will need to design the page using a tool other than JDeveloper, a JSP page is a better choice.

NOTE
If you use JSP documents and decide that your application will only support HTML web browsers, you can embed HTML inside a JSP document by enclosing it inside the f:verbatim tag.

Why Do We Use JSP Pages in This Book?   As you may have gathered from the preceding discussion, the choice of whether to use JSP pages or JSP documents is almost arbitrary. No compelling reasons exist for using either type for any application, especially in applications that will only support an HTML display device (web browser). The *Oracle ADF Developer's Guide* (available in the JDeveloper Help system and as a separate file from otn.oracle.com) promotes the use of JSP documents.

This book shows all examples in the JSP page (.jsp) style because it is more universal to all editors. In addition, the applications you develop in this part of the book target users who are only running HTML. That said, we demonstrate the best practice of creating well-formed code and minimizing the use of HTML so that support for other display devices will be possible in the future. For example, instead of using HTML tables to lay out a set of objects on the screen, we use the powerful layout capabilities of the ADF Faces container components.

NOTE
If you use the Create JSF JSP Wizard to create a JSP file of either type, the wizard will preload html, head, and body tags, as shown later in this practice. If you then drop an ADF Faces component onto that page, JDeveloper will convert the HTML tags to their equivalent ADF Faces tags—adf:html, adf:head, and adf:body, respectively. At that point, the JSP file becomes an XML file, regardless of the extension (.jsp or .jspx).

Create the JSP Pages
The following steps create files corresponding to the symbols you dropped onto the diagram.

1. Be sure the Diagram tab of the JSF Navigation Diagram is visible. Double click the /login.jsp page icon. The Create JSF JSP Wizard will open. Click Next if the Welcome page appears.

TIP
You can select the "Skip this Page Next Time" checkbox on the Welcome page of any wizard to specify that it will not be displayed the next time you start that wizard. You can still return to the Welcome page in any wizard by clicking the Back button on the second page of the dialog.

2. On the JSP File page, ensure that the *File Name* is "login.jsp," and select the *Type* as "JSP Page (*.jsp)" (the default).

NOTE
Notice (but do not select) the "Add Mobile Support" checkbox at the bottom of this page. This allows you to configure the file to use libraries that support a wireless (PDA) or TELNET client in case the file needs to be displayed on such a device.

3. Click Next. On the Component Binding page, select "Automatically Expose UI Components in a New Managed Bean," and leave the default in *Name* as "backing_login" and in *Class* as "Login." Change *Package* from its default (application package plus "backing" package) to "login.view.backing." This will allow us to place other files in the view package if needed but still keep the backing beans in a separate package (view.backing).

Additional Information: The backing bean containing a private class variable and accessors for each component on this page is created from this dialog selection, but you can also create it later and associate it with the JSP file using the Overview tab (Managed Beans page) of the faces-config.xml file. The backing bean will also house the event methods for buttons and other logic needed to process the page.

NOTE
*You can write the code for more than one page inside a single
managed bean. Some developers prefer this style because it allows for
a centralized point for all action code.*

4. Click Next to display the Tag Libraries page. Be sure the ADF Faces libraries (Cache, Components, and HTML) and two JSF libraries (Core and HTML) appear in the *Selected Libraries* area (move them if they do not).

5. Click Next to display the HTML Options page. In *Title* enter "Login". This value will be written into the HTML `title` tag in the JSP page heading section. When you run the JSP file, this title displays in the browser's window title.

6. Click Next and then click Finish to create the JSP file. Click Save All.

   Additional Information: The JSP file will open in the visual editor. Expanding the nodes in the Application Navigator will display the login.jsp file and its backing bean file, Login.java, as shown here:

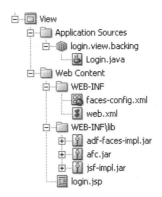

7. In the Diagram tab of the faces-config.xml file, notice that the yellow information triangle icon for login.jsp has disappeared, indicating that a real JSP page file has been associated with this symbol.

8. Double click the /home.jsp symbol on the diagram to start the process again for the home page. When you reach the Component Binding page, change *Package* to "login.view .backing" (you can select it from the pulldown that appears when you click this field).

9. On the HTML Options page, in *Title* enter "Home" and click Finish. The file will be created and will be visible in the navigator as well as in the visual editor.

10. Click Save All.

What Did You Just Do?   You used the JSF Navigation Diagram to create two JSP page files. The process of creating each JSP file linked it to a backing bean, which will hold processing logic and data access logic for the page. It is useful to pause and take a brief look at the contents and style of code in one of the JSP files (the other contains similar elements), the application configuration resource, and the backing bean file.

JSP File

The home.jsp file should already be open in the visual editor. If it is not, double click its node in the Application Navigator. This view of the file shows the visual elements and represents some of the HTML elements on the page. At this point, you have not added anything to the page, but you will see a red, dotted rectangle on the page. Hold the mouse cursor over one of the lines, and you should see the hint shown on the right.

This hint identifies the dotted line as a form element from a tag library aliased as "h." Therefore, this is a JSF HTML form tag. This tag works similarly to a standard HTML form (described in Chapter 5), because it submits values in its child controls (for example, input fields or pulldown lists). Now click the Source tab. You will see code like the following (without the line numbers):

```
01: <!DOCTYPE HTML PUBLIC "-//W3C//DTD HTML 4.01 Transitional//EN"
02:                    "http://www.w3.org/TR/html4/loose.dtd">
03: <%@ page contentType="text/html;charset=windows-1252"%>
04: <%@ taglib uri="http://java.sun.com/jsf/html" prefix="h"%>
05: <%@ taglib uri="http://java.sun.com/jsf/core" prefix="f"%>
06: <%@ taglib uri="http://xmlns.oracle.com/adf/faces" prefix="af"%>
07: <%@ taglib uri="http://xmlns.oracle.com/adf/faces/html" prefix="afh"%>
08: <f:view>
09:   <html>
10:     <head>
11:       <meta http-equiv="Content-Type"
12:             content="text/html; charset=windows-1252"/>
13:       <title>Home</title>
14:     </head>
15:     <body><h:form binding="#{backing_home.form1}"
                     id="form1"></h:form></body>
16:   </html>
17: </f:view>
18:<%-- oracle-jdev-comment:auto-binding-backing-bean-name:backing_home--%>
```

The Structure window displays the hierarchy of the tags in this file, as shown:

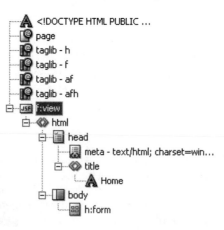

This JSF code stub contains the following elements:

- **Lines 01–02** identify the page as an HTML file and specify its Document Tag Definition, loose.dtd (called "HTML 4.01 Transitional"), and the HTML version. *HTML Transitional* defines tags that can be used until a new version of HTML is available. You use it when you need support for special presentation elements and attributes.

- **Line 03** identifies the MIME type of the file.

- **Lines 04–07** declare the tag libraries (JSF HTML, JSF Core, ADF Faces Core, and ADF Faces HTML) and their namespace prefixes—h, f, af, and afh, respectively. Tag names will start with the prefix, for example, `f:view` in line 08 represents the view tag in the ADF Faces Core library.

- **Lines 08 and 17** define the JSF tag container (`f:view`) used for all the other elements in the page. This tag identifies the file as a JSF page.

- **Lines 09 and 16** declare the HTML page boundaries. The `html` element is the top-level container for HTML tags.

- **Lines 10 and 14** identify the HTML page heading area. The heading will typically include page-level definitions, such as JavaScript, and links to cascading style sheets, as well as the page `title` and `meta` tags.

- **Lines 11–12** define a `meta` tag that again identifies the content of the page as HTML (for the browser this time). Other `meta` tags can supply keywords from which web search engines build their indexes and links to your page.

- **Line 13** defines the text that appears in the title bar of the browser window. In some operating systems, such as Microsoft Windows, the window title also appears as the label of the open window in the taskbar.

- **Line 15** starts the HTML body and defines a JSF HTML form tag. This `h:form` tag specifies the name of the component. It also uses Expression Language (described later) to define the binding to the component in the backing bean (referenced by "backing_home" here and in the faces-config.xml file). In addition, this line names the form ("form1").

- **Line 18** is a JSP comment line used at design time only. It identifies the backing bean name that is associated with this page in the faces-config.xml file. This line declares that JDeveloper should update the backing bean's members when the *Id* property for an element in the JSP changes or when you add or delete components in the page. You will see this automatic renaming process in action later on.

TIP
You can use several methods to view help for a code element in JDeveloper. For Java files, position the cursor in a class name or method name and select **Go to Javadoc** *from the right-click menu.* **Go to Declaration** *in that same menu shows you where the code element is defined (master class or variable declaration).* **Quick Javadoc** *in the right-click menu displays a popup window containing an excerpt from the class's Javadoc. For non-Java sources (such as the faces-config.xml or JSP files), press* F1 *when the cursor is positioned in the element and the Help window will load with applicable reference material.*

Application Configuration Resource (faces-config.xml)

The faces-config.xml file was automatically modified when you created the JSP files so that it contains references to the backing beans. Adding a reference to an application file is known as *registering* the file to the application. At this point in the development of the sample application, we have registered two backing beans with the application. Click the Source tab for the faces-config .xml file. You will see that JDeveloper added the following (without the line numbers):

```
20:    <managed-bean>
21:      <managed-bean-name>backing_login</managed-bean-name>
22:      <managed-bean-class>login.view.backing.Login</managed-bean-class>
23:      <managed-bean-scope>request</managed-bean-scope>
24:      <!--oracle-jdev-comment:managed-bean-jsp-link:1login.jsp-->
25:    </managed-bean>
26:    <managed-bean>
27:      <managed-bean-name>backing_home</managed-bean-name>
28:      <managed-bean-class>login.view.backing.Home</managed-bean-class>
29:      <managed-bean-scope>request</managed-bean-scope>
30:      <!--oracle-jdev-comment:managed-bean-jsp-link:1home.jsp-->
31:    </managed-bean>
```

Each page contains a similar managed-bean entry, as described here for the login.jsp page:

- **Lines 20 and 25** surround a managed (backing) bean declaration. JDeveloper added this entry because you specified in the wizard that the login.jsp file would use a backing bean for its data and logic.

- **Line 21** defines the name of the bean (backing_login) that you specified in the JDeveloper Create JSF JSP Wizard. This name will be used as a prefix when you refer to the elements inside the backing bean. For example, to access the form1 element in the backing bean for the login.jsp file, you would use the token `backing_login.form1`.

- **Line 22** specifies the fully qualified class name for this backing bean.

- **Line 23** declares the *scope*, that is, how long the bean will be retained in memory. The sidebar "About Scope" briefly describes the available scope values.

- **Line 24** is a comment JDeveloper uses to define that this backing bean is linked to the JSP file. When you change a name (*Id* property) of an element in the JSP file, JDeveloper rewrites the backing bean so that its variables and accessor methods use the new name. This comment corresponds to the special comment described earlier for the JSP file.

- **Lines 26–31** follow the same pattern to declare the backing bean for the home page.

The Backing Bean (Login.java)

The faces-config.xml file registers the backing bean (managed bean), Login.java, that is used to hold code for the JSP file, login.jsp. The Home.java file is registered similarly for the home.jsp file. The contents of the Login.java file follow. As before, line numbers appear only in this listing. Expand the Application Sources\login.view.backing node in the navigator, and double click the Login.java file if you want to follow along in the Code Editor. (In order to see all lines, you may need to expand any collapsed structures using the "+" signs in the editor's margin.)

About Scope

The *scope setting* for a bean instance (or variable) determines how long that element will remain in memory. The JSF framework offers three scopes: request, session, and application. The *request scope* signifies that the bean will be retained in memory only for the HTTP request and response; the data held in the bean will not be available after that time. In the *session scope*, the bean will be retained across requests for the same client session. When the client disconnects (logs out) or times out, the bean will be destroyed. The *application scope* setting retains the bean across client sessions. This setting is good for beans that need to hold globally available data. In addition to the standard JSF scopes, ADF offers a *process scope*, which is retained across pages. It is a longer scope than request scope but shorter than session scope, because process scope ends when a new window is opened in the same session. Therefore, process scope is active only for a series of requests that share a window.

```
01: package view.view.backing;
02:
03: import javax.faces.component.html.HtmlForm;
04:
05: public class Login
06: {
07:    private HtmlForm form1;
08:
09:    public void setForm1(HtmlForm form1)
10:    {
11:      this.form1 = form1;
12:    }
13:
14:    public HtmlForm getForm1()
15:    {
16:      return form1;
17:    }
18: }
```

NOTE
JDeveloper will format curly brackets (end of line or new line) according to a preference you set. Select **Tools | Preferences***, navigate to the Code Editor\Code Style node, and set the "Profile" to "JDeveloper Classic" to match examples shown throughout this book.*

This file is a standard class file that contains the following elements:

- **Line 01** is a package instruction.
- **Line 03** is an import for the Faces form element.
- **Line 05** is the class declaration.
- **Lines 06 and 18** are class block delimiters.

■ **Line 07** defines a private variable, form1, declared as an HtmlForm type.

■ **Lines 09–17** are added by JDeveloper as accessor methods for each component that you add to the JSP file. In this case, you have not yet added any components, but creating the JSP file automatically created a form component from the JSF HTML library. The accessor methods setForm1() and getForm1() support this element.

A name such as "form1" is not very descriptive, and for production-level code, you will want to change the default names of components that you add to the JSP file if you think you will need to write code that references them. JDeveloper maintains the link between a JSP file element and its code in the backing bean. As a demonstration of this feature, follow these steps:

1. Open the login.jsp file in the editor, and click the Design tab, if it is not already active.

2. Select the form object by clicking its node (h:form) in the Structure window (under f:view\html\body). This will display the form properties in the Property Inspector.

   Additional Information: If the Property Inspector is not open, select it in the View menu. You can also select an element by clicking it in the visual editor, but some components, such as the h:form element, are a bit easier to select in the Structure window.

3. Change the *Id* property to "loginForm" and press ENTER to register the change. A dialog will appear, indicating that the rename operation is being propagated to other components.

4. Click the Source tab and notice that the *id* attribute of the form element has been renamed.

5. Click the Login.java tab in the Editor window to display the code (or open the file from the navigator, if it is not already open).

   Additional Information: Notice that the private variable and accessor method names have been renamed to loginForm, setLoginForm(), and getLoginForm(), although the arguments used by the methods have not been renamed. As you add elements to the JSP file, you will be able to rename them so that you can distinguish the elements more easily and the code will automatically synchronize to the new names.

6. Repeat this renaming operation for the form1 element in home.jsp. Call this element "homeForm."

7. Click Save All.

CAUTION
If you rename the form in the Source view of the file, the name change will not cascade to other elements.

IV. Add Components to the Login Page

This phase demonstrates how to add containers, messages, fields, and a button to the login page. Since this application is only concerned with showing how to develop simple JSF JSP files in JDeveloper, it does not connect the pages to the database.

In this phase, you select components from the Component Palette. These components are not automatically bound to data sources, so you need to add mechanisms to load data into and read data from the components.

Applications that require database access normally contain one or more Model layer projects that represent tables. When Model layer code is available, you select components from the Data Control Palette instead of the Component Palette. This action adds ADF Faces components that are automatically bound to the Model layer objects. Other practices in this part of this book demonstrate adding components using the Data Control Palette.

When designing a screen layout, it is important to consider the arrangement of container components and their child components. When starting with ADF Faces, it is important to scan the documentation (such as the list of ADF Faces tags available in the JSF section of otn.oracle.com) to find appropriate container components and other components. Drawing a layout arrangement with notes about the component types will assist when it comes time to add components to the file. For example, you could draw this layout using nested boxes (as shown in Figure 9-1a) or using a hierarchy (as shown in Figure 9-1b) to indicate how you will place components within containers.

In this diagram, the h:form container component is the parent for the other components. It corresponds to the HTML form tag and must enclose all components whose values are submitted to the server. The child components for h:form are af:messages, which displays messages returned as errors or warnings as the page is processed, and af:panelHeader which allows you to place a title on the page and place components under that title. Inside af:panelHeader is af:panelForm, which lays out its child components in rows and columns. The user interacts with or uses these child components within af:panelForm: af:inputText (for the two text fields), af:commandButton (the submit button for the page), af:inputHidden (a hidden field for values not seen by the user but included in the request), and af:objectLegend (a read-only text message inside the footer facet that displays an icon and hint text about required fields).

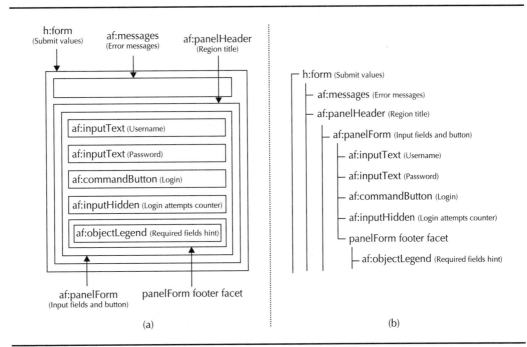

FIGURE 9-1. *Two representations of an ADF Faces JSP component layout*

Add the Container Components

After designing the page, the next step when creating a JSF project is working out templates so that all pages can share a look and feel. Although this example ignores the template step, the practice in Chapter 11 demonstrates the principles of copying templates as a starting point for a page file.

In this section, you add container components that will hold other objects. When you drag in the first ADF Faces component, the page will be rewritten to focus on ADF Faces components instead of HTML components. In addition, you will copy a cascading style sheet into the project and reference it in the JSP file.

The steps in this example use the Structure window to position components. A JSF or ADF Faces file (and even a standard HTML file) is laid out hierarchically. Sometimes, it is easier to lay out a component in a specific position in this hierarchy using the visual representation of that hierarchy in the Structure window. It is also usually possible to perform a layout task by dragging and dropping directly into the visual editor, but you will still need to check the Structure window to be sure that the component is in the correct place in the hierarchy.

1. Open the login.jsp file (by double clicking the login.jsp file in the navigator), or select its tab in the editor, if it is already open. Be sure the Design tab is selected.

2. Be sure the Component Palette is accessible. It usually appears in the upper-right corner of the JDeveloper window. If it is not displayed, select it using **View | Component Palette**.

3. Be sure the Structure window is displayed. This usually appears in the lower-left corner of the JDeveloper window, but you can display it using **View | Structure**.

4. Select the ADF Faces Core page from the Component Palette pulldown. Drag and drop a PanelHeader component on top of the h:form tag in the Structure window, as shown here:

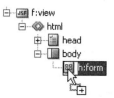

Additional Information: The code will change in a number of ways that are most easily visible in the Structure window, as shown here:

All raw HTML tags are replaced with their ADF Faces equivalents. For example, the html, head, and body tags now appear as the ADF Faces tags afh:html, afh:head, and afh:body, respectively.

NOTE
The label for your af:panelHeader component may be slightly different. JDeveloper generates default labels and names for components you drop into the editor based on the component name and a running index number. This is similar to the naming scheme that Oracle Forms uses when creating objects.

5. If your Structure window nodes do not appear in the same order as in the illustration, use drag-and-drop operations to rearrange them until they match. Click the Source tab, and you will not see any standard HTML tags. Click the Design tab. The Visual Editor should appear as follows:

panelHeader 1

TIP
*You can correct a drag-and-drop operation by selecting **Edit** / **Undo** (CTRL-Z) or by dragging components around in the Structure window.*

Additional Information: The af:panelHeader component is an ADF Faces container that displays a heading and can contain stacked child components. It has no other inherent layout capabilities.

TIP
Another way to reorder the components is to drag a component on top of its parent container. Components dropped onto containers always appear below all other child components in that container.

6. The af:panelHeader tag should now appear nested under the h:form tag. Be sure the af:panelHeader is selected. Click the Inspector tab (or select **View** / **Property Inspector** if that tab is not available).

Additional Information: We will not change the *Id* property of this component because we do not need to reference it in code.

7. Change the *Text* property to "Enter Login Information" and press ENTER. This text will now appear as the main heading for the page.

TIP
You can alternatively type some text changes such as this directly in the visual editor. However, you will probably find it faster and easier to use the Property Inspector.

8. You now need a component to display messages to the user. The ADF Faces `af:messages` component is designed for this purpose. Select Messages (not Message) in the ADF Faces Core page of the Component Palette, and drag it between the `af:panelHeader` and `h:form` tags in the Structure window. It should appear as a child node under the `h:form` tag, as shown next. If it does not, drag it until it appears in the proper location.

9. Change the *Id* property of the `af:messages` component to "loginMessages." Press ENTER to register the change.

CAUTION
Component names (the "Id" property) should start with lowercase, as is a convention for Java object names. You may receive errors when running an application that does not use this naming scheme.

10. You now need a container to hold the form's objects. ADF Faces offers an `af:panelForm` component that stacks fields and keeps their prompts aligned. Select PanelForm in the Component Palette, and drop it on top of the `af:panelHeader` tag in the Structure window.

11. Expand this tag and you will see the following arrangement:

Additional Information: As mentioned in Chapter 5, some ADF Faces containers, such as `af:panelForm`, come with *facets*—predefined areas into which you can place child objects. Usually, the child component appears in a specific location on the page within the parent component. In this case, a facet exists for footer elements. When you place a component inside this facet, it will automatically be placed at the bottom of all child components.

12. Click Save All.

Add the Form Components

You are now ready to add the form fields, button, and a footer message. ADF Faces offers `af:inputText`, an improvement on the standard JSF input field, `h:inputText`. The ADF Faces component adds a prompt, a rich set of validators, and default messages to the JSF component. ADF Faces also supplies an `af:commandButton` component used to submit the form. All components use a default style defined in the ADF Faces libraries, and you do not need to apply styles manually.

TIP
You can change the style sheet if the default styles are not suitable for your environment. Look for white papers about altering the look-and-feel definitions (skins) of ADF Faces at otn.oracle.com. In addition, the help system contains a topic, "Working with Skins in ADF Faces," that will assist (enter "skins" in the Search page to find this topic).

As mentioned in the explanation of the HTML form in Chapter 5, the form tag (`h:form`) must surround the fields and buttons it submits to the server.

1. Select the `af:panelForm` tag in the Structure window. Click InputText in the ADF Faces Core page of the Component Palette. (This is an alternative layout technique to the drag-and-drop operation you have used before.) A field and label will appear in the visual editor and the tag will be nested under the `af:panelForm` in the Structure window.

    Additional Information: `af:inputText` allows the user to enter data that will be sent to the server when the form is submitted. This field will hold the user's name.

2. Repeat the preceding step to add another InputText component. Another field and label will appear in the visual editor. This field will hold the login password.

3. Drag and drop a CommandButton on top of the `af:panelForm` node of the Structure Window. A button will appear in the visual editor. This button will be used to submit the login values.

TIP
You can hold the mouse cursor above a Component Palette item, such as InputText, to view a tooltip containing a description of the component.

4. The logic you will write later requires a hidden field to hold information (the number of login attempts) for a message on the home page. You may not know ahead of time that a hidden field is required, so you would add one when you find you need it. However, in this case, you know you will need this field. Drag an InputHidden component on top of `af:panelForm` in the Structure window.

    Additional Information: The Structure window should now appear as follows:

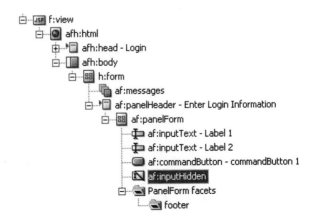

5. Both fields will be required. You can make changes to both fields at the same time. Select the two fields by clicking one and CTRL-clicking the other. (You may need to wait a couple of seconds for the Property Inspector to merge the properties.) In the Property Inspector, set the *Required* property to "true."

    Additional Information: Setting the *Required* property to "true" for an ADF Faces field causes an asterisk to display in the label. For example, the field label for the first field appears as "* Label 1." This suggests to the user that this field requires input.

6. With both fields still selected, set the following properties. (Be sure to press ENTER after entering each value so JDeveloper can register the change.)
    Columns as "15" (the width on the page)
    RequiredMessageDetail as "is required" (this text will appear as an error message if the user submits the form without a value in this field)
    MaximumLength as "20" (the limit of the number of characters a user can type in the field)

7. Click the page outside of a field to deselect the two fields.

8. ADF Faces supplies a component that contains a message explaining the meaning of the required icon—`af:objectLegend`. Select ObjectLegend in the Component Palette, and drop it on top of the footer tag in the Visual Editor. (This is yet another way to add components to the page.) The object will replace the placeholder for the footer facet and the Structure window will appear as shown in Figure 9-2.

9. Click Save All.

10. You can now fine-tune more properties on each component. Select the first `af:inputText` item ("Label 1") in the Structure window. You have set some of its properties before. Now set the following properties:
    Id as "usernameField"
    LabelAndAccessKey as "&Username"
    Tip (under the Message category) as "Your name" (this appears as a hint under the field)

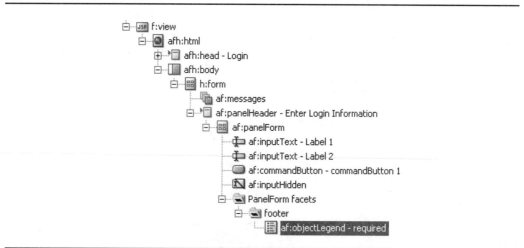

FIGURE 9-2. *Structure window excerpt after all components are in place*

Additional Information: The *LabelAndAccessKey* property combines a field prompt with an access key assignment. (An *AccessKey* property just assigns the access key.) The access key allows the user to navigate to a field by pressing ALT-<LETTER>, where "<LETTER>" is the letter that appears in the label after an ampersand character. For example, the *LabelAndAccessKey* value "&Username" will be displayed as follows:

<u>U</u>sername

The letter following the ampersand ("U") is underscored to signify that the user can press ALT-U to move the cursor to that field. The access key need not be the first letter in the label, but it does need to appear in the label. This is the same concept as the *Access Key* property for an Oracle Forms button item.

TIP
You can view reference information about a component and its properties by selecting the component in the visual editor, clicking the Source tab, and pressing F1. The reference page for the component will appear. This page should give you additional clues for the component's use. You can view help for properties by selecting the property in the Property Inspector and dragging the hint panel at the bottom of the window into view, as shown here:

11. Select the second field and set its properties as follows:
    Id as "passwordField" (press ENTER)
    LabelAndAccessKey as "&Password" (This value overrides the *Label* property value—currently "Label 2.")
    Secret as "true" (This setting causes the characters the user enters in this field to appear as dots so that an onlooker cannot see the password, like the *Conceal Data* property on an Oracle Forms item.)
    Tip as "Just Something Fun"

TIP
Get into the habit of pressing ENTER *after typing a property so that the value will register before you navigate the cursor to a different place. This keypress is not required for values set using pulldown lists or popup dialogs.*

12. Select the af:commandButton component and set its properties as follows:
     TextAndAccessKey as "&Login"
     Id as "loginButton"

13. Select the af:inputHidden field in the Structure window, set its *Id* as "loginCountField," and press ENTER. The page should appear in the visual editor as follows:

> Messages
>
> **Enter Login Information**
>
> * Username [   ]
>   Your name
> * Password [   ]
>   Just Something Fun
> (Login)
>   * Indicates required field

14. Click Save All.

Test the Page

Although the logic to process input and navigate to the home page is not in place, you can run this page in the Embedded OC4J Server to view its appearance in the browser.

1. Be sure the login.jsp file is active (click its tab if you are not certain). Click Run (the green arrowhead icon in the JDeveloper main toolbar).

2. The Embedded OC4J Server will start, and the page will appear in your browser. Without entering data, click Login to submit the form. Since you did not fill in mandatory fields, the following dialog will appear:

> **Microsoft Internet Explorer** [X]
>
> ⚠ Form validation failures:
>   Username - is required
>   Password - is required
>
>   [OK]

NOTE
Different browsers display alerts in different ways, but the message and buttons will be the same in all browsers.

3. Notice that the dialog contains the field labels from the *LabelAndAccessKey* property and the text from the *RequiredMessageDetail* property.

Additional Information: You may also notice that this dialog did not require a roundtrip request to the server; you can usually tell if the page submits to the server because part or all of the page is redrawn. In this case, JavaScript on the page checked the values before submitting the page to the server. The dialog you are viewing is a JavaScript alert dialog. JSF reference implementation (RI) controls allow you to set the *Required* property, but they require a roundtrip to the server to return an error message for a missing value.

4.   Click OK to dismiss the validation error dialog.

5.   Enter a value in the *Username* field value, and click Login again. The same dialog will appear but it will contain only one message (for the Password field). Click OK to dismiss the dialog.

6.   Press ALT-P and ALT-U to test the navigation to the fields based on the access key. This navigation aid is useful for assisting users who prefer or require keyboard navigation. ALT-L navigates to the button and activates it as if you clicked it.

7.   Close the browser window. Stop the Embedded OC4J Server by clicking the red Terminate button in the Log window at the bottom of the JDeveloper IDE window.

Additional Information: You do not need to stop the Embedded OC4J Server each time you test the application, but doing so ensures that no information or error states are held in server memory between test runs. Also, in the following chapters in this book, changes you make to database access code (using ADF Business Components) may not take effect until the server is restarted to clear out any objects cached in memory.

What Did You Just Do?   In this phase, you added ADF Faces container components to the login JSP file. These container components abstract the HTML layout so that you do not need to worry about coding HTML structures such as tables and rows. Some ADF Faces containers also offer facets—prebuilt slots into which you can add components. The work with container components parallels work in Oracle Forms, where you create windows and canvases as containers and then add objects such as items and boilerplate to those containers.

In addition, you added components to the login page and set their properties; then you tested the page. Many properties you set for the ADF Faces field items (such as *LabelAndAccessKey*, *Required, Columns, Secret,* and *MaximumLength*) should be familiar to an Oracle Forms developer. The property set offered by ADF Faces is richer than most other J2EE-oriented component sets, including the JSF RI components.

It is time to take another quick look at the JSP file and the backing bean. The faces-config.xml file has not changed since you last examined it.

Login JSP File   Click the Source tab for login.jsp, and locate the HTML-oriented ADF Faces tags, such as afh:html, afh:head, and afh:body. Identify the tags for the ADF Faces containers— af:panelHeader and af:panelForm. Find the af:panelForm's facet, as shown in Lines 23–27 of the following code (your line numbers and the location of other components may differ):

```
22: <af:panelForm binding="#{backing_login.panelForm1}" id="panelForm1">
23:    <f:facet name="footer">
24:      <af:objectLegend name="required"
25:                       binding="#{backing_login.objectLegend1}"
26:                       id="objectLegend1"/>
27:    </f:facet>
      <!-- more components here -->
46: </af:panelForm>
```

NOTE
The af:objectLegend component is still set to its default "Id" property value. As mentioned, it is not necessary to reassign the "Id" property of all components you use in a JSF JSP. However, you will find descriptive names useful if you write backing bean code. In this code, you need to distinguish between multiple occurrences of text fields or other components in the same file, and descriptive names make this identification easier.

The af:objectLegend element is assigned to this facet, so it will appear in the footer area. Remember that all ADF Faces components will be sent as HTML to the web browser (or in another language to other display devices such as PDAs). For the HTML display, container components will create HTML tables with specific properties. Components such as af: inputText and af:commandButton will create HTML form elements such as fields and buttons, respectively.

If you run this file, view its HTML source in the browser, save the source to an HTML file in the file system, and open the file in JDeveloper, the Structure window will appear as shown in Figure 9-3. Compare this complex and large HTML structure (for a relatively simple user interface) with the ADF Faces structure in Figure 9-2. The structure display in Figure 9-3 is not fully expanded and is too tall to print in a single column. In other words, using JSF and ADF Faces tags supplies a large amount of HTML output, which provides sophisticated layouts. In addition, you do not code much, if any, HTML; the JSF code—or, more correctly, the JSF render kit—is responsible for generating HTML to the browser.

Spend a bit more time familiarizing yourself with the components in the source code. Identify the property values you set in the Property Inspector. Remember that you can always view the help page for a component by clicking inside the tag in the Code Editor and pressing F1.

The Backing Bean File   The Login.java backing bean for this page has grown substantially since you last viewed it. Each time you drop a component onto the visual editor, JDeveloper creates accessor methods and a private variable for the object. When you change the *Id* property, JDeveloper sweeps through the backing bean and changes the accessors and private variable to match the new component name. Open the editor for the Login.java file, and scan through it to find the private variable and accessors for usernameField, for example. All other objects in the JSP file have similar code units. Browse the contents a bit further using the Structure window. You may need to click the Show Methods or Show Fields button in the Structure window toolbar to see these elements.

V. Add Components to the Home Page

The intent of the home page in this example is to demonstrate page navigation and value passing, and, therefore, it contains very few components.

Add ADF Faces Components

The first steps in completing the home page are to add components to the page:

1. Double click the home.jsp node in the navigator if the home.jsp file is not already open. Click the Design tab.

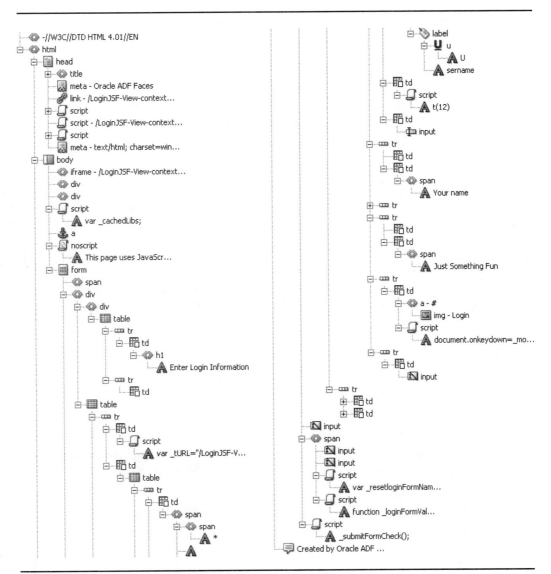

FIGURE 9-3. *Runtime HTML structure of the login.jsp file*

2. As with the login page, drag a PanelHeader element from the Component Palette, and drop it on top of the h:form tag in the Structure window. As before, the HTML tags will be rewritten as ADF Faces tags. The structure should appear as shown to the right:

3. With the `af:panelHeader` tag selected, select the *Text* property and click "Bind to data" (shown next).

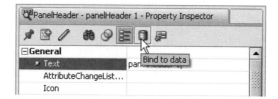

4. The Text (bind to data) dialog shown in Figure 9-4 will appear. As mentioned in Chapter 8, this dialog assists in building an expression used to supply a value to a property. Delete the contents of the *Expression* field and type "Home Page for " (including the trailing space). In the next step, you will fill in that phrase with an expression that contains the value of the Username field on the login page.

Additional Information: Since the username value is loaded into a field on the login page and that field is controlled by a backing bean with accessors for the field's value, you can build an expression that will call the accessor for that field. You build this expression using Expression Language (EL), as introduced in the sidebar "About Expression Language." This dialog will help you build a proper expression, so you do not need to master EL right away.

NOTE
EL is also known as "Variable Binding Language (VBL)" because EL allows you to bind component attributes to variable values. However, EL also allows you to bind to methods, so it is technically more inclusive than VBL.

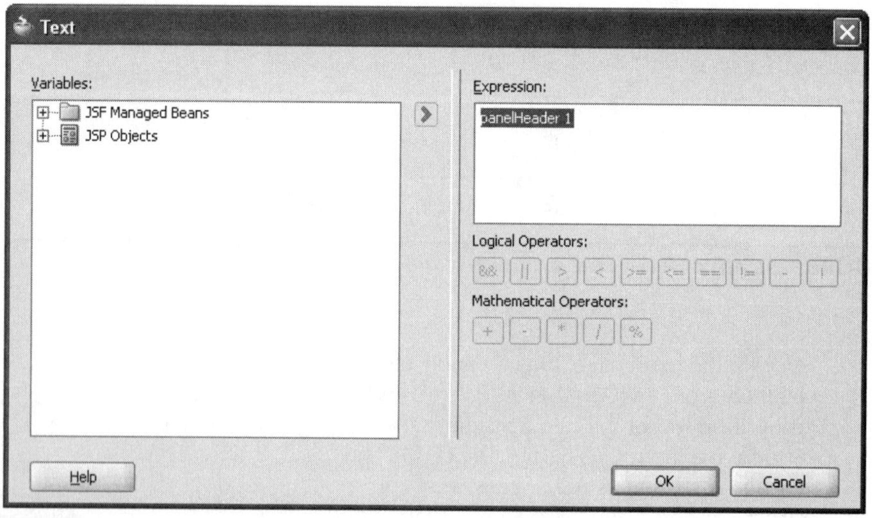

FIGURE 9-4.   *The bind to data dialog for the* Text *property*

About Expression Language

In an effort to reduce the amount of scriptlet and non-tag Java language in JSP files, Sun Microsystems introduced *JavaServer Pages Standard Tag Language (JSTL)* with the JSP 1.2 specification. This language includes JSP tags for procedural processing operations, such as conditional statements and iterative structures. In addition, it contains *Expression Language (EL)*, which defines syntax for accessing dynamic values.

JSF adopted and adapted EL. You use EL in JDeveloper to define data binding and other dynamic values for attributes of various JSF elements. The standard syntax for an EL expression is as follows:

```
#{object.attribute}
```

JSF prefixes the expression with "#," to make the destinction from JSTL expressions, which use the "$" prefix. Unlike JSTL expressions, JSF expressions can define both bindings to method calls and read-write data.

For example, the expression "#{backing_login.usernameField}" represents an object instantiated from the backing bean for the login.jsp file ("backing_login" is defined as the name of the Login class file in the faces-config.xml file). The expression accesses the *usernameField* attribute of that object. You can build expressions most easily using the "Bind to data" dialog, as described in this section of the hands-on practice. In addition to attributes, you can express methods for the object.

EL also allows you to build more complex expressions using mathematical and logical operators. The "Bind to data" dialog can help you create these expressions. More information about JSF EL is available in Chapter 12 of The J2EE 1.4 Tutorial (currently at java.sun.com/j2ee/1.4/docs/tutorial/doc/).

5. You need to select something that will represent the value of the Username field, which has an *Id* property of "usernameField" in login.jsp. Remember that the data for login.jsp is supplied by a managed bean, known to the controller as backing_login. These clues will lead you to the correct expression. Start the search by expanding the JSF Managed Beans node.

6. Find the backing_login node and expand it. You will see a node for the usernameField element. Expand that node and scroll down until you find the value node. Select the value node.

   Additional Information: Reading backwards in the object hierarchy, the *value* property is supplied for the usernameField element contained in the managed bean backing_login.

7. Be sure the cursor is sitting after the final space in the *Expression* area. Move the value node to the *Expression* field by clicking the right arrow button. The expression `#{backing_login.usernameField.value}` will be added. Click OK. The expression and literal text will appear in the *Text* property and also in the visual editor.

8. As with the login page, drop a PanelForm on top of the `af:panelHeader` node in the Structure window. Although you will not use the footer facet, this container offers the appropriate component stacking behavior.

   Additional Information: As you saw when creating the Login page, you can add components in the correct location in the structure by selecting the parent object and then clicking the new child object type in the Component Palette. A child component will appear under the parent component with no drag-and-drop operation. The next several steps use this technique again.

9. Select the new `af:panelForm` node in the Structure window, and click OutputText in the Component Palette. An `af:outputText` node will appear under `af:panelForm`.

   Additional Information: The `af:outputText` component displays read-only text much like an item defined as a "Display Item" item type in Oracle Forms. In an HTML display, it will be rendered as plain text.

10. Select the `af:panelForm` and click CommandButton in the Component Palette to add an `af:commandButton` within the `af:panelForm`.

    Additional Information: This button will be used to send control back to the Controller layer so that the login page can be redisplayed. This is an alternative to the browser's Back button, which can cause the problems mentioned in the sidebar "The Back and Refresh Button Problem."

The Back and Refresh Button Problem

Users may be accustomed to clicking the browser's Back button to return to the preceding page or the Refresh button to reload the page. This can cause problems with web applications that use a Controller layer, like the JSF controller or Struts, because the browser Back button returns to the preceding page in the browser's page history without calling code in the Controller layer. The Controller will, therefore, not know the state of the application's data, and the preceding page will either not load properly or may place the application into an inconsistent or unstable state. The same problem occurs with the browser's Refresh button, which just reloads the same page, again without calling Controller layer code. This is a problem in all web applications, not only those using J2EE technology or ADF libraries.

Frameworks do not offer programmatic solutions for this problem yet. At this point in web technologies, the solutions consist of user education (to warn them of incorrect results when using these buttons) and hiding the browser's buttons (using a JavaScript window call that specifies no toolbars), although users can still press the keyboard shortcut to perform the Back and Refresh functions. Other solutions, such as those built into JHeadstart, check a timestamp on the page and issue a warning about an inconsistent state. Another partial solution is to provide the equivalent of the Back button, as with the Logout button on this page that performs standard Controller actions so the user can perform the same function as the browser's Back button.

11. Click Save All. The structure should appear as follows:

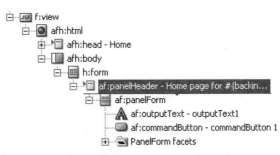

Set the Component Properties and Test the Page

You can now set properties on the new components.

1. Set the following properties for the af:outputText component:
Id as "loginCountText" (press ENTER)
Value as "Number of login attempts: " (including the trailing space), plus an expression representing the value of the login page's hidden field loginCountField.

Additional Information: You can set this expression as before: select the *Value* property and click "Bind to data;" remove the contents of the *Expression* field, add the literal value with a trailing space, navigate to the JSF Managed Beans\backing_login\loginCountField\ value node, move it to the right, and click OK. The expression "#{backing_login .loginCountField.value}" will be added to the static message and will display in the visual editor as follows:

Number of login attempts: #{backing_login.loginCountField.value}

2. Set the following properties for the af:commandButton:
TextAndAccessKey as "&Logout"
Id as "logoutButton" (press ENTER)

Additional Information: As you saw for the Login button on the Login page, the *TextAndAccessKey* property for the af:commandButton works similarly to the *LabelAndAccessKey* property for the af:textInput component. It underscores the letter following the "&" in the property, in this example "L." When the user presses ALT-L, the button will be activated as if the user had clicked it.

3. Click Save All.

4. Although you have not connected this page to the login page, you can now run this page to check its visual elements. Click the mouse cursor in the home.jsp editor window and click Run.

Additional Information: The home page will appear in your browser without the user name and login count. Notice that the browser window title is set to "Home"—the text you entered in the Create JSF JSP Wizard (this is the afh:head *Title* property).

5. Close the browser.

6. End the server session by clicking Terminate in the Log window.

What Did You Just Do?   You added home page components to show the user name, a message about logins, and a button to return to the login page. Using the bind to data dialog for the Text property, you defined the `af:panelHeader` and `af:outputText` values using an EL expression. You also ran the JSP pages to check that they appear correctly. You will specify the navigation and logic to check and process values entered by the user in the next phase.

Examine the home.jsp file's code to identify its elements. Notice that the EL data bindings appear as property values, as you would expect, because you entered the expressions in the Property Inspector.

VI. Add Navigation and Validation Logic to the Application

This phase specifies the page navigation and adds logic in the backing bean for the validation and other required functionality.

Add the Navigation and Validation Code

Navigation, validation, and other logic are initiated by a user event, for example, a Login button click. Event logic is coded in a managed bean listener method named, by convention, "<element>_ action," where "<element>" is the name (*Id* property value) of the element, such as the command button. For example, you would use a method called "loginButton_action" to run code when the user clicks the `af:loginButton` component. JDeveloper can add a method stub for this event, as you will see in this section. This method serves as a place to enter any code that applies to the navigation. We will use this technique to define the navigation from the login page to the home page, because we need to check the number of logins and to validate the password.

The event code validates the user name and password values and returns a value to the controller. If the login is successful, the event code will return "login" (the name of the navigation case in the struts-config.xml diagram) and the home.jsp page will load. If the login is unsuccessful, the event code will return null, a message will be added to the `af:messages` item, and control will remain on the login page.

If you have no code to run for a particular navigation, you can define navigation in the *action* property for an `af:commandButton` (or link). We will use this technique for the navigation from the home page back to the login page. No additional logic is required for this type of navigation.

As you saw earlier, error messages for required values are displayed in a JavaScript alert. The code you will add in this section issues error messages to the `af:messages` component so they may be shown on the page. Loading the messages component requires a small amount of Java code, as explained in the sidebar "About Messages in the af:messages Component."

1.   Display the Design page of the home.jsp file. Select the Logout button. In the *Action* property, select "logout" from the pulldown.

   Additional Information: The *Action* pulldown contains a list of all navigation cases you have defined from this page. In this case, you only defined one called "logout," so that is the only value preloaded into the property's pulldown. You do not need any conditional or validation logic for this navigation, because the framework performs the navigation based on the *Action* property setting.

2.   Click Save All.

3.   Display the Design tab of the login.jsp file. Double click the Login button. A Bind Action Property dialog will appear so that you can identify the managed bean name and method name for this button. The defaults will work, so click OK. The Login.java file will appear

About Messages in the af:messages Component

The `af:messages` component automatically displays messages that you or the controller loads into the FacesContext area. To access the FacesContext area, you create a `FacesContext` object that represents the current instance of the context using code similar to the following:

```
FacesContext messageContext = FacesContext.getCurrentInstance();
```

You can then load messages into the context area using the `addMessage()` method. The string passed to `addMessage()` must be of type `FacesMessage`. You can combine these requirements into a single line of code that calls `addMessage()` on the current context object and that passes it a new `FacesMessage` object loaded with the desired text. The following shows an example of how you would place the "Hello JSF World" message into the FacesContext area so that it will be displayed in the messages component:

```
messageContext.addMessage(null, new FacesMessage("Hello JSF World"));
```

in the editor, and the cursor will navigate to the code stub for a newly added method, `loginButton_action()`.

4. Delete the following lines in this method stub:

```
// Add event code here...
return null;
```

5. In their place, enter the following code. The line numbers are for reference purposes and should not appear in the code text.

```
01: FacesContext messageContext = FacesContext.getCurrentInstance();
02:
03: String returnResult = "login";
04: loginAttempts++;
05:
06: if (!passwordField.getValue().toString().equals("JSF"))
07: {
08:    returnResult = null;
09:    if (loginAttempts >= 3)
10:    {
11:      // message displayed in the messages tag
12:      messageContext.addMessage(null, new FacesMessage("You seem " +
13:          " to have forgotten that the password is \"JSF.\""));
14:    }
15:    else
16:    {
17:       messageContext.addMessage(null,
18:          new FacesMessage("Incorrect login. Try again."));
19:    }
```

```
20: }
21: else
22: {
23:    loginCountField.setValue(loginAttempts);
24:    loginAttempts = 0;
25:    passwordField.setValue(null);
26: }
27:
28: return returnResult;
```

6. In addition, outside of this and any other method (at the top of the class where the private variables are declared), declare the variable to hold the number of login attempts as follows:

    ```
    int loginAttempts = 0;
    ```

    Additional Information: We will explain how this code works a little later.

7. In `loginButton_action()`, several code lines will display wavy red underlines, indicating that a class cannot be found. The editor window's left margin will also display a Quick Fixes lightbulb symbol, as shown here:

8. Since the class cannot be found, you need to add an `import` statement. Hold the mouse cursor above the `FacesContext` class name. The following hints will appear:

9. Click the Quick Fixes icon, and select "Import 'javax.faces.context.FacesContext'" to add the class import statement at the top of the file. The wavy red lines under the class name will disappear.

    Additional Information: You can alternatively press ALT-ENTER after the hint appears above the class name to add the import statement. You can expand the import statement node at the top of the file (or hold the mouse cursor over the "+" expansion symbol in the margin to display a tooltip) to check this addition.

10. Repeat this action for the `FacesMessage` class (`javax.faces.application.FacesMessage`).

11. Select **Make** from the right-click menu in the Code Editor to compile the class file.

12. The variable that stores the number of login attempts is incremented across multiple requests (command button clicks); therefore, you need to set the backing bean's scope. It is set to "request" by default, but this would reset the value each time the page is submitted. Select the Overview tab of the faces-config.xml file.

NOTE
*Normally, backing beans are left at their default scope of "request."
By convention, you would use a managed bean that is shared among
pages to code functionality required across requests (application or
session scopes). For simplicity in illustrating the concept of scope, this
example sets the backing bean's scope directly and does not create a
separate managed bean.*

13. On the Managed Beans page, double click the backing_login bean name. The managed-bean
Properties dialog will open. Change *Scope* to "session" and click OK. This action resets the
scope of the backing bean so the login attempts counter will persist across requests.

14. Click Save All.

15. Select the Login.java backing bean file tab in the editor to examine the code you just
entered. This block of code performs the following actions:

- **Line 01** creates the context variable that represents messages you will display in the
  `af:messages` component.

- **Line 03** declares and initializes a return variable with the value "login." Returning
  this value will instruct the controller to forward to the home page. The code reassigns
  this variable to null if the validation fails. In that case, the controller will not forward
  to the home page.

- **Line 04** increments the login counter variable. This variable is retained throughout
  the user session, but is reset to zero if a login attempt is successful (in line 24).

- **Lines 06–15** test if the password is not "JSF." The `getValue()` method calls the getter
  method for the component's variable in the backing bean. For example, the value of
  the passwordField component is accessed in the Login.java backing bean using the
  `getPasswordField()` method, declared by the following method signature:

  ```
  public CoreInputText getPasswordField()
  ```

  Notice that `getPasswordField()` returns a `CoreInputText` type. However, the
  `getValue()` method that calls `getPasswordField()` returns an `Object` type.
  To compare this `Object` type with a null string, you need to convert it to a string
  (using the `toString()` method available to all Objects). Finally, a null pointer
  exception can result from a comparison with a null string, so you need to use the
  `equals()` method to compare the value with the desired password. (Don't worry;
  you will soon be able to construct expressions like this faster than you can explain
  them.)

- **Line 08** sets the return variable to null so that the controller will not forward to the
  home page.

- **Lines 09–14** check if the user has attempted three or more logins. If so, it sets a
  message into the context area in Lines 12–13 using `addMessage()`. This message
  shows the user the password (although you would never show a password in a real-
  world situation). The error message shows the user's correct password inside quotes;

the backslash characters in the string escape the double quotes that follow, so they can appear as a literal inside the string delimited by double quotes. For example, `"\"JSF.\""` will appear as `"JSF."` on the page.

- **Lines 15–19** are reached if the number of login attempts is fewer than three. This code sets a message indicating an unsuccessful login.

- **Lines 23–25** are reached if the password is correct ("JSF").

- **Line 23** sets the hidden variable with the number of invalid logins. The home page `af:outputText` component displays a message, including an EL statement that references this hidden field value.

- **Line 24** resets the number of login attempts to zero in case the user returns to the login page to attempt another login.

- **Line 25** clears the password field in case the user returns to the login page. The password must be reentered each time the login page appears.

- **Line 28** returns the value that has been set in the logic before it. If all validation succeeds, the value will still be set to "login," which causes the controller to forward to the home page. If any validation fails, the return value passed to the controller will be null and no page navigation will occur.

Test the Validation and Navigation Logic

This section tests the validation and navigation code you just created.

1. Before testing the login.jsp file again, set it to run when any non-JSP file in the project is run. Be sure the faces-config.xml Diagram tab is active, and, on the login.jsp icon, select **Set as Default Run Target** from the right-click menu.

   Additional Information: Notice that an asterisk appears to the left of the login.jsp file name in the diagram, indicating that it is the default run target. Now, whenever you run any non-JSP file in the ViewController project, JDeveloper will automatically run login.jsp.

2. Press F11 to run the project. The login.jsp file will display.

3. You have already tested the JavaScript error alert that indicates whether either field is blank when you click Login, but you may test other combinations of null values if you wish.

4. Enter a user name. Enter a password other than "JSF". Notice that the password is converted to dots so it cannot be read. Click Login and the messages area will appear, indicating that the login is incorrect, as shown here:

5. Try two more times without the correct password. The third unsuccessful login attempt will show a different message and display the required password.

6. Enter the password as "JSF" (using uppercase) and be sure the user name is still filled in. Click Login and the home page will load with a title containing the user's name and a message indicating the number of logins, as shown here:

7. Click Logout to return to the login page. The login page will reappear with no messages and no password (although the user name will be retained).

8. Close the browser. Stop the OC4J server.

What Did You Just Do?   In this phase, you defined the page navigation from login to home and from home to login. Both navigation cases were triggered by button clicks. The former navigation case required validating the user name and password fields and returning success if the values were valid; returning "login" caused the controller to follow the navigation case and forward to the home page. The logic returned null and displayed a message on the login page if the password was invalid.

The home page Logout button is connected to the navigation case "logout" through the *action* property, and this navigation will occur regardless of data values. Therefore, clicking Logout will always redisplay the login page.

What Could You Do Next?   Although this is a simple example, it demonstrates many of the basic operations you perform when developing JSF and ADF Faces applications. A few areas you can explore follow:

- **Support for wireless and TELNET displays**   You can build in support for other display devices, such as TELNET or wireless devices. The JSF JSP Create Wizard contains a checkbox to include this support. You can then run the same application in the other devices. This demonstrates how specific render kits are activated to support special devices. To test this feature on your local computer, you need an emulator for the alternative device. Start your search for the required code and emulators on the otn.oracle.com JDeveloper home page.

- **Centralize messages**   You can place messages shown to the user in all JSP pages inside a single file. The next section explores this topic a bit more.

Centralizing Messages

JSF offers a facility to store *messages*—text such as prompts, errors and warnings, button labels, and tab labels as text strings inside a *message bundle*, a Java file or properties file that contains key-value pairs defining the text displayed to users. You can access this file programmatically in the backing bean (or other controller) code. The benefits of message bundles are as follows:

- **They centralize messages.**   That way, you can change any message in the application by editing a single file.

■ **You can replace default validation messages.** The JSF framework allows you to code validators for each component by embedding a child tag, such as `f:validateLength minimum="8" maximum="20"`, inside the opening and closing tags of the component (for example, `af:inputText`). This validator calls default functionality and displays a default error message under the component (such as a field). You can replace the default error message using message bundles. The sidebar "Using a Message Bundle for JSF Error Messages" describes this a bit more.

■ **They allow you to internationalize (localize) the application.** You can create separate message bundle files for each language you need to support. Each message bundle would contain all messages used in the application translated into the local language. These language files share the same file name prefix and a suffix indicating the language. The JSF runtime engine retrieves the locale information from the browser and uses the appropriate file to supply messages to the application.

Using a Message Bundle for JSF Error Messages

Default JSF messages are not very user-friendly. For example, the standard JSF message for a required field (and InputText component with the *Required* property set to "true"), which the user has left blank, is "Validation Error: Value is required." This message does not indicate the problem field name and the wording may not be as descriptive as you might like.

To replace messages such as these, you create entries with predefined names in the message bundle file. For example, naming the message "javax.faces.component.UIInput .REQUIRED" will cause the JSF runtime to replace the default error message for required text with whatever you have assigned to that message. The JSF error message names appear in the JSF specification (available from www.jcp.org; search for "JSR 127") or by searching the Web (for example, a list appears currently at www.jsf-faq.com/faqs/faces-messages.html#126). This will only redefine the default message that the framework provides. You will need EL and other customizations (such as the techniques described in this practice) to provide field-specific messages.

You also need to register the message bundle file with the application. In JDeveloper, you would open the Overview tab of the faces-config.xml file, select the Application page, and set the *Message Bundle* property to "resources.Messages" (if your file were Messages .properties inside a directory called "resources"); the framework will fill in the file extension ".properties" by default. When that is in place and an error is raised, the JSF runtime will find the message bundle file, read the appropriate named message, and display its text instead of the default. This entry is only required if you are overriding a default JSF error.

ADF Faces replaces a number of standard JSF validations, such as *Required*, and presents more user-friendly messages in their place. Therefore, the application described in this book does not override default JSF error messages.

Hands-on Practice: Create and Call a Message Bundle

You can try out this concept using the code in the following example. This example adds messages to a single message file for the application developed in the earlier section. It also adds the code to extract the messages in the backing bean. If you required international support, you would create additional message files in the same way, using the same message key names. The exercise of creating additional files is left to you, but it follows the same pattern as the next steps.

You need to create a file that JDeveloper does not create by default—the message bundle file. This example will demonstrate how to create a properties (text) file with key-value pairs for the message. Alternatively, you can create a Java file that loads key-value pairs into a collection object, as shown in Chapter 7.

1. On the ViewController node in the navigator, select **New** from the right-click menu. In the New Gallery, select the General category, and double click the File item.

    Additional Information: This New Gallery item allows you to create a plain file in any location and of any type, but it will not preload code into that file.

2. In *File Name* enter "Messages.properties." For the *Directory Name* value, add "\resources" (including the backslash) to the end of the existing name. This will create a subdirectory that you can use to store all message files. Click OK.

3. The Messages.properties file will open in the editor and will appear under the Resources node in the navigator. Enter the following lines in this file:

    ```
    incorrectLogin=Incorrect login. Try again.
    loginHint=You seem to have forgotten that the password is "JSF."
    ```

4. Click Save All.

5. You can now add code to read these messages. You need to add an object that represents the contents of the message bundle file. Then you can reference specific messages from that bundle. Open Login.java in the editor.

6. In the `loginButton_action()` method, in the blank line under the declaration of `messageContext` (Line 01 in the listing shown earlier in the "Add the Navigation and Validation Code" section of this chapter), add the following code:

    ```
    ResourceBundle messageBundle = ResourceBundle.getBundle(
            "resources.Messages",
            messageContext.getViewRoot().getLocale());
    ```

    Additional Information: This statement declares a message bundle object of type `ResourceBundle`. It references the Messages.properties file you just created in the resources directory and specifies that you need to obtain the locale from the context area. (Notice that you do not need to enter the file extension ".properties.") The context area stores information about the session, including the user's preferred language. *Locale* specifies a language and includes the concept that a language may be used in one way by a certain region and in another way by another region. For example, the English language can be used in U.K. or U.S. form, and that form (the region) would be stored as a user preference available to the browser. Message bundle files can use a locale suffix of language (for example, Messages_en.properties) or a locale suffix of both language and region (for example, Messages_en_us.properties). If your application only offers one message file, that file will be used regardless of the user's locale preference.

7. As before, a wavy red line will appear under `ResourceBundle`. Hold the cursor over that class name and press ALT-ENTER to add the import (`java.util.ResourceBundle`).

8. Replace the `addMessage()` call for the message that displays the "JSF" password (Lines 12 and 13 in the previous listing) with the following:

   ```
   messageContext.addMessage(null, new FacesMessage(
       messageBundle.getString("loginHint")));
   ```

   Additional Information: This code refers to the loginHint key in the message bundle file (the file is now represented as the messageBundle object in the code).

9. Replace the `addMessage()` call that indicates to the user to try again (Lines 17 and 18 in the earlier listing) with this:

   ```
   messageContext.addMessage(null, new FacesMessage(
       messageBundle.getString("incorrectLogin")));
   ```

10. Click Save All.

11. Run the application and login incorrectly three times to see the two login error messages stored in the message bundle file.

    Additional Information: If you would like more practice with this concept, work on replacing the "Home Page for " and "Enter Login Information" strings with text in the Messages.properties file.

12. Close the browser and stop the server process. The next section describes another method.

Hands-on Practice: Access Message Bundle Messages with EL

You can retrieve messages from the message bundle without writing Java code by using a JSF component, `f:loadBundle`; this component creates a token (variable) that represents all messages and you can access this token in EL expressions. The following steps demonstrate how this method works.

1. In the home.jsp file, drag LoadBundle from the JSF Core page of the Component Palette on top of the `f:view` node of the Structure window.

2. In the Insert LoadBundle dialog, click "…" next to the *Basename* field. Select the Properties File option, and the dialog will change to a file browser display.

3. Navigate to the ..\ViewController\resources directory, and select "Messages.properties." Click OK.

4. For *Var*, type "msg". Click OK. The messages will now be available to the JSF components using EL that references the variable "msg."

Additional Information: If this dialog returns a message about a missing value that is not missing, type a space after the value, delete the space, and click OK again.

5. In the Structure window, move `f:loadBundle` directly under the `f:view` node above `afh:html` so that the variable will be available to all components.

6. Add the following to the Messages.properties file:

```
loginAttempts=Number of login attempts:
```

7. Select ViewController in the navigator, and then click Rebuild in the JDeveloper toolbar to recompile the project so that the new message is available. Select the `af:outputText` component of the home page, open the Property Inspector, and click the "..." button in the *Value* property field. Remove the hard-coded string "Number of login attempts:".

8. Expand the JSP Objects node and the msg node under it. Select loginAttempts and move it to the *Expression* field. Click OK. The `af:outputText` component should appear in the visual editor as "#{msg.loginAttempts} #{backing_login .loginCountField.value}".

9. Click Save All. Run the application and enter a correct login. You will see the message from the message bundle file on the home page. Close the browser and stop the OC4J process.

This chapter demonstrated JSF concepts and how the development process works for a simple, non-database-oriented JSF JSP. Although this may seem a bit complex at this point, with more use, you will become accustomed to working with the JDeveloper editors and visual tools. These tools offer better productivity for creating and managing code than is possible by using simpler IDEs. In addition, using JSF and ADF Faces offloads a significant amount of HTML layout code that you would need to write otherwise.

CHAPTER
10

Application Design Principles and Sample Application Overview

Good design keeps the user happy,
the manufacturer in the black
and the aesthete unoffended.

—Raymond Loewy (1893–1986), industrial designer

 efore launching into development of a sample application that interacts with the database, we need to set the stage by explaining the design of the application. Even before that, we need to prepare for this discussion by briefly reviewing the principles and concepts of system design for a web application. The hands-on practice at the end of this chapter begins the application by creating the workspace and projects in JDeveloper.

System Design

The goal of system design is to outline details of system components that will fulfill requirements of the business. Business requirements are implemented in two different but integrated areas within a system design:

- **Database design**   The data model determines what data structures (tables and views) you will need to create in the database. Some business rules and requirements derived from requirements analysis can be implemented as database design elements. For example, the system could require datatypes, sizes, and NOT NULL characteristics for specific columns. It could also require foreign key constraints. All of these would be implemented in the database.

- **Application design**   The functional process model helps form the application design. The application design consists of the user interface and back-end database (or application server) code to enforce business rules that implement the business requirements. Application design includes defining standard layout features that are common to all pages. It also includes *process flow*—the steps the user and system follow to complete a business function. These definitions translate to the elements available on the page as well as the functional responsibility of each page.

Design tools can assist with the process of capturing business requirements into database and application definitions that you can use to build the application.

System Design Tools and the SDLC

The term "system design" evokes thoughts of a *system development life cycle (SDLC)*—a process by which system development is divided into phases, for example, Strategy, Analysis, Design, Development, and Deployment (Implementation). SDLCs guide the system through these phases in some order, such as sequential (known as a *waterfall approach*), iterative (as with Rapid Application Development, or RAD, approaches, discussed in Chapter 3), or "middle out" (Development at the same time as Analysis and Design).

Various software tools can support the SDLC. In the past, *computer-aided software engineering (CASE)* software tools assisted the process by providing a repository for all information about the system's data and processes, and by generating some front-end and database code. Although JDeveloper contains a number of Unified Modeling Language (UML) diagramming tools that can be used for analysis and design, Oracle Designer still holds the niche as the full-system life cycle tool for the Oracle product line.

Oracle Designer

Oracle Designer, once categorized as a CASE tool, stores information about processes and data throughout an SDLC; it can generate application code in Oracle Forms, Oracle Reports, Web PL/SQL, and Visual Basic styles, as well as database Data Definition Language (DDL) code for any kind of Oracle database object, such as a table, view, PL/SQL package, or sequence. Oracle Designer is still available, and Oracle still supports it. Oracle Designer still offers the most complete design support for Oracle database objects.

Although Oracle Designer can store information and generate code for Java code stored in the database, it cannot generate front-end J2EE code or Business Tier code, such as ADF BC. Also, Oracle Designer does not support object-oriented analysis and design.

NOTE
Oracle JHeadstart (described in Chapter 16) can generate starting ADF View and Model layer code from Oracle Designer definitions. This tool generates ADF code as a one-way migration from Oracle Designer, unlike the code generators in Oracle Designer, which you can run each time you make a change to Designer definitions.

Unified Modeling Language Tools

Recently, many organizations have chosen newer *Unified Modeling Language (UML)* tools to assist with the SDLC phases. UML standardizes a symbolic syntax for diagramming system design in various ways; UML offers a richer symbol set and better support for object-oriented analysis and design than the traditional tools, such as those available in Oracle Designer.

JDeveloper's Diagrams   JDeveloper offers the ability to create the following UML diagrams:

- **Activity Diagram**   This modeling tool looks similar to the Process Modeler in Oracle Designer. It represents activities (processes) and the transitions (flows) between activities within partitions (swim lanes or organizational units). You cannot generate code from this diagram.

- **Class Diagram**   This diagram can represent various domains of information, such as conceptual classes (not connected to code), Java classes and interfaces, EJBs (Enterprise JavaBeans), database objects, and business components. You can build this type of diagram from existing code (or database objects) and can also generate code from the diagram.

- **Sequence Diagram**   This diagram shows the messages exchanged between classes. You do not generate code from this diagram.

- **Use Case Diagram**   This diagram represents actors and their use cases (actions). It is used to represent details of how a system task (or process) is accomplished. You do not generate code from this diagram either.

In addition to these diagrams, JDeveloper contains two diagrams to assist in creating code: the *XML Schema Diagram*—for coding XML schemas—and the *JSF Navigation Diagram*—for defining the navigation rules and navigation cases between JSF pages and coding the faces-config .xml file.

The JDeveloper diagrammers help greatly with the Development phase of the system life cycle because they provide the ability to graphically represent the components in your system. However, they do not store information in a central repository, do not provide features for the Strategy and Analysis phases, and, except as noted, do not generate code.

Which Oracle Design Tool to Use

Currently, no one Oracle tool supports the complete system life cycle for a typical J2EE web project. If you want to stay with all Oracle development tools and feel that SDLC tools are important, you can use Oracle Designer's Strategy and Analysis tools for the early stages of the system life cycle; then you can use JDeveloper's tools for the Design, Development, and Deployment stages.

NOTE
Since this book focuses on the use of JDeveloper for web application development, it bypasses the question of how to use Oracle Designer and JDeveloper's diagramming tools within a full life system life cycle.

Application Design Considerations

Application design consists of planning how to implement a user interface and other code to fulfill a set of business requirements. You need to consider several areas when designing an application's user interface.

Setting a Standard for Scrolling and Screen Resolution

The user's monitor resolution will affect the amount of content you can place on a page. Although it is best to place all content so that a user does not need to use the browser scrollbars to view parts of the screen, this is not always possible. A good guideline for web applications is to expect the user to use the vertical scrollbar but not the horizontal scrollbar. Scrolling to the right and left to see additional content is not a standard action for web applications because content is often grouped horizontally. That means, if the user is viewing a field, other fields with related information may be to the left or right and the user would not be able to see all related information at the same time. However, expecting the user to scroll the browser window up or down is reasonable and, in fact, common in web applications.

After setting the standard about avoiding horizontal scrolling, you can then set a standard on what monitor resolution size your application will support. This decision will affect the amount of content you can place horizontally on the page. These days, many applications standardize on support for a 1024 × 768 resolution, but it is always good to do some research to ensure that the majority of users can accommodate that standard. You need to publish whatever standard you choose for the minimum screen resolution so that users can be aware that anything under it could require horizontal scrolling.

Some JSF container components allow you to set a width that represents a percentage of the screen width. For example, setting the width of a container that displays a table layout to "100%" will fill the screen horizontally regardless of the size of the screen. However, if a window is narrowed, the text within the container may wrap to more than one line to accommodate the contents. Therefore, setting the width of a container is only part of a solution that includes a design based on the user's screen resolution.

Achieving a Common Look and Feel

One of the steps in system design is creating a common look and feel for the user interface. A well-designed user interface is important from the standpoint of aesthetics. It is also a key to efficient use of the application. It, therefore, expresses both art and science. The page should be pleasant to look at with colors and graphics that do not distract from the functional purpose of the page.

Applications available on the Web are usually aimed at users who can teach themselves how the application function should be accomplished. Often, no formal training other than a help system is available for a web application. Clarity in the design allows users to quickly understand how to accomplish the intended business function. Consistency of this design means that the user needs to learn a particular interface design only once for the entire application. Therefore, to achieve user friendliness, the user interface and screen design should be clear and consistent.

NOTE
You may also need to plan your application for use by those who cannot see the screen or who cannot use a mouse. You will need to plan early in the application process if you want to use web component features such as access keys and alt text for these users.

Using Templates

One of the ways to provide consistency among your pages is through the use of *templates*, files containing elements that are common to all pages. Oracle Forms developers, particularly those who generate Oracle Forms using Oracle Designer, are likely to be experienced with the use of templates for Oracle Forms work. Once you have defined the common elements in a template file, you can apply the template in two primary ways:

- ■ **Copying**   You make a copy of the template file for each new page you create. This method provides each page with a separate copy of the template. The benefit of this method is that you can alter a common element on any page so that it works best for that page. The drawback of this method is that the common elements are copied; if the common design changes, the changes must be applied to each page.

- ■ **Referencing**   The pages in your application include one or more files containing the common elements. For example, you might create a template file containing menus and logos. This template would be referenced to appear in the header area of each page in the application. You would create similar template files for other shared areas, such as the footer and message areas.

The benefit of the referencing approach is that all pages share common files. If you need to make a change to one of the common elements (for example, a new entry in the menu), you change one file and all pages in the application will automatically use the new element. The drawback of this method is that you cannot change a shared element for one page without making that change to a copy of the shared file and referencing the copy.

You will need to decide which template method to use. The hands-on practices in this book use the copy method because, at this writing, there is no standard support within JDeveloper for templates for JSF JSP pages.

Approaching the User Interface Design

One approach to take when designing page flow for the user interface is to create a storyboard or sketch that shows the pages and action items (buttons or links) that will cause navigation to other pages. You use this sketch to communicate your design to users so they can provide feedback before the application is started. Also, this storyboard sketch guides you while developing the pages. A full user interface design will also include mockups of the screens so that you can prove the concepts.

This sketch can be drawn using any tool (software or manual). Although the JDeveloper JSF Navigation Diagram is intended as a visual editor to assist in building the faces-config.xml file used to define page flow, you can also use it to create an application page flow sketch. A JDeveloper JSF Navigation Diagram can only contain pages, navigation cases, *notes* (boxes containing text), or *attachments* (dotted lines drawn from one attachment to another or from one page to an attachment). However, with smart use of notes and attachments, you can represent non-page items (such as tab bars and tab items); these items will not become part of the code, so you can add any kind of documentation or note to them.

The benefit of using JDeveloper's JSF Navigation Diagram for the page flow sketch is that drawing page and navigation case symbols on the diagram will create code in the faces-config.xml file. This code can be used as is or refined later to define navigation. As mentioned in the Chapter 9 practice, when you define a JSP file for a page represented on the diagram, the yellow "undefined" triangle symbol will disappear.

NOTE
Since undefined pages on the diagram do not affect functionality of defined pages, you can wait until the end of the project to delete undefined pages from the diagram.

Approaching ADF Business Components Design

An effective design method for the ADF BC layer is driving its design from the user interface screens as they are planned. View objects and view links should be developed to support the data requirements for each screen. In addition, entity objects are created to support the data needs of the view objects. This iterative approach needs constant monitoring to check for and consolidate any duplication, but the final design will fit the application requirements much more effectively than the alternate approach of generating default entity objects and view objects from the database schema and trying to force the user interface into using them.

When planning the view objects for a screen, take full advantage of the capability of the view objects to join entities. For example, ADF applications don't have the luxury of the Oracle Forms POST-QUERY trigger to manage foreign key lookups for reference data. Such lookups should be encapsulated in the view objects as a standard approach. This can actually be more efficient because the cursor OPEN and CLOSE operations commonly coded into an Oracle Forms POST-QUERY trigger causes more network traffic and uses more database resources than a simple lookup join in a view object or database view.

Additionally, determine if a particular view object needs to be read-only. If a view object is only ever used for populating dropdown lists or query-only screens, then marking it as read-only can save resources on the application server.

Finally, look for opportunities to reuse objects. The view link and bind variable mechanisms discussed in Chapter 6 can be used to adapt a single view object for use in several different contexts, for example, to serve a standalone data entry form and as part of a master-detail screen.

Implementing Business Rules and Validation

One of the most discussed areas of J2EE application design is where to locate application logic. We have seen how ADF Business Components provides places for both declarative and coded validation, and this will be the natural place for the majority of your logic. However, we also appreciate that a proven technique for implementing business rules is the *database-centric approach* that keeps as much of the business rule code in the database as possible, implemented through views and PL/SQL triggers. There are other approaches. The approach you use depends upon how much you want to rely on database code to enforce business rules.

A Database-centric Approach   The authors have had success with the database-centric approach to business rules, which stores all business rules code in the database and calls this code from database triggers. That way, the application front-end layer can be changed more easily with less recoding. In addition, any application—past, present, or future—will pass through the same validation rules.

This is the idea behind the Table API that Oracle Designer generates. The Table API is a PL/SQL package of procedures that handle INSERT, UPDATE, DELETE, SELECT, and LOCK operations for a table. A full set of table triggers ensures that access to the table (for INSERT, UPDATE, DELETE, and LOCK) is only allowed by calling these procedures. By adding to this system fine-grained access control (also called virtual private database) policies to restrict access to specific rows of data, the table is effectively protected with a code layer that allows business rules code to be applied to any type of operation. If rules error messages from this layer are handled in a user-friendly way, this system can, theoretically, serve any type of user interface layer.

A Modified Database-centric Approach   Using the database-centric approach, the application layer can, also theoretically, be devoid of business rules code. This situation is rarely completely practical, because some validations, such as datatype, format, and mandatory values, as well as JSF validators and converters, are most user-friendly when they occur immediately on the user interface level before the page is submitted to the application server and from there to the database. Therefore, you may opt for a modified database-centric approach where you repeat business rules, such as those just mentioned in the user interface layer. Validation in the UI layer has the advantage of providing more immediate feedback to users when they are in error. However, such code should always be used in addition to checks in the business or database layers, and should not be the only form of validation.

CAUTION
Always assume that any validation in the user interface layer can be bypassed by alternative interfaces into the business service or malicious users, so it should not be relied upon.

In addition, some business rules, such as field value comparisons and conditional logic based on cached data, can be easily handled on the application server side. Validation errors from this level of code would appear to the user faster than the corresponding errors coded in database triggers. In addition, enforcing these business rules on the application server level would not require database processing time or network messages to and from the database. In this case, the business rules code that implements these business rules would also be duplicated in the application server layers (such as ADF BC code).

NOTE
ADF wraps error messages from the database (such as those from explicit RAISE_APPLICATION_ERROR statements) inside several layers of Oracle and business components error messages. These messages are unfriendly to end users. Translating them (or just stripping out the unfriendly parts, such as error numbers) requires custom coding within the ADFm (ADF model) life cycle. An example code required to modify the ADFm life cycle can be found in the Oracle SRDemo Sample application available in the JDeveloper Update Center.

Duplicating business rules code in more than one layer does require extra coding as well as extra work in synchronizing the code that is duplicated between layers. Therefore, you need to seriously consider whether the benefits of this duplication—namely, saving database processing, saving network traffic, and providing friendlier feedback to users—are worthwhile.

TIP
If you are concerned about the extra processing time needed to run database trigger code that validates a value already checked in the UI, set a context variable as described in the audit columns practice in Chapter 15. Then read this context variable in the trigger code to determine whether the value (or a set of values) has already been validated by the UI.

Which Approach to Take?   In addition to the database-centric approaches mentioned, you can select variations on coding all business rules in the application server and all business rules in the database. These variations would code a particular business rule in one place or the other.

The approach that you take will depend partially on your preference for Java or PL/SQL code; both types of code are valid and both will be required at some level in each application. The important thing to remember, though, is that ultimate responsibility for the integrity of data must remain with the database. At the minimum, your approach should take full advantage of the relational integrity capability offered by database constraints (primary key, foreign key, and check) to ensure that data has a valid structure.

Designing Security

Most applications will need some security, even if it is just to determine the identity of a user. In the traditional Oracle Forms and PL/SQL worlds, this user information is generally gathered from the Oracle database account that connects the application to the database. However, as we discussed in Chapter 6, for scalability reasons, Java enterprise applications do not work this way and usually use a shared database account to connect the application to the database.

The important thing about a security strategy is to think about it from the start. Base your thinking on application roles rather than on specific user identities. As you lay out the user interface and the page flow, consider which pages need to be restricted and which logical user roles are required. In some cases, you may need to hide regions of the page or make them read-only based on these roles, so plan out these requirements as you design the pages. Once the application is deployed, the logical application roles can be mapped to real users without having to make changes to the application. In Chapter 14, we look at how the standard security provided by J2EE containers can be used to provide authentication for users, to give access to the roles that these users belong to, and to provide an identity (for data manipulations) to the connected user.

Best Practices

As you build more ADF-based applications, you will start to establish work patterns and toolkits to speed up the process. In this section, we highlight some of the habits that it's best to adopt from the outset. You will see these in use throughout the sample application discussed in the remainder of Part II. This advice is intended to be a good starting point. As adoption of the ADF platform grows, the body of knowledge and best practices will evolve.

Use Framework Buffer Classes

Frameworks, such as ADF Business Components and the ADF Model, provide comprehensive framework extension points. You should use these capabilities to create *framework buffer classes*—Java classes that provide a layer between the framework implementation and any code that you write using that framework.

As an example, let's look at how this works for ADF Business Components. In Chapter 6, you saw how to add validation code to an entity object by choosing the *Generate Java File* option in the entity object properties. This creates an *Impl* (implementation) class, which subclasses the framework `EntityImpl` class, for example:

```
public class DepartmentsImpl extends EntityImpl
{
}
```

Your specific entity Impl class (`DepartmentsImpl`, in this case) should not directly extend the framework `EntityImpl` class, but rather should extend a framework buffer class that you create that, in turn, extends the framework-supplied `EntityImpl`, as shown in the following illustration.

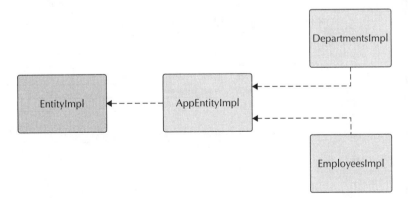

In this example, `DepartmentsImpl` and `EmployeesImpl` extend `AppEntityImpl`, which, in turn, extends the framework class, `EntityImpl`. The `AppEntityImpl` class does not initially need to contain any extra functionality; it just extends the `EntityImpl` class as follows:

```
public class AppEntityImpl extends EntityImpl
{
}
```

You would then change your code to extend the framework buffer class as follows:

```
public class DepartmentsImpl extends AppEntityImpl
{
}
```

Adding your own buffer classes between the application and the framework provides two benefits. First, as the application evolves, you will identify certain bits of reusable functionality or functionality that modifies the default way that the framework operates. These can be moved into the buffer class with a minimum of disruption and immediately become available to all your classes, since your classes will extend this framework buffer class. Second, the buffer class provides a good patching point. If you encounter a problem in the way that the base framework works, you can patch workarounds into the single buffer class, rather than having to make the change in every implementation.

Setting Up Framework Extensions   JDeveloper provides excellent support for layering in buffer classes with ADF Business Components. You can configure the IDE to automatically use your extension when creating new objects. You can define these buffer classes on a project-by-project basis (in the Project Properties screen) or from the Preferences dialog (**Tools | Preferences**). In the Preferences dialog, select Business Components\Base Classes in the preferences tree, and the following screen will display:

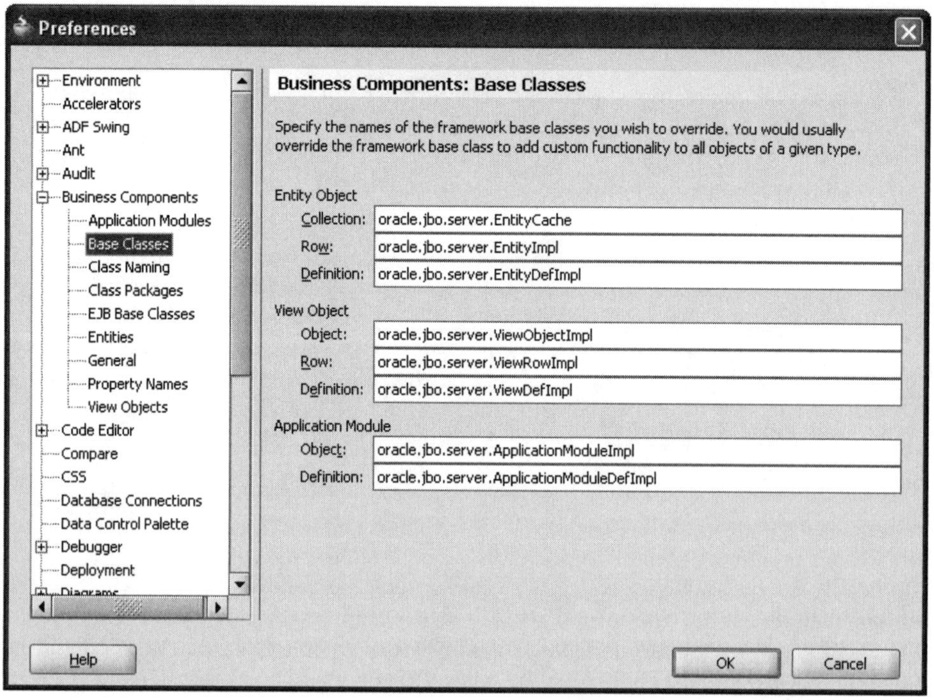

Each of the base classes shown in this dialog can be replaced with an application-specific subclass at the very start of the project build. For most applications, it will be sufficient to provide framework buffer classes for `EntityImpl`, `ViewObjectImpl`, `ViewRowImpl`, and `ApplicationModuleImpl` because they are the most commonly used extension points. When an ADF BC wizard creates a business component class, it will use the class of the appropriate type defined on this page as the superclass.

For other parts of the application that wire into the frameworks, such as backing beans for JSF pages, you will not be directly subclassing framework classes, but it is still useful to put a superclass in place that all your implementations subclass. This superclass will provide you with a place to put common functionality.

Use Java Packaging

In Chapter 6, we mentioned how it was sensible to create your entity objects and view objects in separate packages within the model project to ease maintenance. This same principle can be extended to the ViewController project as well. Keep page backing beans, PageDef files, and other files partitioned into their own package structures.

Write Tests

Although we won't spend any time discussing test-driven development, if you examine the application in the sample files on the website, you will find a ModelTesting project within the Tuhra workspace. This project contains JUnit (junit.org) tests that can be run repeatedly against the ADF Business Components model to verify its functionality. JUnit is a comprehensive testing framework that makes it easier to automate such repeatable tests. It is available as an extension for JDeveloper from the update menu option (**Help | Check For Updates**).

With a testing framework in place, you can ensure that changes made to the application model as the application evolves do not break the user interface. You should also use tests to validate your implementation of all business rules.

Stick to JSF and Only JSF

In the design of the user interface, don't mix HTML markup with JSF components. Doing so can lead to unexpected results because of the different page-creation life cycles of JSF and normal JSP/HTML. Using HTML markup in a JSF page will also make it harder to migrate the application to use the templating technologies that are emerging for JSF, such as Facelets, or to deploy to devices other than a standard web browser. Use the power of the JSF layout containers, such as `af:panelPage`, to position your components in a portable and consistent manner. It is important, therefore, to take the time to understand the layout capabilities of the various container components available.

NOTE
When you drop the first ADF Faces component onto a JSP page, JDeveloper converts the raw HTML tags in the JSP file (html, head, and body) to their ADF Faces equivalents (afh:html, afh:head, and afh:body). These ADF Faces HTML tags will be ignored by render kits that do not generate HTML-specific tags.

Sample Application System Design

The sample application developed in this book is called *The Ultimate Human Resources Application (TUHRA)* (pronounced "too-rah"). As discussed in the Introduction, this application uses the database objects installed in the HR schema in Oracle9*i* and Oracle 10*g*. The purpose of the application is to allow access to and modification of the data in the HR tables. The Security Administrator for the company assigns one of three application roles—user, admin, and manager—to each user by entering the user and role in a security file (described in Chapter 14).

Users assigned the user role are allowed to search for any employee record, but will not be able to edit any employee record but their own. Users assigned the manager role have the same access, but are also able to edit or create any other employee record, too. Users assigned the admin role have the same access as managers, but can also display the screens used to maintain reference data, such as job types.

Database Design

This sample application starts development work by assuming that all analysis and design has been completed. That is, the business requirements are known, the business rules have been documented, and the page flows and screens have been designed. In addition, the database design has been worked out and the system's tables, views, constraints, and sequences have been created and proven to fulfill the business requirements.

Since the system design and database development is complete, the scope of the rest of this part of the book is limited to describing how to accomplish the development tasks required to implement the application design. Therefore, a quick look and brief description of the database tables and their relationships will suffice. The database tables used in this application are shown in the JDeveloper database diagram in Figure 10-1.

This diagram depicts the following design:

- **A hierarchy of tables** from REGIONS to COUNTRIES to LOCATIONS to DEPARTMENTS to EMPLOYEES. Each pair of tables represents a master-detail (parent-child) relationship.

- **An optional lookup relationship** between a single DEPARTMENTS record and the EMPLOYEES table to associate a manager with the department.

- **An optional self-referencing relationship** in EMPLOYEES to associate a manager record with an employee record.

- **A lookup table**, JOBS, that provides a job code for the EMPLOYEES and JOB_HISTORY tables.

- **A history table**, JOB_HISTORY, that stores a record for each time an employee changes jobs or departments.

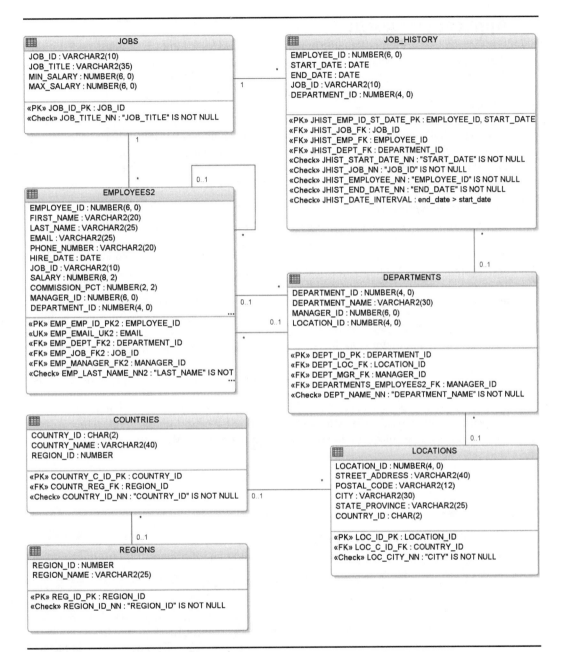

FIGURE 10-1. *HR database design diagram*

Application Design

The TUHRA application design implements a common look and feel. Development of each page starts by copying a template to ensure that this look and feel is applied consistently. The following describes this look and feel before describing each page and the flows between pages.

Look and Feel

We base the application's appearance on Oracle's Browser Look and Feel (BLAF) standards, as described briefly in the sidebar "About Browser Look and Feel." We feel that a solid user interface requires a large amount of thought and effort as well as some artistic input, and BLAF supplies this. The main design elements this application derives from BLAF are the color schemes and the page layout (for example, the header, footer, and menu tabs).

Pages and Navigation

The page flow and main design elements for all pages in the application are depicted in the JDeveloper JSF Navigation diagram in Figure 10-2. This diagram uses note symbols to hold descriptions of each page as well as to represent tab bars and navigation items. Attachment lines connect note boxes to other elements. You will notice the page names include directory names. This application uses container-based security (as described in Chapter 14), which enforces access privileges on a *URL pattern*—a set of characters in the web address for a set of pages that match an entry in web.xml. This entry specifies how the URL will be handled for a purpose such as processing or handling security. For example, you can define that the admin role can access pages that match the URL pattern "faces/pages/admin/*"; this pattern refers to all pages in the faces/pages/admin virtual directory, which maps to a physical directory. These pages will be available to users in the admin role. Therefore, the directory name (corresponding to this URL pattern) is important to the security design.

   This diagram shows the pages for the entire application. The remaining hands-on practices in this part of the book describe how to create some of these pages. Samples and technical notes for the other pages are available on the websites mentioned in the "Websites for Sample Code" section of the Introduction.

About Browser Look and Feel

Oracle's *Browser Look and Feel* (BLAF) is an extensive set of standards for designing the appearance and workings of the user interface layer of an application. Oracle develops and maintains these standards primarily to support the E-Business Suite (Oracle Applications) modules that present web interfaces.

   The detailed BLAF standards are available in hundreds of pages of web files (www.oracle .com/technology/tech/blaf). Although Oracle online applications apply the BLAF standards to ADF UIX user interface code, the standards are perfectly suitable to ADF Faces. In fact, ADF Faces uses BLAF standards for its default look and feel.

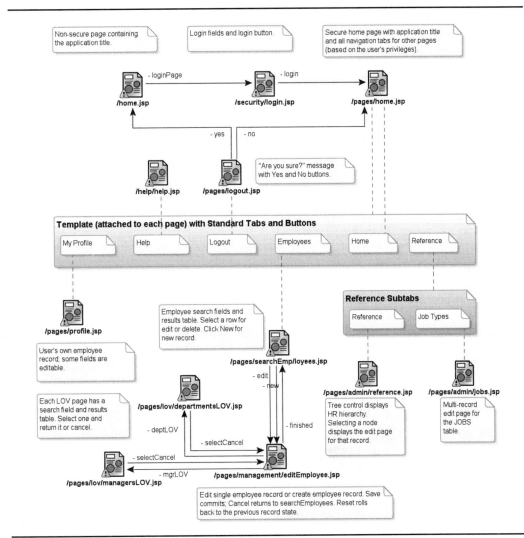

FIGURE 10-2. *Application design sketch as a JDeveloper JSF Navigation Diagram*

Pages Created in This Book

The following page descriptions summarize the functionality and contents of the pages you will create in the following chapters. In the application development stage, you would normally base your coding work on mockups (or a storyboard sketch) of the page designs. The following descriptions also show the finalized screens instead of these mockups.

Home (public)   The user accesses the application using a link or URL. The first page that displays is home.jsp, a page containing the application name and a Login button as shown here.

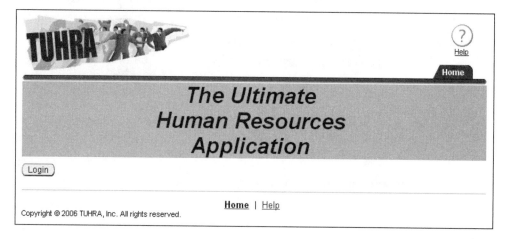

No login is required to access this page. It does not contain any application-specific links or data. Those will appear after the user logs in.

Login   The login.jsp page appears when the user clicks Login on the Home page. It presents fields for entering the application user name and password. This application authenticates the user with container security (as described in Chapter 14) so that, if the user is not logged in, any secure page the user accesses will automatically display the Login page. After the login is successful, no additional logins will be necessary. This Login page is shown here:

Home (secure) In the normal page flow (the page flow initiated by accessing a secure page when logged in), the secure Home page that follows will appear after a successful login:

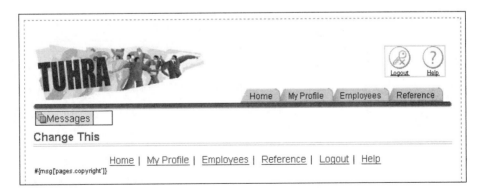

This page displays navigation tabs and buttons appropriate to the user. In this case, an admin user (TFOX) is logged in and sees all tabs. The page displays the user name and a welcome message.

Template The home page shows a standard container component used in the BLAF design, the `af:panelPage`. This component offers prebuilt facets for areas such as graphical "branding" logos, a global button area in the upper-right corner, a tab navigation bar area, a content area, and a footer area with navigation links and a copyright line. These elements are built into each page from the template. Then, when a new page is created, the branding, global button, tab bar, content, and footer areas are copied to the new page file. The following illustration shows the main template in the JDeveloper Visual Editor:

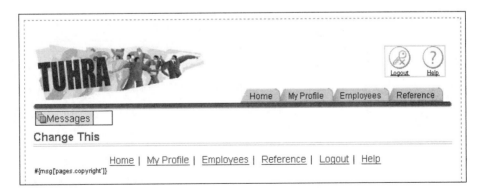

Employees Search   Clicking the Employees tab on any screen displays the searchEmployees.jsp page shown here:

TUHRA

Logout Help

Home | My Profile | **Employees** | Reference

Signed in as TFOX

Employees Search

ID		Department ID	
First Name		Job ID	
Last Name		Manager ID	

Search   Clear

☑ **TIP** Enter employee search criteria and click Search.

Home | My Profile | **Employees** | Reference | Logout | Help
Copyright © 2006 TUHRA, Inc. All rights reserved.

This page allows the user to search for employee records based on some details about the employee. Users in any role can access this screen and perform queries. No personal information, such as salary or commission, is displayed or is queriable.

The user enters query criteria in the fields and clicks Search. Records that match the query criteria are displayed in a table below the criteria fields, as shown here:

TUHRA

Logout Help

Home | My Profile | **Employees** | Reference

Signed in as TFOX

Employees Search

ID		Department ID	
First Name	S%	Job ID	
Last Name		Manager ID	

Search   Clear

Matching Employees

Select and Edit Delete New   ⊘ Previous 1-10 of 12 ▾ Next 2 ⊛

Select	ID	First Name	Last Name	Department	Job ID	Manager ID
⦿	166	Sundar	Andes	80	SA_REP	147
○	116	Shelli	Baida	30	PU_CLERK	114
○	192	Sarah	Bell	50	SH_CLERK	123
○	205	Shelley	Higgins	110	AC_MGR	101
○	100	Steven	King	90	AD_PRES	
○	173	Sundita	Kumar	80	SA_REP	148
○	128	Steven	Markle	50	ST_CLERK	120
○	203	Susan	Mavris	40	HR_REP	101
○	194	Samuel	McCain	50	SH_CLERK	123
○	161	Sarath	Sewall	80	SA_REP	146

Select and Edit Delete New   ⊘ Previous 1-10 of 12 ▾ Next 2 ⊛

Home | My Profile | **Employees** | Reference | Logout | Help
Copyright © 2006 TUHRA, Inc. All rights reserved.

This results table displays 10 records at a time and contains navigation controls to scroll to different record sets. Users in the manager and admin roles will see Edit, Delete, and New buttons. Delete removes the selected record. Edit loads another screen with a single record for the purposes of modifying it. New loads the single-record screen with blank fields so that a new employee record can be entered. Users who see these buttons will also see an edit link in the EmployeeId column; clicking this link loads the same screen as the Edit button.

Employee Edit   Users in the manager and admin roles can click the Edit button or the edit link on the search page to load editEmployee.jsp, as shown here:

Clicking New on the Search page will load this same page but with a blank record and no EmployeeId value displayed.

This page allows the user to create or edit an employee record. Notice that, unlike other pages in this application, no tabs are selected for this page. This page is only accessible from the Search page, so clicking a tab will not display it. To return to the Search page, the user clicks the Employees tab again.

This page contains buttons for Save (commit), Cancel (rollback and return to the Search page), and Reset (rollback without leaving the page). It also contains a pulldown list for JobId and lists of values (LOVs) for Department and Manager.

LOVs for Department and Manager   Clicking an LOV (flashlight) button next to the *Department* field on the employee edit page pops up this page (departmentsLOV.jsp):

This window allows the user to search on a department name using the *Department Name* field and Search button. The user then selects a department and clicks Select. The department number for the department is returned to the edit page. Clicking Close in the LOV window closes the window and does not select a department. While the LOV window is displayed, the user cannot interact with the edit page. When the LOV window closes, the edit page is again enabled.

Clicking the LOV button next to the *Manager* field on the Edit page displays a similar LOV window for manager. This LOV window works the same way, but searches for a manager last name or first name and returns the manager (employee) ID to the edit page.

Logout   Clicking the Logout global button or footer link on any page displays the following page:

This page displays a confirmation message with two buttons: Yes and No. Clicking Yes logs the user out of the application and returns him or her to the public Home page. Clicking No (or the Cancel button at the top of the page) returns the user to the secure Home page.

Pages Available on the Sample Code Websites

In addition to the functionality just discussed, the application is designed to contain the following pages, which are documented on the sample code websites.

My Profile   The user clicks the My Profile tab on any page to access profile.jsp, shown here:

This page automatically loads the user's employee record and allows the user to modify First Name, Last Name, Email, and Phone. Save and Clear buttons allow the user to commit or rollback the changes, respectively. Users in all roles can access their own profiles.

Reference The Reference tab is available only for users in the admin role. Clicking this tab displays the reference.jsp page, as shown here:

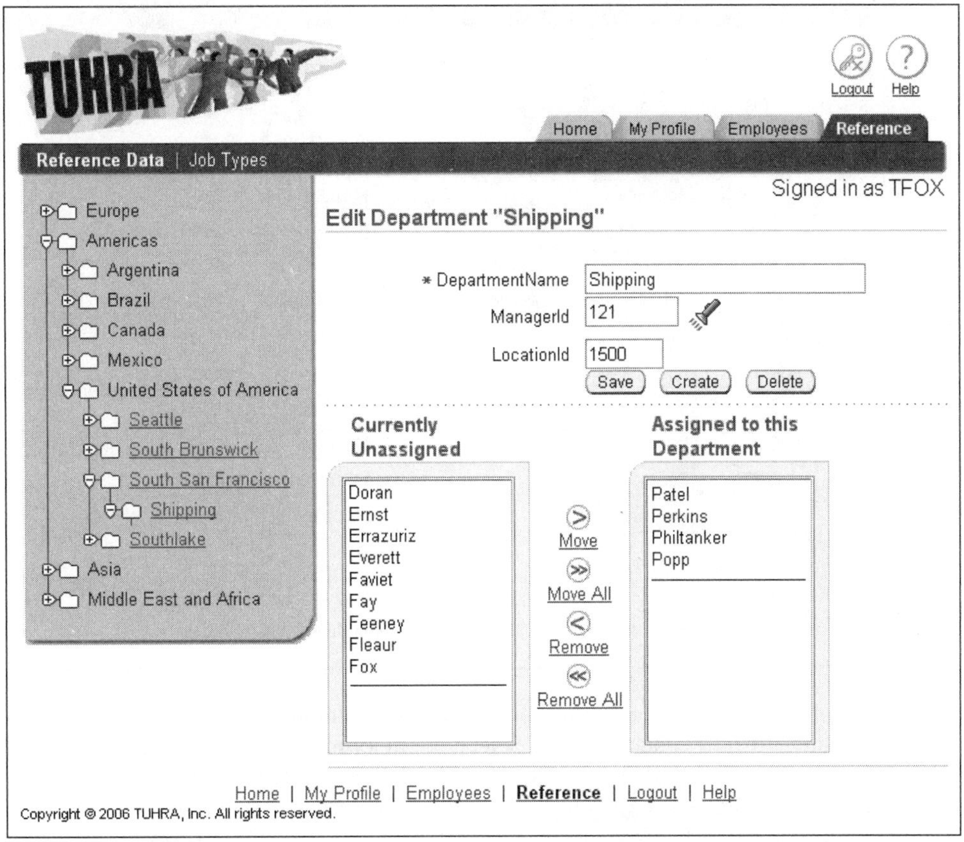

This page displays a subtab for Reference Data and for Job Types.

The tree component on the left side of the screen allows the user to drill down to a specific level of the HR hierarchy. Selecting a node will display an edit page for that node on the right side of the screen. This allows administrative users to quickly find and edit a lookup record, such as a country or region.

Jobs   After clicking the Reference tab (visible to admin users only) and the Job Types subtab, the jobs.jsp file will appear, as follows:

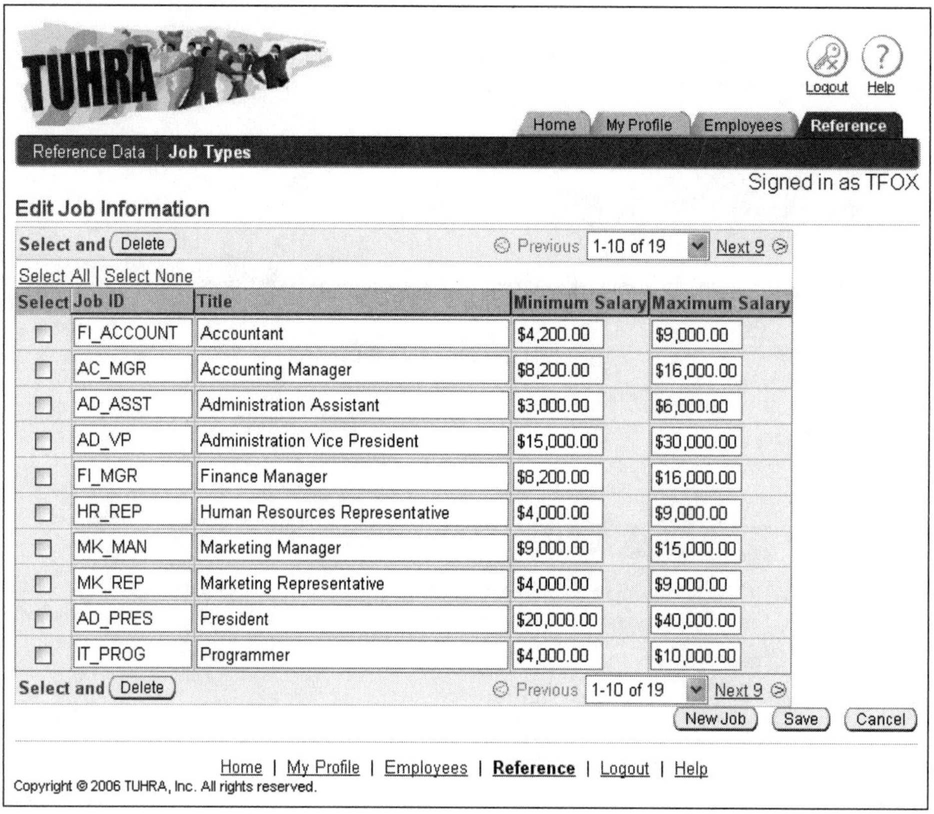

This page allows the user to edit multiple records and commit all changes (using the Save button). Clicking Cancel will roll back changes. Selecting one or more records using the checkboxes in the Select column and then clicking Delete will delete the selected records. Clicking the Select All or Select None links will add checkmarks to all rows on the page or will remove checkmarks from all rows on the page, respectively. Clicking New Job adds a blank row at the bottom of the first page. You can then fill in this blank row and click Save to add JOBS records.

Clicking the Reference Data subtab on this page loads the reference.jsp file described in the preceding section.

Help   The sample application includes a single page (shown next) that is available to all users and that contains documentation about all aspects of the system.

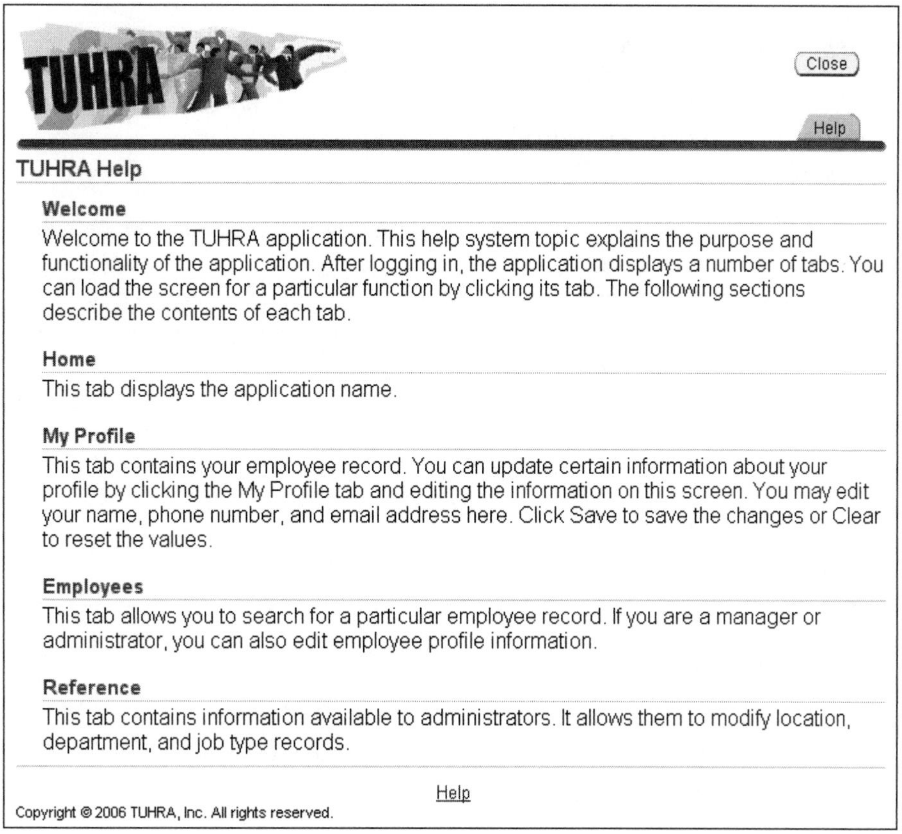

TUHRA Help

Welcome

Welcome to the TUHRA application. This help system topic explains the purpose and functionality of the application. After logging in, the application displays a number of tabs. You can load the screen for a particular function by clicking its tab. The following sections describe the contents of each tab.

Home

This tab displays the application name.

My Profile

This tab contains your employee record. You can update certain information about your profile by clicking the My Profile tab and editing the information on this screen. You may edit your name, phone number, and email address here. Click Save to save the changes or Clear to reset the values.

Employees

This tab allows you to search for a particular employee record. If you are a manager or administrator, you can also edit employee profile information.

Reference

This tab contains information available to administrators. It allows them to modify location, department, and job type records.

Help

Copyright © 2006 TUHRA, Inc. All rights reserved.

This page appears in a separate modal window when the user clicks the Help button on any page. Although the sample shown here is a single page that briefly introduces the contents of the system, it could be expanded to a fuller help system with context-sensitive contents, embedded graphics, and text queried from the database.

Hands-on Practice: Create the Workspace and Projects

With that brief view of the system design, we are ready to start building the application. The steps in this section create the application workspace and default projects. The process is similar to the one you used in Chapter 9, but this time you use an application template specific to JSF work.

Before starting, be sure you have followed the guidelines in the "Accessing the Sample Database Schema" section of this book's Introduction to prepare the database schema.

TIP
As mentioned in Chapter 9, be sure to look through the "Ensuring Success with the Hands-On Practices" section of this book's Introduction for hints about what to do if something does not work correctly. The Introduction also contains information about the supported version of JDeveloper.

1. On the Applications node of the navigator, select **New Application** from the right-click menu.

2. In the Create Application dialog, fill in the *Application Name* as "Tuhra," the *Application Package Prefix* as "tuhra," and the *Application Template* as "Web Application [JSF, ADF BC]." Accept the default directory name. Click OK.

    Additional Information: The application and two projects (Model and ViewController) will appear in the navigator, as shown here:

NOTE
This example simplifies the package name for the sake of faster reading. For an enterprise application, you would follow the corporate standard for package names. Often, this standard will include the domain extension (such as com, gov, net, or org), the company name or abbreviation, and the project name. For example, if the company name were JDev Tools, Inc., the package name for the TUHRA application would be "com.jdevtools.tuhra" or, more simply, "jdevtools.tuhra."

3. Click Save All.

What Did You Just Do? You created a workspace and two projects, Model and ViewController. You selected an application workspace template assigned to JSF and ADF BC work, so the projects are configured for work with those technologies. The ViewController project will contain all user interface code and configuration files, such as the faces-config.xml file, which defines the page flow and event handling. The Model project will contain ADF Business Components objects that represent database structures, such as tables. You will add to both projects throughout the remaining chapters in this part of the book.

CHAPTER
11

Home Page and Menus

*The best way to keep children at home
is to make the home atmosphere pleasant,
and let the air out of their tires.*

—Dorothy Parker (1893–1967)

ow that you have an idea about the application design and have defined the
workspace and projects, you can develop the rest of the application. This chapter
explains how to prepare the starting files for most of the user interface pages and
how to complete the home pages.

As in all chapters in Part II of this book, this chapter discusses key concepts as it shows you
how to develop the application. Therefore, it is important to read the discussions as well as to
follow the hands-on practice steps.

Hands-on Practice: Create the Home Page and Menus

The work in this chapter is divided into the following phases:

I. Prepare the Model project

- Define a database connection
- Set up the framework buffer layer
- Create the application module

II. Prepare the ViewController project

- Reset project properties
- Set up the framework buffer layer
- Add the message bundle file

III. Create a template

- Create the template file
- Add components to the template
- Add menu tabs and other components
- Declare JSF pages in the JSF Navigation Diagram
- Define navigation actions

IV. Copy the template file and customize the copies

- Create all page files
- Customize the page files
- Add subtab navigation
- Test the navigation

V. Complete the home pages

■ Add components

■ Create a CSS file and apply it

I. Prepare the Model Project

This phase creates the connection to the database and adds buffer classes and an application module to the Model project. All work from this chapter forward in this part of the book assumes that you have completed the hands-on practice in the preceding chapter. Starting files for each chapter are available on the sample code websites mentioned in the "Websites for Sample Code" section in the Introduction.

Define a Database Connection

ADF BC communicates to the database using a connection object that you need to define and use for each project that requires a database connection. The connection object contains information about the database user, host, and database identifier, and you can use it for any application you create in the future. You can switch these connection objects when you deploy code to another server without changing anything other than a property that associates an application module with the connection object. This section sets up the connection object to the sample schema. It assumes that you have a database running on your desktop as described in the Introduction. If you are accessing a remote database server, you will need to adjust the values in these steps appropriately.

1. Close all editor windows (on any editor tab, select **Close All** from the right-click menu).

2. In the navigator area, click the Connections tab. If the Connections tab is not displayed, select **View | Connection Navigator**.

3. Expand the Database node to determine if you have created a connection called "HR." If so, open it by double clicking it, and check that the values in the dialog correspond to values in the wizard described in this section.

4. If you have no HR connection, double click the Database node to start the Create Database Connection Wizard. Click Next if the Welcome page appears.

5. Enter the *Connection Name* as "HR" and click Next. Enter the *Username* ("HR") and *Password* ("HR" by default). This is the user account that ADF BC will connect to. Leave *Role* blank, select the *Deploy Password* checkbox, and click Next.

TIP
The Help button on any wizard page in JDeveloper shows a help topic that describes the fields and contents of that wizard page.

6. Enter the *Host Name* (for a database on your desktop computer, use "localhost") and *JDBC Port* ("1521" by default). Enter the *SID* (the database name, for example, "XE" for Oracle Express or "ORCL" for Oracle Enterprise Edition). Click Next.

7. On the Test page, click Test Connection. If the test fails, check the settings in the wizard pages with your DBA and correct any problem settings. When the test succeeds, click Finish to dismiss the wizard and create the connection.

8. You can browse objects granted to or owned by the HR user by opening the nodes under the HR connection node of the Connections Navigator.

9. When you are finished browsing, click the Applications Navigator tab.

Set Up the Framework Buffer Layer

As Chapter 10 describes, adding a buffer layer between the framework code and your application code offers benefits such as the ability to work around framework bugs and to provide additional functionality that is shared with all your application code. This buffer layer is made of Java class files that extend the base framework classes. The buffer classes are then used as parent classes to all classes you create in the project. This section sets up JDeveloper to use a buffer layer for ADF BC objects in the Model project and then creates the required class files.

Although you may not need to supplement or override the behavior of the ADF BC base classes, the JDeveloper entity object, view object, and application module wizards create Java class files for you to modify. These default classes are necessary so that your framework buffer classes will be used. For example, if you created an entity object for the EMPLOYEES table but specified that the wizard should not create a specific Java class file, the framework would access the table using only the ADF BC base class for entity objects. This would bypass your entity object framework buffer class. However, if you allow the wizard to create the specific entity object Java class file, you can declare that it will use your framework buffer class.

The following steps modify the wizard defaults so that it will create only the Java class files you require (the entity object's row class, the view object's object class, and the application module's object class).

1. The wizard's default properties are available in the Preferences dialog. Select **Tools** | **Preferences** and click the Business Components node. Ensure that the checkmarks for only these class types are selected: *Entity Object: Row Class*, *View Object: Object Class*, and *Application Module: Object Class*.

   Additional Information: This will cause the corresponding checkboxes to be selected in the Entity Object Wizard, View Object Wizard, and Application Module Wizard, respectively. You can always override these defaults for a particular object. The framework buffer classes that you create will serve as superclasses for these automatically generated classes. You will also create a framework buffer class for the view object row class.

2. Click OK.

3. You now need to add the ADF BC library to the project. Normally, the ADF BC wizards will add this library, but you will be setting up Java class files before running these wizards, so you need to add the library manually. Double click the Model project node in the navigator.

4. Select the Libraries node and click Add Library. Select the BC4J Runtime node and click OK. Click OK to dismiss the Project Properties dialog. (*BC4J* stands for "Business Components for Java," the old name for ADF BC.)

5. To create a framework buffer class for the application module object, on the Model node, select **New** from the right-click menu. Select the General category and double click the Java Class item to display the Create Java Class dialog.

6. Enter the *Name* as "TuhraApplicationModuleImpl" and enter "tuhra.model.framework" in the *Package* field. Click Browse next to the *Extends* property and, in the Class Browser's

Search tab, type "ApplicationM" in the *Match Class Name* field. The classes with matching names will appear in the bottom pane. Note that two `ApplicationModuleImpl` classes appear. Select "ApplicationModuleImpl (oracle.jbo.server)" and click OK. The *Extends* property will fill in with the fully qualified class name.

Additional Information: The oracle.jbo.server package contains most of the ADF BC base classes. You can also use the Hierarchy tab of the Class Browser to find the class if you know the package name. ("*JBO*" in the library path and in some error messages stands for "Java Business Objects," a previous name used for the ADF BC framework.)

7.   In the Create Java Class dialog, leave *Public* and *Generate Default Constructor* selected and *Generate Main Method* unselected. Click OK to create the class file and its package.

8.   The TuhraApplicationModuleImpl.java file should open in the editor. If it is not open, double click it (under Model\Application Sources\tuhra.model.framework) to open it. Notice that JDeveloper added the proper package and import statements, as well as filling in the class signature with the name of the superclass (`ApplicationModuleImpl`). You will add to this code as required during the development process.

NOTE
If you see an src folder under the project folder in the navigator, click the Toggle Directories button in the navigator toolbar so that your display matches the illustrations in the book.

9.   Repeat steps 5–8 for the following classes. All Java files are placed in the tuhra.model .framework package. You may spot-check any of these classes in the editor along the way.

Class Name	Extends
TuhraEntityImpl	oracle.jbo.server.EntityImpl
TuhraViewObjectImpl	oracle.jbo.server.ViewObjectImpl
TuhraViewRowImpl	oracle.jbo.server.ViewRowImpl

10.   Click Save All.

11.   Select the Model node in the navigator, and click Rebuild in the JDeveloper toolbar to be sure all code compiles. Fix problems that occur, and recompile. Repeat until the code compiles.

Additional Information: These class files will serve as the application-level framework buffer layer through which code in the Model project will pass. The next steps will define the Model project so that it uses these classes as the parent classes for ADF BC objects in this project.

12.   Double click the Model project to display its properties. Select the Business Components\ Base Classes node in the Project Properties navigator.

13.   If you do not see Browse buttons next to the fields on this page, select the Business Components node and select the *Initialize Project for Business Components* checkbox. Be sure the HR connection is selected in the *Connection* pulldown. Click OK and reopen

the Project Properties dialog. Return to the Base Classes node. The Browse buttons should now appear as shown here:

14. Click Browse next to the *Application Module: Object* field and, in the Search tab, enter "Tu" to search for "TuhraApplicationModuleImpl." Select it and click OK.

    Additional Information: Notice that, although you have defined four class files that begin with "Tu," JDeveloper's class browser selects files of the relevant type. For example, you only see `TuhraApplicationModuleImpl` for the application module object because it shares the same parent class as the default application module object class (`oracle.jbo.server.ApplicationModuleImpl`).

15. Repeat the preceding step to fill in the following base classes:
    Entity Object:Row as "tuhra.model.framework.TuhraEntityImpl"
    View Object: Object as "tuhra.model.framework.TuhraViewObjectImpl"
    View Object: Row as "tuhra.model.framework.TuhraViewRowImpl"

    Additional Information: You can set these properties on a more global level using the Preferences dialog. (Select **Tools | Preferences** and navigate to the Business Components\ Base Classes node.) Setting these properties at the JDeveloper level in this way will make these buffer classes available to all future projects. However, this example uses application-level buffer files, so they are set at the project level instead of the global level. Since you did not change the corresponding properties in the Preferences dialog, these specific buffer classes will not be available outside the Model project.

16. Click OK. Click Save All. If you expand the nodes under Model, the navigator will now appear as follows:

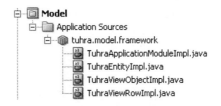

Using the Business Components Diagram for ADF BC and Database Objects

Although you will likely know from the design phase which tables will be required in the Model layer, you will probably develop and refine Model components iteratively with the View and Controller code. This iterative approach is in line with *Rapid Application Development (RAD)* principles described in Chapter 3 that guide system development through a process of initial analysis, quick prototyping and checking requirements, and then looping in the code refinements and requirements testing stages until the application is complete.

You may prefer a different system life cycle approach. For example, as we mentioned in Chapter 10, JDeveloper allows you to diagram ADF Business Components (select Business Components Diagram from the General\Diagrams category in the New Gallery). After laying out entity objects, view objects, application modules, and other ADF BC objects, you can choose to generate database tables from the entity objects; you can also choose to generate ADF BC code from the diagram. Using JDeveloper's diagrammer in this way supports a *waterfall* approach to the application life cycle, where you move from an analysis phase to a design phase and then to development and deployment phases with little or no returning to preceding phases.

You can also use the Business Components Diagram to represent existing database tables and views. As before, you can generate ADF BC code from the diagram after dropping tables from the Connections navigator onto the diagram. In this situation, you would not generate database structures from the diagram.

NOTE
Creating ADF BC objects from database tables or views is best if the database structures are completely (or almost completely) designed. Since most Oracle Forms and PL/SQL developers are accustomed to creating user interface code after the database structures have been finalized, the steps in this book use this method.

Create the Application Module

This section sets up an application module that will expose the view objects to the application. Each phase of the development will add to this application module and to the Model project.

1. On the Model node, select **New** from the right-click menu to display the New Gallery.

2. Select the Business Tier\ADF Business Components node in the *Categories* area. Double click the Application Module item in the *Items* area. The Create Application Module dialog will appear. Click Next if the Welcome page appears.

NOTE
As mentioned in Chapter 9, if you would rather not see the Welcome page for a particular wizard, select the "Skip this Page Next Time" checkbox on that wizard's Welcome page. The wizard will then display the second page the next time you run it; you can click Back from this page to return to the Welcome page, if needed.

3. On the Name page, enter the following:
   Package as "tuhra.model" (this might be the default)
   Name as "TuhraService"

4. Click Next three times to proceed to the Java page. Notice that the *Generate Java File(s)* checkbox for creating the application module object class, TuhraServiceImpl, is selected. This checkbox is selected because you set up the Model project property to create a Java class for the application module object.

5. Click Class Extends. The Extends dialog will appear. Notice that the *Object* value contains the name of the framework buffer file, `tuhra.model.framework` `.TuhraApplicationModuleImpl`. You set this up for the Model project a bit earlier in this practice. Click Cancel to dismiss the Extends dialog.

6. In the Create Application Module Wizard, click Next to navigate to the Finish page. The application module name will appear in the list of objects to be created. Click Finish.

7. Expand the tuhra.model package node in the navigator, and select the TuhraService node. The following will display in the Structure window:

Additional Information: The Structure window shows the TuhraService.xml file (the application module definition), the TuhraServiceImpl.java file (the application module object class), and *bc4j.xcfg* (the ADF BC configurations file containing information about the database connection). You can open bc4j.xcfg in the code editor by double clicking it in the Structure window. Alternatively, on the application module node (TuhraService), in the navigator, select **Configurations** from the right-click menu to open the properties editor for this configuration file.

8. Select TuhraService (under the tuhra.model node) in the navigator, and double click the TuhraService.xml file in the Structure window to open it in the code editor. The status bar at the bottom of the JDeveloper IDE window will display "Protected," which means you cannot edit this file directly.

   Additional Information: At this point, this file contains little information, but you will notice the root level tag "AppModule" and the name of the application module "TuhraService".

9. Double click the TuhraService node in the navigator to display the Application Module Editor. This editor, a version of the Create Application Module Wizard, stores its entries in the TuhraService.xml file, so you are not responsible for editing the XML file directly. Click Cancel to dismiss this editor.

10. Double click the TuhraServiceImpl.java node in the Structure window to display the class file in the code editor. Notice that TuhraServiceImpl extends `TuhraApplicationModuleImpl`, as you defined earlier in the Project Properties.

11. Click Save All. Close all code editor windows.

What Did You Just Do?   In this phase, you set up framework buffer classes for selected objects in the ADF BC layer. You modified the project properties so the ADF BC wizards will create only the most frequently used Java files. Then you created and examined the application module files that will be used to interface between ADF BC objects and the View objects.

II. Prepare the ViewController Project

This phase customizes the ViewController project by resetting some project properties, adding a framework buffer layer, and adding a message bundle file.

Reset Project Properties

The default project properties are sufficient in most cases. With some experience, you will collect some properties that should be reset when starting a project. This section resets some of these properties.

1. Double click the ViewController project, and select the J2EE Application node. The *J2EE Web Application Name* property is copied into the relevant configuration files when the application is deployed. The default value consists of the workspace name, project name, and "webapp"; this is longer than you need. Change this property to "tuhra".

2. Change the *J2EE Web Context Root* property to "tuhra". This property is used as the *context root*—that is, the application directory name in the URL. As before, the default value is longer than you need.

3. Select the Dependencies node. This page defines the other projects that are required by this project. The deployment utilities will use this information to package all required projects when you deploy this project.

   Additional Information: When you drag a control from the Data Control Palette to a page in this project, the ViewController project will depend upon objects in the Model project. Therefore, JDeveloper will automatically select this checkbox when you perform the first drag-and-drop operation from the Data Control Palette. Alternatively, you can select this checkbox yourself to define the dependency.

4. Click OK to dismiss the Project Properties dialog. Click Save All.

Set Up the Framework Buffer Layer

Just as framework buffer classes are useful for ADF BC classes, they are also useful for backing beans created for the ViewController code. You only need one backing bean buffer class for all pages. As with the ADF BC buffer classes, the file starts as a stub (no active code).

1. On the ViewController node in the navigator, select **New** from the right-click menu. In the New Gallery, select the General category and double click the Java Class item. The Create Java Class dialog will appear.

2. Enter the *Name* as "TuhraBackingBean" and the *Package* as "tuhra.view.framework". Leave *Extends* as "java.lang.Object," leave the *Public* and *Generate Default Constructor* checkboxes selected, and leave the *Generate Main Method* checkbox unselected.

NOTE
ADF BC framework buffer classes subclass ADF BC base classes. However, this View layer framework buffer class has no base class to act as a parent, so it subclasses the default parent java.lang.Object.

3. Click OK. The file will be created and you will see it in the ViewController project node for Application Sources\tuhra.view.framework.

4. Click Save All.

Add the Message Bundle File

This section adds a message bundle file, as demonstrated in the hands-on practice in Chapter 9. The *message bundle file* provides a central location for text the user sees on the page. It also allows you to localize and internationalize these messages for the user's language. This application does not use the localization and internationalization features, but it does demonstrate how to work with the message file.

1. On the ViewController node in the navigator, select **New** from the right-click menu. In the New Gallery, select the General category, and double click the File item. The Create File dialog will appear.

2. Enter the *File Name* as "Messages.properties". For the *Directory Name* value, after "ViewController," add "\src\tuhra\view\messages" (including the leading backslash) to the end of the existing name. This will create a subdirectory that you can use to store all message files. Click OK.

3. The Messages.properties file will open in the editor and will appear under the Resources node in the navigator. Enter the following lines in this file:

```
###
### Messages for pages
###
# Home page
pages.home.messageLine1=The Ultimate
pages.home.messageLine2=Human Resources
pages.home.messageLine3=Application
```

Additional Information: These messages will be used to display the application name on the Home page. You can construct different levels for your messages using names separated with periods (such as "pages.home.messageLine1"). The idea in this example is to place messages for all pages under the "pages" level. Under the pages level, you would construct a level for each page. In this code example, messages are available for the Home page ("pages.home"). The organization levels are up to you, but using some kind of structure can make the messages easier to find and use.

TIP
Inserting messages into a message file and referring to them using EL (Expression Language) in the components can slow down development. One strategy for developing an application that uses a message bundle file is to hard-code message text on the page but make entries in the message bundle file as you develop. In a later step, you can replace all hard-coded messages with EL referring to the message bundle file.

4. Click Save All.

What Did You Just Do? You just reset some default project properties for the ViewController project. You also set up the framework buffer file for the backing bean classes. Lastly, you set up the message bundle file so that the messages may be maintained locally. To make these messages available for all pages, you will add an `f:loadBundle` component to the template later on.

NOTE
Although this application does not override default JSF error messages, you can also use the message bundle file for these messages. The sidebar "Using a Message Bundle for JSF Error Messages" in Chapter 9 explains this technique.

III. Create a Template

In this phase, you create a file containing components that all pages in the application will share, including a menu system that defines navigation between pages. Ideally, you decide on the page design and navigation before beginning to work on the template. That way, you will be able to code all shared objects into the template before you copy it to the page files. Should you find, after copying the template, that you missed placing a common object, you will need to copy the object to all page files. This can be a relatively simple operation, because the JDeveloper Structure window allows you to copy and paste objects (including their properties) between pages.

Create the Template File

In this section, you create the template file using Oracle's Browser Look and Feel (BLAF) as the guiding design principle. (Both templates and BLAF are discussed in Chapter 10.) Therefore, color and layout choices are based on the BLAF scheme.

1. On the ViewController project node in the navigator, select **New** from the right-click menu (you can also press CTRL-N) to display the New Gallery.

2. Select the Web Tier\JSF category, and double click the JSF JSP item. The Create JSF JSP Wizard will start. Click Next if the Welcome page appears.

3. In the JSP File page, enter the *File Name* as "template.jsp". Add to the end of the *Directory Name* value, "\WEB-INF\template" (including the leading backslash)—for example, "C:\Tuhra\ViewController\public_html\WEB-INF\template". Select the *Type* as "JSP Page."

   Additional Information: The directory structure for files you create in JDeveloper closely resembles the deployment directory structure. By convention, the public_html directory stores all runtime user interface files, such as JSP page files. The wizard will create the WEB-INF\template directory under the public_html directory. Users will not see this template.jsp file. You use it only to develop new pages; therefore, you store it in a separate directory. As mentioned in Chapter 9, this application uses JSP pages (.jsp files) instead of JSP documents (.jspx files), although both styles work equally well with JSF code.

4. Click Next. As Chapter 9 describes, if you select "Automatically Expose UI Components in a New Managed Bean" on this page, JDeveloper will create accessor methods for each component on the page. It is likely that you will not use most of these accessor methods, so although the practice in Chapter 9 created the default backing bean as a demonstration, it is a best practice to build backing beans from scratch and add methods as needed. Therefore, select "Do Not Automatically Expose UI Components in a Managed Bean" if it is not already selected, and click Next.

5. Be sure the Selected Libraries list includes ADF Faces Components, ADF Faces HTML, JSF Core, and JSF HTML (each will display a version number after its name). Click Next.

6. On the HTML Options page, enter the *Title* as "template" (if it is not already filled in), and click Finish. The JSF JSP file will be created and will open in the visual editor. You will see the template.jsp file inside a WEB-INF\template directory under Web Content in the navigator.

7. Click Save All.

Add Components to the Template

As mentioned in Chapter 5, ADF Faces offers a large number of container components. One of these components, `af:panelPage`, contains facets for page areas that support the BLAF layout standards. Although this practice will not use all facets of `af:panelPage`, this component will provide the main layout elements for this application. The aim is to produce something that looks like the page shown in Figure 11-1.

1. Select template.jsp in the navigator. Be sure the Component Palette, visual editor for template.jsp, and the Structure window are displayed. In the ADF Faces Core page of the Component Palette, select PanelPage and drop it on top of the `h:form` tag. It should appear nested within the `h:form` tag in the Structure window, as shown here:

![Template displayed in the visual editor]

FIGURE 11-1. *Template displayed in the visual editor*

NOTE
*If you lose access to the ADF Faces pages on the Component Palette
and ADF Faces components do not render correctly in the visual
editor, close JDeveloper and reopen it. The ADF Faces functionality
should then be restored.*

2. In the Property Inspector, change the *Title* property of af:panelPage to "Change This".
   This text will remind you to change the heading on each page.

3. Select the afh:head node in the Structure window, and change the *Title* property to
   "TUHRA". This title will appear in the window title bar when the browser displays
   the page. All pages will share the same window title. The visual editor will appear
   as follows:

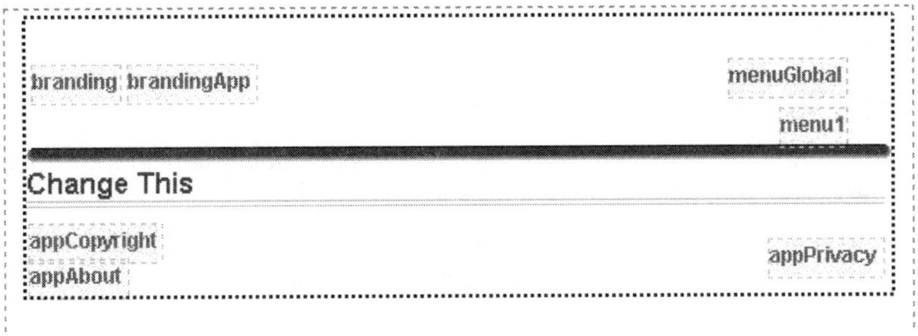

4. Notice that this panel contains a number of facets into which you can place components. Expand the `af:panelPage` node and the PanelPage facets node in the Structure window, and you will see the following:

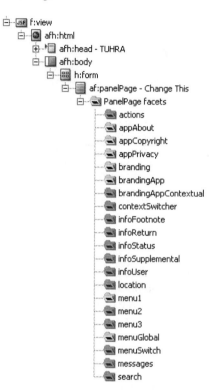

Additional Information: This application will use the branding facet for the application logo, the menuGlobal facet for global buttons (buttons on each page that are responsible for application-level navigation), menu1 and menu2 for tabs and subtabs, and appCopyright for the copyright message.

5. The sidebar "Obtaining the Sample Image Files" explains the three files you will need to supply images to the template. Identify and make a note of the location of these image files.

6. In the ADF Faces Core page of the Component Palette, select ObjectImage, and drop it into the branding facet in the visual editor. The Insert ObjectImage dialog will appear.

Additional Information: This item creates an `af:objectImage` component, which will embed the image in the page using an HTML image tag.

7. Click the browse button "…" next to the *Source* field, and find the logo image file in the file system using the Advanced Editor dialog that appears.

8. Click OK after selecting the file. The Image Location Problem dialog will appear, indicating that the file is not in the project directories. Since you will need to deploy this file with the application, it will be more convenient to copy it into the project directories. Click Yes.

Obtaining the Sample Image Files
The template requires three image files in either JPEG or GIF format: one for the logo and one for each of the two global buttons (Logout and Help). You may download these image files (tuhra.gif—the logo—and help.gif and logout.gif—the Help and Logout button images, respectively) from the sample code websites. Alternatively, you can use any graphics file you choose for these images, for example, from the JDEV_HOME\jdev\doc\welcome\ welcomeImages directory or from the BLAF Icon Repository at www.oracle.com/technology/ tech/blaf/specs/iconlist.html. This directory contains a gb-help.gif, a getstartedicon_stpg.gif, and a jdeveloper10g_clr.gif that you could use for the help, logout, and logo image files, respectively (although the logout and logo images will not match the sample screens shown in this book).

9. The Save Image dialog will appear, prompting you to find a directory. Navigate to the ViewController\public_html directory if it is not already the current directory. Click the "Create new subdirectory" button in the upper-right corner of this dialog, and enter a *Directory Name* of "images". Click OK to add the directory, and navigate into it.

10. In the Save Image dialog, click Save to save the file (tuhra.gif) into the new images directory. The file name will be added to the Source field in the Insert ObjectImage dialog.

11. Click OK. The image file will be displayed in the navigator node for images, and the visual editor will display the logo in the branding facet location.

    Additional Information: The steps just described use JDeveloper to add the image file and set up an images subdirectory. You could alternatively use a file system utility, such as Microsoft Windows Explorer, to create the subdirectory and copy files into it. This method would substitute for steps 8–10.

12. You can now build the menu container for the global buttons (Logout and Help). The af:menuButtons component is designed to hold menu items such as the global buttons. Drag a MenuButtons component from the Component Palette, and drop it in the menuGlobal facet in the visual editor. A dotted square box will appear, identifying the af:menuButtons component.

13. The af:commandMenuItem component provides navigation functionality for a specific purpose (such as a logout). Drag a CommandMenuItem from the Component Palette into the Structure window on top of the af:menuButtons component. The af:commandMenuItem component will appear as a child of af:menuButtons. Repeat this drag-and-drop procedure for another af:commandMenuItem component.

14. Select the left-most global button (the commandMenuItem1 link) in the visual editor. In the Property Inspector, change *Text* to "Logout". Change the *Text* property of the global button on the right side to "Help".

Additional Information: Notice that the links in the upper-right corner of the page change, as do the links in the center of the footer. These footer links are a function of the combination of these components.

15. The *Icon* property of these items allows you to attach an image file. Select the Logout link, and click the browse ("…") button in the *Icon* property of the Property Inspector. If you have already copied the image files to the images directory, select the logout file (logout.gif), click OK, and skip the next step.

16. In the Icon dialog, navigate to the directory in which you placed the logout image file. Select the file and click OK. As before, the Image Location Problem dialog will appear. Click Yes, navigate to the images directory, and then click Save.

17. Notice that the image appears in the visual editor above the corresponding link.

18. Repeat steps 15–17 for the Help menu item and image file (help.gif).

19. You need to be sure the *Icon* properties reference the directory in a generic way. Set the *Icon* property for Logout to "/images/logout.gif" (removing the "../.." prefix). Repeat this edit for the Help link icon. The visual editor should appear as follows:

20. Click Save All.

Add Menu Tabs and Other Components

Tab navigation is a standard feature in the BLAF standards and is a familiar and easy-to-understand user interface. Clicking a tab loads the page associated with that tab and acts as the page-to-page menu system. ADF Faces provides a menu container component, af:menuTabs, into which you place af:commandMenuItem components (the same components you used for the global buttons). This section adds this tabbed menu system, as well as a messages component and an outputFormatted component for the copyright message.

1. Drag a MenuTabs component on top of the menu1 facet in the Structure window. The visual editor will display a single tab.

2. Drop four CommandMenuItem components, one at a time, onto the top of the af:menuTabs component in the Structure window. Four tabs will appear in the visual editor and the menu1 node of the Structure window will appear as follows (although the number suffixes on the labels may be different):

3. Change the *Text* property of each tab so that the tabs read "Home", "My Profile", "Employees", and "Reference" from left to right.

4. The `af:panelPage` component contains a `messages` facet where you can place an `af:messages` component to display the message queue loaded during the JSF runtime process. Find the `messages` facet for the `af:panelPage` component in the Structure window, and drop a Messages (not Message) component into it from the Component Palette.

5. An `f:loadBundle` component must appear before any components that refer to the message bundle file's messages. Find the `afh:html` node in the Structure window.

6. Select LoadBundle from the JSF Core page of the Component Palette. Holding down the mouse button, position the component above the `afh:html` node in the Structure window until a line with an up arrow appears above `afh:html`. Drop the component after the display appears, as follows:

7. In the Insert LoadBundle dialog that appears, enter the *Basename* as "tuhra.view.messages .Messages" (or use the "…" browse button to find the file name in ViewController\src\ view\messages) and the *Var* as "msg". Click OK.

8. Check that the `f:loadBundle` node appears in Structure window in the following position; drag it to this position if it does not:

Additional Information: As discussed in Chapter 9, the *Var* setting ("msg") is used as the top-level object to build an EL expression for a message in the message bundle. You will use this for the copyright message.

9. Open the Messages.properties file (under Application Sources\tuhra.view.messages), and add the following above the comment for the Home page:

```
pages.copyright=Copyright &copy; 2006 TUHRA, Inc. All rights reserved.
```

Additional Information: This entry refers to a token used on all pages—the copyright.

10. Click Save All.

11. Return to the template.jsp visual editor. Drop an OutputFormatted component from the ADF Faces Core page of the Component Palette into the appCopyright facet in the visual editor.

Additional Information: The `af:outputFormatted` component renders HTML tags that you place in its *Value* property as HTML. Therefore, it will display the copyright symbol, ©, for the HTML entity, "©" in the message file.

12. In the *Value* property, click "Bind to data" (in the Property Inspector toolbar) to display the Value binding dialog. Drill down to the JSP Objects\msg node, and select pages .copyright. Move the selection to the right, and click OK to accept the value change.

Additional Information: The visual editor will show the copyright message expression.

13. Click Save All. You can run the template.jsp now if you want to see it displayed in the browser. With the Design tab selected, click Run in the JDeveloper toolbar. You will see the copyright message with text from the message bundle file in the lower-left corner of the screen. Close the browser and stop the server when you have reviewed the page.

Declare JSF Pages in the JSF Navigation Diagram

You will probably switch back and forth between work in the JSF Navigation Diagram and work in tools that create the JSF JSP files represented on that diagram. However, it is usually best to start with the diagram so that you have a clear picture of the flow of the application. Also, setting up navigation rules and navigation cases is just a matter of drawing lines instead of setting properties in the diagram's Overview tab. In addition, if you define the navigation cases before the pages, the navigation case outcome names will then appear in the *Action* property pulldown for command items such as buttons. This will allow you to quickly connect one page to another as you are working with these components.

This section creates page symbols in the JSF Navigation Diagram. The tab menu you defined in the template provides the main navigation method for all pages. Therefore, your work in the JSF Navigation Diagram for this application consists primarily of adding symbols for each page. The page flow sketch you created earlier (as described in Chapter 10) can help supply names and paths for these symbols.

1. On the ViewController project node in the navigator, select **Open JSF Navigation** from the right-click menu. Select the Diagram tab if it is not active.

2. Select a JSF Page from the Component Palette, and drop it on the diagram. Type the name as "home" and press ENTER. JDeveloper will add a ".jsp" extension and a leading slash.

3. Add the following pages to the diagram in an arrangement such as that shown in Figure 11-2.

   - /help/help.jsp
   - /pages/home.jsp
   - /pages/profile.jsp
   - /pages/searchEmployees.jsp
   - /pages/logout.jsp

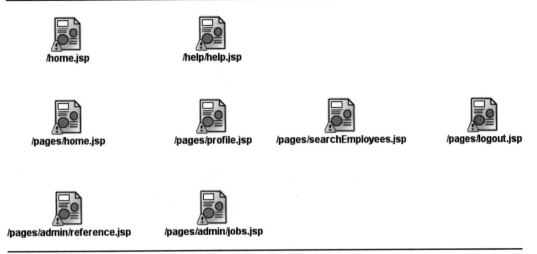

FIGURE 11-2.   *Pages declared in the JSF Navigation Diagram*

- ■ /pages/admin/reference.jsp
- ■ /pages/admin/jobs.jsp

4. Click Save All.

Define Navigation Actions

Now that you have all visual and other components on the page, you can turn to defining the actions that will allow users to navigate through the application. The JSF framework supplies default behavior for handling page navigation. Components built from the UICommand class (such as `af:commandMenuItem`) include a default action listener to navigate from one page to another when the component is clicked. To define this navigation, you set the *Action* property to the outcome name of the navigation case; you do not need to define your own action listener method (as you did for loginButton_action in the practice in Chapter 9).

Navigation Rules and Navigation Cases   JSF defines navigation from these command components using navigation rules and navigation cases, both of which are stored in the faces-config.xml file. You can always define navigation rules and navigation cases during the development of specific pages. However, if you know the overall navigation for the application (for example, which page will load when the user clicks a tab or global button), you can define it in the template so that all copies of the template will receive the navigation definition.

A *navigation rule* declares the starting point for the page navigation. The *navigation case* declares the target point for the navigation. For example, if you wanted to declare navigation from the Home page to the Profile page, you would code a navigation rule for the Home page by entering a navigation rule tag, such as the following:

```
<navigation-rule>
  <from-view-id>/pages/home.jsp</from-view-id>
  <navigation-case>
    <from-outcome>Profile</from-outcome>
```

```
      <to-view-id>/pages/profile.jsp</to-view-id>
   </navigation-case>
</navigation-rule>
```

This code defines a navigation rule for actions initiated by commands on the home.jsp page (in the pages directory). Within the navigation rule is a navigation case that declares profile.jsp as the target page. The navigation rule is initiated when the controller receives an action outcome of "Profile." In the login page you created in Chapter 9, you defined an *outcome*, the return value from the action listener method on a button, and this outcome was sent to the Controller. The navigation cases were identified as "login," so if the code returned the string "login," navigation to the target page occurred. Although you did not enter these in the faces-config.xml file, the diagrammer added them for you when you drew navigation case lines.

You can declare more than one navigation case for a page. For example, in addition to the navigation case for profile.jsp, the home.jsp page might have a navigation rule to forward to the employees search page, searchEmployees.jsp. This code would appear as follows:

```
<navigation-rule>
   <from-view-id>/pages/home.jsp</from-view-id>
   <navigation-case>
      <from-outcome>Profile</from-outcome>
      <to-view-id>/pages/profile.jsp</to-view-id>
   </navigation-case>
   <navigation-case>
      <from-outcome>EmpSearch</from-outcome>
      <to-view-id>/pages/searchEmployees.jsp</to-view-id>
   </navigation-case>
</navigation-rule>
```

Both navigation cases declare different targets and have different outcomes but appear within the same navigation rule. Therefore, if an action listener from a button component returned the value of "EmpSearch," navigation would proceed to the searchEmployees.jsp page.

In this application, the tabs and global buttons always navigate to the same pages, regardless of the starting page. You might think that you need to write a navigation rule for each page, with three navigation cases to define the other target pages accessed by the tab buttons. However, JSF offers a shortcut so that many pages can share the same navigation cases. You just define the navigation from "*" instead of from a specific page. For example, you can change the preceding code snippet to allow all pages to navigate to the profile.jsp and searchEmployees.jsp pages by using the "*" for from-view-id, as in the following:

```
<navigation-rule>
   <from-view-id>*</from-view-id>
   <navigation-case>
      <from-outcome>Profile</from-outcome>
      <to-view-id>/pages/profile.jsp</to-view-id>
   </navigation-case>
   <navigation-case>
      <from-outcome>EmpSearch</from-outcome>
      <to-view-id>/pages/searchEmployees.jsp</to-view-id>
   </navigation-case>
</navigation-rule>
```

Although you can enter navigation cases for pages by drawing lines between JSF pages in the JSF Navigation Diagram, the global navigation cases are available on all pages. No symbol on the diagram represents a global navigation rule, so we will use the Overview tab of the faces-config .xml file to enter the global navigation rules and cases. You are aiming at navigation from the tabs and global buttons, as represented in Figure 11-3. Follow these steps to define the navigation.

1. You need a navigation case to define the flow between the Reference Data subtab and the Job Types subtab. If the JSF Navigation Diagram is not open, on the ViewController node, select **Open JSF Navigation** from the right-click menu. Click the navigation diagram and then click JSF Navigation Case in the Component Palette.

2. Draw the navigation case line from /pages/admin/reference.jsp to /pages/admin/jobs.jsp. Change the navigation outcome name to "jobs" by clicking "success" to open the field for editing, typing "jobs", and clicking outside the field. (Although it is not represented in the application flow diagram in Chapter 10, this navigation case is required as a value for the *Action* property of the Job Types subtab.) These two symbols will appear as follows:

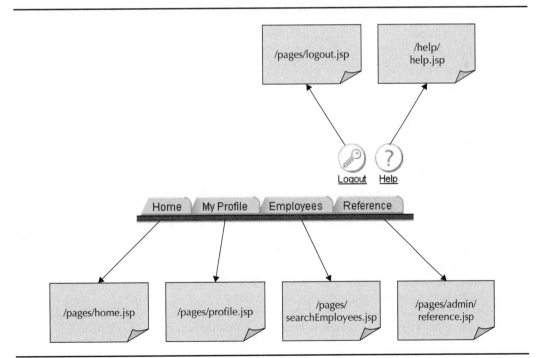

FIGURE 11-3. *Navigation from global command components to application pages*

3. Since you cannot define global navigation cases in the JSF Navigation Diagram, you need to use the Overview tab for these definitions. This tab allows you to interact with elements in the file without worrying about tags and syntax. Select the Overview tab for the faces-config.xml file.

4. On the Overview tab, select the Navigation Rules page. Notice that one navigation case has already been defined for one navigation rule to define the flow from reference.jsp to jobs.jsp. This navigation rule and navigation case were created when you drew the navigation case line in the diagram. Select that navigation rule.

5. In the Navigation Cases area, be sure "/pages/admin/jobs.jsp" is selected, and click Edit in that area. The navigation-case Properties dialog will appear. Set *Redirect* to "true" and click OK. Check that "true" is displayed in the Redirect column.

   Additional Information: Setting *Redirect* to "true" instructs the Controller to send a redirect command to the browser so that it will load this page. The sidebar "About Forward and Redirect" explains redirect and its alternative: forward.

6. Click New in the Navigation Rules area. The Create Navigation Rule dialog will appear. In the *From View ID* field, enter "*" and click OK.

   Additional Information: An asterisk ("*") will be displayed in the *From Rule ID* list and the code will contain a navigation rule tag with no ID. You can alternatively select "<Global Navigation Rule>" in the *From View ID* pulldown to enter a global rule. Although this provides the Controller with the same information, the rule will be

---

About Forward and Redirect

At the end of processing a request, the Controller layer code can perform either a forward or a redirect. A *forward* passes control to the View layer code that constructs a second page. Since the call to the second page is handled by Controller code on the server, the user's URL address line does not change. In effect, the user requests and receives one page, issues a request by clicking a button or performing some action on that page (other than clicking a link), and receives a different page as a response. Since the URL in the user's browser does not change, the identity of the second page is hidden. If the user clicks the Refresh button, the original page (not the second page) will reload. (As mentioned in Chapter 9, use of the Refresh button can cause other problems in a J2EE application.)

A *redirect* sends the URL of the second page to the browser using a command that causes the browser to issue another request to the second page's URL. In this situation, the browser's address line will identify the URL of the second page. Since redirect requires another response-and-request message to return the page, it is slower than the forward. After the second page is displayed, with the second page's URL in the address line, clicking the browser Refresh button will reload the second page (again with the same problems associated with that button and J2EE applications).

For this application, you want to cause a redirect for the JSP files because these pages need to be protected by security. These protected directory names in the URL will activate the container security mechanism explained in Chapter 14.

displayed as "<Global Navigation Rule>" in the Overview tab and no code will result until you create the navigation case. In addition, in the current version of JDeveloper, using "*" rather than "<Global Navigation Rule>" allows the Property Inspector to display a list of target outcomes; using "<Global Navigation Rule>" does not. Therefore, at this point, "*" is preferable to "<Global Navigation Rule>."

7. With the global navigation rule ("*") selected, click New in the Navigation Cases area (under Navigation Rules). The Create Navigation Case dialog will appear.

8. Enter the *To View ID* value as "/pages/home.jsp." Enter the *From Outcome* as "GlobalHome" (a name that suggests that all pages will access the Home page when this navigation case is specified). Leave the *Redirect* checkbox unselected in this case. You will change this in the hands-on practice in Chapter 14. Click OK.

9. The navigation case will appear in the list. Click the Source tab. You should see familiar code to define this navigation case. Return to the Overview tab.

10. Repeat steps 7–8 to create additional navigation cases on the "*" navigation rule. Use the following entries for these navigation cases:

To View ID	From Outcome	Redirect
/pages/searchEmployees.jsp	GlobalSearch	(selected)
/pages/logout.jsp	GlobalLogout	(selected)
/pages/admin/reference.jsp	GlobalRef	(selected)
/pages/profile.jsp	GlobalProfile	(selected)
/help/help.jsp	dialog:GlobalHelp	(unselected)

Additional Information: These entries closely follow the patterns for the Home page. The logout page and its code are discussed in Chapter 14. The reference.jsp file will be stored in the admin subdirectory of the pages directory, and the help.jsp for the help global button will be stored in the help directory that is parallel to the pages directory. The "dialog:" prefix for the GlobalHelp outcome causes the Help page to open in a separate modal dialog window. The Chapter 13 sidebar "About ADF Faces Dialogs" explains the dialog window feature a bit further, and you will use this feature again when defining LOV (list of values) windows for the employee Edit page. Note that you leave the *Redirect* checkbox unselected for the help.jsp file because this will open in a new window; if you were to select the *Redirect* checkbox, the help file would load in the same browser window.

11. Click the Source tab to briefly review the code. Examine a few properties in the navigation rules under the global navigation case ("*"). Notice that the file names within the to-view-id tags are underlined with wavy lines indicating that they do not yet refer to real JSP page files. When you are finished, click the Overview tab.

12. Click Save All.

13. Now you need to hook up the command components to these actions. Open the Design tab for the template.jsp file.

14. Select the Home tab and, in the Property Inspector, select "GlobalHome" from the *Action* property pulldown. Repeat this step for the following tabs and global buttons:

Tab or Button	Action
My Profile	GlobalProfile
Employees	GlobalSearch
Reference	GlobalRef
Logout	GlobalLogout
Help	dialog:GlobalHelp

Additional Information: The actions connect the buttons or menu items to the navigation cases you defined in the faces-config.xml Overview tab.

15. Select the Help global button, and set the *UseWindow* property to "true." This property works with the "dialog:" prefix to open the Help page in a separate modal window.

16. The last task in working with the template is to remove all facet markers for the `af:panelPage` that you are not using so that they do not clutter the files and the visual editor. Open the template.jsp file. In the Structure window, on the PanelPage facets node, under `af:panelPage`, select **Facets – Panel Page** from the right-click menu to display the list of visible facets.

17. Unselect AppAbout. The placeholder for this facet will disappear from the visual editor. You can still place components in this facet later, if needed.

18. Repeat the preceding step for App Privacy and Branding App.

Additional Information: You can alternatively select the facet node in the Structure window and press DELETE to remove the facet placeholder in the visual editor.

19. Click Save All.

TIP
The Source tab of the Structure window will show only the facets that you have used.

What Did You Just Do? In this phase, you created a template file that will supply a common look and feel to all pages in your application. The template is built around an `af:panelPage` component that provides a large number of prebuilt facets into which you can place other components. You added a menu system consisting of tabs and global buttons. In addition, you used two methods to define navigation between pages using navigation rules and navigation cases—the diagram and the Overview tab editor. You also defined the action property of the buttons and tabs so that they follow the navigation cases you set up.

IV. Copy the Template File and Customize the Copies

In this phase, you will copy the template file to each file required for the application. At the end of this phase, you will have one JSP file for each page in the application. You will add content to some of these files in later chapters. Pages in the application are protected by security defined for

URL patterns (directories). The pages directory in this application holds all the page files available to a user who is logged in. The files in the admin directory under the pages directory are available only to administrative users. The help directory is available to all users.

NOTE
Although you will create page files in this phase for all pages in the application, this part of the book only finishes the pages available in the Home and Employees tabs. As mentioned in Chapter 10, samples of techniques to create the pages in the My Profile and Reference tabs can be found on the sample code websites mentioned in the "Websites for Sample Code" section of the Introduction.

Create All Page Files

Before making copies of the template, double-check that the design is complete and the template is correct. You can run the template file to check its appearance if you wish. The buttons will not work, but you will be able to view the page in the browser. After reviewing the contents of the file at runtime, close the browser and the server, and proceed to the next steps.

1. Select template.jsp under ViewController\Web Content\WEB-INF\template in the navigator. Select **File** I **Save As** and navigate to the ViewController\public_html directory.

2. You need to create a pages directory that is inside public_html. Click the "Create new subdirectory" button in the Save As dialog. Enter the *Directory Name* as "pages". Click OK. The focus will change to the new pages directory. Repeat the directory creation for an "admin" directory under ViewController\public_html\pages\.

3. Navigate back to the public_html directory. Repeat the directory creation action to create a directory called "help." Navigate back to public_html. (Alternatively, you can create any of these directories outside of JDeveloper.)

4. Double click the pages directory to navigate into it. Change the *File name* to "home" and click Save. JDeveloper will fill in the .jsp extension.

NOTE
The public_html directory does not appear in the navigator. The pages node will display under the Web Content node.

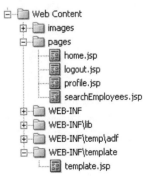

5. Expand the pages node in the navigator, and copy the home.jsp file using **File** I **Save As** to a file called "logout.jsp" in the same public_html\pages directory. Repeat the steps to copy the file, and create profile.jsp, and searchEmployees.jsp files inside the same directory. If you expand the pages directory, the navigator's Web Content node will appear as shown here:

6. Repeat the copy procedure to create the following files in the following directories:

File Name	Directory
jobs.jsp	public_html\pages\admin
reference.jsp	public_html\pages\admin
help.jsp	public_html\help
home.jsp	public_html

Additional Information: You will now have several copies of the same file in various directories. The Web Content node of the navigator should look like this:

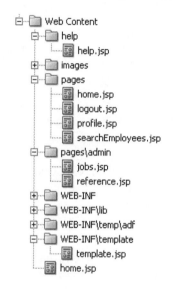

7. Open the Diagram tab of the JSF Navigation Diagram, and notice that all the page icons no longer contain the yellow triangle symbol (as they do in Figure 11-2). This indicates that the pages on the diagram represent files.

Additional Information: If the diagram page icons still contain yellow triangles, the pages you created are probably in the wrong subdirectories. Check that pages appear under the nodes in the navigator as shown in the preceding illustration. If they do not, delete the misplaced files (other than the template) by selecting them one at a time and selecting **File | Erase from Disk**. Then recopy the files using the earlier instructions.

Customize the Page Files

You can now customize the files for specific content. The rest of the chapters in this part of the book step through creating the content in the Home and Employees tabs, but in this section, we will modify the template components for all pages. The properties we need to modify for each pages are the page heading and the active tab.

1. Open the help.jsp file under the help node of the navigator. Select the title "Change This" in the visual editor (the `af:panelPage` component will be selected, not the text) and, in the Property Inspector, change the *Title* property to "TUHRA Help". (The *Title* property appears under the General category in the Property Inspector.)

2. Open home.jsp under the pages node. Change the title to "Welcome to TUHRA". Select the Home tab and change the *Selected* property to "true." The tab will darken to indicate that it identifies the current page.

3. Open the other pages and make the same changes, as specified in the following table:

JSP File	Title	Tab for *Selected* = "true"
logout.jsp	Logout Confirmation	(None)
profile.jsp	Edit Your Profile	My Profile
searchEmployees.jsp	Employees Search	Employees
jobs.jsp	Edit Job Information	Reference
reference.jsp	Select Location or Department	Reference
home.jsp (under Web Content)	(delete the title)	Home

4. Click Save All.

Add Subtab Navigation

The Reference tab contains two pages—reference.jsp (for departments and locations) and jobs.jsp (for job types). To navigate between these pages, you will create subtabs in the menu2 facet and use the navigation rule for reference.jsp with its navigation case to jobs.jsp.

1. Open the reference.jsp file in the editor. In the Structure window, drill down to the PanelPage facets.

   Additional Information: You want to add an `af:menuBar` component, which defines a blue bar area under the tab bar, into which you will place two `af:commandMenuItem` components.

2. Drag MenuBar from the ADF Faces Core page of the Property Inspector, and drop it on the menu2 facet in the Structure window. The visual editor will display a dotted outline for the `af:menuBar` component.

3. Select CommandMenuItem in the Component Palette, and drop it onto the `af:menuBar` node of the Structure window. Repeat this action to add another CommandMenuItem.

NOTE
You are now using the af:commandMenuItem inside three different container components: af:menuButtons for the global buttons, af:menuTabs for the tab controls, and af:menuBar for the subtabs. The appearance of af:commandMenuItem depends upon the container in which it is placed.

4. Select the af:commandMenuItem on the left. Change the *Text* property to "Reference Data" and *Selected* to "true." The button label will then appear in boldface.

5. Select the second af:commentMenuItem component. Change its *Text* property to "Job Types".

6. Select the af:menuBar node (under menu2) in the Structure window. Copy it to the clipboard (CTRL-C).

7. Open the jobs.jsp file. Select the menu2 node in the Structure window for jobs.jsp, and press CTRL-V to paste menu2. The visual editor will display the menu bar with its buttons.

8. Select the Job Types command menu item in the jobs.jsp file, and change *Selected* to "true." Change *Selected* for the Reference Data command menu item to "false." The proper subtab will be boldfaced only for Job Types.

9. Click Save All.

Additional Information: Earlier in this practice, you defined navigation cases to all main pages; you also connected the global buttons and tabs to those cases using the *Action* property. That way, when the user clicks a global button or tab defined in the template, the JSF controller will forward or redirect to the page defined in the navigation case named in the *Action* property. You now need to set up navigation for the subtabs on the Reference tab pages in a similar way.

10. In the visual editor for jobs.jsp, select the Reference Data command menu item and, in the *Action* property, select "GlobalRef." This will cause navigation to occur back to the reference.jsp page using the navigation case you defined for all pages ("***").

11. Open the visual editor for reference.jsp. Select the Job Types menu item and, in the *Action* property, select "jobs." This defines navigation from reference.jsp to jobs.jsp.

12. Click Save All.

Test the Navigation

Even though you have not added any data components to these pages, you can run this set of files to verify that navigation works. (You may need to disable popup blockers and firewall filters to run these pages.)

NOTE
The logout link is not active yet, so you do not need to test it. The hands-on practice in Chapter 14 develops the logout function.

1. On the home.jsp file, under the pages node of the navigator, select **Run** from the right-click menu.

2. The browser will open and display the Home page. For each tab, check navigation to the other tabs, be sure the proper heading appears on the page, and confirm that the proper tab appears selected for that page.

3. Click the Help button to check that it displays a separate window containing the Help page. (Do not bother testing navigation from this page because you will delete its navigation elements later.) Close the help topic window to return to the main browser window.

4. Click the Reference tab, and try navigating between its subtabs. Notice that the selected top tab does not change when you navigate between subtab pages.

5. Close the browser and stop the server.

What Did You Just Do?   You just copied the template file to all other files you know will be in the application. You then reset the page title and activated a menu tab for each page. You also defined subtab navigation for the Reference and Jobs pages. Finally, you tested the navigation by running the application. While developing the application, you will likely find the need to create other pages. However, you should find that creating all pages from your design in this way as a first step in development will speed up later work.

While performing development work, you may also need to add common elements to more than one page. Usually, it is easiest to perform this task by using copy and paste operations on container nodes in the Structure window as you did with the subtab elements in the Reference Data and Job Types pages. It is important to keep the template up to date with global changes you make to the other page files in case you need to create another page from it in the future.

V. Complete the Home Pages
The home pages provide a visual starting point for the application. This section adds elements to the two home pages—the home page that appears when the user is not logged in (the unprotected Home page in the public_html directory) and the home page that appears when the user is logged in (the Home page in the protected pages directory). The proper navigation path for the application displays the public Home page first. The user clicks the Login button on that page to display the Login page. Upon a successful login, the protected Home page is displayed.

Add Components

1. Open the home.jsp file under Web Content (not under the pages node) in the editor. This is the unprotected version of this file, so delete all tabs except the Home tab by selecting each one and pressing DELETE.

2. Delete the Logout global button. Check that the *Selected* property of the remaining Home tab is set to "true."

3. Select a PanelGroup component from the ADF Faces Core Component Palette page, and drop it on the `af:panelPage` node in the Structure window. Set its *Layout* property to "vertical."

   Additional Information: This component organizes its child objects in a column (vertical) or in a row (horizontal).

4. You now need to add three `af:outputText` components inside this container. These components will display the opening message. Drop an OutputText item from the Component Palette on top of the new `af:panelGroup` component in the Structure window.

5. Copy the new `af:outputText` node (CTRL-C), select the `af:panelGroup` node, and press paste (CTRL-V). Select the `af:panelGroup` node again and paste again.

6. Select the top `af:outputText` item and select its *Value* property. Click "Bind to data" to display the Value binding editor. Expand the JSP Objects\msg node, and select pages.home.messageLine1.

7. Move that node to the right, and click OK to dismiss the dialog and write the expression into the *Value* property.

8. Repeat this for the other two `af:outputText` items for messageLine2 and messageLine3.

9. In the Structure window, select the `af:panelPage` node and click ObjectSpacer in the ADF Faces Core page of the Component Palette. This will add the component as a child of the `af:panelPage` element.

10. Repeat the previous step for a CommandButton. Repeat the step again for another ObjectSpacer. The Structure window should appear as follows:

11. Set the *Text* property of the `af:commandButton` as "Login". Set its *Action* property from the pulldown as "GlobalHome." The button will navigate to the home page in the protected pages directory; after you define security in the hands-on practice in Chapter 14, this navigation will activate a login dialog.

Create a CSS File and Apply It

You now need to apply color and font changes to these elements. The most universal way to accomplish this task with HTML controls is by using a CSS file containing a style you want to use. Although you could attach the blaf.css style sheet and use its selectors, this section demonstrates how to create a style sheet and reference it. The CSS file is not required for other pages. If it were, you would add it to the template before copying the template to the other pages.

NOTE
As mentioned in Chapter 5, JSF technology supports multiple display devices, but using HTML-specific code, such as a CSS file, limits the ability to use the same file on multiple device types. Of course, this is not a problem for an application whose users will only be running web browsers.

1. On the ViewController node in the navigator, select **New** from the right-click menu. Select the Web Tier\HTML category, and double click the CSS item to open the Create Cascading Style Sheet dialog.

2. Enter the *File Name* as "tuhra" and leave the Directory Name as its default. Click OK to create the file (and directory, if the directory does not exist). The file will open in the editor.

3. Delete the existing code (none of those styles will be useful to this application) and add the following code:

```
.homePageText
{
    font-size: 200%;
    font-weight: bold;
    font-style: italic;
    font-family: Arial, Helvetica, sans-serif;;
    background-color: rgb(204,204,153);
    color: Black;
    text-align: center;
}
```

   Additional Information: This code defines a single CSS selector, homePageText, with an increased font size, bold, italic, and the Arial font family. It mixes red, green, and blue color intensities for a light tan (specified by the BLAF standards) as the background. The font text is black, and the components will be centered.

4. Click Save All. You now need to apply this style to the af:panelGroup component so its members are formatted. Drop the tuhra.css file from the Web Content\css node of the navigator onto the visual editor for the public Home.jsp page.

5. Click the Source tab of the editor, and notice that a link tag was added inside the afh:head tag to reference the CSS file. Click the Design tab.

6. Select the af:panelGroup component in the Structure window and, in the *StyleClass* property, type "homePageText". The font and background color of the message components will change.

7. Click Save All.

8. Run this file to test it. Try the Login button. At this point, it will navigate to the protected Home page (with all tabs displayed). In Chapter 14, you will change that navigation to require a login.

9. Close the browser. You need to apply the same changes to the protected Home page. You can use copy and paste for most of this task. Open the home.jsp file from the pages node of the navigator.

10. Navigate back to the public Home page (where you changed the font and color), and, in the Structure window under af:panelPage, select as a group af:panelGroup, af:objectSpacer, af:commandButton, and af:objectSpacer (using CTRL-click). Copy them to the clipboard (CTRL-C).

11. In the Structure window for the protected Home page (under the pages node in the navigator), paste these items onto the af:panelPage node (CTRL-V). All objects (and their child objects) that you copied will be inserted into the protected Home page.

12. As before, drop the tuhra.css file onto the visual editor. The font and color will change.

13. Select the Login button, and set its *Text* property to "Logout" and *Action* property to "GlobalLogout."

14. Click Save All.

15. Now run the public Home page, and try navigating to the protected Home page again (using the Login button). You will see the new components on the protected Home page this time.

16. Close the browser and stop the server.

What Did You Just Do?   You finished the home pages by adding messages from the message bundle file and by applying a style sheet selector to the message. The public Home page that is available to users who are not logged in contains no content except a link to help and a button to log into the application. After logging in, all content appropriate to the user will be available.

CHAPTER
12

Search Page

The search for truth is more precious than its possession.

—Albert Einstein (1879–1955),
The American Mathematical Monthly, v. 100, no. 3

Research is what I'm doing when I don't know what I'm doing.

—Wernher von Braun (1912–1977)

 roviding the ability to enter data into a database using an application user interface is important. However, the ability to quickly find and be able to modify data is the other critical function of all data-oriented systems. The hands-on practice in this chapter explains how to create a Query-by-Example Search page for the EMPLOYEES table. The Search page you develop in this chapter, and an Edit page you will develop in the next chapter, offer a complete set of data functions for search, browse, create, update, and delete to administrators and managers. Other users will be able to search and browse records but not create, update, or delete them.

After briefly reviewing how Query-by-Example works, this chapter steps through the hands-on practice to create the Search page.

Search and Edit Functions

The Search page in this hands-on practice provides a classic *Query-by-Example* (QBE) screen, with a search block at the top and a tabular results block at the bottom. QBE screens are often used as the start of a navigation path to an edit screen. Oracle Forms developers (particularly those who developed extensions for Oracle E-Business Suite applications) will likely have experience with this style because Oracle Forms applications offer native functions for Enter Query and Execute Query. QBE is also a classic design for web applications.

The processing sequence for a set of QBE screens consists of the following:

1. **Display the search criteria fields.** These are usually fields representing columns in the table containing the data, although they may represent data in another table. For example, when searching for an employee, the user might want to enter the department name instead of its number. The department name is not in the employee table.

2. **The user fills in search criteria and clicks Search.** The application queries the data based on the search criteria and presents a list of results. The list of results contains fields that the user searched, along with others that will help the user identify a record.

3. **The user finds the correct record.** The results list may be lengthy, so the user may need to scroll through multiple pages to find the relevant record. Sort buttons on the search results list can help the user find a record. Once the user finds the record, she or he can edit or delete it using an interface item such as a link, checkbox, or radio button.

    a. **The user clicks Delete.** The system will delete the record.

    b. **The user clicks Edit.** An edit page will display containing all fields preloaded with the selected record values. After editing the record, the user clicks Save (to commit the changes) or Reset (to roll back any changes to the database). A Cancel button navigates back to the Search page.

4. **Alternatively, the user can click New.** The New button displays the Edit page with empty fields so that a new record can be entered. After filling in the fields, the user clicks Save to insert the record or Cancel to roll back the insert. The Search page will redisplay.

Web search engines use this style of information mining, although their search criteria are usually entered in only one field. The QBE search you will build in the next section contains multiple search fields. As with web search engines, the results are displayed under the search fields.

Hands-on Practice: Develop the Employee Search Page

This hands-on practice concentrates on developing the QBE search page for employees. Throughout, you will use the principles of binding, actions, and iterators introduced in Chapters 7 and 8.

This hands-on practice follows these phases:

I. Prepare the Model objects

- ■ Set up the Employees business components

- ■ Define Employees control hints and validation rules

- ■ Set up Jobs and Departments business components

- ■ Add lookup attributes to the Employees view object

- ■ Create the Managers view object

- ■ Update and test the application module

II. Add components to the Search page

- ■ Add the ADF Search Form

- ■ Add the ADF Read-only Table

III. Refine the Search page functionality

- ■ Keep the form in Find mode

- ■ Separate the search form from the results table

- ■ Hide the results table if no rows are returned

- ■ Add a Clear button to the search form

- ■ Add Edit, Delete, and New buttons

- ■ Define actions for the Delete button

TIP

As mentioned in the "Ensuring Success with the Hands-On Practices" section of the Introduction, after you have completed a large amount of work and successfully tested the application, save a copy of the application workspace directory (outside of JDeveloper) so you can return to that point later if you want to restart a section. Application workspaces and other sample code are available on the websites mentioned in the "Websites for Sample Code" section of the Introduction.

I. Prepare the Model Objects

The ADF Business Components require an entity object for INSERT, UPDATE, and DELETE operations as well as a view object for SELECT statement queries. JDeveloper offers a shortcut for creating a related entity object and view object, as explained in this phase. You will create business components for the EMPLOYEES table, which is the main table used for the query and edit pages. You also need business components for the DEPARTMENTS and JOBS tables used to provide lookup lists for fields representing the foreign key fields of the EMPLOYEES table.

In addition, this phase provides examples of how to use ADF BC declarative features—control hints and declarative validation rules—to provide additional functionality.

Control Hints

You can declare *control hints*—additional properties for an entity object or view object that will be used by ADF user interface libraries, such as Swing, JSP, and ADF Faces. For example, by default, user interface components render a field label as the name of the attribute on which the field is based. You can define a *Label Text* control hint that changes this default. Also, control hints allow you to declare display types, sizes, and format masks in much the same way that properties for an Oracle Forms item modify the item's appearance and behavior.

NOTE
Control hints only affect View layer user interface functionality.

You can write control hints for the entity object so that all view objects built from that entity object will inherit the control hints. This means that you can build multiple pages on the same or different view objects based on the same entity object, and all will use the same control hints. You can also write control hints on the view object if you want to override entity object control hints or if the view object is read-only and has no entity object.

Control hints are available on a separate tab in the attribute page of the Entity Object Editor and View Object Editor.

TIP
The best practice for control hints is to always set them on the entity object. That way, if you create any view object for the entity object, you will not need to set the control hints. You can always override control hints for a specific view object. Naturally, if a view object is based on a SELECT statement instead of an entity object, you will need to set control hints for that view object.

Declarative Validation Rules

As mentioned in Chapter 6, you can declare simple validations in ADF BC entity objects that require no coding. These validations allow the application to test input before sending the record to the database. This section steps through several examples of this type of validation for the Employees entity object. A handful of validation types are prebuilt into ADF BC to validate a value based on a comparison, a fixed list, a range, a specific length, a regular expression, or a Boolean method that you write in the entity object. You can also create your own validations. (Refer to the JDeveloper help system for details about creating validations.)

Declarative validation rules are available on the Validation page of the Entity Object Editor.

Set Up the Employees Business Components

The Search page needs access to the EMPLOYEES table. This section sets up the entity object and view object business components for this table.

1. Expand the Model\Application Sources node, and on the tuhra.model (package-level) node, select **New Entity Object** from the right-click menu. The Create Entity Object Wizard will display. Click Next if the Welcome page appears.

2. In the Name page, select the *Schema Object* as "EMPLOYEES." The *Entity Object:Name* will automatically change to "Employees." Change the *Package* to "tuhra.model.entities".

   Additional Information: Creating separate packages for entity objects, view objects, and application module components allows you to more quickly navigate to an object in the JDeveloper navigator and in the file system.

   NOTE
   The ADF BC creation wizards fill in the package name based on the node in the navigator from which you start the wizard. In this case, you started from "tuhra.model" because no entity object package has been created. Future entity objects will be created from the tuhra.model.entities node that this wizard will create.

3. Click Next. The Attributes page lists attributes for all columns in the EMPLOYEES table. Allowing all attributes to be available in the entity object assists with flexibility for creating view objects from the entity object.

   NOTE
   If you have added audit columns (for create and modify users and dates), select those columns and click Remove on the Attributes page.

4. Click Next to skip this page. You can further refine the attribute properties later, so click Next to skip the Attribute Settings page as well.

   NOTE
   If the database table on which you are basing the entity object does not contain any primary key columns, this wizard will create an attribute called "RowId" (after a confirmation dialog) and select the "Primary Key" checkbox for that attribute when you leave this page.

5. On the Java page, be sure that the default for generating the entity object class with accessors is selected. This is a default you set up for the project. As mentioned in Chapter 6, should you need another Java file to add custom code after first visiting this page, you can add it later by returning to the editor and selecting the relevant checkbox. Click Next.

6. You need to create a view object for this entity object so that you can query the EMPLOYEES table. On the Generate page, select the *Generate Default View Object* checkbox to activate the other fields. Change *Package* to "tuhra.model.views" and *Name* to "AllEmployees". The view will be stored in a separate package from the application module and entity object.

TIP
This book uses a naming convention that entity object names match the database tables or views upon which they are based. View object names describe the contents of the view object.

7. Click Next to review the settings you applied in the preceding pages. Click Finish to generate the entity object and view object as well as the packages to contain them. Click Save All. The expanded Model project should look like the following illustration:

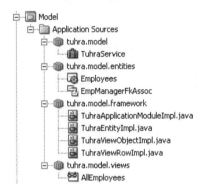

8. Notice that an entity object association, EmpManagerFkAssoc, was also added to the tuhra.model.entities node. Select this association in the navigator, and view the Structure window. The Create Entity Object Wizard created this association from the foreign key constraint for MANAGER_ID (represented by the Destination End node) that points to EMPLOYEE_ID (represented by the Source End node).

9. The AllEmployees view object (under tuhra.model.views) should return its results sorted by LAST_NAME and FIRST_NAME. Double click the AllEmployees node to display the View Object Editor. Select the SQL Statement page, and click Edit next to the *Order By* field.

10. In the Order By dialog, click "+" to add an ORDER BY clause. Expand the Employees node of the Expression Palette to display the columns; select "LAST_NAME." (As with most dialogs in JDeveloper, you can resize this dialog to provide larger selection panels.) In the *Order* field, select "ASC" and click the "<" button to move the column to the *Expression* field.

11. Click the "+" button again to add a row. Move FIRST_NAME (with ASC) to the left. Click OK. The *Order By* field will read "Employees.LAST_NAME ASC , Employees.FIRST_NAME ASC".

TIP
You will probably find it easier to set the Order By field by typing in the column names.

12. Click Test to check the query. Then click OK in the notification dialog. Click OK to dismiss the editor, and click Save All.

13. Select the Employees entity object in the navigator, and double click the entity object file EmployeesImpl.java in the Structure window to open the Java file in the editor. Notice that the class definition extends (subclasses) `TuhraEntityImpl`, the framework buffer class, as the superclass. You specified this superclass when you set the project properties in the practice in Chapter 11.

14. Close this file (by clicking the "x" icon in the editor window tab or by clicking the middle mouse button or wheel on the file's editor tab), and open the view object file AllEmployeesImpl.java for the AllEmployees view object in the same way to see its framework buffer class reference. Close the view object file.

Define Employees Control Hints and Validation Rules

This section sets the label control hints and defines declarative validation rules for attributes in the Employees entity object.

1. In the Model project, under the Application Sources\tuhra.model.entities node, double click Employees to open the Entity Object Editor.

2. Expand the Attributes node in the navigator, and select the EmployeeId attribute. Select the Control Hints tab and set *Label Text* as "ID" and *Display Width* as "10". Click Apply to save the change, but leave the editor open.

Additional Information: The *Label Text* property becomes the prompt, and *Display Width* is used to set the visual size for fields based on this attribute. UI components, such as af:inputText, also offer a *Columns* property that defines the visual width of the component. If you use the Data Control Palette to create a component for this attribute, the *Columns* property will be set to the expression #{bindings.EmployeeId .displayWidth}, which refers to the control hint setting. You can also override this width and set the *Columns* property of the component to a literal value. This principle applies to the *Label Text* control hint, too. If the control hints are not set, the expressions resolve to properties of the attribute (for example, the attribute name for the label, and column size for width).

3. Select the following attributes one at a time, and set the *Label Text* property as follows:

Attribute	Label Text
FirstName	First Name
LastName	Last Name
Email	Email
PhoneNumber	Phone
HireDate	Hire Date
JobID	Job ID
Salary	Salary
CommissionPct	% Commission
ManagerID	Manager ID
DepartmentID	Department ID

4. You can also use control hints to set a date format mask for input and output of the value. Return to the Control Hints tab for HireDate. In the *Format Type* property, select "Simple Date," and for *Format*, enter "MM/dd/yyyy". Date format masks in Java are case-sensitive, so be sure to match the example shown exactly.

NOTE
The examples used in this book format dates in the American style, "MM/dd/yyyy" but you are free to change this to a style that is more familiar. Date format masks are documented in the Javadoc for the SimpleDateFormat class (in the core Java library).

5. Select the Validation page.

Additional Information: This page contains a list of attributes in the entity object. You can create validations on the entity object level or on the attribute level. The validation will occur when the ADF BC framework attempts to set a value for insert or update.

6. Select FirstName and click New. The "Add Validation Rule for: FirstName" dialog will appear. Pull down the list in the *Rule* field. You will see a number of prebuilt validation types. Select "Length Validator." The dialog will change to display relevant properties for this validator.

NOTE
You can define input lengths in the attribute's database column type, but the error that occurs if the input value exceeds the specified length is generic. Validation rules allow you to specify the error message displayed if the validation fails. For example, using a length validation rule, you could designate an attribute as mandatory (length greater than zero) and specify the error message text. The mandatory attribute setting on an attribute will provide a generic error message.

7. Select an *Operator* of "LessOrEqualTo" and an *Enter Length* of "15". Enter the *Error Message* as "The maximum length for First Name is 15 characters." Click OK to accept the validation rule. The rule will be summarized under the *FirstName* attribute.

Additional Information: The database column for FIRST_NAME holds a maximum of 20 characters, but you want to restrict this even further because of a business requirement. Defining the ADF BC validator allows code in the application server tier to check the value before it is sent to the database.

8. Repeat steps 6 and 7 to specify length validators for some other attributes as follows:

Attribute	Operator	Length	Error Message
PhoneNumber	GreaterThan	0	The Phone is required.
PhoneNumber	LessOrEqualTo	15	The maximum length for Phone is 15 characters.

9. Check that the validations page appears as follows:

Entity Object Editor: Employees

- Name
- Attributes
  - EmployeeId
  - FirstName
  - LastName
  - Email
  - PhoneNumber
  - HireDate
  - JobId
  - Salary
  - CommissionPct
  - ManagerId
  - DepartmentId
- Tuning
- Java
- Validation
- Publish
- Subscribe
- Authorization
- Custom Properties

Validation

Select the Entity Object or one of its attributes and click the New button to apply a new validation rule.

Declared Validation Rules:

- Employees
  - EmployeeId
  - FirstName
    - FirstName Character length Less than or equals 15
  - LastName
  - Email
  - PhoneNumber
    - PhoneNumber Character length Greater than 0
    - PhoneNumber Character length Less than or equals 15
  - HireDate
  - JobId
  - Salary
  - CommissionPct
  - ManagerId
  - DepartmentId

New...   Edit...   Remove

Help   Apply   OK   Cancel

10. Click OK to close the editor and write the validations into the entity object. Click Save All. You will test these validations later.

11. Select the Employees entity object in the navigator. In the Structure window, notice that the declarative validation rules appear under the relevant attributes. Double click EmployeesImplMsgBundle.java under the Sources node of the Structure window. Browse the code in the editor, and identify the control hints and validator messages in the object array, sMessageStrings. Close this file.

NOTE
As Chapters 5 and 9 explain, JSF message bundle files allow you to change messages centrally and provide the ability to internationalize your messages. You can also centralize and internationalize Model layer messages, such as the message bundle you just examined. Since the messages are loaded into a Java class file array, you can supplement the Java code with code that extracts the message from a properties file instead.

Where to Put the SELECT Statement Logic?

View objects are closely coupled to SELECT statements, and are designed to handle any simple or complex query. For example, in the AllEmployees view object, you need to join the EMPLOYEES table to the DEPARTMENTS table for the department name and to the EMPLOYEES table again for the manager name. You have several choices for how to define a multi-table view object based on where to locate the logic for SELECT statements.

Base the View Object on an Entity Object Built from a Database View   Rather than basing the entity object on a single table, you can base it on a database view. The database view contains the multi-table SELECT statement with all necessary join and other statements (such as subqueries or UNION statements). You then create an entity object based on the database view and a view object based on the entity object.

The benefit of this method is that code other than ADF BC (such as PL/SQL stored package code and other database views) can share the SELECT statement definition represented by the database view. In addition, simple, updateable database views allow INSERT, UPDATE, and DELETE statements to be issued directly to the view from any source, including ADF BC entity objects.

If your database view represents a complex query, you can write INSTEAD OF database triggers for the view to handle the INSERT, UPDATE, and DELETE statements issued from the entity object (or any other source). INSTEAD OF triggers act the same way as Oracle Forms ON- triggers (such as ON-INSERT, ON-UPDATE, and ON-DELETE). They trap the SQL statement sent to the database view and replace it with logic you have written to perform the required action.

Another advantage to basing the view object on an entity object that represents a database view is that changes to the logic in the view are made in the database. This can be a benefit for an application in production mode, because a simple change in the database view's logic (without changing the numbers or types of queried columns) can change the behavior of the application, with no changes required on the application code side. Changes on the application side often require a redeployment, which is a bit more effort than changing the view's logic.

NOTE
If you have decided to place business rules validation code in the middle tier, you can define declarative validation rules or write Java code in the entity object class for an ADF BC entity object based on a database view.

Base It on a Query—the Read-Only View Object   If the view object will only be used for queries, it is a best practice to represent it as a read-only view object. Read-only view objects, by definition, are based on a SELECT statement, not on an entity object. This means that you will not be able to issue INSERT, UPDATE, or DELETE statements to the view object. However, if you are certain that you will not need the entity object, coding a read-only view object adds a bit of efficiency to the ADF BC code because it eliminates processing associated entity object code and the entity object cache.

You still have a choice when coding a read-only view object of whether to write the join and other complex statements in the view object or in a database view upon which the view object is based. The same consideration for the location of the logic applies here. If a production application requires a change in SELECT statement logic (but not in the number or types of columns), a database view change may not require an ADF BC change (and a redeployment of the application). You always need to consider the efficiency of SELECT statements you write regardless of where they appear in the application. The sidebar "Tuning the View Object" explains some techniques you can use to tune SELECT statements used in view objects.

Base the View Object on Multiple Entity Objects   For this strategy, each entity object represents one of the tables in the view. The View Object Editor allows you to create the required joins easily if the tables have entity associations between them. If the entity associations are not in place, you will

Tuning the View Object

You can build the same complexity into the SELECT statement for a view object as you can for a database view. However, you can also build in the same inefficiencies. Although the SQL Statement page of the View Object Editor allows you to see the query tuning path of the view object's query by using the Explain Plan button, you might want to tune the SELECT statement coded into a view object in an external tool. The SQL Statement page of the View Object Editor allows you to copy the SELECT statement to the clipboard. You can paste it into your favorite SQL tuning tool, including JDeveloper's SQL Worksheet, which contains an EXPLAIN PLAN button. Then copy the tuned query back into the view object.

In addition, the View Object Editor contains some ADF BC properties that you can use to optimize the view object's performance, including a field for an optimizer hint.

need to type the join statements into the *Where* field. If the SELECT statement requires subqueries or other non-join syntactical elements, you will need to place the view object in expert mode and manually enter the additional elements.

This technique is useful if you cannot easily create database views, if you have no other non-ADF BC code or applications that need to share the view (the statement is built into the ADF BC view object only), or if you want to maintain code (for example, for validations) in the ADF BC layer instead of in the database. In addition, you can mark a lookup entity object (such as Departments for an AllEmployees view object that includes Department Name) as a *reference* so that it is not used for INSERT, UPDATE, and DELETE. This means that you do not need to write database INSTEAD OF view triggers. All INSERT, UPDATE, and DELETE statements will go to the entity objects that are not specified as reference types.

If you need to make changes to the underlying logic supporting the query after the application is in production, you will need to modify the view object and redeploy the application.

NOTE
Redeploying an application is not a difficult task, but it can require a restart of the Java runtime container on the server. Users who are logged into the application will lose their sessions if this occurs.

This is the solution we will use for the AllEmployees view. After defining the departments and employees (managers) entity objects, you will redefine the AllEmployees view object as a join from the required entity objects.

Set Up Jobs and Departments Business Components

In Oracle Forms, you can build a pulldown list (poplist) or LOV (list of values) that is loaded from a database query by defining a record group. For pulldown lists, you then populate a list item programmatically from that record group. For LOVs, you associate the record group with an LOV object that is attached to the item (or you just use the LOV Wizard to create the record group and the LOV). In JDeveloper and ADF BC work, the Oracle Forms record group role is played by the ADF BC view object. As in Oracle Forms, you need some code on the UI side to display the view object data in a pulldown list or separate LOV window. With ADF BC, this additional code can be created declaratively.

NOTE
Oracle Forms developers are accustomed to making a distinction between a poplist (pulldown list) and an LOV window. In JDeveloper work, you will sometimes see the term "LOV" used to refer to both pulldown lists and LOV windows.

This section sets up entity objects and view objects for the pulldown list (Jobs) and one of the LOVs (Departments). This section assumes that you have completed the earlier section for setting up the Employees business components. Therefore, the instructions are task-oriented and a bit abbreviated, rather than step-oriented. If you need help with a particular task, refer to the detailed steps in the earlier section.

The Jobs pulldown will display all rows from the Jobs table, so no additional WHERE clause is required. The Departments LOV will allow the user to query using part or all of the department name. This type of functionality requires a *bind variable*, a placeholder in the WHERE clause that substitutes for a value entered by the user. In this section, you will create a bind variable, `searchDepartment`, that is used in a WHERE clause, as follows:

```
WHERE UPPER(Departments.DEPARTMENT_NAME) LIKE
    CONCAT(UPPER(:searchDepartment), '%')
```

When the query is issued, the `searchDepartment` variable is replaced by the value entered by the user, and the WHERE clause is completed.

1. From the tuhra.model.entities node in the navigator, create an entity object for the JOBS table with a default view object called "AllJobs." Create the view object in the tuhra.model.views package. The wizard will also create an association representing the foreign key on JOB_ID from EMPLOYEES to JOBS.

2. Click Finish in the wizard, and click Save All. The Model project will appear in the navigator as follows:

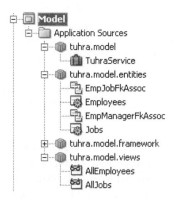

3. Create the following validations with the Range Validator rule for the Jobs entity object:

Attribute	Operator	Minimum Value	Maximum Value	Error Message
MinSalary	Between	1000	10000	Minimum Salary must be at least 1,000.
MaxSalary	Between	1000	10000	Maximum Salary must be 10,000 or less.

4. Click OK. Double click the AllJobs view object node in the navigator to display the View Object Editor. On the SQL Statement page, enter the *Order By* field as "Jobs.JOB_TITLE ASC" so that the LOV built from this view object will be sorted by job title.

5. Click OK.

6. Open the Entity Object Editor for Jobs, and add the following control hints:

Attribute	Label Text	Format Type	Format
JobId	Job ID	<none>	<none>
JobTitle	Title	<none>	<none>
MinSalary	Minimum Salary	Number	$##,###
MaxSalary	Maximum Salary	Number	$##,###

Additional Information: The *Format Type* control hint for the salary amounts specifies that the number will be displayed with a dollar sign and no decimal places (the database columns are typed as NUMBER(6,0)). For a number format type, the *Format* pulldown also contains a "Currency" format, but this will display the number with the currency setting that is local to the server. The prebuilt formatters (Number and Currency) are defined in the JDEV_HOME\jdev\system\oracle.BC4J.10.1.3.x\formatinfo.xml file and are available at runtime in an ADF BC library class referenced by the JobsImplMsgBundle.java file.

7. Click OK. Click Save All.

8. Add an entity object, Departments, for the DEPARTMENTS table with a default view object called "DepartmentsByName." Start the Create Entity Object Wizard from the tuhra.model.entities package node of the navigator. As before, be sure to specify the view object package as "tuhra.model.views". Click Finish to complete the wizard.

9. Open the Entity Object Editor for Departments and set the following Label Text control hints:

Attribute	Label Text
DepartmentId	ID
DepartmentName	Name
ManagerId	Manager ID
LocationId	Location ID

10. Click OK and then click Save All. The Model project will appear in the navigator as follows:

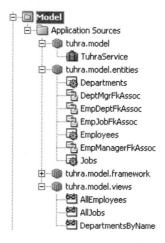

Additional Information: The wizard added an entity object association, EmpDeptFkAssoc, for the foreign key on EMPLOYEE_ID from EMPLOYEES to DEPARTMENTS and DeptMgrFkAssoc for the foreign key on MANAGER ID from DEPARTMENTS to EMPLOYEES (EMPLOYEE_ID).

11. Double click DepartmentsByName in the navigator to open the View Object Editor.

    Additional Information: The DepartmentsByName view object will be the source of data for the Departments LOV. Since you want to allow users to search this view object, you need to add a WHERE clause containing a bind variable (bind parameter). The bind variable will be filled in with the value that the user enters in the LOV *Department Name* search field.

12. Select the Bind Variables page. Click New under the *Variables* area. In the Variable tab below, enter the *Name* as "searchDepartment", the *Type* as "String," and the *Default* as "%".

13. Select the *Updateable* checkbox (if it is not already selected) so that the user can enter values into this parameter. Click Control Hints and enter *Label Text* as "Department Name". This text will be used as the prompt for the search field in the LOV.

14. Select the SQL Statement page, and enter *Where* as follows:

```
UPPER(Departments.DEPARTMENT_NAME) LIKE CONCAT(UPPER(
    :searchDepartment), '%')
```

15. Use the Order By dialog (by clicking Edit), or type in the *Order By* field as follows:

```
Departments.DEPARTMENT_NAME ASC
```

    Additional Information: Notice that the WHERE clause appears in the *Generated Statement* area but the ORDER BY clause does not.

16. Click Test to check the syntax and fix any errors. Click OK. Click Save All.

Additional Information: You will add code to load the `searchDepartment` bind variable later. The code will load the value the user types in the search field into this bind variable; the WHERE clause will then be constructed with a value substituted for the bind variable name. An alternative approach to using a bind variable is to concatenate the value to the end of a WHERE clause snippet. However, Oracle recommends using bind variables because they allow parsed SQL to be reused in the shared SQL area of the database and because they are more resistant to SQL injection, which allows users to enter SQL (and possibly even DDL—Data Definition Language—statements) inside query parameters. The "SQL Injection" section at the end of this phase explains this topic a bit more.

Add Lookup Attributes to the Employees View Object

You need to display the department name and manager name in the AllEmployees view object. Now that you have definitions for the department object, you can proceed with this requirement. You can use any of the techniques discussed previously to add the required DEPARTMENTS and EMPLOYEES (manager) table to this query. Since the view object will be used for viewing records as well as for updating records (on the Edit page), you need to base the view object on entity objects. Using the multiple entity object techniques described earlier, we can declare that only the Employees entity object is writeable.

1. Double click AllEmployees under tuhra.model.views to open it in the View Object Editor. On the Entity Objects page, notice that the selected entity object is Employees. We need to add Departments (for the department name) and Employees again (for the manager name).

2. Select Departments (under tuhra.model.entities), and move it to the *Selected* area. Change its *Alias* to "EmployeeDepartment". Ensure that the *Reference* checkbox is selected (so that changing a key value (DepartmentId) will automatically query the referenced value, DepartmentName) and that *Updatable* is unselected (so that no INSERT, UPDATE, or DELETE statement will be issued to the entity object). Notice that the *Association* property is automatically filled in as the EmpDeptFkAssoc (foreign key) association.

3. Select Employees and move it to the *Selected* area. Change its *Alias* to "EmployeeManager". *Reference* should be selected, and *Updatable* should be unselected.

4. Navigate to the SQL Statement page. The WHERE clause to join the tables will be filled in from the associations between the entity objects you selected. Since you want to show all employee records, even if they have no manager ID or department ID, you need to modify the clause to include outer joins. Change the *Where* property field to read as follows:

   ```
   (Employees.DEPARTMENT_ID = EmployeeDepartment.DEPARTMENT_ID (+)) AND
      (Employees.MANAGER_ID = EmployeeManager.EMPLOYEE_ID (+))
   ```

   Additional Information: You can also click the Edit button and use the Where Clause dialog to change this property, but it requires the same amount of typing. The inner parentheses will be removed if you use this dialog, but the statement will still work.

5. Click Test and fix any errors. Click Apply to save the changes, but leave the editor open. Select the Attributes page. You will see the new entity usages for EmployeeDepartment and EmployeeManager in the *Available* area.

6. Select DepartmentName under the EmployeeDepartment node, and move it to the *Selected* area. The EmployeeDepartment.DepartmentId will also move to *Selected* as DepartmentId1, because the view object already contains a DepartmentId attribute. The view object requires this attribute for the lookup feature. The Department Name is now an attribute of the view object.

7. Under EmployeeManager, select *FirstName* and *LastName* as a group, and move them to the *Selected* area. As before, the key, EmployeeId, will also move (and appear as EmployeeId1).

8. Notice that the DepartmentId and EmployeeId keys that moved contain a number suffix. Expand the Attributes node and select the DepartmentId1 attribute. Change its *Name* property to "DepartmentDepartmentId". Change *Query Column: Alias* to "DEPARTMENT_DEPARTMENT_ID".

   Additional Information: The *Query Column: Type* property is disabled because this database datatype is inherited from the entity object.

9. Change the following attributes in the same way:

Attribute	Attribute: Name	Query Column: Alias
EmployeeId1	ManagerEmployeeId	MANAGER_EMPLOYEE_ID
FirstName1	ManagerFirstName	MANAGER_FIRST_NAME
LastName1	ManagerLastName	MANAGER_LAST_NAME

10. Click Apply. You can now set the values for some control hints as follows:

Attribute	Control Hint	Value
ManagerEmployeeId	Display Hint	Hide
DepartmentDepartmentId	Display Hint	Hide
ManagerFirstName	Label Text	Manager's First Name
ManagerLastName	Label Text	Manager's Last Name
DepartmentName	Label Text	Department

Additional Information: The ID attributes are used for lookups only and, therefore, you will not need to build user interface components from it. Notice that you are setting these control hints on the view object level not on the entity object level, even though it is usually better to set them on the entity object level. All view object attributes inherit control hints from the entities in which they are declared. However, this will not work for the manager lookup usage of the Employees entity object. For example, the EmployeeId entity object label is "First Name." This label works for the base usage of Employee in AllEmployees, but it needs a manager-specific version in the lookup usage of the Employees entity object. Therefore, it is necessary to set this label control hint on the view object level.

11. Select the Attributes node in the View Object Editor navigator, and compare it with the following display. If needed, use the up and down arrow buttons to reorder the attributes.

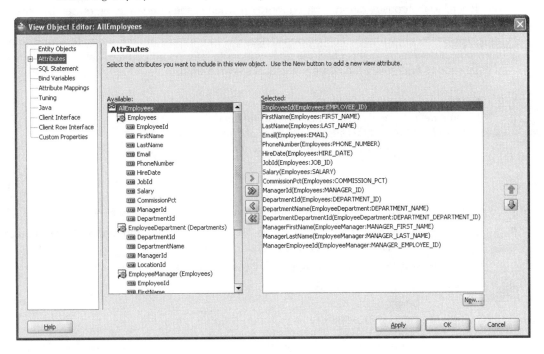

12. Click OK. Click Save All.

Create the Managers View Object

You now need to create a view object for the Managers LOV that shows all managers in the system. Since there is no indicator on the Job record or the Employee record to identify a manager, we assume (and have, of course, confirmed with the business users) that managers are individuals who have been assigned as the manager for one or more departments (using the MANAGER_ID column in the DEPARTMENTS table) or who have been assigned as a manager for an employee (the MANAGER_ID column in the EMPLOYEES table). Therefore, the screens in this system will only display employees as managers if they have been assigned employees or departments.

We would like to display the manager's name and, if appropriate, the department name for the department he or she is assigned to manage; these two features require joining the EMPLOYEES table (for the manager name) and outer joining to the DEPARTMENTS table (for the department name, if the manager is associated with that DEPARTMENTS record).

As mentioned before, you have a choice about what style of view object to create (read-only or entity-based) and whether the view object will be backed by an entity object. Since the view object will only be used to select a manager ID for the employee search and edit pages, it will never have an INSERT, UPDATE, or DELETE statement issued to it. Therefore a read-only view object is the logical choice because it avoids the minor programming and runtime overheads of processing entity object code.

The choice of whether to create a database view for this view object or to embed the SELECT logic in the view object is more difficult. The two methods have no significant performance difference, so the consideration is based more on whether the query may be reused by other applications. We will assume that the query is not likely to be reused, so the example places the join logic in the view object. This demonstrates how to embed a multi-table statement inside a view object definition. In this case, the code you write later on will create a bind variable that will be used to filter using the name entered in a search field.

NOTE
In some development environments, creating database views is restricted to DBAs. In this situation, you might find coding the SELECT statement in the view object more convenient than requesting a new database view.

1. On the tuhra.model.views node, select **New View Object** from the right-click menu. In the Create View Object Wizard, click Next if the Welcome page appears.

2. On the Name page, enter the *Name* as "ManagersByName" and, under "Rows Populated by a SQL Query, with:" radio group option, select *Read-only Access*. Click Next.

3. On the SQL Statement page, enter the *Query Statement* as follows:

```
SELECT emp.employee_id,
       emp.first_name,
       emp.last_name,
       managed_dept.department_name,
       managed_dept.department_id
FROM   (
          SELECT DISTINCT manager_id FROM employees
          UNION
          SELECT DISTINCT manager_id FROM departments
       ) mgr,
       departments managed_dept,
       employees emp
WHERE mgr.manager_id = emp.employee_id
AND   managed_dept.manager_id (+) = mgr.manager_id
AND   (
          UPPER(emp.first_name) LIKE CONCAT(UPPER(:searchMgrName), '%') OR
          UPPER(emp.last_name) LIKE CONCAT(UPPER(:searchMgrName), '%')
      )
```

Additional Information: You would have developed and confirmed this statement (with literal values instead of the bind variable names) before starting up the wizard. On the database connection node, you can select SQL Worksheet to run a SQL command-line tool inside JDeveloper. This will assist you in working out the query. You can alternatively use a SQL editing tool of your choice. The important consideration is to be able to paste a working query into this page because the SELECT statement debugging capabilities on this page are limited to standard database error messages. If you are unclear about the relationships between tables and column names of the tables, you can possibly use the Query Builder (accessed using the Query Builder button on this page). This tool is restricted to queries that do not contain SQL set operators (UNION, INTERSECT, and MINUS).

4. Enter *Order By* as "LAST_NAME ASC, FIRST_NAME ASC". (The Order By dialog accessed from the Edit button is also not accessible if you use set operators in the query.) Click Test to confirm that the query is properly entered. The wizard should appear as follows:

View Object Editor: ManagersByName

- Entity Objects
- Attributes
- SQL Statement
- Bind Variables
- Attribute Mappings
- Tuning
- Java
- Client Interface
- Client Row Interface
- Custom Properties

SQL Statement

Enter your custom SELECT statement and click Test to check its syntax. Provide the ORDER BY clause separately.

Query Statement

```
SELECT emp.employee_id,
       emp.first_name,
       emp.last_name,
       managed_dept.department_name,
       managed_dept.department_id
FROM   (
           SELECT DISTINCT manager_id FROM employees
           UNION
           SELECT DISTINCT manager_id FROM departments
       ) mgr,
       departments managed_dept,
       employees emp
WHERE mgr.manager_id = emp.employee_id
AND   managed_dept.manager_id (+) = mgr.manager_id
AND   (
           UPPER(emp.first_name) LIKE CONCAT(UPPER(:searchMgrName), '%') OR
           UPPER(emp.last_name) LIKE CONCAT(UPPER(:searchMgrName), '%')
       )
```

Query Clauses

Order By: LAST_NAME ASC, FIRST_NAME ASC   Edit...

☑ Expert Mode   Query Builder... Explain Plan... Test

Binding Style: Oracle Named ▼

Help   Apply   OK   Cancel

NOTE
Remember that most dialogs in JDeveloper are resizable.

5. You will notice that the query includes references to the searchMgrName bind variable. Click Next. As before, click New and enter the *Name* as "searchMgrName". Be sure the *Type* is "String" and *Updateable* is selected. Enter the *Default* as "%".

6. On the Control Hints tab, enter the *Label Text* as "Manager First or Last Name". Click Next.

7. The attribute mappings show the attributes associated with the query columns. The defaults are fine, so click Next.

8. The Attributes page shows the existing attributes and allows you to create other attributes. Each attribute is marked as "Calculated" because it is derived from the query. Click Next.

9. On the Attribute Settings page, you need to specify a primary key attribute. Normally, the view object inherits its primary key attribute assignment from the entity object, but this view object has no entity object. Be sure the EmployeeId attribute is selected, and select the *Key Attribute* checkbox.

10. Scroll through the attributes, and notice they are all marked as "Mapped to Column or SQL." Click Next. The default Java files will work for this view object, so click Next.

11. Review the options you have chosen, and click Finish to create the view object. Click Save All.

12. You can now set the control hints for the fields so that their prompts will appear correctly in the LOV. Double click ManagersByName in the navigator. The View Object Editor will appear.

13. Expand the Attributes node and, on the Control Hints tab for each attribute, set the *Label Text* control hint as before (select the attribute and click the Control Hints tab) using the following labels:

Attribute	Label Text
EmployeeId	Manager ID
FirstName	First Name
LastName	Last Name
DepartmentName	Department Managed
DepartmentID	Department ID

14. Click OK and click Save All.

Update and Test the Application Module

Now that you have all view objects created for this practice, you can add them to the application module. The application module manages database transactions and provides the main connection point between the View and Model code.

1. Double click TuhraService under the tuhra.model node in the navigator. The Application Module Editor will appear.

2. Expand the tuhra.model.views node in the *Available View Objects* area, and move each view object to the *Selected* area.

3. Select each view object in the *Data Model* area, and remove the numbered suffix from the *Instance Name* so that the view object instance name matches the view object name. The editor should appear as follows:

4.   Click OK to accept the changes. Click Save All.

5.   On the TuhraService application module node, select **Test** from the right-click menu. Select the HR connection in the Connect dialog, and click Connect. The Oracle Business Component Browser will open.

6.   Double click AllEmployees to open the tester's browse window. Notice that the prompts reflect the control hint labels you set and that the reference attributes from Departments (Name, Manager's First Name, and Manager's Last Name) are disabled because the lookup entity object usages are marked as reference usages.

7.   Change a first name to contain 16 characters. Navigate out of the field, and you will see the error message you defined for the length validator on FirstName.

   Additional Information: This validation is immediate in an application client such as the Oracle Business Component Browser. When you run an application in a web browser, the page would need to be submitted so that the Controller can pass the values to the Model layer validator.

8.   Dismiss the error dialog. Fix the value for first name, and delete the phone number value. Navigate out of that field to check the error message. Type a phone number with 16 characters, and check that error message.

9.   Dismiss the error dialog and fix the phone number. Double click the AllJobs node in the browser. Notice that the prompts are set to the control hint text and that the format mask for the salary fields is used to display the values.

10.   Double click DepartmentsByName. A Bind Variables dialog will appear, showing the prompt of the bind variable ("Department Name") and the name of the variable

("searchDepartment"). Enter the *Value* as "S%" and click OK. The browser will show all departments whose names start with "S." (You can use the navigation buttons in the toolbar to scroll through records in the result set.) Check that the field prompts show your control hint text.

11. Double click ManagersByName. The Bind Variables window will open for the searchMgrName variable. Enter the *Value* as "M%" and click OK. The query will retrieve all managers with first or last names starting with "M." Notice that all fields are disabled because this is a read-only view object.

12. Close the Oracle Business Component Browser window.

TIP
Click Save All and use your favorite file system utility to copy the workspace directory to another directory as a backup of your work up to this point. If you experience problems later, you can restore the backup copy and start from this point.

What Did You Just Do?   You prepared the ADF BC objects needed by the JSF code. You cannot develop user interface code that uses the ADF automatic data binding tools, such as the Data Control Palette, unless the data model is prepared. Therefore, when you use ADF tools, steps such as those in this phase will precede the work you perform in the user interface layer.

The AllEmployees view object will be the main business component used on the Search page and its related edit page. The AllJobs view object will be used for the Jobs pulldown. The DepartmentsByName and ManagersByName view objects will be used for Departments and Managers LOVs, respectively. You created ManagersByName as a read-only view object. After setting up the entity objects and view objects, you refined some control hints to make the field labels (prompts) more user-friendly. Finally, you tested the control hints, validations, and other aspects of the components using the Oracle Business Component Browser.

As mentioned before, SQL injection is a problem for all web applications that allow users to submit information. You need to think about this in an early stage of the project, so a brief description here is appropriate.

SQL Injection
SQL injection is the ability to execute undesired SQL snippets or full statements by including code inside fields presented to the user (or in other input streams such as parameters in URLs). For example, a web form could display a Last Name field to query employee records. The SELECT statement executed when the form is submitted could be the following:

```
SELECT * FROM employees
WHERE last_name LIKE '<field_value>%'
```

In this example, "<field_value>" is the value the user typed in the search field. The intended use of this field is to allow the user to enter a string (such as "Kin"). The code then executes the query based on this value; in this example, the WHERE clause would expand to the following:

```
WHERE last_name LIKE 'Kin%'
```

If no value is entered, the WHERE clause would become this:

```
WHERE last_name LIKE '%'
```

In this case, all rows would be retrieved.

A smart user could exploit this mechanism for unintended and possible risky uses. For example, although the application may not allow queries based on salary, a user could enter something like the following in a Last Name query field to view records for employees whose salaries are over 10,000:

```
%' and salary > 10000 --
```

The starting percent sign and quote ends the last name component of the WHERE clause and will return all employee records. The "salary > 10000" component adds an unintended filter to show only those employees with salaries over 10,000. The closing dashes "--" comment out the final percent sign and quote automatically added by the code.

Moreover, if the user could determine names and parameters for PL/SQL functions that performed unwanted actions, such as clearing tables, the user could embed the functions in the WHERE clause components injected into the query field.

The user may need to do some tests to find out the type of syntax and names used, but non-intuitive names and syntax additions, such as wrapping each WHERE clause component inside parentheses, will only slow down determined users, not stop them from performing undesired operations.

Sometimes, ADF BC can provide clues about the SQL and database object names used if a syntax error occurs. For example, in a web page created from the AllEmployees view object, entering "--" as the value for *Department* in the Employees Search page displays the following error on the page:

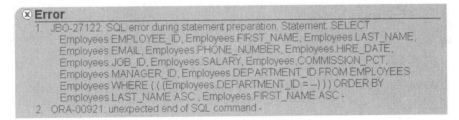

This kind of message is helpful to developers and confusing to normal users. However, it also provides valuable information to malicious users about the syntax of the generated SQL statement and the database object names. It makes it easier for them to work out unintended statements.

An excellent guard against SQL insertion is the use of bind variables like those you created for the Managers and Departments LOV view objects. The bind variable is just a placeholder in a preformatted SQL statement, and its semantics are, therefore, quite limited. This is different from adding to a SQL statement from SQL snippets and string variables, as shown in the previous examples.

Another guard against SQL injection, particularly for QBE functions such as the search form you develop in this chapter, is a validation method for each field, where the user can type data. The validation filters out DDL, logical and comparison operators, and comment markers. This book assumes that you have coded and incorporated such validations. Chapter 15 contains an example of validation code used to safeguard ADF BC from SQL injection.

NOTE
In addition to normal SQL injection concerns, it is helpful to implement a design guideline stating that the database user account used to connect an ADF BC application to the database be different from the schema object owner. The connection user would be granted only minimal privileges. This strategy helps you closely control access privileges on the database side and will restrict the operations attempted in any SQL injection that slips through your SQL injection safeguards.

II. Add Components to the Search Page

You created a page for searchEmployees.jsp in Chapter 11 by copying the template and changing the tab selection and title. This phase adds data-aware user interface components to the Search page. All work takes place in the ViewController project. You will drop in an ADF Search Form to present the query criteria fields; you will also drop in an ADF Read-only Table to hold the search results list.

Layout Containers and Tab Order

Designing the layout for components in an ADF Faces application requires a bit of thought. Since ADF Faces and JSF, in general, are component-oriented technologies, you need to consider the capabilities of various container components into which you drop user interface components, such as `af:inputText` and `af:outputText`. Different container components offer different capabilities. Here are some examples:

- **af:panelForm**   This container allows you to lay out fields in columns without requiring any other embedded containers. The fields are left-aligned and their prompts are right-aligned. All fields are stacked on top of one another, but you can specify the number of columns and rows for a columnar arrangement. This provides a familiar appearance for data entry needs. The fields are rendered down one column and then down the next column. This ordering implements a *tab order* (the order in which the cursor navigates fields when the TAB key is pressed) of down and across.

- **af:panelHeader**   This container provides a title and horizontal line to denote a grouping of elements on the page. Nesting components within this container will display them stacked vertically on the page. The tab order is down.

- **af:panelHorizontal**   This container lays out components in a single row. You do not and cannot specify the number of rows or columns. The tab order is across.

- **af:panelGrid**   This container lays out nested components in rows and columns. You can specify the number of columns, and the component will calculate the number of rows automatically. The tab order is across and down.

As with other tag languages, such as HTML, you can embed containers within containers to take advantage of more than one type of layout arrangement. For example, the next illustration shows a single-column `af:panelForm` container that contains six `af:panelHorizontal` components, each of which contains two `af:inputText` components (except the first `af:panelHorizontal`, which contains an `af:inputText` and an `af:outputText` that is not assigned a value).

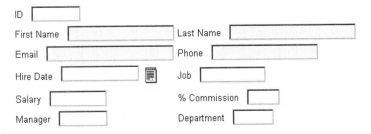

Notice that the fields and prompts are only left-aligned. The ability of the surrounding
af:panelForm to align prompts and fields is lost because the components stacked within the
af:panelForm are af:panelHorizontal containers. This arrangement implements a tab order
of across and down.

The next example shows an af:panelGrid component in a two-column format containing
af:inputText components (with one blank af:outputText field after the ID field).

You will notice that the prompts in the column on the right are left-aligned. However, there is no
ability to align prompts and fields separately within the same column using this arrangement. As a
variation, you could create an af:outputText item for each field and remove the prompt on the
af:inputText component. This technique requires twice as many components and does not
use the prompt capability of the component. The tab order for this type of arrangement is across
and down.

In this phase, you drop an ADF Search Form onto the page. This data control uses the native
capabilities of the af:panelForm to lay out components in two columns, where prompts and
fields are aligned in an arrangement such as in the following illustration:

The tab order for this arrangement is down and across, so you will place the Last Name field
under the First Name field in case the user tabs between fields.

More About Containers The JDeveloper help system contains a topic, "Laying Out Pages with
ADF Faces," that provides some details about various layout techniques. Use the help system
Search tab to look for "laying out pages." In addition, it is useful to learn the capabilities of the
various container components. A good way to start learning about containers is to drag a container
component into the code editor and press F1 to show the tag's documentation. In addition,

container components are subclasses of the `UIXPanel` class, so you can navigate to the Javadoc for UIXPanel (search for "UIXPanel" in the Search tab of the help system). Then navigate one at a time to classes in the "Direct Known Subclasses" list.

TIP
The JDeveloper help system contains a list of ADF Faces components, including the container components. In the Table of Contents, navigate to Reference\Oracle ADF Faces and double click "Oracle ADF Faces Core Tag Documentation" to view this topic.

Add the ADF Search Form

The *ADF Search Form* (*search form*) consists of a set of fields, one for each attribute in the view object. These fields allow the user to enter query criteria used in a search. Like Oracle Forms, the form allows query and data modification on the same form. The search form uses the concept of *Find mode*, in which data the user enters will be used as query criteria, not as input to the database. Find mode is similar to Enter Query mode in Oracle Forms. The search form provides Find and Execute buttons (for Enter Query and Execute Query functions), as well as an indicator specifying if the form is in Find mode.

Although the search form provides all this functionality, you will want to change its behavior to be more user-friendly. For example, most users do not know or care about Find mode, so you want to hide much of the modality of the form. Later sections in this practice will modify the default functionality of the search form you create in this section.

1. Double click the searchEmployees.jsp file (under ViewController\Web Content\pages) to open it in the visual editor (select the Design tab if it does not appear).

2. If the Data Control Palette is not displayed (usually on the right side of the JDeveloper window), select it from the View menu.

3. Expand the TuhraServiceDataControl node. Select AllEmployees and drag it to the title line "Employees Search." The entire area will be selected with a black rectangle, as shown here:

![Screenshot of the TUHRA application showing the Employees Search page with navigation tabs Home, My Profile, Employees, Reference, and Logout/Help icons]

4. Drop the component when the selection appears as shown. A context menu will appear, and you can expand its Forms menu, as in the following illustration:

Additional Information: This menu contains all ADF data controls available for the selected collection, in this case, the AllEmployees view object instance. (Chapter 7 discusses these data controls in detail.)

5.   Select **Forms | ADF Search Form** from this context menu. A set of fields and prompts corresponding to the attributes in this view object will appear on the page in the visual editor.

   Additional Information: The prompts and fields contain EL expressions pointing to the Model bindings. The result of this drag-and-drop operation is akin to the results you achieve using the Oracle Forms Data Block Wizard and Layout Wizard.

6.   Select the top (EmployeeId) field, and, in the Structure window, notice that the fields are contained within an `af:panelForm` component, which you used in the practice in Chapter 9. Under all attribute fields are buttons for Find and Execute, as well as an `af:outputText` element to indicate when the form is in Find mode.

7.   In the visual editor, select the `af:outputText` item that represents the Find mode indicator (above the buttons). Use the Structure window, if needed, to select the proper component. Press DELETE to remove this component.

   Additional Information: This indicator field is unnecessary. Later on, you will set properties so that the form will always be in Find mode so that the user does not need to know about it.

8.   Notice that the HireDate field includes a calendar icon, as shown here:

#{bindings.HireDate.label}

   Additional Information: Although you are about to delete this field, it is useful to note that it appears as an `af:selectInputDate` component; JDeveloper added this component based on the attribute's datatype. This component displays this calendar icon by default. If the user clicks the button, a calendar window will appear. (You can run the page now if you would like to test this icon. After testing it, close the browser and stop the server.) The user can navigate to the correct day and double click it to set the value of the *HireDate* field.

9.   Delete the *HireDate, Salary, CommissionPct, DepartmentDepartmentId, DepartmentName, ManagerFirstName, ManagerLastName, Email, PhoneNumber*, and *ManagerEmployeeId* fields by selecting each field in the visual editor or Structure window and pressing DELETE. You do not want the user to search using those values. You can now perform some layout tasks on this page.

10.   Select the `af:panelForm` component in the Structure window and, in the Property Inspector, set *MaxColumns* to "2" and *Rows* to "3." The fields will rearrange into two columns.

TIP
Double click the center of an editor tab (at the top of the editor window) to maximize the window. Double click it again to restore the window to its previous size.

11. In the Structure window, drag and drop the fields under the `af:panelForm` to rearrange the order in which they appear on the page to match the following:

```
af:panelForm
    af:inputText - #{bindings.EmployeeId....
    af:inputText - #{bindings.FirstName.I...
    af:inputText - #{bindings.LastName.la...
    af:inputText - #{bindings.DepartmentI...
    af:inputText - #{bindings.JobId.label}
    af:inputText - #{bindings.ManagerId.I...
    PanelForm facets
```

Additional Information: As you drag and drop components in the Structure window, you will see the visual editor updating.

Add the ADF Read-Only Table

You are now ready to add the search results table using an ADF Read-only Table data control. This data control displays a grid of multiple columns and multiple rows. It provides a scrolling feature so the user can navigate through many pages of records.

Several layout components will assist the appearance of the page. The `af:objectSpacer` component provides some control over where the objects display on the browser page. It inserts a blank image that is sized using the height and width property values you specify; this component forces a specific layout for other objects around or below it. As mentioned earlier, the `af:panelHeader` component adds a container that you can use to provide a heading for an area of the screen. You place components (such as the table of results) into this container.

You need to decide which columns to display in a results table such as this. Since the user will need to verify that the results match the query criteria fields, you will need to include the same columns in both search form and results table. However, sometimes you might also need to include additional columns in the results to help the user identify a record. Keep in mind the general guideline of not requiring the user to scroll horizontally. This will limit the number of columns you display in the results table, which will also limit the number of search fields.

1. Open the Structure window nodes so that the `af:panelPage` component is visible. Drag an ObjectSpacer component from the ADF Faces Core page of the Component Palette, and drop it on top of the `af:panelPage` node. The `af:objectSpacer` component should appear directly under the `af:panelForm` component as shown on the right:

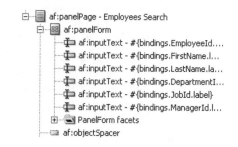

2. Set the objectSpacer's *Height* property to "20" (this measurement is in pixels).

3. Drop a PanelHeader component on top of the af:panelPage component in the Structure window so that the component appears under the af:objectSpacer component. Set its *Text* property to "Matching Employees". The region's heading will change in the visual editor.

4. From the Data Control Palette, drop AllEmployees onto the af:panelHeader component in the Structure window or visual editor and select **Tables | ADF Read-only Table**.

5. In the Edit Table Columns dialog, click Delete for all columns except EmployeeId, FirstName, LastName, JobId, ManagerId, and DepartmentId—the attributes used for the query criteria. (You can group columns together by holding the CTRL key while clicking the column; then press DELETE to delete the group.) Using the Up and Down buttons, reorder the fields so they match the attribute order in the Structure window. Select the *Enable selection* and *Enable sorting* checkboxes.

   Additional Information: The *Enable selection* checkbox specifies that a facet will be added for a selection column so that the user can select a record to delete or edit. The *Enable sorting* checkbox specifies that buttons will be created in the header of each column in the table; when the user clicks a header button, the table rows will re-sort based in ascending or descending order (alternatively for each click of the button).

6. Click OK to accept the definition. Click Save All. The visual editor will contain the components shown in Figure 12-1.

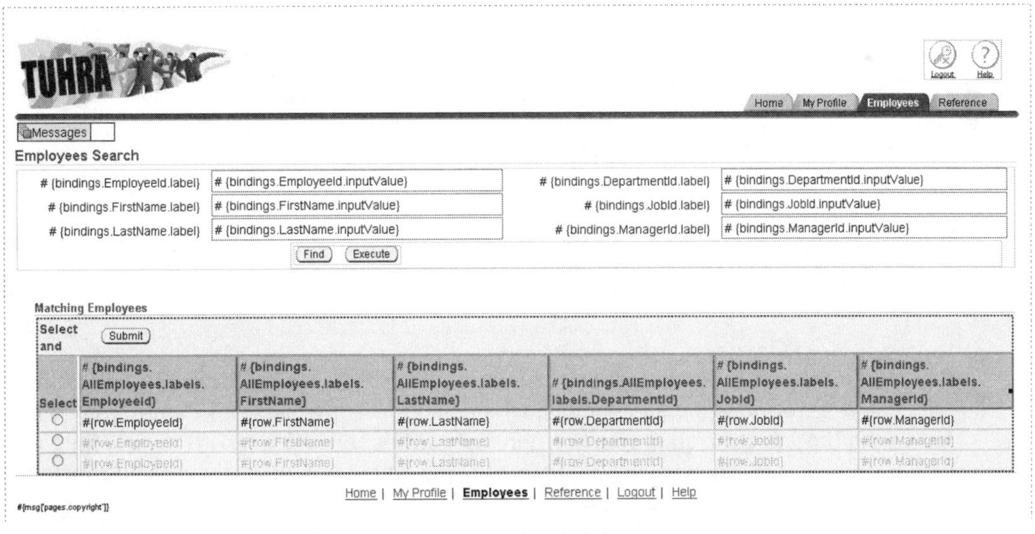

FIGURE 12-1. *Employees Search page with search form and read-only table*

Additional Information: Expand the Table facets node under the new `af:table` node in the Structure window. Under the selection facet, you will see an `af:tableSelectOne` component representing the radio group in the first column of the table. You will use this component later to pass a row identifier to the Edit page. The sidebar "About Current Record Selection with af:tableSelectOne" explains this concept further.

7. Select `af:table` in the Structure window, and change its *Width* property to "100%".

Additional Information: This will cause the table to fill the available width of the browser window. To test this effect, maximize the visual editor (double click the searchEmployees.jsp tab in the editor window), and narrow and widen the JDeveloper window. You will see the results table grow and shrink appropriately. (Double click the tab again to restore the view.)

About Current Record Selection with af:tableSelectOne

In this section, you dropped onto the page a read-only table with the *Enable selection* checkbox selected. This checkbox causes an `af:tableSelectOne` container component to be added to the selection facet of the `af:table`. As mentioned in Chapter 7, the `af:tableSelectOne` component renders a prompt ("Select and" by default), a button area, and a "Select" radio group column that appears on the left side of the table, as shown here:

Select and	Edit Delete New	
Select	# {bindings. AllEmployees. labels. EmployeeId}	# {bindings. AllEmployees. labels. FirstName}
◉	#{row. EmployeeId}	#{row. FirstName}
◉	#{row. EmployeeId}	#{row. FirstName}
◉	#{row. EmployeeId}	#{row. FirstName}

When the user selects a radio button in this column, the command items nested in the `af:tableSelectOne` component will, when clicked, set the iterator's current row to the row with the selected radio button. Therefore, after choosing a record by selecting its corresponding radio button, the user can click the Edit button to set the current row to the selected row and to navigate to the Edit page. The Edit page's context will be that of the current row in the iterator, which is the row represented by the selection in the radio group column.

Chapter 13 shows how you can alternatively or additionally use a link to set the current row and navigate to another page in a single click.

8. Click Save All.

9. The page is complete enough that you can test its basic search features. With the searchEmployees.jsp selected, click Run. The form will appear in the browser with data already queried and sorted according to last name (as you specified for the AllEmployees view object). The automatic query is a default behavior for these data controls. You will also see the label text you set in the business components' control hints.

10. Notice that the read-only table displays a page navigation control in the upper-right and lower-right corners of the table, as shown here:

$$\circledcirc \text{ Previous 10 } \boxed{\text{11-20 of 107}} \text{ Next 10 } \circledcirc$$

This control allows the user to view a different page of results by clicking the links or buttons or by selecting a range of records from the pulldown.

11. Navigate to another page of records using this control, and notice that the page does not refresh; only the contents of the table refresh. This is a demonstration of the ADF Faces feature, *partial page rendering*, introduced in Chapter 5. Partial page rendering allows only part of the display to be redrawn when the form is submitted.

12. Click the *sort button* (column heading) of one of the table columns, and the results will sort based on that column. An arrow in the sort button indicates whether the sort is ascending or descending. This is another feature of this ADF Faces component.

TIP

At this stage in development, you may receive an error (JBO-25013) when you click sort buttons more than once or when you click Find after clicking a sort button. You will fix this problem later. If you receive an error now, close the browser and run the page again to clear the error state.

13. The form is not in Find mode at this point. Click Find to clear the form and activate Find mode (like Enter Query mode in Oracle Forms). (As mentioned in the preceding Tip, if you receive an error, close the browser and restart the page.) Enter "M%" in the *Last Name* field, and click Execute. The results table will fill with data for employees whose last names begin with "M." You can repeat this cycle (clicking Find, entering query criteria, and then clicking Execute) with other values.

NOTE

You can modify the default Find mode behavior so the user does not need to add the "%" wildcard. Although this is beyond the scope of this book, it is similar to the attribute value filtering technique for preventing SQL injection described in Chapter 15.

14. Notice that the search fields are filled in with the details of the first record selected in the table. Select a record other than the first one (using the Select radio group column), and click Submit. The search fields are filled in with details of the selected record. This demonstrates the synchronization of components that share an iterator.

15. Close the browser and stop the OC4J server by clicking the red, square Terminate button in the Log window.

What Did You Just Do?   You added a search form and read-only table data control to the searchEmployees.jsp page. You also added other components to provide a spacer and heading. At this point, you have only used the declarative and visual tools, but the page already performs a basic search function. The ADF data controls offer this basic functionality without adding code. The next phase requires refining Search page functionality to make it more user-friendly.

III. Refine the Search Page Functionality

Now that you have placed the default data controls on the page, you can focus on non-default functionality. Although much of the work consists of adding code to the components, you still use declarative and visual tools heavily.

In addition to the LOVs and pulldown lists you will add in the next phase, you want to add the following functions to this screen:

■ **Ensure that the page stays in Find mode.**

■ **Separate the results table from the search form** so that the table is not in Find mode.

■ **Hide the results table** if it is empty, including when the page first loads.

■ **Offer the user a Clear button** to reset the search fields.

■ **Add Delete, Edit, and New buttons to the results table** so that the user can delete a record or navigate to the Edit page for a particular employee record or for a new record.

Keep the Form in Find Mode

The default ADF Faces Search Form requires the user to click Find to enter Find mode, enter query criteria, and click Execute. We would like to avoid the first of those steps so that the user can just enter query criteria and click a button called Search. In addition, a default search form returns to non-Find mode after a query. We would like the search form to automatically switch back to Find mode after the query. These changes require modifying the default behavior using actions and invoke actions defined in the PageDef file. Although Chapter 7 introduces these concepts, a brief review and further explanation of those concepts are in order.

Actions   In Chapter 11 you defined *actions*, named commands that execute from a page navigation or other event, in the faces-config.xml file for tab command items. An action is similar to a call to a built-in in Oracle Forms. In this example, the Find operation corresponds to the ENTER_QUERY built-in in Oracle Forms. If you want to place an Oracle Forms block into Enter Query mode, you call the ENTER_QUERY built-in.

Expand Operations under the AllEmployees node in the Data Control Palette. You will see something like the following:

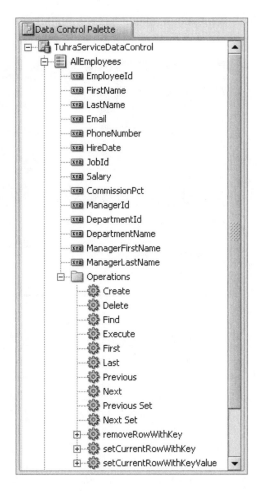

Find is one of the operations available for the AllEmployees collection. You will create an action associated with this operation, which will make the operation available to the page. The action will be defined in the context of the AllEmployees iterator, which represents the AllEmployees data collection.

NOTE
Just as you can create PL/SQL procedures and functions in Oracle Forms and call them from any trigger, you can also define methods on the application module or view object and make them available as operations in the Data Control Palette.

Invoke Actions   Actions do not execute automatically. For example, to activate the Find mode action, you need to create an *invoke action*, a definition for an action to be executed during the page life cycle. For example, you will define a refresh condition for the invoke action indicating that the page should switch to Find mode if it is not in Find mode. The invoke action dialog displays properties on two tabs, as follows:

The properties in this dialog represent the following:

- **id** is a name that you define for the invoke action (similar to a trigger name in Oracle Forms, such as WHEN-NEW-BLOCK-INSTANCE), but the name is not meaningful to the JSF life cycle controller.

- **Binds** declares the action that will be executed. The pulldown list shows actions that are already coded into the PageDef file. This defines the call to the action as a trigger in Oracle Forms would call a built-in.

- **Refresh** allows you to specify at which point in the ADF page life cycle, the action is called. In this example, "ifNeeded" is the default; it signifies the point in the life cycle when the invoke action is first encountered, or when a commit or rollback occurs, or when a page returns from running a query. There is no real parallel in Oracle Forms other than naming the trigger based on when you want Forms to run its code. Oracle Forms trigger names define when the triggers are run in the Oracle Forms runtime life cycle.

- **RefreshCondition** allows you to declare a Boolean expression. If the expression evaluates to "false," the action will not be invoked; if the expression evaluates to "true," the action will be invoked.

PageDef File   The PageDef (page definition) file, introduced in Chapter 7, contains details about the page, including bindings (such as attributes from iterators and actions) and executables (such as iterators and invoke actions). You can edit this file by opening it in the code editor (from a pageDefs package in the ViewController project's Application Source node).

An easy and safe way to edit this file is through the use of the property dialogs available from the right-click menu in the Structure window. The following shows sample contents of a PageDef file as depicted in the Structure window:

TIP
Although this illustration shows only one executable, a page will typically have many executables. The order of elements in the executables section signifies the order in which the invoke actions and iterators are run. You can fix problems that occur due to the order of execution by dragging and dropping elements in the Structure window or moving the code in the code editor.

1. In the visual editor for searchEmployees.jsp, select the Find button and delete it. Select the Execute button and change its *Text* property to "Search".

   Additional Information: The default search form Execute button runs the query with the criteria that the user enters. This is the effect the user would expect when clicking a button called "Search."

2. In the visual editor for the Search page, select **Go to Page Definition** from the right-click menu. The pages_searchEmployeesPageDef.xml file will open in the code editor.

3. You need to add an action for Find mode. Be sure the cursor is somewhere in the PageDef file. In the Structure window, on the `bindings` node, select **Insert inside bindings | action** from the right-click menu.

   Additional Information: The right-click menus for the PageDef file allow you to add elements within the XML file without actually editing the XML code. You interact with property editors that write their contents into the XML file. These property editors are also available to edit the definitions after you create them.

4. The Action Binding Editor will appear. Select AllEmployeesIterator in the *Select an Iterator* pulldown. In the *Select an Action* pulldown, select "Find." Click OK to dismiss the editor.

   Additional Information: This step adds an action tag to the PageDef file to define the action, Find, which is associated with the AllEmployeesIterator. As you saw in the last illustration, Find is one of the operations available to the AllEmployees collection.

5. Now you need to create the invokeAction, which will call the Find action. In the Structure window, on the `executables` node, select **Insert inside executables | invokeAction** from the right-click menu.

6. In the Insert invokeAction dialog, enter the *id* field as "AlwaysFind" and the *Binds* field as "Find."

   Additional Information: The *id* property, as well as the others in this dialog, were described earlier in this section.

7. Click the Advanced Properties tab. Leave Refresh as "ifNeeded," and click the "..." button next to the *RefreshCondition* field to display the Advanced Editor expression-builder dialog.

8. Expand the ADF Bindings\bindings\AllEmployeesIterator node, and select "findMode." Click the right arrow button to move the expression into the *Expression* field. After the opening curly bracket, type " !" so that the expression reads as follows:

   ```
   ${ !bindings.AllEmployeesIterator.findMode}
   ```

   Additional Information: You can also add the not symbol ("!") by positioning the cursor after the curly bracket and clicking the "!" button. This expression returns true if the AllEmployees iterator is not in Find mode. Although the non-Find mode condition normally occurs after a query is executed, it can also occur at other times, such as when the page is first loaded or after a commit or rollback. The expression you just entered ensures that the invoke action will occur whenever the page is not in Find mode.

NOTE
Instead of using the "Advanced Editor" expression editor, you can just type the value in the Insert invokeAction dialog.

9. Click OK to set the expression, and click OK to dismiss the invoke action dialog and add the invokeAction tag to the PageDef file. Click Save All. This page is not ready to run yet.

NOTE
The expression editor for invokeAction prefixes the statement with a "$" instead of a "#." These two EL prefixes are equivalent in this case, but JSF expressions must use the "#" prefix.

10. In the code editor for the PageDef file, find the action you just added for Find. Notice that this element contains an attribute, *Action*, which is assigned "3." This number indicates to ADF that this action is the Find mode. All predefined operations are associated with a number in this way. Operations you define and declare for data controls are assigned "999." The list of available operations and their number keys appears in Chapter 8 (Table 8-3).

Separate the Search Form from the Results Table

The next modification you will work on is separating the search form from the results table. You added the search form and results table by dropping them from the Data Control Palette. At this point, both use the same iterator (AllEmployeesIterator, shown in the executables section of the PageDef file). This means that when one *UI block* (table or form, further described in the "About the UI Block" sidebar) shows a record, the other UI block will show the same record. Interacting with one item will affect another that has the same data source. Since we just defined the action and invoke action to keep the iterator in Find mode, both UI blocks will always be in Find mode (and no records will ever display).

About the UI Block

In this book, *UI block* (user interface block) refers to a group of data-bound components in a container that is associated with an iterator (for example, the search form fields or results table data). The components (for example, input fields) are bound to attributes in the iterator. In Oracle Forms, the base-table block serves this role. However, the Oracle Forms block also serves as the Model layer where SQL is generated to interact with the database. This role is filled in an ADF application workspace by the ADF BC objects in the Model project. ADF code separates the UI block functionality from the model functionality; Oracle Forms does not.

NOTE
In Oracle Forms, a mirror item shares data with another item in the form. Changing one item's data changes the mirror item's data. This Oracle Forms feature is similar to multiple fields on the JSP page based on the same iterator attribute.

Defining a separate iterator for the search results' UI block breaks the synchronization effect and allows the UI blocks to independently use the same data collection (AllEmployees).

The search form will continue to use the AllEmployeesIterator. To clarify this concept, Figure 12-2 summarizes the relationship between ADF BC objects, iterators, and UI blocks. In this diagram, the application module contains three view object instances. The top PageDef file is associated with the deptEmployees.jsp file. It declares two iterators—one for AllDepartmentsIterator and another for DeptEmployeesIterator. AllDepartments is the master view object, and DeptEmployees is the detail view object. When a record is current in the AllDepartmentsIterator, only employee records associated with that department will be available

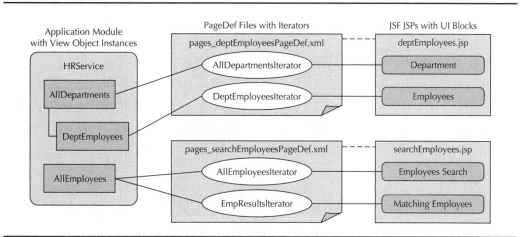

FIGURE 12-2. *Relationships between ADF BC, PageDef files, and JSP pages*

in the DeptEmployeesIterator. Each iterator is presented on the page by a UI block—one for Departments and one for Employees within the selected department.

The bottom PageDef file also contains two iterators—AllEmployeesIterator and EmpResultsIterator, to which the UI blocks for the Search form and the results table are bound, respectively. Although both iterators share a view object instance, AllEmployees, they are functionally separate. The data in each iterator can be traversed separately. This is the situation we need to create in the Search page. Although the search form components will not display data, they need to be bound to an iterator for the purpose of constructing a query.

Current State of searchEmployees.jsp   As shown in the Before section of Figure 12-3, the PageDef file currently holds one iterator, AllEmployeesIterator, which returns data rows for the AllEmployees collection in the data controls model. This iterator acts as the source for attributes

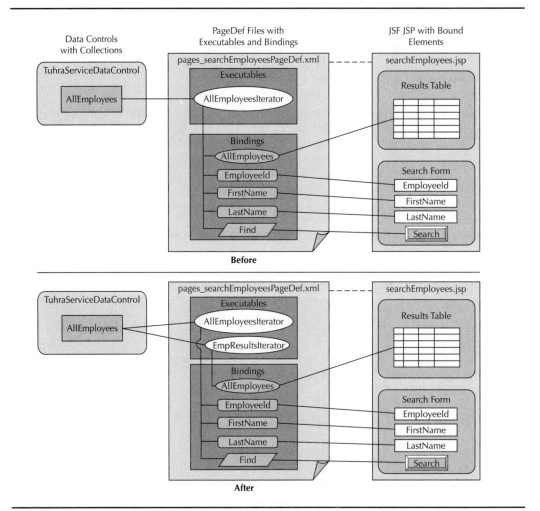

FIGURE 12-3.   *Search page and its source objects before and after an iterator addition*

(such as EmployeeId, FirstName, and LastName), actions (such as Find), and range bindings (such as AllEmployees). As described in Chapter 8, a *table binding* (or *range binding*) is used to retrieve multiple attributes for each value in the range (for example, multiple rows from a database table). In this PageDef file, the binding is a *table* element that supplies separate data values for each column in the row of the results table. The attachment of a table binding to a UI block element is performed at the collection level (AllEmployees), not the attribute level (such as EmployeeId).

Columns within the table UI block are bound to attributes in the iterator (not displayed in this diagram). We will create another iterator, EmpResultsIterator, on the same AllEmployees collection to serve the results table. The After section of Figure 12-3 represents this additional iterator.

1. Open the Structure window and code editor for the pages_searchEmployees PageDef file. In the Structure window, select the EmployeeId node under the `bindings` node. The element will be selected in the code editor. If it is not, on the EmployeeId node, select **Go to Source** from the right-click menu.

2. Find the property, *IterBinding*, and notice that it is set to "AllEmployeesIterator" and the *value* property of the item is "EmployeeId"; this means that the value for this binding attribute is derived from the EmployeeId attribute of the AllEmployeesIterator iterator. This iterator was created when you dragged the first data control, the Search form, onto the page. You can view the iterator definition in the executables section of this file.

3. Examine other attributes in the `bindings` section, and notice that each is linked to an attribute in the AllEmployeesIterator iterator in the same way as EmployeeId. The Find action is also linked to the same iterator.

4. In the Structure window, select the `AllEmployees` node under the `bindings` node. The code editor will select the `table` element (if it does not, on the AllEmployees node, select **Go to Source** from the right-click menu).

5. In the Structure window, expand the `AllEmployees\AttrNames` node to view the individual attributes that make up the table binding. As mentioned, the binding from the JSF component occurs at the table level, but each column in the table will refer to an individual attribute in the table binding's `AttrNames` node.

NOTE
By default, table bindings are named the same as the view object instance that they reference. If it is clearer, you can change this name (for example, to "AllEmployeesTable") in the "id" property of the Property Inspector after clicking the range binding name in the Structure window. You also need to rename references in the af:table (and all its child tags) in the page file. This practice assumes that you do not rename this binding.

6. Open the searchEmployees.jsp file in the code editor. Click the Matching Employees heading to open the Structure window nodes. Select the `af:table` node. Click the Source tab in the visual editor. The table element with all its child elements will be selected. Notice that the table element contains the binding to the range binding, AllEmployees.

7. Look for the column elements within the table element, and notice that the binding occurs to an attribute of the row (one record from the query). These attributes are defined in the AttrNames section of the range binding.

8. With that brief background in how bindings and components relate, you can define the second iterator. Return to the Structure window for the PageDef file.

9. On the `executables` node, select **Insert inside executables | iterator** from the right-click menu. In the Iterator Binding Editor, enter the *Iterator Id* field as "EmpResultsIterator". In the *Data Collection* area, select "AllEmployees" under TuhraServiceDataControl. Click OK.

   Additional Information: This creates an iterator that you can associate with the results table. The original iterator, AllEmployeesIterator, will serve the search form.

10. Under the `bindings` node in the Structure window, select AllEmployees. In the Property Inspector, replace the value in *IterBinding* with "EmpResultsIterator". This switches the source of the range binding for the table to the new iterator.

11. Click Save All.

New State of searchEmployees.jsp   As shown in the After section of Figure 12-3, the search form and results table are now bound to separate iterators, which allows the UI blocks to maintain separate views of data for the same data collection (a view object, in this case). The new iterator, EmpResultsIterator, now supplies data to the results table. You can run the searchEmployees page now if you would like to see how this separation works. Enter "M%" in the *Last Name* field, and click Search to retrieve the matching records. You can also click a header sort button more than once now without causing an error state. Close the browser and stop the server.

Hide the Results Table If No Rows Are Returned

This section describes how to modify the page so that the results table is not rendered when the page is first loaded and when no rows are returned after a query. You will create a session variable and assign it when the user clicks the Search button. Then you will use this variable to determine whether to refresh EmpResultsIterator. If EmpResultsIterator is not refreshed, no query will occur. You will use the same variable to determine whether to show a hint explaining how to perform searches. This hint will disappear after the first query.

   We want to hide the results table if it is empty (that is, the number of rows is <= 0). We accomplish this by setting the *Rendered* property of the `af:panelHeader` container that surrounds the results table. This property will be set to "true" if the *estimatedRowCount* (an attribute of the iterator) is greater than zero. It is set to "false" otherwise.

1. Display the visual editor for the searchEmployees.jsp file. Select the Search button. The Structure window will expand so that the button's node is selected.

2. Drop a SetActionListener from the ADF Faces Core page of the Component Palette on top of the `af:commandButton` – `Search` node in the Structure window. In the Insert SetActionListener dialog, enter the following and click OK. (You will not be able to use the expression dialog to build these expressions.)
   From as "#{true}"
   To as "#{sessionScope.displaySearchResults}"

Additional Information: The *setActionListener* child component allows you to assign a value to a variable. The sidebar "About af:setActionListener" describes this component further.

TIP
If clicking OK in this dialog displays an error about a required value that is already filled in, type a space at the end of the value, delete the space, and click OK again. (You can alternatively select the problem value and press CTRL-C and then CTRL-V before clicking OK.)

3. The displaySearchResults variable will be null when the page is first loaded, because the Search button sets the value and the Search button has not been clicked. You can use this condition to determine whether to refresh the iterator for the results table. Load the PageDef file into the code editor and Structure window.

4. Select EmpResultsIterator under the executables node in the Structure window. In the Property Inspector, click the "…" button in the *RefreshCondition* property to display the RefreshCondition EL dialog. Under the JSP Objects node, select sessionScope and move it to the right. Complete the expression so it reads as follows:

```
${sessionScope.displaySearchResults != null}
```

Additional Information: The displaySearchResults variable does not show under the sessionScope node because you are creating it dynamically. Session variables are similar to Oracle Forms global variables (for example, :GLOBAL.USERNAME) that are available in all applications run in the same Oracle Forms session.

About af:setActionListener
The af:setActionListener component is an ADF Faces element that you can nest in a parent action component, such as an af:commandButton or af:commandLink. You can use it to pass values from one page to another by placing the value in the sessionScope domain, for example, in a variable called "sessionScope.employeeIdToQuery." You can also use this component to insert values into managed beans, HTTP sessions, HTTP requests, or even cookies. (Chapter 9 introduces scope settings in the "About Scope" sidebar.)

A single command component can contain multiple af:setActionListener tags, and their actions will be triggered in addition to the main action of the command item. The order of execution for multiple af:setActionListener tags will be the order in which they are nested within the command component. af:setActionListener is often used to set flags or store reference values without having to resort to writing Java code.

The *From* property indicates the value, and the *To* property represents the name of the variable. Therefore, this component sets a variable we are creating here, displaySearchResults, in the session scope (until the user disconnects) to "true." Both properties must be set using EL. If you need to set a literal string value into the variable, you can use a quoted string, for example, "#{'Tuhra'}". Other literal values do not need to use the quoted string, for example, "#{1}" or "{true}" for int or boolean values, respectively.

NOTE
Variables in the session, request, process, and application scopes are created when you first assign them. You do not need to declare them separately. If you refer to a variable that has not been assigned (that is, has not been created), you will receive a null value, not an error. This is a different behavior from Oracle Forms global variables, because Oracle Forms will return an error if you refer to a non-existent global variable.

5. Click OK to write the expression into the file. Click Save All.

6. You can now add a hint that uses this same variable. An ADF Faces component, `af:panelTip`, is designed to display hints to the user. Display the searchEmployees.jsp file in the visual editor and Structure window. Expand the Structure window nodes, and select the `af:PanelPage` node. On the ADF Faces Core page of the Component Palette, click the PanelTip component to add it below the `af:panelHeader`. The Structure window will appear as shown:

7. Select the `af:panelTip` in the Structure window. In the Property Inspector, click the "Bind to data" button for the *Rendered* property, and set the value to the following (optionally using the EL editor as before):

   `#{ !sessionScope.displaySearchResults}`

8. Click OK if you used the EL editor. Drag an OutputText component on top of the `af:panelTip` component. This component will hold the message to the user. As with all messages, you will eventually place this message in the message bundle file, but, for now, enter the *Value* property as "Enter employee search criteria and click Search."

9. Now you can declare that the table be hidden if no rows are returned. In the Structure window, select the `af:panelHeader - Matching Employees` node (this container encloses the read-only table). In the *Rendered* property, click "Bind to data," and compose the following expression:

   `#{bindings.EmpResultsIterator.estimatedRowCount > 0}`

   Additional Information: The `estimatedRowCount` variable for an iterator indicates the number of rows returned from the query.

TIP
In the EL editor, you can double click the variable name in the ADF Bindings node of the Variables area to enter the expression for that variable into the Expression area.

10. Click OK. Click Save All.

11. Run the searchEmployees.jsp file again. The page should look something like this:

12. Notice the results table is not initially displayed, but the user hint appears. Enter the *Last Name* as "M%" and click Search. The results table will appear and the hint will disappear. You can test any number of clicks for the sort buttons if you did not test them before.

13. Enter the *Last Name* as "Z" and click Search. The results table will disappear because there are no employees with that last name.

14. Close the browser and stop the server.

NOTE
If you change or remove the query conditions and click a sort button, the query will be re-run with the new query conditions. This occurs because the query will be reissued to the database and the WHERE clause is built from the search block fields.

Add a Clear Button to the Search Form

Many web query pages offer the user a Clear or Reset button to clear the search fields. This button makes starting a new query easier. This function requires writing some Java code in a backing bean for the page. We have not created a backing bean yet, so these steps will use some automated property dialogs to create that file.

Dragging an operation onto the page allows you to create a button whose logic automatically binds the button click to an operation on the iterator. In the case of a search form in Find mode, a Delete operation will clear the criteria, as mentioned in Chapter 8. Therefore, this section creates a button called "Clear" for the Delete operation. In addition to the Delete operation, you need to set the form back into Find mode. Therefore, you will need to modify the Delete code that the data control creates in the backing bean.

Calling an operation from backing bean code requires three steps: create a binding container programmatically, create a binding for the operation, and execute the operation for that binding. For example:

```
BindingContainer bindings = getBindings();
OperationBinding operationBinding = bindings.getOperationBinding("Delete");
Object result = operationBinding.execute();
```

Notice that this code works on an operation called "Delete." Delete for the search form refers to the iterator relevant to the UI block. You will be creating a Delete button for the results table later on. This button will also call the Delete operation. The button does not call the operation directly. Rather, it accesses an action in the PageDef file that defines on which iterator the operation will run. Therefore, we need two actions for the Delete buttons: one for each UI block.

1. In the Data Control Palette, expand AllEmployees\Operations. Select Delete, and drag and drop it as an ADF Command Button to the right of the Search button inside the button bar container. If the button does not appear in the correct location, find it in the Structure window and drag it to the proper location, as shown here:

2. In the Property Inspector, change *Text* to "Clear."

3. Double click the button in the visual editor. If you had created a backing bean for this page, this action would load the backing bean Java file into the code editor. However, you have not created the backing bean yet, so the Bind Action Property dialog appears.

4. Click New to display the Create Managed Bean dialog. Enter the *Name* field as "backing_searchEmployees" (the name to be registered in faces-config.xml) and the *Class* as "tuhra.view.backing.SearchEmployees". Ensure that the *Generate Class If It Does Not Exist* checkbox is selected (to create the backing bean), and click OK.

5. The Bind Action Property dialog will fill with the values you entered. Change *Method* to "clearButton_action". Ensure that the *Generate ADF Binding Code* checkbox is selected (so that sample code will be created). Click OK to create the backing bean, register it in the faces-config.xml file, and open it in the editor.

   Additional Information: The `clearButton_action()` method will contain sample binding code.

6. Change the class declaration to use the framework buffer class:

   ```
   public class SearchEmployees extends TuhraBackingBean
   ```

   Additional Information: In the practice in Chapter 11, you created the backing bean framework buffer class used to act as a superclass for all managed beans.

7. You need to indicate where the framework buffer class is located using an import. Move the mouse over the TuhraBackingBean class name and press ALT-ENTER. Alternatively, you can select **Import 'tuhra.view.framework.TuhraBackingBean'** from the right-click menu on the quick fixes icon in the gutter of the code editor, as shown here:

8. Find the `clearButton_action()` method in the editor. It will look like this:

```
public String clearButton_action()
{
  BindingContainer bindings = getBindings();
  OperationBinding operationBinding =
    bindings.getOperationBinding("Delete");
  Object result = operationBinding.execute();
  if (!operationBinding.getErrors().isEmpty())
  {
    return null;
  }
  return null;
}
```

9. This code accesses the binding to call the Delete operation on the data control. The conditional test that uses `operationBinding.getErrors().isEmpty()` is not required. Remove the `if` statement with its curly brackets and the `return null` statement directly under it (leaving one `return null` statement).

10. Change the `bindings.getOperationBinding()` call from "Delete" to "ClearSearch". You will create a ClearSearch binding later. The line of code you just modified should like this:

```
OperationBinding operationBinding =
  bindings.getOperationBinding("ClearSearch");
```

11. Also, you need to return the form to Find mode after the Delete operation. Add the following code before the `return null` statement at the end of the method:

```
operationBinding = bindings.getOperationBinding("Find");
result = operationBinding.execute();
```

Additional Information: This code sets the binding to the Find operation and executes it.

12. Check that the method matches the following code:

```
public String clearButton_action()
{
  BindingContainer bindings = getBindings();
  OperationBinding operationBinding =
    bindings.getOperationBinding("ClearSearch");
  Object result = operationBinding.execute();
  operationBinding = bindings.getOperationBinding("Find");
  result = operationBinding.execute();
  return null;
}
```

13. Compile the file (using Make) to check syntax.

14. Open the PageDef file in the editor (by clicking its tab in the editor window). In the Structure window, on the `bindings` node, select **Insert inside bindings | action** from the right-click menu.

15. In the *Select an Iterator* pulldown, select AllEmployeesIterator. (AllEmployees should be selected in the *Data Collections* list.) In the *Select an Action* pulldown, select "Delete." Click OK.

Additional Information: A binding will be added to the PageDef file. Notice that the code editor shows the *id* for the new action as "Delete1." Change that *id* in the code editor or Property Inspector to "ClearSearch".

TIP
Remember to press ENTER *after typing a value into the Property Inspector. This will save the value in the property.*

16. Click Save All.

17. Run the searchEmployees.jsp file. Enter query criteria and click Search. Then click Clear. The form will clear and return to Find mode, although the results will remain in the table area. Close the browser and stop the server.

Add Edit, Delete, and New Buttons

In addition to querying and browsing records, managers and administrators need to edit, delete, and add employee records. Only users who are in the manager or administrator roles will have access to these functions. This section adds Edit, Delete, and New buttons to the results table area. It completes the actions for Delete but leaves the Edit and New functions for the next chapter.

1. With the searchEmployees.jsp in the visual editor (Design tab), select the Submit button in the table header. The Structure window node for the `af:commandButton` will be selected.

2. This button is contained within an `af:tableSelectOne` component that acts on a record selected using the Select radio group column in the read-only table. Select the `af:tableSelectOne` node. In the Property Inspector, click "Bind to data" for the *Rendered* property to display the Rendered dialog. Enter the Expression as "#{true}". Click OK.

Additional Information: You will add the application's security layer in the practice in Chapter 14; at that time, you'll replace this expression with one that interrogates the user's role and hides the buttons inside this container component if the user is not a manager or an administrator.

3. Select the Submit button and change its *Text* property to "Edit" and its *Action* property to "editEmp".

   Additional Information: This *Action* property will match a navigation case, "editEmp," to load the Edit page from the Search page. You have not defined the navigation case yet, so this value is not available in the *Action* pulldown.

4. Expand the Data Control Palette AllEmployees\Operations node. Drop Delete under that node to the right of the Edit button, and specify an ADF Command Button.

5. Repeat the preceding step for the Create operation. Change the button's *Text* property to "New" and *Action* to "createEmp".

Define Actions for the Delete Button

This section completes the Delete button code by adding definitions for the Delete action and for a commit.

1. Open the PageDef file for searchEmployees.jsp. As before, the button components you just dropped onto the page refer to the default iterator, AllEmployeesIterator. However, you need to have the Delete button action execute on the current record in the results block, which now uses another iterator: EmpResultsIterator.

2. In the Structure window, on Delete under the `bindings` node, select **Properties** from the right-click menu. The Action Binding Editor will appear as follows:

3. In the *Select an Iterator* pulldown, select "EmpResultsIterator" and click OK. Now the Delete action will occur on the selected record in the results table.

   Additional Information: The Delete operation removes the record from the ADF BC model area but it does not issue a COMMIT to the database. You could add another button for the commit operation, but the two-step process of deleting and then committing may not be familiar to the user. The user will find it more intuitive if clicking the Delete button removes the record from the database. Since the Delete button needs to perform two actions, you need to write a bit of code like the code for the Clear button.

4. First, you need to declare an action binding in the PageDef file for the Commit operation in the data controls. In the Structure window for the PageDef file, on the `bindings` node, select **Insert inside bindings | action** from the right-click menu.

5. In the Action Binding Editor, select the top node, TuhraServiceDataControl. The commit operation is performed on the service (application module) level of the data controls; this level represents the database transaction.

6. For *Select an Action*, select "Commit." Leave the *Select an Iterator* dropdown list blank; it is not applicable to the data control level. Commit operates on all data in the same database transaction, regardless of the iterators used. Click OK. You will see a Commit action appear in the `bindings` node.

   Additional Information: Now that the action to call the Commit data control operation is in place, you can write the required code. The sequence for creating the code is the same as with the Clear button. You will create the listener method for the Delete button, and then add a call to the Commit action to that code.

7. In the visual editor for searchEmployees.jsp, double click the Delete button. The Bind Action Property dialog will appear. In the *Managed Bean* pulldown, select the value "backing_searchEmployees."

8. Change *Method* to "deleteButton_action". Click OK. The backing bean code will appear in the code editor.

9. Change the code generated in the `deleteButton_action()` method by adding a binding and execute for the Commit action and removing the conditional statement to process errors. (Refer to the earlier section, "Add a Clear Button to the Search Form," for explanations of these changes.) The code should read as follows:

```
public String deleteButton_action() {
    BindingContainer bindings = getBindings();
    OperationBinding operationBinding =
        bindings.getOperationBinding("Delete");
    Object result = operationBinding.execute();

    operationBinding = bindings.getOperationBinding("Commit");
    result = operationBinding.execute();

    return null;
}
```

10. Since clicking the button will permanently remove the record, you want to present a confirmation dialog to the user. You can use event properties on the button to add JavaScript code. Click the Delete button in the visual editor, and open its properties in the Property Inspector.

CAUTION
JavaScript events for a JSF component are the closest thing to triggers in Oracle Forms because they are written for a specific object. Including JavaScript in your code will require the code to be run in an environment that supports JavaScript, such as a web browser. Certain client environments, such as a cell phone, may not support this type of event code.

11. In the *Onclick* property, enter the following (all on one line):

```
javascript:if(confirm('You are about to delete the selected record.'))
    {return true;} else {return false;}
```

TIP
Remember that you can double click the tab of any window (such as the Property Inspector) to maximize it within the JDeveloper main window. Double click the tab to restore the window.

Additional Information: This code presents an OK-Cancel confirmation dialog. If the user clicks OK, the code returns "true" and the action continues. If the user clicks Cancel, the code returns "false" and the action stops. If you need this type of confirmation on several pages, you could code it into a JavaScript function in an external file, attach that file to each page in the head section, and call the function in the *Onclick* property.

12. Click Save All. Run the searchEmployees.jsp file. Click Search to query all records. Select a record and click Delete. A dialog such as the following will appear.

13. Click Cancel. The record will remain on the screen. Click Delete again. This time, click OK in the confirmation dialog. The record will be deleted from the database. You can verify the deletion with the Table Viewer in JDeveloper (in the Connections tab, under Database\HR\HR\Tables) or in your favorite SQL tool.

14. Close the browser and stop the server.

What Did You Just Do?   In this phase, you added components and modified the default behavior of the Search page. The ADF Search Form component works the same way as the Enter Query/Execute

Query mechanism in Oracle Forms. This is not the friendliest interface for novice users, so many applications written in Oracle Forms, including those in the Oracle E-Business Suite, have customized this behavior by using Enter Query/Execute Query behind the scenes and presenting the user with a block used only for entering query conditions. This phase performed the customizations required to keep the query criteria form in Find mode.

The block in Oracle Forms applications represents the data model—the link between the user interface items and a database table. It also represents the user interface items. ADF separates these functions so that a single data model can be rendered in multiple UI blocks. By default, all UI blocks built from the same view object instance use the same iterator and share a current record and a result set. In this phase, you modified the default behavior by supplying separate iterators on the same view object instance for each UI block so that you could handle the records in each UI block separately.

In Oracle Forms, you can programmatically set a property on a canvas to hide it when no data is retrieved. As with all customizations, this requires some trigger logic to set the *Visible* property of the canvas and to ensure that the user cannot navigate to the items on the block (which would reveal the canvas). In this phase, you wrote code to perform a similar action by basing the *Rendered* property of a container component on a conditional statement that evaluates the number of rows returned from the query.

Oracle Forms includes built-ins to perform basic screen functions, such as Clear Block, Delete Record, and New Record. ADF offers default operations for functions such as Find, Delete, Create, and Commit. In this phase, you used these operations and added a button to clear the search block, as well as a button to delete a record and commit that delete. You also added Edit and New buttons that perform navigation to the Edit page for the purposes of editing an existing record or adding a record, respectively. You will fill in the code for Edit and New in the next chapter when you develop the Edit page.

CHAPTER
13

Edit Page

No passion in the world, no love or hate,
is equal to the passion to change someone else's draft.

—H. G. Wells (1866–1946)

I can't write five words but that I change seven.

—Dorothy Parker (1893–1967)

 ow that you have coded and tested the Search page, you can complete the functionality for the Employees tab by working on the Edit page. This chapter concentrates on creating the page, then completing the navigation for the Edit and New buttons on the Search page. The Edit page loads the current record when you click the Edit button on the Search page. It will load with a blank set of fields when you click the New button on the Search page. This page will contain examples of a pulldown (Jobs) and LOVs (Managers and Departments) that are loaded from queries in view objects you set up in Chapter 12.

NOTE
You can, on your own, apply the pulldown and LOV techniques demonstrated in this chapter to the Search page as well.

Hands-on Practice: Complete the Edit Page

You start adding components to the Edit page by dropping in an ADF Form based on AllEmployees. The AllEmployees view object represents a query that joins EMPLOYEES and EMPLOYEES (for the manager) tables and also joins the EMPLOYEES and DEPARTMENTS tables. Because the EMPLOYEES (managers) and DEPARTMENTS tables were marked as reference only, ADF BC will not issue INSERT, UPDATE, or DELETE statements to those tables.

This is comparable to the behavior we would see if this query were a database view; we would only be able to update columns in the base table (EMPLOYEES), not columns in the lookup tables (EMPLOYEES, for managers, and DEPARTMENTS).

This hands-on practice follows these phases:

I. Prepare the Model components

- Add a Manager Full Name attribute
- Create an INSERT trigger
- Set up the Employees entity object

II. Create the Employees Edit page

- Create the page file
- Hide the *EmployeeId* attribute
- Add navigation cases
- Add action buttons
- Add a success message

III. **Finish navigation from the Search page**
  ■ Complete the New button code
  ■ Add an Edit link
  ■ Test the Search and Edit pages

IV. **Build a pulldown list and LOVs**
  ■ Add a pulldown list for job titles
  ■ Create the LOV template and copy it
  ■ Set up navigation to the LOVs
  ■ Add components to the Departments LOV
  ■ Create the Managers LOV page

NOTE
As mentioned, completed application workspaces and code snippets are available from the websites mentioned in the "Websites for Sample Code" section of the Introduction.

I. Prepare the Model Components

You set up ADF BC components for querying employees in the preceding chapter. These components work for querying records, but we have a specific requirement for creating an employee record. The requirement states that the user should not be responsible for assigning an Employee ID for a new employee record. A database trigger can easily generate a unique ID from the existing sequence object, EMPLOYEES_SEQ. Since the database trigger to load this column does not exist in the demonstration application, this section adds it. It also sets up the Employees entity object to not require data entry for the EmployeeId attribute.

You will also further refine the Model by adding an attribute to the AllEmployees view object to display the manager's full name.

Add a Manager Full Name Attribute

You would like to show the manager name in a single field on the employee Edit page. This section adds a view object attribute for this purpose.

1. In the Model project, under the Application Sources\tuhra.model.views node, double click AllEmployees to open the View Object Editor.

2. Select the SQL Statement node. Note the table alias used for the EMPLOYEES table that supplies manager information ("EmployeeManager").

3. Select the Attributes node and click New. In the New View Object Attribute dialog, enter the following:
   Name as "ManagerFullName"
   Type as "String"

> *Mapped to Column or SQL* selected
> *Selected in Query* and *Queryable* selected
> *Updatable* as "Never"
> *Query Column: Alias* as "MANAGER_FULL_NAME"
> *Query Column: Type* as "VARCHAR2(100)"
> *Query Column: Expression* as "EmployeeManager.FIRST_NAME || ' ' || EmployeeManager.LAST_NAME"

4. Click OK. Select the SQL Statement node, and view the query. You will see the new column added to the SELECT list. Click Test to check the SQL statement. Click OK in the confirmation dialog.

5. Click OK again to apply the view object definition and dismiss the dialog.

6. Click Save All.

Create an INSERT Trigger

You can use your favorite PL/SQL editing tool to create the required database trigger. However, you might be interested in some of the PL/SQL editing features of JDeveloper. Therefore, this section shows how to use the JDeveloper tools to create a database trigger that sets the value of the EMPLOYEE_ID column from a database sequence upon INSERT.

CAUTION
In the demonstration HR schema for some database versions, the EMPLOYEE_SEQ sequence is set to start with 1. The first employee ID value in the EMPLOYEES table is 100. Therefore, you can use this sequence for new employee records until it reaches 100. Then the database trigger will fail with a primary key violation when it tries to assign the already-used ID (100). You can fix this problem by dropping and re-creating this sequence with a starting number that is greater than the maximum employee ID. Be sure to restore grants, if any, when you drop and re-create the sequence.

1. Click the Connections tab in the navigator area. If this tab is not visible, select **View | Connection Navigator**.

2. Expand the Database\HR\HR node. Expand the Sequences node, and make sure the EMPLOYEES_SEQ sequence exists.

    Additional Information: If the sequence does not exist, you can create it by selecting **New Sequence** from the right-click menu on the Sequences node.

3. Expand the Triggers node, and make sure EMPLOYEES_BI (before INSERT trigger on the EMPLOYEES table) does not exist. If it does exist, you can skip to the next section.

4. On the Triggers node, select **New Trigger** from the right-click menu. The Create Trigger dialog shown here will appear:

5. Fill in *Name* as "EMPLOYEES_BI". Leave the default *Trigger Type* ("TABLE"), and select a *Table Name* as "EMPLOYEES."

6. Leave the default *Before* option selected for timing; select the *Row Level* radio button; and select the *Insert* checkbox. Click OK. This will create a trigger stub, and the trigger will appear in the navigator.

7. Double click EMPLOYEES_BI, if it is not already open in the editor. Replace the NULL statement between BEGIN and END with the following:

```
SELECT employees_seq.nextval
INTO   :new.employee_id
FROM   dual;
```

8. Click Save. This will compile the trigger in the database. Check the Log window for compile errors, and correct any errors.

   Additional Information: This trigger will load the next sequence number from EMPLOYEES_SEQ into the EMPLOYEE_ID column for any INSERT statement on the Employees table. This overrides any value for EMPLOYEE_ID in the INSERT statement. It is cleaner to perform this SELECT statement in a trigger than in application code, because you only need to code it once rather than in every application that performs an INSERT on the EMPLOYEES table.

Set Up the Employees Entity Object

Now that we have a trigger to set the EmployeeId value, we need to make a change to the Employees entity object. Since this attribute is marked as a primary key, it is also required, so ADF BC will validate that it contains a value before an INSERT or UPDATE is sent to the database. This required property will not work for the proposed design wherein we do not allow users to enter this value. However, we want to leave this attribute assigned as the primary key so that it correctly reflects the database design; therefore, we need an alternative. As described in Chapter 6, ADF BC provides a special way to mark a primary key attribute based on a column populated by a database trigger from a database sequence using the DBSequence domain.

1. Select the Applications Navigator tab, if it is not visible. Double click the Employees entity object in the navigator (under tuhra.model.entities).

2. Expand the Attributes node and select EmployeeId. You will see the following properties:

Additional Information: Remember that most properties that represent database characteristics, such as datatype, primary key, and mandatory, appear on the entity object because these properties are required by INSERT, UPDATE, and DELETE statements issued for the entity object.

3. In the *Type* field, replace "Number" with "DBSequence" (you can use the pulldown for this field). A new tab will appear at the bottom of the screen for Sequence. This tab contains a definition of a database sequence to be created in the database. Our database already contains a database sequence, so filling out this tab is not required.

Additional Information: Chapter 6 discusses the result of setting an attribute as a DBSequence. You will notice that *While New* in the Updatable section is automatically selected and *Always* is disabled, as are the checkboxes for *Persistent*, *Mandatory*, *Primary Key*, and several others.

4. Click OK to accept the changes in the entity object, and click Save All.

5. You can now test this trigger and DBSequence using the Oracle Business Component Browser. On the TuhraService node, under Model\Application Sources\tuhra.model, select **Test** from the right-click menu. Click Connect in the Connection dialog.

6. In the Oracle Business Component Browser, double click AllEmployees to display the test page for Employees. Click the "Insert a new record" icon (green plus sign) to open a new record. Notice that the *ID* field is filled with a negative number because you set that attribute as a DBSequence type.

7. You need to add a value for at least the required columns in the EMPLOYEES table. Fill in a *Last Name, Email*, and *Hire Date* in the format you set in the control hint, for example, "MM/dd/yyyy." Fill in *Job ID* as "AD_ASST" and *Manager ID* as "103".

8. Navigate out of the *Manager ID* field, and the *Manager's First Name* and *Manager's Last Name* fields will fill in (with "Alexander" and "Hunold," respectively). ADF BC uses the view link defined in AllEmployees to look up this information.

    Additional Information: This effect occurs automatically with an application client interface such as this tester but will not automatically occur in a web client interface.

9. Fill in *Department ID* as "90". Navigate out of the *Department ID* field, and you will see the Department (description) fill in as "Executive" because ADF BC looks up the related information based on a view link.

10. Click the commit (curved green arrow) icon in the top toolbar of the browser. The record will be saved to the database. Notice that the ID has been filled in with the next number in the database sequence.

NOTE
If you receive an error because of a duplicate primary key value, as mentioned earlier, you need to drop and re-create the sequence with a number greater than the largest EMPLOYEE_ID value in the table.

11. Close the Oracle Business Component Browser.

12. Open searchEmployees.jsp (under ViewController\Web Content\pages) again, and run it. Click the Search button.

13. If you receive an IllegalArgumentException error, close the browser. In the visual editor, select the EmployeeId column in the results table. In the Structure window, expand the `af:outputText` node under the `af:column` node for EmployeeId. Delete the `f:convertNumber` node. Run the searchEmployees.jsp file, and test the search again.

    Additional Information: This workaround may not be required in later builds of JDeveloper. It is not required if you assign the DBSequence domain to the attribute before creating the ADF Faces Read-only Table.

14. Close browser and stop the server.

What Did You Just Do?   In this phase, you added an attribute to the AllEmployees view object to display the manager's full name. This attribute will be handy when showing the manager's information on the employee edit page.

In addition, you added a trigger to the EMPLOYEES table that will load the EMPLOYEE_ID column from a database sequence upon INSERT. You also modified the Employees entity object to handle the non-standard action of a missing primary key value.

As depicted in Figure 13-1, the EmployeeId attribute uses the DBSequence domain as its datatype. When the ADF BC framework creates a blank record to be filled in by the user, the DBSequence type fills in a placeholder negative number value (−1) for the EmployeesId attribute (which would be hidden or disabled in the user interface). This placeholder number satisfies the unique and mandatory validation requirements for a primary key. This placeholder value is also used within the ADF BC transaction to set any foreign key values based on the DBSequence attribute. When the transaction is committed, the ADF BC framework ignores the placeholder value and creates an INSERT statement with a NULL value in place of the placeholder. This INSERT statement is sent through JDBC (Java Database Connectivity) to the database. The EMPLOYEES_BI trigger intercepts the INSERT statement and loads the next number from the EMPLOYEES_SEQ sequence. The database inserts the record and returns the sequence number (301) through JDBC, the ADF BC classes, and the entity object to the page.

II. Create the Employees Edit Page

The Edit page uses an ADF Form data control for data entry. This data control offers a field and prompt for each attribute in the view object. Therefore, the edit form looks much the same as the search form, but includes buttons for data entry functions instead of search functions. The mechanics of adding this data control to the page are the same as with the search form.

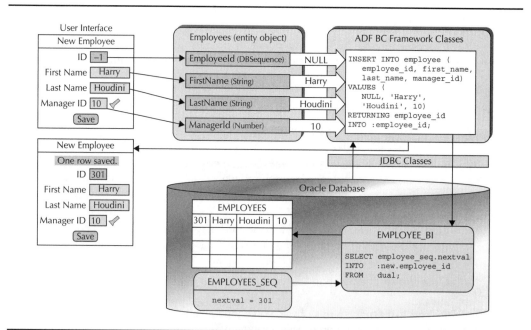

FIGURE 13-1. *DBSequence and database trigger interaction*

Create the Page File

This section creates this edit page as a copy of the template you set up in Chapter 11.

1. In the Applications Navigator tab, select template.jsp in the WEB-INF\template node, and select **File | Save As**. In the Save As dialog, navigate to ViewController\public_html\ pages. Click the "Create new subdirectory" button, and fill in the *Directory Name* as "management".

   Additional Information: The management directory will hold pages that only management and administrative users can access.

2. Click OK to create the directory, and navigate to it. Enter the *File name* as "editEmployee.jsp", and click Save.

3. Open the new JSP in the visual editor (under the pages\management node).

   Additional Information: Since this is not one of the main pages accessible from the top-level tabs, you do not need to change a tab to selected (highlighted) as you did with other pages. The user will click the Employees tab or click a Cancel button to return to the searchEmployees.jsp page.

4. In the Data Control Palette, select AllEmployees and drag and drop it onto the page. Be sure that the `af:panelPage` component is outlined so that the control will be placed inside that component. You can check this in the Structure window. Select **Forms | ADF Form** from the menu.

   Additional Information: The set of data controls available to this page is the same as the set of data controls available to the Search page. When you drag a data control onto the page, an iterator is created in the PageDef file. The default name for the iterator is the name of the collection with an "Iterator" suffix. Therefore, when you drag AllEmployees onto the page the first time, an iterator called "AllEmployeesIterator" is created. This iterator is the same name as the iterator on the Search page, but iterator names are unique only within the scope of a page. Therefore, this AllEmployeesIterator will be treated separately from the AllEmployeesIterator on the Search page.

5. The Edit Form Fields dialog will appear. Delete the following fields:
   DepartmentDepartmentId
   ManagerEmployeeId
   ManagerFirstName
   ManagerLastName

   Additional Information: These fields map to attributes of the lookup tables, and the user will not enter values for these attributes.

6. Rearrange the items in the following order using the move buttons on the right. You can group fields (click and CTRL-click) and move the group to save some time.
   EmployeeId
   FirstName
   LastName
   Email
   PhoneNumber
   HireDate
   JobId

DepartmentId
DepartmentName
ManagerId
ManagerFullName
Salary
CommissionPct

NOTE

If you know you will create more than one page from the same view object, you might want to consider reordering the attributes in the view object so that all pages you create afterwards will have the desired order. The Attributes page of the View Object Editor contains buttons that allow you to move attributes up and down in the list.

7. Do not select the Include Submit Button or Include Navigation Controls checkboxes. Click OK.

Additional Information: This adds a bound UI block to the page. You can now rearrange it in the same way as you rearranged the Search form in the Search Employees page.

8. Change the `af:panelForm` properties for *MaxColumns* to "2" and *Rows* to "7". The component will arrange the fields into two columns.

Additional Information: Notice that you need to set both *MaxColumns* and *Rows* properties before the component rearranges the fields.

9. Select the *DepartmentName* field, and remove the text in the *Label* property. Change *ReadOnly* to "true." This field will store the name retrieved from the department lookup; you will not allow the user to enter or change this value.

10. Repeat the preceding step for the *ManagerFullName* field.

11. Drop a PanelTip component on top of the `af:panelPage` node in the Structure window to add this container under the `af:panelForm` component. Drop an OutputText component from the ADF Faces Core page of the Component Palette into the node for `af:panelTip`. Set the *Value* of the `af:outputText` component to "Fields marked with * are required." (without quotes).

Additional Information: You could alternatively use an ObjectLegend component, as in the practice in Chapter 9. That component automatically writes the text for icons such as the "*" marker for required fields. The difference between using `af:objectLegend` and `af:panelTip` (with `af:outputText`) components is that you can change the message text for the `af:outputText` inside the `af:panelTip`.

NOTE

Remember that it is a best practice to place all text displayed on the page in the message bundle file so that it can be easily modified from a central location and so that you can internationalize the application, if required. You may find it more expedient to code text directly into the page initially, then sweep through the files and move messages to the message bundle file later.

12. This page will be used for create and edit functions, and you want the page heading to appear differently in each case. As you might suspect, this requires a bit of conditional logic in Expression Language (EL). Click the "Change This" heading. Select the af:PanelPage node in the Structure window, if it is not selected. In the *Title* property, click "Bind to data" to open the Title EL dialog.

13. The DBSequence domain you set on the EmployeeId attribute in the preceding phase will cause a negative number to appear for EmployeeId if the page contains a new record. You can use that fact to modify the title. In the *Expression* field, enter the following (you can use the ADF Bindings\bindings\EmployeeId\inputValue node to start the expression if you want):

```
#{bindings.EmployeeId.inputValue.value > 0 ? 'Edit Employee' :
  'New Employee'}
```

Additional Information: This expression uses the *ternary operator* ("? :") described in the sidebar "What is a Ternary Expression?"in Chapter 8. This expression checks the value in the EmployeeId that will be passed to the page. If the EmployeeId is negative, the page is displaying a new record. The EmployeeId will be positive for existing records. The EmployeeId will never be null.

14. Click OK and click Save All. The visual editor will now show something like Figure 13-2.

15. You can test the page now. With the visual editor selected, click Run. You will see the current record in the iterator and the region label of "Edit Employee." Notice the read-only fields for *EmployeeId*, *DepartmentName*, and *ManagerFullName*. You cannot manipulate data with this page yet, so once you have verified the layout, exit the browser and stop the server.

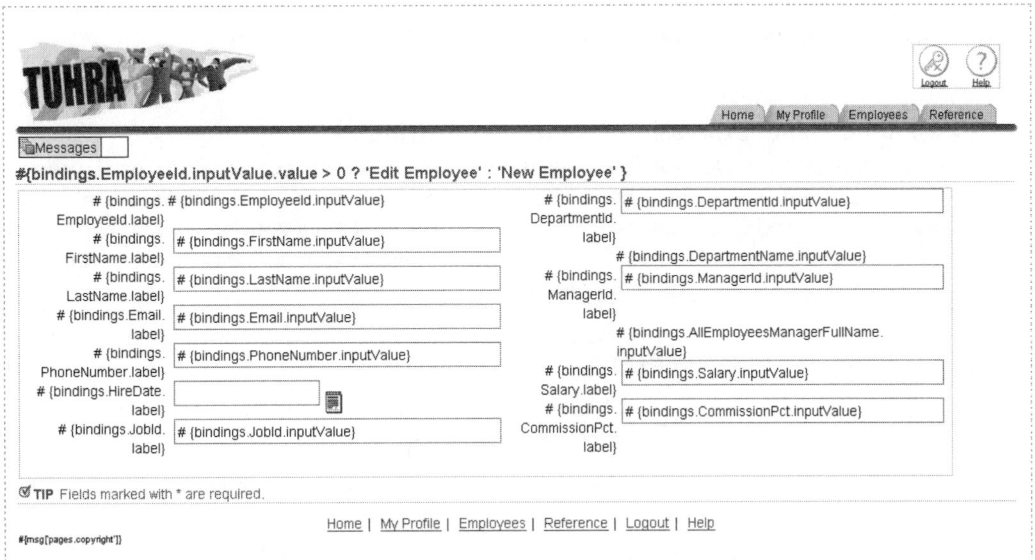

FIGURE 13-2. *Employee Edit page*

Hide the EmployeeId Attribute

We do not want users to supply an employee ID for new records, because this value will be overwritten by the database trigger. Also, we do not want them to view the negative placeholder number that the DBSequence domain defines for new employee records.

We cannot just delete the field, because the *EmployeeId* attribute in the entity object is required. In addition, we want to use this page for editing existing records, and the Employee ID should be visible for that purpose. HTML allows you to add *hidden fields*—form elements, which are not displayed but whose values will be submitted with other fields in the form.

We want users to be able to see the employee ID for existing records. However, they should not be able to update it because it is the primary key and may have foreign key values referencing it. This section converts the *EmployeeId* field to a read-only field that is hidden for new records. This feature uses the *rendered* property of the `af:inputText` component.

1. Select the *EmployeeId* field in the visual editor. In the Property Inspector, change *ReadOnly* to "true."

2. In the *Rendered* property, click "Bind to data," and add the following expression:
   `#{bindings.EmployeeId.inputValue.value > 0}`

   Additional Information: The return type of `inputValue` is an `Object`. Although you can compare this `Object` with a `String`, you cannot compare it with an integer or number. This expression converts the inputValue attribute of *EmployeeId* to a number (using the method "value") so that it can be compared to a number (0). The expression will evaluate to "true" if the *EmployeeId* is a positive number (an existing record). In this situation, the field will be displayed. If the *EmployeeId* is negative, the expression will evaluate to "false" and the field will be hidden. The sidebar "Understanding Expression Language in Attributes" describes how the expression is interpreted.

3. Click OK. Test this page again and be sure that the *Employee ID* is not editable but is still displayed for the existing record that appears. You will test the display for a new record later.

4. Close the browser and stop the server.

Understanding Expression Language in Attributes

The expression used for the EmployeeId rendered property (`#{bindings.EmployeeId.inputValue.value}`) is an example of a complex expression in which several different methods are used by the JSF framework to obtain a final value. Starting with the top level object (`bindings`, in this case) the JSF framework will examine the next segment of the expression (`EmployeeId`) and try to evaluate it in one of two ways:

- If the parent object (`bindings`) has a getter method that corresponds to this string (for example, `getEmployeeId()`), use that method.

- If it does not have the string's getter method, but it does have a `get()` method, call that method with the supplied segment as a key.

This evaluation takes place for each segment of the expression to complete the resolution. In this example, the expression would resolve to this Java statement:

```
bindings.get("EmployeeId").getInputValue().getValue();
```

Add Navigation Cases

Now that the Edit page is created, you can define the navigation to it. This phase declares a navigation rule and navigation cases for the New and Edit functions on the Search page.

1. Open the faces-config.xml file. (On the ViewController node, select **Open JSF Navigation** from the right-click menu.) Click the Overview tab.

2. On the Navigation Rules page, click New in the Navigation Rules area. In the *From View ID* pulldown, select "/pages/searchEmployees.jsp." Click OK to create the rule.

3. With the new rule selected, click New in the Navigation Cases area. Fill in *To View ID* as "/pages/management/editEmployee.jsp" (from the pulldown) and fill in *From Outcome* as "createEmp". Leave *Redirect* unselected. Click OK.

   Additional Information: For simplicity, the Search page will call the Create operation on the Employees collection. This will only work if the link between the Search page and the Edit page is a forward, so *redirect* must be set to "false." Otherwise, the new record that is created will be discarded. If a redirect is needed in conjunction with a Create operation, the Create operation should be invoked in the called page (editEmployee.jsp, in this case), not from the calling page. To make this call, you would use an invokeAction in the PageDef file on the Edit page. (See Chapter 8 for a refresher on invoking operations on page startup.) Because the same page is used for both editing and creating employees, this invokeAction call needs to be made conditional using a refreshCondition in conjunction with a flag set by the calling button.

4. Repeat the preceding step, but fill in *From Outcome* as "editEmp" (*To View ID* is the same).

   Additional Information: This defines the navigation from the Search page to the Edit page for two different purposes—editing a record or creating a record.

5. Click the Diagram tab to review your work. You will see two navigation cases from searchEmployees.jsp to editEmployee.jsp. Click Save All.

   Additional Information: In Chapter 11, you set up one navigation rule for reference.jsp with a navigation case to jobs.jsp and another navigation rule for global navigation to all main pages in the application. In this section, you added a navigation rule for searchEmployees.jsp, with one navigation case for the create function and another for the edit function. Each of these new navigation cases will have a different calling mechanism. If you rearrange the page and navigation case symbols, the diagram should now contain something like this:

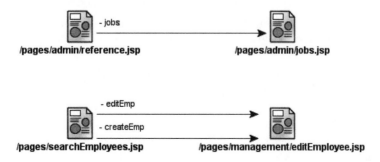

TIP
*You can use the Thumbnail window to find an area of the JSF
Navigation Diagram. If the Thumbnail window is not visible, select
it from the View menu. Then, drag the box in the thumbnail to
reposition the view in the diagram.*

Add Action Buttons

This section adds buttons to the Edit page for Save, Cancel, and Reset. Fortunately, you can drag
buttons to the page with the appropriate functions without writing any code. The Save button
represents a standard Commit operation; the Cancel button navigates back to the Search page (as
does the Employees tab); and the Reset button clears all fields in the form.

1. Open the visual editor for editEmployee.jsp. In the Structure window, expand the
   PanelForm facets node so that the footer node under it is visible. From the Data Control
   Palette, drag the Commit operation from the TuhraServiceDataControl\Operations node
   to the footer facet as an ADF Command Button.

2. Change the button's *Text* property to "Save", and remove the expression from the
   Disabled property.

   Additional Information: The expression you just removed from *Disabled*
   ("#{!bindings.Commit.enabled}") evaluates to "true" if a change is made to the record in
   the Model layer and the page is refreshed. However, changes to the page do not register
   as a change in the Model layer until the page is submitted. We could create a submit
   button (called "Post Changes") to submit changes to the Model layer, but the user would
   then need to click this button (so Save would be enabled) and then click Save to commit
   the record to the database. A single Save button that performs the commit is more intuitive.
   Therefore, we want the Save (commit) button to be enabled even if the Model layer does
   not know the record has been changed.

3. For the Cancel button, you need a new navigation rule with one navigation case. Return
   to the editor window for faces-config.xml (or select **Open JSF Navigation** from the right-
   click menu on the ViewController project).

4. You have created navigation rules and cases by drawing in the diagram and defining
   them in the Overview tab. As with all XML code in JDeveloper, you can alternatively use
   the Structure window to edit the file. On the Faces Config node of the Structure window,
   select **Insert inside Faces Config | navigation-rule** from the right-click menu.

5. In the *From View ID* field, select "/pages/management/editEmployee.jsp," and click OK.

6. The new navigation rule will be selected in the Structure window. Select **Insert inside
   navigation-rule - /pages/management/editEmployee.jsp | navigation-case** from the right-
   click menu on this new navigation rule.

7. For *To View ID*, select "/pages/searchEmployees.jsp." For *From Outcome*, enter
   "cancelEditEmp". Click OK. The navigation case will be displayed.

TIP
You may find it easier to draw a navigation case on the diagram rather than define the rule using the Structure window or Overview tab. All three methods accomplish the same task. The Outcome property mentioned before becomes the navigation case label on the diagram.

8. Click Save All.

9. With the editEmployee.jsp page in the visual editor, drag a Rollback operation from the Data Control Palette to the right of the Save button (on top of the af:panelForm's footer facet), and specify an ADF Command Button. Change the button's *Text* property to "Cancel", and select the *Action* property as "cancelEditEmp." Remove the expression in *Disabled* by clicking the "Reset to Default" button. Be sure that *Immediate* is set to "true" (as it should be for a Rollback button).

Additional Information: The Rollback operation will remove the blank record (with the negative EmployeeId) from the EmpResultsIterator. The *Action* setting navigates back to the Search page using the navigation case you created earlier. If you had defined the button to cause the navigation without a rollback, a blank record (with a negative Employee Id) would appear in the Search page results table. The *Immediate* property value defaults to "false." An *Immediate* value of "true" for a command item such as a button signals to the JSF framework that modified data on the page should be ignored and only the code associated with the command item should be executed.

Notice in the Structure window that JDeveloper added an h:panelGroup node in the footer facet around the two buttons. The rule is that you can only place one component inside a facet; the second button broke this rule. Therefore, JDeveloper added a container component as the single component within the facet and placed the button components inside it.

10. You need to modify the Logout button so that any changes made to the record are rolled back before the navigation occurs to the logout page. The Rollback function is already defined for the page and bound to the existing Cancel button. To connect the same call to the global Logout button, select the Cancel button and copy its *ActionListener* property value. Then select the Logout global button, and paste the value into its *ActionListener* property. When the user clicks this global button, a Rollback operation will occur before navigation to the logout page occurs.

11. Drag a ResetButton from the ADF Faces Core page of the Component Palette on top of the h:panelGroup node in the Structure window. Change its *Text* property to "Reset". The *reset button* initiates a standard form reset, such as that defined for HTML forms. This will allow the user to undo changes that have not been committed.

Additional Information: If you double click the JSP's editor tab to maximize it in the JDeveloper window, you will see something like the screen shown in Figure 13-3. Double click the editor tab to restore the window after you have examined the screen.

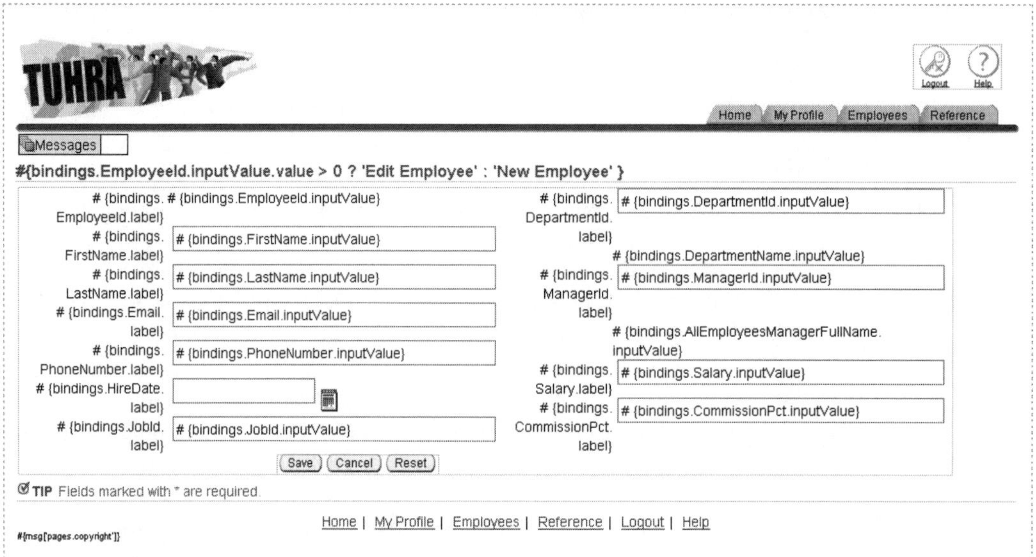

FIGURE 13-3. *Edit form with action buttons*

12. Although you haven't fully defined the navigation from the Search page, you can try the actions on the Edit page. Click Run when the editEmployee.jsp file is active in the editor.

13. The first record will appear. Change the *Last Name* value, and click Reset. The change will be discarded.

14. Repeat the change to the *Last Name* value, and click Save. Verify that this change was committed to the database (you can use the JDeveloper table browser to view the data).

15. Click Cancel. The searchEmployees.jsp page will appear.

16. Close the browser and stop the server.

Add a Success Message

You set up an `af:messages` component in the template so that text returned by the page life cycle would be displayed on the page. If an operation fails, messages will appear in this messages area. As you may have noticed, by default, no notification message will be displayed when a record is committed successfully. The following steps describe how to add a message to notify the user of success. This technique requires customizing the Save operation using a backing bean for the Edit page.

1. In the visual editor for the editEmployee.jsp page, select the Save button. Notice that the *ActionListener* property is set to "#{bindings.Commit.execute}" so that the button will call the default Commit operation in the TuhraService application module.

   Additional Information: You will be adding code to the *Action* property that calls a method in a new backing bean file; this method will load a success message into the context area. The *ActionListener* property will still be required so that the commit still occurs. As mentioned in Chapter 8, the function defined in the *ActionListener* property will execute before the function defined in the *Action* property. You could write both functions into the same *Action* property method, but you would need to write more Java code. The method we use here leverages the framework's ability to perform two separate functions defined in these two properties.

2. Double click the Save button. The Bind Action Property dialog will appear. No backing bean exists for this page, so click New.

3. In the Create Managed Bean dialog, enter the *Name* as "backing_editEmployee" and enter the *Class* as "tuhra.view.backing.EditEmployee". Be sure that *Scope* is "request" and *Generate Class If It Does Not* Exist is selected. Click OK to create the class file.

4. In the Bind Action Property dialog, change *Method* to "saveButton_action". Be sure that *Generate ADF Binding Code* is selected, and click OK. The file will open in the code editor.

Additional Information: You can also add a backing bean by copying an existing bean (**Refactor | Duplicate**), but this utility will not insert a reference to the new class in the faces-config.xml. The double click method creates such a reference. It also allows you to load default code for the new method (by selecting the *Generate ADF Binding Code* checkbox).

If you view the properties for the Save button at this point, you will see that the *ActionListener* property has been cleared. This occurs as a result of creating the action method. You will restore the *ActionListener* property in a later step. Return to the EditEmployee.java file code editor tab if it is not visible at this point.

5. Subclass the framework class by changing the class declaration to the following:

```
public class EditEmployee extends TuhraBackingBean
```

6. When the message about a missing import for the superclass appears, press ALT-ENTER to add the following import line:

```
import tuhra.view.framework.TuhraBackingBean;
```

7. Change the saveButton_action() method to look like the following:

```
public String saveButton_action() {
  FacesContext ctx = FacesContext.getCurrentInstance();
  FacesMessage saveMsg = new FacesMessage("Record saved successfully.");
  ctx.addMessage(null,saveMsg);
  return null;
}
```

Additional Information: You have seen this type of code for displaying messages in the hands-on practice in Chapter 9. The code creates a FacesMessage object and adds it to the FacesContext object that represents the current runtime session. The FacesContext object will then display the message inside the af:messages component at the proper point in the life cycle. As with the example in Chapter 9, you can write the code to retrieve the message from a message bundle file instead of hard-coding the message in the backing bean. The Save operation occurs because the *ActionListener* property for the button will be reset to the commit operation (#{bindings.Commit.execute}).

8. Import the FacesContext and FacesMessage classes by selecting their imports from the quick fixes (light bulb icon) pulldown next to the relevant line in the code editor gutter. The wavy red lines under the class references will disappear.

9. Select **Make** from the right-click menu to compile the class. Fix any compilation errors.

10. In the visual editor for the editEmployee.jsp file, select the Save button and view the properties. You will see that the *Action* property is filled with an expression pointing to the saveButton_action() method.

11. The *ActionListener* property is now blank, but you still want to commit the record, so you will need to restore the call to the operation. Fill in the *ActionListener* property with #{bindings.Commit.execute} (the original value you saw in this property in step 1). This expression references the Commit operation.

12. Click Save All.

13. Run editEmployee.jsp again. Make a change to the Last Name, and click Save. You will see the message you added to the backing bean. Check the EMPLOYEES table to verify that the record was changed.

14. Close the browser and stop the server.

TIP
You might want to take this opportunity to copy the application directory to another name in case you need to roll back to this point in the hands-on practice.

What Did You Just Do?   You created the Edit page in this phase by copying the template JSP file and dropping in an ADF Form containing fields for the attributes in AllEmployees. You wrote conditional expressions to display the title and employee ID differently, depending upon whether the page is used for editing an existing record or for creating a record. Then you defined the navigation case for page flow from Search to Edit pages and added buttons for Save, Cancel, and Reset. Lastly, you added a message to indicate a successful save.

What Could You Do Next?   As with the Delete button on the Search page, you can add a JavaScript confirmation dialog to the Logout button on this page to inform the user that changes will be discarded.

The technique described in this phase for adding a success message to the Save button demonstrates the functionality of the *Action* and *ActionListener* properties for an action item. However, this code will produce a success message in some cases when the record does not save correctly. For example, if you enter a value in the *First Name* field that contains more than the maximum number of characters (20), you will see an error message accompanied by a success message. To prevent this from occurring, you can use the following code inside the *Action* method (saveButton_action()) in this way:

```
public String saveButton_action()
{
  BindingContainer bindings = getBindings();
  OperationBinding operationBinding =
    bindings.getOperationBinding("Commit");
  Object result = operationBinding.execute();
  // note that the "!" operator has been removed from the default code
  if (operationBinding.getErrors().isEmpty())
  {
    FacesContext ctx = FacesContext.getCurrentInstance();
    FacesMessage saveMsg = new FacesMessage("Record saved successfully.");
    ctx.addMessage(null,saveMsg);
  }
  return null;
}
```

This code merges the default Commit code (created when you double click the button in the visual editor) with the code you added for the message in this phase of the practice. With these two functions (Commit and success message) in one *Action* method, you do not need to restore an *ActionListener* value and the success message will not be displayed if an error (such as exceeding the maximum number of characters) occurs.

III. Finish Navigation from the Search Page

Before you add the pulldown list and LOVs (lists of values), you need to complete the navigation from the Search page to the Edit page. This phase finishes off the Edit and New button code on the Search page. It also adds a link in the results table on the Search page for calling the Edit page for a selected employee record.

Complete the New Button Code

This section completes code for the New button in the Search page.

TIP
*To clear the window of all open editor windows, select **Close All** from the right-click menu on any editor tab.*

1. Open searchEmployees.jsp in the visual editor. On the New button, select **Edit Binding** from the right-click menu.

   Additional Information: Notice that the Select an Action pulldown contains "Create" because this is the operation you dragged onto the form. However, the drag-and-drop operation assigned the default iterator for the AllEmployees collection (AllEmployeesIterator).

2. The action should occur on the results iterator you added in the preceding chapter, so, in the Select an Iterator pulldown, select "EmpResultsIterator," if it is not selected, and click OK.

   Additional Information: These steps demonstrate the shortcut way to access the binding for a screen item. Instead of loading the PageDef file in the editor and finding the appropriate binding in the Structure window, you can use the binding editor for a specific component.

Add an Edit Link

As mentioned in Chapter 12, dragging and dropping a read-only table with selection enabled into a page adds an `af:tableSelectOne` component in the selection facet of the `af:table` component, as shown in the Structure window here:

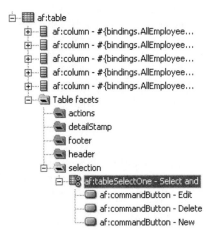

This component adds a radio group column that allows users to select a record. This will set the current row in the iterator to the selected record when the page is submitted. This works, but it requires the user to perform two actions: selecting a record and clicking a button.

This section creates a link in the table that accomplishes both tasks—in this case, setting the current row and navigating to the Edit page. Collections in the Data Control Palette offer these two features that you can use to assist with the row selection:

- **rowKeyStr** This is a pseudo-column available in the collection that defines the unique identifier for each row in the collection.

- **setCurrentRowWithKey** This is an operation available to the collection that uses rowKeyStr to set an iterator's current row.

1. Open or set focus to the searchEmployees.jsp visual editor. In the Data Control Palette, expand the TuhraServiceDataControl\AllEmployees\Operations node.

2. In the visual editor, drop setCurrentRowWithKey onto the EmployeeId column heading in the results table. Select **Operations | ADF Command Link** from the context menu. This link will call the `setCurrentRowWithKey()` method. The link will appear inside the EmployeeId column.

3. In the Structure window, drag the `af:outputText` for EmployeeId on top of the `af:commandLink` so it is embedded inside the link, as shown here:

4. For the `af:commandLink` component, remove the text in the *Text* property. Change the *Action* property to "editEmp". This link will call the same navigation rule as the Edit button.

5. The *ActionListener* property will call the `setCurrentRowWithKey()` method. The drag-and-drop operation also added a binding for this method. Open the PageDef file, and find this binding under the `bindings` node of the Structure window. Select setCurrentRowWithKey to select the source code.

TIP
If the code editor does not select code for a selected node in the Structure window, click another node and then click the desired node again.

6. In the code editor, examine the selected section of code. Notice that the child element, `NamedData` element, for the `rowKey` holds a parameter value for the action. This is a default parameter that we need to replace with the `rowKeyStr` column.

7. In the Structure window, double click `rowKey` under `setCurrentRowWithKey` to open the NamedData Properties dialog.

8. Replace the value of *NDValue* with `${row.rowKeyStr}`, and click OK. This expression uses the rowKeyStr pseudo-column to set the current record. The prefix "row" is used to identify a collection of columns in the table (one row in the results table).

9. Double click the `setCurrentRowWithKey` node above `rowKey` to display the Action Binding Editor for this binding, and set the iterator to "EmpResultsIterator."

    Additional Information: As before, you need to use the results table iterator as the target for the current row setting operation.

10. Click OK. Click Save All.

    Additional Information: As a summary, clicking a link calls the associated action binding, `setCurrentRowWithKey`. This binding evaluates the contents of its parameter, `rowKey` (the `NamedData` element), which represents a unique identifier for the row. The `setCurrentRowWithKey()` method uses this row to set the current row in the iterator. The action on the link component specifies navigation to the Edit page (the "editEmp" navigation case), which displays the current record in the iterator.

Test the Search and Edit Pages

You can now test the Search page's New button; you can also check that the Edit button and link navigate to the Edit page and load the selected record.

1. Run the Search page. Click Search to display the results table. Choose a record other than the first one by selecting the Select radio button in the relevant row.

2. Remember the selected employee ID and last name, and click Edit. The Edit page will load with that record displayed, as shown in the following illustration:

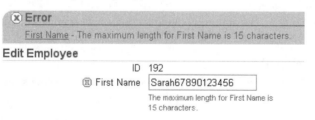

3. Verify the following features:

    ■   The page heading reads "Edit Employee" because you defined an EL expression to display this message if the Employee ID was a positive number.

    ■   The Employee ID is the one you selected on the Search page and is read-only as you defined in the *ReadOnly* property.

    ■   The date format for HireDate appears as you set it in the Employees entity object control hint.

4. Fill in the *First Name* field so it contains between 16 and 20 characters, and click Save. You will see the following message appear:

> ⊗ **Error**
>
> First Name - The maximum length for First Name is 15 characters.
>
> **Edit Employee**
>
>   ID 192
>
> ⊠ First Name   Sarah67890123456
>
>   The maximum length for First Name is
>   15 characters.

Additional Information: This message was defined in the Employees entity object declarative validation rules. The message is stored in a message bundle file specific to that entity object. The ADF BC layer handles the length problem before it reaches the database. Notice that the field label appears in the error message as a link. Clicking that link scrolls through the page to that field (although this will have minimal effect in this layout because the first name already appears on the screen). In addition, the field is specially marked with an icon and the error message is repeated under the field. This additional error handling is a feature of ADF Faces.

5. Correct the *First Name* field, and click Save. You can also try the validations for *Phone Number* (more than zero characters and less than or equal to 15 characters) if you are interested in examining those messages.

   Additional Information: The maximum limit on the phone number is contrived to demonstrate the validators. Some phone numbers in the HR sample data exceed this length, and you may need to truncate phone numbers for records you edit in this application.

6. Note the value of *Job ID,* and change it to "−10"; click Save. You will see an Oracle SQL error that is not very user-friendly. Later phases will add a pulldown list to this field so that users can only select valid job IDs.

7. Restore the *Job ID* and click Save.

8. Change the *Salary* so that it begins with an "*" (for example, "*1000"). Click Save. An error message indicating an invalid number will appear in the messages area and an error indicator with error message will appear by the field, as shown here:

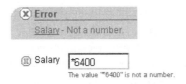

   Additional Information: This error message is generated from the framework and it is friendly enough for most applications. You can use a custom method and the declarative validation rules if you want to replace this message.

9. Click Cancel to return to the Search page. You will now see changes you made in the results table.

10. Click New. The Edit page will load again with a blank record. The heading appears as "New Employee" and the Employee ID is hidden. Enter something for *Email, Hire Date,* and *Job ID* (such as "AD_ASST").

11. Leave *Last Name* blank and click Save. A JavaScript dialog will appear indicating that *Last Name* is required. This event occurs on the page before the form is submitted. Click OK in response to that dialog.

12. Enter a *Last Name* and click Reset. The form will clear. Enter the required fields again (marked with an "*"), and click Save. The success message will appear, and the page will shift to edit mode (the *Employee ID* will appear and the heading will change to "Edit Employee"). Note the *Employee ID value.*

13. Click Cancel to return to the Search page. The new record will appear in the results table (if the query conditions allow it to be displayed). You may need to scroll or sort the records to find the new record. Check the database to ensure that the commit occurred and that the record appears in the EMPLOYEES table (using the Connections window and viewing the EMPLOYEES table under the database connection).

14. Close the browser and stop the server.

What Did You Just Do? In this phase, you completed the New button code in the Search page by changing the iterator assigned to the button action. You also added a link that serves the same purpose as the Select radio button column and the Edit button—that is, it navigates to the Edit page and loads the selected record into the Edit page fields. Part of your application design will need to address the question of which type of navigation to use; you may decide to use both methods, as in this example, or you may decide to use one or the other method.

IV. Build a Pulldown List and LOVs

Pulldown lists and LOVs allow the user to correctly enter lookup information for foreign key values. This phase shows how to build these features into the Edit page.

Add a Pulldown List for Job Titles

This section replaces the *Job ID* field on the Edit page with a list component. You then define this component as a list of job types from the JOBS table. If you know Oracle Forms, you will find many parallels between this technique and the Oracle Forms' record group and poplist item. Both ADF and Oracle Forms use the principles of displaying a list of titles (*JobTitle*) queried from a table but returning a code value (*JobId*) to the field on the form.

1. Open the editEmployee.jsp file in the visual editor. Select and delete the *JobId* field.

2. In the Data Control Palette, expand AllEmployees and select JobId. Drag and drop it into the visual editor (or drop it into place in the Structure window) before the *DepartmentId* field. Specify **Single Selections | ADF Select One Choice** in the context menu.

3. The List Binding Editor shown next will appear. This dialog allows you to specify the data sources for the list.

Additional Information: This editor somewhat resembles the Form Builder Editor for record groups. As in Oracle Forms, you can define a dynamic list for values from a collection.

You can also define a static list for hard-coded values. Chapter 8 describes details about list bindings and this editor.

4. Be sure the *Dynamic List* button is selected. The *Base Data Source* pulldown should contain "TuhraServiceDataControl.AllEmployees." This represents the collection you will be updating with this selection list.

5. The *List Data Source* pulldown provides a list of available source collections. AllJobs does not appear in this list, so click Add to the right of this field. The Add Data Source dialog will appear. Select AllJobs. The *Iterator Name* will automatically fill in as "AllJobsIterator." Click OK.

6. The *List Data Source* field will fill in as "TuhraServiceDataControl.AllJobs." Now you can map the *Base Data Source Attribute* to the *List Data Source Attribute*. Select JobId for both fields (if it is not already selected).

7. In the List Items area, select the *Display Attribute* as JobTitle. This value will appear in the selection list, although the value of the field will be JobId.

8. For the *"No Selection" Item* value, select "Include Labeled Item." The field to the right of the pulldown will be enabled and appear as "<No Selection>." Change this text to "<No Job Title Yet>". If the user selects this value in the pulldown, a NULL will be assigned to the JobId attribute.

9. Click OK. The list item will appear (in a compressed form) under the *HireDate* field.

10. In the Property Inspector for the JobId list component, change *Required* to "true." Notice that a mandatory flag ("*") then appears next to the *JobId* field in the visual editor to indicate this property.

11. Click Save All.

12. Run the searchEmployees.jsp file, and click New after querying employee records. The pulldown list will appear as follows (although yours may display fewer titles with a scrollbar):

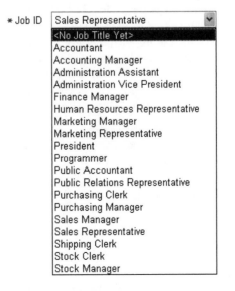

13. Notice that the list is in alphabetical order because you defined an ORDER BY clause on the view object when creating the AllJobs view object.

14. Close the browser and stop the server.

Create the LOV Template and Copy It

LOVs require more setup steps than pulldown lists. An LOV pops up in a separate window when a button is clicked. This window displays a page with a search field and results table much like the searchEmployees page. LOVs do not need the same menu or visual components as the main application pages, so before launching into creating LOVs, we will build a template that you can use for many LOVs. The components we need for this page will be arranged in the order shown in the Structure window excerpt here:

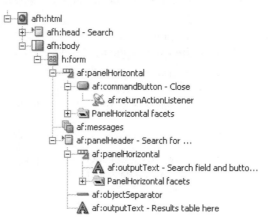

This section builds a template for the LOV windows and copies it to create two page files.

1. Copy the template.jsp file to templateLOV.jsp in the same directory (select template.jsp under WEB-INF\template, select **File | Save As**, name the file, and click Save).

2. Open templateLOV.jsp in the visual editor. In the Structure window, delete the `af:panelPage` node. This will remove almost all elements on the page. It will retain the `f:loadBundle` and basic JSF and ADF Faces page structure elements, however.

3. Select the `afh:head` node in the Structure window, and change the *Title* to "Search". You will fill this in appropriately for each LOV.

4. Drop a PanelHorizontal from the Component Palette on top of the `h:form` node in the Structure window. Change its *Halign* property to "right." This will right-justify any buttons we will place in this component.

   Additional Information: Building a JSF page usually consists of adding containers before adding components. The `af:panelHorizontal` container component arranges its child objects horizontally.

TIP
If you want to add a container around an existing component, in the visual editor, on the component you wish to enclose, select Surround With from the right-click menu and select a specific container.

5. Drop a CommandButton on top of the `af:panelHorizontal` node.

6. Change the `af:commandButton` *Text* to "Close" and *Immediate* to "true." This button will be used to close the LOV window.

7. The Close button will cancel the LOV window without returning a value. The `af:returnActionListener` component closes the dialog and can return a value to the calling window, although you will not need the return value in this case. Drop the ReturnActionListener component on top of the `af:commandButton` component.

8. Drop a Messages (not Message) component on top of the `h:form` node in the Structure window. This component will display messages from the JSF message system.

9. Drop a PanelHeader component onto the `h:form` node. Change its *Text* to "Search for...". You will replace the ellipses with a specific subject when you use this template.

10. Drop another PanelHorizontal onto the `af:panelHeader` node.

11. Drop an OutputText component onto the `af:panelHorizontal` node. Change its *Value* to "Search field and button here." This component acts as a hint for the developer to add a search field and button.

12. Drop an ObjectSeparator onto the `af:panelHeader` node. A dotted box will appear under the `af:outputText` component in the visual editor.

13. Drop an OutputText component onto the `af:panelHeader` node. Change its *Value* to "Results table here." This is another reminder to the developer.

14. Click Save All.

    Additional Information: Compare the Structure window with the illustration at the start of this section, and make corrections if needed. The visual editor should look like this:

15. Select templateLOV in the navigator. Select **File | Save As**. Navigate to the ViewController\public_html\pages directory. If no subdirectory exists for "lov," create it in the Save dialog by clicking "Create new subdirectory," entering the name as "lov", and clicking OK. This will navigate to the new directory. If the directory already exists, navigate to it.

16. Name the file "departmentsLOV" (JDeveloper will fill in the .jsp extension) and click Save. The file will appear under the pages\lov node of the navigator.

17. Repeat the preceding two steps for the managersLOV.jsp file.

Set Up Navigation to the LOVs

You now have two page files for the LOVs. This section defines the navigation cases for displaying these from the Edit page.

1. Open the JSF Navigation Diagram (by selecting **Open JSF Navigation** from the right-click menu on the ViewController project), and click the Diagram tab if it is not already in focus.

2. Since the departmentsLOV.jsp page you want to add already exists, drag it from the navigator onto the diagram next to "/pages/management/editEmployee.jsp" and name it "/pages/lov/departmentsLOV.jsp".

   Additional Information: The LOV pages will be stored in a subdirectory of the pages directory. The LOVs could be reused (for example, on the Search page), and will not be restricted by the security imposed on the management directory.

3. Draw a JSF Navigation Case from /pages/management/editEmployee.jsp to /pages/lov/departmentsLOV.jsp. Change the name for the navigation case to "dialog: departmentsSearch".

   Additional Information: This name will be available as an action for the LOV button on the *DepartmentId field.* The prefix "dialog" indicates a popup window, as described in the sidebar "About ADF Faces Dialogs."

4. Drag the managersLOV.jsp from the Applications Navigator onto the JSF Navigation Diagram above the departmentsLOV page.

5. Draw a JSF Navigation Case from /pages/management/editEmployee.jsp to /pages/lov/managersLOV.jsp. Change the name for the navigation case to "dialog:managersSearch".

   Additional Information: Since the page files exist for these page symbols, no yellow "unfinished" triangle will appear on the page symbols.

NOTE
So far, we have added JSF pages using the Create JSF JSP Wizard or using a copy of a template. The JSF Navigation Diagram is another starting point for creating JSF JSP pages. If you were to double click the page symbol you create on the diagram (which has no file created), the Create JSF JSP Wizard would appear and you could create the JSP file.

6. Click Save All.

7. In the visual editor for editEmployee.jsp, on the *DepartmentId* field, select **Convert** from the right-click menu. In the Convert InputText dialog, select the category as "ADF Faces Core" and select the SelectInputText item. Click OK.

   Additional Information: The `af:selectInputText` component is an entry field that also displays an LOV (flashlight) image for which you can define a popup dialog, such as an LOV window. The field will be displayed as follows:

8. In the component's *Action* property, select "dialog:departmentsSearch."

9. Repeat steps 7 and 8 for the *ManagerId* field. Specify "dialog:managersSearch" as the *Action* property.

About ADF Faces Dialogs

The examples in this section use the prefix "dialog:" to call LOV pages. This prefix designates that the navigation will use an *ADF Faces dialog*, a mechanism for displaying a popup window that can transfer a value back to the calling page. The popup dialog window takes control, so the calling window is disabled until the user dismisses the popup dialog. Normally, this would require using JavaScript for this functionality, but the ADF Faces dialog provides this ability with no additional coding.

This feature requires you to create a page that will be displayed in the popup window. It also requires you to use the "dialog:" prefix when specifying navigation to the dialog page from a command link or command button. The *useWindow* property of these components must be set to "true" and the *Action* property must be set to the navigation case (for example, "dialog:departmentsLOV"). List components can also pop up a dialog. The *useWindow* property is only available on command components such as buttons.

The window automatically sizes to fit its contents, although, for some command components (such as af:commandButton), you can specify a *WindowHeight* and *WindowWidth* property that will set the window size. The window appears in the upper-left corner of the screen; you do not have control over this location.

Searching for "Popup Dialogs" in the help system's Search tab should yield a topic entitled "Using Complex UI Components." That topic contains further information about using popup dialogs.

Add Components to the Departments LOV

This section explains how to add components to the Departments LOV page. Laying out the Managers LOV is similar, so detailed steps are only provided for the Departments LOV. The LOV windows implement standard search and results functionality. In Chapter 12, you set up the DepartmentsByName view object with a bind variable so that the WHERE clause reads as follows:

```
WHERE UPPER(Departments.DEPARTMENT_NAME) LIKE
    CONCAT(UPPER(:searchDepartment), '%')
```

In addition, you added an *Order By* property to sort by Department Name.

1. Open departmentsLOV.jsp in the visual editor.

2. Change the afh:head *Title* to read "Search Departments". Change the af:panelHeader *Text* property to read "Search for a Department".

3. In the Data Control Palette, expand the DepartmentsByName\Operations\ ExecuteWithParams\Parameters nodes. The searchDepartment bind variable you created in the DepartmentsByName View Object Editor will appear as a data control parameter.

4. Drop searchDepartment onto the af:panelHorizontal under the af:panelHeader in the Structure window. Select **Texts | ADF Input Text w/ Label**. The field will appear in the visual editor.

5. Delete the af:outputText placeholder component (labeled "Search field and button here") inside this af:panelHorizontal component.

6. In the Data Control Palette, select the ExecuteWithParams node above the parameter. Drag it onto the same af:panelHorizontal node in the Structure Window, and select **Operations | ADF Command Button**. A button will appear to the right of the field. This operation will cause the view object to requery using a parameter value of the search field's contents.

7. Change the button's *Text* property to "Search." The Structure window will show the following components. (Rearrange your structure if it does not match.)

8. Drag the DepartmentsByName collection from the Data Control Palette onto the af:panelHeader node in the Structure window. Select **Tables | ADF Read-only Table**. The Edit Table Columns dialog will appear.

9. Delete all fields except *DepartmentId* and *DepartmentName*. Select the *Enable selection* and *Enable sorting* checkboxes, and click OK.

10. Delete the af:outputText placeholder above the table. Expand the af:table\Table facets\selection node. Under that node, change the af:tableSelectOne *Text* property to "Select Department and."

11. Click Save All.

12. In the departmentsLOV.jsp visual editor, change the Submit button *Text* to "Select". On the Select button, select **Insert inside CommandButton - Select | ADF Faces Core | ReturnActionListener**.

    Additional Information: The context menu for inserting a component works the same way in the visual editor and the Structure window. It is an alternative to dragging a component from the Component Palette into either of those windows. Although it accomplishes the same task as dragging and dropping from the Component Palette, it allows you to have more control over the exact positioning of a component than a drag-and-drop operation offers.

13. With the af:returnActionListener selected in the Structure window, set the *Value* as #{row.DepartmentId}. (Be sure to press ENTER when setting properties before you navigate to a different window.)

    Additional Information: The af:returnActionListener specifies the value that will be sent back to the Edit page. The expression "row.DepartmentId" represents the value as the selected row's DepartmentId. This component also triggers the window to close.

14. Click Save All. The finished layout should appear as follows in the visual editor:

15. Run the editEmployee.jsp page. Click the LOV button next to the *Department* field. The LOV window will appear as follows. (As mentioned, you need to turn off popup blockers when running ADF Faces pages such as this.)

Additional Information: Notice that the records are automatically queried. You could stop this window from automatically querying by setting the *refreshCondition* property for the DepartmentsByNameIterator binding in the LOV's PageDef file to `#{adfFacesContext.postback}`. If you did not want an empty results table to display, you would set the *rendered* property to `#{bindings.DepartmentsByName .estimatedRowCount > 0}`.

Notice, too, that the LOV window is sized automatically to the content. The Edit page is disabled, so you cannot enter text or otherwise interact with it until the LOV is dismissed. Both of these effects are native features provided by the `af:selectInputText` component calling an ADF Faces dialog.

16. Notice that the window title is "Search Departments," as you set it in the `afh:head` component. The search field label is loaded from the control hint on the view object bind variable.

17. In the *Department Name* field, enter "s" and click Search.

18. All departments that start with "s" will appear. Notice that the query is not case-sensitive and requires no "%" wildcard. This feature is due to the WHERE clause you added to the view object; this WHERE clause converts the value to uppercase and adds the wildcard character.

19. Enter a department name of "XYZ" and click Search. No rows will be retrieved and a message will be displayed. You can change this message by modifying the expression in the *EmptyText* property of the `af:table` component.

20. Remove the search criteria and click Search. Try the sort and scroll buttons to verify their effects.

21. Select a Department ID that is different from the one in the record. Click the close ("x") icon in the upper-right corner of the window. The LOV window will close, and control will be returned to the Edit page. The *Department* field value will not change.

22. Display the LOV window again, select a different department, and click Close. This button has the same effect as closing the window. No change will occur in the department.

23. Display the LOV window and select a different department. Click Select. This time, the selected ID will be returned to the *Department* field.

Additional Information: Notice that the Department Name output text does not change. An LOV can return only one value by default. To refresh the department name, you would need to trigger a Partial Page Rendering (PPR) event. Chapter 15 contains a basic example of how to work with PPR.

24. Close the browser and stop the server.

Create the Managers LOV Page

The Managers LOV page is set up in the same way as the Departments LOV, so you can follow the steps in the preceding section to set it up. Several notes about specific names and other settings follow:

- In general, change all text referencing "Department" to "Manager."
- The JSP page name is "managersLOV.jsp."

- Use "searchManagerName" instead of "searchDepartment" for the bind variable (parameter).

- After dragging the read-only table, delete only the *DepartmentId* field, and leave *EmployeeId*, *FirstName*, *LastName*, and *DepartmentName*.

- In the returnActionListener for the Select button, set the *Value* to #{row.EmployeeId}.

What Did You Just Do?   You defined the pulldown list for Jobs using a dialog similar to the record group dialogs in Oracle Forms. You also created an LOV template and copied it to the Department and Manager LOV page files. In addition, you defined a navigation case to each LOV. Then you added components to the LOV pages. The result is a fully featured Edit page containing LOVs, a pulldown, and lookup data in read-only fields (department name and manager name).

What Could You Do Next?   You can make several enhancements to these pages:

- **You could change the Department and Manager fields** on the Search page to af:selectInputText components, and define them to use the same LOVs you just created. You would also need to add the navigation cases.

- **You can improve the layout of the Edit page** by positioning the description components to the right of the code fields they describe. The af:panelLabelAndMessage component allows you to place items inside a container that has a label. Therefore, you can place more than one component inside this container and place this container inside an af:panelForm. The af:panelForm will align the prompt for the af:panelLabelAndMessage component with its other fields. For example, you can change the *DepartmentId* and *DepartmentName* fields so that they appear inside an af:panelHorizontal, which is inside an af:panelLabelAndMessage between the *JobId* af:selectOneChoice and the *ManagerId* af:selectInputText. This structure is shown here:

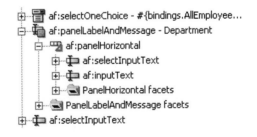

The af:panelLabelAndMessage acts like a field, so its *Label* property must be set to "Department" and the *Label* property for DepartmentId must be blank. The af:panelLabelAndMessage label lines up with the labels of the other fields. Notice that the af:selectInputText (for the field with the LOV button) and af:selectInput (set to read-only for the department name) are placed within the af:panelHorizontal so they appear on the same line. You can create this code by dragging and dropping and rearranging components within the Structure window. When you run the JSP file with this modification, the *DepartmentId* and *Department* Name will appear next to the other fields, as shown:

Department [80]   Sales

■ **You can reset the LOV so it does not automatically query** by changing the *refreshCondition* of the iterator to "never." The default value of "ifNeeded" shows all rows the first time the LOV is displayed. If you enter search criteria and click Search, the list is reduced and that list will show the next time you display the LOV. In addition, the value in the field will be preselected in the LOV's list.

CHAPTER
14

Adding Security

Distrust and caution are the parents of security.
> —Ben Franklin (1706–1790), *Poor Richard's Almanack* (1733)

We will bankrupt ourselves in the vain search for absolute security.
> —Dwight David Eisenhower (1890–1969)

ata is the lifeblood of an organization. Decisions are made; customers and clients are served; and careers are made because of data. Therefore, securing data from unauthorized access is an important requirement for any database system. This chapter briefly examines the security needs of a J2EE web application. It then explores one strategy for implementing security and follows with a hands-on practice that demonstrates how to incorporate this strategy (container-managed security) into the TUHRA sample application.

Application Security

Application security is an important component of system design. You must carefully plan which users should have access to particular application functions that manage specific data sets. Coding and testing this access is part of a complete system-development effort. Security considerations are slightly different in Oracle Forms and Oracle Reports applications than in J2EE web applications.

Security in Oracle Forms and Oracle Reports Applications

Applications developed using Oracle tools, such as Oracle Forms and Oracle Reports, often manage database security by requiring each user to obtain a database login account and password. This strategy requires the database administrator to set up the account and its password and the system administrator to set up global names or to make the TNSNAMES.ORA SQL*Net configuration file available to the user or server (if using web-deployed Oracle Forms). However, with this policy of issuing individual database accounts to set up global names or to control access, users could often access the database using tools other than the approved application, unless special policy code blocked this type of access.

Another common strategy (used by Oracle E-Business Suite) uses a single database login user and requires users to log in using an application account. Privileges to application functions and data are granted through application groups, and users assigned to the groups inherit the privileges of the group (in the same way that database users assigned a database role inherit the privileges granted to the role). With this strategy, the user never knows or cares about the database login account and cannot access data using tools other than the application. This strategy also requires access to the network so that the application can find the database.

Security in Web Applications

Web applications, especially those with Internet audiences, need a publicly available web server that responds to HTTP requests. The application code and file privileges on this server can be limited to read-only. However, unlike Oracle Forms and Oracle Reports applications that require the user to establish a database login session to access the application, web applications handle the database connection automatically in the Model layer code. As with the E-Business Suite applications, a single database user account is used for all users accessing the database. This means that application user accounts must be established outside of the database.

The Oracle Application Server 10*g* provides authentication features that require users to log into an application session. The user accounts on the application server serve as user accounts for a specific application. Application logic then manages specific application privileges to these users. However, this strategy requires application user setup, and this may duplicate existing user lists on a network.

Authentication and Authorization

Logging into a J2EE application using the Oracle Application Server requires two stages—both of which are provided by the OC4J container. These stages follow:

1. Authentication   The security service validates the user's credentials based upon a user name and password or, potentially, a token-based mechanism, such as a Secure Socket Layer (SSL) certificate, or a biometric device, such as a fingerprint scanner. The user name and password approach is the most familiar and common implementation of authentication. The user's name, password, and a definition of the groups to which he or she belongs are stored in a *user repository* (also called an *identity store* or *credentials store*). The user repository can be in the form of an XML file or a directory service (such as an LDAP server). The security service verifies the identity of the user based on entries in the user repository.

2. Authorization   After passing the authentication stage to verify the user, the security service provides access to information about the user to the application. This information may take the form of a list of roles to which the user belongs. These roles are then mapped to the *logical roles* within the application. The application's logical roles are used in the definition of rules that allow access for parts of the application. In a J2EE application, the rules are stored in one deployment descriptor file and the roles are mapped in another descriptor file to users and user groups. The logged-in user and the user's roles from the authentication stage are given access based on this mapping.

In addition, the application can read the logged-in user's name and role, and hide or disable restricted parts of the application appropriately. In the hands-on practice at the end of this chapter, you will set up the files to provide user authentication and authorization. You will also define some application code to provide access based on the user's role.

JAAS

Java Authentication and Authorization Services (JAAS) provides security services for Java-based applications from a library in the Java JDK (J2SE Development Kit). It offers functionality that you can use by calling its APIs to verify user logins and restrict access to resources. This library also provides an industry-standard method for authentication and authorization. The JAAS features are available to application client (desktop) applications as well as web client applications.

JAZN

JAZN, the Oracle JAAS provider, is the facility inside the OC4J server that allows OC4J to use the JAAS library and its standards. Oracle Application Server provides security services through JAZN as well as services such as single sign-on and network encryption. JAZN also provides the ability to authorize based on container security and, thus, supplies the authentication and authorization functions for OC4J. JAZN offers two providers for these services: JAZN-XML and JAZN-LDAP.

JAZN-XML   *JAZN-XML* provides JAAS services to OC4J using XML files for user information. It offers a fast and easy way to code user information into files rather than using an enterprise-wide service.

Therefore, it is well suited to development work. The user repository resides inside an XML file, *jazn-data.xml*, which stores user names and encrypted passwords as well as the names of groups to which the users belong. JDeveloper offers a property editor to assist in setting up users and roles; you will use this editor in the hands-on practice at the end of this chapter.

JAZN-LDAP   *JAZN-LDAP* provides JAAS services to OC4J using a Lightweight Directory Access Protocol (LDAP) directory access system. The *Oracle Internet Directory* (OID) component of Oracle Application Server provides LDAP services, but JAZN-LDAP can use other LDAP systems as well. JAZN-LDAP supports OracleAS Single Sign-On (a facility for passing user login information between applications). It is intended as a provider for an enterprise-ready production environment.

Alternative Providers   Because JAZN uses JAAS under the covers to implement authentication, it is possible to leverage the *Pluggable Authentication Module* (PAM) mechanism defined by the JAAS standard. The idea behind PAM is to provide a standard way of plugging in alternative authentication mechanisms using a LoginModule. A *LoginModule* is a JAAS API you can use to interface with existing security systems. This is of particular interest to many Oracle Forms customers who have an existing security infrastructure using a credential store based on database tables and PL/SQL packages. PAMs allow these existing mechanisms to be reused to secure J2EE applications. The Oracle technology network contains resources that discuss how to write a custom LoginModule. Of particular interest is the paper "Declarative J2EE authentication and authorization with JAAS" available at www.oracle.com/technology/products/jdev/howtos/10g/ jaassec/index.htm.

Switching JAZN Providers   The hands-on practice in this chapter uses the JAZN-XML provider. By default, the OC4J container is configured to use the XML-based user repository, jazn-data.xml, for each application. This user repository is configured through a file, which can be found in the /j2ee/home/config directory within an OC4J installation—application.xml for the application. The application.xml file specifies the type of security provider through the JAZN XML element. Typically, the entry would look something like this:

```
<jazn provider="XML" location="jazn-data.xml" default-realm="jazn.com"/>
```

In order to switch to using LDAP to provide user information, this element would change to something like:

```
<jazn provider="LDAP" location="ldap://ldap.tuhra.com:389">
```

Notice how it is relatively simple to switch the security provider without having to change the application. You might modify the code in this way if you were moving from testing the application within a local OC4J instance (or the JDeveloper Embedded OC4J Server) that used an XML-based user repository to deploying the application into production using an LDAP-based user repository.

NOTE
Oracle Application Server 10g, Release 3 (10.1.3) uses the system-wide JAZN files system-jazn-data.xml and system-application.xml. These files are located in the J2EE_HOME/config directory on the server.

Directory Services

Directory services software, an application server feature, provides a link between the application server and an established user access control list that is external to the application server. This allows an application to use the directory services from the application server to access the external user list. In Oracle Application Server 10*g*, Release 3, any LDAP server can supply these directory services. The examples that follow use LDAP services from Oracle Internet Directory, which can tap into the user list in an existing *Lightweight Directory Access Protocol (LDAP)* system (such as Windows Active Directory). LDAP repositories are used to validate network users for file and directory access privileges outside of web (and other) applications. The communication path for this strategy is shown in Figure 14-1.

The process flow for the application server login in this diagram is as follows:

1. The user issues an HTTP request to the application server. This request includes a context root indicating a particular application, TUHRA in this example.

2. The authentication service in the application server reads a configuration file and determines that access to this application must be authenticated by a particular security strategy—LDAP in this example. It then presents a login page.

3. The user enters an ID and password and submits the page.

4. The authentication service passes the LDAP authentication request to OID to verify the user and password.

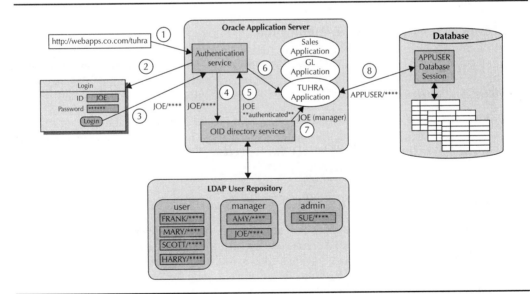

FIGURE 14-1. *Directory services used for a J2EE web application*

5. OID looks up the user in the LDAP repository and verifies the password. It indicates to the authentication service that the user and password are valid.

6. The application server authentication service places the user name into the HTTP session and passes control to the application. The application can read the HTTP session at any time to determine the user's name.

7. The application can also request the group or role (in this example, "manager") to which the user belongs from OID at any point, using standard servlet APIs provided for the purpose.

8. The application connects to the database using the application database user account (the same database account for all web users), in this example, APPUSER. It starts a connection session in the database for that user. The user name and password are written into a configuration file that the application can access. This file is not available to any user, but (with JDeveloper connection files) the password can be encrypted within the file using a feature called *password indirection*.

NOTE
Figure 14-1 represents the LDAP-based user repository. The sample TUHRA application uses the XML-based user repository to demonstrate security within an OC4J server. The documentation for OC4J—for example, the "Oracle Application Server Containers for J2EE Security Guide 10g Release 3 (10.1.3)" online book—provides further overviews and details of security implementations in OC4J.

Levels of Security in a Web Application
Due to the nature of the World Wide Web, web applications are often more widely available than traditional Oracle Forms and Oracle Reports applications. Since more people can potentially access an application with only a web browser, an approach that addresses multiple layers is necessary. Based on the strategies discussed earlier, security can be provided at the following levels:

- **Database user** All web application users connect to the database using a single database user account. This application database user account would be different from the application database object owner account. It would be granted access to only the required application objects.

NOTE
To simplify the database setup, TUHRA uses the schema owner database account as the application database user account. However, implementing an application database user account would only require creating the database account, granting it access to the required database objects, creating synonyms to those objects, and changing the JDeveloper connection to refer to that account.

- **Application user account** Just as database grants must be in place so that the application user account can access the application owner account's objects, the application needs to set and interrogate privileges when presenting menu options, pages, or components on a page.

■ **Application user data access**   Access to pages and components can provide security at the table level. However, this level may not be sufficient. Your application may also require restriction to specific rows within a table. You can accomplish this by adding WHERE clause components that read the database user or by using table policies.

■ **Data query restrictions**   As mentioned in Chapter 12, Query-By-Example (Find mode) screens may give the user the ability to query data in an unintended way using SQL injection. Chapter 15 contains some hints and examples of how to guard against SQL injection.

Matching the Authorized User to the Database

Although the preceding discussion mentions authentication and authorization as being separate from the traditional database login we are accustomed to in Oracle Forms and PL/SQL, some applications will still need to maintain some form of mapping between the authenticated user account on the application server and the database data. For example, the application may need to display the logged-in user on the screen or write audit information about the logged-in user to audit columns in a table.

In the case of the TUHRA application, we need the "My Profile" screen to display the logged-in user. In order to keep things as simple as possible and to remove the requirement to make schema changes, we have chosen, in TUHRA, to use the EMAIL value in the EMPLOYEES table as the container-managed security user ID. In reality, this is not a good way to associate the authenticated user with the identity in the database because changing the database user's email address becomes more complex. Any such change would have to be cascaded into the security system outside of the database—an unnecessary complication. In your own system designs, you would instead use a separate column or lookup table to map the two different types of identity (email address and web user account name) if you require that feature.

Logging Data Modifications

Although they are not unique to web applications, two techniques familiar to Oracle developers can identify who modified data and what they modified. This information can help you research questions about security breaches or security holes.

Data Journaling   Data journaling (also called "archiving") refers to saving a copy of each record that is modified or deleted. Typically, this copy is placed in a separate journal table that is designed with the same structure as the original table. Row-level BEFORE triggers on UPDATE and DELETE save the entire record in its pre-operation state. They also save information about who performed the action and when the action was performed.

Data Audit Columns   You can add columns to each table to store the name of the user who created the record and the date of creation, as well as the name of the user who last modified the data and the date the record was last modified. This information will not provide the same detailed history of changes as the preceding technique, but it is simpler to implement.

As mentioned in Chapter 6, ADF Business Components contains a declarative mechanism for carrying out this form of auditing: the entity object attribute *History Column* property.

The following illustration shows an entity object attribute called CreatedBy in the Entity Object Editor:

Selecting the *History Column* checkbox enables a dropdown list containing a list of audit operations. Once you assign an audit operation to an entity attribute using this mechanism, ADF Business Components will automatically maintain the audit content columns for you without the need to write database triggers.

TIP
If you have JAZN security turned on in the application (as described in this chapter), the "modified by" and "created by" history column values are set to the application user name, not the connection user name. If you do not have JAZN security turned on, all history column values will be NULL.

The Problem with USER   The history column technique will ensure that the application writes audit information to the associated database columns. However, if your table data can be updated outside of the application (for example, by IT staff), you might choose to audit on a more global level using database triggers to capture user information.

The problem you face when implementing these techniques for a web application is in identifying the user. When users log into an application with separate database accounts, the database triggers can use the pseudo-column USER to capture the user name. However, when users log in with an application user name and connect to the database with a common database user name, the pseudo-column USER will be the application database user account. However, you need to record the user name set in the application server session. One solution to this problem is to write the application user name into a database context. Database triggers and other PL/SQL code can then read the application user name from the context instead of using the USER pseudo-column. This technique is detailed in Chapter 15.

Hands-on Practice: Set Up Security in the Sample Application

As Chapter 10 explains, security within the TUHRA application is based around several logical roles—user, admin, and manager. It is important to understand that these roles are private to the application and do not directly represent roles in the database or any user repository, such as OID. The reason for this approach is that it provides us with a security abstraction. We can hook up a security-provider implementation that has its own concept of roles, which may or may not match those within the TUHRA application. If the roles do not match directly, then a mapping can be made between the security-provider role name and the application role name once the application is installed into a J2EE runtime container.

In the sample application, we will simplify the security implementation by using a file-based security provider built into the OC4J container and by defining identical role names in this provider to eliminate the need for any mapping. All security within the application is then based on these logical roles. Although the identity of the logged-in user is available to the developer, general tasks, such as access control to screens, should always be controlled by role.

We use the role information in two ways, first within the user interface to hide or display elements conditionally. For example, a normal user should not see a menu item that leads to administration screens. This is an effective first level of security. However, one of the weaknesses of browser-based applications is the browser's location (address) bar. There is nothing to stop a user from manually altering the URL to access a different part of the application directly. Even if you go to great lengths to customize the browser to hide the location bar, this will not prevent any serious security attack. Fortunately, container security allows us to use the role information to protect specific URL patterns.

Therefore, as a second level of defense, we can partition the application into various subdirectories under the root and protect sensitive pages accordingly.

This hands-on practice will add these types of security. The work follows these phases:

I. **Configure container security**
   - Define users and passwords
   - Set up the user roles
   - Browse the security data

II. **Define application security settings**
   - Set up the logical application roles
   - Define the protected URLs with security constraints
   - Set up a login page
   - Detect multiple login attempts

- Set up a logout page
- Set up the application entry page
- Switch security on
- Ensure that security is triggered

III. Add security to the user interface

- Install JSF-Security
- Add a user ID indicator
- Control access for the admin role
- Control access for the manager role

NOTE
As with all practices in this book, sample application files and code snippets are available from the websites mentioned in the "Websites for Sample Code" in the Introduction.

I. Configure Container Security

Although you can set up application security before container security, it is best to set up the container security first. That way, the user repository will be ready, so you can test the application right after you code security hooks into the application. In this phase, we set up the OC4J container with a user repository that will be used to both authenticate users and provide the list of roles granted to them.

Define Users and Passwords

Each user that can log into the system needs to be defined in the jazn-data.xml file.

1. With the cursor selecting a file in the workspace, select **Tools | Embedded OC4J Server Preferences**. The Embedded OC4J Server Preferences for Tuhra dialog will appear. This dialog allows you to control many aspects of the internal OC4J server within JDeveloper, including the security parameters we need to set.

2. Expand the Current Workspace\Authentication\Realms nodes in the preference tree. There should already be a realm within this node called jazn.com. If not, select Realms, click *New*, and in the Create Realm dialog, specify the *Name* as "jazn.com." Click OK.

   Additional Information: A *realm*, also called a *protection domain*, is just a namespace within the jazn-data.xml. An application can specify that authentication and authorization should take place for users in a specified realm. The default realm is called jazn.com.

3. Two nodes will appear beneath jazn.com in the navigator—Users and Roles. Select the Users node.

   Additional Information: JDeveloper stores some credential information of its own within the User node of the jazn.com realm. Therefore, in the Users area, you may see names like "DataBase_User_5-S5QS0zCT7P7WqAyij6RN4NL8FtF2ZF." Leave any existing entries unchanged.

4. Click Add. The Add User dialog shown here will appear. We are using email addresses from the EMPLOYEES table as user names, so enter the *Name* as "TFOX" and, for *Credentials*, enter the password as "tuhra". Click OK.

CAUTION
JAZN user names and passwords are case sensitive.

5. Repeat step 4 for CDAVIES and NKOCHHAR. Use the same password for simplicity. Leave the Embedded OC4J Preferences for Tuhra dialog open.

Set Up the User Roles

Now that the user entries are created, you can enter the three roles and assign users to those roles:

1. Select the Roles node under the jazn.com realm, and click Add.

2. In the Create Role dialog, enter the *Name* as "admin". As before, case sensitivity is important. Click OK.

3. Repeat step 2 for roles named "user" and "manager".

4. Select the admin role in the *Roles* list, click the Member Users tab, and using the shuttle control, move TFOX to the *Selected* pane. This assigns TFOX to the admin role. In the same way, assign CDAVIES to the user role and NKOCHHAR to the manager role.

   Additional Information: Many users can belong to a role, and a user can belong to zero, one, or more roles, but this example is kept simple to demonstrate security principles.

NOTE
You will notice that you can also associate member roles within a role, so you could make admin a member role for manager. In that situation, any user assigned to admin would automatically have privileges assigned to the manager role as well.

5. Click OK to dismiss the OC4J preferences dialog.

6. Click Save All.

Browse the Security Data

Now that you have defined users and roles, you can take a look at the jazn-data.xml file that contains this information. We mentioned that the normal location for the jazn-data.xml file is the j2ee/home/config directory under your OC4J installation. However, this can be overridden if required. In fact, when you define security information for an application workspace through the JDeveloper editor, you are overriding the files in the J2EE home configuration. JDeveloper needs each application workspace to have its own version of the file, so rather than updating the central copy in j2ee\home, a workspace-specific file, prefixed with the workspace name, is created in the workspace root folder and used when running the application from JDeveloper's Embedded OC4J Server.

1. Select the workspace node (Tuhra) in the navigator, and select **File | Open**. You should see the Tuhra.jws workspace file in this directory.

2. Select the file Tuhra-jazn-data.xml, and click Open. Identify the user, role, and member information you entered in the editor.

    Additional Information: Depending on your JDeveloper version, the passwords may be encrypted (shown with a "(903)" prefix) or may be shown prefixed with an exclamation point "!" inside the credentials element of the user element. The "!" signals the server to encrypt them the first time that the application is run. This encryption demonstrates the password indirection feature mentioned previously.

3. In the same way, open the Tuhra-oc4j-app.xml file. You will see that the jazn element identifies the Tuhra-jazn-data.xml file as the location of the user repository and defines the provider as XML. If you wanted to use a different source of credentials, you would change these attributes as described earlier.

4. Close the editor windows for these two files.

What Did You Just Do?   Using the interfaces provided by the JDeveloper IDE, you configured security for the internal J2EE container, the Embedded OC4J Server, which JDeveloper uses to run J2EE code. You added a set of valid users and passwords, as well as roles for the users. These roles match the names of the logical roles that you will be using within the application, so no further mapping will be required. When you test security later in this practice, you will test these credentials. In addition, you also examined the JAZN file and the OC4J file that points to it. This demonstrates how the security is configured for a workspace and how the code that defines users and roles appears.

What Could You Do Next?   Now that you have defined a few users one by one, and are familiar with the format of the XML that the editor generates, you could write a SQL script to generate the XML tags required to define user account information; for example, something like this:

```
SELECT '<user>' || CHR(10) ||
       '  <name>' || email || '</name> '
       -- add the credentials and closing user tags here
FROM employees
```

You can then paste this XML into the JAZN data file. You can generate a password with a leading "!" so that it is automatically encrypted, for example, "!tuhra." Here is an example of the following XML code you would generate and then paste into the users section of the data file:

```
<user>
  <name>NKOCHHAR</name>
  <credentials>!tuhra</credentials>
</user>
```

Similarly, you would also generate something like the following code and paste it into the role\ members section of the data file:

```
<member>
  <type>user</type>
  <name>NKOCHHAR</name>
</member>
```

II. Define Application Security Settings

In this phase of the practice, you will add security to the TUHRA application. With the exception of creating the logon and logout pages, all work in this phase will take place in the ViewController project's web.xml file.

Set Up the Logical Application Roles

Remember that we need three roles for the application: admin, manager, and user. Use these steps to create the logical roles.

1. On the web.xml node under ViewController\Web Content\WEB-INF, select **Properties** from the right-click menu. The Web Application Deployment Descriptor dialog will appear, as shown here:

2. Scroll to and select the Security Roles node in the navigator, and click Add.

3. In the Create Security Role dialog, enter the *Security Role Name* as "admin" (pay attention to case sensitivity) and *Description* as "Administrative users". Click OK.

4. Repeat steps 2 and 3 for the manager (Management users) and user (Employees and other limited-access users) roles. Click OK to dismiss the descriptor dialog.

5. Click Save All.

Define the Protected URLs with Security Constraints

The security model of the application divides the pages into several sets, depending upon the user groups to which each page is available:

- **Non-logged-in users** The initial home page is available to users who are not logged into the application.

- **Logged-in users** The logged-in home page, profile, and employee search pages are available to any authenticated user.

- **Managers** The employees Edit page is available only to managers and administrators.

- **Administrators** The reference and jobs pages (on the Reference tab) are available only to administrative users.

The access restriction to pages is accomplished by partitioning different functional areas of the application into different physical directories under the web root. You have already placed the pages in various physical directories. The next step is to apply permissions for specific roles to the relevant URL patterns that specify each directory. In this section, you will apply that protection.

1. Open the property dialog for the web.xml file again.

2. In the navigator, select the Security Constraints node, and click New. The new constraint node will be added and the dialog will now look like this:

3. Click Add and in the Create Web Resource Collection dialog, enter the *Web Resource Name* as "AdminZone". Click OK.

4. Click the Authorization tab at the top of the dialog, and select the admin security role checkbox, as shown here:

5. Click the Web Resources tab, and select AdminZone in the *Web Resource Collections* area. Click Add next to the lower set of tabs.

6. In the Create URL Pattern dialog, enter the *URL Pattern* as "faces/pages/admin/*". Click OK.

Additional Information: This setting protects the AdminZone pages so that when the application requests the container to display a page in this location—for example, the "faces/pages/admin/jobs.jsp" page—the container will check if the user is already authenticated. If the user is not yet authenticated, he or she will be challenged to authenticate with a login screen before proceeding. If the user is already authenticated, the container will check the user's roles against the authorized roles for this resource—in this case, admin. It will allow the user access to the page only if the user is a member of that role.

Notice that the URL pattern we use here does not exactly mimic the file system directory location of the page file under the context root of the application. For example, the actual location of the jobs.jsp page is ../pages/admin/jobs.jsp. The extra "faces/" prefix is required, because all page requests are going through the JSF servlet, which is triggered by the use of this faces prefix. This prefix is specified in the web.xml. Click the Servlet Mappings node in the navigator to see this mapping. Return to the AdminZone constraint node.

As you would expect, the trailing "*" is a wildcard matching any page in that directory. You could add the exact URL of each page to protect them individually. However, partitioning the application into directories and using wildcard mappings is simpler.

TIP
If you need to modify the URL pattern, you can double click the value in the URL Patterns tab to open the field for editing. Press ENTER *when you are finished editing.*

7. Repeat steps 2–6 to create a second security constraint called "ManagerZone," which is available to the manager and admin roles, and protects the URL pattern "faces/pages/ management/*." (Be sure to reselect the Web Resource Collection value before trying to add the URL Pattern value.)

8. Repeat steps 2–6 to create a third security constraint called "UserZone," which is available to all three roles and protects the URL pattern "faces/pages/*."

   Additional Information: J2EE container security supports a flat security model and has no provision for creating hierarchical security rules. This is why we define three separate security constraint elements for the application.

9. Click OK to dismiss the dialog. Click Save All.

Constraint Order Is Important   When applying security, always define the most restricted access first, in this case, the admin pages (the AdminZone constraint). If a user is a member of several roles, she or he will be authenticated at the most powerful level. The container evaluates the security constraints in the order that they are defined in the web.xml, so using the wrong ordering could result in a user being authenticated at a lower privilege level than to which he or she is entitled. For example, in this application, we defined AdminZone above ManagerZone. To verify the generated XML, you can open the web.xml file and browse for the security-constraint tags.

The web.xml editor has no provision for re-ordering the constraints. If you need to change the ordering, drag and drop the nodes in the Structure window or edit the source code.

Set Up a Login Page
When using container-managed security, you can use several approaches to authenticate the user. The two most common approaches are: basic authentication, where you allow the browser to generate a default popup login dialog; and a custom login form, which is coded as part of the application. TUHRA uses a custom login page that is branded to fit in with the rest of the application. For the login page, you will be using a normal JSP page, not a JSF JSP of the type that you have been using so far. The normal JSP file is required for two reasons. First, the container calls the login page (using a definition in the web.xml file that you will define later) and, in the process, bypasses the various servlet mechanisms that an ADF Faces page needs to work correctly. Second, JSF cannot be configured to call the special URL that the container uses to accept authentication requests. Fortunately, the login page uses a simple design that does not require sophisticated JSF components.

1. On the ViewController project node, select **New** from the right-click menu. In the Web Tier\JSP category of the New Gallery, double click the JSP item. The Create JSP Wizard dialog will appear. Click Next if the Welcome page appears.

2. In the Step 1 page, set the *File Name* to "login.jsp" and add "\security" to the *Directory Name* so it reads "TUHRA_HOME\ViewController\public_html\security." For "TUHRA_HOME," indicate the exact drive and directory you specified when creating the application.

3. Click Next.

4. Click Next on the Step 2 page. On the Step 3 Libraries page, select "All Libraries" in the *Filter By* pulldown, and move the JSTL Core 1.1 library to the *Selected Libraries* list.

CAUTION
You may see JSTL Core 1.0 in the list, but be sure to select JSTL Core 1.1.

Additional Information: The *JSP Standard Tag Library (JSTL)* is a set of tags that supplies iterative and conditional control as well as other functionality. It is defined by the JSP specification, and is considered easier to read and easier to use than native JSP tags, such as scriptlets and expressions. JSTL tags use a "c" prefix; for example, c:choose. You will be using JSTL expressions to detect if the user is on the first or subsequent login attempts. JSTL tags allow you to write simple procedural code within the body of your JSP page. You will write JSTL code to conditionally display a message about invalid login credentials if the user has more than one unsuccessful login attempt.

5. Confirm that you have selected JSTL Core 1.1 (not JSTL Core 1.0) and click Next. In the Step 4 HTML Options page of the wizard, set the *Title* to "Login." Click Finish. The page will be created and will appear in the visual editor.

6. You can now lay out components on the page. From the HTML Forms Component Palette page, drop a Form tag onto the page. The Insert Form dialog will appear.

7. In this dialog, enter the *Action* as "j_security_check" and select the *Method* as "post". Click OK. A form box will appear on the page.

Additional Information: The *j_security_check* action is a magic action that every J2EE container is required to implement for developers to use. This will hook into whatever authentication mechanism is currently selected for the container. As you will see, some special field names are also required to complement this action.

8. From the HTML Common Component Palette page, drop a Table inside the Form tag area that has just been created. Set *Rows* as "7", *Columns* as "2", *Width* as "100" percent, *Border Size* as "0", and *Header* as "None". Click OK.

9. You will be using this table to lay out the various parts of the login screen, such as the logo, title, and input fields. Start this process by selecting as a group the two cells in the top row of the table, and then select **Table | Merge Cells** from the right-click menu. This will combine the cells into a single two-column cell, which we will use to hold the logo.

10. Repeat the cell-merging process for the second, third, and last rows of the table. The table should now look like this in the visual editor:

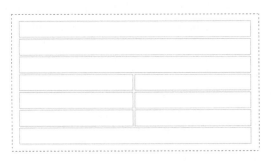

11. In the navigator, expand the Web Content\images folder, select "tuhra.gif" or your own selected logo, and drag it into the top row. Select the image in the editor, and in the Property Inspector, change the *Src* attribute of the image to the path "/tuhra/images/tuhra.gif". The image will disappear from the visual editor.

    Additional Information: In this page, we make a compromise on the specification of the logo location. If the image location is defined as " ../images/tuhra.gif," it will display correctly at design time; however, this path using the "../" prefix is relative to the invoking page. In the special case of the login screen, the page may be invoked from several locations, so relative URLs cannot be used safely. Therefore, a fixed URL needs to be used for the correct behavior at runtime. The JDeveloper design time editors cannot understand this location, so the image item containing the TUHRA logo now shows as a broken image in the visual editor; the correct image will appear at runtime.

12. Set the *Alt* property of the image to "TUHRA logo." The *Alt* property defines the text for the mouseover hint that appears when the mouse hovers over the image. Set *Align* to "top."

13. Select the logo image. In the Structure window, select the td node above the image. Click Horizontal Rule in the HTML Common Component Palette page to add a horizontal line under the logo. Drop another Horizontal Rule into the last row of the table. These elements display decorative lines that emulate the ADF Faces layout containers used on the other pages.

14. In the second row of the table, enter the heading for the page: "Sign on to TUHRA". Set the style to Heading 2 using the toolbar style pulldown.

15. From the CSS Component Palette, drag and drop the JDeveloper style sheet onto the page. The title font will change and a horizontal rule will appear under the text because of the style properties in the CSS file.

16. In the Structure window, expand the html\head node, and select the link tag for the CSS reference. In the Property Inspector, change *HRef* to "/tuhra/css/jdeveloper.css". The fonts will revert to their default appearance (although the style sheet will be used at runtime).

    Additional Information: Changing the reference to use the absolute path is required for the same reason as for the logo image file.

17. In the leftmost cell of the fourth row, enter "* Username"; in the leftmost cell of the fifth row, enter "* Password".

Additional Information: As with prompts for required fields in the application, the "*" symbol signals to the user that these fields are required.

18. From the HTML Forms page of the Component Palette, drag a Text Field into the rightmost cell in the fourth row. In the Insert Text Field dialog, enter the *Name* as "j_username". Click OK. Drop a Password Field into the rightmost cell of the fifth row. Enter the field's *Name* as "j_password".

    Additional Information: These two fields names are also magic values that the container expects when a j_security_check form is submitted. The Password Field will hide the characters the user types.

19. Click OK to close the dialog. Drop a Submit Button into the rightmost cell of the sixth row. Set its *Name* property to "login" and its *Value* property to "Login." This will be used to submit the form to the container so it can validate the credentials. Click OK.

    Additional Information: If you want to make this button look like a JSF command button as on the non-logged-in home page, follow the steps in the sidebar "Using an Image Button in a JSP File."

Using an Image Button in a JSP File

You can use the Image Button component to make the Login button look like a JSF command button. The following steps describe this task.

1. Delete the button you just added. You now need to find an image for the button. Fortunately, this image has been generated by the Login button on the home page you created in Chapter 11. You just need to find the image.

2. In Windows Explorer, or any image viewer utility, navigate to TUHRA_HOME\ ViewController\ public_html\WEB-INF\temp\adf\images\cache\en.

3. Modify the display to thumbnails (**View | Thumbnails** in Windows Explorer); browse until you find the Login button image file.

   Additional Information: If the image is not yet available, you can create a JSF JSP file and add a command button to it. The image for that button will be generated automatically and be placed in the directory described in step 2.

4. Still using the file utility, copy the login button image file, and paste it into the directory TUHRA_HOME\ViewController\ public_html\images. Rename the file to login-button.gif.

5. In JDeveloper, drop an Image Button from the HTML Forms page of the Component Palette into the rightmost cell of the fifth row.

6. In the *Src* field of the dialog, browse for the login-button.gif (now in the "..\public_html\images" directory); select it and click Open. Enter the *Name* as "login". Click OK. The button will appear selected in the table as shown on the right.

7. Select the image button, and change its Src property to "/tuhra/images/images/ login-button.gif" (for the same reason as mentioned before for the logo image). Press ENTER and the image will disappear from the visual editor.

20. Click in the Username prompt cell. In the Structure window, select the td node above the Username prompt. Set its *Width* property to "10%". This will resize the column for all three rows. Also set its *Align* property to "right" so that the prompt is right-aligned. (This will more closely emulate the layout of an ADF Faces field with its prompt.) Repeat the alignment setting for the Password prompt's td tag.

Additional Information: These settings modify the default behavior so that the prompts are right-aligned and stay close to the fields when the browser window is widened or narrowed. The login form should look something like this (if you applied the image button technique):

Sign on to TUHRA	
|	
* User ID	
* Password	
⊠	

21. Click Save All. Although the security functionality is not yet complete, run this page so you can check its appearance. If the logo and images do not appear, check their *Src* properties.

22. Close the browser and stop the server.

Detect Multiple Login Attempts

As a final polish to the login page, you will add some JSTL code to detect if the user has visited the login page more than once; this would indicate that a login attempt failed and that an error message should be displayed.

1. In the visual editor for the login page, switch to the JSTL 1.1 Core page of the Component Palette, and drag a Choose tag into the empty third row of the table. The Insert Choose dialog will appear.

NOTE
If the JSTL 1.1 Core page does not appear in the Component Palette, double click the ViewController node and be sure JSTL 1.1 is listed on the Libraries page. If it is not, click Add Library and add it. Click OK. If the JSTL 1.1 Core page still does not appear, click Save All. Then close and reopen JDeveloper. The JSTL 1.1 Core page should now be available.

Additional Information: JSTL tags are displayed uppercased without their prefix in the visual editor. The JSTL c:choose tag allows you to embed a conditional test in the page. Each test condition starts with a when tag. It provides similar functionality to an IF...THEN...ELSIF...ELSE...END IF structure in PL/SQL.

2. Click New to add a when condition, and enter the *Value* as the following:

   ```
   ${sessionScope.attemptsAtLogin == null}
   ```

   This statement checks if a session variable, attemptsAtLogin, does not exist.

3. Select the *Add c:otherwise* checkbox, and click OK. The Choose tag will appear in the visual editor, as shown next. (This tag will not be displayed at runtime.)

Additional Information: JSTL supports both c:if statements and c:choose statements. The c:if statement only allows testing of a single condition and does not provide an else option. In this situation, a single outcome is not sufficient, so c:choose is best.

4. Click the Source tab to view this code and to double-check the expression with the instruction in step 2. If it is the first time that the login screen has been displayed, the attemptsAtLogin variable will not be assigned (and will therefore have a null value). You want to initialize it so that next time around (if the login fails) the c:otherwise statement will be executed.

5. You can set session variables from JSTL using the set tag. In the Design tab, drag a Set tag from the Component Palette and drop it into the empty box to the right of the c:when tag. This will nest the c:set tag within the c:when tag, and the c:choose tag will appear as follows:

6. With the c:set tag selected, set the *Var* property as "attemptsAtLogin," the *Scope* as "session" (using the pulldown), and the *Value* to "0" (zero).

7. If the user returns to the screen for a second time, the attemptsAtLogin session variable will have been set to "0" (not "null"), so the c:otherwise statement will be triggered. In the c:otherwise tag, you will print out an error message and maintain a count of how many attempts the user has actually made. Click inside the box to the right of the c:otherwise tag, and type the error message "Error: Invalid Username or Password."

8. Select the text and, with the font color picker button in the toolbar of the visual editor, set the font color to red. Select the word "Error" and click the "B" button to boldface the word.

9. Drag a Set tag from the Component Palette and drop it after the error message in the c:otherwise tag. In the Property Inspector, set the c:set tag's *Var* as "attemptsAtLogin" and the *Scope* to "session" as before. Set the *Value* to the following expression:
   ${sessionScope.attemptsAtLogin + 1}

   Additional Information: JSTL allows you to apply simple calculations like this within your markup. In this case, you are incrementing the value that is currently held in the attemptsAtLogin variable, maintaining it as a running count of login attempts. Since the scope is set to "session" for both instances of setting the variable, the value will carry through between page reloads.

10. Switch to the Source tab in the visual editor, and check that the code for this row in the table reads as follows (although the code formatting may vary):

```
<tr>
  <td colspan="2">
    <c:choose>
      <c:when test="${sessionScope.attemptsAtLogin == null}">
        <c:set var="attemptsAtLogin"
               scope="session"
               value="0"/>
      </c:when>
      <c:otherwise>
        <font color="#ff0000">
          <strong>Error:</strong>
          Invalid User ID or Password.
        </font>
        <c:set var="attemptsAtLogin"
               scope="session"
               value="${sessionScope.attemptsAtLogin + 1}"/>
      </c:otherwise>
    </c:choose>
  </td>
</tr>
```

11. Correct any errors. Click the Design tab. Click Save All.

12. Run this page again. Click the Login button and you will see the error message. You haven't set up navigation for this button, so after viewing the error message, close the browser and stop the server.

TIP
You might want to copy the application workspace directory as a backup at this point.

Set Up a Logout Page

Now that you have a login page for the application, you also need to provide a way to log out. Logging out of a web application requires invalidating the session using Java code. Invalidating the session throws away all of the data saved at the session level, including the authenticated credentials and variables such as attemptsAtLogin. As soon as the session is invalidated, the OC4J container will start over with a blank state and the user will have to reauthenticate in the same way as the initial login. This section implements the session invalidation and creates a logout confirmation page to check that the user really wants to log out.

1. You created the logout page file in Chapter 11, but you need to remove some of the template content before the logout code can be added.

2. Open the logout.jsp file under the pages node. Select a tab to expand the tag hierarchy in the Structure window. In the Structure window, select the menu1 facet of the PanelPage. Press DELETE to remove this facet and all menu tabs.

3. Delete the two global buttons for Logout and Help, and drag a CommandMenuItem from the ADF Faces Core page of the Component Palette into the af:menuButtons container. Set its *Text* as "Cancel" and *Action* as "GlobalHome" (from the pulldown). Type the *Icon* property as "../images/return.gif" and set *Immediate* to "true."

   Additional Information: As mentioned in Chapter 11, you can use any icon you have at hand for the global button icons in this project. If you would like to match the examples in this book, you can download the return.gif file from the websites mentioned in the "Websites for Sample Code" section of the Introduction (or save equivalent files from the Icon Repository for BLAF available at www.oracle.com/technology/tech/blaf/specs/iconlist.html). Name the file return.gif, and place it in the TUHRA_HOME\ViewController\public_html\images directory.

4. Next, you need to create a bit of explanatory text and buttons to confirm or cancel the logout and return to the home page. One at a time, drag two PanelHorizontal tags on top of the af:panelPage in the Structure window. Add an ObjectSpacer and move it between the two af:panelHorizontal tags so that the components will have a bit of space between them. Be sure the components are arranged in the Structure window as follows:

   ```
   ⊟──▣ af:panelPage - Logout Confirmation
      ⊞──▩ af:panelHorizontal
         ┈┈▦ af:objectSpacer
      ⊞──▩ af:panelHorizontal
      ⊞──▩ PanelPage facets
   ```

5. Select both of the af:panelHorizontal components, and set *Halign* to "center."

NOTE
When you first group select elements (using CTRL click), the Property Inspector may display the properties in a collapsed form. If this occurs, move down the drag bar (the horizontal separator at the top of the Property Inspector window) in the Property Inspector to reveal the properties.

6. In the first af:panelHorizontal, drop an OutputText component and set its *Value* to "Are you sure you want to log out?" This text will appear on the page after you press ENTER.

7. In the second af:panelHorizontal component, drop a PanelButtonBar. Drop two CommandButton components inside the af:panelButtonBar. Set the *Text* of the first to "Yes" and the *Text* of the second to "No". Add another ObjectSpacer component

under the af:panelButtonBar component by dropping it on top of the af:panelPage component. The screen will now look like this:

8. The No button will repeat the functionality of the Cancel global button, so select its *Action* property as "GlobalHome." Clicking either button will return the user to the logged-in home page.

9. We need to add code to the Yes button to invalidate the session. Double click the Yes button in the visual editor. The Bind Action Property dialog will appear.

10. Click New to display the Create Managed Bean dialog. Set the *Name* as "backing_logout" and the *Class* as "tuhra.view.backing.Logout". This class does not yet exist, so select the *Generate Class If It Does Not Exist* checkbox. Click OK.

11. In the Bind Action Property dialog, set the *Method* to "logoutButton_action" and click OK to create the Java class, register it in the faces-config.xml file, and open it in the editor.

12. Change the declaration of the class to extend the framework class (TuhraBackingBean). Import the superclass using ALT-ENTER as you have done on previous occasions. The class declaration should appear as follows:

```
public class Logout extends TuhraBackingBean
```

13. In the logoutButton_action() method, set the code to the following to invalidate the session and hence log off the user. As usual, do not enter the line numbers.

```
01: public String logoutButton_action() throws IOException
02: {
03:    ExternalContext ectx = FacesContext.getCurrentInstance().getExternalContext();
04:    HttpServletResponse response = (HttpServletResponse)ectx.getResponse();
05:    HttpSession session = (HttpSession)ectx.getSession(false);
06:    session.invalidate();
07:    response.sendRedirect("home.jsp");
08:    return null;
09: }
```

Additional Information: **Line 03** is similar to code you have seen before to create a FacesContext object for the current instance, but it is extended to retrieve the ExternalContext object from the JSF framework. The *ExternalContext* object provides direct access to the HTTP session and response objects that are needed to log out and return to the home page, respectively. **Line 04** creates a response object from the ExternalContext object. **Line 05** creates a session object from the External Context object. **Line 06** invalidates the session (effectively logging off). Finally, in **Line 07**, the code uses the response object to direct the browser to redisplay the protected home page. Because the existing account has been logged off by the session invalidation, the login page will be presented to force another logon.

14. As before, import the required classes (`IOException`, `FacesContext`, `ExternalContext`, `HttpServletResponse`, and `HttpSession`) using the quick fixes (light bulb) icon in the left gutter of the code editor. (Use `javax.faces.context.FacesContext`, `javax.faces.context.ExternalContext`, `javax.servlet.http.HttpServletResponse`, and `javax.servlet.http.HttpSession` if given choices.) The import section should appear something like the following:

```
import java.io.IOException;
import javax.faces.context.ExternalContext;
import javax.faces.context.FacesContext;
import javax.servlet.http.HttpServletResponse;
import javax.servlet.http.HttpSession;
import tuhra.view.framework.TuhraBackingBean;
```

15. Click Make to compile the file. Click Save All.

16. You can now test this page to verify its layout. With the cursor in the logout.jsp page, click Run.

17. If a security "Connect to" dialog appears, enter the *user name* as "TFOX" and the *Password* as "tuhra". Click OK. The Logout Confirmation page will appear.

18. Check the layout of the Logout page. The Yes and No buttons will both forward to the protected home page at this point. Close the browser and stop the server.

Set Up the Application Entry Page

You need to have the OC4J container automatically load the non-logged-in home page when a user accesses the application's context root (http://host:port/tuhra). This involves setting up the home page as a welcome page for the application. *Welcome pages* are a servlet mechanism whereby if the application root is accessed directly, without a page being specified, the servlet knows what default page to supply. First, you will check the context root that you set up in Chapter 11.

1. Double click the ViewController project node in the navigator to display the project properties. Select the J2EE Application node in the properties navigator, and verify that both the *J2EE Web Application Name* and *J2EE Web Context Root* are set to "tuhra."

    Additional Information: *J2EE Web Context Root* defines the URL that will be used to access the application once it is deployed. The *J2EE Web Application Name* property is used internally in the deployment descriptor and configuration files.

2. Click OK. On the web.xml file under the ViewController\Web Content\WEB-INF node, select **Properties** from the right-click menu.

3. Select the Welcome File Lists node in the navigator, and click New.

4. Click Add and enter the path "/faces/home.jsp" in the Create Welcome File dialog. Click OK.

5. Click OK to dismiss the descriptor dialog. Click Save All.

6. Run the home.jsp page under Web Content (not under Web Content\pages). Change the URL in the Address (Location) field of the browser to "http://<host:port>/tuhra" (replacing "<host:port>" with the computer and port already in the URL), and press ENTER. The home page will load again, because this context root URL sends control to the file defined in the Welcome File List node of web.xml.

7. Close the browser and stop the server.

Switch Security On

Even though all the roles, security constraints, and physical pages are in place to secure the application, you still need to switch on the security mechanism to use your login form instead of the default security dialog. This is also defined in the application's web.xml file:

1. Open the properties dialog for web.xml, and select the Login Configuration node in the navigator.

2. Select the *Form-Based Authentication* radio button. Enter "security/login.jsp" for both *Login Page* and *Error Page*.

   Additional Information: The implication of using the same page for both purposes is that if the first attempt to log in fails, the user will be able to try again immediately, rather than by having to navigate back to the login page. The JSTL code you added to the login page will detect that the user is trying again and will print the error message relating to the first failed attempt. If you don't specify an error page, the container will use a default authorization failed page.

3. Click OK. Click Save All.

CAUTION
The form-based authentication used here is only truly secure when used in conjunction with secure HTTP (HTTPS). This ensures that the login information will be encrypted when it is posted to the server. Without this additional layer of security, it is possible for someone to obtain the login credentials by monitoring the network traffic between the browser and the server. For information on how to set up HTTPS, refer to Chapter 10 of the Oracle Application Server Administrator's Guide—"Overview of Secure Sockets Layer (SSL) in Oracle Application Server."

Ensure That Security Is Triggered

This section tests the application and makes another required setting to the redirect properties of some pages.

1. Run home.jsp (under Web Content) to test the application. Click Login, and you will forward to the logged-in home page (/pages/home.jsp with the tabs) without being challenged for your user name and password.

NOTE
If clicking the Login button displays the login page, return to the Overview tab of the faces-config.xml file, select the global navigation rule, and set the "Redirect" property for home.jsp to "false." Then run the home page again. You can now follow the next explanation and steps.

Additional Information: This is not what you would expect. The problem lies in the way that the need for authentication and authorization is detected by the container. You have secured certain paths in the application, such as "/faces/pages/*," but if you look at the URL in the browser now, you will see that it is still showing "faces/home.jsp" even though the protected "faces/pages/home.jsp" page shows in the browser.

This situation reflects the way that JSF navigation works. A navigation rule will, by default, act as a forward within the container. As mentioned in Chapter 11, a *forward* occurs when a servlet transparently rewrites the URL for a page to a new value and then sends the output of that new page to the screen without informing the browser. Therefore, the browser still shows the old URL. In this case, however, this is not good, because we want to explicitly issue a request to a protected URL to trigger the container security mechanisms. Fortunately, we can alter the JSF navigation behavior to explicitly request the key protected pages and trigger security.

2. Close the browser and stop the server.

3. Open the faces-config.xml file in the editor, and switch to the Overview tab. Select Navigation Rules and select the "*" entry in the *From View ID* list. Select the GlobalHome navigation case (home.jsp) and, in the Property Inspector, set *Redirect* to "true," as shown here:

Additional Information: This value forces the browser to re-request the explicit URL defined by the GlobalHome rule, and this will trigger the security check.

4. Check that all navigation cases for the "*" navigation rule except for help.jsp show *Redirect* as "true" in the summary list on the Overview tab. (The help.jsp file is a popup dialog and requires a forward instead of a redirect.)

5. Select each of the other navigation rules and examine their navigation cases. Be sure the *Redirect* property is set to "true" for all but the popup windows (LOVs and help page) and the createEmp rule from editEmployee.jsp.

6. Click Save All.

7. Run home.jsp (under Web Content) again. Click Login. The login page will display instead of the protected home page and the URL in the Address line of the browser will show "../faces/pages/home.jsp."

8. Log in as TFOX with a password of "tuhra." Click Login. The protected home page will display.

9. Click Logout to view the Logout Confirmation page. Click No to return to the protected home page.

10. Click Logout again and, on the logout page, click Yes. The login page will display. This is the full login and logout cycle. You can try logging in with an invalid user name or password to display the error message.

11. Close the browser and stop the server.

What Did You Just Do?   You defined the logical roles that are used within the application to judge the privilege level of each user and then used those roles to protect certain pages based on their location under the web root. When a user is authenticated, he or she will only be allowed to access pages in locations granted to the role to which he or she belongs.

You also defined a custom login page for use by the J2EE container using the magic form name (j_security_check) and field names that inform any J2EE container that the form will call authentication and authorization services. In addition, you added logic to display an error message if the user has made more than one attempt to log in.

Then you implemented a logout page and its accompanying backing bean that invalidates the user's session. Once the session has been invalidated, the browser will be redirected back to the initial home page using a navigation rule that you created in the JSF navigation diagram. This allows the user to log in again, possibly using different credentials. Because the old session was invalidated, any state associated with it, such as the count of login attempts, will be discarded.

Lastly, you switched on security for the application in the web.xml file and ensured that key navigation rules within the application trigger security-checking by redirecting rather than forwarding.

What Could You Do Next?   You probably noticed that the attemptsAtLogin session variable is maintaining a running count of the login attempts. Try using this information to restrict the user to just three tries. As a hint: the type of conditional JSTL statement that you have already used can be applied anywhere in the page to hide or display much more than an error message.

III. Add Security to the User Interface

You have now set up role-based access to pages in the application using container- and application-level settings. This final phase examines how you can apply security attributes within these pages to gain a deeper level of control over what the user sees and to access relevant security information, such as the user ID of the authenticated user.

NOTE
Several of the tasks defined in this practice apply to multiple pages throughout the application. To help with the logical flow of the preceding practices, we have gathered these tasks into this section. However, in real application development, these tasks should be worked into the initial application template development process.

The Servlet API provides various calls that can be used to extract information such as the authenticated user (the getRemoteUser() method in the HttpSession class) and the roles of that user. These API calls are straightforward to use in code, and the JSF ExternalContext object provides a shortcut for you to use. For example, the following code fragment will assign the user ID to a code object, userName:

```
FacesContext ctx = FacesContext.getCurrentInstance();
ExternalContext ectx = ctx.getExternalContext();
userName = ectx.getRemoteUser();
```

Accessing this information within the structure of a page is a bit different from accessing it in backing bean code. JSF screens use Expression Language to bind attributes to useful information and, therefore, Expression Language is the key to accessing this information.

The JSF-Security Project

The *JSF-Security Project* is an open-source effort to simplify the use of security information in JSF. The JSF-Security Project offers a framework that extends the JSF Expression Language, adding a scope called "securityScope." *securityScope* provides access to information such as the authenticated user ID and the roles of that user from within standard expressions.

NOTE
The home page for this project is sourceforge.net/projects/jsf-security. Details about the expression syntax and functionality are available at jsf-security.sourceforge.net/.

The JSF-Security extension is not the only way to achieve Expression Language access to security information. You can alternatively create a JSF-managed bean that exposes properties to Expression Language. However, using the JSF-Security extension in this practice means that you won't have to write code and you can concentrate on the job of applying security rather than accessing it.

Install JSF-Security

To use the JSF-Security expressions, you will need to connect to sourceforge.net/projects/jsf-security, and then download and install the extension using these steps.

1. Click the "Download Java Server Faces Security Extensions" link.
2. On the next page, click the "Download" link associated with the jsf-security package.

3. Find the latest release and select the .zip file, if you are working in Windows, or tar.gz if you are on Linux, Macintosh, or Unix.

   Additional Information: The files with "-src" in the name include the source code as well as the final JAR file. You do not need this version unless you are interested in seeing how the code works.

4. On the next page, select a download mirror close to your location.

5. Once the archive is downloaded, open it and extract the jsf-security.jar file to your desktop (without using folder names in the extract process). Drop this .jar file from the desktop into your application's TUHRA_HOME\ViewController\public-html\WEB-INF\ lib directory using Windows Explorer or another file utility.

CAUTION
The .jar file must reside directly in this lib directory, not in a subdirectory of lib.

Add a User ID Indicator

The first task in this section is to display the name of the authenticated user at the top of each page. The steps that follow describe how to set this up on a single page and then copy this component to other pages. (This tag would have been part of the template that you copied to each page if security had been turned on earlier in the development process.)

1. Open the /pages/home.jsp page from the navigator. Select a tab to expand the Structure window to the PanelPage facets area of the structure.

2. In the Structure window, under the PanelPage facets, locate the infoUser facet. On this node, select **Insert inside infoUser | OutputFormatted** from the right-click menu.

   Additional Information: As you have seen in other hands-on practices, the af:panelPage layout component provides many facets, such as infoUser, for standardizing the layout of your screens. Of course, you do not have to use these facets to display this kind of information—you can display it anywhere. However, the facets provide a useful way of ensuring a consistent appearance for all of your pages.

3. Set the *Value* property of the new af:outputFormatted component to the following:
   `Signed in as #{securityScope.remoteUser}`
   At runtime, this will display the authenticated user ID.

4. Click Save All.

5. Before copying this to all other pages, run this home page, log in, and verify that the logged-in user name appears in this component. If it does not, check your work with the preceding steps and fix any problems. Close the browser but leave the server running.

6. Select the af:outputFormatted node under infoUser in the Structure window, and copy it to the clipboard (CTRL-C).

7. Open help/help.jsp. Expand the Structure window by clicking the Home tab then find the infoUser facet. Select that facet, and press CTRL-V to paste the customized af:outputFormatted component from the clipboard. The component will appear in the userInfo area in the visual editor.

8. Repeat the preceding step for pages/profile.jsp, pages/searchEmployees.jsp, pages/admin/jobs.jsp, pages/admin/reference.jsp, and pages/management/editEmployee.jsp.

9. Click Save All. Close all editor windows (on any editor tab, select **Close All** from the right-click menu).

10. Run the pages/home page and log in. Check the pages to be sure the user name appears.

11. Close the browser and stop the server. The sidebar "When Should I Restart the Embedded OC4J Server?" describes some guidelines for server handling when testing code in JDeveloper.

Control Access for the Admin Role

Within the TUHRA application, the reference screens (/pages/admin/jobs.jsp and /pages/admin/reference.jsp) should be available only to authenticated users with the "admin" role. Although you have not defined content for these pages, you can set up their security now. You have already configured the application to prevent unauthorized users from accessing these pages using a security constraint. However, it would be nice to remove the Reference tab so that only admin users know these pages exist. This section configures the Reference tab so it appears based on the role of the user.

1. Open the /pages/home.jsp page from the navigator and, in the visual editor, select the Reference tab. The corresponding `af:commandMenuItem` in the `af:menuTabs` container component will be selected in the Structure window.

2. In the Property Inspector, select the *Rendered* property in the Core section of the Property Inspector. This property can accept an expression that will evaluate to a Boolean. If it evaluates to "true," the component will display; otherwise, it will not. Click "Bind to data" in that property.

When Should I Restart the Embedded OC4J Server?

You may have noticed that we did not stop the server after testing the page in step 5. Although it is always cleaner to stop the server so that any cached objects are cleared out, if you do not stop the server, the next time you run a page in JDeveloper, the startup time will be a bit shorter.

You can get a feeling for when you need to restart the server by not stopping it before making modifications. If, upon your next test after the modification, you do not see the results of those changes, you know you need to stop and restart the server. With some experimentation, you will be able to determine when the server needs to be restarted after a modification. You can start with these rules-of-thumb:

- You do not need to restart the server for most modifications to a JSF JSP page.
- You need to restart the server if you change Model project objects.
- If you do not see the results of a change you made, restart the server.

Experience with which changes require a restart can serve you well if you need to make changes to production code. Stopping and restarting an OC4J instance in a production situation can affect many users, but you may be able to avoid that impact if the change does not require a restart.

3. In the Rendered binding dialog, enter the following expression:

```
#{securityScope.userInRole['admin']}
```

4. A return value of "true" will ensure that only users with the admin role (for example, TFOX) will see this tab. Double check the expression and copy it to the clipboard (so that you can copy it to other pages). Click OK.

5. Click Save All.

6. Run the home.jsp file, log in as CDAVIES (password of "tuhra"). CDAVIES belongs to the user role and cannot see the Reference tab.

7. Log out and log in again as NKOCHHAR (same password). This user belongs to the manager role and also cannot see the Reference tab.

8. Repeat the logout and log in once more as TFOX. You will see the Reference tab because this user belongs to the admin role.

9. Copy this expression into the Reference tab's *Rendered* property for profile.jsp, searchEmployees.jsp, and editEmployee.jsp. You do not need to copy this value for the reference.jsp and jobs.jsp pages because they appear when that tab is selected. Click Save All and test these three pages in the same way you tested the Home page.

10. Close the browser.

Control Access for the Manager Role

We also need conditional logic based on the role of the user to display buttons to edit, delete, and create employee records in the search results table on the Employees Search page, as shown here:

Matching Employees

Action buttons

Select and (Edit)(Delete)(New)

Select	ID	First Name	Last Name	Email Address	Telephone
⦿	105	David	Austin	DAUSTIN	590.423.4569
○	104	Bruce	Ernst	BERNST	590.423.4568
○	103	Alexander	Hunold	AHUNOLD	590.423.4567
○	107	Diana	Lorentz	DLORENTZ	590.423.5567
○	106	Valli	Pataballa	VPATABAL	590.423.4560

In Chapter 12, you created the af:tableSelectOne component in the results table and set the *Rendered* property to the explicit expression value #{true}. This causes the contents of that component—the selection radio group column, "Select and" prompt, and header action buttons—to appear. Now that you have access to information about the authenticated user, you can replace this expression with an expression that displays the buttons only for users in the admin or manager roles.

1. Open the pages/searchEmployees.jsp and select the Edit button to open the nodes in the Structure window. In the Structure window, select the af:tableSelectOne component within the selection facet.

2. Change the existing value of the *Rendered* property from #{true} to the following expression:

```
#{securityScope.userInRole['admin,manager']}
```

Additional Information: This expression will return "true" if the user is a member of the admin or the manager (or both) roles. By setting the *Rendered* property on the `af:tableSelectOne`, you will automatically hide (or display) all of its children, including the selection radio buttons shown in each row of the table.

3. Click OK. Click Save All.

4. Run the application. Log in as CDAVIES. After querying records on the Search page, you will not see the buttons or radio group column. Both TFOX and NKOCHHAR will be able to see the buttons because of the role to which they are assigned.

TIP
As mentioned in Chapter 9, you can set the run target for an application so that clicking Run from non-JSP files will always run a specified JSP. In the faces-config.xml navigation diagram, select **Set as Run Target** *from the right-click menu on the page you would like to be the default startup page (in this application, it is home.jsp, not pages/home.jsp).*

5. Close the browser and stop the server.

What Did You Just Do? In this final phase for setting up security, you incorporated security details into the pages. You first added a security library that assists with JSF page control by adding a security scope containing user and role information. You then added a user indicator on the pages to demonstrate how this security information could be available to the components on the page. You also set up security for a menu tab so that only the admin role will see the Reference tab. Lastly, you modified an expression on the `af:tableSelectOne` component of the Search page so that the buttons for adding, modifying, and deleting employee records are only shown to managers and administrators.

This hands-on practice has shown how to set up container-based security and how you can access security information through Expression Language. EL can be used both for the purposes of display, as in the case of the authenticated user, and also to dynamically control the display of areas of the screen using the combination of expressions and the *Rendered* property.

PART
III

Additional Techniques

Whenever you are asked if you can do a job,
tell 'em, "Certainly I can!"
Then get busy and find out how to do it.

—Theodore Roosevelt (1858–1919)

CHAPTER
15

Sample Application
Enhancements

Few things are harder to put up with
than the annoyance of a good example.

—Mark Twain (1835–1910), *Pudd'nhead Wilson* (1894)

 s mentioned in the Introduction, we think of work in user-interface development tools in different levels: wizards, declarative tools, and writing code. You have worked mainly in the second level, but you have also used the wizards and have written a bit of code. To set your expectations correctly, it is likely that your first project using ADF in JDeveloper will require techniques we have not mentioned. A real-world application development project requires many techniques and, although we have shown some of the frequently used techniques, you will need many more.

Along with the application development techniques, we have spent time introducing the technologies in use and explaining why you are doing what you are doing so that you can learn the principles and apply these principles in other ways to solve other needs. Should you require examples of other techniques, you can refer to these sources:

- **The JDeveloper sample application** (SR Demo) is located on otn.oracle.com. You can also load it using the **Help | Check for Updates** menu item. Two versions of the demo exist; you will be most interested in the version that uses ADF BC.

- **The Oracle ADF Developer's Guide** that appears in the Help Center tab of the JDeveloper help system. It is also available on the Oracle Technology Network (OTN) in a PDF file. As mentioned, this comes in two flavors, one of which is specific to ADF BC.

- **The JDeveloper home page** on otn.oracle.com contains links to many how-to's and other technical white papers. It also contains links to other resources, such as blogs by Oracle technologists who focus on ADF techniques.

- **The JDeveloper discussion forum**, also available from a link on the JDeveloper home page.

- **The www.tuhra.com website**, which contains some samples from these authors and additional techniques for the TUHRA application.

- **User group conference papers** that focus on ADF techniques.

Closer to home, we have dedicated the final two chapters of the book to explaining some additional techniques you can use for ADF web development in JDeveloper. This chapter explains features that you may want to add to the sample application. Chapter 16 provides a brief overview of the JHeadstart add-on to JDeveloper, which you can use to generate a number of fully functional pages and controller code to begin developing an ADF application.

Some of the techniques in this chapter are described in the same style as the hands-on practices in preceding chapters—that is, through a step-by-step explanation. Other techniques are more discursive and provide a basic direction and thought pattern rather than a step-by-step guide. The techniques explained in this chapter follow:

- **Load audit columns using a database procedure and application context**
- **Rename an ADF-oriented JSF JSP file**

- **Prevent SQL injection attacks**
- **Invoke Partial Page Rendering**
- **Define global format masks**

NOTE
As usual, all scripts and code snippets for these techniques are available from the websites mentioned in the "Websites for Sample Code" section in the Introduction.

Hands-on Practice: Load Audit Columns Using a Database Procedure and Application Context

A common requirement for database designs is to record the name of the user who created the record, as well as the name of the user who last modified the record, in separate columns (CREATED_BY and MODIFIED_BY, respectively) in each table. In addition, the creation date and last modified date are stored in two more columns (CREATED_DATE and MODIFIED_DATE, respectively). Although this information does not provide a complete history of the record, it helps track some of the activity. For a complete history, you would create a journal table for each table that requires operation-level audits. This journal table would store details about every INSERT, UPDATE, and DELETE operation issued to the table.

In Chapter 14, we saw how this form of auditing can be implemented declaratively using the history column attribute properties in ADF BC. Now we will look at a different approach to the same problem implemented within the database itself. As we mentioned before, you may choose to take this approach if you have other applications accessing the same data or requirements that are not covered by the basic history column functionality of ADF BC.

Implementing audit columns or a journal table in PL/SQL requires BEFORE row-level triggers for each operation. The row-level trigger updates an audit column or inserts the values of the old (or new) row in the journal table; alternatively, the journal table could hold just the data that has been changed. The problem, mentioned in Chapter 14, is that if your application uses a single database user account to connect to the database (as do most J2EE web applications), the table triggers cannot use the USER pseudo-column to assign the created or modified user columns. For example, in an Oracle Forms application where the user logs in using his or her own database account, a BEFORE INSERT row-level database trigger would contain the following:

```
:NEW.created_by := USER;
:NEW.created_date := SYSDATE;
```

If this trigger was created for an application that uses a single database user login, the CREATED_BY would always be the database connection user, regardless of the user who was logged into the application. It would be better to store the name of the user who logged into the application. The audit columns technique demonstrated in this section solves this problem by adding some application module Impl file code, which reads the user name for the logged-in user from the OC4J container and writes it to a database context area. Table triggers assign the user name from the context area to the table's journal columns.

This technique consists of the following phases:

I.   Create the database objects

II.   Set the context from the application

- Call the database procedure from `prepareSession()`
- Test the method call
- Move the code to the framework class

I. Create the Database Objects

Although this section describes how to implement the audit column technique, you could apply many of the same principles to inserting a row into a journal table. Although the PL/SQL triggers and tables will differ between the two requirements, the problem is the same—how to access the logged-in user name from within PL/SQL code.

The key to the solution is an *application context*, an Oracle database feature that allows you to store and query information for a specific user session. You need to create the context and associate it with a PL/SQL package that will manage writing and reading from the context. You can think of the application context as a memory area, which you can write to and read from throughout a user's database session.

You can create named values (like variables) that you store in the application context by assigning a value to a name. You can then read the values by accessing the value name within that same database session. Since you declare these variables at runtime (not in explicit declarative code), context name-value pairs are akin to global variables in Oracle Forms. In Oracle Forms, you create global variables by assigning them, and you can then read the value throughout the same database session.

The entire solution requires the following elements:

- **An application context**   You access a context by a name; the same context can provide session-specific information for many database sessions, although the values assigned into the context in one session will be readable only within that session. Therefore, you only need one application context for this purpose.

- **A PL/SQL context package**   This package contains procedures and functions that write and read to the context area.

- **J2EE code to write to the context**   The J2EE code will call a procedure in the context package to write a value for the logged-in user name to the application context.

- **Table trigger code to read the context**   The built-in database function SYS_CONTEXT can access the context in the trigger. For example, you could create a context called HR_CONTEXT; application code would write a value called APP_USERNAME into that context with the logged-in user name. The snippet shown earlier from the BEFORE INSERT table trigger would then become this:

```
:NEW.created_by := SYS_CONTEXT('HR_CONTEXT', 'APP_USERNAME');
:NEW.created_date := SYSDATE;
```

You need to follow the steps in this section to make the required database changes.

1. Log in to the database as SYS, or a DBA account connected as sysdba, and grant access to the application object owner (HR) using the following statements:

```
GRANT EXECUTE ON SYS.dbms_session TO hr;
GRANT CREATE ANY CONTEXT TO hr;
GRANT DROP ANY CONTEXT TO hr;
GRANT SELECT ON SYS.v_$session TO hr;
```

2. Log in as HR, and add audit columns to the table. This example uses the EMPLOYEES table, so you would run the following:

```
ALTER TABLE employees
ADD (
    created_by      VARCHAR2(30),
    created_date    DATE,
    modified_by     VARCHAR2(30),
    modified_date   DATE);
```

3. Update the CREATED_BY and CREATED_DATE columns with appropriate values, and change those columns to NOT NULL, as follows:

```
UPDATE employees
SET created_by = 'HR',
    created_date = TO_DATE('01/01/1980 12:12','MM/DD/YYYY HH24:MI');

ALTER TABLE employees
MODIFY ( created_by NOT NULL,
         created_date NOT NULL);
```

4. Create the context and refer to a package (even though this package is not yet created):

```
CREATE CONTEXT hr_context USING security_pkg;
```

5. Create the SECURITY_PKG using the following SQL:

```
CREATE OR REPLACE PACKAGE security_pkg
IS
    PROCEDURE set_security_context (
        p_username    IN VARCHAR2,
        p_application IN VARCHAR2 DEFAULT 'TUHRA');

    FUNCTION logged_in_user
        RETURN VARCHAR2;

END security_pkg;

CREATE OR REPLACE PACKAGE BODY security_pkg
IS
    PROCEDURE set_security_context (
        p_username    IN VARCHAR2,
        p_application IN VARCHAR2 DEFAULT 'TUHRA')
    IS
```

```
BEGIN
   -- Write the user info into the context area
   -- The application name is used later
   SYS.DBMS_SESSION.set_context ('HR_CONTEXT', 'APP_USERNAME', p_username);
EXCEPTION
   WHEN OTHERS
   THEN RAISE_APPLICATION_ERROR(-20001,
          'Error in SECURITY_PKG.SET_SECURITY_CONTEXT: ' || SQLERRM);
END;

FUNCTION logged_in_user
   RETURN VARCHAR2
IS
   v_username   VARCHAR2(100);
BEGIN
   v_username := UPPER(SYS_CONTEXT('HR_CONTEXT', 'APP_USERNAME'));
   RETURN v_username;
EXCEPTION
   WHEN OTHERS
   THEN RETURN 'Error in LOGGED_IN_USER';
END;

END security_pkg;
```

Additional Information: The Java code you write later will pass the logged-in user name to the `set_security_context` procedure. It will also pass the application name. Although the code just shown does not use this parameter, the section "What Could You Do Next?" later in this chapter explains its possible use.

6. Create the trigger to set the audit columns as follows:

```
CREATE OR REPLACE TRIGGER employees_audit_biu
   BEFORE INSERT OR UPDATE
   ON employees
   FOR EACH ROW
DECLARE
   v_user   VARCHAR2(30);
BEGIN
   v_user := security_pkg.logged_in_user;

   IF INSERTING
   THEN
      :NEW.created_by := v_user;
      :NEW.created_date := SYSDATE;
   ELSIF UPDATING
   THEN
      :NEW.modified_by := v_user;
      :NEW.modified_date := SYSDATE;
   END IF;
END;
/
```

7. You can test your code in the SQL tool of your choice (for example, JDeveloper's SQL Worksheet). First note the contents of the audit columns for a particular row in the EMPLOYEES table:

```
SELECT employee_id,
       first_name, last_name,
       created_by,
       TO_CHAR(created_date, 'mm/dd/yyyy hh24:mi:ss') created_date,
       modified_by,
       TO_CHAR(modified_date, 'mm/dd/yyyy hh24:mi:ss') modified_date
FROM   employees
WHERE  employee_id = 100;
```

8. Set the application context parameter for the session as follows:

```
BEGIN
    security_pkg.set_security_context('TFOX', 'TUHRA');
END;
```

9. Check that the application context parameter is set:

```
SELECT security_pkg.logged_in_user
FROM dual;
```

10. Issue an UPDATE statement. The following does not change anything, but it will cause the trigger to fire:

```
UPDATE employees
SET    last_name = last_name
WHERE  employee_id = 100;
```

11. Check the audit column values by re-running the SELECT statement from step 7. You should see a MODIFIED_BY value of "TFOX" and the MODIFIED_DATE of today.

What Did You Just Do?   You added audit columns to the EMPLOYEES table and created an application context to hold the value of the user name, which will be passed to the application context. You also created a package associated with the application context. This package contains a procedure to add the user name to the application context and a function to read the user name from the context. In addition, you created a trigger on the EMPLOYEES table that loads the user name into an audit column during an INSERT or UPDATE. Finally, you tested these database components by updating the EMPLOYEES table and viewing the resulting audit column values.

What Could You Do Next?   Naturally, you can add this kind of functionality to more than one table. Each table requires audit columns and a trigger to load the user name and dates for INSERT and UPDATE operations. The package and application context would be shared by all these triggers.

  You could use a similar technique to implement a journal table system by creating a duplicate of the main table (for example, EMPLOYEES_JN), with additional columns for OPERATION ("INSERT" or "UPDATE"), OPERATION_DATE, and OPERATION_USER. The trigger would be modified to insert a record with the old values and values for the additional columns into this table. Again, the package and application context would be the same as before.

You might want to add a condition to the audit columns trigger so that if a user is not logged in through the web application, the trigger will record the database login user name instead of the web application login name. This requires the following changes:

- **An additional context value** IS_WEB_USER that you assign as "Y" in the set_security_context function.

- **Additional trigger logic** to check if the context variable IS_WEB_USER is set to "Y." If so, the user name column is set to the user name in the context. Otherwise, it is set to USER (the logged-in database user).

Since all web users log in as the same database user, there is no way to distinguish their sessions when viewing the virtual view, V$SESSION. However, V$SESSION contains two columns, CLIENT_INFO and ACTION, into which you can write information such as the logged-in user name. To add user-specific information to these columns, you would add these two lines to the security_pkg.set_security_context procedure:

```
DBMS_APPLICATION_INFO.SET_CLIENT_INFO(p_username);
DBMS_APPLICATION_INFO.SET_ACTION(p_application || ' - ' ||
      TO_CHAR(SYSDATE,'MM/DD/YYYY HH24:MI'));
```

You must also grant the connection user EXECUTE privilege on DBMS_APPLICATION. The first line writes the user name into the CLIENT_INFO column, and the second line writes the value of the p_application parameter (set to "TUHRA" by the application code) and the date and time into the ACTION column.

> **NOTE**
> *V$SESSION displays information about database connections. Since a J2EE web application has no persistent database connection and since ADF BC pools database connections, you do not know the state of user sessions that appear to be connected in V$SESSION. For example, a user name may appear in V$SESSION even though the user has closed the browser, because the database connection in the application module pool may not have been reused.*

II. Set the Context from the Application

Now that the PL/SQL and database objects are in place, all that remains is to write code in the application to call the database function that sets the application context value for the user name. This phase uses the technique explained in Chapter 6 to call a database procedure and to define code that will be executed automatically as the ADF Business Components layer establishes the user session with the database.

Call the Database Procedure from prepareSession( )

This section extends the functionality of the application module prepareSession() method, which the ADF BC will automatically call as the database connection is established (for each interaction with the database). The advantages of adding the context initialization code to this method follow:

- **The framework will execute the context setting code for you.** You do not need to explicitly execute the call from the user interface code.

- **The `prepareSession()` method will automatically be reinvoked** and the context set correctly if the application employs connection pooling or application module pooling,

- **The context will be reset with the new ID** if the user logs out of the application and connects using another ID.

The following steps start with the sample Tuhra application workspace. In addition to the database code described in Phase I of this practice, they require an Employees Edit page and the security features worked into the application in Chapter 14.

1. Select the TuhraService application module node under Model\Application Sources\ tuhra.model. Double click TuhraServiceImpl.java in the Structure window to open the Java file in the editor.

2. Select **Source | Override Methods** and select the checkbox for the prepareSession(oracle.jbo.Session) method. (This method will display an open lock icon, indicating that it is public.) Click OK. The method code stub will be inserted into the code file.

3. Modify the generated prepareSession() method so it includes the following code:

```
public void prepareSession(Session session)
{
  super.prepareSession(session);
  // Retrieve the J2EE user ID
  String authenticatedUser = getUserPrincipalName();

  if ( (authenticatedUser != null) &&
       (authenticatedUser.trim().length() > 0))
  {
    DBTransactionImpl dbTransaction = (DBTransactionImpl)getDBTransaction();
    // Parameter for application name
    String pApplication = "TUHRA";
    // Transaction statement with procedure call
    CallableStatement callableStmt = dbTransaction.createCallableStatement(
      ("BEGIN " +
         "security_pkg.set_security_context(?, ?); " +
       "END;"), 0);
    try
    {
      // Register parameters and call procedure
      callableStmt.setString(1, authenticatedUser);
      callableStmt.setString(2, pApplication);
      callableStmt.execute();
    } catch (SQLException sqlExcept)
    {
      throw new JboException(sqlExcept);
    }
```

```
        finally
        {
          try
          {
            if (callableStmt != null)
            {
              callableStmt.close();
            }
          } catch (SQLException closeExcept)
          {
            throw new JboException(closeExcept);
          }
        }
      }
    }
```

Additional Information: This code uses an API function provided by the
ApplicationModuleImpl superclass—getUserPrincipalName(), which returns the
ID of the user that is authenticated by the J2EE container. If the user name is not null,
the code then creates a database transaction object, dbTransaction, and prepares a
statement with two replaceable parameters (user name and application name) to call the
database procedure. Next, the code registers the parameters and executes the PL/SQL
statement. Chapter 6 contains more detailed explanations of this type of code.

4. You will see many class names with wavy underlines. These indicate missing imports.
   Hold the mouse cursor over DBTransactionImpl, and press ALT-ENTER to add the
   import (oracle.jbo.server.DBTransactionImpl). Repeat this operation for
   CallableStatement.

5. Hold the mouse cursor over one of the callableStmt lines, and import SQLException.
   Repeat this for JboException (select oracle.jbo.JboException from the pulldown).

6. Compile the code (using **Make** from the right-click menu in the editor). Fix any problems
   and recompile.

7. Click Save All. The method is now defined and will execute automatically when a new
   session is created.

Test the Method Call
Now that the setup is complete, you can run a test in the application.

1. Open the Table Viewer in JDeveloper for the EMPLOYEES table (in the Connections
   Navigator, open the Database, HR, HR, and Tables nodes; and double click the EMPLOYEES
   node). Select the Data tab.

2. Select an employee record, and note the values for the columns MODIFIED_BY and
   MODIFIED_DATE (probably NULL).

3. Return to the Applications tab, and run the application. Log in as TFOX. On the
   Employees tab, query and edit the employee record you noted in the preceding step.
   Change the phone number, and click Save.

4. Close the Table Viewer in JDeveloper, and reopen it. The MODIFIED_BY and
   MODIFIED_DATE for the record should now be TFOX and the current date.

5. Log out and log in again as NKOCHHAR. Update the same record, and note the change in the audit column values.

6. Close the browser and stop the server.

Move the Code to the Framework Class

Although this application only contains one application module at this stage of development, you expect the project to grow so that it contains more than one application module. You will need to apply the same context-setting procedure call to all application modules. Instead of repeating the method in each application module, you can code it on the application framework level so that one method is available to all application modules. In this section, you will move the method call to the framework code level.

1. Open the TuhraServiceImpl.java file if it is closed. (Select the application module and double click the file name in the Structure window.)

2. Place the cursor in the `prepareSession()` method, and select **Refactor | Pull Members Up**. The Pull Members Up dialog will appear, as shown here:

3. Be sure the `prepareSession()` method checkbox is selected.

4. Notice the *Target* pulldown contains the name of the superclass `TuhraApplicationModuleImpl`. Click OK. The method will disappear from the editor.

5. Scroll to the class declaration line (`public class TuhraServiceImpl`) and, on the `TuhraApplicationModuleImpl` class name (in the `extends` `TuhraApplicationModuleImpl` clause), select Go to Declaration from the right-click menu. The superclass file will open in the editor. Verify that `prepareSession()` was moved. This method will now be available to all application modules in the same project.

6. Click Save All.

7. Run the application. Log in as TFOX again. Make a change to a record, and check that the audit columns are updated.

8. Close the browser and stop the server.

What Did You Just Do?   You wrote code in the application layer to call the `security_pkg` `.set_security_context` procedure so the logged-in user name would be placed in the application context and the INSERT and UPDATE trigger could write the proper user name into the table's audit columns. You did this by overriding and adding functionality to a framework method, which is called as the database session is established. Then you tested this code and moved the method to the framework class so that all application modules in the same project will be able to take advantage of it.

TIP
Should you wish to share this code among projects, you can create a cross-application framework file that extends the ADF class. The new cross-application framework file would be distributed in a library that you attach to each Model project you create. Your project-level framework class would then subclass the cross-application framework class.

You could also implement *Virtual Private Database (VPD)* features that restrict a user's access to specific rows. The technique just described writes the logged-in user name to the application context. You can write functions that return WHERE clause predicates using the user name in the context to restrict rows. You then attach the functions to tables by setting up *policies*, definitions that cause a policy function to be executed when any SELECT statement is issued to its attached table. More information about VPD can be found in the *Oracle Application Developer's Guide– Fundamentals*, available in the Oracle database documentation.

Hands-on Practice: Rename an ADF-Oriented JSF JSP File

JDeveloper offers a large number of utilities (for example, Pull Members Up) for *refactoring* (moving, renaming, or reorganizing) Java code. These utilities (available in the Refactor menu) save time because they synchronize all dependent classes as well as rename the class file, its signature, and its constructors. No refactoring utility exists for renaming a JSP file at this writing. JSF JSP files that use ADF controls and ADF Faces have several dependent files, so merely renaming the JSF JSP file using **File | Rename** is not sufficient. The following steps explain how to rename this type of file.

CAUTION
So you do not jeapordize the integrity of the full Tuhra sample application, copy the Tuhra application workspace directory and use that copy to practice this renaming process. Alternatively, create a simple application (such as Employees_Ch15 in the sample files) with an Employees browse page, an Employees edit page (or other data-oriented block), backing beans, and navigation rules between the pages.

1.   Select the JSP file in the navigator, and select **File | Save As**. Enter the new name. (Copying the file maintains the navigation rules for the old file.)

2.   Click Save. In the faces-config.xml file, change the navigation rules and navigation cases to route to or from the new name as appropriate.

3. Select the associated backing bean file, if any, in the navigator, and select **Refactor |
   Rename**. Enter the new backing bean name. The refactor utility will also modify the
   faces-config.xml file to reference the new name.

4. Select the JSP file's PageDef file. Select **File | Save As** and specify the new file name.
   Click Save All.

5. Open the new PageDef file, and locate the `pageDefinition` element. Change the *id*
   attribute to reference the new PageDef file name.

6. Open the DataBindings.cpx file in the editor under the ViewController project's main
   model node (for example, Application Sources\tuhra.view). Under the `pageMap` element,
   change the relevant `page` element's `path` and `usageId` properties to reference the new
   JSP and PageDef names.

7. Under the DataBindings.cpx's `pageDefinitionUsages` element, change the relevant
   page element's `id` and `path` properties to the new PageDef name.

8. If you have associated a message bundle file, rename that file using the Refactor menu.

9. Delete the old page's symbol from the JSF Navigation Diagram.

10. Delete the old JSP and PageDef files (using **File | Erase from Disk**).

11. Click Save All

12. Run the application to be sure it still works. If you run into problems, examine all files
    mentioned in this technique to be sure you have made the correct changes.

NOTE
*If the JSP page was defined as the application's target page, change
the name in the Welcome File List in web.xml (on the web.xml node
under WebContent\WEB-INF in the navigator, select **Properties** from
the right-click menu and look for the Welcome File Lists node).*

Prevent SQL Injection Attacks

One of the most common vulnerabilities in relational database applications is leaving the
application open to SQL injection (described in Chapter 12). *SQL injection* is a technique that
users can employ to insert SQL statements inside a string variable that is meant to hold query
criteria values such that unintended results occur. For example, imagine a query screen that allows
a customer to track an order. The screen exposes an Order Number field called q_ordernum. The
user can enter a number and click the Find button to retrieve details of that order. Usually, the
programmer or the framework code would include a SQL statement that uses the parameter value,
such as:

```
stmt = "SELECT order_total, status FROM orders WHERE order_number = " +
    q_ordernum;
```

This statement will work as expected if the user enters valid data. For example, a value of "101"
will generate the following statement:

```
SELECT order_total, status FROM orders WHERE order_number = 101
```

Using SQL injection techniques, the user could insert SQL language snippets within the criteria; in the previous example, entering a value of "`=order_number and order_total > 1000`" in the `q_ordernum` field will result in the following SQL statement:

```
SELECT order_total, status FROM orders WHERE order_number = order_number and
order_total > 1000
```

The screen was intended to allow queries on item numbers only, but a query such as this reveals data that is potentially proprietary.

SQL Injection Exposure for ADF Web Applications

For ADF web applications, SQL injection is a concern wherever the framework generates a SQL statement by concatenating values the user enters. In the sample application, you used two techniques to allow users to enter values for queries, and these techniques react differently to SQL injection.

Bind Variables and SQL Injection   The first technique you used (for the departments and managers LOVs) added bind variables inside the WHERE clause of the view object. This type of query is a fixed statement that the ADF BC framework passes to the database as a normal bind variable SELECT statement. The database processes the statement and resolves the datatype of the bind variable value. This type of user input is impervious to SQL injection because of the way the database processes and substitutes the bind variable values in the statement.

NOTE
As a bonus, queries that use bind variables are more likely to be cached by the database parser and will be more efficient as a result.

Find Mode and SQL Injection   The second technique you used to allow users to enter values for queries was Find mode (in the searchEmployees.jsp). The ADF BC framework processes this type of user input by constructing a dynamic query which concatenates the column names associated with the fields with the values entered by the user. ADF BC also performs some smart parsing to determine the operator appropriate for the value. For example, the user can enter a WHERE clause predicate such as "> 200" in the EmployeeId field, and the framework will construct a WHERE clause containing "AND EMPLOYEE_ID > 200." If the user were to enter "200" as the value, the framework would construct the clause "AND EMPLOYEE_ID = 200."

A problem related to the smart parsing in Find mode is detailed in the sidebar "A QBE Find Mode Parsing Problem."

Find mode is open to SQL injection because the values the user enters can be concatenated with the column names in the WHERE clause that the framework constructs. Therefore, the SQL injection query using `q_ordernum` mentioned earlier would be possible using native ADF BC with no filters for SQL injection.

TIP
The key rule when constructing dynamic queries in your application is to use bind variables whenever possible rather than building statements by concatenating user-input values.

A QBE Find Mode Parsing Problem

The QBE implementation in ADF BC has another known problem that results from its smart parsing, and this problem does not exist in the QBE mechanism in Oracle Forms. That is, instead of wrapping the field values with a "LIKE" and "%'" in all cases, it looks to see if the user has entered a keyword and constructs the WHERE clause differently. For example, in a QBE form for Countries, if you enter a *RegionId* value of "1," the QBE mechanism correctly constructs a WHERE clause component as "(Countries.REGION_ID = 1)." However, if you enter a CountryId of "IN" (for "India"), the framework detects a SQL keyword and assumes the user is entering valid WHERE clause syntax. It removes the "=" (equals) operator and constructs the WHERE clause component as "(Countries.COUNTRY_ID IN)." This is an incomplete statement, so the query fails.

You can work around this effect in several ways:

- **Restrict the values in the tables** you query with QBE so they do not contain SQL keywords.

- **Request that users enter query conditions** for columns that contain keywords with correct SQL syntax, for example, "IN ('IN')."

- **Write a filter** such as that described in this section to account for keyword values in the data.

Securing Find Mode

Despite its vulnerability to SQL injection, ADF BC Find mode is useful because it provides easy development of highly functional Query-By-Example screens. Users are not confined to simple equality comparisons; they can use wildcards or operators such as ">" (greater than) in the query criteria fields.

Guarding against SQL injection in Find mode requires adding some logic to the view object's Java coding. The method we use in this example is the view object's `getViewCriteriaClause()` method. The ADF BC framework calls this method when constructing a SQL WHERE clause to incorporate the values entered by a user in a form in Find mode. We can override the method in our view object implementation class and add some validation code to reduce the risk of a user entering unintended criteria values.

In the code example that follows, we implement the following simple rules that attempt to balance user functionality with safety:

- **Reject query criteria that contain the name of one of the attributes** the view object contains.

- **Reject query criteria that contain SQL operations** such as "BETWEEN," ">=," or "=" for columns that are not dates or numbers. These operators are allowed for dates and numbers because a user might want to use such comparisons in a legitimate way.

NOTE
These simple rules will defeat the most obvious attacks. However, they may also give rise to false results, depending on your data set and database column names. Consider this and tailor the code to suit your needs and satisfy your security requirements and testing. In addition, consider your data when thinking about other possible SQL injection possibilities.

getViewCriteriaClause( ) Method

Enter the following method in your `AllEmployeesImpl` view object class. As before, the line numbers are for reference in this text and should not be included in the code. This code is split by explanations, but you can use the line numbers to ensure you code the entire method.

```
01: public String getViewCriteriaClause(boolean forQuery)
02: {
03:   ViewCriteria viewCriteria = getViewCriteria();
04:   if (viewCriteria != null)
05:   {
06:     AttributeDef[] attrs = viewCriteria.getViewObject().getAttributeDefs();
07:     StringBuffer columnNameListBuff = new StringBuffer();
08:     for (AttributeDef attr: attrs)
09:     {
10:       columnNameListBuff.append(attr.getColumnName().toUpperCase());
11:       columnNameListBuff.append("|");
12:     }
13:     String columnNameList =
14:         columnNameListBuff.substring(0, columnNameListBuff.length() - 1);
```

Check for Criteria   **Line 01** defines the method for `getViewCriteriaClause()`. The base framework class, `ViewObjectImpl`, contains this method and performs default ADF BC behavior when Query-By-Example (Find mode) functionality is required. We override this method in the ADF BC base framework class and call the superclass' corresponding method at the end of our method. The base class requires a boolean argument, and we pass that value back to the framework class without changing it at the end of the method.

   Line 03 obtains the `ViewCriteria` object from the view object. This object contains values for all Find mode fields the user entered.

   Line 04 bypasses the rest of the code if no criteria exist.

Obtain a List of Column Names   **Line 06** uses the `getAttributeDefs()` view criteria method to gather a list of column names used by the view object's attributes. We need this to implement the rule to reject any query criteria that contain one of these column names.

   Lines 07–12 convert the array of `AttributeDef` objects returned by line 06 into a single long string (columnNameListBuff, defined in line 07) containing column names, with each column name separated by a "|" (pipe symbol). This long string of column names will be used later for the pattern matching that searches for possible SQL injections.

NOTE
We use a StringBuffer instead of a String for the column name list,
because, as you may recall from Chapter 4, reassigning a String uses
more memory than appending to a StringBuffer.

Lines 13–14 strip the unwanted extra "|" from the end of the column name string.

```
15:      ViewCriteriaRow vcr = (ViewCriteriaRow)viewCriteria.first();
16:      while (vcr != null)
17:      {
18:        for (AttributeDef attr : attrs)
19:        {
20:          int index = attr.getIndex();
21:          String criteria = (String)vcr.getAttribute(index);
```

Process Criteria Rows and Attributes in Each Row   The `ViewCriteria` object contains a row for each set of criteria field values. Therefore, one row will contain values for the EmployeeID, FirstName, LastName, Email, PhoneNumber, DepartmentId, JobId, and other AllEmployees attributes. The Find mode capability of ADF BC allows the user to create multiple rows of criteria by invoking an insert action on the View Object while in Find mode. Each of the query attributes would appear in each row of the `ViewCriteria` object. Although we have not coded the page to allow for multiple criteria rows, the code in Lines 15–21 accounts for adding this capability in the future.

When the query criteria are processed, all attribute values entered for the first row are assembled into a WHERE clause condition with an AND operator between each field-value set. The values entered in the second row would be assembled in the same way into a second condition, which is then joined to the first row's condition using the OR operator.

Line 15 retrieves the first criteria row into the object "`vcr`."

Line 16 starts a loop through each criteria row. The page we created for searching employees only contains one row of query criteria but the loop is created in case other rows are added in the future.

Line 18 starts a loop through all attributes in the query criteria row. In a typical Query-By-Example screen, the user enters criteria in several fields, so the code needs to examine each attribute.

Lines 20–21 retrieve the index number associated with the attribute and use the index number to extract the criteria value entered by the user for that attribute. Each column or attribute can be identified by index number or column name; since the column name can vary, the index number is more reliable.

```
22:          if (criteria != null)
23:          {
24:            boolean restricted = true;
25:            switch (attr.getSQLType())
26:            {
27:              case (Types.INTEGER):
28:              case (Types.NUMERIC):
29:              case (Types.DECIMAL):
30:              case (Types.DATE):
31:              case (Types.TIMESTAMP):
```

```
32:                    {
33:                      restricted = false;
34:                    }
35:                    break;
36:                  }  // end of switch
37:                  String newCriteria =
38:                        detectInjection(criteria,columnNameList,restricted);
39:                  vcr.setAttribute(index, newCriteria);
40:                }  // end of if (criteria != null)
41:              }  // end of for (AttributeDef attr: attrs)
42:            vcr = (ViewCriteriaRow)viewCriteria.next();
43:          }  // end of while (vcr != null)
44:      }  // end of if (viewCriteria != null)
45:      return super.getViewCriteriaClause(forQuery);
46: }  // end of method
```

Test the Criteria   Line 22 determines if something has been entered in this attribute and, if so, processing continues; otherwise, the code continues with Line 41, which retrieves the next criteria row and passes control back to the top of the attribute loop.

   Lines 24–36 retrieve the SQL datatype of the attribute and decide how restrictive the check should be. The mode is initially restrictive, as defined by the boolean variable `restricted`, but if the datatype of the attribute turns out to be a number or a date, `restricted` is set to "false," because our design rule states that we will allow operators in these fields in case the user wants to search a range of numbers or dates (using BETWEEN, >, <, and so on).

   Lines 37–38 call another method, `detectInjection()`, that checks for possible injection. This method returns a `String` into the `newCriteria` variable. If the criteria entered by the user is deemed to be safe, the criteria is returned unchanged. If the criteria is suspect, then "null" will be returned instead; this code effectively removes the criteria from the WHERE clause. (See the sidebar "Why Suppress SQL Injection Errors?" for the reason.) The variable, `restricted`, is passed into this method (explained later).

   Line 39 resets the criteria to the value passed back from `detectInjection()`. After all attributes are processed in this way, the attribute loop is exhausted and control passes to Line 42.

   Line 42 retrieves the next criteria row. The query criteria row loop and nested attribute loop continues until no view criteria rows remain.

   Line 45 calls back to the superclass to perform its normal processing using the now-corrected set of query criteria.

NOTE
You will need to import oracle.jbo.ViewCriteria, oracle.jbo
.AttributeDef, oracle.jbo.ViewCriteriaRow, and java.sql.Types.

The detectInjection( ) Filter Method

The `getViewCriteria()` method is only half of the story. We also need a method that performs the hard work—`detectInjection()`. This method uses regular expressions to look for suspicious patterns in the supplied criteria. *Regular expression* is a powerful string manipulation feature that is available in most programming languages, including native PL/SQL (with Oracle 10*g*) and the Oracle Application Server PL/SQL Web Toolkit package OWA_PATTERN. A regular expression

Why Suppress SQL Injection Errors?

You might be wondering why the check for SQL injection does not raise some kind of error. A general principle to adopt when implementing restrictions against hacking attempts is to give away as little as possible. If a procedure such as this quietly throws away suspicious query criteria, the hacker will have no clue why the SQL injection did not return the expected results. It could be because no rows matched the altered statement, or maybe there was a mistake in the injected string.

If, on the other hand, an application blurts out an error message reporting the detection of a particular restricted keyword (as shown in the example of SQL injection in Chapter 12), the hacker will know that the site is filtering in some way. Even worse: the error message might enable her or him to better understand how to bypass the filter.

Even though you would not display the detected hacking attempt, you would want to internally log it in some way.

allows the code to check for matches against multiple patterns in one pass, which removes the need to use multiple conditions with different patterns.

The code for detectInjection() follows, with line numbers that would not appear in the code. Add this method to the view object Impl class, AllEmployeesImpl.

NOTE
Both methods would be reasonable candidates for refactoring to the framework buffer class.

```
01: protected String detectInjection(String criteria,
02:                                  String columnNames,
03:                                  boolean restrictive)
04: {
05:   boolean reject = false;
06:   String testPattern;
07:   if (restrictive)
08:   {
09:     testPattern = "^(>=|<=|<|>|<>|!=|=|BETWEEN|IN|LIKE|IS)";
10:   }
11:   else
12:   {
13:     StringBuffer constructLooseTestPattern =
14:                     new StringBuffer("(^(=|!=|LIKE))|(");
15:     constructLooseTestPattern.append(columnNames);
16:     constructLooseTestPattern.append(")");
17:     testPattern = constructLooseTestPattern.toString();
18:   }
19:   String testCriteria = criteria.trim().toUpperCase();
20:   if (testCriteria != null && testCriteria.length() > 0)
```

```
21:   {
22:      Pattern sqliPattern = Pattern.compile(testPattern);
23:      Matcher matcher = sqliPattern.matcher(testCriteria);
24:      if (matcher.find())
25:      {
26:         reject = true;
27:      }
28:   }
29:   return reject?null:criteria;
30: }
```

Lines 01 and 30 define the method block. Lines 01–03 declare the method signature with arguments of the criteria string to be tested, the list of column names for this view object, and the boolean flag indicating if the check needs to be more or less restrictive.

Lines 05–06 set up variables for the rejection flag and test pattern string.

Lines 07–18 create the appropriate regular expression-matching pattern based on whether the check is restrictive.

Line 09 loads the testPattern variable with operators that are not allowed for criteria values that are not number or date datatypes.

Lines 13–16 set up a StringBuffer, constructLooseTestPattern, containing some operators and the names of the columns represented by the view object.

Line 17 assigns the StringBuffer to the testPattern variable so it can be used in later code.

Line 19 removes any trailing and leading white spaces from the criteria string and converts the value to uppercase for ease of comparison.

Line 20 determines if there is anything to check now that white space has been removed. If so, it processes the values in Lines 22–27.

Line 22 invokes Java's regular expression engine to compile the expression pattern object, testPattern, just constructed.

Line 23 performs the pattern match between the compiled test pattern and the criteria that the user entered.

Lines 24–27 check if the criteria matched the filter pattern; if so, the reject flag is set to "true."

Line 29 returns "null," if the regular expression test found a matching string, or the original criteria string, if the expression test did not find a match.

NOTE
As always, you will need to import classes required for this code, such as java.util.regex.Pattern and java.util.regex.Matcher.

You can now test the code using the searchEmployee.jsp file. First try a SQL injection violation. Comment out the new getViewCriteriaClause() method before running the application (press CTRL-/ after selecting the method text). Run the application and, in the Search page, enter the following in the First Name field:

```
=employees.first_name and employees.salary > 10000
```

You will see a subset of the records—just those employees with a salary over 10,000. This is a violation of the intended design, which was to not allow users to determine the employee earnings. Even though the salary amount is not displayed, you could repeat the queries to hone in on the exact amount for a particular employee.

Close the browser and stop the server. Then uncomment the method in the view object code (pressing CTRL-Z should reverse the comments) and re-run the application. Try that search clause again to see the effect of the filter. The filter will ignore the query value because it contains an attribute name (*Salary*), so you should see all rows. With this filter, the confidentiality of employees' salaries is secure. Close the browser and stop the server.

Invoke Partial Page Rendering

Partial Page Rendering (PPR) is one of the most powerful features of the ADF Faces component set that TUHRA uses. PPR appears as smart components that work in the background. It asynchronously performs tasks, such as sending or fetching data from the view object (or other business tier model component), without having to refresh the entire page in the browser. A standard, browser-based application interacts with the server only when the user clicks a button or a hyperlink. At that time, the entire page is returned from the server with an associated time delay and bandwidth cost. PPR uses the same concepts as *Asynchronous JavaScript and XML (Ajax)*, a new trend in web development, named for the underlying technologies used to achieve the effect. The core principle underlying Ajax and PPR is that pages with suitably crafted scripting can carry out conversations with the server that are outside of the normal full-page submit-and-redraw paradigm. This, in turn, can yield smarter and more interactive user interfaces.

The downside of this technology is its reliance on scripting in the browser; the popular browsers don't implement scripting in exactly the same way, which causes complexities when coding JavaScript event code. Fortunately, when using PPR with JSF, the component developer is responsible for this scripting, and you do not need to worry about the details of the JavaScript code.

Using PPR

As demonstrated in Chapter 12, you are already using PPR. The ADF Faces table component used in the employee search results UI block uses background transactions to fetch data as you scroll through the results table. Only the table portion is redrawn, not the page, as you scroll through pages.

However, you can do more than just passively use PPR in this way. ADF Faces components also expose PPR attributes in a way that you can directly control. The first concern is deciding where PPR might be useful. Some typical examples follow:

- **List of values** When a user invokes an LOV window and selects a value in that window, a description for the returned value needs to appear on the main screen. The user may be halfway through creating a new record, so we would not want the whole screen to be submitted to the server to retrieve that value.

- **Validation and calculation** In response to a changed value in a field, you might want to carry out some middle-tier validation or operation on the data that has been entered (for example, calculating a line total when an order item quantity is modified).

- **Customizing the user interface** You can also use PPR for dynamic user interface changes, such as conditionally hiding and displaying fields at runtime.

These operations have two requirements: first, the PPR event needs to be triggered in some way; and second, the components that require the results need to be listening in some way. For example, your page contains an input column of number values and a field for a column total. The number input field needs to trigger a PPR event, and the total field needs to be listening so it knows when to update the total value.

Triggering a PPR Event

The component type determines how you raise a PPR event. Command items, such as `af:commandButton` and `af:commandLink`, provide a property called *partialSubmit*. The default value for this property is "false," so clicking the component at runtime will submit the entire page for processing in the traditional way. If you set this property to "true," the entire page will not be submitted; instead, only the code associated with that command item's action will execute. A typical use for this partial submit is to cause a pop-up window to appear for a list of values.

CAUTION
Because the entire page has not been submitted, the data in the business components layer is not necessarily in sync with any changes the user has made on the screen. Keep this in mind when using values in both page-level and model-level areas.

Editable items, such as `af:inputText` and `af:selectOneChoice`, provide an *autoSubmit* property that you can set to "true." If this is set to "true," the items will fire a PPR event as soon as the user tabs out of the field or clicks another field. In the case of list items and radio groups, selecting a new choice will trigger an event. The data change for input using these UI components is passed to the Model layer once the event is fired so that the contents of the associated attribute in the Model are up to date.

Listening for a PPR Event

Because PPR events do not explicitly trigger a full-page update, other components on the screen will not be aware of PPR unless you code them to listen for these events. A property available on all components, *partialTriggers*, fills this need. It accepts a list of component IDs in a space-separated list. The property inspector for the *partialTriggers* property pops up a dialog to help you select the correct component IDs. A component that has *partialTriggers* set in this way will listen for PPR events from all of the listed sources. This means that in order for a PPR-raising component to be detected, it must have its *Id* property set so that other components can list this ID in *partialTriggers*.

Once a component is listening for a PPR source, any PPR event will cause that component to reevaluate its properties, for example, its value and other expression-derived attributes. An example follows.

NOTE
For some components, you will need to set the "partialTriggers" property for the component's parent, not for the component itself. An example is a menu where the menuBar, not the individual menu items, should be listening for the PPR sources. If you find that components are ignoring PPR events when they should be reacting, try setting "partialTriggers" on their parent container.

Hands-on Practice: Use PPR to Disable the Menu Until Outstanding Changes Are Committed

As an example of how PPR can be used to create a richer end-user experience, we will enhance the Edit page (editEmployee.jsp) to disable all tabs to prevent navigation from that screen if changes are outstanding. The only way to allow navigation will be to click the Save (commit) button. The tabs will then be enabled.

1. In the Tuhra workspace, open the editEmployee.jsp page under ViewController\Web Content\pages\management node.

2. One at a time, select each input item (except *EmployeeId*), and set its *AutoSubmit* property to "true" and its *Id* to an appropriate value, such as "firstName" for the *First Name* field.

   Additional Information: Assigning values to the *Id* properties will allow you to set the *partialTriggers* property on other components so they can listen for changes raised by these fields.

3. Select the af:menuTabs component in the menu1 facet of the page (for example, by clicking a tab in the visual editor and selecting af:menuTabs in the Structure window). Click the "…" button in the *partialTriggers* property. You will see the following dialog:

4. Click New to add a line, and select one of the field IDs that appears in the pulldown when you select the highlighted line. Repeat this for all fields (except *EmployeeId*, which should not appear). Click OK. The property will show a space-separated list of IDs.

   Additional Information: You can also just type the names, but you will not be sure their *Id* properties are properly set that way. This will create code in the JSP file such as this excerpt:

   ```
   <af:menuTabs partialTriggers="firstName email lastName phoneNumber">
   ```

5. Copy the space-separated list of IDs, and paste it into the *partialTriggers* property of the af:menuButtons component under the menuGlobal facet.

6. Copy the IDs to the *partialTriggers* property of the Save button (af:commandButton).

7. In the Structure window, under `af:menuTabs` (under the menu1 facet) and `af:menuButtons` (under the menuGlobal facet), select as a group (CTRL-click) the six `af:commandMenuItem` components (Home, My Profile, Employees, Reference, Logout, and Help).

8. In the Property Inspector, click the "Bind to data" icon on the toolbar for the *Disabled* property, and set the expression as `#{bindings.Commit.enabled}`. This will change all six items, so be sure not to change any other properties.

   Additional Information: When a change is made to the record, ADF BC will set an internal flag indicating that changes need to be committed. This flag is exposed as the *Enabled* property on the Commit operation. The menu items containing the expression will be enabled or disabled based on this property. If you are an Oracle Forms user, this is analogous to the :SYSTEM.FORM_STATUS variable, which also indicates that at least one change needs committing.

9. Click OK. Returning to the Save button, set *Disabled* to the inverse of the other command items—"`#{!bindings.Commit.enabled}`" (without the quotation marks).

10. Run the page and observe that as soon as you make a change in one of the enterable fields and navigate out of it, the Save button becomes enabled and the various menu items become disabled. Save the change, and the enabling should reverse.

11. Close the browser and stop the server.

NOTE
Global buttons are effectively disabled using this PPR technique, but, at this writing, a bug with the Oracle Browser Look And Feel (BLAF) allows navigation to occur for menu tab clicks. The current workaround is to use the minimal look and feel. Alternatively, you can implement a check in the menu command items' action that prevents navigation. The online sample of the Tuhra application contains the latter example.

What Did You Just Do? Setting the *autoSubmit* property on the input fields causes them to post any data changes to the view object as soon as you navigate to another field. The command menu items listen to these fields as defined by their *partialTriggers* property. When the menu items sense a change, they reevaluate their properties, including the *disabled* property. If a change has been made to the record, the commit enabled check will evaluate to "true" and the menu item will be disabled.

When the user clicks Save, the entire page is submitted, and the record's changed flag is cleared in ADF BC. When the menu items reevaluate, they will be enabled again and the user can navigate to another page.

NOTE
The Reset button does not change the disabling. You cannot attach events to this button, but you could delete the Reset button if you use this disabling feature.

Define Global Format Masks

Many systems have a requirement to standardize various key presentation formats, such as dates or currency amounts. You would like a standard format mask to be easily changeable and available in one place so that a single change can affect the entire application.

Within ADF BC, we have seen how you can apply control hints to all usages of a particular entity object attribute. However, it would be better if the format mask were applied to every applicable field in the application, not just to those related to a single entity object.

If you examine one of the Salary fields in the TUHRA system, you will see something like the following definition:

```
<af:outputText value="#{bindings.Salary.inputValue}">
  <f:convertNumber groupingUsed="false"
                   pattern="#{bindings.Salary.format}"/>
</af:outputText>
```

Notice how the formatting of the salary value is managed by a nested `f:convertNumber` component. This tag offers attributes that define the way in which the number is formatted, including, as we see here, a pattern. Another thing you will notice in this example is that the value for pattern is not hard-coded; it is set to an expression—"#{bindings.Salary.format}." This EL is a reference to the format control hint defined for the view object or its entity object. There is no reason why the expression needs to point to this control hint. Instead, you can use an expression that points to a global configuration setting and have all similar fields use that global format mask. The following brief exercise illustrates this concept.

Hands-on Practice: Apply Standard Formatting to the Salary Field

The following steps will apply this principle to the sample application.

1. In the Application navigator, under ViewController\Web Content\WEB-INF, locate and open the properties web.xml file in the code editor. After the `description` tag, near the top of the file, enter the following XML:

    ```
    <context-param>
        <param-name>CURRENCY_FORMAT</param-name>
        <param-value>$######</param-value>
    </context-param>
    ```

    This defines a global mask that you can use throughout the application.

2. Open the editEmployee.jsp page and select the *Salary* field. In the Structure window, select the `f:convertNumber` component nested under the salary `af:outputText` component. The *Pattern* property will be set to the default of "#{bindings.Salary.format}" (the control hint value). Replace this with a new expression, "#{initParam['CURRENCY_FORMAT']}". Click OK.

    Additional Information: You can type in this value or use the EL binding editor; `initParam` appears under the JSP Objects node, but you will need to type the parameter name after shuttling the parameter to the expression area.

3. Save and run the application; navigate to the Edit page. Notice how the salary field now shows six digits, prefixed with the dollar sign and with no decimal places. (This pattern overrides the value of the *IntegerOnly* property for this item.)

4. Experiment with changing the pattern defined in the web.xml configuration parameter and showing it by running the application. When you are finished, close the browser and stop the server.

What Did You Just Do?   You have seen how to define a global format mask that can be referenced from every applicable field in the system. Also, of more general value, you've seen how to define a global variable (as an initialization parameter in web.xml), which can be referenced in any EL expression.

NOTE
Seed patterns, such as this one for formats, do not need to be defined in the web.xml. The expression used to reference a pattern could alternatively relate to a managed bean that you would define in the faces-config.xml file, or even a binding expression for a format stored in a database table.

This chapter has provided a number of techniques you may want to use to enhance the sample application. In addition, the techniques just described can act as patterns for code you need to write that has similar requirements.

CHAPTER
16

Oracle JHeadstart

Any sufficiently advanced technology is indistinguishable from magic.
—Arthur C. Clarke (1917–),*Profiles of the Future* (1973),
Clarke's third law

 n this book, you have learned how to build web applications using ADF in a visual and declarative way. For readers with an Oracle Forms background, we have mapped some ADF concepts to Oracle Forms. We manually created the TUHRA web application page by page, just as you create forms one by one using the Oracle Forms Builder. The subject of this chapter, Oracle JHeadstart, allows you to generate a complete and feature-rich ADF application using metadata that can be maintained using the same ADF tools. It can generate pages similar to those you developed manually in the TUHRA application. For readers with an Oracle Designer background, JHeadstart can be seen as the J2EE equivalent of the Oracle Forms Generator. The Oracle Forms Generator generates Oracle Forms applications; JHeadstart generates J2EE web pages.

This chapter explains what JHeadstart is, the features it provides, how it works, and how you can use it to migrate Oracle Forms applications to a J2EE environment. It also provides some guidelines about how to evaluate Oracle Forms migration tools.

What Is JHeadstart?

JHeadstart is a product that is developed and maintained by Oracle Consulting; it is a development toolkit built on top of ADF that uses JDeveloper's extension API to fully integrate with the JDeveloper Integrated Development Environment (IDE). JHeadstart generates fully functional, ADF-based web applications with features such as wizards, trees, shuttles (multi-select fields), lists of values (LOVs) with validation, advanced search, quick search, and role-based security. You coded some of these features manually in the sample application in Part II, but JHeadstart generates them from metadata properties.

JHeadstart Benefits

JHeadstart can deliver the following benefits:

- **Higher productivity**   It offers a significant productivity advantage in creating sophisticated web-based, J2EE, ADF business applications.

- **Easier transition to J2EE**   It will ease the transition to J2EE and ADF since it builds on concepts familiar to people with an Oracle Designer and/or Oracle Forms background. You use wizards and property editors to declaratively specify advanced behaviors that are generated into your application.

- **Consistent look and feel**   Using an application generator such as JHeadstart results in a highly consistent look and feel for your application.

- **Ability to leverage Oracle Designer work**   JHeadstart protects your investment in Oracle Designer since it can migrate Oracle Designer metadata to build ADF applications.

- **Ability to leverage Oracle Forms work**   JHeadstart can be used to migrate Oracle Forms applications generated using Oracle Designer or hand-built using Oracle Forms.

- **Technology-agnostic metadata layer** JHeadstart defines the application in a metadata format that is not specific to any technology. Therefore, your application becomes more future-proof. For example, if you used JDeveloper 10.1.2 and JHeadstart 10.1.2 to build an application using Struts and ADF UIX, you can upgrade to JSF and ADF Faces by regenerating your application using JHeadstart 10.1.3. The JHeadstart metadata model changed in version 10.1.3, but a 10.1.2 model will automatically be upgraded to the 10.1.3 format before you regenerate your application. The total effort of such an upgrade will depend on the number of post-generation changes you made. These changes will have to be reapplied manually if they are not natively supported in the new release.

Using JHeadstart

JHeadstart can be used in these two ways:

- **Build from scratch** In this method, you do not use or need to know Oracle Designer and Oracle Forms.
- **Build from Oracle Designer metadata** You can build ADF web applications by migrating them from existing Oracle Designer metadata. These metadata might already exist because you have previously generated your Oracle Forms applications from Designer. If your Oracle Forms applications are not defined in Designer, you can reverse-engineer (also called "design-capture") them into Oracle Designer, and then migrate them to ADF using JHeadstart.

This chapter discusses the second method in more detail in the section "JHeadstart Designer Generator." For now, we will concentrate on the first method, illustrated in Figure 16-1.

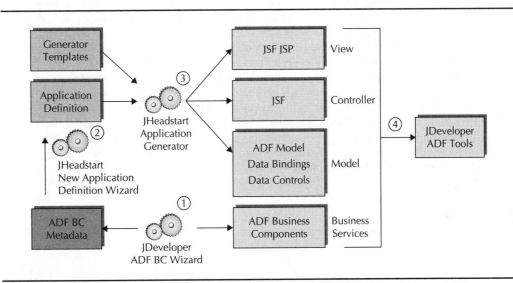

FIGURE 16-1. *Building an application from scratch using JHeadstart*

The high-level development process shown in this diagram is as follows:

1. Create the business service using ADF Business Components wizards in JDeveloper as described in Chapter 6. This step is independent of JHeadstart.

2. Use the JHeadstart New Application Definition Wizard to create a first-cut of the *application definition,* the metadata file in XML format required to generate the application. Then, although it is not shown on the diagram, you would refine the metadata using the Application Definition Editor and customize the generator templates using the JDeveloper code editor.

3. Generate the Model (data bindings), View, and Controller layer code using the JHeadstart Application Generator. This is a highly iterative process, where you refine the metadata and templates based on previous generation results.

4. If the results from the JHeadstart generator do not fully match your functional requirements, you can enhance the generated pages using the JDeveloper ADF tools (visual editors, property inspectors, and drag-and-drop facilities) described earlier in this book. There are several ways to preserve post-generation changes, as we will discuss later.

NOTE

In addition to modifying the pages you generate using the visual and declarative editors, you will also likely write some Java code to provide specific functionality using the managed bean classes and, perhaps, extending the JHeadstart framework classes. The documentation set included with JHeadstart will assist with these types of modifications.

While the main benefit of JHeadstart is in the Design and Build phases of your project, it can be a great help during analysis as well, particularly when you use an iterative, or agile development, approach. The New Application Definition Wizard, together with the ADF Business Components wizards, allows you to create feature-rich, working prototypes in minutes. These prototypes help you validate user requirements gathered in an analysis workshop.

Embedding JHeadstart in the development process increases your productivity without jeopardizing the flexibility, maintainability, and openness of J2EE development using ADF. This is an important point to make, since many people have negative associations with code generators. Generated code can be hard to understand and tedious to modify when you need functionality not provided by the generator. These disadvantages do not normally apply to JHeadstart because it does not generate Java code. Rather than generating Java code, JHeadstart includes generic, reusable runtime components that are configured and wired together through the generated faces-config.xml file and JSF JSP files.

NOTE

The JHeadstart runtime is described further in the section "The Role of the JHeadstart Runtime" later in this chapter.

To give you a more thorough understanding on how this works, we will discuss the following topics in more detail:

- **The JHeadstart application definition file** structure and how to create and refine it
- **The JHeadstart Application Generator** output and how to customize the result using generator templates
- **The JHeadstart runtime** libraries and examples of generated screens

Understanding the Application Definition

The main input to the JHeadstart Application Generator is the *application definition,* an XML file that defines the data collections to use, the page layout styles, query behaviors, transactional behaviors, and the user interface components to be generated.

This section discusses how to create and edit the application definition in addition to describing the elements defined in this file.

Creating an Application Definition

You use the JHeadstart New Application Definition Wizard to create an initial application definition file. In this wizard, you select an ADF BC application module and specify default layout settings to be used for all groups, as shown in the following wizard page:

Results of the New Application Definition Wizard

The wizard will create an application definition file (visible in the Resources node of the navigator) that contains a group for each view object instance in the application module you select. Nested (parent-child) view object instances will be represented as nested groups. Dynamic domains for allowable values (with the item *Display Type* as "dropDownList") or LOV groups (with the item *Display Type* as "lov" and a List of Values element added to the item) will be created for "lookup" view links between view objects.

NOTE
You specify the generation of pulldown lists or LOVs with the checkbox "Generate all lookup attributes with display type 'lov' instead of 'pulldownList'?" as shown in the preceding illustration.

For example, the RegionCountriesFKLink view link represents the one-to-many link between Region.RegionId and Country.RegionId. If the application module contains a top-level view object instance named "Countries," the wizard will create a group named "Countries." In this group, the RegionId item will have a *Display Type* of "dropDownList" or "lov" (with an associated LOV group or dynamic domain, respectively).

If the application module contains a top-level view object instance "Regions" and a nested view object instance "CountriesInRegion" using the same view link RegionCountriesFKLink, the wizard will create a master group "Regions" and a detail group "CountriesInRegion." In the CountriesInRegions detail group, the wizard will not assign the *Display Type* of the RegionId item as "lov" or "dropDownList" because the RegionCountriesFKLink is already used as the link to the parent group "Regions." Therefore, it would not make any sense to have a "lookup" to regions, because the country is always accessed in the context of a region and the link mechanism populates the RegionId value automatically for a new Countries detail row.

For example, a DeptEmpFKLink view link represents the link between Departments.ManagerId and Employees.EmployeeId. In this situation, Departments is a detail of Employees because Departments contains the foreign key on ManagerId. For the detail group, Departments, the wizard assigns a *Display Type* for the ManagerId as "lov" or "dropDownList" (with associated LOV group or dynamic domain, respectively). This allows the user to select a master Employees record to supply a value for the Departments.ManagerId attribute.

The Application Definition Editor

Although you can directly edit the raw XML of the application definition file, JHeadstart provides a properties editor, which you can invoke through the right-click menu on the project node in JDeveloper's navigator. If the project contains multiple application definition files, a submenu will appear that lists them all.

The left side of the Application Definition Editor, shown in Figure 16-2, contains the tree structure of the application definition elements, and the right side displays the properties of the selected node. All information required to drive the JHeadstart Application Generator is shown in this editor, which provides a complete overview of the application.

The properties are logically grouped, and a description of the selected property is displayed at the bottom of the Property Inspector.

Main features of the Application Definition Editor include the following:

- **Copying and moving** elements using a drag-and-drop action. For example, you can drag and drop one or more items into an item region.

- **Switching between novice mode and expert mode.** In novice mode, advanced properties are hidden, as are properties that currently do not apply because of values chosen for dependent properties. Expert mode shows all properties.

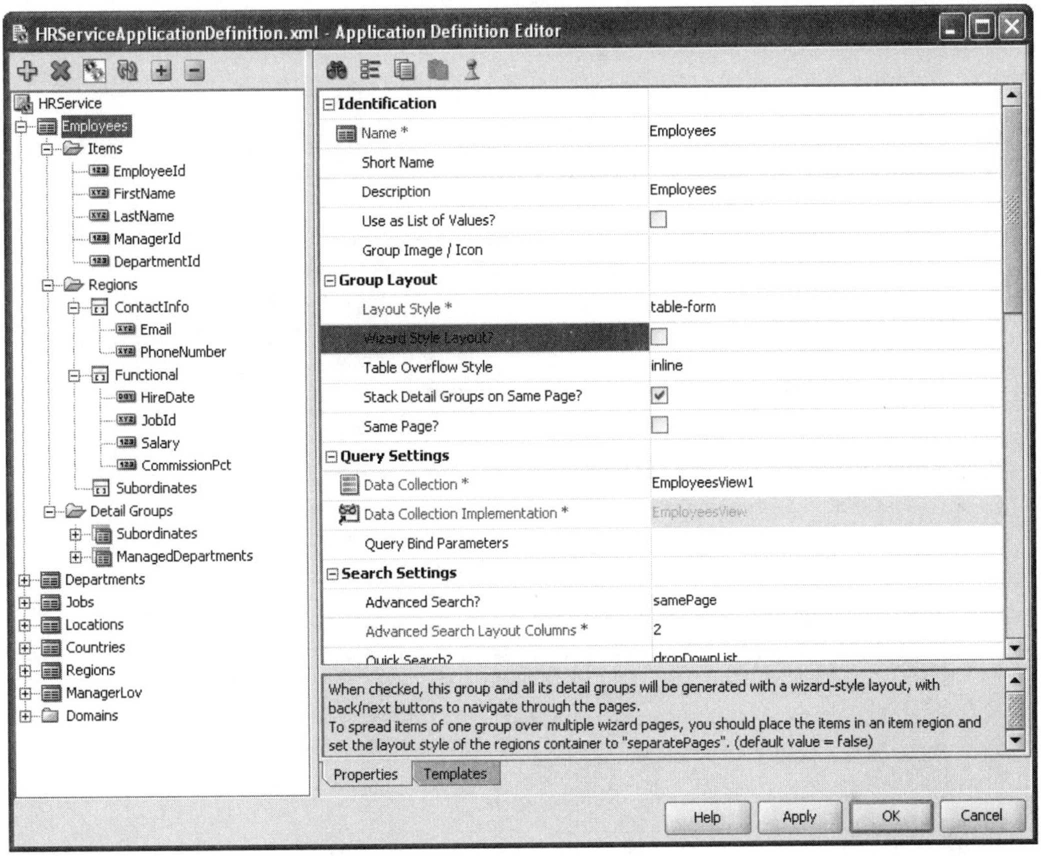

FIGURE 16-2. *Application Definition Editor*

- **Multi-selecting properties to copy and paste property values** to other objects of the same type.

- **Displaying the relevant editor** for a particular property, as in the rest of JDeveloper. Depending on the property type, you might see a text input field, a checkbox, a dropdown or pulldown list, or a file browse button.

Contents of the Application Definition

The application definition contains several elements that you can manipulate (as shown in the Application Definition Editor navigator in Figure 16-3): a service, groups, items, LOV, region containers, item regions, group regions, detail groups, and domains. Each element has a number of properties.

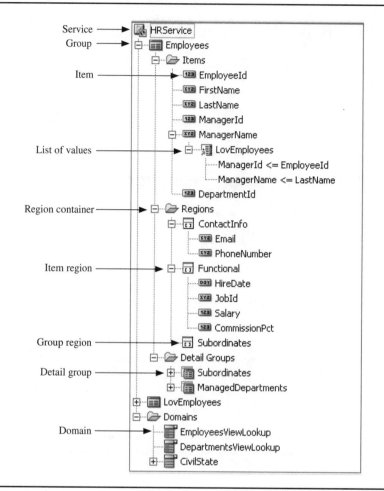

FIGURE 16-3. *Application Definition Editor navigator showing metadata elements*

Service

The top-level node in the application definition is the *service* —a functional subsystem of the application. It includes logically related functionality on which a user performs tasks that are logically linked together. The service level contains definitions for, among other things, the ADF data control that will be used (the application module, in the case of ADF Business Components). You use the same considerations to create one or more application definition files as you do to create one or more application modules in the Business Tier.

The service includes properties to specify file locations, general UI settings (for example, date and date-time formats), authorization, and internationalization settings, as shown next in an excerpt of the service-level Property Inspector window.

⊟ **Identification**	
🔲 Name *	HRService
Description	Application Definition for HRService
⊟ **Generator Flavours**	
View Type *	ADF Faces
JSP Version *	2.0
⊟ **File Locations**	
🔲 Main Faces Config *	/WEB-INF/faces-config.xml
🔲 Common Beans Faces Config *	/WEB-INF/JhsCommon-beans.xml
🔲 Group Beans Faces Config Directory *	/WEB-INF/
UI Pages Directory *	/WEB-INF/page/
UI Page Regions Directory *	/regions/
⊞ **Java**	
⊞ **Supporting Files**	
⊟ **UI Settings**	
Show Hint Text As Popup?	☑
Date Format *	dd-MMM-yyyy
DateTime Format *	dd-MMM-yyyy HH:mm
Unselected Label in Dropdown List	
Allow Partial Last Page in ViewObject Page ...	☑
⊟ **Authorization**	
Use Role-based Authorization	☐
Use Group Name As (Default) Role	☑
Role/Function Prefix	
Insert Allowed EL Expression	
Update Allowed EL Expression	
Delete Allowed EL Expression	

JSF EL Expression used to conditionally render the Create button and new rows in a table.
If the Insert Allowed Expression is set at the group level, this property is ignored for such a group.
Occurrences of $GROUP_NAME$ and $PARENT_GROUP_NAME$ in this expression will be replaced by the name
of the group (or name of parent group) for which the expression is applied. Example:
#{jhsUserRoles['GROUP_NAME.create']}

Group

A service consists of one or more groups. A *group* is tied to one data collection within the data control, which maps to a view object instance when using ADF BC. The group contains properties to set the layout, the allowable operations (insert, update, delete), and the ability to specify the query and search behaviors.

A group is similar to the concept of an Oracle Forms block; however, a group definition can result in multiple pages, whereas an Oracle Forms block usually appears on a single canvas. The number of pages generated for a group depends on the *Layout Style* property (form, table, table-form, select-form, tree, tree-form, parent-shuttle, intersection-shuttle) and the *Advanced Search* setting (samePage, separatePage, or none). Groups can be nested to represent parent-child relationships, and child groups are called *detail groups.*

The *Wizard Style* property can be used to generate wizard-style navigation with Back and Next buttons to navigate through the pages of the group and all its detail groups.

The *Same Page* property for detail groups can be used to indicate whether the detail group should be generated on the same page as its parent. The following illustration shows some of the properties for a group:

⊟ **Identification**	
🔲 Name *	Employees
Short Name	
Description	Employees
Use as List of Values?	☐
Group Image / Icon	
⊟ **Group Layout**	
Layout Style *	table-form
Wizard Style Layout?	☐
Table Overflow Style	inline
Stack Detail Groups on Same Page?	☑
Same Page?	☐
⊞ **Query Settings**	
⊟ **Search Settings**	
Advanced Search?	samePage
Advanced Search Layout Columns *	2
Quick Search?	dropDownList
🔲 Single or Default Search Item	
Maximum Number of Search Hits	
Auto Query?	☑
⊞ **Labels**	
⊟ **Operations**	
Single-Row Insert allowed?	☑
Single-Row Update allowed?	☑
Single-Row Delete allowed?	☑
Multi-Row Insert allowed?	☑
Multi-Row Update allowed?	☑
Multi-Row Delete allowed?	☑
New Rows	2
Show New Rows At Top?	☐
⊞ **Form Layout**	
⊞ **Table Layout**	
⊞ **Authorization**	

Comparing this to an Oracle Forms module defined through Oracle Designer, you would typically create one JHeadstart group for each top-level module component you define in Designer. For detail module components in a master-detail relationship, you would use detail groups in JHeadstart.

Item

A group contains one or more *items*, components that represent single data elements. Items can be databound or unbound. *Databound items* are based on an attribute of the data collection associated with the group. *Unbound items* can be used to generate buttons, hyperlinks, or "control" fields. The *Display Type* property of an item defines the user interface widget that is generated—for example, text input, dropdown list, checkbox, radio group, or file download link.

Other properties that can be set include *Prompt in Form Layout, Prompt in Table Layout, Display in Table Layout, Display in Form Layout, Width, Maximum Length, Height, Required, Update Allowed, Default Display Value, Depends On Item,* and *Disabled*, as shown in the next illustration. Where appropriate, you can use a JSF expression as the value of a property. For example, you can make an item read-only based on the user's security roles, or you can make an item disabled conditionally based on a JSF expression that evaluates the value of another item.

General	
Bound to Model Attribute?	☑
Name *	LastName
Attribute Name	LastName
Value	
Java Type *	String
Display Type *	textInput
Display Settings	
Display in Form Layout? *	true
Display in Table Layout? *	true
Display in Table Overflow Area? *	false
Prompt in Form Layout	LastName
Prompt in Table Layout	
Width	#{bindings.EmployeesLastName.displayWidth}
Height	#{bindings.EmployeesLastName.displayHeight}
Maximum Length	25
Column Alignment	
Default Display Value	
Column Sortable?	☑
Column Wrap?	☐
Hint (Tooltip)	
Depends On Item	
Operations	
Update Allowed?	true
Disabled	
Validation	
Required?	#{bindings.EmployeesLastName.mandatory}
Validator Binding	
Regular Expression	
Regular Expression Error Message	
⊞ Query Settings	
⊞ File Upload/Download Settings	

The JHeadstart Application Definition Editor contains a button to synchronize the group items with the underlying data collection. New attributes added to the data collection will be added as databound items.

Region Container, Item Region, and Group Region
Items can be grouped in an item region—a logical grouping of attributes with an optional title. Multiple regions can be grouped in a *region container*. The region container *Layout Style* property specifies the layout of the regions in the container: horizontally, vertically, stacked, or on separate pages. The last option ("separatePages") is useful when you have selected the *Wizard Style* checkbox on the group level. By creating item regions within a region container with a *Layout*

Style value of "separatePages," you can generate a wizard with the items of one group spread over multiple wizard pages. Region containers can be nested to generate nested stacked regions. A region container can also contain a *group region*—a region container for a single detail group. A group region has one property, *Detail Group Name,* which specifies the name of a detail group that should be placed in the region. Items within the detail group will be placed in the location of the region. Figure 16-2 shows item regions for ContactInfo and Functional, as well as a group region for Subordinates.

Without JHeadstart, you would use container components, such as af:panelHeader and af:panelForm, to group input components or other container components. The container component supplies layout behavior such as vertical or horizontal stacking.

List of Values

You can associate a list of values (LOV) with an item. In JHeadstart, a *list of values* displays values from a view object in a popup window. The *LOV Group Name* property of the LOV specifies the name of the group used to generate the list of values page. Only groups that have the property *Use as List of Values* set to "true" can be chosen. A list of values element contains one or more *return value* elements. A *return value* defines a lookup-base attribute pair—that is, the attribute of the selected row in the LOV group's data collection and the attribute of the current row of the base group data collection to which the value will be copied.

In the hands-on practice in Chapter 13, you created LOV windows that correspond to the LOVs that JHeadstart generates. However, JHeadstart can also return multiple values from the LOV and can generate multiple selections, using LOVs for validation and LOVs on read-only attributes.

A powerful property of the list of values element is *Use LOV for Validation,* shown in the LOV Property Inspector in the following illustration. When selected ("true"), the LOV will automatically appear when the user tabs out of the field with the LOV, if the value entered matches either none or multiple rows in the lookup data collection. When the value matches exactly one row, the LOV is not shown and the value will be auto-completed, if required. This type of validation and auto-completion is a well-known feature to Oracle Forms developers.

Multi-select LOVs (where the user can select more than one value) can be generated by selecting the *Allow multiple selection in LOV?* property. When this property is selected, and the user selects multiple rows in the LOV, new rows will be created in the base page. A typical example is a page containing a master order and order lines details; on this page, a multi-select LOV for products will create new order line records, one for each selected product.

Domain

The *domain* element (shown in the next illustration) specifies a static or dynamic list of allowable values. When the *Domain Type* property is set to "Dynamic," you can use the *Data Collection* property to specify the data source of the allowable values. When the *Type* property is set to "Static," you can specify allowable value child elements (in the same way you add allowable values to a Designer domain). The allowable value element has two properties: *Value* and *Meaning*. Domains can be used to generate items with a type of radio group, dropdown list, or checkbox. Domains are not used for Lists of Values, as they have no properties to specify how the LOV page should look and behave. Lists of values are defined using the Group element, as explained before.

You associate a domain with one or more items through the *Domain* property of the items. The *Display Type* property of the item determines if the list of allowable values is presented to the user as a radio group, a checkbox, a dropdown list, or a list box (text list). Domains provide the same functionality you created in the pulldown list for job titles that you created in the hands-on practice in Chapter 13.

Running the JHeadstart Application Generator

You can run the JHeadstart Application Generator (JAG) in two ways: using the iconic button in the Application Definition Editor or using a right-click menu option on the application definition file in the JDeveloper navigator.

This section discusses the outputs of the JAG in more detail and describes how you can preserve changes to these outputs made after generation. First, we will briefly introduce you to the powerful concept of generator templates.

Generator Templates

The content of the generated JSP pages and faces-config.xml file is driven by templates. These templates can contain static content that will be included without being changed in the generated page, as well as dynamic content. Dynamic content is defined using the *Velocity Template Language* (VTL). *Velocity* is an open-source Java-based template engine, which is an effort of the Apache Jakarta Project (jakarta.apache.org/velocity). It permits anyone to use a simple yet powerful template language to reference objects defined in Java code. When running the JAG, JHeadstart creates Java objects for the various elements of the application definition and calls the Velocity Template Engine to resolve the VTL constructs in the various generator templates.

JHeadstart ships with a large set of default templates for generating the faces-config.xml file, menus, overall page layout, search regions, item regions, various group layout styles (tree, form, table, parent-shuttle, intersection-shuttle, select list), and all item types. The JHeadstart page-level templates are comparable to the Oracle Designer Forms Generator templates; all JHeadstart lower-level templates roughly correspond to objects specified in the Oracle Forms object library. Like the Oracle Designer Forms Generator, you can create custom generator templates, and configure the JAG to use your custom template instead of the default one. Once you become familiar with the template structure and VTL, you will be able to customize the generator outputs any way you want.

NOTE
You can find VTL documentation, including a reference of all constructs, at jakarta.apache.org/velocity/docs.

Generator Outputs

The JHeadstart Application Generator is capable of generating the following types of output:

- **JSF JSP Pages** in XML format (.jspx files)
- **faces-config.xml file** for the JSF Controller
- **PageDef files** containing the ADF Model bindings for the generated pages
- **Resource bundles** for internationalization

JSF JSP Pages

The structure of a generated JSF JSP page is identical to the pages that you create manually using drag-and-drop actions. This means that you can open a generated page in the visual editor and add or modify functionality manually. See the section "Making and Preserving Post-Generation Changes" for more information.

faces-config.xml

The main contents generated into the faces-config.xml file are the navigation rules and the managed bean definitions. As mentioned in Chapter 5, the managed beans used to hold code for the application's pages are defined in the faces-config.xml file.

Classes from the JHeadstart runtime library are used as the managed bean classes. One library class can serve as a managed bean for multiple pages because the classes are highly configurable. Each instance of the managed bean class is configured for usage in a specific page. For example, many pages in the generated application might offer a quick and/or advanced search region (as explained and shown later in the "Examples of Generated Screens" section).

For each search region in each page, a managed bean definition such as the following is added to the faces-config.xml file, reusing the same generic `JhsSearchBean` class:

```
<managed-bean>
  <managed-bean-name>searchEmployee</managed-bean-name>
  <managed-bean-class>oracle.jheadstart.controller.bean.JhsSearchBean
  </managed-bean-class>
  <managed-bean-scope>session</managed-bean-scope>
  <managed-property>
    <property-name>bindings</property-name>
    <value>#{data.EmployeeTablePageDef}</value>
  </managed-property>
  <managed-property>
    <property-name>searchBinding</property-name>
    <value>#{data.EmployeeTablePageDef.advancedSearch}</value>
  </managed-property>
  <managed-property>
    <property-name>dataCollection</property-name>
    <value>EmployeesView1</value>
  </managed-property>
  <managed-property>
    <property-name>maxQueryHits</property-name>
    <value>50</value>
  </managed-property>
</managed-bean>
```

As you will notice, the `JhsSearchBean` JHeadstart runtime class acts as the managed bean for the search region in the EmployeeTable page. Various properties (parameters) are passed to this class using the managed property elements. In this way, you can reuse the `JhsSearchBean` for search regions in different pages and define page-specific values in the managed-property elements to customize its behavior.

This same concept is used to implement other JHeadstart runtime features, such as LOV functionality, the shuttle functionality, query parameter binding, tree forms, and multi-row insert and delete. All these features rely on generic classes included in the JHeadstart runtime library; the classes are configured as managed beans in the faces-config.xml. This architecture makes it easy to customize or extend the default behavior of the JHeadstart managed beans. You can extend a managed bean class, and, to ensure your custom class is used, you customize the generator template used for the specific managed bean definition.

PageDef files
As discussed in Chapter 7, ADF creates a PageDef file when you drag and drop objects from the Data Control Palette to your page. The PageDef file holds the executables and bindings of your page, and is required to run your pages. JHeadstart-generated pages work in the same way.

For each page, the JAG will create a PageDef file containing executables and bindings based on the information in the application definition.

Resource Bundles (Message Bundle)

The JHeadstart Application Generator creates a resource bundle (message bundle) for text used on the screens. As described in Chapter 5, you can use different resource bundles to hold text translated into different languages. You specify the name of the resource bundle in the service-level property *NLS Resource Bundle*. The *Resource Bundle Type* property defines whether the generator creates a property file (as in the hands-on practice in Chapter 9) or a Java class.

The JAG writes text into this file for boilerplate text and for button labels and page header titles. You can use the service-level checkbox *Generate NLS-enabled Prompts and Tabs* to load prompts, tab names, and display titles. This is also useful if you need to translate this text. The Internationalization section of the service node in the application definition appears here:

⊟ **Internationalization**	
NLS Resource Bundle *	view.ApplicationResources
Resource Bundle Type *	propertyFile
Override NLS Resource Bundle Entries?	☑
Generate NLS-enabled prompts and tabs?	☑
Generator Default Locale *	en
Generator Locales	

Using the *Generator Locales* property, you can specify which locales are supported by your application. A resource bundle will be generated for each locale.

Making and Preserving Post-Generation Changes

The JHeadstart Application Generator is a powerful generator, and by customizing the generator templates, you have a lot of control over the functionality and look and feel of the generated application. It is probably not realistic for most web applications to expect 100 percent generation (as some shops were able to attain with Oracle Designer Forms Generator), and too much focus on trying to generate a feature that is not supported out of the box might be counterproductive.

If you have experience using the Oracle Designer Forms Generator, you might remember how hard it can be to make the fields lay out properly. Various generator preferences and the *Relative Tab Stop* property can be used to govern the layout. Real Oracle Designer Forms Generator gurus can generate any layout they want, but using Oracle Forms Builder to change the generated layout is much faster.

The same principle applies to JHeadstart. The more skilled you are in JHeadstart, the more likely you are to stretch the capabilities of the JHeadstart Application Generator. But remember, JHeadstart is there to help you work faster. The moment you get the feeling that JHeadstart hinders you in implementing functionality, you should abandon generation and build the remaining functionality manually using the visual editors, code editors, and drag-and-drop action from the Data Control Palette.

Some people just stick to generation because they lack an understanding of how to build things manually using ADF. Since you have reached this point in the book, we certainly hope this does not apply to you. All the knowledge you gained in the previous chapters is also applicable when performing post-generation changes. After all, the runtime architecture, the JSP pages, the PageDef files, and the faces-config.xml file produced by JHeadstart, are all similar to applications that are hand-built.

Ideally, you start applying post-generation changes when the data model and the system requirements are fairly stable. But we do not live in an ideal world, and certainly now with the increasing popularity of agile development approaches, it is hard to tell when the system functionality has become stable (if it ever does).

Options for Preserving Post-Generation Changes

More often than not, you will be confronted with changing requirements that are easily implemented using the JHeadstart Application Generator. However, what happens if the requirements change and you have already made post-generation changes? You basically have three options:

- **Do not regenerate the parts of the system** that have been changed.
- **Regenerate the entire system** and reapply the post-generation changes afterwards.
- **Define all your post-generation changes in custom templates** so that nothing gets lost after regenerating.

Do Not Regenerate Parts of the System   The first option is supported by a number of properties called *generator switches* that govern the files or parts of files that will be regenerated. These switches appear at two levels:

- **The service level** offers coarse-grained switches you can set to prevent regeneration of the faces-config.xml file, the NLS (National Language Support) resource bundle(s), and the menu bar.
- **The group level** supplies switches to prevent regeneration of group-specific JSF JSP pages, the PageDef files, and the managed beans and navigation rules in the faces-config.xml file.

Custom managed beans and navigation rules that you add manually to the faces-config.xml file will never be removed or overridden, regardless of the generator switch settings. This also holds true for custom executables and bindings that you add manually to the PageDef file or that are added when you drag and drop onto the visual editor.

Regenerate the Entire System   The second option of reapplying post-generation changes sounds less attractive, but might be useful when the generator switches are too coarse-grained and the post-generation changes are quickly and easily reapplied. For example, you have a master-detail page where the detail UI block needs to be regenerated because of new requirements, and the master "block" has post-generation changes. In this case, it might be much faster to regenerate the whole page and reapply the post-generation changes to the master block. Of course, this approach requires discipline: you need to carefully document your post-generation changes step by step.

Define Post-Generation Changes in Custom Templates   If you have chosen the second option, and you find yourself reapplying the same post-generation changes over and over again, you might actually go for a third option that merges the first two options. JHeadstart provides an extremely fine-grained template mechanism—that is, each UI component on the page has its own template that you can customize. Using the example explained before, you could create a custom template that only contains static content: the code of the master "block," including the post-generation changes. Using the Templates tab of the Application Definition Editor (shown in Figure 16-2), you can configure JHeadstart to use this custom template for the master block. When you then regenerate the page, the code in the custom template is copied into the generated page. This technique is the Holy Grail of 100 percent generation: you can move any post-generation change into a custom template if you like. Experiences in real-world projects indicate that this approach works well, particularly in a Rapid Application Development (RAD) environment with customized modules that are expected to change often.

NOTE
The JHeadstart Blog contains an interesting post about documenting post-generation changes. Although a bit out-of-date (the post was written for the JHeadstart 10.1.2 release compliant with JDeveloper 10.1.2), the technique described is still useful. This post can currently be found at www.orablogs.com/jheadstart/archives/001391.html.

Running the Generated Application

The generator outputs, together with the JHeadstart runtime, provide a fully functional application.

Examples of Generated Screens

Rather than providing a long list of feature descriptions, we will show you several generated screens and describe the generator settings that were used to create these screens. This will give you a feeling for what is feasible with JHeadstart, as well as how to use the JHeadstart application definition to specify these features.

Advanced Search, Editable Table, and Inline Overflow

Figure 16-4 shows a screen containing a search region, multi-row editable table, details region, and pulldown lists. This section describes how these features were defined.

Search Region   The search region is placed on the page because the *Advanced Search* property of the group is set to "samePage." Items displayed in the advanced search page have the *Show in Advanced Search* checkbox selected. The dropdown list in the search field *Last Name* allows the user to set the type of SQL operator and wildcard usage in an intuitive way; this behavior is generated because the item property *Query Operator* is set to "setByUser." The Quick Search button is generated because the group *Quick Search* property is set to "dropDownList." When clicking this button, the advanced search region will be hidden and the quick search region will be displayed, as shown here:

Filter By | Last Name ▾ | k | (Go) (Advanced Search)

The quick search field displays differently, depending on the quick search item. For example, when the quick search attribute is set to Department, a dropdown list with all departments will be displayed instead of a text input field.

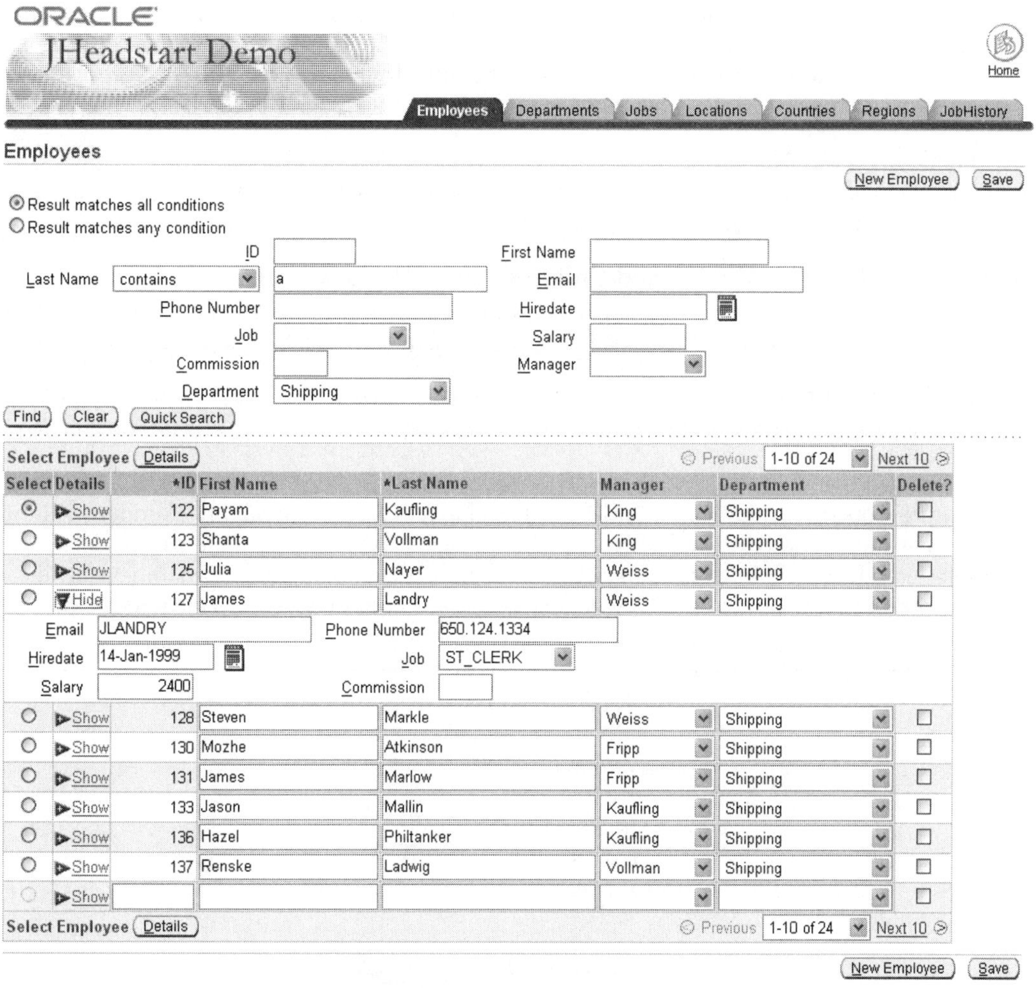

ORACLE
JHeadstart Demo

Home

Employees | Departments | Jobs | Locations | Countries | Regions | JobHistory

Employees

New Employee | Save

⦿ Result matches all conditions
○ Result matches any condition

ID		First Name		
Last Name	contains ▾	a	Email	
Phone Number		Hiredate		
Job	▾	Salary		
Commission		Manager	▾	
Department	Shipping ▾			

Find | Clear | Quick Search

Select Employee (Details)   ○ Previous 1-10 of 24 ▾ Next 10 ⊙

Select	Details	*ID	First Name	*Last Name	Manager	Department	Delete?
⦿	▶Show	122	Payam	Kaufling	King ▾	Shipping ▾	☐
○	▶Show	123	Shanta	Vollman	King ▾	Shipping ▾	☐
○	▶Show	125	Julia	Nayer	Weiss ▾	Shipping ▾	☐
○	▼Hide	127	James	Landry	Weiss ▾	Shipping ▾	☐

Email JLANDRY   Phone Number 650.124.1334
Hiredate 14-Jan-1999   Job ST_CLERK ▾
Salary 2400   Commission

○	▶Show	128	Steven	Markle	Weiss ▾	Shipping ▾	☐
○	▶Show	130	Mozhe	Atkinson	Fripp ▾	Shipping ▾	☐
○	▶Show	131	James	Marlow	Fripp ▾	Shipping ▾	☐
○	▶Show	133	Jason	Mallin	Kaufling ▾	Shipping ▾	☐
○	▶Show	136	Hazel	Philtanker	Kaufling ▾	Shipping ▾	☐
○	▶Show	137	Renske	Ladwig	Vollman ▾	Shipping ▾	☐
○	▶Show				▾	▾	☐

Select Employee (Details)   ○ Previous 1-10 of 24 ▾ Next 10 ⊙

New Employee | Save

FIGURE 16-4. *Generated page with advanced search, editable table, and inline overflow*

Multi-row Editable Table   The table is generated because the group *Layout Style* is set to "table-form." The Details button will display the Employee form page, which will show the selected employee record in single-row format. The table displays 10 rows at a time because the group *Table Range Size* property has been set to "10." The rows are updateable because the group checkbox *Multi-Row Update Allowed* is selected. The delete checkbox is generated because the group checkbox *Multi-Row Delete Allowed* is selected. The new row at the bottom is generated because the group checkbox *Multi-Row Insert Allowed* is selected and the group property *New Rows* is set to "1." The ID field in the table is only editable in a new row because the item property *Update Allowed* is set to "while_new."

Details Region   The Show/Hide icons and the employee details that are subsequently shown when clicking the Show icon are generated because the group *Table Overflow Style* property is set to "inline." The items displayed in the table row have the item property *Display in Table Layout* set to "true." The items displayed in the inline overflow area have that property set to "false" and property *Display in Table Overflow Area* set to "true."

Pulldown Lists   The items rendered as pulldown lists have the *Display Type* property set to "dropDownList" and an associated dynamic domain element with a *Data Collection* property that specifies the data shown in the dropdown list.

Parent UI Block with Stacked Children, List of Values, and Shuttle
The screen shown in Figure 16-5 contains a form-style UI block, shuttle control, editable UI block, stacked detail groups, and a list of values. It was generated with the settings described next.

Form-Style UI Block   The parent group Department *Layout Style* property is set to "table-form." The page shown represents the form layout that displays after selecting a record on a table page and clicking Details.

Shuttle Control   The detail group TransferEmployees has its *Layout Style* property set to "parent-shuttle" and the *Same Page* checkbox selected. When saving the changes, detail rows selected on the right side of the shuttle component in the parent group (Departments) will cause the foreign key value of a detail row (Employees) to be updated to refer to the selected parent row;

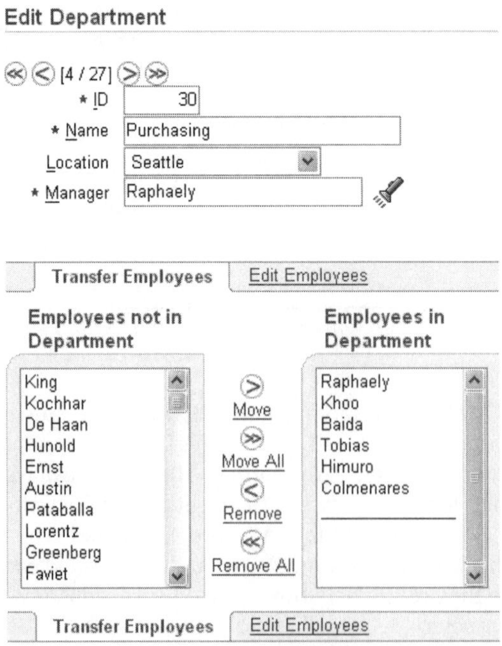

FIGURE 16-5.   *Generated page with stacked children, list of values, and shuttle*

the foreign key value for detail rows that have been deselected (moved to the left shuttle area) will be nullified. JHeadstart also supports an *intersection shuttle*, which will insert and delete entries in an intersection table.

Editable UI Block   The detail group EditEmployees, not shown in Figure 16-5, has *Layout Style* set to "table" and the *Same Page* checkbox selected.

Stacked Detail Groups   The detail groups (that form the tabs) are stacked into tabs because the master group Departments has a *Region Container* named "Regions" with *Layout Style* set to "Stacked." This region container includes two detail group regions, as shown in the following illustration. The *Detail Group Name* property of the group region is set to the detail group inside the region (shown next for TransferEmployees).

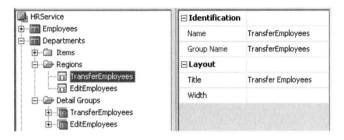

List of Values   The Manager item displays an LOV icon that invokes a separate list of values window because its *Display Type* property is set to "lov." The data shown in the LOV window and the query capabilities in the LOV are defined through the group element that supplies the values for the LOV. This group is associated with this item using the property *LOV Group Name* for the associated list of values.

Tree, Form, and Detail Table with Stacked Overflow

The screen shown in Figure 16-6 contains a tree component, a table area, and stacked overflow tabs. These features were defined using the settings described in this section.

Tree Component   The group structure is nested five levels deep to represent Regions, Countries, Locations, Departments, and Employees. All groups except Employees have the *Layout Style* set to "tree-form." The *Layout Style* of the Employees group is set to "table" and the *Same Page* checkbox is selected.

Table and Overflow Area   The *Layout Style* property of the Employees group is set to "table" and *Table Overflow Style* is set to "right." The overflow area shows items you do not want to display in the table because they would make the table too wide. Only EmployeeId, FirstName, and LastName items have the property *Display in Table Layout* set to "true." All other items have this property set to "false" and the property *Display in Table Overflow Area* set to "true."

Stacked Overflow Tabs   The items in the overflow region appear stacked because the Employees group has a RegionContainer named Regions with the property *Layout Style* set to "stacked." This RegionContainer contains two ItemRegions with the *Title* property respectively set to "Functional" and "Contact Info."

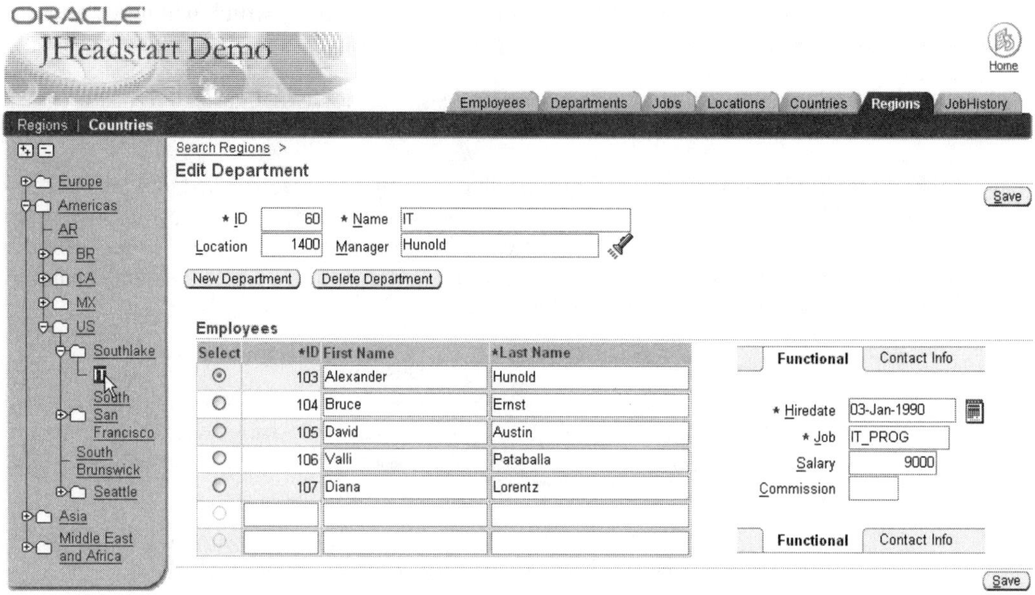

FIGURE 16-6. *Generated page with a tree, form, and detail table with stacked overflow*

The Role of the JHeadstart Runtime

The JHeadstart runtime consists of a set of Java classes (the sources are included), a JavaScript library, and a cascading style sheet that together provide application functionality for all tiers of a J2EE web application. The JHeadstart runtime provides you with a host of ADF best practices, as described in this book and on Oracle's Technology Network website (otn.oracle.com).

Some examples of runtime components and the features they provide are as follows:

- **The JhsApplicationModuleImpl class** extends the standard ADF BC `ApplicationModuleImpl` class. It includes generic methods to perform advanced searches on a view object, to execute a query on a view object when bind parameter values have changed, and to handle shuttle selections.

- **The JhsPageLifecycle class** extends the default ADF page life cycle (mentioned in Chapter 8) to add additional behavior to standard ADF operations, for example:

  - In the `onCreate()` method, default display values, which you can define as JSF expressions in the application definition, are set on the new row.

  - In the `onDelete()` method, the deletion is auto-committed, as the end user would expect when clicking a Delete button.

- In the `onCommit()` method, user feedback similar to that in Oracle Forms will be displayed. For example, the user will see either a "No Changes to Save" or "Transaction Completed Successfully" message as a result of a save operation.

- In the `onRollback()` method, the row currency and range start positions of all iterator bindings are restored to the values prior to the rollback. This means that query results will be displayed with the same current row and sort order as before the operation.

■ **The JhsListOfValues class** is used as a JSF managed bean that provides LOV features like multi-select, copying multiple values back to the base page, and using the LOV to validate the value entered in the field that has the LOV attached.

■ **The ReportingUtils class** enhances standard ADF error reporting. Container exceptions are filtered out, and only error messages that make sense to the user are displayed. Database constraint violations are handled gracefully, allowing the developer to specify a user-friendly error message in the resource bundle using the constraint name as the key.

■ **The alertForChanges() function** in the JHeadstart JavaScript library displays a JavaScript alert (shown in the next illustration) when the user abandons a page that has unsaved changes.

This list is not exhaustive by any means, but it should give you an idea of the types of functionality provided by the JHeadstart runtime.

JHeadstart Designer Generator

If you are familiar with generating Oracle Forms applications using Oracle Designer, you may have noticed in the preceding discussion that the metadata structures you can specify in the JHeadstart application definition are inspired by the Oracle Designer metadata model. Some properties even have identical names, such as the group properties *Table Overflow Style* and *Descriptor Attribute*.

A major difference between Oracle Designer and JHeadstart is the storage format: JHeadstart uses an XML file, and Oracle Designer uses relational tables. The *JHeadstart Designer Generator (JDG)* allows you to convert the Oracle Designer metadata to the XML format required by JHeadstart, and it creates the ADF Business Components metadata. This effectively allows you to reuse Oracle Designer metadata to generate ADF applications. It is a two-step process, as shown in Figure 16-7.

In the first step, you run the JHeadstart Designer Generator to create the ADF Business Components, the ADF BC metadata, and the application definition. The second step is to run the JHeadstart Application Generator to create the Model, View, and Controller files required to create a fully functional ADF web application.

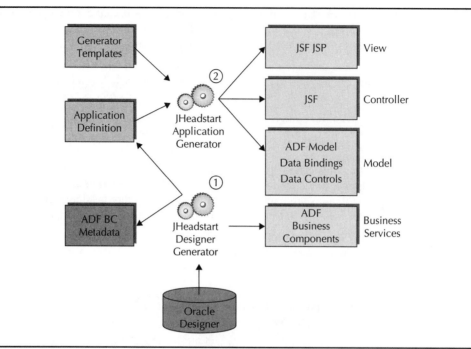

FIGURE 16-7. *JHeadstart Designer Generator migration process*

The business components are created as follows:

■ **Designer table definitions** are implemented as ADF BC entity objects.

■ **Designer module components** are implemented as ADF BC view objects.

■ **Designer modules** are implemented as ADF BC application modules.

You will typically run the JDG only once for a set of Designer modules. If, for some reason, you change the definitions in Oracle Designer after running the JDG, you will need to re-run the JDG. After running the JDG, if you make changes to a group in the application definition file that you do not want to lose when re-running the JDG, you can select the *JDG Protected* checkbox at the group level.

NOTE
JHeadstart includes an "Oracle JHeadstart Designer Generator Reference," which lists how each metadata element in Designer is converted to its JHeadstart equivalent.

Design-Capturing Oracle Forms in Oracle Designer

You might wonder how the JHeadstart Designer Generator can help you when you have not used Oracle Designer to generate your forms, or you did generate your forms but customized them heavily afterwards using Oracle Forms Builder. If this is the case, you can first design-capture (reverse-engineer) your database and Oracle Forms definitions into the Oracle Designer repository by using Designer's Design Capture Wizard. This wizard creates the metadata in the repository according to the following list from the Oracle Designer online help system:

- **A new module definition** for the form being captured. If the module definition already exists, you can merge the results of the design capture with the existing form definition.
- **Window definitions** for windows in the form
- **Module components** for blocks in the form
- **Base table usages** for base table blocks in the form
- **Lookup table usages** when capturing generated forms containing LOV usages
- **Bound and unbound items** for all items in the form except control block items displayed on vertical or horizontal toolbar canvases
- **Item groups** for items on different tab pages of a tab canvas in the form
- **Module arguments** for each parameter in the form

Migrating Oracle Forms Applications

We intentionally used the phrase "reuse Oracle Designer metadata" when describing the purpose of the JDG. Why didn't we write "migrate Oracle Designer metadata"? You can certainly migrate Oracle Forms applications from Oracle Designer to JHeadstart, but there is more to such a migration than just running the JDG and JAG. Chapter 1 discusses questions you should ask yourself when making a decision between Oracle Forms or J2EE. To a large degree, the same considerations apply when you decide whether to migrate Oracle Forms to J2EE, for example:

- Are the users familiar with web browser applications or able to adjust to the new front-end?
- Do I need to migrate an existing application to J2EE?
- Does the application require high interactivity? If so, can we provide a user interface experience using JSF components that meets the high interactivity requirements?
- Are our infrastructure and development teams ready for the J2EE technology stack?
- Is the application large, mission-critical, or time-sensitive?

Chapter 1 discusses these questions. In this section, we discuss two additional questions you need to answer before migrating forms to J2EE:

- Is the application suitable for a partial migration?
- How do I select a migration tool?

NOTE
It is good to keep in mind that migration from Oracle Forms to J2EE might not be needed. It is also good to keep in mind that, should you decide to migrate existing applications from Oracle Forms to ADF web applications, you need to consider if it would be better to start from scratch using JDeveloper or JDeveloper with JHeadstart. For example, starting from scratch is a good idea when the functionality of the existing Oracle Forms application is out of date and does not match the current requirements.

Is the Application Suitable for a Partial Migration?

Larger Oracle Forms applications can often be divided into functional subsystems that have their own user groups. Each user group might use the system differently and have different backgrounds. Subsequently, the questions about familiarity with web browsers and high interactivity requirements need to be answered for each user group. The user groups might also have different satisfaction levels with the functionality of the current system.

In addition, web-based, self-service intranet and Internet applications are becoming more and more popular in organizations because the applications can save a considerable amount in administrative overhead. This trend leads to a shift of functionality traditionally performed by back-office, data-entry staff (who have frequent use and need high interactivity) to all employees of an organization (who might have infrequent use and are satisfied with lower interactivity) or, for Internet applications, even to customers and suppliers of the organization.

If the trend just mentioned applies to your organization, we recommend starting with a partial migration of your application. This migration has a number of benefits that together greatly reduce the risks associated with forms migration, for example:

- **You can start on a small scale** by migrating a small subsystem that is not mission-critical that serves end users who are accustomed to web applications.

- **You can evaluate the migration tool** you have selected. Does it meet your expectations?

- **You can collect metrics on the effort** involved in migrating a number of forms. You can extrapolate these numbers to make more reliable estimates of the costs involved in migrating other, bigger subsystems.

How Do I Select a Migration Tool?

The Oracle Forms migration market is expected to grow significantly in the coming years. So, not surprisingly, more and more companies have offerings in this space. Oracle helps you in selecting a company by validating the products that help with migrating forms to J2EE and ADF.

Oracle has validated a number of partner products as being viable for its customers to use when migrating Oracle Forms applications. Although it is beyond the scope of this book to directly compare product features, we will provide some considerations you can use when making the decision about a product.

NOTE
An up-to-date list of validated migration products can be found at www.oracle.com/technology/products/forms/htdocs/ Oracle_Forms_Migration_Partners.htm.

Main Technical Considerations

Apart from non-technical criteria, like price, support, documentation, and references, we see two main technical aspects to take into account when making this choice:

- The amount of functionality that is migrated automatically
- The architecture of the migrated application

Without comparing JHeadstart to other commercial products, we can mention the functionality JHeadstart provides against the functionality that another tool might provide. Once you have identified a short list of products to consider, you will then be able to plug in specifics about those products.

Migrating Oracle Forms' PL/SQL Code

With JHeadstart, the runtime architecture of the migrated application is identical to a hand-built ADF-JSF application. Everything you learned in this book about JSF and ADF is applicable to a JHeadstart-migrated application. However, by design, JHeadstart does not migrate the PL/SQL logic that is coded in the forms. PL/SQL logic should be migrated manually using the following process:

1. Evaluate the type of logic in each trigger and procedure.
2. Determine in which tier or tiers (database, business service, Model, Controller, or View) the functionality should be implemented.
3. Implement the functionality using best practices that apply to the technology used for that tier.

How Much Oracle Forms Code Is Converted?

That is, will the resulting application have the same appearance as the original Oracle Forms application, and will it retain the same business logic and code structure as the original? Some products essentially just rebuilt Oracle Forms in Java; for example, a Java method is available in a library for each Oracle Forms built-in procedure. The appearance remains the same, because other products may use a Swing-based Java applet to convert the Oracle Forms user interface, which allows them to support typical Oracle Forms features, like Enter Query mode.

Advantages of JHeadstart for Migration

JHeadstart offers the following advantages:

- JHeadstart-migrated applications are as easy to maintain as applications built from scratch using ADF and JSF.
- Developers can reuse the same skills required for building ADF-JSF applications to maintain and extend JHeadstart-migrated applications.
- JHeadstart-migrated applications can easily be enriched with additional features supported by the JHeadstart Application Generator. This only requires changes to the migrated application definition.

Advantages of Other Products for Migration

Other products may offer the following advantages over JHeadstart:

- Migrating applications is fast and low-risk, because close to 100 percent of the functionality is migrated.

- Applications are relatively easy to understand and maintain for Oracle Forms developers because the structure is similar to Oracle Forms. Oracle Forms developers only need to learn the Java language syntax and how to work with the migration tool.

- End users do not need retraining because the appearance is the same as the original form.

Disadvantages of JHeadstart for Migration

Consider the following disadvantages of migrating Oracle Forms applications using JHeadstart within JDeveloper:

- A JHeadstart migration can be time-consuming, depending on the amount and complexity of PL/SQL logic in the forms.

- JHeadstart requires Oracle Designer metadata to perform the migration of Oracle Forms applications, and this might require the reverse-engineering of hand-built forms into Oracle Designer prior to the migration.

- Functionality and appearance of the application will most likely be different. Therefore, users will need to become accustomed to the new interface, although the JSF JSP file using ADF Faces that it generates contains more user-friendly features than many applications on the Web now.

Disadvantages of Other Products for Migration

Other products may have other disadvantages, as follows:

- They may not use the JSF standard, which allows the application to be run in a browser without the Java runtime. Instead, they may use a proprietary Swing-based applet that requires the Java Virtual Machine (JVM) to run in the browser.

- A Java developer without a background in Oracle Forms may require training in understanding the runtime architecture. This is necessary for development as well as for maintenance.

- If your organization builds other J2EE web applications from scratch—for example, using JDeveloper, ADF, and JHeadstart—these applications will have a different architecture than the migrated application. This means that you must invest in two separate skill sets to maintain both types of J2EE web applications.

Your choice will depend on how you value the various pros and cons of each migration product.

Licensing, Support, and Other Resources

As mentioned, JHeadstart is a separate product and, as such, it must be purchased separately. As an Oracle Consulting product, it is not yet handled by Oracle Support Services or Metalink. However, you can use the JHeadstart Discussion Forum on the OTN website to ask questions, raise issues, and log enhancement requests. The JHeadstart Product Center on the OTN website contains all information related to JHeadstart. You can view and/or download the following:

- **An evaluation copy** of the JHeadstart software. This copy contains all functionality and can be used for pilot projects to evaluate JHeadstart.

- **An end-to-end tutorial,** which showcases the main JHeadstart features.

- **Extensive documentation**, consisting of the *Oracle JHeadstart for ADF Developer's Guide, Installation Guide, Release Notes, Migration Guide, Runtime Javadoc*, and *Designer Generator Reference.*

- **Viewlets** that demonstrate the usage of the JHeadstart Application Generator and the JHeadstart Designer Generator.

- **Frequently Asked Questions**, including information about the price and purchase details.

The JHeadstart Product Center can be found at www.oracle.com/technology/consulting/9iservices/jheadstart.html (or by searching www.google.com for "jheadstart product center"). Additional information sources are as follows:

- **JHeadstart Discussion Forum** at forums.oracle.com/forums/forum.jspa?forumID=38
- **JHeadstart Blog** at blogs.oracle.com/jheadstart/

Index